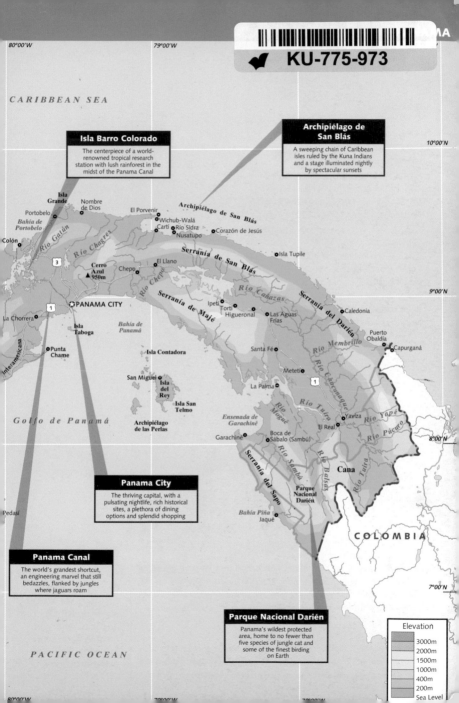

KU-775-973

CARIBBEAN SEA

80°00'W
79°00'W

10°00'N

9°00'N

8°00'N

7°00'N

Isla Barro Colorado
The centerpiece of a world-renowned tropical research station with lush rainforest in the midst of the Panama Canal

Archipiélago de San Blás
A sweeping chain of Caribbean isles ruled by the Kuna Indians and a stage illuminated nightly by spectacular sunsets

Isla Grande
Nombre de Dios
Portobelo
Bahía de Portobelo
Colón
Río Gatún
Río Chagres
El Porvenir
Wichub-Walá
Cartí
Río Sidra
Nusatupo
Corazón de Jesús
Archipiélago de San Blás
Isla Tupile
Serranía de San Blás

Cerro Azul ▲950m
Chepo
El Llano
Río Chepo
Serranía de Majé
Río Cañazas
Serranía del Darién
Caledonia

PANAMA CITY
Ipetí
Torti
Higueronal
Las Aguas Frías
Río Membrillo
Puerto Obaldía
Capurganá

La Chorrera
Santa Fé
Río Tuira
Metetí
Río Chucunaque

Isla Taboga
Bahía de Panamá
La Palma
Río Mogué
Río Tuira
Yaviza
Río Yapé

Punta Chame
Isla Contadora
Río Púcuro

San Miguel
Isla del Rey
Ensenada de Garachiné
Boca de Sábalo (Sambú)
El Real
Río Balsas
Cana

Isla San Telmo
Garachiné
Río Sambú
Río Tuira

Golfo de Panamá
Archipiélago de las Perlas
Serranía del Sapo

Panama City
The thriving capital, with a pulsating nightlife, rich historical sites, a plethora of dining options and splendid shopping

Parque Nacional Darién

Bahía Piña
Jaqué

COLOMBIA

Panama Canal
The world's grandest shortcut, an engineering marvel that still bedazzles, flanked by jungles where jaguars roam

Pedasí

Parque Nacional Darién
Panama's wildest protected area, home to no fewer than five species of jungle cat and some of the finest birding on Earth

PACIFIC OCEAN

Interamericana

La Chorrera

Elevation	
	3000m
	2000m
	1500m
	1000m
	400m
	200m
	Sea Level

80°00'W
79°00'W

Panama
2nd edition – November 2001
First published – January 1999

Published by
Lonely Planet Publications Pty Ltd ABN 36 005 607 983
90 Maribyrnong St, Footscray, Victoria 3011, Australia

Lonely Planet Offices
Australia Locked Bag 1, Footscray, Victoria 3011
USA 150 Linden St, Oakland, CA 94607
UK 10a Spring Place, London NW5 3BH
France 1 rue du Dahomey, 75011 Paris

Photographs
Many of the images in this guide are available for licensing from
Lonely Planet Images.
email: lpi@lonelyplanet.com.au

Front cover photograph
Miraflores Locks, Panama Canal, Panama (Alfredo Maiquez)

ISBN 1 86450 307 6

text & maps © Lonely Planet Publications Pty Ltd 2001
photos © photographers as indicated 2001

Printed by Colorcraft Ltd, Hong Kong

**Although the authors
and Lonely Planet try
to make the informa-
tion as accurate as
possible, we accept
no responsibility for
any loss, injury or
inconvenience sus-
tained by anyone
using this book.**

Contents

2   Contents

MAP INDEX

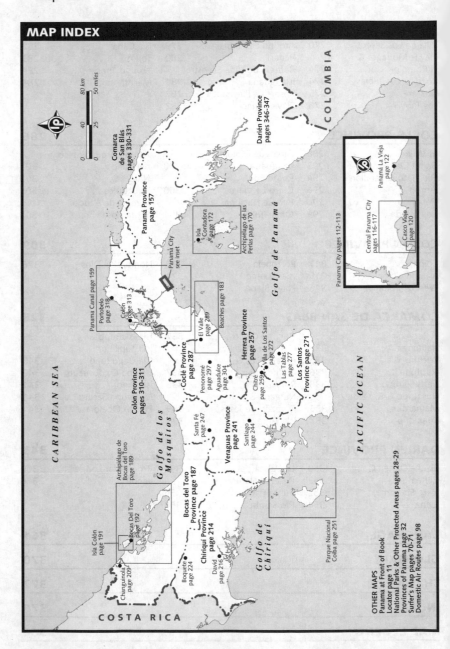

COLOMBIA

COSTA RICA

CARIBBEAN SEA

PACIFIC OCEAN

Golfo de los Mosquitos

Golfo de Panamá

Golfo de Chiriquí

80 km
50 miles

Comarca de San Blás pages 330-331

Darién Province pages 346-347

Panamá La Vieja page 122

Central Panama City pages 116-117

Casco Viejo page 120

Panama City pages 112-113

Panamá Province page 157

Archipiélago de las Perlas page 170

Isla Contadora page 172

Panamá City see inset

Panama Canal page 159

Portobelo page 318

Colón page 313

Colón Province pages 310-311

Beaches page 183

El Valle page 289

Herrera Province page 257

Villa de Los Santos page 272

Las Tablas page 277

Los Santos Province page 271

Chitré page 259

Coclé Province page 287

Penonomé page 297

Aguadulce page 304

Santa Fé page 247

Veraguas Province page 241

Santiago page 244

Archipiélago de Bocas del Toro page 189

Isla Colón page 191

Bocas Del Toro page 192

Bocas del Toro Province page 187

Changuinola page 209

Boquete page 224

Chiriquí Province page 216

David page 216

Parque Nacional Coiba page 251

OTHER MAPS
Panama at Front of Book
Locator page 11
National Parks & Other Protected Areas pages 28-29
Provinces of Panama page 32
Surfer's Map pages 70-71
Domestic Air Routes page 98

The Author

SCOTT DOGGETT

A New York City native, Scott spent most of his childhood in California. He graduated from UC Berkeley in June of 1983 and began his professional life six weeks later as a freelance photographer covering wars in Central America. That death-wishy behavior, as he now views it, was followed by postgraduate work at Stanford University; crime reporting in Los Angeles and war reporting in Afghanistan for United Press International ('more lunacy,' he says); and, from 1989 through 1996, seven years as a staff editor for the *Los Angeles Times* ('the payoff for all the lunacy'). Anxious to see more of the world, Scott began writing for Lonely Planet in 1997. Today, he is the author of Lonely Planet's *Las Vegas* and *Yucatán* guides and coauthor of Lonely Planet's *Havana*, *Mexico* and *Dominican Republic & Haiti* guides. Scott has also written guidebooks to Amsterdam and Los Angeles, and he is an author and coeditor of the award-winning anthology *Travelers' Tales: Brazil.* In 1999 and 2000, Scott briefly rekindled his love affair with the *Times*, writing a weekly business column for the newspaper with his wife, Annette Haddad.

FROM THE AUTHOR

This book is dedicated to the woman of my dreams, Annette.

Quite a number of people assisted me with this labor of love. In Panama, historian Amado Araúz made available to me his extensive library. Eric Jackson, editor of *The Panama News*, proved an invaluable source of information. The same can be said for Nancy Hanna, president of the super-informative www.panamainfo.com. Adrienne Samos, director of *Talingo*, the Sunday arts supplement of *La Prensa*, offered excellent suggestions concerning the initial chapters of this book. John Miller, who teaches instructors at US-based Nantahala Outdoor Center, the world's premier kayaking school, provided the expert information contained in the 'Chiriquí Is for Kayakers' boxed text. Monica E Kupfer, a widely recognized authority on painting and sculpture in Central America, deserves credit for much of the information appearing in the Arts section of the Facts about Panama chapter. Roberto Sarmiento, administrative librarian at the Panama Canal Commission's Technical Resources Center, was of tremendous help in locating historical documents I could find nowhere else. Professor Vladimir Berrío-Lemm, the country's foremost expert on Panamá La Vieja, taught me a great deal about the early history of Panama City. Jon Hanna, administrator of www.panamasurftours.com, offered terrific information on Panama's surfing scene. Paul Winder, a captive guest of Colombian rebels for nine months, gave me insight into the horrors of going too far.

When conducting research for a Lonely Planet guidebook, I often rely on local guides to apprise me of recent developments, remote facilities and hidden attractions. Guides Hernán Araúz, Richard Cahill, Rick Morales, Jonathan Parris, Guido Berguido, Mario Bernal and Alberto

5

Castillo were particularly helpful. Upon occasion Panama's tourism agency, IPAT, made available to me a car and a driver to facilitate my work. To IPAT marketing and advertising advisor Americo de la Guardia and driver Omar Dubos, I exuberantly raise a pair of *baja panties* and toast to your health. A great many other people assisted me in my quest to learn all things Panamanian, and I would be remiss if I failed to mention the most helpful of them: Julie Gómez, Marco A Gandásegui, Jane Walker, Charlotte Elton, Sara R Jalil, Julie and Emanuel González-Revilla, Cameron Forsyth, Claudio Talley, Danny Poirier, Kristen Weibe and James Schreiber. Thank you all very much.

Every guidebook has had its share of problems, and this guidebook was no exception. The fact that it appears in your hands without so much as a missing period or a misplaced modifier is due to Christine Lee, the hawk-eye editor of this book. I also take my Panama hat off to Mariah Bear, Lonely Planet's publisher for the Americas; senior editor Tom Downs; cartographer Justin Colgan; and designer Lora Santiago, plus the illustrators of this book. Of course, we'd all be out washing cars if it wasn't for Eric Kettunen, who does a superlative job managing Lonely Planet's business operations for the Northern Hemisphere.

This Book

Scott Doggett researched and wrote this 2nd edition of *Panama*, which was based to some extent on his fine 1st edition.

FROM THE PUBLISHER

This book was edited by Christine Lee, with help from Emily Wolman and Susannah Farfor and plenty of support from managing editor Kate Hoffman and senior editors Maria Donohoe, Tom Downs and Wade Fox. Emily, Susannah Farfor, Kanani Kauka and Susan Shook-Malloy proofread the book. Ken DellaPenta created the index. Cartographer Justin Colgan led the mapping team, which included Matt DeMartini, Mary Hagemann, Patrick Huerta, Brad Lodge and Kat Smith. Senior cartographers Monica Lepe and Sean Brandt oversaw the show, with help from cartography manager Alex Guilbert. Lora Santiago designed both the book and the color pages, and Margaret Livingston created the cover, all under the careful eyes of design manager Susan Rimerman. Hugh D'Andrade, Mark Butler, Hayden Foell, Beca Lafore, Justin Marler, Henia Miedzinski, Hannah Reineck, Jim Swanson and Wendy Yanagihara provided the illustrations for this book.

ACKNOWLEDGMENTS

The Panamá La Vieja map appearing in the Panama City chapter was partially prepared from a map provided by Professor Vladimir Berrío-Lemm.

Foreword

ABOUT LONELY PLANET GUIDEBOOKS

The story begins with a classic travel adventure: Tony and Maureen Wheeler's 1972 journey across Europe and Asia to Australia. Useful information about the overland trail did not exist at that time, so Tony and Maureen published the first Lonely Planet guidebook to meet a growing need.

From a kitchen table, then from a tiny office in Melbourne (Australia), Lonely Planet has become the largest independent travel publisher in the world, an international company with offices in Melbourne, Oakland (USA), London (UK) and Paris (France).

Today Lonely Planet guidebooks cover the globe. There is an ever-growing list of books, and there's information in a variety of forms and media. Some things haven't changed. The main aim is still to help make it possible for adventurous travelers to get out there – to explore and better understand the world.

At Lonely Planet we believe travelers can make a positive contribution to the countries they visit – if they respect their host communities and spend their money wisely. Since 1986 a percentage of the income from each book has been donated to aid projects and human-rights campaigns.

Updates Lonely Planet thoroughly updates each guidebook as often as possible. This usually means there are around two years between editions, although for more unusual or more stable destinations the gap can be longer. Check the imprint page (usually following the color map at the beginning of the book) for publication dates.

Between editions up-to-date information is available in two free newsletters – the paper *Planet Talk* and email *Comet* (to subscribe, contact any Lonely Planet office) – and on our Web site at www.lonelyplanet.com. The *Upgrades* section of the Web site covers a number of important and volatile destinations and is regularly updated by Lonely Planet authors. *Scoop* covers news and current affairs relevant to travelers. And, lastly, the *Thorn Tree* bulletin board and *Postcards* section of the site carry unverified, but fascinating, reports from travelers.

Correspondence The process of creating new editions begins with the letters, postcards and emails received from travelers. This correspondence often includes suggestions, criticisms and comments about the current editions. Interesting excerpts are immediately passed on via newsletters and the Web site, and everything goes to our authors to be verified when they're researching on the road. We're keen to get more feedback from organizations or individuals who represent communities visited by travelers.

Lonely Planet gathers information for everyone who's curious about the planet – and especially for those who explore it first-hand. Through guidebooks, phrasebooks, activity guides, maps, literature, newsletters, image library, TV series and Web site we act as an information exchange for a worldwide community of travelers.

Research Authors aim to gather sufficient practical information to enable travelers to make informed choices and to make the mechanics of a journey run smoothly. They also research historical and cultural background to help enrich the travel experience and allow travelers to understand and respond appropriately to cultural and environmental issues.

Authors don't stay in every hotel because that would mean spending a couple of months in each medium-size city and, no, they don't eat at every restaurant because that would mean stretching belts beyond capacity. They do visit hotels and restaurants to check standards and prices, but feedback based on readers' direct experiences can be very helpful.

Many of our authors work undercover; others aren't so secretive. None of them accept freebies in exchange for positive write-ups. And none of our guidebooks contain any advertising.

Production Authors submit their raw manuscripts and maps to offices in Australia, the USA, UK or France. Editors and cartographers – all experienced travelers themselves – then begin the process of assembling the pieces. When the book finally hits the shops, some things are already out of date, we start getting feedback from readers and the process begins again...

WARNING & REQUEST

Things change – prices go up, schedules change, good places go bad and bad places go bankrupt – nothing stays the same. So, if you find things better or worse, recently opened or long since closed, please tell us and help make the next edition even more accurate and useful. We genuinely value all the feedback we receive. A well-traveled team reads and acknowledges every letter, postcard and email and ensures that every morsel of information finds its way to the appropriate authors, editors and cartographers for verification.

Everyone who writes to us will find their name in the next edition of the appropriate guidebook. They will also receive the latest issue of *Planet Talk*, our quarterly printed newsletter, or *Comet*, our monthly email newsletter. Subscriptions to both newsletters are free. The very best contributions will be rewarded with a free guidebook.

Excerpts from your correspondence may appear in new editions of Lonely Planet guidebooks, the Lonely Planet Web site, *Planet Talk* or *Comet*, so please let us know if you *don't* want your letter published or your name acknowledged.

Send all correspondence to the Lonely Planet office closest to you:

Australia: Locked Bag 1, Footscray, Victoria 3011
USA: 150 Linden St, Oakland, CA 94607
UK: 10a Spring Place, London NW5 3BH
France: 1 rue du Dahomey, 75011 Paris

Or email us at: talk2us@lonelyplanet.com.au

For news, views and updates, see our Web site: www.lonelyplanet.com

HOW TO USE A LONELY PLANET GUIDEBOOK

The best way to use a Lonely Planet guidebook is any way you choose. At Lonely Planet, we believe the most memorable travel experiences are often those that are unexpected, and the finest discoveries are those you make yourself. Guidebooks are not intended to be used as if they provided a detailed set of infallible instructions!

Contents All Lonely Planet guidebooks follow roughly the same format. The Facts about the Destination chapters or sections give background information ranging from history to weather. Facts for the Visitor gives practical information on issues like visas and health. Getting There & Away gives a brief starting point for researching travel to and from the destination. Getting Around gives an overview of the transport options when you arrive.

The peculiar demands of each destination determine how subsequent chapters are broken up, but some things remain constant. We always start with background, then proceed to sights, places to stay, places to eat, entertainment, getting there and away, and getting around information – in that order.

Heading Hierarchy Lonely Planet headings are used in a strict hierarchical structure that can be visualized as a set of Russian dolls. Each heading (and its following text) is encompassed by any preceding heading that is higher on the hierarchical ladder.

Entry Points We do not assume guidebooks will be read from beginning to end, but that people will dip into them. The traditional entry points are the list of contents and the index. In addition, however, some books have a complete list of maps and an index map illustrating map coverage.

There may also be a color map that shows highlights. These highlights are dealt with in greater detail in the Facts for the Visitor chapter, along with planning questions and suggested itineraries. Each chapter covering a geographical region usually begins with a locator map and another list of highlights. Once you find something of interest in a list of highlights, turn to the index.

Maps Maps play a crucial role in Lonely Planet guidebooks and include a huge amount of information. A legend is printed on the back page. We seek to have complete consistency between maps and text and to have every important place in the text captured on a map. Map key numbers usually start in the top left corner.

Although inclusion in a guidebook usually implies a recommendation, we cannot list every good place. Exclusion does not necessarily imply criticism. In fact there are a number of reasons why we might exclude a place – sometimes it is simply inappropriate to encourage an influx of travelers.

Introduction

Panama offers some of the finest birding, snorkeling and deep-sea fishing in the Americas, but most foreigners know the country only for its famous canal. Indeed, Panama is a proud nation that offers astounding wildlife adventures, that respects its seven indigenous peoples and that celebrates its Spanish heritage with frequent and colorful festivals. It's difficult to leave the country without feeling you're in on a secret the rest of the traveling world has yet to discover.

Located at the southern end of Central America, Panama is an 800km land bridge where the wildlife of North and South America meet and intermingle. It is largely because of its geographical position that Panama is home to a recorded 940 bird species – more than in all of North America. Panama is the only country where jaguars and pumas prowl a short drive from the capital. It is home to some of the most remote and some of the most accessible rain forest in the world.

This country, whose Indian name means 'abundance of fish,' has mostly evaded the tourist's radar screen despite having much more to offer than its wildly popular western neighbor, Costa Rica. Tour guides in Panama are fond of saying that in Costa Rica 20 birders would be lucky to see one resplendent quetzal, while in Panama one birder might see 20 quetzals. There's truth in what they say: The crush of tourists who pass through Costa Rica's national parks tends to scare off wildlife, while in Panama's national parks tourists are as scarce as harpy eagles, and wildlife abounds.

There are rivers in Panama where rafters can ride 20 sets of rapids in a single afternoon. There are scores of picturesque palm-lined beaches with hardly a human on them. There are several peaks from which travelers can see the Pacific Ocean over one shoulder and the Caribbean Sea over the other. There are mangrove swamps on both Panamanian coasts that transport imaginative souls to times when dinosaurs roamed the Earth. In

fact, the dinosaurs' closest living relative – the crocodile – still lurks in many Panamanian swamps.

There are 1518 islands off the coasts of Panama and, because the coasts are less than an hour's drive apart, you can easily spend the morning snorkeling in the Caribbean and the afternoon swimming in the Pacific. Some of the best snorkeling and scuba diving in Central America can be found near Panama's Isla de Coiba, which is both a national park and home to a penal colony. If you stay on Coiba, your boatman will likely be a tough-looking policeman and your cook a soft-spoken prisoner.

Surfers from all points on the globe have discovered Playa Santa Catalina in Veraguas Province, which periodically hosts waves with 5m faces, and the breaks near Isla Colón in Bocas del Toro Province are comparable to those along Costa Rica's eastern shore but lack the crowds. Orchid lovers can see some of the world's largest and smallest in Santa Fé, an easygoing town set amid spectacular jungle three hours' drive from Playa Santa Catalina.

More deep-sea fishing records have been broken in Bahía Piña, off the Pacific coast of Panama, than anywhere else in the world. You can see sea turtles by the dozen much of the year along both Panamanian coasts. Cana, at the heart of Parque Nacional Darién, is birding nirvana, where four species of macaw – including great greens and blue-and-yellows – shriek across the sky with astonishing frequency.

As for culture, Panama beams with it. The Península de Azuero in central Panama is like a slice of Spain dropped into the Americas, with traditional Spanish festivals celebrated often and with great gusto. Unlike some places where locals put on a show for tourists, on the Azuero the people perform for themselves. Likewise, the country's indigenous peoples share a desire to maintain their traditions. They are a pleasure to encounter on an island or in a jungle, as long as you don't hound them with cameras or otherwise behave badly.

Historically, Panama is a story of riches, of Peruvian gold carried by Spaniards across the isthmus from Panama City on the Pacific coast to Nombre de Dios and (later) to nearby Portobelo on the Caribbean coast, where the precious metal was stored until it could be shipped to Spain. Huge forts were built from blocks of rock and coral to protect the gold from marauders, but the bastions failed to deter pirates. Ruins from those days of yore, complete with cannons and moats, make for fascinating touring.

Then there's the canal. Its construction by the USA during the early 20th century is, like the pyramids of Egypt, a stunning testament to what humans can accomplish. Almost 90 years after the SS *Ancon* became the first ship to traverse the lock-and-lake waterway, the Panama Canal remains one of the engineering marvels of the world. Whether they are seen from the deck of a boat or from a viewing stand, the great locks of the canal leave no visitor unimpressed.

It is difficult to write an introduction to a guidebook on Panama without sounding a bit like a tourism official; the country truly is an unpolished gem. But Panama isn't tourist-perfect. Because the country's tourism industry is now in its infancy, travelers expecting to find five-star accommodations a stone's throw from a pristine rain forest will generally be disappointed. And reaching destinations can be a pain; for starters, the country could do with a few thousand more road signs.

But if you have ever found yourself saying, 'Oh, you should have seen this place 10 years ago, before it was overrun with tourists,' chances are you would leave Panama today feeling you'd visited at just the right time. As John le Carré writes in his novel *The Tailor of Panama*, 'We've got everything God needed to make paradise. Great farming, beaches, mountains, wildlife you wouldn't believe, put a stick in the ground you get a fruit tree, people so beautiful you could cry.' It's the voice of a fictional character, but it's also the attitude of most Panamanians, who take great pride in their country. As well they should.

Facts about Panama

HISTORY
Pre-Columbian History

Archaeological evidence shows that people have been living in Panama for at least 11,000 years, and that agriculture arose here as early as 1500 BC. Panama's first peoples lived beside the Pacific and fished in mangrove swamps and estuaries, just as many of the country's Indians do today. Archaeological sites dating from 5000 BC contain remains of large fish, but they lack obvious fishing artifacts, such as hooks and sinkers. This suggests the people probably caught fish using traps near shore.

Fishing was still the main occupation of the Indians as late as 1500 BC. By this time the Pacific communities were taking larger numbers of very small fish that swim farther from shore. Instead of using shore traps, they were probably using gill nets tossed from boats. By 400 BC villagers living 10 to 20km inland were using marine fish from a wide variety of habitats, suggesting that the coastal villages were each catching particular types of fish and trading them. Evidence also shows that the fishermen were going farther out than before.

By AD 1600 European colonists had introduced new methods of fishing, but the ancient techniques used by the region's first inhabitants have continued to be used to the present day. Given the tremendous importance fish have had in the lives of isthmians since humans arrived 13 millennia ago, it seems only fitting that the country's name means 'abundance of fish' in an Indian language.

Archaeologists divide pre-Columbian Panama into three distinct cultural zones – western, central and eastern – based on the types of pottery and other artifacts found at archaeological sites. None of these zones was culturally isolated; evidence of trading shows ties not only among the zones but between them and Colombia, other parts of Central America and even Mexico and Peru. In addition to commercial trade and

fishing, the economies of all of Panama's early societies were based on extensive agriculture and hunting. It is believed that these societies were hierarchical and headed by chiefs, and that war played a significant role.

In western Panama on the slopes of the Barú volcano, Barriles is an important archaeological center where finds have included unusual life-size stone statues of human figures, some with one figure sitting astride another's shoulders. Giant *metates* – flat stone platforms that were used for grinding corn – have also been found here.

Archaeologists estimate that the early civilization represented at Barriles was established around the 4th or 5th century BC when settlers arrived from the west (now Costa Rica). This culture came to an abrupt end when Volcán Barú erupted violently in the 5th century AD. Later, the region was inhabited again, this time by two different groups whose archaeological remnants include a great variety of distinctive types of pottery.

Between Penonomé and Natá in the central region, Sitio Conte is an important archaeological zone and ancient ceremonial center where thousands of pieces of pottery, as well as tombs and many other items of interest, have been unearthed.

Another central archaeological zone, Cerro Juan Díaz, near Villa de Los Santos on the Península de Azuero, is believed to have been inhabited from about 300 BC until the time of the Spanish conquest. Pre-Columbian pottery and other artifacts have also been found at sites in Parque Nacional Sarigua on the Península de Azuero.

Not as much is known about the early peoples of the eastern region of Panama, because archaeologists have yet to conduct extensive studies there. Most knowledge of the area's history and its peoples' hierarchical social structure has been gleaned from accounts by the first Spanish explorers, who arrived in the Darién region of present-day eastern Panama and western Colombia during the 16th century.

Gold objects appeared in Panama suddenly, with a sophisticated and completely developed technology. Metallurgy was practiced in Peru as early as the 2nd century BC; by the 1st century AD it had arrived in Panama. Archaeologists believe it probably arrived from the Sinú, Quimbaya and Tairona regions of Colombia, with the Urabá area as the point of contact and interchange.

Colombia, Panama and Costa Rica all became metallurgic provinces, and objects of gold and other metals were exchanged all the way from Mesoamerica to the Andes. Gold was made into ornaments (necklaces, nose rings and so on) and animal, human and other figures, and it was also used for ceremonial purposes; it probably did not connote wealth to the Indians in the same way that it did to the Spaniards.

Spanish Colonization

When Spaniards first arrived on the isthmus of Panama in the early 16th century, they found it inhabited by various indigenous peoples. The population may have been as large then as it is now, but it was rapidly decimated by European diseases and Spanish swords. Several dozen Indian tribes lived in the region at the time of the Spaniards' arrival, but only seven of these exist today: the Kuna, the Ngöbe-Buglé (also known as Guaymís), the Emberá, the Wounaan, the Bokatá, the Bribri and the Naso (also known as the Teribe Indians).

The first Europeans in the area were led by the Spanish explorer Rodrigo de Bastidas, who sailed along Panama's Caribbean coast in 1501 with Vasco Núñez de Balboa and Juan de la Cosa as his first mates. The following year, Christopher Columbus sailed along the coast on his fourth and final New World voyage. An attempt by him to establish a colony at the mouth of the Río Belén in 1503 ended when he fled an imminent Indian attack.

In 1510 Diego de Nicuesa, attempting to do what Columbus couldn't, was also driven by Indians and hunger from the Río Belén. Leading a small fleet with 280 starving men aboard, the weary explorer looked upon a protected bay 23km east of what is now Portobelo and exclaimed: *'¡Paremos aqui, en nombre de Dios!'* ('Let us stop here, in the name of God!') Thus was named the town of Nombre de Dios, one of the first Spanish settlements in the continental New World. It was soon abandoned, then was resettled in 1519. For many decades thereafter, the town was the main Caribbean port for commerce along the isthmus, as well as the beginning of the trail leading to the city of Panamá on the Pacific side. Nombre de Dios was finally abandoned in 1597 by order of King Félipe II of Spain.

Nearly 300km southeast of Nombre de Dios, on the eastern side of the Golfo de Urabá in what is now Colombia, Spanish explorer Alonso de Ojeda founded San Sebastian de Urabá in 1510. Ojeda named the settlement in honor of the arrow-martyred saint whose protection the harried captain craved against the venomous darts of the natives. But the saint's protection was ineffective, and all the colonists could do was await reinforcements, which Ojeda had requested from Hispaniola.

When the rescue ship eventually reached San Sebastian, the fort and 30 houses that Ojeda had erected were in ashes and his men slain. Several of the rescue party came across Indians while foraging and were themselves struck with poisoned arrows. They died tortuous deaths that terrified the remaining would-be rescuers, who included Balboa.

Balboa had sailed with Bastidas and told the frightened men around him that the western shore of the Golfo de Urabá was fertile and rich with gold, and though the Indians there were warlike, they did not use poisoned arrows. This was great news to their ears, and the conquistadors eagerly sailed to the western side of the gulf, to the mouth of the Río Atrato. The new settlement, within present-day Colombia, was named Santa María la Antigua del Darién.

In time Indians told Balboa of a large sea and a wealthy, gold-producing civilization – almost certainly referring to the Inca empire of Peru – across the mountains of the isthmus. Balboa subsequently scaled the mountains and on September 26, 1513, became the first European to set eyes upon the Pacific, claiming it and the lands it touched for the king of Spain. He named the ocean the Mar del Sur (South Sea) because he had crossed Panama from north to south. The Caribbean was likewise known as the Mar del Norte (North Sea) for many years.

In 1519 a cruel and vindictive man named Pedro Arias de Ávila (or Pedrarias, as many of his contemporaries called him) founded the city of Panamá on the Pacific side, near where Panama City stands today. The governor is also remembered for ordering the beheading of Balboa in 1517 on a trumped-up charge of treason and for ordering murderous attacks against Indians, whom he roasted alive or fed to dogs when opportunity permitted. Panamá became an important Spanish settlement, commercial center and the springboard for further explorations, including the conquest of Peru and some expeditions north into Central America. The ruins of this old settlement, now known as Panamá La Vieja, can still be seen today.

Goods from Panamá and Peru were transported across the isthmus by foot to the town of Venta de Cruces, and then by boat from there to Nombre de Dios via the Río Chagres. This route was called the Sendero Las Cruces (Las Cruces Trail, also known as the Camino de Cruces), vestiges of which can still be found. Goods moved between the two ports until late in the 16th century, when Nombre de Dios was destroyed by the English pirate Sir Francis Drake. The small nearby bay of Portobelo then became the chief Caribbean connection. The Sendero Las Cruces continued to be used until the mid-19th century, when the Panama Railroad was completed.

Also used to transport goods across the isthmus during the early Spanish days was the Camino Real (King's Highway), a series of trails that linked Panamá with Portobelo. Indeed, from the late 16th century until the advent of the Americans in 1904, the Camino Real was the only semblance of a roadway across the isthmus. Peruvian gold and other natural products were brought to Portobelo along the Camino Real by mule train from Panamá. The products were then held for an annual trading fair that lured Spanish galleons laden with European goods.

All this wealth concentrated in one small bay naturally attracted English, French, Dutch and other pirates who were plying the Caribbean at the time. The Spaniards built large stone fortresses to try to ward off attack; the ones at Portobelo and at Fuerte San Lorenzo, at the mouth of the Río Chagres, can still be visited today.

These fortifications weren't enough, however. In 1671 the Welsh buccaneer Sir Henry Morgan overpowered Fuerte San Lorenzo, sailed up the Río Chagres and crossed the isthmus. His forces sacked the city of Panamá, making off with its entire treasure and arriving back on the Caribbean coast with 200 mules loaded with loot. The city burned down during Morgan's stay there, but no one knows for certain whether it was his men or fleeing Spaniards who put it to the torch. The town was rebuilt a few years later on a cape several kilometers west of its original site, on the spot where the Casco Viejo district of Panama City is today.

In 1739 Portobelo was destroyed by British Admiral Edward Vernon, finally forcing Spain to abandon the Panamanian crossing in favor of sailing the long way around Cape Horn to the western coast of South America. Panama declined in importance, and it eventually became part of the Viceroyalty of Nueva Andalucía, later called Nueva Granada and thereafter Colombia.

Independence

In 1821 Colombia, including Panama, gained its independence from Spanish rule. Panama joined Gran Colombia, which included Bolivia, Colombia, Ecuador, Peru and Venezuela, forming the united Latin American nation that had long been the dream of Simón Bolívar. Later Gran Colombia split up, but Panama remained a province of Colombia.

Panama Railroad

From the moment that the world's major powers learned that the isthmus of Panama was the narrowest point between the Atlantic and Pacific Oceans, they focused attention on the region.

In 1846 Colombia signed a treaty permitting the USA to construct a railway across the isthmus. The treaty guaranteed the USA rights of free transit across the isthmus and the right to protect the railway with military force. This was a time of great political turbulence in Panama. Construction of the railroad began in 1850 and concluded in 1855; during that time Panama had 20 governors.

The California gold rush of 1848, which resulted in thousands of people traveling from the East Coast of the USA to the West Coast via Panama (to avoid hostile Indians living in the central states), helped to make the railway a profitable venture, and it also spurred efforts to construct an interoceanic canal across Central America.

Panama Canal & the French

The idea of a canal across the isthmus was first broached in 1524, when King Charles V of Spain ordered that a survey be undertaken to determine the feasibility of constructing such a waterway. In 1878 the Colombian government awarded a contract to build a canal to French lieutenant Lucien NB Wyse, who sold the concession to the French diplomat Ferdinand de Lesseps, who was then basking in his success as the contractor-builder of the Suez Canal.

Lesseps' Compagnie Universelle du Canal Interocéanique began work in 1881. Lesseps was determined to build a sea-level canal alongside the interoceanic railway, but the project proved more difficult than anyone had expected. Yellow fever and malaria killed some 22,000 workers, there were insurmountable construction problems and financial mismanagement drove the company bankrupt by 1889.

One of Lesseps' chief engineers, Philippe Bunau-Varilla, formed a new canal company, but at the same time the USA was seriously considering putting its own canal somewhere through Central America. Nica-ragua seemed the most likely site, but taking over the canal in Panama was also a possibility. The French, unable to complete the canal, finally agreed to sell the concession to the USA. In 1903 Bunau-Varilla asked the Colombian government for permission to conclude the sale. Colombia refused.

Panama Becomes a Nation

Revolutionary sentiments had been brewing in Panama for many years, but repeated attempts to break away from Colombia had met with no success. In 1903 a civil war in Colombia created fresh discontent as Panamanians were drafted to fight and Panamanians' property was confiscated by the Colombian government for the war effort.

When the Colombian government refused to allow the transfer of the canal treaty to the USA, it thwarted US and French interests as well as Panama's own. Bunau-Varilla, who had a lot to gain financially if the sale went through, approached the US government to back Panama if it declared its independence from Colombia.

A revolutionary junta declared Panama independent on November 3, 1903, with the support of the USA, which immediately recognized the new government. Colombia sent troops by sea to try to regain control of the province, but US battleships prevented them from reaching land.

The First Canal Treaty

Bunau-Varilla, who became Panamanian ambassador to the USA, moved quickly to preempt the arrival in Washington, DC, of an official delegation from Panama that was slated to negotiate the terms of the canal treaty. On November 18, before the delegation arrived, he signed the Hay-Bunau-Varilla Treaty with US Secretary of State John Hay. It gave the USA far more than had been offered in the original treaty rejected by the Colombian government. The treaty's 26 articles awarded the USA 'sovereign rights in perpetuity over the Canal Zone,' an area extending 8km on either side of the canal, and a broad right of intervention in Panamanian affairs. The treaty was ratified over the Panamanian delegation's protests.

The treaty led to friction between the USA and Panama for decades, partly because it was overly favorable to the USA at the expense of Panama and partly due to lingering questions about its legality. Colombia did not recognize Panama as a legitimately separate nation until 1921, when the USA paid Colombia US$25 million in 'compensation.'

The USA Builds the Canal

Construction began again on the canal in 1904. The project, one of the greatest engineering feats in the world, was completed despite disease, landslides and many other difficulties. More than 75,000 workers took part in its construction. Canal heroes included Colonel William Crawford Gorgas, who managed a massive campaign to eliminate yellow fever and malaria, and two chief engineers, John F Stevens and Colonel George Washington Goethals. Construction took 10 years. The first ship sailed through the canal on August 15, 1914.

See the Panama Canal section in the Panamá Province chapter for more details on the canal.

Rise of the Military

The US military intervened repeatedly in Panama's political affairs until 1936, when the Hay-Bunau-Varilla Treaty was replaced by the Hull-Alfaro Treaty. The USA relinquished its rights to use its troops outside the Canal Zone and to seize land for canal purposes, and the annual sum paid to Panama for use of the Canal Zone was increased.

With the new restrictions on US military activity, the Panamanian army grew more powerful. In 1968 the Guardia Nacional deposed the elected president and took control of the government; the constitution was suspended, the national assembly was dissolved and the press censored. The Guardia's General Omar Torrijos Herrera emerged as the new leader.

Torrijos conducted public-works programs on a grand scale, including a massive modernization of Panama City, which won him the support of much of the populace but also plunged Panama into huge debt.

1977 Canal Treaty

US dominion over the Canal Zone, and the canal itself, were continuing sources of conflict between Panama and the USA. After years of negotiation that foundered in a series of stalemates, a new treaty was finally accepted by both sides in 1977. It was signed by Torrijos and US President Jimmy Carter.

The treaty provided that US control of the canal would be phased out, with Panama assuming ownership and control of the canal on December 31, 1999. It also provided for the phasing out of US military bases in Panama. In 1978 the US Senate attached extenuating conditions that grant the USA the right of limited intervention and rights to defend the canal beyond the 1999 date. The treaty finally went into effect on October 1, 1979. A separate treaty ensures that the canal shall remain open and neutral for all nations, during both peace and war.

Manuel Noriega

Torrijos was killed in a plane crash in 1981. In September 1983, after a brief period of leadership by Colonel Rubén Darío Paredes, Colonel Manuel Antonio Noriega took control of the Guardia Nacional and then of the country itself.

Noriega, a former head of Panama's secret police and a former CIA operative, quickly began to consolidate his power. He enlarged the Guardia Nacional, significantly expanded its authority and renamed it the Panama Defense Forces. He also closed down all media that criticized him, and he created a paramilitary 'Dignity Battalion' in every city,

Noriega, nicknamed The Pineapple (for his bad skin), is serving time in a Florida jail.

town and village, its members armed and ready to inform on any of their neighbors showing less than complete loyalty to the Noriega regime.

The first presidential election in 16 years was held in 1984. Although the count was challenged, Noriega's candidate, respected economist Nicolás Ardito Barletta, was declared the winner. A year later Barletta was removed by Noriega for insisting on a top-level investigation into the murder of a popular Panamanian political leader, Dr Hugo Spadafora.

In early 1987 Noriega became the center of an international scandal. He was publicly accused of involvement in drug trafficking with Colombian drug cartels, murdering his opponents and rigging elections. According to a *New York Times* article published in June 1986, he was also involved in clandestine arms trading and the sale of high-technology equipment to Cuba. Many Panamanians demanded Noriega's dismissal, protesting with general strikes and street demonstrations that resulted in violent clashes with the Panama Defense Forces.

Relations with the USA went from bad to worse. By February 1988 the USA had indicted Noriega for drug trafficking and involvement in organized crime. In the same month, Barletta's successor as president, Eric Arturo Delvalle, attempted to dismiss Noriega, but Noriega still held the reins of power, and Delvalle ended up fleeing Panama after being deposed himself. Noriega appointed a substitute president.

Noriega's regime became an international embarrassment. In March 1988 the USA imposed economic sanctions against Panama, ending a preferential trade agreement, freezing Panamanian assets in US banks and refusing to pay canal fees. Panama's international offshore banking industry, which the USA had asserted was deeply involved with drug cartels and with laundering money for organized crime, buckled under the strain of the American sanctions.

A few days after the sanctions were imposed, there was an unsuccessful military coup. Noriega responded by stepping up violent repression of his critics, including the increasing numbers of antigovernment demonstrators.

Presidential elections were held once again in May 1989. When Noriega's candidate failed to win, Noriega declared the entire election null and void. Meanwhile, Guillermo Endara, the winning candidate, and his two vice-presidential running mates were badly beaten by some of Noriega's thugs; the bloody scene was captured by a TV crew and its broadcast infuriated the nation. An attempted coup in October 1989 was followed by even more repressive measures.

On December 15, 1989, Noriega's legislature declared him president. At the same time Noriega announced that Panama was at war with the USA. The following day, an unarmed US Marine dressed in civilian clothes was killed by Panamanian soldiers.

Operation Just Cause

US reaction was swift and unrelenting. In the first hour of December 20, 1989, Panama City was attacked by aircraft, tanks and 26,000 US troops in a mission they called 'Operation Just Cause.' US President George Bush (the first one; not the current US president) said the invasion had four objectives: to protect US lives, to maintain the security of the Panama Canal, to restore democracy to Panama and to capture Noriega and bring him to justice.

Shortly before the invasion, there had been an attempt to kidnap Noriega, but he had gone into hiding. On Christmas Day, the fifth day of the invasion, he went to the Vatican nuncio to request asylum. He remained in the Vatican Embassy for 10 days. Outside, US soldiers reinforced diplomatic pressure on the Vatican to expel him by setting up loudspeakers in front of the embassy and blaring rock music to unnerve those inside. Meanwhile, angry crowds near the blocked-off embassy urged Noriega's ousting.

The chief of the Vatican Embassy finally persuaded Noriega to give himself up by threatening to cancel his asylum. Noriega surrendered to US forces on January 3, 1990. He was flown immediately to Miami, where he was tried on numerous criminal charges and convicted in April 1992 on eight charges of conspiracy to manufacture and distribute cocaine. In July 1992 he was sentenced to 40 years in prison.

Today Noriega is serving his sentence in a Florida prison. A relative of the once-arrogant dictator told Lonely Planet in early 2001 that Noriega had sunk into depression, certain that he would never again be free.

Post-Invasion Panama

After Noriega's ouster, Guillermo Endara, the legitimate winner of the 1989 election, was sworn in as president, and Panama attempted to put itself back together. The country's image and economy were in shambles, and its capital had suffered damage not only from the invasion itself but from widespread looting.

The Endara government did not turn out to be a panacea. There was public concern over Endara's involvement with the USA – which many considered excessive – his handling of the military and his inability to create economic well-being. The public was also concerned with the future of the canal.

In the next presidential election, held on May 8, 1994, Ernesto Pérez Balladares, candidate of a political alliance that included the Partido Revolucionario Democrático (Noriega's old party), won by a narrow margin. Mireya Moscoso placed a surprisingly strong second by riding a wave of loyalty toward her late husband – he was in his late 60s and she was 23 when they were married – Arnulfo Arias, a legendary autocrat who was elected president three times in the 1940s and 1960s and overthrown by the army each time (indeed, he was cheated out of a fourth victory in 1984). Rubén Blades, an internationally renowned salsa star, came in third.

During his five years in office, Pérez Balladares allocated unprecedented levels of funding for education, health care, housing projects and infrastructure improvements. The US-trained banker also attracted much-needed foreign investment. But he was widely viewed as corrupt, and in the spring of 1999 voters rejected his attempt to change constitutional limits barring a president from serving two consecutive terms.

A Female President

On May 2, 1999, Panama held its second democratic elections since the 1989 US invasion. This time Moscoso came out on top, beating Martin Torrijos, the son of strongman General Omar Torrijos. Moscoso promised to improve education, health care and housing for the 36% of Panama's 2.8 million people who live in poverty. She also vowed to generate jobs to reduce the 12.8% unemployment and 20% underemployment rates.

But even before she took power four months later, Moscoso was roundly attacked for her lack of qualifications. Indeed, she had not previously held a government office, her formal education is limited to a degree in interior design from a lowly community college, and insiders say her former husband, three-time president Arnulfo Arias, asked her to leave the room whenever he engaged in political discussions.

At the time this was written – 18 months into her presidency – Moscoso had earned the nickname 'the ribbon-cutting president' because she seemed to spend most of her time attending opening ceremonies for new businesses. She had no economic plan. Her government was strictly reactive, and her popularity had sputtered. Whether Moscoso would accomplish much during her term remained to be seen.

The Canal Changes Hands

Meanwhile, in accordance with the Carter-Torrijos treaty of 1977, in late 1999 the USA relinquished to Panama control of the world's most important shortcut. The USA also closed all of its military bases in Panama. In the first year under Panamanian control, the Panama Canal Authority reported that the average transit time for ships passing through the 80-km canal fell by almost 10 percent and the number of collisions involving transiting vessels had decreased.

However, many were the allegations that the Authority had already fallen behind on canal maintenance. What's more, forest surrounding the big ditch, which is vital to canal operations, was being cleared. Under American control, the canal watershed was strictly protected. But within year one of Panamanian control, a portion of the watershed had been carved away to build the sprawling Gamboa Rainforest Resort and another chunk was felled to add nine holes to a nine-hole golf course.

Far worse, the Moscoso government approved the request of a politically influential group to log 10,000 hectares of virgin forest within the Panama Canal's supposedly protected watershed. Timber permits such as this are often granted in return for campaign contributions, political favors or outright bribes.

As if these attacks on the watershed weren't enough, the government in 2001 was considering plans to turn over to developers a wide swath of forest near the eastern end of the canal.

In light of these ominous events only a year after Panamanians received control of the canal, they clearly were not taking the steps needed to maintain the very thing that put Panama on the world map. Indeed, due to the corruption of a few at the expense of many, they were well on their way to destroying it.

GEOGRAPHY

Panama is the southernmost of the Central American countries. It is a long, narrow country in the shape of an S, bordered on the west by Costa Rica, on the east by Colombia, on the north by a 1160km Caribbean coastline and on the south by a 1690km Pacific coastline. The total land area is 78,046 sq km. By comparison, Panama is slightly bigger than Ireland or Austria, one-fifth the size of Japan or California, more than three times the size of Belize or Israel, one-hundredth the size of Australia, and 2½ times bigger than Belgium or Vancouver Island, Canada.

While traveling about Panama, one must remember that the isthmus of the Western Hemisphere runs west to east; that Colón, on the Caribbean Sea, is not only north but also west of Panama City; and that in the capital city the sun appears to rise out of the Pacific Ocean. Most visitors, cognizant that Panama's land boundaries are *North* and *South* America, find it difficult to grasp that Panama runs west to east. As historian Tracy Robinson once said, 'There is a suspicion of something crooked about this.'

The isthmus of Panama is the narrowest landmass between the Atlantic and Pacific Oceans. At its narrowest point it is less than 50km wide. The Panama Canal, which is about 80km long, effectively divides the country into eastern and western regions. The provinces of Herrera, Los Santos and Veraguas are often referred to as the 'central provinces' or as 'the interior' – as in the interior of the country.

Two mountain chains run along Panama's spine, one in the east and one in the west. The highest point in the country is 3478m Volcán Barú, in western Chiriquí Province. Barú, Panama's only volcano, is dormant, although hot springs around its flanks testify to continuing activity under the ground.

Like all the Central American countries, Panama has large, flat coastal lowlands. In some places these lowlands are covered in huge banana plantations, particularly in the area from Changuinola to Almirante in Bocas del Toro Province. These plantations are owned by the Chiriquí Land Company, a subsidiary of the Chiquita Brands International corporation.

There are about 480 rivers in Panama that drain into the Pacific Ocean or Caribbean Sea, and 1518 islands off its coasts. The two main island groups, both in the Caribbean, are the San Blás and Bocas del Toro archipelagos, but most of Panama's islands are in fact on the Pacific side, small and often unmapped. Even the Panama Canal has islands, including Isla Barro Colorado, which is home to a world-renowned rain forest research station operated by the Smithsonian Tropical Research Institute.

GEOLOGY

The surface of the Earth is covered with 13 tectonic plates which, over many millions of years, have moved to create the planet's surface as we know it. Central America began to be formed only 20 million years ago, when the Cocos Plate began its north-eastern shift and collided with the Antilles Plate. This collision forced the edge of the Cocos Plate up and the edge of the Antilles Plate underneath it. Gradually the edge of the Cocos Plate rose from the ocean to form most of Central America.

From a geological perspective, Panama is a youngster. The country began to emerge from the sea only 3 million to 4 million years ago, and the Cocos Plate is continuing to slide over the Antilles Plate at a rate of about 10cm every year – quite fast by geological standards. The movement of one huge landmass shoving another huge landmass out of its way creates a tremendous amount of friction, which we observe in the form of earthquakes and volcanic activity throughout Central America.

The emergence of Panama created a land bridge between the American continents, which until then were separated. That bridge remained intact for at least 200,000 human generations until a wee nine decades ago, when people cut a canal across the isthmus. Before humans intervened, some mammals in South America wandered into North America and vice versa. It is because of this wandering that such originally South American creatures as armadillos, anteaters and sloths can be found in North America, and North American natives such as tapirs, jaguars and deer can be found in South America (see Flora & Fauna, later in this chapter).

CLIMATE

Most of Panama has two seasons: the dry and the rainy. On the Pacific slope of Panama – to the south of the major mountain ranges – *erano* (summer), the dry season, lasts from around mid-December to mid-April; *in ierno* (winter), the rainy season, lasts from mid-April to mid-December. Even at the height of the rainy season,

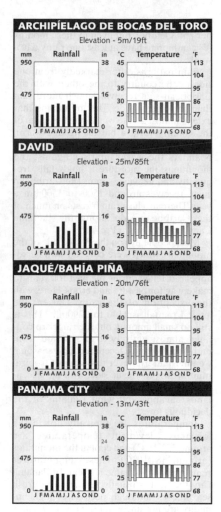

all-day rains are rare in the southern half of Panama. Typically rain arrives here in downpours lasting less than an hour.

North of the mountain ranges, on what naturalists call the 'Caribbean slope,' the climate can best be described as wet and wetter. Here, as you can see by looking at the rainfall chart for the Archipiélago de Bocas del Toro, it rains a lot all year long. There's a little letup during the months of

February and March and again in September and October, but even in these months it's common to have at least one rainy day a week.

Rain patterns differ markedly from one side of the country to the other, with the Caribbean side receiving much more rain than the Pacific side. The mountains that extend almost all the way along the spine of the country form a barrier against warm, moist trade winds that blow from the Caribbean. As the warm air rises against the mountains, the moisture it holds falls, frequently and heavily, as rain. The Caribbean coast receives around 1500 to 3500mm a year. There are lush rain forests on much of the Caribbean side, along the Panama Canal and in Darién Province.

Most people live on the Pacific side of the mountains, which were covered with deciduous forest; today that forest has all but disappeared, felled during the past 100 years to make way for pasture and crops. Here, with the exception of the rainy Darién, the annual rainfall is 1140 to 2290mm. This is still no small amount, but the rains are confined almost entirely to the period from mid-April to mid-December. This seasonal weather pattern never did support tropical rain forest; the Pacific side, with the exception of the Darién, is lined with broad grasslands, savanna and what remains of the deciduous forests.

Temperatures are typically hot in the lowlands (day/night temperatures are around 32°/21°C) and cool in the mountains (around 18°/10°C). These temperatures remain about the same all year. In Panama City the heat is usually tempered by fresh sea breezes, although periods of high humidity are not uncommon. Storm watchers will be glad to know that Panama lies below the hurricane track, though occasionally a weak tropical depression will skirt the Caribbean coast.

ECOLOGY & ENVIRONMENT

With about 30% of its total land placed in areas set aside for conservation, Panama *is* making an effort to protect some of its remaining natural resources. In fact, Panama has set aside more land for habitat protection than any other Central American country, and Panama's forests contain the greatest number of species of all the New World countries north of Colombia. But it's doubtful whether Panamanians will be able to live in harmony with their wilderness areas in the years to come.

For one thing, a significant sector of Panamanian society believes it's manly to cut down trees. If you listen in on conversations among common folk in Los Santos Province, for example, it won't be long before you overhear talk about the good old days when you could cut down trees as wide as cars. The urge to log goes well beyond economic welfare. In this province women compete with trees for men's hearts. As a result, there's hardly a patch of forest remaining there, and the *hombres* are so anxious to fell more trees that they're moving to the Darién, where big trees still abound.

Additionally, Panama's national parks are staffed by few park rangers, and many of the rangers aren't given patrol vehicles or radios, although their areas of coverage are colossal. In Parque Nacional Darién, for instance, there are never more than 20 rangers assigned to protect 576,000 hectares – an area larger than some countries. These rangers are unarmed, poorly paid and spend most of the day trying to figure out what they are going to eat for dinner. Meanwhile illegal hunting, settling and logging take place in their park. Unless the Panamanian government gets serious, it may not be long before the country's 'protected' areas are nothing more than paper parks.

Environmental Problems

Deforestation The major problem facing the nation's environment is deforestation. Panama's natural vegetation was originally almost all forest, but most of this has been cleared, mainly for pasture and agriculture. The destruction of a rain forest not only wipes out the animals that had inhabited it but also kills many migratory animals (among them bats, butterflies and birds) who move with their seasonal food supplies.

Tree plantations are being developed nationwide, and as the trees mature the availability of commercially grown timber will lessen the pressure to log natural forests. But by the time these trees are ready for harvesting (between 2015 and 2020), the destruction will be done; at the current rate of deforestation, less than 20% of Panama's natural forests will exist by the year 2005.

Moreover, even the land that has been set aside for preservation is under attack. Inadequate funding, indifference and corruption have allowed logging and hunting to occur virtually unabated in supposedly protected areas. Also, laws prohibiting the killing of endangered animals are not enforced and are widely ignored; *tortuga* (sea turtle) often appears on Panamanian menus, for example, and some restaurants and hotels display jaguars, ocelots and margays in tiny cages, knowing that the agency responsible for apprehending perpetrators of such crimes likely won't intervene.

Soil Erosion Deforestation has resulted in yet another serious problem for Panama: soil erosion. Huge, exposed tree roots prevent heavy rains from washing away the thin layer of nutrient-rich topsoil found in tropical forests. Take out the trees and the next big storm to hit the denuded area will carry the topsoil into rivers and out to sea, leaving only the nutrient-deficient lower soil where the vibrant jungle once stood.

When you consider that 50% of the country's soil is of poor quality to begin with and that 75% of it is on hillsides, the seriousness of the problem becomes apparent. And yet ranchers, who have deforested most of the Pacific slope from the Costa Rican border to Yaviza, are still allowed to clearcut forest to create pasture for their cattle.

Water Pollution Panama has some serious water-pollution problems. They are most apparent in and around Panama City and Colón – areas where 90% of Panamanians live. Most of the sewage from these cities is discharged untreated directly into coastal waters or canals that flow through the cities. Skin afflictions among children who swim in the Bahía de Panamá are common. Regardless, the efforts by Panama City Mayor Juan Carlos Navarro to construct a new water-treatment plant next to the bay were stymied by a national agency.

The water-pollution crisis is also evident in the central provinces, where rivers are widely used as garbage dumps. Likewise, throughout the Archipiélago de San Blás, the Kuna Indians view the ocean around them as a natural toilet and build their outhouses on the water. In sharp contrast with the common belief that Indians are environmentalists, the Kunas think nothing of tossing cans, bottles and plastic containers into the sea.

Heartless Fishing Practices Countries worldwide have increasingly adopted tuna fishing methods that do not kill dolphins, but Panama isn't one of them. Indeed, despite a US ban on imports of Panamanian yellowfin tuna because of Panama's dolphin-killing practices, the country refuses to join Mexico and other Latin American countries in this area.

Worse than the country's atrocious tuna-catching practices are its widespread use of drag nets. If you ever have the chance to be on a Panamanian boat that uses drag nets, you will witness the following: An enormous net is lowered from the deck to the sea floor and dragged along it for an hour or so, then pulled back onto the deck. As the net is brought up, everything it trapped as it raked the ocean floor spills onto the deck. From this haul the crew sorts out commercially valuable creatures such as large fish, lobsters and large crabs, and everything else – usually about 80% of the catch – dies in the hot sun before the crew shovels it back into the sea.

Mangrove Destruction Another major environmental problem in Panama today is the destruction of mangrove swamps, which play an important role in stemming beach erosion and in maintaining balance in delicate marine ecosystems. Mangrove destruction also takes a heavy toll on the country's important seafood industry, because many species of fish need mangrove swamps to survive. Regardless, mangroves throughout Panama are being cut down to make room for shrimp farms, resorts and urban development. Red-mangrove bark, which is used by the tanning industry, is being exported to Costa Rica, where harvesting of the bark is prohibited.

Conservation Organizations

The Panamanian government has forbidden development on about one-third of the country's land, which is good, and it has given responsibility for protection of that land to the Autoridad Nacional de Ambiente (ANAM; National Environmental Authority), which is bad. As manager of Panama's national park system, ANAM has proved impotent at curbing encroachment on the parks by squatters and at preventing logging and hunting within them.

In its defense, ANAM faces some major obstacles in its role as protector of lands set aside for conservation. For one thing, many of these lands were inhabited at the time they were designated protected areas, and

those inhabitants were permitted to stay where they were despite the many inherent problems associated with allowing people to live in environmentally sensitive regions.

But one of ANAM's functions is the allocation of unprotected state lands for private uses, and in this capacity the agency's record is indefensible. The agency still allows loggers, ranchers and settlers to fell rain forest, despite the now widely known environmental damage that results. Furthermore, Panamanian law states that logging companies must plant trees to replace the ones they cut down, but in reality this is seldom done; it is a law that ANAM is supposed to enforce.

As impotent as ANAM is today, it is better than it would be if not for the private Asociación Nacional para la Conservación de la Naturaleza (ANCON; National Association for the Conservation of Nature; ☎ 314-0060, fax 314-0061, ancon@ancon.com, www.ancon.org), Apartado 1387, Panamá 1, República de Panamá. Founded in 1985 by academic and business leaders, Ancon has played a major role in

Panama's Marvelous Mangroves

If you have the good fortune of visiting either of Panama's coasts, you're likely too see stretches of mangrove, which is the common name applied to several kinds of tropical trees and shrubs belonging to three families that flourish in brackish water or shallow, muddy salt water. All three families of mangrove abound in Panama.

Mangrove swamps (also called mangrove forests, or shortened to mangroves) are easy to spot due to their tangled masses of arching roots and, typically, their location along beachless shorelines and in estuaries. For years Panama's Indians used to chop down mangrove trees for charcoal, but today it is illegal to fell these trees in most parts of the country. That's because mangrove forests, by acting as a barrier between waves and shoreline, prevent erosion, and because they are home to many species of bird and reptile, including boa constrictors, alligators and crocodiles (all of which can also be found in Panama). Sure, windswept beaches are lovely, but for wildlife lovers, no beach can compare to a healthy mangrove swamp.

the creation of national parks and on many occasions has spurred ANAM into action.

In addition, with money donated primarily by US conservation groups and wealthy Panamanians, ANCON has purchased several large tracts of rain forest for preservation. Through a subsidiary, Ancon Expeditions of Panama, it is making these and other biologically rich areas more accessible to tourists; without question, the country's finest nature guides work for Ancon Expeditions. It also organizes nationwide litter-removal campaigns and sponsors programs that show farmers how they can utilize their land in a sustainable manner.

Panama's many less significant conservation organizations include the Student Association for the Conservation of the Environment (ACECAP) and the Project for the Study and Management of Wild Areas of the Kuna Yala (PEMASKY). The student group's main achievement has been successfully pressuring the government to protect two endangered areas along the Caribbean coast. PEMASKY is a grassroots movement led by the Kuna, and its primary aim is to prevent outsiders from settling on their land.

FLORA & FAUNA

Panama's position as a narrow land bridge between two huge continents has given it a remarkable variety of plant and animal life. Its great biodiversity is directly attributable to the fact that it is home to North and Central American species at their southernmost range and South American species at their northernmost range.

Panama's geographical position also makes it a crossroads for migratory birds. Out of the country's 940 recorded bird species, 122 occur only as long-distance migrants (that is, they don't breed in Panama). These migrants can be amazing to watch. As this was penned in a hotel room in Panama City in November, literally millions of hawks passed overhead en route to South America. There are so many hawks that they made a black streak across an otherwise blue sky.

The migration of turkey vultures over the islands of Bocas del Toro in early March and again in October is another striking sight. These big, black-bodied, red-necked birds can streak the sky and are able to soar for long periods without a single flap as they migrate between southern Canada and Tierra del Fuego.

Panama's biodiversity is also a product of the size of its wilderness regions. Jaguars and cougars, for example, need large tracts of forest to survive. Without them, the big cats gradually exhaust their food supply and perish. In Panama there are no fewer than five protected areas large enough to sustain jaguar and cougar populations. Just how big are these areas? In the Darién and La Amistad parks, for instance, you can hike in one direction for a week and not cross a road.

Additionally, Panama has no fewer than 125 animal species found nowhere else in the world; these endemic species include 56 types of freshwater fish, 25 types of amphibian, 22 types of reptile, 12 types of mammal and 10 types of bird.

Panama's offshore waters host a fascinating assortment of creatures. Reefs are found off both coasts, and aquatic species in Panamanian waters include jack, snappers, jewfish, eel, sailfish, sea bass, puffer fish, rays, lobsters, caimans and octopi. Visitors to the national marine parks might spot humpback whales, reef sharks, bottlenose dolphins, or killer or sperm whales. Sea turtles, whale sharks and white-tip sharks also visit.

Tropical rain forest is the dominant vegetation in the canal area, along the Caribbean coast and in most of the eastern half of the country. Parque Nacional Darién protects much of Panama's largest tropical rain forest region. Other vegetation zones include grassland on the Pacific coast, mountain forest in the highlands, alpine vegetation on the highest peaks and mangrove forest on both coasts and around many islands.

Endangered Species

According to the World Conservation Monitoring Centre, there are at least 105 species threatened with extinction within Panama.

Among the animals appearing on its 'red list' for Panama are the jaguar, the spectacled bear, the Central American tapir, the American crocodile, all five species of sea turtle that nest on Panamanian beaches, and dozens of birds, including several eagle species and the military and scarlet macaws.

The Panamanian legislature has implemented laws to curb illegal hunting and logging, but the laws are widely ignored due to an absence of enforcement. For example, keeping a parrot, toucan or macaw in a cage is a fineable offense in Panama. Yet not only can you see them in cages outside many residences, but many hotel managers apparently believe that tourists enjoy seeing large tropical birds in itty-bitty cages.

You can help reduce the threat to Panama's endangered species. If you see caged animals at a hotel, complain to the manager, take your business elsewhere and report the crime to ANCON (☎ 314-0060). Also, please don't eat *tortuga* (sea turtle), *hue os de tortuga* (turtle eggs), *cazón* (shark), *conejo pintado* (paca), *ñeque* (agouti), *enado* (deer) or iguana if you see them on a menu.

Obviously, buying jaguar teeth, ocelot skins or objects made from turtle shells directly contributes to these animals' extinction. If a sense of moral outrage doesn't stop you from considering such a purchase, you might like to know that the penalty for trying to leave Panama with any of these products is a fine typically accompanied by jail time.

NATIONAL PARKS

The development of wildlife sanctuaries in Panama began in 1966 with the establishment of the Parque Nacional Altos de Campana. It was not until 1975 that a second park was created. Today Panama has 11 national parks and more than two dozen other officially protected areas (see details below in the Other Protected Areas section).

To enter a national park, travelers must pay US$3 (US$10 if it's a national marine park) at ANAM headquarters, at a regional ANAM office or at an ANAM ranger station inside the park being visited. ANAM has its headquarters (☎ 315-0855 or 315-0903) inside Building 804 in the Albrook district of Panama City; Spanish and some English are spoken.

Permits to stay at an ANAM ranger station or to camp in a national park can be obtained at the headquarters, regional offices or an ANAM ranger station. If you believe you'll be visiting numerous national parks, you would be wise to obtain permits for them all at once at ANAM's headquarters; this can save you headaches later, as the regional offices are often closed.

The cost of the permits varies. A permit for camping in an ANAM-protected area or to stay at an ANAM ranger station is US$5 per night. However, ANAM also maintains four scientific stations – at Boca Chica (Chiriquí Province), Cayo Zapatilla Sur (Bocas del Toro Province), Isla de Coiba (Veraguas Province) and Pirre (Darién Province) – and the cost of a permit to stay at any of them is US$10 per night.

Generally, food is not available for visitors at the ranger stations; if you intend to eat, you should bring food with you. If the food requires cooking, most rangers are happy to cook for you for a tip (US$2 per person per meal is most appreciated). You'd be wise to bring extra food and a six-pack of beer for the rangers. After all, if they like you they'll be more willing to help you in the event you need help.

Panama's national parks, from west to east, are as follows:

Parque Nacional Volcán Barú – This park contains the giant Barú volcano, which soars to the highest elevation in Panama (3478m above sea level). From its usually cloud-shrouded summit, it is occasionally possible to glimpse the Pacific Ocean and the Caribbean Sea. The resplendent quetzal, a world-class find, is here. Endemic bird species include the volcano junco and the baru burbit. Access is from Boquete and Volcán. (14,300 hectares, Chiriquí Province)

Parque Nacional Coiba – This remote park protects marine and coastal ecosystems in an almost virgin setting. It is the last refuge in Panama for the scarlet macaw, and the waters around the island are breeding grounds for several species of whale. Visitors' movements are restricted due to the presence of a penal colony on the island. (270,000 hectares, of which 216,543 are oceanic; Veraguas Province)

Parque Nacional Cerro Hoya – This park, on the southwestern side of the Península de Azuero, protects the headwaters of three rivers. It also protects many endemic plant species and animals like the carato parakeet. Within the confines of the park is some of the last remaining forest on the peninsula. (32,577 hectares, Veraguas and Los Santos Provinces)

Parque Nacional Omar Torrijos – Near the center of the isthmus, this park includes cloud forest, rubber trees and the watersheds of the Ríos Bermejo, Marta, Blanco, Guabal and Lajas. It's of particular interest to ecotourists for its foothill birds and golden frogs. There are some fine hiking opportunities near the summit. Access is from the town of El Copé. (6000 hectares, Coclé and Colón Provinces)

Parque Nacional Sarigua – On the northeastern side of the Península de Azuero, this park contains some dry forest, salt marsh and mangrove swamps, and an archaeological zone. With its salt pans, windblown sand and cacti, most of the park resembles desert, but it's not; Sarigua receives more than a meter of rain each year. Instead, what you will see here is environmental devastation – the product of overgrazing, loss of topsoil and erosion. Access is from Chitré. (8000 hectares, Herrera Province)

Parque Nacional y Reser a Biológica Altos de Campana – This park protects two watersheds, the Río Sajalices, which empties into the Pacific, and the Ríos Cirí and Trinidad, which flow into the Río Chagres basin, the water catchment system for the Panama Canal. Endemic species include Panama's famous golden frogs, the common vampire bat and the colored rabbit, a local variety of wild rabbit. There's also a great variety of native conifers. Picturesque cliffs abound. (4816 hectares, Panamá Province)

Parque Nacional Soberanía – Also protecting the watershed of the Panama Canal, this park contains excellent hiking trails, including the famous Camino del Oleoducto (Pipeline Road), one of the world's top birding sites, and the short Sendero El Charco nature trail. At last count 525 species of bird and 105 species of mammal, including the jaguar, resided here. Morpho butterflies are common in this park. Access is from Panama City. (22,104 hectares, Colón Province)

Parque Nacional Portobelo – East of Colón, this World Heritage Site protects 70km of coastal areas with rich coral reefs, and the ruins of the historic Spanish forts and of the settlement at Portobelo. In colonial times it was the site of storehouses for gold and silver stolen from the Inca empire. It was here that Spanish galleons loaded on treasure for their voyage back to Europe. Access is from Colón. (35,929 hectares, Colón Province)

Parque Nacional Camino de Cruces – On the old Camino Real – the cobblestone road by which stolen Peruvian gold was taken on its way to Spain – this park forms an ecological corridor connecting Parque Nacional Soberanía and Parque Natural Metropolitano. There are waterfalls and a great variety of flora and fauna, including marmosets, armadillos, green iguanas and three-toed sloths. Access is from Panama City. (4000 hectares, Panamá Province)

Parque Nacional Chagres – This park preserves the main watershed of the Panama Canal. About 80% of the water needed for the canal's operation and all of the drinking water for Panama City comes from this watershed. The park includes the Río Chagres, Lago Alajuela, much of El Camino Real and traditional settlements of the Emberá. This park is also the site of elfin forests. Access is from Panama City. (129,000 hectares, Panamá Province)

Parque Nacional Darién – A UNESCO World Heritage Site and a biosphere reserve, Panama's largest national park contains the greatest tropical rain forest wilderness in Central America and forms an effective barrier between Panama and Colombia. At its heart is Cana, a former mining valley that is the top birding site in Central America. Access to the park is by air or trail from El Real, Yaviza and other places; no roads lead into or out of Cana. (576,000 hectares, Darién Province)

Additional details on many of these national parks can be found in the regional chapters.

OTHER PROTECTED AREAS

In addition to the national parks, there are 27 other areas under ANAM management. These include: two national marine parks, seven wildlife refuges, five forest reserves, three wetlands, two natural monuments, one natural recreation area, one recreation area, one wilderness area, one biological corridor, one hydroelectric forest reserve, one nature park, one nature reserve and one protected forest. Additionally, Panama shares an international park with Costa

NATIONAL PARKS & OTHER PROTECTED AREAS

1 Parque Internacional La Amistad
2 Humedal de San-San Pond Sak
3 Bosque Protector de Palo Seco
4 Parque Nacional Marino Isla Bastimentos
5 Humedal Lagunas de Volcán
6 Parque Nacional Volcán Barú
7 Reserva Forestal Fortuna
8 Refugio de Vida Silvestre Playa de La Barqueta Agrícola
9 Parque Nacional Marino Golfo de Chiriquí
10 Refugio de Vida Silvestre Playa Boca Vieja
11 Área Natural Recreativa Salto de Las Palmas
12 Reserva Forestal La Laguna de La Yeguada
13 Monumento Natural de Los Pozos de Calobre
14 Parque Nacional Omar Torrijos
15 Parque Nacional Coiba
16 Humedal El Golfo de Montijo
17 Reserva Forestal El Montuoso
18 Refugio de Vida Silvestre Cenegón del Mangle
19 Parque Nacional Sarigua
20 Parque Nacional Cerro Hoya
21 Reserva Forestal La Tronosa
22 Refugio de Vida Silvestre Isla de Cañas

Rica. From west to east, these protected areas are:

Parque Internacional La Amistad – Shared by Panama and Costa Rica, this park contains seven of the 12 classified life zones, with great biodiversity and numerous endemic species. Quetzals and harpy eagles reside here. It is also home to members of three indigenous groups and is a UNESCO World Heritage Site. The park can be entered from the Río Teribe near Changuinola and Las Nubes near Cerro Punta. (407,000 hectares, Bocas del Toro and Chiriquí Provinces)

Bosque Protector de Palo Seco – The Palo Seco protected forest joins Parque Internacional La Amistad, Parque Nacional Volcán Barú and the Reserva Forestal Fortuna as part of the large complex of protected area established specifically to serve as a refuge for Panama's Caribbean slopes and the plants and animals that live there. Access is difficult and there are no tourist facilities. (244,000 hectares, Bocas del Toro Province)

Humedal Lagunas de Volcán – These wetlands consist of lagoons in the area of Volcán Barú in the highlands of Chiriquí Province and they represent the highest marsh ecosystem in Panama. In the native forest adjacent to the wetland, birdwatchers will want to remain hawk-eyed for the rose-throated becard and the pale-billed woodpecker. Access is from Volcán or David. (143 hectares, Chiriquí Province)

NATIONAL PARKS & OTHER PROTECTED AREAS

23	Refugio de Vida Silvestre Peñón de la Honda
24	Refugio de Vida Silvestre Isla Iguana
25	Parque Nacional Portobelo
26	Área Recreativa Lago Gatún
27	Parque Nacional Chagres
28	Área Silvestre de Narganá
29	Monumento Natural Isla Barro Colorado
30	Parque Nacional Soberanía
31	Parque Nacional Camino de Cruces
32	Parque Natural Metropolitano
33	Parque Nacional y Reserva Biológica Altos de Campana
34	Refugio de Vida Silvestre Islas Taboga y Urabá
35	Reserva Natural Punta Patiño
36	Reserva Hidológica Serranía Filo del Tallo
37	Reserva Forestal Canglón
38	Corredor Biológico de la Serranía Bagre
39	Parque Nacional Darién

Refugio de Vida Sil estre Playa de La Barqueta Agrícola – The welfare of nesting birds and sea turtles spurred conservation-minded Panamanians to keep the beaches and mangroves in this part of western Panama beyond the reach of land developers. (5935 hectares, Chiriquí Province)

Humedal de San-San Pond Sak – This wetland along the western end of Panama's Caribbean coast contains lush swamps and long stretches of beach used by no fewer than four species of sea turtles. It's a terrific place for adventurous souls who have a sense of humor. See the Bocas del Toro Province chapter for details. Access is from Changuinola. (16,125 hectares, Bocas del Toro Province)

Parque Nacional Marino Golfo de Chiriquí – On and around Isla Parida, the Golfo de Chiriquí marine park protects insular, marine and coastal areas. It is used as a nesting site by five species of sea turtle and the scarlet macaw. Several species of monkey inhabit Isla Boca Brava, which borders the park. Snorkeling and diving here can be excellent. Access is from Boca Chica. (14,740 hectares, Chiriquí Province)

Reser a Forestal Fortuna – This mountainous forest reserve was established to ensure a steady flow of rain runoff for the Fortuna hydroelectric plant, which generates about 30% of Panama's electricity. Situated on the Pacific slope with a picturesque lake in the middle of it, this forest reserve consists chiefly of premontane rain forest and montane rain forest, ie, it's usually cloudy and very wet up there. There are no less than 70 known amphibians and reptiles there, as well as 1136 plant species. Access is an hour's drive from David. (19,500 hectares, Chiriquí Province)

Parque Nacional Marina Isla Bastimentos – On the Caribbean coast of western Panama, the Isla Bastimentos marine park conserves marine and coastal ecosystems, including wetlands, mangrove swamps, coral reefs, white-sand beaches and more than 200 species of tropical fish. The diving and snorkeling here are excellent when the visibility is good – about half the time. Access is from Bocas del Toro town on Isla Colón. (13,235 hectares, of which 1639 hectares are of land on Isla Bastimentos and 11,596 hectares are marine zones, Bocas del Toro Province)

Refugio de Vida Sil estre Playa Boca Vieja – Sea turtles were the main reason the government took particular interest in protecting the beaches, mangrove swamps and coast in the Remedios area of Chiriquí Province. Turtles tend to arrive in the area in large numbers from May through September to lay their eggs in the sand. (3740 hectares, Chiriquí Province)

Área Natural Recreati a Salto de Las Palmas – This little natural recreation area consists of a very-seldom-visited waterfall that's quite lovely. At the base of the forest-flanked falls is a fine swimming pool. Due to the steep and poorly maintained road leading to it, visitors should anticipate about a fairly sloping 100m walk to it. *Salto* means 'waterfall,' the site has nothing to do with salt. (One hectare, Veraguas Province)

Humedal El Golfo de Montijo – This large wetlands is internationally recognized for its importance to many species of water birds that visit the area during lengthy north-south migrations. (89,452 hectares, Veraguas Province)

Reser a Forestal La Laguna de La Yeguada – This forest reserve was established to permit a steady flow of rain runoff to work its way down to a large hydroelectric project. And indeed there's still a good amount of native forest in the area, but most of the original forest is gone and in its place are thousands of pine trees planted by the government. (7090 hectares, Veraguas Province)

Reser a Forestal El Montuoso – This forest reserve was created to protect the watershed serving the vast agricultural region below it, but that hasn't kept lots of people from moving in and felling many trees. In the jargon of psychiatrists and environmentalists, this reserve is very disturbed. (10,375 hectares, Herrera Province)

Monumento Natural de Los Pozos de Calobre – Los Pozos means 'the springs,' as in hot thermal springs, and this natural monument was established to ensure that anyone who wanted to gaze upon them, could. These occasionally hot springs are given names that grossly exaggerate their personalities, such Cañon del Tigre (canyon of the tiger) and La Gloria (the glory). (3.5 hectares, Veraguas Province)

Reser a Forestal La Tronosa – This forest reserve near Parque Nacional Cerro Hoya protects the headwaters and hydrographic basin of the Río Tonosí. Though very disturbed by farmers, hunters and settlers, it continues to conserve some of the fauna and flora found in the southern portion of the Azuero Peninsula. (20,579 hectares, Los Santos Province)

Refugio de Vida Sil estre Cenegón del Mangle – What this coastal wildlife refuge lacks in size it makes up for in character. There, most any time of year, visitors can expect to see scores of migratory birds roosting in mangrove trees and feeding in wetlands. (776 hectares, Herrera Province)

Refugio de Vida Sil estre Isla de Cañas – In his excellent book 'Panama: National Parks,' Panama City Mayor Juan Carlos Navarro states that 'Cañas Island is the most important nesting site for sea turtles in Panama and one of the most important in the American Pacific. Every year about 30,000 turtles return to its beaches to lay their eggs.' This author isn't going to argue with the mayor, who is also one of Panama's chief conservationists. See the Los Santos Province chapter for details on visiting the island. (25,453 hectares, Los Santos Province)

Refugio de Vida Sil estre Peñón de la Honda -The main feature of this island refuge is, well, the Peñón (rock) at its heart. Many thousands of birds nest on the thing, including great egrets, snowy egrets and cattle egrets. It's a wonder it wasn't named Egret Refuge, but there you have it. In addition to the rock and its nests, the refuge keeps out of man's way lots of mangrove swamp, plenty of beaches and dunes, and even some thermal waters. (3900 hectares, Los Santos Province)

Refugio de Vida Sil estre Isla Iguana – This nesting site popular with sea turtles and water birds was once used for target practice by the US Navy. Unexploded bombs are still being found on it from time to time, so it's best not to stray from the few trails on the small island. Some fine (and some rather beaten-up) coral reefs can be found in the vicinity of this wildlife sanctuary. (53 hectares, Los Santos Province)

Monumento Natural Isla Barro Colorado – This monument consists of the most-studied tropical forests in the world. Administered by the Smithsonian Tropical Research Institute and located near the midway point of the Panama Canal, Isla Barro Colorado was formed when the Río Chagres was dammed back in 1914 to create Lago Gatún, which in turn permits the canal to operate. It's teeming with wildlife and important ecological experiments and is open to visitors. (5346 hectares, Panamá Province).

Área Recreati a Lago Gatún – This recreational area was created in 1914 with water diverted from the Río Chagres, forming a giant reservoir that ensures the working of the massive sluices of the Panama Canal. Today, the lake offers pretty fine fishing, and the lakeside offers protected moist tropical forest. (348 hectares, Colón Province)

Refugio de Vida Sil estre Islas Taboga y Urabá – The wildlife refuge protects the southern section of Isla Taboga and all of Isla Urabá. Its chief purpose is to protect the nesting sites of brown pelicans, as well as other plants and animals that call these little islands home. Access is from Panama City. (258 hectares, Panamá Province)

Parque Natural Metropolitano – This park, 15 minutes' drive from central Panama City, has nature trails and is the site of scientific tropical rain forest research. Although close to the city, it is home to more than 250 species of bird and 40 species of mammal. The view from atop Cerro Mono Tití is spectacular, offering a panoramic vista of the city, the port of Balboa and neighboring Parque Nacional Camino de Cruces. (265 hectares, Panamá Province)

Área Sil estre de Narganá – This large wildlife reserve was created and is administered by the Kuna people who inhabit the coastline and islands within the Comarca de San Blás. While Parque Nacional Darién is widely regarded as offering the best birding in Panama, Narganá often comes in a close second. There, birders will want to keep their binocs trained for the black-crowned antpitta, the speckled antshrike and, of course, the red-throated caracara. (98,999 hectares, Comarca de San Blás)

Reser a Forestal Canglón – The Canglón Forest Reserve is, like many of Panama's forests, under attack from loggers. But while much of the 'reserve' has been felled, some fairly spectacular lowland tropical forest can still been seen here, including the vast flooded wetlands that border the Río Tuira, Panama's longest river. (31,650 hectares, Darién Province)

Corredor Biológico de la Serranía de Bagre – This is perhaps the most important biological corridor in Central America, ensuring that thousands of species are able to move back and forth between Parque Nacional Darién and the Reserva Natural Punta Patiño. In other words, creatures that need to migrate between the two enormous reserves to find food are able to do so because some folks in the government elected to protect the wilderness in between. (31,275 hectares, Darién Province)

Reser a Hidológica Serranía Filo del Tallo – Much of the forest in northern Darién Province has been felled by greedy loggers, but this forest reserve serving a hydroelectric plant is still very much intact. It was this forest that explorer Vasco Nuñez de Balboa crossed in 1513 on his way to finding the reputed Southern Sea, which he spied and renamed the Pacific Ocean. (24,722 hectares, Darién Province)

In addition to the areas administered by ANAM, there are several vast areas owned and protected by the private environmental group Ancon. The largest of these is the 26,315-hectare Reserva Natural Punta Patiño, Panama's first private nature preserve. In Darién Province, it harbors a variety of ecosystems: mangrove swamps, beaches, dry land forests, rain forests and cloud forests. See the Darién Province chapter for more details on the preserve.

Panama also has one *parque municipal* (municipal park), the Summit Botanical Gardens & Zoo (46 hectares, Panamá Province). Lastly, commercial fishing is not allowed in Bahía Piña, which is home to some of the world's finest sport fishing.

GOVERNMENT & POLITICS

Panama is governed as a constitutional democracy. The executive branch is led by a president, elected by popular vote to a five-year term. The president is assisted by two elected vice presidents and an appointed cabinet.

The victory of Mireya Moscoso in 1999 marked the first time in Panamanian history that a woman held the highest office in the land. Her campaign promises to improve the lives of the poor had created expectations that, at the time this was penned, 18 months into her presidency, she was having a difficult time fulfilling.

The legislative assembly has 72 members, also elected by popular vote to five-year

PROVINCES OF PANAMA

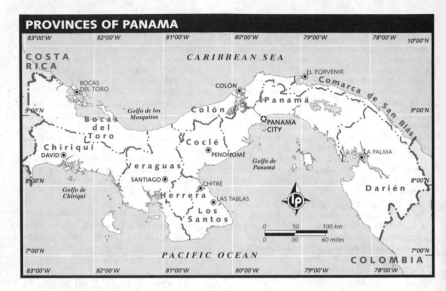

terms. The judiciary consists of a nine-member supreme court, appointed to 10-year terms by the president and approved by the legislature and various lower courts.

Panama consists of nine provinces and an autonomous region – the Kuna Yala, also known as the Comarca de San Blás – governed by Kuna tribal leaders, or *caciques*. Each province has a governor appointed by the president, and each is divided into municipal districts.

ECONOMY

At US$3070 per worker per year, Panama has the highest per-capita income of the Central American countries, but half of its households still do not have enough income to meet their basic living needs. Critical poverty (income insufficient to buy the basic food basket) affects about one-third of households, according to the World Bank. Unemployment hovers around 13%, while underemployment lingers around 20%.

Moreover, Panama's income distribution is extremely skewed. The disparity between rich and poor is obvious in the country's two largest cities. Panama City is home to both a financial district of gleaming sky-scrapers *and* two slummy districts (Chorrillo and Calidonia) that are unsafe to walk at night. The contrast is even more striking between Colón's free-trade zone and the poverty that lies just outside the zone's walls.

On the day she became president (September 1, 1999), Mireya Moscoso told the inaugural crowd, 'I promise today that together we will wipe out poverty in our Panama.' Yet less than a year later she rejected cries from labor unions to decree a minimum monthly wage of US$500. Panama's minimum wage varies according to location and industry, but for Panama City industrial workers, for example, the raise imposed by Moscoso amounted to only 14¢ an hour, or a pay hike from US$224.64 to $253.76 per month. So much for taking a major step toward narrowing the money gap.

According to a World Bank report released in April 2000, 'disparities in education cause most of the poverty, malnutrition and inequality' in Panama. Yet in the summer of 2000 a court voided a law prohibiting the reduction of the University of Panama's budget from one year to the next. When 5000 of the university's students and

Toucan, Darién Province

Kuna girl with friend, Comarca de San Blás

Beware the poison-dart frog, Bocas del Toro Province

Girl with pet parrot, Bocas del Toro Province

'¿Hablas español?' blue and gold macaw

Stream in the Pirre Mountains, Darién Province

Heliconia flower, Bocas del Toro Province

Rubber tree, Darién Province

View from the Río Sambú, Darién Province

An idyllic beach in the Comarca de San Blás

professors led by the rector marched on the presidential palace in protest of the ruling, neither Moscoso nor her education minister would meet with the rector.

The structure of Panama's economy is heavily weighted toward services (chiefly banking, commerce and tourism), which account for a whopping 76.5% of the country's gross domestic product. Industry makes up 16.5% of the GDP, while agriculture comprises 7%.

The Panamanian economy was faltering at the time this was penned on account of the loss of revenue (about US$300 million annually) that accompanied the withdrawal of US soldiers from Panama in 1998 and 1999. The country's leading exports – bananas and shrimp – were way down on account of a worldwide glut of bananas and a disease that plagued Panamanian shrimp, and an unexplained decline in tourism also exacted heavy tolls.

POPULATION & PEOPLE

Panama's population was 2,839,177 in 2000, based on a census taken that year (all population figures in this book are based on the 2000 census). The majority of the population (65%) are *mestizos* of mixed indigenous and Spanish descent, but there are also a number of other sizable groups. Blacks make up 14% of the population, whites comprise 10% and Indians 10%.

The blacks are mostly descendants of English-speaking West Indians, such as Jamaicans and Trinidadians, who were brought to Panama as cheap labor on various projects. West Indians worked on banana plantations in Bocas del Toro Province during the late 19th century and first half of the 20th, the transisthmian railway in the 1850s, the French canal project in the 1880s and the US construction of the canal from 1904 to 1914. Many Panamanian blacks speak English and Spanish; on the islands of Bocas del Toro many also speak Patois, a blend of English, Spanish and Gali-Gali (a local dialect).

Of the several dozen Indian tribes that inhabited Panama when the Spanish arrived, seven now remain: the Kuna, the Guaymís (or Ngöbé-Buglé), the Emberá, the Wounaan, the Bokatá, the Bribri and the Teribe (or Naso). Each of these groups maintains its own language and culture. The Guaymís number about 125,000 and are Panama's largest tribe; the Kuna, who govern their ancestral territory as the autonomous region of the Comarca de San Blás and send representatives to the legislature, are the most politically organized.

EDUCATION

Panama's educational system is composed of elementary, secondary and university levels, each lasting six years. Officially, education is compulsory for six years between the ages of six and 15. Actual enrollment in elementary school is high (over 90%), but there's a drop-off at the secondary level (about 50% enrollment). Education is free up to the university level.

According to 2000 figures, the most current that were available at the time of writing, the median number of years spent in school by the typical adult Panamanian was 6.7. The illiteracy rate was said to be 8% nationwide, but a staggering 50% among the country's indigenous populations.

Education for students with disabilities is the responsibility of the Panamanian Institute of Special Rehabilitation. Among the many schools under its authority are the National School for the Deaf, the Special Education School, the Helen Keller School for the Blind, the School for Premature Growth and the Vocational School.

Panama has three primary universities: the Universidad de Panamá, the Technological University and the Universidad Santa María la Antigua. All three offer programs in the arts and sciences and offer bachelor's and master's degrees, with total enrollment ranging from approximately 32,000 students at the Universidad de Panamá to 6100 students at Universidad Santa María la Antigua.

In addition, there are foreign-run universities – La Universidad del Istmo of Colombia and the Universidad Latinoamericana de Ciencia y Tecnología of Costa Rica – with campuses in Panama.

Two Florida-based universities also teach courses in Panama, though on a much more limited basis: Florida State University and Nova University.

Despite the abundance of universities in Panama and their affordability (tuition at the Universidad de Panamá, for example, is a mere US$30 per semester), most Panamanians who can afford to and have good grades attend universities in the USA.

Besides the universities, higher education is offered in educational centers such as the International Banking Institute, the Institute of Management, the Center for Higher Management Studies, the Hotel and Tourism College, the Nautical School of Panama and the National Agriculture Institute.

ARTS

Panama's arts scene reflects its ethnic mix. A slow spin on the radio dial or a hard look at Panamanian nightclubs will reveal salsa, Latin and American jazz, traditional Panamanian music from the central provinces, reggae, and Latin, British and American rock 'n' roll.

Traditional Panamanian products include wood carvings, textiles, ceramics, masks, straw goods and other handicrafts. Some of the more famous include *molas* (colorful hand-stitched appliqué textiles made by Kuna women) and the *pollera* (the intricately stitched, lacy, Spanish-influenced dress of the Península de Azuero, which is the national dress of Panama for festive occasions).

The country has quite a few impressive painters and writers, some of whom are internationally recognized and have won major competitions. There is also fair representation in dance, theater and other performance arts, which are managed by the Instituto Nacional de Cultura (INAC; the National Institute of Culture). INAC also manages the country's museums, exhibition halls and schools of fine art.

Music

Salsa is the most popular music in Panama, and live salsa is easy to find, particularly in Panama City (see the Panama City chapter for details). The country's most renowned salsa singer, Rubén Blades, is something of a national hero. A kid from the barrio, Blades has had several international hits and has appeared in *Fatal Beauty, Dead Man Out, The Milagro Beanfield War* and other motion pictures. He ran for president in 1994, finishing third.

Jazz, which was brought to Panama from the US, and calypso music from the West Indies can also be heard in clubs in Panama. Rock 'n' roll, in both English and Spanish, is played on most Panamanian FM radio stations, and some very decent bands play it in Panama City clubs. Venues for jazz and rock bands appear in the Panama City chapter.

The jazz composer and pianist Danilo Pérez, trained at the prestigious Berklee College of Music in Boston, is widely acclaimed by American and European jazz critics. His CD *Panamonk*, which puts a Latin spin on many Thelonius Monk compositions, makes for some very pleasurable listening.

Los Rabanes is the most popular rock 'n' roll group in the country. The most talented rock group in Panama is Cage 9, which plays alternative rock and often performs in Panama City. A third rock group to look out for is Santos y Demonios, which cranks out hard rock with spiritual themes. Hasta Que Katy Venga (When Katy Shows Up) is an up-and-coming rock band.

Panamanian folkloric music *(típico)*, in which the accordion is dominant, is well

Danilo Pérez rocks the house.

represented by Dorindo Cárdenas, the late Victorio Vergara (whose band lives on as Nenito Vargas y los Plumas Negras), Osvaldo Ayala, Manuel de Jesús Abrego and the enormously popular brother-sister pair of Sammy and Sandra Sandoval.

Panama's classical music scene is dismal. Only one of Panama's 90 or so radio stations plays any classical music, and the Panama National Orchestra, created in 1941, gives only irregular and infrequent performances. However, a private organization, the Asociación Nacional de Conciertos, does periodically organize excellent concerts by local and foreign artists.

See *The Panama News*, *The Visitor* or the Sunday supplement of *La Prensa* called Talingo for information on upcoming musical performances. The *News* and *Visitor* can often be found in hotel lobbies.

Handicrafts

Panama's handicrafts are varied and often of excellent quality. The Wounaan and Emberá Indians in Darién Province produce some beautiful woven baskets, most of which are exported to the USA and Europe, although many of high quality can be found in Panama. These tribes also sell life-size images of snakes, parrots, toucans and other jungle wildlife carved from cocobolo, a handsome tropical hardwood, and they carve tiny figurines (typically of iguanas, turtles, crocodiles and birds) from the ivory-colored tagua nut. Both tribes also make, and to a lesser degree sell, silver jewelry.

The Kuna of the Comarca de San Blás are known worldwide for their molas – the blouse panels used by women in their traditional dress and sold as crafts. Molas symbolize the identity of the Kuna people to outsiders, and their designs may be very elaborate; they are always colorful and typically depict sea turtles, birds and fish. If you visit an inhabited San Blás island, you will likely see at least a few women making molas.

A variety of handicrafts and curios are available on the Península de Azuero as well. The towns of Ocú and Penonomé produce superior Panama hats, the finest of which are so tightly woven they can hold water. Polleras – elaborate outfits of Spanish origin that consist of an intricately embroidered white skirt with an off-the-shoulder flounced blouse, contrasting petticoats edged with lace, and many pairs of shimmering filigree ornaments worn in the hair with a large comb – are handmade in Guararé and in villages around Las Tablas. Also found on the Azuero are festival masks (in Villa de Los Santos and Parita) and pottery (in La Arena).

Many of the handicrafts mentioned here can be purchased in Panama City. See the Shopping sections in the Facts for the Visitor and Panama City chapters for additional information.

Painting

Trained in France, Roberto Lewis (1874-1949) became the first prominent figure on Panama's art scene. He painted portraits of the nation's leaders and allegorical images to decorate public buildings; among his most notable works are those in the Palacio de las Garzas in Panama City.

In 1913 Lewis became the director of Panama's first art academy, where he and his successor, Humberto Ivaldi (1909-47), educated a generation of artists. Among the school's students were Juan Manuel Cedeño and Isaac Benítez, as well as the painters who would come to the fore in the 1950s and 1960s. This group includes Alfredo Sinclair, Guillermo Trujillo, Ciro Oduber, Eudoro

Panama's Super Stamps

In the world of stamp collecting, Panama is a top producer. The teams of engravers and painters, lithographic artists and graphic designers who create the nation's postal issues are widely regarded as among the world's best. Panamanian stamps not only capture the country's history, places, people and nature but also honor world events and figures.

Silvera and others. Most of these artists are still active today, and their works are occasionally shown in local galleries.

Of this group, Trujillo is the most celebrated. As Latin American arts expert Monica E Kupfer noted in an article that appeared in the excellent compendium *Latin American Art in the Twentieth Century*, Trujillo's 'personal iconography is rooted in Panama's pre-Columbian history and Indian mythology, its landscapes and flora. (…) With a rich and versatile *oeu re* ranging from social satires to imagined landscapes and delicate semiabstractions, Trujillo has achieved international success as a painter. As a professor, he promoted a lasting interest in watercolor painting, ceramics and printmaking in Panama.'

Although there are some exceptions, most contemporary Panamanian artists have not concentrated on political subjects. However, during the 1980s many artists turned to figuration and focused on the human condition. Among them is Brooke Alfaro, whose nightmarish images and disturbing visions of common people and authority figures have achieved international recognition.

Other valuable contemporary painters are Antonio Alvarado (abstract), Isabel de Obaldía, Raúl Vásquez, Roosevelt Díaz, Tabo Toral, Guillermo Mezza, Ana Elena Garuz (abstract), Teresa Icaza, Vicky Suescum (abstract) and Julio Zachrisson (a winner of Spain's prestigious Goya Award). The work of these and other fine artists can be seen and bought in the best galleries in Panama City; see Artwork in the Shopping section of the Panama City chapter for details.

The largest Panamanian art exposition – the Bienal de Arte – is held every two years at the Museo de Arte Contemporáneo, on Avenida San Blás at Avenida de los Mártires in the Ancón district of Panama City (see the listing under Museums in the Panama City chapter for details). The paintings and sculptures on exhibit are selected by a reputable international jury. The monthlong exposition will be held in October 2000 and October 2002, and it is very worthwhile.

Sculpture

Sculpture is not a strong tradition in Panama, but there are a few extraordinary artists in the trade: Guillermo Trujillo is doing beautiful, elegant bronze sculptures; Isabel de Obaldía is an internationally acclaimed glass sculptor; Raúl Vásquez creates totemlike wooden pieces; and Susie Arias has done several public sculptures in California, where she resides (but some of her small pieces can be bought in Panama). Other fine sculptors are Donna Conlon (working in marble), Emily Zhukov (cast aluminum) and Lezlie Milson (a hybrid between painting and sculpture). Coincidentally, these last three are Americans who have lived in Panama for many years. Sculpture can be seen at galleries in Panama City. See details in that chapter.

Photography

Panama has several gifted photographers, including Iraida Icaza, Stuart GR Warner W and Sandra Eleta. Icaza, who lived for many years in Tokyo and now resides in New York, makes abstract art using photographic equipment. Her work is very bold and innovative.

Warner, who has spent much of his life in Asia, the Middle East, Europe and the USA, captures the human spirit in beautiful landscapes and portraits. Unlike many professionals, Warner never relies on artificial lighting or lens filters.

Sandra Eleta's portraits of black inhabitants of Panama's Caribbean coast (particularly of Portobelo, where she resides part of the year) have made her one of the most important photographers in Latin America. A book of her work can be found at Librería Argosy in Panama City (see Bookstores in the Panama City chapter).

Literature

Unfortunately, many of Panama's greatest written works, such as those of Roque Javier Laurenza and José de Jesus Martínez, are no longer available in most of the country's bookstores. However, there are still good things in stock at some stores, mainly at Librería Cultural Panameña (☎ 223-6267).

near the western end of Vía España, near Colejio Javier (a well-known school) in Panama City. Here you can find what many consider to be five of Panama's best novels:

El ahogado – The drowned man, a 1937 novel by Tristán Solarte (pen name for Guillermo Sánchez Borbón, a poet, novelist and journalist of international recognition), ingeniously blends elements of the detective, gothic and psychological genres, along with a famous local myth, into the narration of the events that lead to the tragic death of Rafael, an attractive but demonic young man.

El des án – In The garret, a 1954 novel with a surprise ending, Ramón H Jurado explores the emotional limits of the human condition through the delirious monologue of a man whose sickness is slowly paralyzing him.

Gamboa Road Gang – This 1960 novel by Joaquín Beleño is the best work of fiction about the political and social events surrounding the Panama Canal. It's in English.

Loma ardiente y estida de sol – Burning and sundrenched hill, a 1974 novel by Rafael Pernett y Morales, is a bold look at Panama City's poor, mainly the squatters, in which the author, armed with considerable wit and imagination, tries to rescue popular urban customs and lingo.

Semana sin iernes – In his 1996 novel A week without Friday, Justo Arroyo writes about a young man whose obsession with mastering the game of pool leads him to the verge of murder.

Some of these works are available in English translations, but they can only be found in Panama.

An excellent short-story writer is José María Sanchez, whose work was first published in the 1940s but has recently been re-released in an anthology titled *Cuentos de Bocas del Toro (Tales of Bocas del Toro)*. Set in the beautiful province of Bocas del Toro (where the author was born and raised), these fun stories, whose protagonists are driven by the sensuous, baroque excesses of the tropical jungle and sea, possess a language charged with powerful imagery.

Another superb collection of short stories is *Inauguración de La Fe (Inauguration of La Fe*, 1995), by writer and poet Consuelo Tomás; the tales are full of her characteristically playful but biting humor and her innate ability to depict the idiosyncrasies of the popular neighborhoods of Panama City. Both collections are available at Panamanian bookstores.

Panama can boast of producing some talented poets, such as Ricardo Miró, Rogelio Sinán (also a fiction writer, perhaps the best known outside Panama), Demetrio Herrera Sevillano, Demetrio Korsi, Tristán Solarte, César Young Núñez, Bertalicia Peralta and Manuel Orestes Nieto, as well as Edison Simmons.

Theater

The theater scene in Panama is limited to the capital city, and even there it's weak. There are no professional theater companies in the country, although there are groups of amateurs who stage various low-budget productions. The Teatro En Circulo (Circular Theater) operates as an organized amateur troupe housed in its own theater, as does the Ancon Theater Guild. Check *Talingo,* the arts supplement in the Sunday edition of *La Prensa,* for a list of cultural events scheduled for the upcoming week.

An experimental theater troupe, Oveja Negra (Black Sheep), periodically puts on productions. When they do, their performances are always excellent and are usually held at the Alianza Francesa Panameña in Panama City. Panama City has several other venues for theater; see that chapter for details.

SOCIETY & CONDUCT
Racial Issues

Panama is home to many ethnic groups. The Indian tribes; the various peoples of the West Indies; the Spanish-Indian mestizos; the Chinese, Middle Eastern, Swiss and Croatian immigrants; the North and South Americans; and others all maintain their own cultures, yet some elements of their cultures have mixed to form new combinations. It is partly because of the mixing that the various groups are able to live together. As one Panamanian friend of mine put it, 'That man there is black, but next to you I am black. I must have some black or Indian in me. So, you see, we're just talking about different shades of the same color.'

But class distinctions *do* exist in Panama. While politicians from the president on down take pride in mingling with the public and maintaining some semblance of a classless society, the whites (who make up only 10% of the population) control the majority of the wealth and nearly all of the power. And within that group are several dozen wealthy families who are above the law – people able to escape arrest by mentioning the names of others who could complicate life for a lowly police officer.

This same group can get hard-to-come-by reservations with a phone call. They generally are able to go right to the front of lines because of who they are and because they ask to speak directly with managers, who are keen to attend to the rich and powerful (and the offspring of the rich and powerful) out of respect, envy and fear. In Panama members of a certain class marry only members of that certain class. And at the almighty Union Club – *the* social club of Panama City – memberships are rarely given to people with dark skin.

Racism is a horrible thing no matter where it's found, but racism in Panama is mild compared to the racism found in many other countries. There's no counterpart to the Ku Klux Klan here; there are no skinheads committing hate crimes. For all its inequities, Panama is closer to the ideal in this respect than most developed nations.

Dos & Don'ts

Because Panama is so diverse, what's acceptable in one part of the country may be totally unacceptable in another part. For example, it's OK to get a full-body tan on Playa de las Suecas (Swedish Women Beach) on Isla Contadora – in fact, it's Panama's only government-approved nude beach – but lie naked on a beach in the Archipiélago de San Blás and you should expect a good scolding. Indeed, although the Kuna tolerate sunbathing on their beaches, they are very offended when foreign women enter their villages in bikini tops or short shorts. Same goes with shirt-

less men, even you Arnold Schwarzenegger lookalikes.

Panama City is a dressy town. The men typically wear business shirts and slacks and the women dresses even when they're just tooting about. At work and when club-hopping, they dress to the nines. Many dance clubs in the city won't let in men who are wearing collarless shirts or tennis shoes. A halter top and shorts are OK during the daytime when it's hot, but Panamanians frown upon people who don't dress better after dark. Strategically ripped jeans, tank tops and the like are much frowned upon.

Panama is a conservative country where people generally have a great deal of respect for one another. If, for example, you have a business meeting with a Panamanian, you can expect the Panamanian to be well dressed out of respect for you. Likewise, out of respect for the Panamanian, you should dress well. Foreign women who are trying to win the respect of Panamanian men will dress smartly, and foreign men trying to win the respect of Panamanian women will do the same. Even on very hot days in Panama, you'll rarely see a laborer working with his shirt off or a woman wearing shorts hemmed above the knee. Leave the grunge behind.

In Panama you are considered guilty until proven innocent. For this reason it's wise to avoid placing yourself in situations where a crime is occurring or is likely to occur. For example, if people near you light up a joint or snort cocaine, get away from them; if police see those people doing drugs, they might presume that you're doing drugs too. Public drinking is illegal in Panama. (See Legal Matters in the Facts for the Visitor chapter for more information on drugs and alcohol.)

You should have a photographic ID on you at all times: It's the law. Preferably this should be a passport, and it should contain a tourist card if applicable (see the Facts for the Visitor chapter for details on tourist cards).

The Kuna Indians are a most attractive people. You may find it tempting to take photographs of them. If you wish to do so, be polite and ask their permission beforehand. Note that there is usually a US$1 fee attached to every photo you take of a Kuna, payable to the subject. This fee was arrived at after a Kuna chief saw a postcard of a Kuna woman, learned that it was selling for US$1 and grew incensed when he realized that the subject was not benefiting from the sale of the postcard.

Greetings are very important to Panamanians, as they are to people in most Latin American countries. In all situations, politeness is a valued habit. A certain degree of formality and floweriness is often used in conversation. Expect total strangers to say, *'Buenas días,' 'Buenas tardes'* and *'Buenas noches'* to you, and be prepared to do likewise. Male friends and casual acquaintances meeting one another in the street shake hands at the beginning and end of even a short meeting; women kiss one another on the cheek in greeting and farewell. Men often kiss women decorously on the cheek, and vice versa.

The well-documented fact that smoking is hazardous to one's health is widely known and respected in Panama. There are nonsmoking sections in restaurants, and many hotels have nonsmoking rooms. In keeping with Panamanians' respect for one another (their driving practices notwithstanding), nonsmoking signs are universally obeyed in Panama.

Punctuality in Panama is very different from punctuality in the USA, Canada, Japan and elsewhere. In Panama people expected to attend a business meeting scheduled for 3 pm may not arrive until 3:30 pm or later – and that's acceptable. If you are short on time and are scheduling a meeting, emphasize the designated time. If you're speaking Spanish, follow the designated time with an *'en punto'* (on the dot), as in, *'Vamos a las dos en punto'* (Let's go at two on the dot).

Other things to remember include the following:

• If you're found in possession of pre-Columbian art, you will go to jail.

• The use of flash equipment in churches and museums is prohibited.

• Shorts, halter tops and tank tops are not permitted in churches.

• Shorts are not permitted in any governmental building.

• It is unlawful to drive without wearing a shirt.

• Drinking on All Souls' Day (November 2) is considered disrespectful.

RELIGION

Freedom of religion is constitutionally guaranteed in Panama, although the preeminence of Roman Catholicism is also officially recognized. The major faiths are Roman Catholicism (85%), Protestant denominations (5%), Islam (5%) and Baha'i (1%). There are also small numbers of Hindus, Jews and other believers. In addition, the various Indian tribes have their own belief systems, although these are fading quickly due to the influence of missionaries preaching Christianity.

Religion is especially mixed in Panama City, home to immigrants from all over the world. The city has many Catholic and Protestant churches, three Jewish synagogues and two Moslem mosques, and the Hindu and Baha'i religions each have a temple.

LANGUAGE

Spanish is the official language of Panama, but no fewer than 14 other languages can also be heard on the isthmus. Eight languages are spoken by Panama's seven Indian tribes (the Kuna living in the villages of Paya and Pucuro, in southeastern Panama, speak a language that's quite different from that of Kuna residing elsewhere). Two Chinese languages, Arabic, Hebrew, San Miguel Creole French and Western Caribbean Creole English are also spoken in Panama.

San Miguel Creole French is spoken by scattered groups whose ancestors came from St Lucia during the mid-19th century as laborers. Western Caribbean Creole English is spoken by an estimated 14% of the population, whose ancestors came from Barbados and Jamaica in the 19th century to work in fruit plantations and later to build the Panama Railroad and Canal. Creole English is commonly heard in Bocas del Toro Province and in Colón. Other Panamanians have learned English at school or from US soldiers and Panama Canal workers.

Many Chinese also came to Panama to work on the railway and the canal, and their descendants speak Cantonese or Hakka. During the 20th century, Chinese immigrants arrived as merchants. There is a hearty Chinatown in Panama City and a substantial Chinese community in Colón. Likewise, many Arabs and Jews came to these two cities to conduct business. Today Arabs from several Middle Eastern coun-

tries and Jews from Israel and the USA comprise two of the most powerful groups in Panama.

Just as most Panamanian immigrants have learned to speak Spanish as a second language, any traveler to Panama would be wise to learn at least a little Spanish as a matter of courtesy and convenience. If you don't already speak some Spanish, please look at the Language section at the back of this book, and at the very least learn how to say 'good morning,' 'good afternoon,' 'good evening,' 'goodbye,' 'thank you' and 'glad to meet you' in Spanish. Generally, if you try speaking Spanish in Panama and the person you are talking to speaks English, that person will respond in English.

Facts for the Visitor

HIGHLIGHTS

Most of Panama's visitors see only a slice of the country, literally. That would be the Big Ditch, the World's Greatest Shortcut – the Panama Canal. No matter what you call it, the canal is a must-see for Panama visitors. The lock-and-lake waterway remains one of mankind's greatest endeavors and an engineering marvel on par with the greatest pyramids of Egypt and Mexico.

Visiting Panama to gaze upon the mother of all canals is a terrific idea. But once on the land bridge of the Americas that is Panama, don't forgo the opportunity to explore this often-transited but usually bypassed country. There's a *lot* to see in Panama. The following places are intended to ease the decision making of adventurous spirits who want to peer past the canal.

For more information on the activities listed below, see Activities, later in this chapter.

Surf & Turf

Isla de Coiba is the centerpiece of a national park, and home to numerous beachside prison camps that are generally open to escorted visitors. The snorkeling and fishing here are terrific, but it's the combination of the island's beauty and guests' intimate association with prisoners and guards that make for particularly lasting memories.

The islands in the Comarca de San Blás are ruled by the Kuna Indians. Their handicrafts are known worldwide, but few outsiders know their world. It is one where the sense of community is so strong that the Kuna generally prefer to live hut against hut on a dozen or so islands rather than spread out across the hundreds of islands in their chain. Those mostly uninhabited islands, the fascinating lifestyle of the Kuna and the Comarca's awesome sunsets make for an appealing package.

Few people visit the Archipiélago de Bocas del Toro and leave it unhappy. It is not home to the finest sand or the best snorkeling in the world, or terrific shopping opportunities or a nightlife that rivals Rio's. It is the islands' pervading tranquility, their intriguing residents, their natural beauty and the thrill of exploring the mostly undeveloped islands by boat that make the archipelago a great place to put worries aside and relax.

Cool Alpine Retreats

If your idea of fun is to go hiking in cool mountains by day and retreat to a cozy inn at sundown, chances are you'd find the alpine hamlets of Cerro Punta, Boquete and El Valle very much to your liking. All three lend themselves well to pleasant strolls as well as to arduous trekking – it's your choice – but Cerro Punta wins top honors among the three as a place to 'get away from it all.'

If you prefer to be somewhere that feels more like a town, with plenty of shops to wander in and out of, Boquete and El Valle are probably better for you. Both towns have thus far managed to maintain their charm, but both are increasingly geared toward tourists. If time and money permit, consider visiting either Boquete or El Valle and spending at least two nights in Cerro Punta.

Bungle in the Jungle

Unless you traipse through jungle with the subtlety of a marching band, chances are you would see some lovely feathered wildlife on Pipeline Road, a rain-forest-flanked route inside Parque Nacional Soberanía and yet conveniently close to Panama City and the Panama Canal. Indeed, Pipeline Road is one of the most accessible tropical forests in the world, but still more than 400 bird species (more than in the entire USA) have been recorded there.

Isla Barro Colorado, home to the world's most prestigious tropical research station, is available for guided tours only. If you're able to get into one, you'll be glad you did. Guides

Floss It

For the cost of a crummy cigar, you can buy a vacation-saving item. It's called dental floss, and its uses are innumerable. Got a fishhook but no line? Four words: green waxed dental floss. Need to secure a mosquito net? Reach for dental floss. Forgot to pack a clothesline? You're in luck if you've packed dental floss. Tear in your jeans, rip in your pack? A little dental floss and a sewing needle and life goes on.

Dental floss comes in 50m and 100m lengths and is sold in nifty little cases complete with built-in cutters. It's cheap, it's light, it's strong and it's outrageously useful. Some say dental floss can even remove decay-causing material from between teeth and under gums. Now in cinnamon, mint and grape flavors. No kidding.

are an option for Parque Nacional Darién, which is spectacular to explore by foot and/or boat, but going alone isn't recommended.

A Room with a View

There's no shortage of memorable places to stay in Panama, but some have views that burn enduring images into the ol' grey matter. The Canopy Tower in Panamá Province is a former radar installation, ringed by dense rain forest, that's been converted into a fancy birding platform with half a dozen charming guestrooms.

The Cabañas Los Quetzales, located inside Parque Internacional La Amistad, consist of three romantic chalets with idyllic near-canopy-level sitting areas. Speaking of romance, the rustic-yet-lovely beachside cabañas of Al Natural Resort on Isla Bastimentos in the Archipiélago de Bocas del Toro aren't for everyone, but they are tonic for incurable romantics. From the El Turega and Chichibaldi rooms at the Posada del Cerro La Vieja near Chiguiri Arrbia in Coclé Province, a guest could see forever if it weren't for the many mist-shrouded peaks that inspire beautiful thoughts.

Several of the Kuna-run hotels in the Comarca de San Blás offer magazine-coverish coconut-trees-on-dreamy-isles images neatly captured by your window frame. Among them is the Sapibenega 'The Kuna Lodge' on the isle of Isla Iskardup. There, at least half of the water's edge cabins offer views that inspire gotta-pinch-myself reality tests.

Few visitors to Panama's capital consider it a beautiful city, but then relatively few of Panama City's visitors have stayed in one of the rooms at the Hotel Caesar Park that look back upon the financial district, Casco Viejo and Bahía de Panamá. But watching the skyscrapers of downtown painted in rays of pastel pinks, oranges and reds at sunset, as you nibble on a chocolate and sip a cocktail in a guestroom of this true five-star hotel, is an undeniably glorious urban experience.

PLANNING
When to Go

Panama's high tourist season corresponds with its Pacific-side dry season – from mid-December to mid-April. During these months, there is relatively little rain in Panama City and elsewhere south of the Continental Divide. North of the mountains, on the Caribbean side of Panama, it rains all year around. However, it tends to rain less in February, March, September and October than it does the rest of the year. (See Climate in the Facts for the Visitor chapter for details.)

The best time to visit Panama really depends on what you intend to do and on personal preference. If you intend to spend most of your time on the Pacific side, you might want to visit in December or January, when there's generally little rain and the weather is pleasant. Bear in mind, however, that hotel prices and airfares are generally higher from mid-December to mid-April.

If you'll be doing any serious hiking, the dry season is the most comfortable time to do it – and the least arduous, because you'll have better traction, no sucking mud to contend with and fewer creeks to cross. For planning purposes, beware that Panama's mountains can get very cold at night; if you're considering camping at altitude (in Boquete, El Valle or Cerro Punta, for example), be sure to bring warm clothing.

If you like to party, try to be in Panama City or on the Península de Azuero for Carnaval (Mardi Gras), held each year during the four days leading up to Ash Wednesday. Panama City's Carnaval celebration is one of the world's largest. On the Península de Azuero it's great fun, too, but the crowds are not as huge. Hotel reservations during Carnaval are a must and should be made well in advance. Panama has a number of other festivals worth catching, especially on the Azuero; see the Herrera Province and Los Santos Province chapters for details.

Maps

International Travel Maps (☎ 604-687-3320, fax 604-687-5925, itmb@itmb.com; 530 W Broadway, Vancouver, BC V5Z 1E9, Canada) publishes an excellent 1:800,000 color map showing the geographical features, cities, towns, national parks, airports and roads of Panama (US$8.95). Website: www.itmb.com

The Instituto Geográfico Nacional (☎ 236-2444), just off Avenida Simón Bolívar in Panama City, sells topographical, nautical, provincial, city and regional maps of Panama. Taxi drivers know the institute simply as 'Tommy Guardia' in honor of the man who founded it.

What to Bring

You can buy anything you are likely to need in Panama and probably more cheaply than you can back home, but if you're short on time, try to bring everything you think you'll need with you. And although the risk of contracting malaria is remote, if you intend to be on antimalaria medication during your trip, you'll want to start taking it before you leave, as it takes a couple of weeks to kick in (see Health, later in this chapter).

If you'll be camping, bring a sweater or jacket for chilly nights. If you're planning on scuba diving or snorkeling while you're in Panama, check the Activities section in this chapter for tips on items to bring.

City & Beach Clothing Panamanians place a lot of importance on appearance. If you want to be treated with respect, don't dress like a bum. Only the poorest Panamanian would wear cut-offs, and no locals strut around in bikini tops except at the beach. Due to the heat, the most appropriate clothing for Panamanian cities is made of 100% cotton fiber or (even better, but pricier) material designed to wick moisture away from the skin; such high-tech wear usually can be found in stores specializing in outdoor apparel.

If the club scene is your scene, keep in mind that casual-to-dressy officewear is the norm here, and collared shirts are preferred to T-shirts. Most clubs deny entry to people in shorts. Entry to government buildings, too, is often denied to people in shorts. Shoewise, Panamanians seem to stop wearing sneakers at about age 16 in favor of leather shoes.

The beach scene ranges from the Brazilian (brief briefs and tiny bikinis) to the American (baggy shorts and enveloping one-pieces). Nudity will attract unwanted attention or detention, except at the country's only official nude beach, on Isla Contadora. Remember, every day of the year a sunburn spoils someone's vacation. Regardless of your other beach apparel, wear sunscreen if you are susceptible to burning. You'll be glad you did.

Jungle Gear If you'll be spending a significant amount of time in the jungle, consider bringing along the following items:

- lightweight hiking boots for short jaunts
- military boots with drainage holes for treks
- medium (30-50% Deet) insect repellent
- heavy-duty rain poncho
- light blanket for lowland, thick for mountain
- air-inflated sleeping pad (Thermarest is best)
- washable tennis, running or walking shoes
- sandals (the strap-on sports-style works well)
- two pairs of cotton-polypropylene/nylon socks
- one pair of wool-blend socks
- two pairs of nylon, quick-dry field pants
- one pair of nylon, quick-dry shorts

- two long-sleeved quick-dry shirts
- lightweight jacket or windbreaker
- sun hat or cap
- swimsuit
- first-aid kit (see Predeparture Preparations, later in this chapter)

Of all the items listed above, the three most important are the boots, the insect repellent and the poncho. US Army boots are terrific. They were perfected for jungle wear during the Vietnam War of the 1960s, and no one's improved upon them since. As for repellent, even if you enjoy inhaling mosquitoes, you ought to apply repellent to protect yourself against insect-transmitted diseases. Strong Deet (60% or more) irritates some skin. A well-made poncho is important for keeping rain and insects off you. The best places to buy jungle boots, bug spray and sturdy ponchos are Army/Navy surplus stores. Your pants and shorts should have built-in netting underwear, which alleviates the need to wash and dry 100% cotton underwear, a time-consuming process in humid conditions.

TOURIST OFFICES
Local Tourist Offices
The Instituto Panameño de Turismo (IPAT), the national tourism agency, has its headquarters (☎ 226-7000, fax 226-4849) in the Centro Atlapa on Vía Israel in the San Francisco neighborhood of Panama City.

IPAT has an information counter at Tocumen International Airport. It also has tourist centers in Bocas del Toro town, Boquete, David, Portobelo, Santiago and Villa de Los Santos. There is also a tourist center in Paso Canoas. Be forewarned: IPAT offices tend to be poorly stocked and staffed by people who speak only Spanish.

Tourist Offices Abroad
Panama has no tourist offices in other countries, but IPAT literature and other information is sometimes available at Panamanian consulates and embassies (see the Embassies & Consulates section in this chapter). Be forewarned: IPAT publications tend to be rich with inaccuracies. Many

Panamanian businesses are developing websites, so the Internet is also a good tool for pre-trip research.

VISAS & DOCUMENTS
Passports, Tourist Cards & Visas
Every visitor needs a valid passport and an onward ticket to enter Panama, but further requirements vary from country to country and occasionally change. Persons planning a trip to Panama would be advised to contact the Panamanian embassy or consulate nearest them to obtain the latest information on entry requirements. Ticketing agents of airlines that fly to Panama and tour operators that send groups there often can provide this information.

At the time of writing, people holding passports from the following countries needed to show only their passports to enter Panama: Argentina, Austria, Belgium, Costa Rica, El Salvador, England, Finland, France, Germany, Guatemala, Honduras, Hungary, Israel, Italy, Luxembourg, Paraguay, Poland, Portugal, Northern Ireland, Scotland, Singapore, Switzerland, Uruguay and Wales.

People from the following countries needed a passport and either a tourist visa or a tourist card: Antigua, Australia, Bahamas, Barbados, Belize, Bermuda, Bolivia, Brazil, Canada, Chile, China, Colombia, Denmark, Granada, Greece, Guyana, Iceland, Ireland, Jamaica, Japan, Malta, Mexico, Monaco, the Netherlands, New Zealand, San Marino, South Korea, Suriname, Taiwan, Tobago, Trinidad, the USA and Venezuela.

People holding passports from the following countries needed to show a passport and a Panamanian tourist visa: Chad, Ecuador, Egypt, the Philippines, Peru, the Dominican Republic and Thailand.

If the name of your country does not appear above, you are advised to contact the Panamanian embassy or consulate nearest you, or call the immigration office (☎ 507-227-1448, 225-8925, fax 227-1227, 225-1641).

A tourist card costs US$5 and is available from Panamanian embassies and consulates (see the list later in this chapter), from most airlines serving Panama, from the Tica Bus company and at the airport or border post upon entry. (See the Air and Land sections in the Getting There & Away chapter for contact details.) Tourist visas are issued at Panamanian embassies and consulates and generally cost US$20.

No matter where you are coming from, you will be given a 90-day stamp in your passport when you enter Panama. This means you are allowed to remain in Panama for 90 days without having to obtain further permission from the authorities. After 90 days, visas and tourist cards can be extended at *migración* (immigration) offices.

Those of you planning to enter Panama overland may need to display an onward ticket, and sometimes a show of cash is also required – US$500 per month is generally sufficient.

In the event that you lose your passport while in Panama, you'll need proof of when you entered the country to be able to leave it. That proof, oddly enough, does not come from an immigration office but from the airline you flew in on. You need to go to the airline's main office in Panama City and request a certification of your entry date *(certificación de uelo)*. There's no charge, but you'll likely be asked to come back the next day to pick it up. When you leave the country, along with your new passport (obtained from your embassy in Panama City) you'll present your certificación de vuelo to an immigrations agent.

Extending Your Stay Staying in the country once your tourist card or visa has expired is not risk free. If, for example, a police officer checks your ID and your tourist card or visa has expired, you may be detained until you can convince the person in charge that you'll remedy the situation as soon as possible. An on-the-spot fine may be levied as well.

If you intend to stay more than 90 days and want to do things by the book, you'll need to obtain a *prologa de turista* from the immigration office in Panama City, David or

Chitré; these are the only offices that issue them. A prologa de turista is a permit that resembles a driver's license, complete with photo. To get one, you must be accompanied by a Panamanian citizen who accepts responsibility for you during your stay; this acceptance must be provided in the form of a letter. You or the resident will need to explain why you want to stay in the country more than 90 days.

Additionally, the Panamanian citizen will be expected to show economic solvency. If this person has a job, that'll suffice. If the Panamanian citizen is unemployed, he or she might need to present a bank receipt showing that he or she has money in the bank. Also, you will need to show an international airline ticket – proof that you don't intend to stay in Panama for years – and you'll need to pay US$15 for the permit. You needn't provide a photo; an immigration agent will take one of you.

Lastly, all persons applying for a prologa de turista need to register at the immigration office. This means that you'll need to pay US$1 and provide a photocopy of your passport and your international airline ticket.

These three immigration offices also issue multiple-entry visas to foreigners working in Panama and possessing residency status and a current visa. Multiple-entry visas cost US$100 and are valid for two years.

Onward Tickets

Travelers officially need onward tickets before they are allowed to enter Panama. This requirement is not often checked at Tocumen International Airport. But travelers arriving by land should anticipate a need to show an onward ticket.

If you're heading to Colombia, Venezuela or another South American country from Panama, you may need an onward or roundtrip ticket before you will be allowed entry into that country or even allowed to board the plane if you're flying. A quick check with the appropriate embassy – easy to do by phone in Panama City – will tell you whether the country that you're heading to has an onward-ticket requirement.

Travel Insurance

No matter how you're traveling, make sure you take out travel insurance. This should cover you not only for medical expenses and luggage theft, but also for unavoidable cancellations or delays in your travel arrangements. Also, everyone should be protected against worst-case scenarios, such as an accident that requires hospital treatment and a flight home.

Coverage depends on your insurance and type of ticket, so ask both your insurer and your ticket-issuing agency to explain the finer points. Council Travel and STA Travel, with offices in many countries (see the Getting There & Away chapter for contact information), offer a variety of travel insurance options at reasonable prices.

Buy travel insurance as early as possible. If you buy it the week before you fly, you may find, for instance, that you're not covered for delays to your flight caused by strikes or other labor actions that may have been in force before you took out the insurance.

Driver's License & Permits

You can drive on a foreign license in Panama for up to 90 days. Drivers should carry their passports in addition to their licenses. To rent a car, your passport, driver's license and credit card are generally required. Also, you must be at least 25 years old to rent a car, or 23 if you have an American Express card.

If you plan on driving down to Panama from points north, you will need all the usual insurance and ownership papers. If you are bringing a vehicle into the country, you must pay US$6 for a vehicle control certificate (tarjeta de circulación) and to have your vehicle fumigated. You and your vehicle can stay in the country for up to 90 days. However, after 90 days you'll need to get a Panamanian driver's license.

You can sell your car in Panama, but you must take it to a customs broker (corredor de aduana) for inspection, valuation and taxation. You'll find some customs brokers listed under aduanas, corredores de in the yellow pages of the phone book. Used-car lots can do all the paperwork for you. Be advised that it's common to negotiate payment of the taxes with the prospective buyer.

It's possible to drive into Panama from the three border posts it shares with Costa Rica. At the time of writing, it was not possible to drive into Panama from Colombia. See the Getting There & Away and Getting Around chapters for more driving information.

Hostel & Student Cards

Sorry, there's only one youth hostel in Panama (ie, flashing a youth-hostel card there won't save you a cent), and it's not affiliated with any youth hostel organizations (ie, YHA). Also, student cards generally don't save their carriers any money in Panama.

EMBASSIES & CONSULATES
Panamanian Embassies & Consulates

If you need a visa, you can get one from a Panamanian embassy or consulate in another country. Some countries have several Panamanian consulates; in the USA, for example, Panama has consulates in Atlanta, Chicago, Honolulu, Houston, Miami, New Orleans, New York, Philadelphia, San Diego and San Francisco, in addition to its embassy in Washington, DC.

Unless otherwise noted, the Panamanian diplomatic missions below are embassies.

Brazil (☎ 21-255-8512, fax 255-9085) Rua Figueredo Magalhaes 122, Copacabana, Rio de Janeiro

Canada (☎ 613-236-7177, fax 236-5775, pancanem@travel-net.com) 130 Albert St, Suite 300, Ottawa, Ontario K1P 564

Colombia (☎ 1-257-5067, 257-4452, fax 257-5068, embpacol@impsat.net.com) Calle 92, No 7-70, El Chico, Santa Fe de Bogotá

Costa Rica (☎ 280-1570, 281-2442, fax 281-2161) Barrio La Granja, del Higueron de San Pedro, 200 Metros al Sur y 25 al Este, San Jose

El Salvador (☎ 298-0884, fax 260-5453) Alameda Roosevelt, No 2838 y 55 Ave Norte, Altos de la Compañia COPA Airlines, San Salvador

France (☎ 01-4566-4244, fax 4567-9943, panaemba@worldnet.fr) 145 Avenue de Suffren, 75015 Paris

Germany (☎ 228-36-1036 or 36-1037, fax 36-35-58) Lutzowstrasse 1, D – 53173, Bonn

Guatemala (☎ 2-333-3835, fax 337-2446) 10 Avenida 18-53, Zona 14, La Cañada, Guatemala

Honduras (☎ 239-5508, fax 232-8147) Palmira Building, 2nd floor, in front of Hotel Honduras Maya, Tegucigalpa

Israel (☎ 3-60-69849, fax 691-0045, panama@ netvision.net.il) Hei Be'Iyar St, No 2 10, 3rd floor, Apartment 3, Kikar Hamedina, Tel Aviv 62093

Italy (☎ 6-4425-2173, fax 4425-2237, panambas@ students.rpilo.it) Viale Regina Margherita, No 239, 4th floor, Interno 11, 00198 Rome

Japan (☎ 3-3499-3741, fax 5485-3548) Kowa Building, Na38, Room 902, 4-12-24 Nishi Azabu, Minato-Ku, Tokyo 105-0031

Mexico (☎ 5557-2793 or 5557-6169; fax 5395-4269, embpanmx@avantel.net) Ave Horacio y Calle Sofocle, Casa No 1501, Colonia Chapultepec, Mexico DF

Nicaragua (☎ 266-2224, fax 266-8633) One block south of Cuartel General de Bomberos, Casa No. 93, Managua

Singapore (☎ 221-8677 or 221-8678, fax 224-0892, pacosin@pacific.net.sg) 16 Raffles Quay, No 41-06, Hong Leong Building, Singapore 048581

Spain (☎ 91-576-7668 or 576-5001, fax 435-4923) Claudio Coello 86, 28006 Madrid

UK (☎ 20-7493-4646, fax 493-4333, emb.pan@ lineone.net) Panama House 40, Hertfor Street, London W1Y 3PD

USA
Embassy: (☎ 202-483-1407, fax 483-8413 or 8416) 2862 McGill Terrace NW, Washington, DC 20008

Consulates: (☎/fax 714-816-1809) 3137 W Ball R. Suite 104, Anaheim, California 92804

(☎ 305-447-3700, fax 447-4142) 2801 Ponce de Leon Blvd, Suite 1050, Coral Gables, Florida 33134

(☎ 212-840-2450, fax 840-2469) 1212 Ave of the Americas, 10th floor, New York City, New York 10036

There is no Panamanian mission in Australia. Australians are encouraged to contact the Panamanian mission in Singapore.

Embassies & Consulates in Panama
Most foreign embassies and consulates are located in Panama City; see the Panama City chapter for contact information for many of them. Costa Rica has a consulate in David, too; see the Chiriquí Province chapter.

CUSTOMS
You may bring up to 200 cigarettes and three bottles of liquor into Panama tax free. If you try to leave Panama with products made from endangered species – such as jaguar teeth, ocelot skins and turtle shell – you'll face a steep fine and jail time.

MONEY
Currency & Exchange Rates
The US dollar has been Panama's currency since 1904, although it is called the *balboa* here for nationalistic reasons; prices appear with either a '$' or a 'B/.' out front. US$1 is equal to B/.1. Panamanian coins are of the same value, size and metal as US coins; both are used. Coins include one, five, 10, 25 and 50 *centesimos*; 100 centesimos equal US$1 (or B/.1, if you prefer).

With the exception of a Banco Nacional de Panamá counter at Tocumen International Airport, not one Panamanian bank will exchange currency (although some foreign banks may exchange US dollars for their home currencies). Not even the country's finest hotels change money. Once you've left the airport, the only place willing to swap your marks, yen or other major currency for US dollars is a *casa de cambio* (exchange house). There are several in Panama City, but few outside the capital.

Exchange rates vary daily. At the time of writing, the US dollar was strong, and the sample rates shown below reflect that. However, the actual exchange rates you will encounter could be considerably higher or lower than these figures. Daily exchange rates can often be found in the financial pages of major newspapers and at larger banks.

country	unit		balboas
Australia	A$1	=	B/.0.516
Canada	C$1	=	B/.0.644
Euro	€1	=	B/.0.855
Japan	Y100	=	B/.0.837
New Zealand	NZ$1	=	B/.0.419
UK	UK£1	=	B/.1.418
USA	US$1	=	B/.1

The Rich History of Panama's Coins

From the time Europeans first laid eyes upon the isthmus until Panama's national coinage was issued in 1904, coins of many nations were used in the country. Initially Spanish money was used, introduced by the conquistadors. Those coins were supplemented from the 17th century until the early 19th century by coinage produced by colonial Spanish-American mints. Colombian coinage was introduced and circulated from 1821 until shortly after Panama issued its own coins as an independent republic.

Panama's independence from Colombia occurred just one year before the USA began work on the Panama Canal. The USA and Panama agreed that the two countries' currencies would be interchangeable to facilitate the buying power of canal workers and to stabilize the new Panamanian currency by linking it to the reliable US dollar. Panama minted its coins in the USA and adopted the US greenback as its paper currency (but it called the US greenback a *balboa*). Although Panama often alters the images on its coinage, the coins are equal in metallic content, denomination, size and weight to US coins.

Two images that have not changed over the years are those of Indian chieftain Urraca, a warrior who resisted the conquistadors, and Vasco Núñez de Balboa, the first European to view the Pacific Ocean. The image of Urraca has appeared on the Panamanian one-*centesimo* coin since 1935, and that of Balboa is on several coins of different denominations. Although Panama has had a great many talented artists over the years, the designer who created the images of Urraca and Balboa was, ironically, William Clark Noble, an American who hailed from Newport, Rhode Island.

Cash

Panama has no paper money of its own, but it does issue an impressive array of coins, the most common of which are on par with US coinage in size, shape, content and denomination. The only paper currency accepted in Panama is the US 'greenback,' and the only coinage accepted is either US or Panamanian.

Large bills can be troublesome in Panama, particularly outside the capital city. Only the priciest hotels and restaurants in Panama City are accustomed to breaking US$50 and US$100 bills. Even US$10 bills can pose problems for small vendors in the country's central provinces. Unless you will be staying at upscale hotels or don't mind changing bills at banks, bring plenty of US$10 and US$20 bills; anything larger will likely prove inconvenient.

Traveler's Checks

Traveler's checks in currencies other than US dollars are not accepted anywhere in Panama. Because of the appearance of high-quality counterfeits, some banks will only accept American Express traveler's checks or traveler's checks issued by one of their branches or presented by their account holders. The banks that do accept traveler's checks typically charge an exchange fee equal to 1% of the amount of the check. Also, traveler's checks are infrequently accepted by Panamanian businesses. In short, traveler's checks are inconvenient to use in Panama.

Credit Cards

Major credit cards are widely accepted at travel agencies, upscale hotels and pricey restaurants nationwide, but they can be problematic elsewhere – though this was rapidly changing at the time of writing.

Receiving cash advances against a credit card can be a headache in Panama, with many banks unwilling to perform the service. When a bank will perform a cash advance against a credit card – and Banco Nacional de Panamá is usually the most reliable – expect a US$1000 per-transaction limit.

Also, a cash advance against a credit card is typically accompanied by a high interest rate from the moment you make the withdrawal. However, you can avoid high interest charges by leaving a positive balance in your account before you travel; in other words, pay off your entire bill and add however much money you think you might need to receive in Panama.

Because mistakes happen, a credit-card user should ask the company that issued his or her card for the non-toll-free telephone number to use in case the card is lost while in Panama. Remember to obtain non-toll-free telephone numbers, because toll-free numbers are limited to domestic calls.

ATMs

ATM cards are widely used throughout Panama. Many Panamanian banks are linked to the worldwide Plus and Cirrus automated teller systems, so even if your home bank does not have a branch in Panama, you will likely be able to use your ATM card here. (Check the back of your credit and debit cards for the Plus and Cirrus symbols; cards that do not show one or the other likely will not be accepted by ATMs in Panama. Also, to be able to use them you must have a personal identification number. If you don't have one, contact the company that issued your card and obtain one.) Credit cards linked to Plus and Cirrus can also be used at many ATMs in Panama, but as noted above, cash withdrawn against credit cards usually carries a hefty interest rate.

Most Panamanian banks charge a US$3 fee for every ATM transaction, and the amount that can be withdrawn at one time varies from bank to bank and even from machine to machine at the same bank. For example, at Banco Nacional de Panamá, which has the largest number of branches, most ATMs will allow the cardholder to withdraw up to US$500 per transaction, but some ATMs have a US$200 limit. Just why that is is a bit of a mystery.

Also, if your home bank has placed a maximum limit on the amount its clients can withdraw, that limit will be honored by Panama's ATMs. Bank of America, for example, limits ATM withdrawals to US$300 per day. That limit applies to Bank of America debit cards used at ATMs in Panama.

International Transfers

If you need money sent to you from home, you'll find that many banks in Panama will accept cash transfers, but you'll also find that you must first open an account with them; they will charge a commission, and the size of the cash transfer is often limited to avoid the appearance of money laundering.

At Banco Nacional de Panamá, for example, in addition to opening an account you must state why you are seeking the money, provide your address in Panama and show your passport (and a valid tourist card or visa, if required for entry). The transfer requires two days, and the bank charges a transfer fee; the sender also has to pay a fee.

You can reduce the inconvenience by transferring the money via Western Union, but its transfer fees are very steep. For example, the fee for transferring US$50 by Western Union is US$13; for transferring US$5000 it's US$200. However, there's lots less paperwork involved and the transfer can take as little as 15 minutes. There are more than 20 Western Union offices in Panama City, and others can be found in Aguadulce, Changuinola, Chitré, Colón, Coronado, David, La Chorrera, Las Tablas, Paso Canoas, Penonomé and Santiago.

Security

Pickpockets prey on easy targets, and unsuspecting tourists fit that bill. Avoid losing your money by following a few precautions: Carry money in inside pockets, money belts or pouches beneath your clothes. Don't carry a wallet in a back pocket or an outside jacket pocket. Don't put all your money in one place. Reports of people having their pockets picked are rare in Panama, but it's best to assume pickpockets are around and to behave accordingly.

Costs

Budget accommodations tend to be slightly more expensive in Panama than in other parts of Central America; a hotel room that might cost only US$6 in Nicaragua or Guatemala might cost US$10 here. In Panama City you can get a very basic room for US$8 a night; a modern room in a better area costs around US$15 to US$20. Away from Panama City, accommodations are less expensive; a modern room may cost around US$12. Die-hard shoestring travelers can still find a room almost anywhere in the country for around US$6. Prices for food and transportation are also reasonable.

Tipping & Bargaining

A tip equal to 10% of the bill is standard in upscale restaurants. In small cafés and other casual places, tipping is not necessary and is seldom done. It is not necessary to tip taxi drivers; however, bellhops are usually tipped.

Haggling over prices is not the custom in Panama. However, if you really want an item at a store where you suspect there are steep price markups – at a watch or camera store, for example – prices may be flexible. It never hurts to make an offer.

Taxes

A tax of 10% is added to the price of hotel rooms in Panama; when you inquire about a hotel price, be sure to determine whether the quoted price includes the tax. Hotel prices given in this book include the 10% tax. There's also a 5% sales tax.

POST & COMMUNICATIONS
Sending Mail

An airmail letter from Panama to the USA weighing 20g or less requires 35¢ postage (25¢ for a postcard) and takes five to 10 days to arrive; an airmail letter to Europe or Australia requires 45¢ postage (40¢ for a postcard) and takes 10 days to arrive; to Japan the letter requires 60¢ postage (45¢ for a postcard) and takes 10 to 14 days to arrive. Parcels can also be mailed; they tend to be rather expensive and always take longer than letters to reach a foreign destination.

The better hotels sell stamps; otherwise you'll need to buy them at a post office. Unfortunately, vending machines selling stamps have yet to appear in Panama. If

you're near an upscale hotel, see if you can stamp and mail your correspondence at the hotel to avoid having to wait in line at a post office. US stamps are not accepted.

Most post offices in Panama are open 7 am to 6 pm weekdays and 7 am to 5 pm Saturday. In addresses, *Apartado* means 'PO Box'; it is not a street or apartment address.

Receiving Mail

Poste restante mail can be addressed to '(name), Entrega General, (town and province), República de Panamá.' Be sure the sender writes the country's name as 'República de Panamá' rather than simply 'Panamá,' or the mail may be sent back. Post offices in Panama will hold mail for 30 days before returning it. There is no fee for this service. You will need to show an ID to receive your mail. It's not possible to pick up other people's mail.

If you have mail sent to the post office, remember that the mail is filed alphabetically; if it's addressed to John Gillis Payson, it could well be filed under 'G' or 'J' instead of 'P.' Ask your correspondents to clearly print your last name and to avoid appending witticisms such as 'World Traveler Extraordinaire' to your name.

Poste restante parcels can also be sent to you. If the parcel weighs less than 2kg and isn't large, it will generally arrive at the post office. If it's heavy or large, it will likely be held at the post office in the El Dorado district of Panama City, where it will have to clear customs. You'll be notified that it's there by personnel at the post office addressed by the sender.

Telephone

Panama's longtime state-run telephone company, Intel, was purchased by a British consortium in 1997 for US$625 million and renamed Cable & Wireless. In the years since, Cable & Wireless has installed more than 10,000 phones across Panama, and the company has honored its promise to install at least one public phone in every Panamanian community with at least 250 residents.

Most of the blue public telephones require plastic cards called *tarjetas*. These can be purchased in US$5, US$10 and US$20 denominations from businesses (usually markets) displaying a small Cable & Wireless sign out front. They can also be purchased from machines located outside every Cable & Wireless building; most cities and towns have at least one Cable & Wireless building.

Tarjetas are the easiest and cheapest way to place a call in Panama. Simply insert the card into the pay phone, punch in 00, then punch in your number, starting with the country code. (The country code for the USA and Canada is 1, for Australia it's 61, for France it's 33, for Germany it's 49, for Italy it's 39, for New Zealand it's 64, for Spain it's 34, and for the UK it's 44. Dial ☎ 106 for a local international operator to inquire about other country codes.)

The number you entered will appear in a window on the telephone along with the amount of money remaining on your card. When an answering machine or a person receives your call, the amount of money remaining on the card as well as the amount of time left will appear in the window.

Local Calls Telephone calls to anywhere within Panama can be made from pay phones. Local calls cost 15¢ for three minutes. Many phones accept 5¢, 10¢ and 25¢ coins (both Panamanian and US coins are OK). Follow the directions given on the phone; some phones require you to insert the coin first, and others instruct you to first wait for the tone and then dial the number. For the latter type, don't deposit the coin until the call has been answered at the other end. In order to speak with a national operator, dial ☎ 101. For directory assistance, dial ☎ 102.

International Calls Using a tarjeta (see Telephone, above) is by far the least expensive way to place an international call, plus callers can see exactly how much they are paying for the call. Operated-assisted international calls are possible, but they can be extremely expensive.

Connecting to an international operator from a residential, business or pay phone is easy. To connect with a local international operator, simply dial ☎ 106. For an international operator in the USA, dial ☎ 108 (MCI), 109 (AT&T), 115 (Sprint) or 117 (TRT). To reach a Costa Rican operator, dial ☎ 107; for a Colombian operator, dial ☎ 116.

Most hotels, however, require that you make international calls through a switchboard so they can charge an outrageous connection fee; in the pricier hotels this fee can be US$4 or more – even if you are simply asking to be connected to an international operator.

Furthermore, many hotels in Panama charge a per-minute fee for international calls that is far in excess of what the telephone company charges them. And on top of that, there is often a three-minute minimum. In short, avoid placing international calls from hotels, or at least ask what the connection fee and per-minute rate are before calling, so that you won't receive a surprisingly high telephone bill at the time you check out. Better yet, use a tarjeta!

At the time of writing, a phone call from a public phone to the USA cost about US$1 per minute, to Europe US$3 per minute, to Australia US$4 per minute and to Japan US$5 per minute.

To call Panama from abroad, use the international code (507) before the seven-digit Panamanian telephone number. There are no city codes in Panama.

eKno Communication Service Lonely Planet's eKno global communication service provides low-cost international calls – for local calls, you're usually better off with a local phone card. eKno also offers free messaging services, email, travel information and an online travel vault, where you can securely store all your important documents. You can join online at www.ekno.lonelyplanet.com, where you will find the local-access numbers for the 24-hour customer-service center. Once you have joined, check the eKno website for the latest access numbers for each country and for updates on new features.

Fax, Email & Internet Access
Fax and sometimes email services are offered at Cable & Wireless offices throughout the country.

Many upscale hotels also offer fax service, and some mid-range and most upscale hotels were offering or planning to offer email service on a per-minute basis at the time this book was written.

Internet cafés can be found in all cities and in many towns. Those that appeared to have a certain future are mentioned in the regional chapters of this book. Hotel clerks can usually advise where the nearest Internet café is located.

INTERNET RESOURCES

The World Wide Web is a rich resource for travelers. You can research your trip, hunt down bargain airfares, book hotels, check on weather conditions or chat with locals and other travelers about the best places to visit (or avoid!).

Panama-Specific Sites

The following websites contain information specific to Panama that might be of interest to you.

The Panama Canal This is the website of the Panama Canal Authority, an entity of the Panamanian government charged with managing, operating and maintaining the canal. The site contains a wealth of canal news and recent and historic photos of the canal. Website: www.pancanal.com

Jungle Operations Training Center The JOTC was the US Army's training center at Fort Sherman, near Colón, for light infantry and special operations units from 1953 to 1999. Fort Sherman was handed over to Panama in June 1999. The site contains lots of history and photos. Website: http://junglefighter.panamanow.net

BOOKS

Many of the books listed below are available outside Panama. A few bookstores in Panama City carry some of the titles; see Bookstores in the Panama City chapter.

Lonely Planet

Lonely Planet's *Central America on a shoestring* is useful for travelers on a tight budget who are visiting several Central American countries. Lonely Planet's *Costa Rica* and *Colombia* are the finest guidebooks on those countries. The company's *Latin American Spanish phrasebook* contains practical words and expressions in Latin-American Spanish.

Guidebooks

When choosing travel guidebooks, try to get a recent edition. The older the guidebook, the greater the likelihood that it contains inaccuracies.

The Panama Guide (Seaworthy Publications, 1996), by Nancy Schwalbe Zydler and Tom Zydler, is *the* cruising guide to the isthmus of Panama. It offers piloting directions, charts, anchorages, history, and even instructions for transiting the Panama Canal. Copies are available in Panama City and from Internet booksellers.

Nature & Wildlife

The 2nd edition of *A Guide to the Birds of Panama* (Princeton University Press, 1989), by Robert S Ridgley and John A Gwynne, Jr, is the foremost field guide to Panama's birds. It's an expensive but very comprehensive volume that also includes a list of the avifauna of Costa Rica, Honduras and Nicaragua. Some sections are in need of updating.

Birds of Tropical America (Chapters Publications, 1994), by Steven Hilty, is subtitled *A Watcher's Introduction to Beha ior, Breeding and Di ersity* and provides plenty of interesting background on the birds that you'll see on your trip. The author is a professional ornithologist.

The Botany and Natural History of Panama (Missouri Botanical Gardens, 1985), edited by William G D'Arcy and Mireya D Correa, is a collection of research papers that covers a wide body of work, including the results of aviary experiments and instructions on how to construct aerial walkways in rain forest canopies.

A Panama Forest and Shore: Natural History and Amerindian Culture in Bocas del Toro (Boxwood Press, 1983), by Burton

L Gordon, is an academic's look at western Panama based on the author's observations of Bocas del Toro during seven field trips.

A Field Guide to the Orchids of Costa Rica and Panama, by Robert Dressler, has 240 photos and almost as many drawings of orchids within its 274 pages.

History

The Sack of Panamá: Sir Henry Morgan's Ad entures on the Spanish Main, by Peter Earle, is a vivid though not particularly well-sourced account of the Welsh pirate's looting of Panamá in 1671.

Old Panama and Castilla Del Oro (The Page Company, 1911), by CLG Anderson, is a narrative history of the discovery, conquest and settlement of Panama by the Spaniards. This hard-to-find but impressive tome also reports on the search for a strait through the New World and early efforts to build a canal.

Panama: Resumen Histórico Ilustrado del Istmo 1501-1994 (Antigua Films, 1996), by Ricardo de la Espriella III, is a well-written and beautifully illustrated history of Panama from the arrival of Rodrigo de Bastidas through the US invasion. It is available in Spanish only.

Panama: Four Hundred Years of Dreams and Cruelty, by David A Howarth, is a readable history of the isthmus from Balboa's 1513 exploration through 1964.

Panama Canal

The Path Between the Seas: The Creation of the Panama Canal is an exciting account of the building of the canal, written by the award-winning historian David McCullough. It is 700 pages long and reads like a suspense novel from cover to cover. It is the best book written about the construction of the canal.

And the Mountains Will Mo e, by Miles P Du Val, is a scholarly account of the digging of the canal from the start of the unsuccessful French effort through the US achievement.

Other books describing the building of the unnatural waterway include *The Impossible Dream: The Building of the Panama Canal*, by Ian Cameron; *The Panama Canal:*

The Crisis in Historical Perspecti e, by Walter LaFeber; and *Portrait of the Panama Canal* (Graphic Arts Center Publishing Company, 1996), by William Friar.

An American Legacy in Panama (US Department of Defense, 1995), by Suzanne P Johnson, was prepared for the US Army to provide an overview of US military installations in the Canal Area, and it does indeed give a very thorough report on former US installations near the canal.

Politics & the Noriega Era

9°N (nine degrees north, Panama News Books, 2000), by Panama's finest reporter and editor of *The Panama News*, Eric Jackson, consists of dozens of insightful dispatches by Jackson about life, politics and business practices in Panama from 1994 to 2000. It's available in Panama.

Inside Panama (Interhemispheric Resource Center, 1995), by Tom Barry and John Lindsay-Poland, is a look at the political, economic and human-rights scenes in Panama, with special emphasis on Panamanian society since the 1960s and on US-Panama relations from that time through the mid-1990s.

The Noriega Mess: The Drugs, the Canal, and Why America In aded, a 1000-page tome by Luis E Murillo, is quite interesting and very readable. It's based on a variety of sources and information that have come to light in the years since 1989.

Panama: The Whole Story, by Kevin Buckley, is another fine book about Noriega and the events that led to the 1989 US invasion; 'as readable as a spy thriller,' the book's jacket proclaims, and it nearly lives up to its billing.

For yet another perspective on the Noriega story, look for his memoir, *America's Prisoner: The Memoirs of Manuel Noriega*, cowritten with Peter Eisner, who has researched Noriega's claims and footnoted the text.

Indians

Secrets of the Cuna Earth Mother: A Contemporary Study of Ancient Religions, by Clyde E Keeler, is a collection of notes on the religion and lives of the Kuna and a comparison of their religion with some in the Far East.

Ancient Arts of the Andes, by Wendell C Bennett, discusses the Indian art of Panama, which is related to the pre-Columbian art of the Andes.

NEWSPAPERS & MAGAZINES

La Prensa (independent centrist) is the most widely circulated daily newspaper in Panama. Other major Spanish-language dailies include *El Siglo* (sensationalist), *El Periódico* (pro-Partido Revolucionaro Democrático), *La Estrella de Panamá* (center-right), and *El Panamá América, Crítica* and *Primera Plana* (all right wing).

The Panama News is published in English twice monthly; it is distributed widely and is often found in hotels and restaurants in Panama City. It's free and it is by far the most intelligent and unbiased newspaper in the country. *The Visitor*, published in English and Spanish and written for foreigners, is another free publication, broadly distributed in tourist haunts.

The *Miami Herald International Edition* is widely available. English-language magazines and newspapers, including the *International Herald Tribune*, are available at Farmacias Arrocha and Gran Morrison stores in Panama City.

RADIO & TV

There are three commercial TV stations in Panama (channels 2, 4 and 13) and two devoted to public broadcasting (channels 5 and 11). Sports programming, including NBA and NFL games, is generally shown on channel 2, while channels 4 and 13 favor national productions, situation comedies and movies. Most hotel rooms are equipped with cable TV.

There are about 90 radio stations in Panama, mostly FM and mostly operated on a commercial basis. Popular FM stations and the music they play include 97.1 and 102.1 for salsa, 94.5 for traditional Panamanian, 88.9 for Latin jazz, 88.1 for reggae, 105.7 for classical, 107.3 for disco, 101.1 and

104.7 for easy listening, 106.7 for Latin rock and 93.9 and 98.9 for US rock.

If you have a portable shortwave radio, you can hear the BBC World Service, Voice of America and Radio Moscow.

PHOTOGRAPHY
Film & Equipment

The prices of high-end camera equipment in Panama are competitive, particularly in the Zona Libre in Colón, although the savings are not terribly impressive. The inventory, however, can be excellent, especially for Nikon equipment.

Filmwise, Panama City has everything, but outside the capital city you'll be hardpressed to find Kodachrome 64 or Fuji Velvia slide films – the really good stuff. At the many Supercolor stores in Panama City (check the phone book for addresses and phone numbers), not only can you find Fuji Velvia, but it's well priced.

Film processors in Panama reportedly do good work. If you're going to be in Panama a while and are anxious to see your photos, consider having one roll developed in Panama and examining the results before submitting additional rolls.

Technical Tips

Tropical shadows are very strong and come out almost black on photographs. Often a bright but hazy day makes for better photographs than a very sunny one. Photography in open shade or using a fill-in flash will help. Polarizing filters reduce glare and accentuate colors.

You will need high-speed (400 ASA or faster) film or flash equipment and/or a tripod if you want to take photographs within a rain forest. Pros prefer highquality but super-slow (50 ASA) Fuji Velvia slide film and a tripod to the convenience of high-speed film that produces grainy images. The amount of light penetrating the layers of vegetation is remarkably low.

As a general rule, the best time for shooting is when the sun is low – the first and last two hours of the day. Remember, too, that flash equipment is forbidden in Panama's churches and museums.

Photographing People

Panamanians make wonderful subjects for photos. However, most people resent having cameras thrust in their faces, and some attach price tags to their mugs (see Dos & Don'ts in the Facts about Panama chapter). As a rule, you should ask for permission if you have an inkling your subject would not approve.

Please be sensitive to people's feelings; remember, you're not simply a tourist, you are a representative of your country when you leave its borders. A 50-something British pervert trying to get a photo of an elderly Kuna woman's private parts in 1994 nearly closed the Archipiélago de San Blás to all travelers once word of his attempt reached Kuna leaders.

Airport Security

The security folks at Panama's Tocumen International Airport insist that their X-ray machines are film safe and computer friendly, but you'd be wise to ask to have your film and computer inspected by hand.

TIME

Panama time is in line with New York and Miami, five hours behind Greenwich Mean Time (GMT) and one hour ahead of the rest of Central America. If you're coming from Costa Rica, be sure to reset your watch.

ELECTRICITY

Beware of variations in electrical currents in Panama. Almost everywhere, voltage will be 110 volts, but there are exceptions; an ordinary two-prong socket may be either 110 or 220 volts. Find out which it is before you plug in your appliance. Many travel gadgets can be adjusted for different voltages.

Also, beware that power surges and brief outages are fairly common in Panama, particularly in Panama City. If you're planning on using a laptop computer in Panama, you'd be wise to hook it up to a surge protector; these are fairly inexpensive (under

US$20) and are widely available in Panama City, David and other major cities.

WEIGHTS & MEASURES

The metric system is the official system for weights and measures, but the US system of pounds, gallons and miles is also used. This book uses the metric system; conversion information is given inside the book's back cover.

LAUNDRY

Laundromats (la amáticos) are abundant and cheap in Panama; usually you drop off your laundry, they wash and dry it, and you pick it up a few hours later. Cost per load is 75¢ to wash, 75¢ to dry and another 25¢ for detergent, unless you bring your own.

Dry cleaners (la anderías) are also widely available but considerably more expensive. Many dry cleaners will not wash undergarments.

If you stay at a luxury hotel, note the price of the laundry service before you use it. It will be outrageous. For example, the cost of having one old pair of blue jeans washed at the Radisson in Panama City is US$7.70 – and you won't get them back the same day!

TOILETS

Panamanian plumbing generally is of high quality, although on some San Blás islands and elsewhere you'll find signs beside the toilets asking you to place your used paper in the trash bins provided instead of flushing it away. That's because narrow piping was used during construction and the owners fear clogging. Putting used toilet paper into a trash bin may not seem sanitary, but it is much better than clogged bowls and overflowing toilet water.

Public toilets can be found mainly in bus terminals, airports and restaurants. In Spanish, restrooms are called baños and are often marked caballeros (gentlemen) and damas (ladies). Outside the cities, toilet paper is not always provided, so you may want to consider carrying a personal supply.

HEALTH

It's true that most people traveling for any length of time in Latin America are likely to have an occasional upset stomach. It's also true that if you take certain precautions before, during and after your trip, it's unlikely that you will become seriously ill.

Dengue fever, which is a mosquito-spread disease, is on the rise in Panama, as is leishmaniasis, a disease spread by sand flies, and malaria is present in most of the country. Despite their presence, few Panamanians are ever afflicted with these diseases, and by taking steps to reduce insect bites you can make the risk of contracting these diseases negligible.

Predeparture Preparations

If, as someone once said, almost anything is easier to get into than to get out of, you might want to give undivided attention to the information in this section – and possibly spare yourself some grief.

Vaccinations Panamanian authorities generally do not require anyone to have an up-to-date international vaccination card to enter the country. However, travelers coming from a country experiencing a cholera epidemic may be asked to show proof that they received vaccinations against the disease. Likewise, travelers coming from areas with a high incidence of malaria may be asked if they are taking antimalaria medication.

Regardless of the entry requirements, you should take steps to protect yourself against these diseases if you know you will be spending time in an area where they pose a real health hazard. Pregnant women should consult with their doctors before receiving any vaccinations.

Travel Insurance Regardless of how fit and healthy you are, *do* take out travel insurance, preferably one with provisions for flying you home in the event of a medical emergency. Even if you don't get sick, you might be involved in an accident. Many are the stories of poor souls who thought they'd save some money by passing on travel insurance only to face enormous medical bills when disaster struck.

Travel Health Guides If you are planning to be away for a long period of time or to travel in remote areas, you should consider taking a more detailed health guide, like Lonely Planet's *Healthy Tra el Central & South America*. These and others usually can be found in the Health section of a general bookstore. There are also a number of excellent travel health websites on the Internet. There are links from the Lonely Planet website (www.lonelyplanet.com) to the World Health Organization and to the US Centers for Disease Control & Prevention.

First-Aid Kit How well stocked your first-aid kit should be depends on your knowledge of first-aid procedures, where you will be going, how long you will need the kit and how many people will be sharing it. The following is a suggested checklist, which you should amend as needed:

- your prescription medications
- antiseptic cream
- anti-itch cream for insect bites
- Tylenol or other non-aspirin painkiller
- Lomotil or Pepto-Bismol for diarrhea
- antibiotics
- throat lozenges
- ear and eye drops
- antacid tablets
- anti-motion-sickness medication
- alcohol swabs
- water purification tablets
- rehydration mixture for severe diarrhea
- lip salve and sunscreen
- sunburn salve (aloe vera gel works well)
- antifungal powder (for foot and groin)
- thermometer (in a case)
- surgical tape, gauze and bandages
- moleskin for blistered feet
- scissors, tweezers and earplugs
- first-aid booklet

A convenient way to carry your first-aid kit so that it doesn't get crushed is in a small plastic container with a sealing lid, such as Tupperware.

Don't use medications indiscriminately, and be aware of their side effects: Some people are allergic to drugs as common as aspirin. Antibiotics such as tetracycline make your skin more susceptible to sunburn. Antibiotics are not recommended unless they're needed; they destroy the body's natural resistance to diarrhea, and some people are allergic to them. Lomotil counteracts the symptoms of diarrhea, but it doesn't cure the problem. Anti-motion-sickness or antihistamine medications can make you very drowsy.

Other Preparations Smart travel begins with preparation, and nothing is more important than your health. Don't belittle this fact. If you wear prescription glasses, make sure you take a spare pair and a copy of the prescription with you to Panama. The tropical sun is strong, so you may want to have a prescription pair of sunglasses made before you leave home. If you are going on a long trip, make sure your teeth and gums are healthy.

Regardless of your natural skin color, play it safe and take sunscreen with you. Sunscreen is readily available in pharmacies throughout Panama, but why wait to buy something you'll likely need? A minimum sun protection factor of 15 is good; 30 is even better.

Water & Food

Tap water is safe to drink throughout Panama. The government agency in charge of water treatment regularly checks the drinking water to ensure compliance with World Health Organization standards. As a rule, you should never drink unfiltered or untreated water from streams, rivers or lakes because of the parasites that lurk within them.

If you're one of those people who always seem to get a tummy ache when no one else does, play it super-safe and drink bottled water, soft drinks or Gatorade instead of tap water in areas where you suspect the water might be hazardous to your health.

Canned and bottled beverages are readily available in Panama.

Use common sense when it comes to food. Roadside stands are never as clean as restaurants, so avoid them. If it's midday and there's no one inside the restaurant you've just entered, assume the locals know something about the place that you don't and back out. If a restaurant seems unhealthy, suppose it is and move along.

The beef in Panama is grass fed and tends to be lean and tough. Inspections are spotty and Panamanian meats are not up to US, European and Canadian standards. To avoid problems, don't eat locally raised meat, poultry and seafood that is undercooked. Eat raw fish only at sushi restaurants.

Medical Problems & Treatments

Cholera Cholera is an acute diarrheal illness caused by infection of the intestine by the bacterium *Vibrio cholerae*. It's transmitted directly through food or water contaminated with fecal material from infected people. The symptoms are severe watery diarrhea and vomiting, which cause massive fluid and electrolyte loss, leading to severe dehydration. The only treatment for cholera is prevention. Get vaccinated against cholera before you travel into Central America, where the disease periodically appears.

Dengue Fever This viral disease is carried by the same mosquito that carries yellow fever. There are several hundred known cases each year in Panama. There is no prophylactic available for dengue. The main preventative measure is to avoid getting mosquito bites by using insect repellent, mosquito netting and bug jackets when they're appropriate (such as in the jungle or at the beach at sunset). The areas of highest risk are Darién, Los Santos and Coclé Provinces, but cases have been reported even in Panama City. Symptoms include any of the following: fever, chills, severe back and joint aches, pain behind the eyes, and rash. There is no treatment except for rest and painkillers. Do not take aspirin; drink plenty of liquids. Dengue sometimes kills. If you think you've got it, go to a hospital.

Insect Repellent

The most effective ingredient in insect repellent is diethyl-metatoluamide, also known as Deet. You can buy repellent with 90% or even more of this ingredient; however, many brands contain less than 15%. I find that the rub-on lotions are the most effective, and pump sprays are good for spraying clothes, especially at the neck, wrist, waist and ankle openings.

Some people find that Deet irritates their skin; consider buying a weaker mix of 40% to 60% Deet to reduce the risk of irritation. All users should avoid getting Deet in their eyes, on their lips and on other sensitive regions. This stuff can dissolve plastic, so keep it off plastic lenses, etc. I know of someone who put Deet on his face, began sweating and got Deet-laden sweat in his eyes. The result: eye irritation *and* ruined contact lenses!

Deet is toxic to children and shouldn't be used on their skin. Instead, try Avon's Skin So Soft, which has insect-repellent properties and is not toxic (get the oil, not the lotion). Camping stores sometimes sell insect repellents with names such as 'Green Ban'; these are made with natural products and are not toxic, but many people find them less effective than repellents with Deet.

You can also sometimes find mosquito coils. They work like incense sticks and are fairly effective at keeping insects away.

Diarrhea Most diarrhea is noninfectious and self-limited and may arise from changes in food, water or altitude, combined with fatigue and emotional stresses. This type of diarrhea often clears up on a bland diet, with particular avoidance of fats and alcohol. The important factor in treating any diarrhea is to replace lost fluids by drinking water, tea, broth or carbonated beverages. Gatorade, diluted half and half with water, is good for replacing lost fluids and electrolytes. A useful drug to relieve excessive diarrhea and cramps is Pepto-Bismol, available throughout Panama.

Dysentery If your diarrhea continues for several days and it is accompanied by nausea, severe abdominal pain and fever, and you find blood in your stools, it's likely that you have contracted dysentery. Fortunately, dysentery is not common in Panama. There are two types: amoebic and bacillary. It is not always obvious which kind you have. Although bacillary responds well to antibiotics, amoebic – which is rarer – involves more complex treatment. If you suspect you have dysentery, you should seek medical advice.

Hepatitis Hepatitis A, the most predominant form in Panama, is caused by ingesting contaminated food or water. Salads, uncooked vegetables, unpeeled fruit and unboiled drinks are the worst offenders. Infection risks can be minimized by using bottled drinks, washing your own fruits and vegetables with purified water and paying scrupulous attention to your toilet habits. If you get the disease, you'll know it. Your skin and especially the whites of your eyes turn yellow, and you feel so tired that it literally takes all your effort to go to the toilet. There is no cure except rest. A series of three vaccines given over a one-year period is available. The incidence of hepatitis A is low in Panama, so many travelers opt not to bother with these shots.

Leishmaniasis There are 76 known species of *chitra* (sand fly) in Panama, and five of them are known to carry the leishmaniasis parasite. Once a victim is bitten by an infected sand fly, the parasite enters the body, where it may remain for up to six months without making itself known. Then a sore can develop anywhere on the body, even on the corneas. At first the sore resembles a pimple, but instead of going away it swells and opens up. Leishmaniasis sores can grow to the size of a half-dollar or larger, and at this size they resemble festering wounds and can be crusty in places. A test for the presence of leishmaniasis exists. Treatment involves a series of injections.

Malaria A parasitic infection, malaria is transmitted to humans by mosquitoes. Signs of infection range from fever to flu-like symptoms, including chills, fever, achiness and fatigue. If left untreated, malaria can cause anemia, kidney failure, coma and death. There is risk of malaria in the rural areas of Darién, Chiriquí and Bocas del Toro Provinces and near Lago Bayano and Lago Gatún. If you plan on spending much time in the infected areas, you might want to consider taking antimalaria medication. It is supplied in the form of pills that must be taken from two weeks before until six weeks after your visit. Be advised that antimalaria medication makes you more susceptible to sunburn, which is something to factor into your decision if you burn easily anyway and if you plan to be taking precautions against mosquito bites (such as using repellent, bug jackets and so on).

Rabies Rabies is a fatal viral infection found in many countries, including Panama. Many animals can be infected (such as dogs, cats, bats and monkeys), and it is their saliva that is infectious. Any bite, scratch or even lick from a warm-blooded, furry animal should be cleaned immediately and thoroughly. Scrub with soap and running water, and then apply alcohol or iodine solution. Medical help should be sought promptly to receive a course of injections to prevent the onset of symptoms. There are vampire bats in many parts of Panama; if you will be sleeping outside, be sure to keep your feet covered and use mosquito netting to keep them off your head. Typically people learn that they have been visited by a vampire bat when they wake up and find blood in their hair or on their toes.

Tetanus Tetanus occurs when a wound becomes infected by a germ that lives in soil and in the feces of various animals. It enters the body via breaks in the skin. All wounds should be cleaned promptly and an antisep-

tic cream or solution applied. Use antibiotics if the wound becomes hot or throbs or pus develops. The first symptom may be discomfort in swallowing or stiffening of the jaw and neck; this is followed by painful convulsions of the jaw and whole body. The disease can be fatal. A tetanus vaccine is available and is strongly recommended.

Yellow Fever Yellow fever is now the only vaccine that is a legal requirement for entry into many countries (it is not required for entrance into Panama). This rule is usually only enforced when visitors are coming from an infected area. Protection lasts 10 years. The Darién is the only area of risk in Panama, and even there the risk is minute. Be advised that the vaccination poses some risk during pregnancy. Also, people allergic to eggs may not be able to have this vaccine. Discuss it with your doctor.

Insect Problems Insect repellents go a long way in preventing bites, but if you do get bitten, avoid scratching. Unfortunately, this is easier said than done.

To alleviate itching, try applying hydrocortisone cream, calamine lotion or some other kind of anti-itch cream, or soaking in baking soda. Scratching will quickly open bites and cause them to become infected. Skin infections are slow to heal in the heat of the Tropics, and all infected bites as well as cuts and grazes should be kept scrupulously clean, treated with antiseptic creams and covered with dressings on a daily basis.

Another insect problem is infestation with lice and scabies. Lice crawl around in your body hair and make you itch. To get rid of them, wash with a shampoo containing benzene hexachloride or shave the affected area. To avoid being reinfected, wash your clothes and bedding in hot water and the shampoo. It's probably best to throw away your underwear if you had body lice. Lice thrive on body warmth; these beasties lurking in clothes will die in about 72 hours if the clothing isn't worn.

Chiggers are mites that burrow into your skin and cause it to become red and intensely itchy. These are also known as sand flies, or *chitras* in Spanish. They are common on Panama's beaches and in the jungle. Once you've got them, you just have to endure them for a few days. They do not pose any serious health threat unless they are leishmaniasis carriers; the chance that they are carrying leishmaniasis is slight, and even then the disease is treatable. The best prevention is sprinkling sulfur powder on socks, shoes and lower legs before walking through grass. Liberal application of insect repellent works pretty well.

Scorpions and spiders can give severely painful – but rarely fatal – stings or bites. A common way to get bitten is to put on your clothes and shoes in the morning without checking them first. Develop the habit of shaking out your clothing before putting it on, especially in the lowlands. Check your bedding before going to sleep. Don't walk barefoot outdoors, and watch where you place your hands when you are reaching for a shelf or branch.

Snakebite This is extremely unlikely. Should you be bitten, the snake may be a nonvenomous one. And even venomous snakes withhold their poison most of the time when they bite. But if you are bitten, assume the worst and try to prevent the circulation of any venom already inside you by following the advice in the next paragraph. Do not try the slash-and-suck routine on the bite, as some of Panama's poisonous snakes contain anticoagulant agents in their venom. Slashing open a snake bite can result in uncontrollable bleeding.

The venom of most dangerous snakes does its nasty work via the lymph system, not the bloodstream, so treatment aimed at reducing the flow of blood or removing venom from the bloodstream is likely to be futile. Aim to immobilize the bitten limb and bandage it tightly and completely (but do not make a tourniquet; this is now considered too dangerous and not particularly effective). Then, with a minimum of disturbance, particularly to the bound limb, get the victim to a hospital as soon as possible (most Panamanian hospitals stock antivenin). Keep calm and reassure the victim.

Sexually Transmitted Diseases Prostitution is legal in Panama, and female prostitutes are required to be registered and receive regular medical checkups. Nevertheless, the incidence of sexually transmitted diseases (STDs) is increasing among Panamanian prostitutes. In addition, some prostitutes are transvestites, who are unlikely to receive the required medical care because of social prejudice against them.

The use of condoms will reduce your chances of contracting an STD. Condoms *(preser ati os)* are available in Panamanian pharmacies. However, while condoms do reduce the risk of contracting the human immunodeficiency virus (HIV), they don't prevent the transmission of herpes, a disease that only requires skin-to-skin contact. Please remember that herpes is forever.

HIV/AIDS HIV leads to acquired immune deficiency syndrome (AIDS, or SIDA in Spanish). Panama is ranked 19th in the world on a per-capita basis for HIV/AIDS cases, with an estimated 40,000 infected people in 2000.

Apart from abstinence, the most effective preventative is to use condoms and avoid sex that involves an exchange of bodily fluids. It is impossible to detect the HIV-positive status of a healthy-looking person without a blood test.

Environmental Hazards
Fungal Infections Fungal infections occur more commonly in hot weather and are usually found on the scalp, between the toes or fingers, in the groin and on the body (ringworm). You get ringworm (which is a fungal infection, not a worm) from infected animals or other people. Moisture encourages these infections.

To prevent fungal infections, wear loose, comfortable clothes, avoid artificial fibers, wash frequently and dry thoroughly. If you do get an infection, wash the infected area at least daily with a disinfectant or medicated soap and water, and rinse and dry well. Apply an antifungal cream or powder such as tolnifate (also known as Tinaderm). Try to expose the infected area to air or sunlight as much as possible, and wash all towels and underwear in hot water, change them often and let them dry in the sun.

Heat Exhaustion Dehydration and salt deficiency can cause heat exhaustion. Take time to acclimatize to high temperatures, drink sufficient amounts of liquids and do not do anything too physically demanding. Salt deficiency is characterized by fatigue, lethargy, headaches, giddiness and muscle cramps; salt tablets may help, but adding salt to your food is better.

Heatstroke This serious, occasionally fatal condition can occur if the body's heat-regulating mechanism breaks down and body temperature rises to dangerous levels. Long, continuous periods of exposure to high temperatures and insufficient fluids can leave you vulnerable to heatstroke.

The symptoms are feeling unwell, little or no sweating and a high body temperature (from 39° to 41°C or 102° to 106°F). Where sweating has ceased, the skin becomes flushed and red. Throbbing headaches and lack of coordination will also occur, and victims may be confused or aggressive. Eventually a victim will become delirious or convulse. Hospitalization is essential, but in the interim get the victim out of the sun, remove his clothing, cover him with a wet towel and fan him continually. Give fluids if the victim is conscious.

Prickly Heat Prickly heat is an itchy rash caused by excessive perspiration trapped under the skin. It usually strikes people who have just arrived in a hot climate. Keeping cool, bathing often, drying the skin and using a mild talcum or prickly heat powder may help, and you can resort to air conditioning.

Sunburn In the Tropics you can get sunburned surprisingly quickly, even through dense cloud cover. Use sunscreen liberally and put barrier cream on your nose and lips. Calamine lotion and aloe vera gel are good for mild sunburns. Protect your eyes with good-quality sunglasses, particularly if you will be near water. A hat can save you pain – and wrinkles.

Women's Health
Antibiotic use, wearing synthetic underwear, sweating and use of contraceptive pills can lead to vaginal infections when you're traveling in hot climates. Wearing loose-fitting clothes and cotton underwear will help to prevent these fungal infections, characterized by a rash, itching and discharge. Such infections can be treated with a vinegar or lemon-juice douche or with yogurt. Nystatin, miconazole or clotrimazole pessaries or vaginal cream are the usual treatments.

Medical Facilities
The best hospital in Panama is the Centro Medico Paitilla (☎ 263-6060), at Calle 53 Este and Avenida Balboa in Panama City, where many of the doctors speak English. See the Information section in the Panama City chapter for details. Every city in Panama has at least one hospital or medical clinic, and many appear on city maps in this guidebook.

WOMEN TRAVELERS
Attitudes Toward Women
In Panama, the penalty for killing a horse is much stiffer than the penalty for wife beating. But that reality is more a sign of some needed changes in Panamanian law than it is a reflection on Panamanian society. A greater reality is that women are highly respected in Panama and, indeed, hold many positions of power in government and in the private sector. At the time of writing, Panama had a female president.

In general, female tourists – particularly American women – are viewed differently than female Panamanians, thanks to American TV programs and Hollywood movies that portray American women as sexually easy. As a result, young foreign women tend to attract more sexual advances in Panama than local women. If you're one of them and don't like the attention, dress conservatively and communicate your disinterest with a firm voice or intentional neglect.

Safety Precautions

Panama is a safe country in general, but conventional wisdom should apply. Women who want to minimize their risk of assault will avoid traveling alone and won't seek out isolated beaches. Being alone is the first step to high physical risk for women in the hunting grounds of sexual predators. That said, a common mistake women make is going together to a nightclub, but leaving separately. This often occurs when one friend decides to leave and the other chooses to stay. By separating, both women increase tenfold their risk of assault on the way back to their hotel rooms.

Other pieces of conventional wisdom that should be applied everywhere: Don't wander unaccompanied into darkness, be it an unlit street, path or parking lot. Look your best, but don't look like a million bucks – unless you want to attract a mugger. And take care in selecting potential friends from total strangers; few sexual predators sport 'Rapist' badges or inform intended victims that they want to brutalize them.

Organizations

There are no social organizations in Panama suitable for foreign women to contact for the express purpose of meeting Panamanian women. However, most of the foreign embassies in Panama City have a cultural attaché, and these people are often willing to connect foreign and Panamanian women who want to network for cultural reasons. See the Panama City chapter for contact information for some of the embassies located there. Others can be found in the yellow pages of the Panama City phone directory under 'Embajadas.'

GAY & LESBIAN TRAVELERS

If you are a gay or lesbian traveler looking to spend time in a country that embraces people regardless of their sexual preference, Panama is not the country for you. In Panama you can lose your job simply because you are gay. There are no gay lobbyists. There are no openly gay politicians. Panama's gay community has no generally accepted leaders. There aren't any local gay publications. Gay-pride parades? Unthinkable.

About the only openly gay things one is likely to come across are Panama City's low-profile gay bars and the transvestite prostitutes who ply several street corners near the city's Casco Viejo district.

As for meeting places, gay bars in Panama are well-kept secrets. The owners, fearing vandalism and worse, never advertise the sexual preference of their patrons, and in some instances they don't even post a sign out front.

Most of Panama City's gay and lesbian clubs are in the Casco Viejo district. Many of these places don't have much in the way of decor – they're just one room with tables, a bar and a jukebox – but they make up for it in atmosphere. There are other gay clubs scattered around the capital city, and they are likewise happening places. See the Entertainment section of the Panama City chapter for names and locations.

Outside Panama City, gay bars are few and far between. In most instances, gays and lesbians just blend in with the straight crowd at the hipper places and avoid cantinas and other conventional lairs of homophobia.

Organizations

Although there are no gay organizations in Panama for foreigners to contact, there are many avenues down which gay foreigners can turn to learn more about the gay scene in Panama and in many other countries. The best medium for this connection is the Internet, and a particularly helpful site is www.gaytravel.com. The site hosts various talk forums where you can seek the very latest information on Panama's gay scene.

Another potentially helpful site is at www.gayscape.com, which, among a great many other things, lists gay organizations in many countries; perhaps it will show one for Panama by the time you investigate the site.

DISABLED TRAVELERS

According to Law 1 of January 28, 1992, all Panamanians and foreigners with

Panamanian residency status who have serious mental or physical impairments are entitled to the same employment and educational opportunities as everyone else and are granted public medical care for their disabilities. Another law specifies that retired disabled Panamanians and foreigners with Panamanian residency status are entitled to discounts such as a break on mortgage, medical and telephone bills.

Additionally, the Instituto Panameño de Habilitación Especial (Panamanian Institute for Special Rehabilitation; IPHE; ☎ 261-0500), on the Camino Real in the Betania district of Panama City and open from 7 am to 4 pm weekdays, was created by the government to assist all disabled people in Panama, including the foreign tourists. However, the law does not require – and Panamanian businesses do not provide – discounts to foreign tourists with disabilities.

Panama is not wheelchair friendly; with the exception of handicapped parking spaces, wheelchair ramps outside a few upscale hotels and perhaps a few dozen oversize bathroom stalls, accommodations for people with physical disabilities do not exist in Panama. Even at the best hotels, you won't find railings in showers or beside toilets.

Organizations

If you have a disability and want to communicate with another disabled person who might have been to Panama recently, consider becoming a member of Travelin' Talk Network (☎ 303-232-2979, fax 303-239-8486; PO Box 1796, Wheat Ridge, CO 80034, USA). TTN offers a worldwide directory of members with various disabilities who communicate among themselves about travel. Membership costs US$20 a year.
Website: www.travelintalk.net

If you have Internet access, you might also find Gimp on the Go helpful. In 2001, it was the most informative of the free Internet-based newsletters written for persons with disabilities who love to travel. A keyword search for 'disabilities and travel' at a major Internet search engine such as www.google.com will turn you on to

many other websites geared toward travelers with disabilities.
Website: www.gimponthego.com

SENIOR TRAVELERS

According to Law 15 of July 13, 1992, all Panamanians and foreigners with Panamanian residency status who are female and 55 years old or older, or are male and 60 years old or older, are entitled to a wide range of discounts, such as the following: 50% off tickets for movies, theater, sports and special events; 25% off tickets for domestic air travel; 25% off the price of restaurant meals; and 15% off medical bills. The list goes on.

However, the law does not require – and Panamanian businesses generally do not offer – discounts to foreign tourists on the basis of age. But if you're a senior, have an identification to prove it and love discounts, you're encouraged to present your ID wherever tickets are sold. Clerks in Panama often would rather provide a discount than disappoint a tourist.

Organizations

In the USA, the American Association of Retired Persons (☎ 800-424-3410; 601 E St NW, Washington, DC 20049) is an advocacy and service group for Americans 50 years and older and a good resource for travel bargains. Membership for one/three years is US$8/20.
Website: www.aarp.org

There is no shortage of organizations catering to seniors who enjoy traveling. To find some in your home country, your best bet is to do an Internet search for 'seniors and travel and (your country's name),' and view the websites that appear.

TRAVEL WITH CHILDREN

Children pay full fare on buses if they occupy a seat, but they often ride for free if they sit on a parent's knee. Children ages two to five pay 75% of the full fare on domestic airline flights and get a seat, while infants under two pay 10% of the fare but don't get a seat. Children's car seats are not always available from Panamanian car-rental agencies, so bring one if you plan on driving with a baby or toddler.

In hotels the general rule is simply to bargain. Children should never have to pay as much as an adult, but whether they stay for half-price or for free is open to discussion.

While 'kids' meals' (small portions at small prices) are not normally offered in restaurants, it is perfectly acceptable to order a meal to split between two children or an adult and a child.

For more suggestions, see Lonely Planet's *Tra el with Children*, by Maureen Wheeler.

DANGERS & ANNOYANCES

Crime is a problem in certain parts of Panama City, namely the districts of Chorrillo and Calidonia. It can also be dangerous to stroll the Casco Viejo district at night. In general, use common sense; stay where it's well lit and there are plenty of people.

Colón has some upscale residential areas, but most of the city is a sad slum widely known for street crime. If you walk around there, even in the middle of the day, well-meaning residents will inform you that you are in danger. Unless you've just got to visit Colón's Zona Libre, it's best to avoid the city altogether.

Parts of Darién Province are extremely dangerous. Many people, including tourists and missionaries, have been kidnapped and/or murdered in the vicinity of the Colombian border.

Plying the waters of the Archipiélago de San Blás are numerous Colombian boats that run back and forth between the Zona Libre in Colón and Cartagena, Colombia. It has been well documented that some of these boats carry cocaine on their northbound voyages. If you decide to ride on one of these slow cargo boats, be forewarned that your crew may be trafficking drugs.

Thefts & Muggings

Tourist-oriented crime is uncommon in Panama, but it does happen, particularly in the districts of Chorrillo and Calidonia. Be smart; avoid carrying all your money in one place, avoid entering areas that appear unsafe, and adhere to the rule 'if a deal seems too good to be true, it probably is.' This last rule is a reference to Panama's confidence artists – people who defraud others after gaining their trust – of which there are many.

If you elect to go bar-hopping in Casco Viejo at night, play it smart and follow this advice: Leave your watch, jewelry and expensive clothing at the hotel; take only the amount of money you think you'll need, and then a little extra tucked away in a shoe; and be sure to carry photographic ID (it's the law). If you look like you don't have anything of value on you, you won't likely interest a mugger.

It is a good idea to carry an emergency packet somewhere separate from all your other valuables. It should contain a photocopy of the important pages of your passport. On the back of the photocopy you should list important numbers, such as your traveler's checks' serial numbers, airline ticket numbers, and credit card and bank account numbers. Also keep one high-denomination bill with this emergency stash.

If you are robbed, you should get a police report as soon as possible. This is a requirement for any insurance claims, although it is unlikely that the police will be able to recover the property. If you don't speak Spanish and are having a hard time making a police report, your embassy can often advise and help.

Panama has a long history of business-related crimes, particularly with regard to real estate. If you want to sink money into any kind of Panamanian business, make sure you check it out *thoroughly*. Don't invest more in Panama than you can afford to lose.

Police

Police corruption is not a big problem in Panama. However, it's not unheard of for a Panamanian police officer to stop a motorist for no obvious reason, accuse him or her of violating a law, and levy a fine to be paid on the spot. If there are people around, making a big scene will sometimes fluster the officer into letting you go. Most of the time, however, you become an unwilling participant in a waiting game.

Traffic control for the Panama Canal

Lobster fishing in the Comarca de San Blás

Slow day at the newsstand, Panama City

Logging old growth in Darién Province

Tourist policeman and his trusty steed, Panama City

Kayaking the Río Chagres, Panamá Province

Bird's-eye view at Gamboa, Panamá Province

Santa Clara beach, Coclé Province

The Parque Nacional Soberanía, Panamá Province

Walk the plank, Bocas del Toro Province

Canopy ride, Bocas del Toro Province

Your best option, unless you want to try to wait out the officer, is to negotiate the fine down. If the officer says the fine is US$50, insist it is US$20. If he says that it's US$20, insist it's US$10. Failure to pay anything can result in your being led to jail with the officer insisting you really did break some law.

Fighting

If you are the sort of person who tends to pick fights or otherwise cause trouble, it may interest you to know that many law enforcement officers in Panama do not wear uniforms. Additionally, because the only requirement for a concealed-weapon permit in Panama is a clean criminal record, more than 70,000 Panamanians legally pack pistols. Panamanians are not a violent people, but if you pick a fight with a local, there's a very good chance you'll find yourself looking down the barrel of a gun.

Swimming Safety

Tourist brochures do not mention the drownings that occur every year in Panamanian waters. Of these, about 80% are caused by rip currents. A rip current is a strong current that pulls the swimmer out to sea. It occurs when two currents that move parallel to the shore meet. When they meet, the opposing waters choose the path of least resistance, which is a path out to sea. It is most important to remember that rip currents will pull you *out but not under*.

If you find yourself caught in a rip current, stay calm and let the current take you away from shore. Rip currents dissipate quickly; you must simply wait them out before you begin to swim back to shore. When the current dissipates, swim back in at a 45° angle to the shore to avoid being caught by the current again. Do not try to swim directly back in, as you would be swimming against the rip current and would only exhaust yourself.

If you feel a rip current while you are wading, try to come back in sideways, thus offering less body surface to the current. If you cannot make headway, walk parallel to the beach so that you can get out of the rip current.

Hiking Safety

Many visitors like to hike in the national parks and wilderness areas. You should be adequately prepared for such trips. Always carry plenty of water, even on short journeys, and always bring adequate clothing; jungles *do* cool down a lot at night, particularly at higher elevations. Hikers have been known to get lost in rain forests – even seemingly user-friendly ones such as Parque Nacional Volcán Barú. A Panamanian hiker who entered that park in 1995 was never seen again; it's assumed that he got lost, died of hypothermia and was fed upon by various creatures.

Never walk in unmarked rain forest; if there's no trail going in, you can assume that there won't be one when you decide to turn around and come back out. Always let someone know where you are going, in order to narrow the search area in the event of an emergency.

EMERGENCIES

Throughout Panama, the police emergency number is ☎ 104; for fire emergencies, call ☎ 103. Telephone numbers for hospitals and ambulances are found on the first page of the national phone directory. In the blue pages of the directory, you'll find a list of service providers that appear under English headings ('attorneys,' 'physicians,' etc).

LEGAL MATTERS

In Panama you are presumed guilty until found innocent. If you are accused of a serious crime, you will be taken to jail, where you will likely spend several years before your case goes before a judge. Some valuable advice: Stay away from people who commit crimes. For example, you can expect to go to jail if the car you are in is stopped and found to contain illegal drugs, even if they aren't yours and you don't do illegal drugs.

More valuable advice: Ignore locals who say these warnings are exaggerated. The fact is that punitive actions taken against a local and a foreigner often vary. It is assumed that if you can afford to travel to Panama, you must have a lot of money and therefore can afford to pay a steep fine. Stories of foreigners paying much larger fines than Panamanians for the same offense are well known.

If you are jailed, your embassy will offer only limited assistance. This may include a visit from an embassy staff member to make sure that your human rights have not been violated, letting your family know where you are and putting you in contact with a lawyer (whom you must pay yourself). Embassy officials will not bail you out.

Remember that you are legally required to carry identification at all times. This should be a photographic ID, preferably a passport.

Drugs

In Panama penalties for possession of even small amounts of illegal drugs are much stricter than in the USA, Europe, Australia and most everywhere else. Defendants often spend years in prison before they are brought to trial and, if convicted (as is usually the case), can expect sentences of several more years in prison. Most lawyers won't even accept drug cases because the outcome is certain: conviction.

Furthermore, if you are convicted, it is the practice of most embassies to notify your country's federal narcotics agency, which can have long-term repercussions. For example, if you are a US citizen convicted of possession of even just one marijuana cigarette, your name will be sent to the US Department of Justice and the US Drug Enforcement Administration, as well as the US Customs Service. Their computers will show only that you were convicted of a drug offense in a foreign country; they do not differentiate between someone who is caught with a single joint and someone who is caught with 1000kg of heroin. At the very least, you and your baggage will be *thoroughly* searched every time you enter the USA.

Alcohol

Public drinking is not tolerated in Panama. If a police officer sees you staggering down the street with a beer in hand, at the very least you will be lectured; most likely you will be handcuffed, searched and led to a jail to sober up.

Strange as it may sound to some people, in Panama it's OK to drink and drive, but driving while legally intoxicated (with a blood alcohol level of 0.1% or above) is a serious offense. If you're drunk and you run over someone and are apprehended, you will be sent to prison for a very long time.

The legal drinking age is 18, and it is strictly enforced in Panama City though generally ignored elsewhere.

BUSINESS HOURS

Business hours are normally 8 am to noon and 1:30 to 5 pm weekdays and 8 am to noon Saturday. Government offices are open 8 am to 4 or 4:30 pm weekdays and don't close for lunch. Most banks are open from 8:30 am to 1 pm Monday to Thursday and 8:30 am to 3 pm Friday; some are open 8:30 am to noon or 1 pm Saturday as well. Stores are generally open 9 or 10 am to 6 or 7 pm Monday to Saturday.

PUBLIC HOLIDAYS & SPECIAL EVENTS

National holidays (*días feriados*) are taken seriously in Panama, and banks, public offices and many stores close. Public transportation tends to be tight on all holidays and the days immediately preceding or following them, so book tickets ahead.

There is no bus service at all on the Thursday afternoon and Friday before Easter, and many businesses are closed for the entire Semana Santa (Holy Week, the week before Easter). From Thursday to Easter Sunday, all bars are closed and alcohol sales are prohibited. Beach hotels are usually booked weeks ahead for the Semana Santa, though a limited choice of rooms is often available.

The week between Christmas and New Year's, along with the first week of the year, tend to be unofficial holidays. In addition, various towns have celebrations for their own particular days. These other holidays and special events are not official holidays, and businesses remain open.

All the official national holidays are listed below, and most are celebrated on Monday to create long weekends: When holidays fall on a Thursday or Friday, they are celebrated on the following Monday; holidays that happen to fall on Tuesday or Wednesday are usually celebrated the prior Monday.

New Year's Day	January 1
Martyrs' Day	January 9
Good Friday, Easter Sunday	March/April
Workers' Day	May 1
Founding of Old Panama (celebrated in Panama City only)	August 15
Hispanic Day	October 12
National Anthem Day	November 1
All Souls' Day	November 2
Independence Day	November 3
First Call for Independence	November 10
Independence from Spain	November 28
Mothers' Day	December 8
Christmas Day	December 25

Carnaval, the Panamanian version of Mardi Gras, is celebrated during the four days leading up to Ash Wednesday. A major holiday in Panama City, it involves costumes, music, dancing, general festivities and a big parade on Shrove Tuesday. Carnaval is also celebrated on the Península de Azuero in Las Tablas, Chitré, Villa de Los Santos and Parita. The celebrations in Panama City and Las Tablas are famous and well worth attending, but hotel reservations must be made well in advance. Upcoming Ash Wednesdays will fall on the following dates:

2002	February 13
2003	March 15
2004	February 25
2005	February 9

Semana Santa is another occasion for special events throughout the country, including the reenactment of the events surrounding the crucifixion and resurrection of Christ; on Good Friday, religious processions are held all over the country.

The famous Corpus Christi celebrations in Villa de Los Santos take place 40 days after Easter. Masked and costumed dancers representing angels, devils, imps and other figures enact dances, acrobatics and dramas.

The Península de Azuero also has a number of other notable festivals; patron saint festivals are held in Ocú (January 20 to 23), Soná (May 15), Chitré (June 24), Las Tablas (July 21) and Guararé (September 23 to 27). The festivals are normally held on the closest Saturday.

The Black Christ celebration held in Portobelo on October 21 attracts tens of thousands of pilgrims from near and far; the celebration for Nuestra Señora del Carmen, which takes place on Isla Taboga on July 16, also attracts large crowds. In western Panama, Boquete's Feria de las Flores y del Café (Fair of Flowers and Coffee), held for 10 days in January, attracts visitors from all over Panama.

Panama's many ethnic groups each have their own cultural events; the Kuna and the descendants of West Indians and Spaniards all have their own special music and dance. If you get a chance to attend any of these occasions, don't miss it. Be aware that while the Kuna allow foreigners to observe their cultural events, they generally do not permit them to be photographed.

ACTIVITIES
There's no shortage of things to do in Panama, as the following pages will indicate. Though some activity sites and tour operators are discussed here, many more can be found in the regional chapters.

Diving & Snorkeling
There are many decent dive spots – and several very good ones – off both coasts of Panama. Panama's three best dive sites are the Archipiélago de San Blás on the Caribbean side and Isla de Coiba and the Archipiélago de las Perlas on the Pacific side. On the Pacific side you'd be looking for reef sharks, groupers and sea turtles near shore, and sailfish, amberjacks and dog-toothed snappers farther out. In the Caribbean the fish tend to be smaller but more colorful,

Why Muddy Beaches Are Best

Odd as it sounds, muddy beaches are more popular with most Panamanians than their country's lovely white-sand beauties. That's because most Panamanians have a real fear of being swept out to sea. Rip currents, which can carry a swimmer away from shore, are usually found in front of beaches covered with fine sand; in fact, currents are needed to create the granular silica that sunbathers love. It's the motion in the ocean that gives sand its size and texture.

Beaches with a lot of mud in their sand are nearly always found beside the mouths of rivers, which dump silt from terra firma into the sea. As silt builds up near a river's mouth, the offshore ocean becomes increasingly shallow. Shallow water prevents hazardous currents from forming, which swimmers really do appreciate, but it also means that the beach is dirty rather than sandy.

the coral is much more appealing and the visibility is better.

The San Blás islands are home to many fine coral reefs, but for years the Kuna prohibited dive operators from taking tourists there following a diving mishap in 1980 that left one Indian dead. Today, diving in the archipelago is again allowed. See the Comarca de San Blás chapter for details.

There are unfenced prison camps on Isla de Coiba and, for obvious reasons, tourists can't just show up there. All trips to the island and all diving nearby must be arranged through a tour or dive operator. Because the island is far from land and the cost of fuel high, an inexpensive dive trip to Coiba and vicinity is not possible. However, there are some fancy dive and snorkel trips available. See the Veraguas Province chapter for details.

The Archipiélago de las Perlas offers excellent snorkeling and scuba diving possibilities. Scuba gear is not necessary here: Sea turtles, white-tipped reef sharks and numerous other intriguing creatures ply the shallow water just off the beach of the Hotel Contadora Resort, a large hotel on Isla Contadora, the most popular of the Pearls. See the Panamá Province chapter for more details.

It's possible to dive the Pacific and Atlantic oceans in one day. Scubapanama (☎ 261-3841, fax 261-9586, renegomez@ scubapanama), at the intersection of Av 6a C Norte and Calle 62 C Oeste in the El Carmen district of Panama City, offers bicoastal dives for US$200 per person (less if there's more than one person in your party). Website: www.scubapanama.com

There's also good diving near Bahía Piña, Punta Mariato and Punta Burica on the Pacific side, and Isla Escudo de Veraguas, Cayos Zapatillas and Portobelo on the Caribbean side. If you've dived some of the world's top spots, these sites won't wow you, but for most divers they're appealing and they can surprise. At Portobelo, for example, it's possible to dive a 110-foot cargo ship and a C-45 twin-engine plane.

When you're making travel plans, bear in mind that the Caribbean Sea is calm during the dry season (mid-December to mid-April). During the rainy season (mid-April to mid-December), the Caribbean can be treacherous due to high winds and strong currents. On the Pacific side strong winds are common during February and March.

Decompression Chambers A warning: Divers, as there are only four decompression chambers in the entire country – one in Colón, one at Lago Gatún and two in Panama City – don't take unnecessary risks. If you stay down too long or come up too fast, you'll be in serious trouble.

Snorkel Gear It's sometimes possible to rent face masks, snorkels and fins, but if snorkeling is an important part of your trip to Panama, you should bring your own gear to ensure comfort and fit. Also, many travelers seem to forget to bring sunscreen, dark glasses and nondrowsy motion-sickness suppressants. If you're fair-skinned, a hat, long-sleeved shirt and baggy lightweight pants are a good idea when you're riding in a boat. Flashlights are not rentable in Panama; if you think you might be doing some night snorkeling, bring an underwater flashlight with you.

Dive Gear Consider bringing all the items listed under Snorkel Gear plus the following: an equipment bag, a regulator and a BCD, gloves, boots and a 3 to 5mm wetsuit if you'll be diving the Pacific or a Lycra suit if you'll be diving the Caribbean only. It's also a good idea to mark all your equipment if you'll be diving with others, to avoid mistaking your equipment for someone else's or vice versa; this is particularly true with regard to charcoal-colored fins, which are so popular among divers.

Good dive equipment is available for rent or purchase at the Scubapanama store; see above for contact details.

Surfing

The best surf breaks in Panama are generally regarded to be out front of Playa Santa Catalina, Playa Teta and Playa Río Mar (all on the Pacific side), though there are some excellent breaks in the Archipiélago de Bocas del Toro and elsewhere. All three Pacific-side breaks are reef breaks, and all three break both ways. The right break at Santa Catalina has no equal in all of Central America when the southern swells appear.

The best months for Santa Catalina are February and March, but the surf breaks here year-round. The face of a typical wave at Santa Catalina is 2m; during February and March waves with 4m faces are fairly common. Like most surfing sites, good waves are hit and miss. But on a particularly good day during medium to high tide, rides approaching 150m are possible. The waves here are at their best during medium to high tide. Surf booties are a must at Santa Catalina due to the volcanic rock beneath the surf and the long walk to the waves during low tide. The water here is never cold, but a Lycra vest is recommended during February and March, due to strong offshore winds. See the Veraguas Province chapter for details on facilities at Santa Catalina.

Playa Teta is very popular with Panamanian surfers due to its beauty and its proximity to Panama City, but its ride is nowhere near as sweet as Santa Catalina's. The face of a typical wave at Teta is 2m, and there are often long stretches between big waves. But when there are big southern swells coming all the way from New Zealand, Teta is a fantastic place for getting barrel. Faces on waves here during this time can reach 4m. The bottom is both rocky and sandy; booties aren't really needed. The best months for Teta are May, June, July and August, but even during these months the waves can be disappointing. Also, there are a lot of people in the water here because the beach is only a 40-minute drive from Panama City.

Playa Río Mar, near Teta in Panamá Province, is only really surfable during medium to low tide, because during high tide the waves generally don't break. What is special about this place is the length of the ride, which can last 100m, and the waves here are easy to ride. The bottom is mostly rocky and there are lots of broken oyster shells in the sand that are as dangerous as broken bottles. Booties are a good idea at low tide. Like Teta, this beach is accessible and popular. The best months to surf Río Mar are May, June, July and August. Beware: If there's little swell, you'll be waiting a long time for a good wave. See the Panamá Province chapter for more details on this beach.

For consistently good breaks, try Playa Venao, also on the Pacific side. Waves there break both ways and are at their best when they are about 2m in height. Any larger and they close out without offering much of a ride. The good news is that the waves at Venao are 2m nearly every day. If you're unsure where to go due to small swell at other Pacific beaches, go to Playa Venao. The bottom is sandy, no booties needed.

On the Caribbean side, the islands of Bocas del Toro offer some of the best and most varied surfing opportunities in Panama. The best time to surf here is December through March. The best breaks in Bocas are Isla Carenero and Silverbacks. Isla Carenero is a reef break near Bocas town that often presents 200m-long peeling

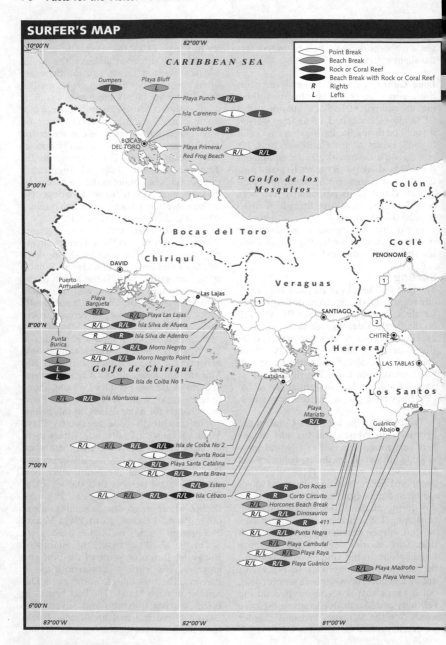

SURFER'S MAP

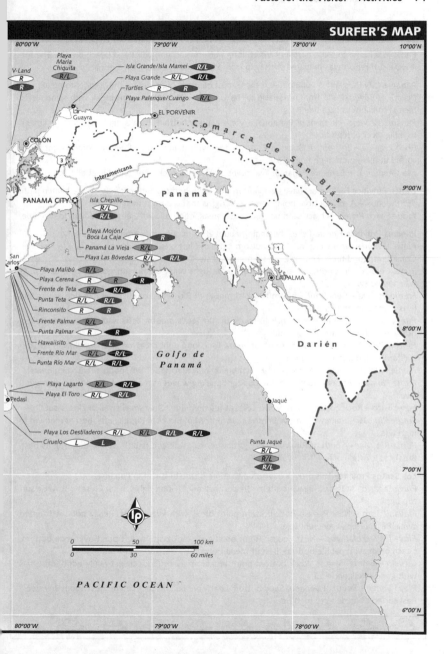

SURFER'S MAP

Panama Surf Report

Panama is home to some excellent tubes, long peelers, and fine point and beach breaks. The following surf report was prepared with help from Panama surf expert Jon Hanna.

Panama City PC's surf is polluted, and there must be really big swell for these spots to break.
Playa Las Bóvedas – In front of Palacio de las Garzas. Rock bottom point break with rights, lefts. Best at medium to high tide.
Panamá La Vieja – In front of Panamá La Vieja. Muddy bottom. Breaks right, left. Surfing limited to a big swell at high tide.
Boca La Caja – In front of Boca La Caja, an area with many thugs. Rock-bottomed right break surfed at medium to high tide.
Isla Chepillo – In Bahía de Panamá. Two point breaks over rocks, one surfable at all tides.

Darién Province Few surfers have ever ventured into this territory, which is way off the beaten path.
Punta Jaqué – A rock bottom point break with rights that is best at medium tide.
Jaqué Beach Break – A black sand bottom beach break, rights and lefts, best at medium to high tide.

Panamá Province Fine surf sites, beginning about a 45-minute drive from Panama City.
Playa Malibu – Near Gorgona. Sand bottom right and left break best during medium to low tide. Consistent, good tubes and long rides when good swell.
Playa Cerena – In Coronado, past security gate. Right point break with good tubes, long rides when good swell.
Frente de Teta – Rock/sand bottom break at mouth of Río Teta. Long lefts at low tide, rights and lefts at medium to high tide.
Punta Teta – Point break over rock to south of Río Teta's mouth. Lefts and rights. Good tubes, rides. Best at medium tide going up.
Rinconsito – Rock bottom point south of Punta Teta, long right break on good swell. Named after California's famous Rincón break.
Frente Palmar – South of San Carlos. Beach break, partial rock bottom, popular with beginners.
Punta Palmar – Rock bottom point break. Right peeling waves at medium to high tide when good swell.
Hawaiisito – Rock bottom point break. Lefts at full high tide. Only small swell or closes out.
Frente Río Mar – Somewhat rocky beach break in front of Río Mar. Rights, lefts. Best at medium to high tide.
Punta Río Mar – South of Río Mar, near jutting rocks. Walk and paddle at low tide. Rights best. Breaks at low tide only.

Los Santos Province This province is home to some of the best surf in Panama.
Playa Lagarto -At Pedasí. Beach bottom. Breaks at all tides. Good rights, lefts. Closes out when surf too big.
Playa El Toro – Near Pedasí. Rock bottom point break with lefts, rights. Really good with good swell. Best surfed at medium tide.
Playa los Destiladeros – Near Pedasí. Right point over rock bottom, left point over rock bottom, beach break with pebble bottom. Best at medium tide.
Ciruelo – Before Venado. Rock bottom point break, rarely surfed, can get really good left tubes with good swell, no wind.
Playa Venao – South of Venado. Sand bottom beach break. This spot catches just about any swell. Best surfed at medium to high tide.

Panama Surf Report

Playa Madroño – Near Venado. 30-minute walk. Surf can get really good, with hollow tubes at low tide. Need to arrive early, before the wind.

Playa Guánico – South of Venado. 45-minute hike. Two rock bottom point breaks with rights, lefts; one beach break with rights and lefts.

Playa Raya – One hour past Venado. The waves 4m to 5m on big swells, with big tubes. Many big sharks here too.

Playa Cambutal – Beyond Tonosí. Beach break with rights, lefts. Catches about any swell. Best at medium to high tide.

Punta Negra – West of Playa Camubtal, around the first point. Point break over rocks, best during medium to high tide.

411 – West of Punta Negra. Locally famous point break with long right over rock ledge. Best during medium to high tide. Can get very big surf.

Dinosaurios – Next to 411. Rock bottom break with rights, lefts at medium to high tide. Can get very big surf.

Horcones Beach Break – West of Dinosaurios. Sand bottom beach break with rights, lefts. Good most tides.

Dos Rocas – Near Horcones. Rock bottom point break beside two jutting boulders. Can get good rights at medium tide.

Corto Circuito – At road's end toward Cerro Hoya. Rock bottom point break with powerful peak. Breaks over a rock ledge and throws a huge tube, then peels for about 100m with a great wall.

Veraguas Province Veraguas has some of the best surf in Central America.

Playa Santa Catalina – South of Sona. Famous surf. Sharp rock bottom right and left break. Main wave is the right. Incredible tubes, long rides with lots of power. Surfed mostly medium to high tide.

Estero Beach Break – Fifteen-minute walk from Santa Catalina. A long beach break, has lefts and rights over sand bottom. Beginners generally surf the beach break at low tide.

Punta Brava – Just west of Estero. Point break breaks at low tide over sharp rock bottom. Has lefts and rights, but the lefts are best. Very powerful. Has a great tube section. Booties needed.

Punta Roca – Thirty minutes' walk from Santa Catalina. Left point break surfed at low tide over a rock bottom ledge, with short rides but big hollow tubes.

Isla Cébaco – Island near Santa Catalina. Four breaks, with rights and lefts. Area known for sharks, huge snapper, grouper.

Playa Mariato – Faces Isla Cebaco. Soft rock bottom break with lefts, rights.

Chiriquí Province Chiriquí has several remote islands with very good surf. Need tour operator to arrange.

Isla de Coiba – Many surf spots, but most are unsurfed and difficult to get to even with a boat.

Isla Montuosa – Isle opposite Hannibal Bank from Coiba. Good right rock bottom point with solid waves and very consistent. Up to 5m. Catches about any swell.

continued on page 74

Panama Surf Report

continued from page 73

Isla Silva de Afuera – Two breaks: one left, one right. Right is big peak breaking over a shallow rock ledge at medium tide; can throw a big tube, with steep drops and no wall. Other break is a good left that breaks over a rock reef at medium tide. This spot catches almost any swell.

Isla Silva de Adentro – A right-hand break over rock reef that can get really good with a good swell.

Morro Negrito – Near Morro Negrito town, difficult access. About 5 breaks, variety of lefts and rights. Good tubes.

Playa Las Lajas – East of David. Beach bottom break with rights and lefts, but in infrequent waves.

La Barqueta – Near David. Beach bottom break with rights and lefts. Breaks at all tides, but medium to high is best.

Punta Burica – On Costa Rican border. Four left points that break along the point for long, tubing rides. Catches any swell. Better wave than Pavones of Costa Rica, and uncrowded.

Archipiélago de Bocas del Toro Excellent surfing with great variety, but limited to December through March.

Dumpers – Isla Colón. Reef bottom left break with a very steep drop, big tube and short ride. Reef is sharp, tricky. Dangerous for beginners.

Playa Punch – Isla Colón. Reef bottom left and right break with good tubes and fun sections to hit the lip and do crazy airs. Popular with beginners, but booties recommended for the reef.

Playa Bluff – Isla Colón, road's end. Long beach renowned for board-breaking powerful surf. The tubes here are incredible.

Carenero – Isla Carenero, 5-minute boat ride from Bocas town. Reef break with 200m peeling lefts, with great tubes. Boat drop-off, pickup at reef. Booties recommended.

Silverbacks – Isla Bastimentos. Reef bottom with waves up to 5m on good swells. Large right with big drop, big tube, but relatively short ride. Not for beginners.

Red Frog Beach & Playa Primera – Isla Bastimentos, walk across island. Both sand and reef bottom breaks with lefts and rights.

Colón-Portobelo Area The best surf for this area is from December through March.

Playa Maria Chiquita – In front of Maria Chiquita. Beach break with lefts and rights, but limited to big swell.

Isla Grande – In front of La Guayra, best reached by water taxi. Reef bottom break with 3 peaks and rights, lefts.

Isla Mamei – Next to Isla Grande, reached by boat or paddling from Isla Grande. Left-hand point break over shallow reef.

Playa Palenque/Cuango – In front of Cuango village. Beach break with rights and lefts. Surfers seldom seen here.

Playa Grande – Mainland, east of Isla Grande. Beach break with some reef. Waves break left and right.

Turtles – Paddling distance from Playa Grande. Waves are great, unreal tubes, if it is glassy with a big swell.

V-Land – Near Devils Beach, in Sherman. Unbelievable right point reef break with great tubes when big swell and glassy.

Visit www.panamasurftours.com for further details.

lefts with great tubes. It breaks over shallow reef and is comparable to the well-known Restaurants break in Tahiti.

Silverbacks, located off Isla Bastimentos, is home to waves up to 5m tall on good swells. Breaking over reef, Silverbacks is known for a large, powerful right with a big drop and big tube but a relatively short ride. Silverbacks compares to Hawaii's big-wave spots; only experienced surfers should surf it.

See the Panama Surf Report and the Surfer's Map for further information on Panamanian surf sites. For even more details and for information on surfing tours available in Panama, contact Panama Surf Tours (☎ 507-672-0089; in the USA, fax and voicemail 800-716-3452; panamasurftours@ hotmail.com). The company is run by Panama native Jon Hanna, a former national champion who knows Panama's surf scene as well as anyone.
Website: www.panamasurftours.com

Hiking

Hiking opportunities abound in Panama. From Boquete, you can hike to the top of Volcán Barú, Panama's highest peak, from which you can see both oceans on a clear day. There are also plenty of other walks around Boquete, where the narrow roads wind up and down slopes among coffee plantations. The Sendero Los Quetzales is a poorly marked trail that leads from Boquete over Volcán Barú to Guadalupe on the other side; it's a six-hour hike through lovely forest. In 2001 there was talk of turning the tail into a road. See the Chiriquí Province chapter for more information.

The little town of El Valle, nestled into the Valle de Antón about a two-hour drive west of Panama City, is a fine place for walking. Many trails lead into the hills around the valley; they are well defined, as the local *campesinos* (peasants) frequently use them.

Near Panama City on the shores of the canal, Parque Nacional Soberanía contains a section of the old Sendero Las Cruces (Las Cruces Trail), used by the Spaniards to cross between the coasts. Here, too, is a short and easy but interesting nature trail, the Sendero El Charco, which is signed

from the highway (see the Panamá Province chapter for details). Parque Natural Metropolitano, on the outskirts of Panama City, also has some good walks, including a nature trail and a 'monkey trail' (see the Panama City chapter for details).

The most famous walk in Panama is the trek of a week or more across the Darién Gap, where the Carretera Interamericana (Panamerican Hwy) comes to a dead end and a jungle wilderness stands between Panama and Colombia. This route can only be undertaken during the dry season and is extremely dangerous, to the point of being suicidal; only idiots try it. Safer Darién treks are described in the Darién Province chapter.

See Hiking Safety, earlier in this chapter, for advice on what to bring on your hike.

Bird Watching

Panama offers magnificent bird watching. The Panama Audubon Society, which does an annual bird count, consistently counts more species of bird in Panama than are recorded anywhere else in Central America. This is due to two factors: Panama's location relative to two continents and its narrow girth. Birds migrating between North and South America tend to be funneled into a small area. Many North and South American species are represented, both native and migratory. Panama also has many endemic species of avifauna.

The famous resplendent quetzal, symbol of Central America, is more abundant in western Panama than anywhere else in the region. It can be seen around Volcán Barú, notably in the hills around Boquete and Cerro Punta, where it is common much of the year.

Other birds of particular interest include the three-wattled bellbird, the harpy eagle, the great green macaw and the king vulture – the list goes on and on. All told, 940 species (native, migratory and endemic) have been identified in Panama.

To see birds in Panama, just get a good set of binoculars and get out on a trail. The Pipeline Road (less commonly known as Camino del Oleoducto) trail near Panama City is a favorite with birders; more than

Look for the rare harpy eagle in Panama.

500 species were sighted there in a single day during a recent Christmas bird count. Most birds are seen around dawn and just afterward, so avid birders will want to arrive just before daylight. (See the Panamá Province chapter for more details.)

A Guide to the Birds of Panama is extremely helpful (see the Books section in this chapter). Helpful organizations include the Panama Audubon Society (☎ 224-9371, fax 224-4740, audupan@pananet.com) in Panama City, which organizes birding expeditions. Companies offering birding services include Ancon Expeditions of Panama, Pesantez Tours and Iguana Tours, which are all based in Panama City (see Tour Companies under Panama in the Getting Around chapter).

Website: www.pananet.com/audubon

Fishing

Panama has 1518 islands, 2988km of coast and 480 major rivers that empty into the oceans, so there's no problem finding a fishing spot.

For deep-sea fishing, Panama offers three world-class areas: Bahía Piña and the Pearl and Coiba archipelagos. All three sites are served by fishing outfits.

Piña is served by Tropic Star Lodge, which boasts more than 50 current world records (see the Darién Province chapter for further details).

The Archipiélago de las Perlas is served by Salvatore Fishing, which features full and half-day trips (see the Panamá Province chapter).

The Coiba group is served by Coiba Adventure Sportfishing and Coiba Explorer Panama; the former offers shipboard lodging, the latter shipboard and beachfront lodging (see the Parque Nacional Isla de Coiba section in the Veraguas Province chapter).

Other angling possibilities include bass fishing in Lago Gatún and trout fishing in the rivers running down Volcán Barú near the towns of Boquete, Volcán, Bambito and Cerro Punta. See the Chiriquí Province chapter for information on trout fishing.

Cycling

Cycling is an excellent way to see most of Panama (although riding in Panama City is not recommended). The roads here are the best in Central America. The Interamericana is in good condition from the Costa Rican border to Panama City and beyond, and most of the roads intersecting it have been or are being improved. The major factor when considering a lengthy bike ride is the weather. No matter what bike you're on, it's not safe to ride in the rain, and it rains quite a lot here – particularly on the Caribbean side.

It is possible to bring your own bike by air and, due to the dearth of bicycle-rental places in Panama (you're limited to one rental outfit in Panama City and another in Bocas del Toro town on Isla Colón), this is definitely the thing to do if you plan on seeing the country by bike. Most airlines will fly a bike as one of your pieces of checked baggage if you box it. However, boxing a bike gives baggage handlers little clue to the contents, and the box is liable to be roughly handled, possibly damaging the bike. An alternative is wrapping it in heavy plastic or bubble wrap – baggage handlers are less likely to drop or throw the bike in this case. Airlines' bicycle carrying policies vary a lot, so ask around.

Be advised that while Panamanians are required to license their bicycles, foreigners are not. However, foreigners are required to be able to demonstrate proof of ownership. Police in Panama have been known to confiscate bikes from foreigners who were unable to show such proof.

River Running

There are three kinds of river running in Panama, all of which are awesome. You can go white-water rafting on the Ríos Chiriquí and Chiriquí Viejo, where trips are offered by the country's top rafting outfit, Chiriquí River Rafting (☎ 720-1505, fax 720-1506, rafting@panama-rafting.com), with its office on Av Central in downtown Boquete. See the Chiriquí Province chapter for details.
Website: www.panama-rafting.com

You can run the same rivers and others in kayaks. Kayak Panama (☎/fax 993-3620, kayakpanama@hotmail.com), based at XS Memories, an American-run hotel and sports bar located in Santa Clara in Coclé Province, offers kayaking tours year round.
Website: www.kayakpanama.com

Nantahala Outdoor Center (in the USA ☎ 828-488-2175, 800-232-7238, fax 828-488-2498; adtrav@noc.com; 13077 Highway 19W, Bryson City, NC 28713) offers several

very popular kayaking adventures in Panama every year.
Website: www.noc.com

The third kind of river running in Panama relies on motorized river boats or motorized dugouts. In Bocas del Toro and Darién Provinces, these boats are the best means of travel by river or sea. Ancon Expeditions of Panama (☎ 269-9414, fax 264-3713, info@anconexpeditions.com), located in Edifio El Dorado No 3 on Calle Elvira Méndez in Panama City, offers numerous tours in the Darién involving travel by river boat and/or dugout, as well as trips up the Río Teribe in Bocas del Toro Province.
Website: www.anconexpeditions.com

LANGUAGE COURSES

There are two Spanish-language programs in Panama that Lonely Planet can recommend. One is located in Bocas del Toro town, the other in Panama City. See the Panama City and Bocas del Toro Province chapters for details.

WORK

It's difficult for foreigners to find work in Panama. The government doesn't want them to take jobs away from Panamanians, and labor laws reflect that sentiment. Basically, the only foreigners legally employed in Panama work for their own businesses, possess skills not found in Panama or work for companies that have special agreements with the Panamanian government (for example, if a French company builds a US$50 million hotel in Panama City, its owners will likely be permitted to fill the general manager's position with a French citizen).

Volunteer Work

The Asociación Nacional para la Conservación de la Naturaleza (ANCON; National Association for the Conservation of Nature; ☎ 314-0060, fax 314-0061, ancon@ancon.com; Apartado 1387, Panamá 1, República de Panamá) offers opportunities for volunteering on projects in national parks and other beautiful natural areas. Volunteers might protect nesting sea turtles near Bocas del

Toro town, do environmental-education work in the Darién or assist national park rangers. You can volunteer for any length of time, from a week up to several months; you won't get paid, but Ancon will supply your basic necessities, such as food and shelter. Contact Ancon for details.
Website: www.ancon.org

ACCOMMODATIONS

Accommodations prices cited in this book are 2001 low-season rates and include Panama's 10% hotel tax. If you'll be traveling during the high season – mid-December through April – you might want to add 15% to the prices shown in this book to adjust for probable price gouging. Also, if you're reading this book toward the end of its shelf life (in 2004 or 2005), count on all of the room rates being 10% higher due to inflation. Remarkably, in 2000 and again in 2001, hotel prices nationwide actually fell due to an unexplained drop-off in foreign visitors.

Hotels

Usually there is no shortage of places to stay in Panama, although getting a hotel room during Carnaval, Easter week and other holiday times can be difficult in some places. Finding a room on a popular island (Isla Contadora or Isla Grande, for example) can be tough on a lovely weekend during the dry season. Hotel accommodations also can be tight if there is a special event going on in a particular town.

Some travelers prefer to make advance reservations everywhere; this is generally possible and recommended in the better places, and in increasingly popular Bocas del Toro town on Isla Colón. Sending faxes and emails to make reservations is becoming more and more common. Airmail is slow and unreliable. The Places to Stay sections in this book give telephone and fax numbers, street addresses, and email and snail-mail addresses for those hotels that have them.

Before accepting a room, ask to see several. The same prices are often charged for rooms of widely differing quality. Even in the US$10-a-night cheapies it's worth looking around. If you are shown a horrible airless box with just a bed and a bare light bulb, you can ask to see a better room without giving offense. You'll often be amazed at the results. Naturally, hotels want you to rent their most expensive rooms; if you're on a tight budget, make a habit of asking if economical rooms are available (some Panamanian hotels have them but don't post their lowest prices).

Hotel Categories Those hotels listed as 'budget' are certainly the cheapest but not necessarily the worst. Although they are usually very basic, with just a bed, a light and four walls, they can nevertheless be well maintained, very clean and an amazing value for the money. They are often good places to meet other travelers, both Panamanian and foreign.

The difference between a bad budget place and a decent economical hotel often cannot be detected from the street. A place may look fine from the roadside, but its rooms might have horrible stains or strong odors. Other places may look like fleabags from the outside, but to your pleasant surprise you'll discover that the rooms are spacious and clean, the beds firm and the shower water hot and available 24 hours.

Also keep in mind that some lower-end lodgings in Panama may be used by locals only as temporary crashpads or as spots for romantic rendezvous. In addition, some budget places do double duty as brothels – the presence of prostitutes and their clients may mean that your room is more likely to be robbed and that you might be mistaken for a prostitute or a client. Check carefully before you take a room. Listings in this book do not include fronts for brothels.

Prices in the budget category begin at about US$5 per person and go up to US$20 for a double room. Almost every town has hotels in this price range. Although you'll usually have to use communal bathrooms in the cheapest hotels, you can sometimes find rooms with private bathrooms for as little as US$10 for two people.

Hotels in the 'mid-range' category usually charge about US$20 to US$40 for a double room, but the cheaper ones are not always better than the best hotels in the budget range. On the whole, you can find some very decent hotels. Even if you're traveling on a tight budget, there may be occasions when you feel like indulging in comparative luxury for a while.

The top-end hotels charge more than US$40 for a double, and rates can go to five times that in Panama City and in the beach resorts. The prices and services in the best places meet international standards.

Hotel Tax A 10% tax is added to hotel prices. Some hotels give prices including the tax, others give prices without the tax, so always clarify this point when asking about room rates. Hotel rates in this book include the tax.

Bathrooms Bathroom facilities in the cheaper hotels are rarely what you may be used to at home. The cheapest hotels don't always have hot water. Even when they do, its availability may be limited to certain hours of the day.

An intriguing device you should know about is the 'electric shower.' This consists of a single cold-water showerhead hooked up to an electric heating element that is switched on when you want a hot (more likely tepid) shower. Don't touch anything metal while you're in the shower or you may discover what an electric shock feels like. The power is never high enough to actually throw you across the room, but it's unpleasant nevertheless.

Flushing a toilet in some of the cheaper hotels can create another hazard – overflow. See the Toilets section in this chapter for details.

Security Most hotels will give you a key to lock your room, and theft from hotel rooms is not as common as it is in some other countries. Once in a while you'll find that a room doesn't look very secure – perhaps there's a window that doesn't close, or the wall doesn't come to the ceiling and can be climbed over. It's worth finding another room. This is another reason why it's always good to look at a room before you rent it.

You should never leave valuables lying around the room; the person cleaning it likely makes less than US$10 a day. Money and passports should be in a secure body pouch; other valuables can usually be kept in the hotel strongbox. Beware of local 'fishermen' – people who poke sticks with hooks on them through unlocked windows to fish out whatever they can get.

B&Bs
Almost unknown in Panama until the start of this millennium, the bed-and-breakfast phenomenon is gaining popularity across the country. Rates at B&Bs range from midrange to top end. B&Bs are mentioned throughout the book.

Camping & Hostels
There is only one youth hostel in Panama, and it doesn't give discounts for members of international youth hostel federations; student IDs and 25¢ will get you only a coffee. Cheap camping facilities *are* available in many of the national parks but in only a few of the towns. At the time of writing, there was only one campground equipped for motor homes (in Santa Clara, Coclé Province).

FOOD
You don't have to eat at a fancy restaurant to enjoy fine food in Panama. A good indication of the quality of food a restaurant serves is the number of locals you see eating there; a restaurant generally isn't empty if its food is delicious and reasonably priced. If you're on a tight budget, eat the set meal offered in most restaurants at lunchtime; it's usually filling and cheap.

You'll find a good range of restaurants at all price levels throughout this book. Remember that tips are rarely included in the check. If you are happy with the service you've received and want to leave a generous tip, leave an amount equal to 10% of the bill. Your tips won't likely do much damage to your budget, as service in Panamanian restaurants usually needs improving.

What to Order

Most restaurants serve *bistec* (beef), *pollo* (chicken) and *pescado* (fish) dishes. Vegetarians should note that *carne* literally means 'meat,' but in Panama it tends to refer to beef. Chicken, *puerco* (pork) and *chi o* (goat) aren't necessarily included in a dish's description, so be specific if you want something without any meat. Try *¿Tienen algún plato egetariano?* (Do you have any vegetarian dishes?); or, *Soy egetariana/o. ¿Me puede preparar este plato sin algún carne?* (I am a vegetarian. Can I get this without any meat?). Generally, Panamanian food is tasty rather than spicy hot.

In keeping with its international and multiethnic character, Panama offers a variety of food. The national dish is *sancocho*, a fairly spicy chicken and vegetable stew. *Ropa ieja* ('old clothes'), a spicy shredded beef combination served over rice, is another common and tasty dish. Other typical Panamanian dishes you are likely to encounter include the following:

carimañola – a roll made from ground and boiled yucca that is filled with chopped meat and then deep-fried.

casado – a set meal that is often filling and always economical. It normally contains *arroz* (rice), *frijoles* (black beans), *plátano* (fried plantain), beef, chopped *repollo* (cabbage) and maybe an egg or an avocado.

ce iche – the classic Panamanian ceviche includes sea bass or *conchas* (shellfish), chopped onion and *ají chombo* (one of the hottest chili peppers in the world), marinated in lemon juice. Increasingly, ceviche in Panama is offered with *langostinos* (shrimp) or *pulpo* (octopus) in lieu of corvina or shellfish.

empanadas – corn turnovers filled with ground meat and fried.

gallo pinto – literally, 'spotted rooster'; a soupy mixture of rice and black beans, often with a pig's tail thrown in for flavor. Gallo pinto is traditionally served at breakfast, sometimes with *natilla* (something like a cross between sour cream and custard) or *hue os fritos/re ueltos* (fried/scrambled eggs). This dish is lightly spiced with herbs and is filling and tasty.

patacones – fried green plantains cut crossways in thin pieces, covered in salt and then pressed and fried.

plátano maduro – also called *plátanos en tentación*; ripe plantains sliced lengthwise and baked or broiled with butter, brown sugar and cinnamon; served hot.

tajadas – ripe plantains sliced lengthwise and fried.

tamales – boiled ground corn with spices and chicken or pork; the tamale is wrapped in banana leaves and boiled.

tasajo – dried meat cooked with vegetables.

tortilla de maíz – a thick, fried cornmeal tortilla.

Seafood is excellent and abundant in Panama. On the Caribbean coast and islands, common everyday foods include lobster, shrimp, Caribbean king crab, octopus and fish such as corvina. Often the seafood is mixed with coconut milk; coconut rice and coconut bread are other Caribbean treats.

The area around Volcán Barú is known for its mountain rainbow trout, coffee, Boquete navel oranges and many other fruits and vegetables.

In Panama City you'll often see men pushing carts and selling *raspados*, cones made of shaved ice topped with fruit syrup and sweetened condensed milk. This is no gourmet dish, but on a hot day nothing is more satisfying.

Many bars serve *bocas*. These are little savory side dishes such as black beans, ceviche, chicken stew, potato chips and sausages, and they are designed to make your drink more pleasurable – maybe you'll have another one! If you have several rounds, you might eat enough bocas to make a light meal.

DRINKS
Nonalcoholic Drinks

Fresh fruit drinks, sweetened with heaping tablespoons of sugar and mixed with water or milk, are called *chichas* and are very common. These drinks originated in Chiriquí Province and are now popular throughout Panama. At Niko's Cafe in Panama City, for example, more than a dozen different chichas are sold. Fruit drinks to try include *piña* (pineapple), *sandía* (watermelon), *melón* (cantaloupe), *mora* (blackberry), *zanahoria* (carrot), *cebada* (barley) and *tamarindo* (a slightly tart but refreshing drink made from the fruit of the tamarind tree).

A nonalcoholic drink found in Panama and nowhere else is the *chicheme*. This delicious concoction consists of milk, sweet corn, cinnamon and vanilla. Many Panamanians believe chicheme has certain health-giving properties and think nothing of driving many kilometers to buy it in La Chorrera, a city in Panamá Province that produces the best chicheme. (See the Panamá Province chapter for more details.)

Perhaps the healthiest drink available in Panama is the one served in its natural container: coconut juice. On certain stretches of the Carretera Nacional (National Hwy) on the Península de Azuero and on some San Blás islands, you'll see people selling coconut juice from little stands. You'll recognize the stands by the piles of coconuts beside them. For 25¢, the vendor will hack a hole in a coconut and serve it to you. The juice is sweet and pure; you needn't worry about bugs. When you're through with the juice, ask the vendor to split the coconut in half. If you're lucky, the meat that it contains will be delicious. Some coconuts have tasty meat, some don't.

Coffee is traditionally served very strong and offered with cream or condensed milk. Café Durán is the most popular of the local brands, and it's quite good. Cappuccinos are increasingly available in Panama City. Tea (including herb tea) is available in the cities but difficult to find in towns. Milk is pasteurized and safe to drink. The usual brands of soft drinks are available.

Alcoholic Drinks

The national alcoholic drink is made of *seco*, milk and ice. Seco, like rum, is distilled from sugar cane, but it doesn't taste anything like the rum you know. This is the drink of campesinos. Order a *seco con leche* in sophisticated Panama City and you'll likely receive some odd looks, but a true world traveler wouldn't leave the country without trying one.

By far the most popular alcoholic beverage in Panama is *cer eza* (beer), and the most popular local brands are Soberana, Panamá, Balboa, Cristal and Atlas. None of these is rich in taste, but served ice cold they're hard to beat on a hot day. A large Atlas at a typical cantina can cost as little as 50¢; the same beer can cost you US$2 at an upscale restaurant.

Just behind cerveza on the popularity index are the hard liquors, often referred to by both sexes as *baja panties* (panty lowerers). Of these, rum, scotch and vodka are the big sellers. The Panamanian label Old Parr scotch tastes a lot like old shoe. Wines are not terribly popular. Those that are offered in most restaurants generally come from Chile, France or the USA and are of mediocre quality. However, quite good wines from California, France, Spain, Italy and Argentina can be found in fine restaurants and wine stores, although the variety is not huge.

There's a drink that peasants in the central provinces particularly like: *ino de palma*, which is sap extracted from the trunk of an odd variety of palm tree called *palma de corozo*. This collected sap can be drunk immediately (it's delicious and sweet) or fermented (which is kind of hard to take for someone not used to its harsh flavor).

Most bars in Panama have a happy hour – drinks are half-price during certain late-afternoon hours, typically 4 to 6 pm or 5 to 7 pm. Some nightclubs offer 'open bars,' which means you pay a certain amount to enter the establishment and thereafter the drinks are free. Generally only local brands, which are far less expensive than imported ones, are served at open bars.

ENTERTAINMENT

Panama City has the best selection of entertainment in Central America. On a typical weekend night visitors have the options of hearing live jazz, rock, salsa or Panamanian music; seeing the newest Hollywood movies in English at any of a number of cinemas; dancing at no fewer than five classy, high-tech dance clubs; drinking in fancy bars, neighborhood pubs or traditional cantinas; gambling at casinos; shooting pool; and/or checking out the strip clubs.

The best place to obtain information about upcoming cultural events in Panama City is *Talingo*, a supplement that appears in the newspaper *La Prensa* every Sunday. On the last inside page of *Talingo*, under the heading 'Nacional,' are lists (in Spanish only) of the art events, concerts, conferences, classes, gallery openings and recommended TV movies for the coming week.

The number of entertainment options drops off dramatically outside the capital city, although it's odd to come across a community that doesn't have at least one watering hole at which to pass the time with some friendly people. Details on local entertainment alternatives are found throughout the regional chapters of this book.

SPECTATOR SPORTS

Panamanians are enthusiastic sports fans. As in all of Latin America, soccer is a favorite; in Panama, baseball, softball and basketball are also all the rage. Boxing is another popular spectator sport; it has been a source of pride to Panamanians (and to Latin Americans in general) ever since Roberto Durán, a Panama City native and boxing legend, won the world championship lightweight title in 1972. He went on to become the world champion in the welterweight (1980), light middleweight (1983) and super middleweight (1989) categories.

SHOPPING

A remarkable variety of imported goods, including cameras, electronic equipment and clothing, is sold in Panama, both in Colón's tax-free Zona Libre and in Panama City. The giant stores in the Zona Libre cater mostly to mass buyers, and most of them will not sell individual items (see the Colón Province chapter for details). Panama City's Avenida Central, however, is a mecca for bargain hunters. Shop around and bargain, as there's a lot of competition.

It's possible to purchase high-quality replicas of *huacas* – golden objects made on the isthmus centuries before the Spanish conquest and placed with Indians at the time of burial. These range in price from

---

Luck of the Draw

Panamanians *love* lotteries, and there are two national lotteries in the country. One allows you to pick your numbers, and the other offers tickets with numbers already on them. As in lotteries everywhere, the goal is to possess those numbers that are randomly selected as winners by the government. No tax is levied on lottery prizes in Panama. Profits from ticket sales go to hospitals and other charitable institutions.

Where can you buy a lottery ticket? Seemingly everywhere. Sellers get a tiny commission for every ticket they sell, so many retired people sell tickets to pick up a little extra money to supplement their pensions. Tickets are also available at most liquor and convenience stores. Winning numbers appear in local newspapers and are often found scribbled on pieces of paper posted in stores that sell tickets.

US$5 to more than US$1000. See the Panama City chapter for details.

The favorite handicraft souvenir from Panama is the *mola*, a colorful, intricate, multilayered appliqué textile sewn by Kuna women of the Archipiélago de San Blás. Small, simple souvenir molas can be bought for as little as US$5, but the best ones are sold on the islands and can fetch several hundred dollars.

Other handicrafts include wood carvings, masks, ceramics and clothing. *Polleras*, the lacy, frilly, intricately sewn dresses that are considered Panama's national dress, are made in Guararé on the Península de Azuero. You can buy one, but they're not cheap; some cost more than US$1000. See the Veraguas, Herrera and Los Santos chapters for details on traditional handicrafts particular to certain villages.

All the Gran Morrison chain department stores have handicraft and traditional art sections. Other places where visitors can shop for handicrafts in the capital city are mentioned in the Panama City chapter.

Getting There & Away

Panama's geographic location between two large continents and two great oceans makes it one of the true crossroads of the world. Each year more than 300 cruise ships transit the Panama Canal. Airlines serving Panama on a regular basis include not only major North and South American carriers, but Taiwanese, Israeli, Russian and Spanish airlines. Overland travelers are entering the country in increasing numbers, and many international tour operators offer Panamanian tours.

AIR

Airlines connect Panama with all the other Central American countries, the Caribbean, and North and South America. If you're traveling a long distance, you can usually arrange a ticket with one or more free stopovers.

The main air connection points in North America for flights to and from Panama are Miami; Houston; Newark, NJ; New York; Washington, DC; Dallas; and Los Angeles. Miami is the principal one. Fares from the USA are competitive, but they generally change seasonally, resulting in higher fares during the peak travel periods of mid-December to mid-January and mid-June to mid-August.

Panama has two international airports (one in Panama City and one in David), and travel agencies can be found in the major cities. There's a US$20 departure tax on international flights. See Visas & Documents in the Facts for the Visitor chapter for entry and exit requirements.

Airports & Airlines

Tocumen International Airport, 35km from downtown Panama City, is where most international flights to Panama arrive. Aeropuerto Enrique Malek, in David, which is 75km southeast of the Costa Rican border, frequently handles flights to and from San José.

Going through immigration, baggage pickup and customs at Tocumen airport usually takes only a matter of minutes. If you need a tourist card and don't have one when you reach the immigration booth, you'll likely be directed to an airline counter 20m away where you can get one for the regular fee of US$5. After you've completed the short form, return to the immigration booth and submit it. You'll then receive an entry stamp valid for 90 days. (See Visas & Documents in the Facts for the Visitor chapter for further details on entry requirements; some visitors don't need tourist cards, while others must obtain a visa.)

Just beyond immigration is an Instituto Panameño de Turismo (IPAT) counter. If you have any questions or want help securing a taxi ride into town, don't hesitate to approach the counter; the people behind it are there to help you. Unfortunately, unless you speak Spanish they likely won't be able to assist you.

Warning

The information in this chapter is particularly vulnerable to change: Prices for international travel are volatile, routes are introduced and canceled, schedules change, special deals come and go, and rules and visa requirements are amended. Airlines and governments seem to take a perverse pleasure in making price structures and regulations as complicated as possible. You should check directly with the airline or a travel agent to make sure you understand how a fare (and any ticket you may buy) works. In addition, the travel industry is highly competitive, and there are many lurks and perks.

The upshot of this is that you should get opinions, quotes and advice from as many airlines and travel agents as possible before you part with your hard-earned cash. The details given in this chapter should be regarded as pointers and are not a substitute for your own careful, up-to-date research.

Remember, Before You Fly...

- Always reconfirm airline reservations, even for short flights.
- Arrive at the airport an hour before departure for domestic flights.
- Arrive at the airport two hours before departure for international flights.

Just beyond the tourist counter you'll come to a conveyor belt where your baggage will appear. After claiming your bags, proceed to customs a few meters away. There you will be asked to press a large red button that will randomly illuminate one of two lights. If you get a green light, you can proceed to the front of the terminal without having your bags checked. If you get a red light, you must present your bags to a customs agent for inspection.

The major airlines flying to Panama come from the USA. These include American Airlines, Aviateca, Continental Airlines, Delta Air Lines, EVA Air, Lacsa, Mexicana, TACA Regional Airways and United Airlines. From Europe, most airlines connect with flights from Miami. Iberia from Spain and LTU International Airways charters from Germany may avoid Miami, but usually stop somewhere in the Caribbean instead. COPA is Panama's national airline, offering flights to and from the USA, numerous Latin and South American countries, and the Caribbean.

Panama also has four domestic carriers, and several charter airlines operate out of Panama City. See the Getting Around chapter for details on domestic air travel.

Buying Tickets

The ordinary economy-class fare is not the most economical way to go. It is convenient, however, because it usually enables you to fly on the next plane out, and your ticket is valid for 12 months. In my experience, contacting the airlines directly is a waste of money. A good travel agent is more likely to find the airline with the best deal for you. If you want to economize further, there are several options, which are discussed below.

Buying Tickets Online The Internet can be a useful source of cheap-fare quotes and even bookings. To buy a ticket on the Internet, you need to use a credit card.

Two websites to check for airline fares from North America are Travelocity (www.travelocity.com) and also Expedia (www.expedia.com). In Britain, try Flifo (www.flifo.com).

For flights from Britain, look at Cheap Tickets (www.cheaptickets.com) and Ebookers (www.ebookers.com). On the Continent, try www.etn.nl. In Australia, try www.travel.com.au. The Lonely Planet website (www.lonelyplanet.com) has more links.

Most airlines also have their own website with online ticket sales, sometimes discounted for online customers. You can find airline websites by going to a major search engine, such as www.google.com, and doing a search for the airline.

Youth & Student Fares People with international student ID cards can get discounts with most major airlines. Student fares are not only cheap, they often include free stopovers, don't require advance purchase and may be valid for up to a year. Although youth and student fares can be arranged through most travel agents and airlines, it is a good idea to go through agents that specialize in student travel.

There are two travel agencies with worldwide offices that provide excellent service to student travelers: STA Travel (www.statravel.com) and Council Travel (www.counciltravel.com). STA Travel is the world's largest travel organization specializing in low-cost travel for students. It has more than 100 offices worldwide. It can get competitive airfares for nonstudents too.

Council Travel is affiliated with the Council on International Educational Exchange and is a well-recommended company for budget travel. It has dozens of sales offices in France, Germany, the UK and the USA. Like STA Travel, Council

Air Travel Glossary

Alliances Many of the world's leading airlines are now intimately involved with each other, sharing everything from reservations systems and check-in to aircraft and frequent-flyer schemes. Opponents say that alliances restrict competition. Whatever the arguments, there is no doubt that big alliances are the way of the future.

Courier Fares Businesses often need to send urgent documents or freight securely and quickly. Courier companies hire people to accompany the package through customs and, in return, offer a discount ticket that is sometimes a bargain. However, you may have to surrender all your baggage allowance and take only carry-on luggage.

Fares Airlines traditionally offer 1st-class (coded F), business-class (coded J) and economy-class (coded Y) tickets. These days, there are so many promotional and discounted fares available that few passengers pay full fare.

Lost Tickets If you lose your airline ticket, an airline will usually treat it as a traveler's check and, after inquiries, issue you with another one. Legally, however, an airline is entitled to treat it as cash, so if you lose it, then it could be gone forever. Take very good care of your tickets.

Onward Tickets An entry requirement for many countries is that you have a ticket out of the country. If you're unsure of your next move, the easiest solution is to buy the cheapest onward ticket to a neighboring country or a ticket (from a reliable airline) that can later be refunded if you do not use it.

Open-Jaw Tickets These are return tickets used to fly out to one place but return from another. If available, this can save you from having to backtrack to your arrival point.

Overbooking Since every flight has some passengers who fail to show up, airlines often book more passengers than they have seats. Usually excess passengers make up for the no-shows, but occasionally somebody gets 'bumped' onto the next available flight. Who is it most likely to be? The passengers who check in late. If you do get 'bumped,' you are normally offered some form of compensation.

Reconfirmation Some airlines require you to reconfirm your flight at least 72 hours prior to departure. Check your travel documents to see if this is the case.

Restrictions Discounted tickets often have various restrictions on them – such as mandatory advance payment and penalties for alterations or cancellations. Others have restrictions on the minimum and maximum period you must be away.

Round-the-World Tickets RTW tickets give you a limited period (usually a year) in which to circumnavigate the globe. You can go anywhere the carrying airlines go, as long as you don't backtrack. The number of stopovers or the total number of separate flights is decided before you set off, and these tickets can offer excellent value.

Ticketless Travel Airlines are gradually realizing that paper tickets are unnecessary encumbrances. On simple one-way or return trips, reservations details can be held on computer, and the passengers merely show identification to claim their seats.

Transferred Tickets Airline tickets cannot be transferred from one person to another. Travelers sometimes try to sell the return half of their tickets, but officials can ask you to prove that you are the person named on the ticket. On an international flight, the name on the ticket is compared with the name on the passport.

Travel can also offer competitive airfares for nonstudents. Several of its offices are listed in this chapter.

Airline Deals Whatever your age, if you can purchase your ticket well in advance and fulfill a minimum length-of-stay requirement, you can find a fare usually about 30% to 40% cheaper than the full economy fare. These are often called 'APEX,' 'excursion' or 'promotional' fares, depending on the country you are flying from and the rules and fare structures that apply there.

Often the following restrictions apply: You must purchase your ticket at least 21 days in advance; you must stay for a minimum period (14 days on average); and you must return within 180 days (sometimes sooner – for example, passengers from the USA must return within 30 days to qualify for the lowest APEX fares). Most of these tickets do not allow stopovers, and there are extra charges if you change your destination or dates of travel. These tickets are often sold out well in advance of departure, so try to book early.

Standby fares are another possibility from some countries. Some airlines will let you travel at the last minute if they have available seats just before the flight. Standby tickets cost less than an economy fare but usually are not as cheap as other discounted tickets.

Discounted Tickets Ticket consolidators, or 'bucket shops,' are allowed to sell discounted tickets to help airlines fill their flights. These tickets are often the cheapest of all, particularly in the low season, but they may sell out fast and you may be limited to only a few available dates.

Discounted, economy and student tickets are available directly from the airlines or from travel agencies, but consolidated discount tickets can be purchased only from the discount-ticket agencies themselves.

Discount-ticket agencies often advertise in the travel sections of newspapers and in travel-oriented magazines. STA Travel and Council Travel, which specialize in inexpensive airline tickets for students, can also offer competitive airfares for nonstudents.

Other Considerations Roundtrip fares are always much cheaper than two one-way tickets. They are also cheaper than 'open-jaw' tickets, which enable you to fly into one city (such as Panama City) and leave from another (such as Guatemala City). However, a few agencies can get some good fares on open-jaw tickets, which are suitable for someone wanting to do a little overland traveling in Central America, so it's a good idea to shop around.

If a late flight (but not a rescheduled one) causes you to miss a connection or forces you to stay overnight, the carrier is responsible for providing you with help in making the earliest possible connection and paying for a room in a hotel of its choice. The airline should also provide you with meal vouchers. If you are seriously delayed on an international flight, you might have to ask for these services.

Travelers are sometimes confused about the meaning of a 'direct flight.' A direct flight goes from your departure point to your destination and does not require that you get off the plane. However, unless it is specifically called a *nonstop* direct flight, the flight can stop in several cities en route to its final destination.

Nonstop direct flights will often cost more than other flights, but money isn't everything. If you're traveling to Panama to relax, avoid a ticket that would have you make many stops before reaching Panama. Be sure to ask about stopovers before purchasing your ticket.

Travelers with Special Needs

If you have special needs of any variety – a broken leg, dietary restrictions, dependence on a wheelchair, responsibility for a baby, fear of flying – you should let the airline know as soon as possible so that they can make arrangements accordingly. You should remind them when you reconfirm your reservation (at least 72 hours before departure) and again when you check in at the airport. It may also be worth calling a few airlines before you make your reservation to find out how each can handle your needs.

Award Yourself Some Space

Gone are the days when you could receive a free trip to an exotic locale as a valued frequent flyer after flying to only a few, albeit distant, destinations. Today you've practically got to fly to another solar system to accrue enough kilometers to qualify for one free airline ticket.

Regardless of the award requirements, there's a very good reason for you to enroll in the frequent-flyer program offered by the airline (or airlines) you'll use for your upcoming trip to Panama: Most carriers allow their frequent-flyer members to board early. Sure, disabled people, 1st-class passengers and families with small children are always allowed to board first. Increasingly, frequent flyers are called immediately afterward, before row-by-row announcements begin.

Boarding early is important because it virtually assures you plenty of overhead cargo space for your carry-on baggage. This may not seem important to you when you're at home selecting your luggage with great care and planning baggage space with utmost efficiency. But you'll be glad to be in front of the herd when you're returning from Panama with newly bought goodies that you'd rather not place in the care of airport baggage handlers.

Joining a frequent-flyer program is easy. You can do it at the time you purchase your ticket, if you obtain the ticket directly from an airline. If you obtain it from a ticket consolidator or travel agent, call the airline and ask to join its program. There's never any charge to join, and most applications can be made simply by calling the airline's toll-free reservations number. Once the application is completed, you'll be mailed a membership card to present at the time you check in. *Bon voyage!*

Airports and airlines can be surprisingly helpful, but they do need advance warning. Most international airports can provide escorts from check-in desk to plane when needed, and there should be ramps, elevators, accessible toilets and reachable phones. Aircraft toilets, on the other hand, are likely to present some problems; travelers should discuss this with the airline at an early stage and, if necessary, with their doctors.

Guide dogs for the blind often have to travel in a specially pressurized baggage compartment with other animals, away from their owners, though smaller dogs may be admitted to the cabin. Guide dogs are not subject to quarantine as long as they have proof of vaccination against rabies.

Deaf travelers can ask that airport and in-flight announcements are written down for them.

Children younger than two travel for 10% of the standard fare (or for free on some airlines) as long as they don't occupy a seat. (They do not receive a baggage allowance, either.) 'Skycots' should be provided by the airline if they're requested in advance; these will take a child weighing up to about 22lbs. Children between the ages of two and 12 can usually occupy a seat for one-half to two-thirds the full fare and do get a baggage allowance. Strollers can often be taken on as hand baggage.

USA & Canada

The following airlines, shown with their North American toll-free telephone numbers, serve Panama from the USA:

American Airlines	☎ 800-433-7300
Continental Airlines	☎ 800-231-0856
COPA	☎ 800-225-2272
Delta Air Lines	☎ 800-221-4141
EVA Air	☎ 800-695-1188
Lacsa	☎ 800-225-2272
Mexicana	☎ 800-531-7921
TACA	☎ 800-225-2272
United Airlines	☎ 800-241-6522

As noted earlier in this chapter, the principal US gateways to and from Panama are Miami; Houston; Newark, NJ; New York; Washington, DC; Dallas; and Los Angeles. At the time of writing, sample roundtrip economy fares for direct flights from

Miami to Panama City ranged between US$375 and US$500. Similar fares from Los Angeles ranged between US$400 and US$675.

Advertisements for ticket consolidators may be found in the Sunday travel sections of the *Los Angeles Times*, *The New York Times* and other major newspapers. An excellent contact for cheap fares from gateway towns is Tico Travel (☎ 954-493-8426, 800-493-8426, fax 954-493-8466, info@ticotravel.com; 161 E Commercial Blvd, Fort Lauderdale, FL 33334), which has discounted fares to anywhere in Central America.
Website: www.ticotravel.com

There were no direct flights from Canada to Panama at the time of writing; travelers needed to connect through one of the gateway cities in the USA. United Airlines, Continental Airlines and American Airlines all have good connections from major Canadian cities. You can also fly with Air Canada and connect to another airline, but it's usually best to try to fly all the way with one airline to reduce the risk of your baggage missing its connection.

A recommended Canadian travel agency is Travel CUTS, with dozens of offices across Canada and a couple in the USA. Though geared for students, it has good deals for nonstudents as well.
Website: www.travelcuts.com

Latin America & the Caribbean

Lacsa, Mexicana and TACA provide services between all the Central American capitals and Panama City. In addition, COPA (the Panamanian airline) offers flights between Panama City and Colombia, Costa Rica, Cuba, the Dominican Republic, Ecuador, El Salvador, Guatemala, Haiti, Jamaica, Mexico and Peru; Aeronica (the Nicaraguan airline) also provides services to and from Panama City.

In South America you'll find that service to and from Panama is offered by Avianca in Colombia; Lacsa in Ecuador, Peru and Venezuela; and Varig in Brazil. American Airlines, Continental Airlines, Delta Air Lines and United Airlines all have connections from Panama City to several South American countries.

These flights tend to be expensive because most Latin American countries tax airfares heavily (usually over 10%), and the number of APEX fares is limited. Ticket consolidators aren't found easily in Latin America and the Caribbean, if at all. If you plan on traveling from outside the region to several Latin American countries by air, it is better to book tickets in advance at home rather than paying as you go.

Students considering a trip to Panama should get in touch with STA Travel (www.statravel.com), which has offices in Buenos Aires, Argentina; Sao Paulo and Rio de Janeiro, Brazil; Santiago, Chile; Bogotá, Colombia; and Caracas, Venezuela.

UK & Ireland

Ticket consolidators generally provide the cheapest fares from Europe to Latin America. Fares from London, where competition is fiercest, are often cheaper than from other European cities; thus some Europeans find it cheaper to fly to Panama via London than directly from their home countries.

Agencies advertise in the classifieds of newspapers ranging from *The Times* to *Time Out*. Journey Latin America (☎ 20-8747-3108, flights@journeylatinamerica .co.uk; 12 & 13 Heathfield Terrace, Chiswick, London W4 4JE) has a healthy reputation. It specializes in cheap fares to Latin American countries as well as arranging itineraries for independent and escorted travel. Journey Latin America also has an office in Manchester.
Website: www.journeylatinamerica.co.uk

Another reputable budget travel agency is Trailfinders (☎ 020-7628-7628; 1 Threadneedle St, London EC2R 8JX). It also maintains branches in Birmingham, Bristol, Glasgow, Manchester and Newcastle; and in Dublin, Ireland.
Website: www.trailfinder.com

Students should consider contacting Council Travel (www.counciltravel.com) and STA Travel (www.statravel.com) for competitive fares.

Continental Europe

Some flights from Europe will take you to Miami, where you can connect with other airlines for flights to Panama. The Spanish airline Iberia has a direct flight to Panama City (with stops in the Caribbean). LTU International Airways has charter flights from Germany. Fares, routes and low/high seasons change frequently; the best information is to be had from travel professionals.

STA Travel (www.statravel.com), Council Travel (www.counciltravel.com) and usit CAMPUS (www.campustravel .co.uk) were designed for students but offer discount travel fares to everyone. Other agencies specializing in cheap tickets and student travel include:

France – Nouvelle Frontières (☎ 08-03-33-3333, www.nouvelles-frontieres.com)

Germany – Alternativ Tours (☎ 030-8-81-2089, www.alternativ-tours.de)

Ireland – usit NOW (☎ 01-679-8833, www.usitnow.ie)

Italy – CTS (☎ 06-462-0431, www.cts.it)

Netherlands – NBBS Reizen (☎ 020-624-0989, www.nbbs.nl)

Norway – Kilroy Travels (☎ 47-815-59633, www.kilroytravels.com)

Spain – Halcón Viajes (☎ 902-300-600, www.halcom-viajes.es)

Australia & New Zealand

Travelers coming from Australia's east coast will usually fly to Panama via the USA or Mexico. Qantas Airways, Air New Zealand and other trans-Pacific carriers fly to Los Angeles via Auckland; Nadi, Fiji; or Honolulu, usually with one stopover allowed on the roundtrip, and connect with various carriers onward to Panama.

Fares from New Zealand via the Pacific will be somewhat lower than those from the east coast of Australia. Routes via Asia are impractical.

Trailfinders Australia (☎ 02-9247-7666; 8 Spring St, Sydney 2000), frequently offers discounted fares to Panama. The company also has offices in Melbourne, Cairns, Brisbane and Perth.

Website: www.trailfinders.com.au

Students would do well to contact STA Travel (STA actually stands for 'Student Travel Australia'), and the company has many offices there. Visit www.statravel.com for contact information for the office nearest you.

Asia

There are few direct flights and no nonstop flights between Asia and Panama, and usually no bargains. Generally the cheapest route is to fly to the West Coast of the USA and connect from there. STA Travel, which has offices throughout Asia, can help.

LAND

If you live in North or Central America, it is possible to travel to Panama overland. The US town nearest Panama is Brownsville, TX, on the Mexican border. From there, it is about 5000km by road to Panama City; nearly half of this distance is through Mexico and the rest through Guatemala, Honduras, Nicaragua and Costa Rica. Panama has land borders with Costa Rica to the west and Colombia to the east. There are no roads linking Panama and Colombia.

You can drive your own car, but the costs of insurance, fuel, border permits, food and accommodations will be much higher than the cost of an airline ticket. Many people opt for flying down and renting cars when they arrive in Panama City.

If you consider driving down, factor in the following: Driving Central American roads at night is not recommended – they are narrow, rarely painted with a center stripe, often potholed and subject to hazards such as cattle and pedestrians in rural areas. Traveling by day from the USA or Canada takes about a week, considerably more if you want to visit some of the fantastic sights en route.

If it's a road trip you want but driving isn't important to you, be advised that public buses can take you all the way from Canada to Panama City. See Lonely Planet's *USA*, *Mexico* and *Central America on a shoestring* guides for details on bus travel to Panama and places to stay en route.

If you decide to drive to Panama, get insurance, have your papers in order and never leave your car unattended (fortunately, guarded lots are common in Latin America). US license plates are attractive to some thieves, so you should display these from inside the car.

If you are bringing a car into Panama, you must pay US$5 for a vehicle control certificate *(tarjeta de circulación)* and another US$1 to have the car fumigated. You will also need to show a driver's license, proof of ownership and insurance papers. Your passport will be stamped to show that you paid the US$6 and followed procedures when you brought the vehicle into the country.

See Visas & Documents in the Facts for the Visitor chapter for entrance requirements.

Costa Rican Border Crossings

There are three road border crossings between Costa Rica and Panama. Border-crossers should note that Panama's time is always one hour ahead of Costa Rica's.

Paso Canoas This crossing is on the Interamericana and is the most frequently used entry and exit point on the border with Costa Rica. Half of the dusty, transient city is in Costa Rica, half in Panama. The border posts are located about the city's waist. For no good reason, the border hours here change frequently; at last check the border was open 7 am to 11 pm daily. Beware: There are hotels on the Costa Rican side of Paso Canoas but none on the Panamanian side.

To enter Panama from Costa Rica, you'll need a passport. Most visitors also need a tourist card, obtainable at the border for US$5, and some people need a visa (see the Visas & Documents section in the Facts for the Visitor chapter). If you bring more than US$4999 into Panama, you'll be asked to pay a 5% tax on it.

There is a Banco Nacional de Panamá just beyond the immigration window. At the bank you can use an ATM, cash traveler's checks and get cash advances against credit cards. However, it's not possible to change Costa Rican colones to US dollars. The bank is open 8 am to 3 pm Monday through Friday and 9 am to noon Saturday. (Men on the street will offer to change money if they see you standing in front of the bank looking perplexed. To lower the risk of being cheated, ask for their exchange rate and calculate how many US dollars you should receive for the amount of colones you intend to unload *before* reaching for your cash.)

Once you have entered Panama, you will see taxis and buses stationed just past the border, on your left and ahead 50m. The nearest Panamanian city with a hotel is David, 1½ hours away by bus. Buses depart Paso Canoas for David from this station every 10 minutes between 5 am and 9:45 pm (US$1.50); look for a bus with 'Frontera – David' on its windshield. There are four buses daily from this station to Panama City, and they depart at 8:30 and 11 am and 4 and 10 pm. The first three buses make numerous stops along the way; travel time is about 10 hours (US$12 for adults, US$6 for kids under 8 years of age). The 10 pm bus makes only a couple of brief food stops and takes about eight hours (US$17 for adults, US$8.50 for kids 7 and younger).

Fifty meters east of that bus station is an unmarked, often-overlooked bus station that features bus rides to Panama City. Except for two express buses, which leave at 9:45 and 10:45 pm and cost US$17, these buses make stops at David and all the other major cities along the way (they'll even stop at a hamlet along the Interamericana or at a turnoff *if* you ask the driver to stop ahead of time). These buses leave at 5:45, 7, 8:30, 10 and 11:30 am and 2, 4 and 6:45 pm (US$12).

There is a taxi stand near the bus station. Taxis are available 24 hours a day. A taxi ride from the border to David will cost US$25 to US$30 per party, depending on the driver and the hour.

If you are entering Costa Rica, you may be required to show a ticket out of the country, although this is rarely requested. If you don't have one, buy a Tracopa bus ticket in David for David to Paso Canoas and the return trip; this is acceptable to the Costa Rican authorities. Buying just the Paso Canoas-to-David section at the border is not acceptable.

There is a Costa Rican consulate in David, and another one in Panama City. IPAT, the Panamanian tourism agency, has a tourist center in Paso Canoas.

Sixaola/Guabito This crossing is on the Caribbean coast. Sixaola is the last town on the Costa Rican side; Guabito is its Panamanian counterpart. There are no hotels or banks in Guabito, but stores there will accept your Costa Rican colones, Panamanian balboas or US dollars. Colones are not accepted south of Guabito.

The border is officially open from 7 am to 11 pm daily. However, immigration and customs officers often don't work past 7 pm, which is when bus service on both sides also grinds to a halt. During the day, there are frequent minibuses from Guabito to Changuinola, 17km away; the fare is US$1. The minibuses can be found on the southern side of the elevated entrance road, just past the immigration office. Taxis are found on the northern side of the road; the fare to Changuinola is US$5.

To enter Guabito, you'll need a passport and you might need a tourist card (see Visas & Documents in the Facts for the Visitor chapter). A tourist card can be obtained for US$5 at the Panamanian Embassy in San José (see Embassies & Consulates in the Facts for the Visitor chapter). Or, in lieu of a tourist card, you can go to the Banco Nacional de Panamá in Changuinola and for US$10 obtain a stamp, which you should then take to Changuinola's immigration office (☎ 758-8651; open 8 am to noon, 1 to 3 pm weekdays) across the street. The office will put the stamp in your passport along with an official signature; this will serve as your tourist card and entry stamp. If the immigration office is closed and you're on your way to Bocas, just return when you can and have the stamp and entry stamp entered into your passport. Don't ignore the importance of the entry stamp, because it's

necessary to have one to be able to leave the country.

The border officials reside in nearby houses, and if it is hot (as it usually is in Guabito), they sometimes go home to sleep when they're supposed to be working. If you arrive at the border and you have a passport that needs stamping or otherwise need their services, look around for them. Even if you don't speak Spanish, if you're wandering around with a passport in your hand and looking confused, it'll only be a matter of minutes before someone takes pity on you and leads you to an official's home. If awakened, he'll return to his post with you and stamp your passport.

In Changuinola there are numerous hotels, several banks, some decent restaurants, and an airstrip with daily service to David and Panama City. Bus and taxi service to Almirante and David exists. See the Bocas del Toro Province chapter for more information on Changuinola.

Río Sereno This little town at the eastern terminus of the scenic Concepción-Volcán road sees so few *gringos* (tourists) that locals often stare at those who pass through. If you arrive here from Costa Rica by small bus (as most people do), you'll be hard pressed to figure out where one country ends and the other begins. There's no fence, not even a 'Now Leaving Costa Rica – Welcome to Panama' sign. The Río Sereno crossing is open from 7:30 am to 5 pm daily.

The immigration officials here can be sticklers on formalities: To enter Panama here, visitors are often required to show a return ticket to their country of origin and show that they are economically solvent (ie, carrying at least US$500 in cash; citizens from the Dominican Republic will be asked to display US$1000). That's in addition to the usual entry requirements (see the Facts for the Visitor chapter). The little immigration office is near the base of a huge police communications tower. The office is identifiable by an orange-and-black 'Migracion' sign.

There's one hotel in this sleepy town nestled amid coffee plantations and patches of forest. The comfortable *Posada Los Andes* (no phone), above the pharmacy at the southeast corner of the town plaza, has 11 rooms with firm mattresses and shared hot-water bathrooms (US$8/10 for one/two people) and three rooms with private bathrooms (US$15 per room).

There is a Banco Nacional de Panamá, which has an ATM. Services at the bank include cashing traveler's checks and offering cash advances against major credit cards. However, foreign currency cannot be exchanged here. The bank is open 8 am to 3 pm Monday through Friday and 9 am to noon Saturday.

There's a bus terminal two blocks northeast of the bank (ie, along the same street and away from the border). Hourly buses depart from Río Sereno to Volcán (US$2.65, 40km) and continue on to David (US$4), with the first bus departing at 5 am and the last at 5 pm.

Bus At all three of these border crossings, you can take a local bus up to the border on either side, cross over, board another local bus and continue on your way. Be aware that, as previously mentioned, the last buses leave the border crossings at Guabito and Río Sereno at 7 pm and 5 pm, respectively; the last bus leaves Paso Canoas for Panama City at 10 pm.

Two companies, Panaline (☎ 227-8648, fax 227-8647) and Tica Bus (☎ 262-2084, fax 262-6275), operate daily direct buses between San José, Costa Rica, and Panama City, traveling by way of the Carretera Interamericana. Both recommend that you make reservations a few days in advance.

In Panama City, Panaline buses arrive at and depart from the Gran Hotel Saloy. They depart Panama City at noon daily and arrive in San José the following morning around 4 am. These are good buses, equipped with air con, bathrooms and video. The fare is US$25/50 one-way/roundtrip.

Tica Bus arrives at and departs from an office beside the Hotel Ideal, Calle 17 Oeste, No 15-55, a block west of Avenida Central in Panama City. These buses depart at 11 am daily and arrive in San José the fol-

lowing day around 4 am. The fare is US$25/50 one-way/roundtrip. You must bring your passport when you reserve your ticket. From San José, these buses continue to Managua (US$40 one-way), Tegucigalpa (US$60), San Salvador (US$75) and Guatemala City (US$83).

Colombian Border Crossing

No roads link Panama and Colombia. The Interamericana does not go all the way from Panama into Colombia, but terminates at the grimy town of Yaviza, in the Darién, and reappears some 150km farther on – far beyond the Colombian border. This break in the highway between Central and South America is known as the Darién Gap. If you wish to take a vehicle into South America from Panama, you must ship it around the Darién Gap.

There is only one place to cross along the entire length of the Panama-Colombia border – a rugged point on the Caribbean coast between rustic Puerto Obaldía (on the Panamanian side) and the resort of Capurganá (on the Colombian side). From either direction, you can reach the other country by boat or by hiking across the point to it. But before you board a boat or put on your walking shoes, you must first obtain the proper passport stamps (see details below).

If you're heading into South America by land or by sea, you must first get to Puerto Obaldía, Panama's official border town (which is actually a few kilometers from the border). The simplest way to do this is to fly from Panama City. Aereo Taxi (☎ 315-0300) and Ansa (☎ 315-7520) have regular flights between Panama City and Puerto Obaldía. The one-way/roundtrip fare is US$46/92.

The alternative is to arrive by boat, usually as the last stop on an island-hopping excursion through the Archipiélago de San Blás. You have three boating options: Pay a Kuna Indian to take you from the San Blás islands to the border in a long, narrow boat – neither comfortable nor very safe. You can catch a ride on one of the slow-moving coconut boats heading for Puerto Obaldía from El Porvenir in the San Blás islands; these boats stop at many islands, picking up coconuts, and for US$30 or less you can often negotiate a ride (you'll want to bring a hammock to sleep in). The third option is to negotiate a ride on a Colombian merchant boat, which is risky; these boats, which travel between Colón and Cartagena, Colombia, are notorious for running drugs and contraband.

Puerto Obaldía is a nine-square-block tropical way station. Its beaches are strewn with litter and there's little to do in the town itself. There are no services, just a police station (you must check in with the police upon arrival), a couple of immigration offices, a basic hotel and a community of black people who live in simple wooden houses. There's one main road, with a soccer field at one end and the police station at the other. In between are the Panamanian and Colombian immigration offices and the *Pensión Conde* (no phone), which offers 15 basic rooms with private bathrooms for US$12 per room.

If you're heading into Colombia, you need to check with the Panamanian immigration office for an exit stamp or, if you're heading into Panama, an entry stamp. Make sure you have all the necessary documents (passport and tourist card or visa if required) and onward tickets, as well as proof of sufficient funds; US$500 per month of your planned stay is usually enough. Although you may not be asked for these, it's a long backtrack if you show up short. The office is open 9 am to 5 pm weekdays; it closes at noon on Saturday and is closed all day Sunday. An entry stamp is supposed to cost US$5, but officers have been known to ask for US$10, US$15 or US$20.

Once you have your exit stamp, you must then go to the Colombian immigration office and obtain a Colombian entry stamp. There's a US$5 charge. Check with the Colombian embassy in Panama City (☎ 264-9266, Oficina 1802, Edificio World Trade Center) or the Colombian embassy or consulate in your home country to learn the entrance requirements for you (requirements vary from country to country).

There are two transportation options between Puerto Obaldía and Capurganá:

Driving to the Darién Gap

The Carretera Interamericana stops near the Colombian border at the Darién Gap, a stretch of unbroken wilderness that divides the continents of North and South America and bisects the otherwise continuous hemispheric highway that winds from Alaska to the tip of Chile.

It is possible to drive from the capital to Yaviza, the Darién town at which the Interamericana finally peters out. The drive – along 266km of mostly bad road – took nine hours during the dry season in late 2000, but efforts to pave the Interamericana all the way to Yaviza were underway and the work should have been completed by the time you read this.

Along the way to Yaviza you'll pass a variety of small towns: Chepo, El Llano, Cañita, Ipetí, Tortí, Las Aguas Frías, Santa Fé and Metetí. For details on facilities in these towns, see those headings in the Panamá Province and Darién Province chapters.

traveling by boat or by foot. Boats depart for Sapzurro (the first community on the Colombian side) when they collect enough people. The ride costs US$10 and lasts 15 minutes. The boats then continue to Capurganá, an additional 10-minute ride; the Puerto Obaldía-Capurganá fare is US$20. The boatmen often try to make foreign travelers pay more by claiming it's an 'international route' or saying that your backpack is heavy. A good laugh often lets them know you're not falling for it. Present what others are paying, and no more.

The alternative is to walk. This option is a dangerous one, but it does exist. The journey by foot from Puerto Obaldía to Sapzurro takes about 2½ hours. The first part of the trail goes from Puerto Obaldía to La Miel, the last Panamanian village; it's a two-hour walk. This part of the track is unsafe for walking due to bandits and smugglers in the area. Also, the trails are so indistinct that you could easily become lost in the jungle. It may be wisest to travel to La Miel by boat; rides can be negotiated in Puerto Obaldía.

Once you reach La Miel, you *should* be fine (the conflict in Colombia is very fluid; this option isn't without risk). From the village, you climb a small hill, pass the border marker on the top and descend to Sapzurro – all that in half an hour. Small and pleasant Sapzurro is beautifully set on the shore of a deep horseshoe-shaped bay. There are a couple of *hospedajes* (guest-houses), several restaurants and a narrow but clean white-sand beach that's shaded by coconut palms.

From Sapzurro, the footpath (there is no road) climbs again and then drops to the next coastal village, Capurganá. This portion can be easily walked in 1½ to two hours; go at a leisurely pace to take in the splendid scenery.

Capurganá, with a strip of fine hotels lining a wide sweep of beach, is the most touristy place in the area and can get crowded from mid-December to the end of January; at other times it's quiet and easygoing. Hotel rates range from US$25 to US$100. Capurganá is a pleasant place to spend a day or two. A few businesses in the village change US dollars, though at a poor rate.

SEA

Every year several hundred cruise ships transit the Panama Canal. Some carry as many as 2000 passengers and are so large that there's scarcely a meter to spare between the ships and the walls of the locks. Most of the cruise ships make the transit during the months of January, February and March, often while returning to the Caribbean from Alaska. A few passenger ships trickle in during April, but by May and June hardly a cruise liner can be found there; it's just too hot and humid to be aboard a ship in the canal. The transcanal cruises pick up again in October and November. December's generally a slow month, then the cycle repeats itself.

Odd as it may seem, prior to year 2000 not a single one of the cruise ships offered a Panama shore excursion. There simply

was no dock for them. Now there are several places for the ships to tie up, giving their passengers the freedom to see some of Panama on foot. All of these ships offer guided tours.

Among the cruise lines that regularly transit the canal (and their US telephone numbers) are: Princess Cruises (☎ 310-553-1770, 800-774-6237), Crystal Cruises (☎ 310-785-9300), Celebrity Cruises (☎ 305-262-6677, 800-437-3111) and Holland America Line (☎ 800-426-0327). These are also the most expensive, with rates ranging from US$250 to US$350 per person per day, excluding airfare and taxes. Down a step in both price and luxury are Costa Cruises (☎ 305-358-7325, 800-462-6782) and Royal Caribbean Cruise Lines (☎ 305-539-6000, 800-327-6700), charging about US$200 per person per day. The most-bang-for-the-buck award would go to the Carnival (☎ 305-599-2600, 800-327-9501) or Norwegian (☎ 305-436-4000, 800-327-7030) cruise lines, charging about US$125 per person per day. Among the sailing ships making the transit, Windstar Cruises (☎ 206-281-3535, 800-426-0327) in Seattle, WA, enjoys a strong reputation.

An excellent resource if you're considering a cruise and have questions is Cruises Inc (☎ 315-463-9695, 800-854-0500, info@cruisesinc.com; 5000 Campuswood Drive, E Syracuse, NY 13057), a US-based travel agency specializing in cruises. The company represents all the major cruise lines, and their representatives are helpful and extremely knowledgeable. If you visit their website (www.cruisesinc.com), you can see their reviews of all the cruise lines mentioned above and many more.

Departure Tax

There is a US$20 departure tax. If you overstay the 90-day limit, you'll need to get an exit stamp before leaving the country (see Visas & Documents in the Facts for the Visitor chapter).

ORGANIZED TOURS

Compared to such beaten-path Latin American countries as Costa Rica and Guatemala, Panama is served by very few tour operators.

Those operators that do send people here typically offer Panama Canal transits, rainforest walks, white-water rafting, river adventures, snorkeling, diving and/or fishing trips, and educational tours to colonial ruins.

Costs for the best-arranged tours can exceed US$200 per person daily, plus airfare to and from Panama City. These tours usually provide an experienced bilingual guide, the best lodging available, all in-country transportation and most meals.

The advantage of a tour is that everything is taken care of from the time you arrive until the time you leave. You don't have to worry about speaking Spanish, figuring out itineraries, finding bus stations, haggling with taxi drivers, locating hotels with available rooms or translating restaurant menus. People on tours have activities scheduled for every day of their trips and don't need to spend time figuring out what to do and how to do it once they get to Panama City. Tours are often preferred by people who have a short vacation period and enough money to afford this kind of care.

Even if you don't want a tour, there's a good reason to contact a tour operator: savings. If you simply walk into a hotel, you will be given what the tourism industry refers to as the 'rack rate.' However, if a tour operator makes the hotel reservation for you, the amount you pay for the room will be less than the rack rate. For example, a hotel with a rack rate of US$150 per night might sell a room to a tour operator for US$90. The operator might offer you the room for US$120, saving you US$30. It never hurts to see what a tour operator can do for you, particularly if it has a toll-free telephone number.

Travelers who would like the advantages of a tour but can't stand the idea of traveling with a tour group are served by several companies that can arrange custom itineraries. These are never cheap, but they aren't necessarily terribly expensive. You can ask for the more economical hotels to keep costs down. Guides can be arranged, but if you go with the custom itinerary route, these can be fairly expensive for just one or two people. If you are traveling with a small group of friends or family members, a guide could be affordable, as the cost would be split among several people.

Tour Companies

The tour operators mentioned below have strong reputations. Most have sliding price scales (a group of four on a two-week trip might pay US$300 per person more than a group of 14, for example). Prices are based on double occupancy, and people sleeping in single rooms may pay considerably more, depending on the hotels used. Prices can be a little lower in the low season.

The tour operators listed here are based outside Panama, and they represent the only foreign companies that were regularly sending tourists to Panama at the time this book went to press. For information on tours offered by Panamanian companies (some of which also have a US address or contact phone), see the Getting Around chapter. For current tour offerings and prices, visit the websites of the companies mentioned or contact them and request a brochure.

The USA Wildland Adventures (☎ 206-365-0686, 800-345-4453, fax 206-363-6615, info@wildland.com; 3516 NE 155th St, Seattle, WA 98155) is a company that does things the right way. Its friendly staff can arrange specialty trips, particularly birding, family travel, honeymoon adventures, trekking adventures and student/teacher study trips in Panama. Its many high-quality, personalized natural history trips on the Isthmus offer cushy accommodations for cushy people, hard-core adventures for hard-core rugged types and lots of in-between. I've received numerous letters in praise of this company from satisfied clients and not a single complaint. Website: www.wildland.com

Preferred Adventures Ltd (☎ 612-222-8131, 800-840-8687, fax 612-222-4221, travel@preferredadventures.com; One W Water St, Suite 300, St Paul, MN 55107) is another top-notch tour operator with many years in the business and excellent Panama offerings. In addition to birding, horticul-

tural, natural history, cultural and special-interest study trips in Panama, this company can arrange customized itineraries.
Website: www.preferredadventures.com

In my opinion, Preferred Adventures and Wildland Adventures are the top US-based tour operators serving Panama. Both rely heavily upon the very reputable Ancon Expeditions of Panama for ground transportation and guides.

The UK Two British tour operators serving Panama enjoy particularly strong reputations. The Travelling Naturalist (☎ 44-1305-267994, fax 44-1305-265506, jamie@naturalist.co.uk; PO Box 3141, Dorchester, DT1 2XD, Dorset) specializes in birding tours limited to small groups, but also looks at general wildlife as well. At the time of writing the company was offering a popular Panama-Costa Rica combination trip and was planning annual Panama-only trips. The Travelling Naturalist boasts that about 60% of its business comes from repeat clients.
Website: www.naturalist.co.uk

Journey Latin America (☎ 0181-747-8315, fax 0181-742-1312, charles@journey-latinamerica.co.uk; 16 Devonshire Rd, Chiswick, London W4 2HD) offers tailor-made programs of flights, hotels and excursions to Panama as well as jungle-lodge packages and canal transits. In addition, JLA features Panama in its 'Alcion Escorted Economy' tour, which also takes in Costa Rica, Nicaragua, Honduras and Guatemala. JLA can arrange discounted 'open-jaw' tickets for you, too.
Website: www.journeylatinamerica.co.uk

Australia Adventure Associates (☎ 02-9389-7466, fax 02-9369-1853, mail@adventureassociates.com; PO Box 612, Bondi Junction, NSW 1355; 197 Oxford Street Mall, Bondi Junction, Sydney, NSW 2022) offers individual tour packages to Panama that range from a three-day stopover in Panama City to in-depth looks at the country. Highlights of their tours to Panama typically include visits to the ruins of Panamá La Vieja and Portobelo, a partial transit of the Panama Canal, and a boat trip up the Río Chagres to visit an Emberá community. Adventure Associates can also arrange customized jungle, beach, island and/or fishing tours to accommodate your particular desires.
Website: www.adventureassociates.com

Taiwan Natural Kingdom Inc (☎ 886-2-2712-2703, fax 2-2712-4668, nki@ms24.hinet.net; 12F, 309 Fu-Hsin N Road, Taipei, Taiwan 105) opened for business in 1995 and quickly made a strong reputation for itself. Today, it specializes in birding and wildlife tours to some of the world's top national parks, including Parque Nacional Darién and South Africa's famous nature preserves. A brief description of its current offerings is provided in English at the website above, but for details you'll need to click to Natural Kingdom's linked Chinese website and read Mandarin.
Website: www.natural.kingdom

Getting Around

Local transportation in Panama is very good. There are airstrips throughout the country, and most receive commercial flights. The domestic airlines are inexpensive, and they are safe; the US Federal Aviation Administration has assessed Panama's civil aviation authority as being in compliance with international aviation safety standards for oversight of the country's air carrier operations.

Because so many Panamanians depend on buses, there's also an excellent bus system serving all the road-accessible parts of the country. Intercity fares are typically in the US$2 to US$5 range, except for long-distance routes, which can run up to US$25 for nonstop rides on very comfortable Mercedes-Benz buses. Bus fares within cities are typically less than 25¢.

Taxis are one of the best deals going in Panama. Despite high gas prices, the most you have to pay to take a taxi from one part of a city to another part of the same city is US$3 – except in Panama City, where you might have to pay US$5 (this does not include the sedan taxis stationed outside Panama City's upscale hotels, which are allowed by law to charge more). For this reason, taxis are very popular in Panama, and they are usually easy to find.

There are no subways in Panama, and train service at the time this was penned in 2001 was nonexistent (although tracks were being laid between Panama City and Colón, with passenger service possible by 2002). Boats are the best way to get around in some parts of the country, and this option is discussed in detail in the regional chapters.

AIR
Domestic Air Services
Panama is well served by its domestic airlines: Aeroperlas, Aereo Taxi, Ansa, Aviatur and Aero Mapiex. All five airlines have their headquarters at the country's chief domestic airport, Aeropuerto Marcos A Gelabert in the Albrook district of Panama City. Most people know the airport only as Aeropuerto Albrook (Albrook Airport).

Before boarding domestic flights, beware that you likely will be asked to present your passport and that your carry-on luggage will be inspected. The total weight of your luggage, including a carry-on bag, is limited to 11.25kg (25 pounds). If your luggage exceeds this limit, you may incur an overweight charge of 25¢ to 45¢ per pound starting with the 26th pound (the fee varies with destination). If the flight is full, you may also

Watch Your Weight

On domestic flights, you're allowed a total of 11.25kg (25 pounds) of luggage. That's checked baggage *and* carry-on items combined. However, nine times out of 10, if you've got a carry-on bag slung over a shoulder, the clerk weighing baggage at the check-in counter will ignore it.

So, if you know or suspect your carry-on and checked bags weigh more than 11.25kg, you'd be wise to put your heaviest items in your carry-on bag and sling it casually over a shoulder. This way you'll likely dodge an overweight-baggage charge.

It should go without saying, but I'll say it anyway: Do your best not to look as though you are about to collapse under the weight of your carry-on bag, or you'll be asked to place it on the scale. (Oddly, sometimes baggage isn't weighed until you've arrived. Regardless, the same advice applies.)

You will be asked your weight before you board. In reply, it's very important that you add the estimated weight of your unweighed carry-on to your body weight. If you weigh 50kg and you believe your carry-on weighs 12kg, say you weigh 62kg. Do not forget to do this. The small domestic plane you'll be boarding has a maximum-weight limit. Don't contribute to exceeding it.

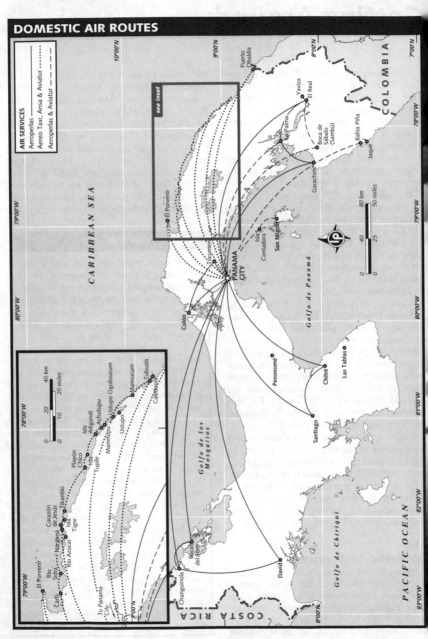

be told that your luggage will be placed on a later flight. Before you board you will also be asked to specify your body weight.

As a general rule, it is a good idea to make your flight reservation as far in advance as possible. Be sure to reconfirm your reservation 72 hours ahead of the scheduled departure time. Furthermore, always arrive at the airport at least an hour early; domestic airline representatives can release reserved seats to standby passengers as early as 45 minutes prior to departure in their quest to fill planes. Air passes are not available in Panama, and student fares don't exist.

The following table lists flights from Aeropuerto Albrook on the country's largest domestic carrier, Aeroperlas (☎ 315-7500, fax 315-7580, iflyap@aeroperlas.com). Website: www.aeroperlas.com

destination	frequency	fare (one-way/roundtrip)
Bahía Piña	Three weekly	US$44/88
Bocas del Toro town	Two daily	US$50/100
Changuinola	Two daily	US$53/106
Chitré	Two daily	US$32/64
Colón	Seven daily	US$36/72
David	Three daily	US$57/114
El Real	Four weekly	US$39/78
Garachiné	Two weekly	US$36/72
Isla Contadora	Two daily	US$27/54
Jaqué	Three weekly	US$44/88
La Palma	One daily	US$36/72
Sambú	Three weekly	US$36/72

Exceptions to the chart: There's only one flight to Chitré on Sunday and only one to Colón on Saturday and Sunday; there are four flights to Isla Contadora on Saturday and three on Sunday, and there's no flight to La Palma on Sunday.

Other Aeroperlas routes include David-Bocas del Toro town (two flights daily Monday through Friday, one on Saturday and Sunday, US$26/52), David-Changuinola (two flights daily Monday through Friday, one on Saturday and Sunday, US$26/52), Santiago-Chitré (two flights daily Monday through Friday, one on Saturday and

Sunday, US$19/38), La Palma-El Real (one flight weekly, US$21/42), La Palma-Garachiné (two flights weekly) and El Real-Sambú (three flights weekly).

Aeroperlas – and all of the airlines listed in these pages – maintain the same frequency of return trips as they do outbound trips. For example, Aeroperlas flies from Panama City to David three times a day. Rest assured Aeroperlas also flies from David to Panama City three times daily.

Three airlines fly between Aeropuerto Albrook and the Comarca de San Blás:

airline	at Aeropuerto Albrook
Aereo Taxi	☎ 315-0300
Ansa	☎ 315-7520
Aviatur	☎ 315-0307

Together, the airlines fly between Panama City and 19 San Blás destinations. From west to east they are: Cartí, El Porvenir, Río Sidra, Río Azucar, Naraganá, Corazón de Jesús, Isla Tigre, Tikantiki, Playón Chico, Isla Tupile, Isla Ailigandí, Achutupu, Mamitupu, Ustupo Ogobsucum, Ustupo, Mansucum, Mulatupo Sasardí, Tubualá, Caledonia and Puerto Obaldía.

Reservations are advised, as the Comarca de San Blás is served by small aircraft and seats fill up quickly. Be aware that an airplane flying from Panama City to the district may stop at several islands before reaching your destination; be sure to ask the name of the island you're on before disembarking. Likewise, it's possible that the aircraft you board in the Comarca de San Blás to return to Panama City will make several stops before it reaches the capital.

Most of the 19 San Blás locations with airline service handle flights to and from Panama City at least six days a week. For prices and further flight information, see the Comarca de San Blás chapter.

In addition to providing service to and from San Blás, Aviatur also flies from Aeropuerto Albrook to: Isla Contadora and Isla del Rey in the Archipiélago de las Perlas; and to Garachiné, Jaqué and Sambú in the Darién.

Aero Mapiex (☎ 315-0888), the smallest of the five airlines, offers limited service from Panama City to David, Changuinola and Bocas del Toro town.

BUS

You can take a bus to just about any community in Panama that is reachable by road. Some of the buses are huge, new Mercedes-Benzes equipped with air con, movie screens and reclining seats. These top-of-the-line buses generally cruise long stretches of highway.

More frequently used – and often seen on the Carretera Interamericana – are Toyota Coaster buses that can seat 28 people. These are not as comfortable as the Mercedes-Benzes, but they aren't bad and they're less expensive. They are an excellent way to visit towns on the Península de Azuero and along the Interamericana.

Also seen on Panamanian roads – particularly within cities – are converted school buses. They are neither comfortable for most adults (they were designed for children) nor convenient (they stop every 10m, or so it seems), and they are usually crowded. Still, they are an extremely cheap way to get around and they beat hoofing it.

See the Getting There & Away section of the Panama City chapter for details on the country's new and terrific central bus station and services to and from the capital city.

TRAIN

The famous old passenger train that once ran along the canal between Panama City and Colón was allowed to fall into ruin during the 1980s. Efforts to get the train up and running again began in 1997, but a dispute soon arose regarding the ownership of property under the tracks. The dispute was settled, and in 2001 new tracks were being laid. There's a fair chance passenger service will resume in 2002.

Trains are still being used to move bananas from the muggy, buggy fields around Changuinola to the docks at Almirante, in Bocas del Toro Province. The only passengers allowed to ride them are banana workers.

Until recently, some wonderful old trains had been used to move bananas from outlying fields to the docks at Puerto Armuelles in Chiriquí Province. Then in 1999, their owner, Chiquita Brands International, stopped using the docks in favor of those at Almirante. Some of the trains were scrapped; the remainder are now hauling bananas in and out of Changuinola.

CAR & MOTORCYCLE

Few tourists drive to Panama in their own vehicles, though it is certainly possible to do so. Renting a car after arrival, on the other hand, is something many travelers do during parts of their trips. A smaller number rent motorcycles.

Road Rules

The universal road signs apply – about half the time. For example, often motorists can only tell which streets are one-way from past experience; one-way signs are as rare as harpy eagles in Panama. Also, during commuter hours some two-way streets suddenly become one-way streets. This is especially true in Panama City. No signs indicate when this changeover occurs. The locals know about such trick streets, but tourists are occasionally spotted taking a wrong turn and confronting several lanes of oncoming traffic.

Another thing to consider before driving in Panama is local disrespect for stop signs. Generally, Panamanians will only come to complete stops at stop signs if they feel there's a good chance they'll collide with an oncoming vehicle. When two vehicles approach an intersection without a traffic signal and are on a collision course, generally the driver of the bigger vehicle blasts through the intersection and the driver of the smaller vehicle brakes.

A really good thing to do before renting a vehicle in Panama is to stand near a busy intersection for a while so you'll know what you'll be getting yourself into. If you do rent a car, beware that Panamanians rarely stop to allow pedestrians to cross the street in front of them. When drivers do stop for this purpose, their kind acts are often followed by bewildered motorists rear-ending them. So be careful before stopping for a pedestrian.

Motorists drive on the right side of the street in Panama. Passing is allowed only on the left. Beware: You can get a traffic ticket for not wearing a seat belt. It is illegal to enter an intersection unless you can also leave it (don't block intersections), and it is illegal to make a right turn on a red light unless a sign indicates that a turn is permitted. At unmarked intersections you're supposed to yield to the car on your right.

Because of difficult driving conditions, there are speed limits of 80kph on all primary roads and 60kph or less on secondary roads. Drivers should carry their passports as well as driver's licenses.

Road Safety

In addition to the concerns expressed in the preceding section, you should be aware of two often overlooked facts about Panama's roads: Animals seem to use them as much as people, and places you can't go by bus are usually inaccessible by other kinds of vehicles (a fact many motorists learn the hard way).

In Panama the immortal question 'Why did the chicken cross the road?' is answered: 'So that its owners can collect US$4.' That's what a driver is expected to pay to the owner of the chicken he or she has just flattened. On the Península de Azuero and throughout Chiriquí Province, chickens often wander onto busy roads – as do dogs, cats, pigs, goats, cows and horses. In Darién Province more sloths are killed by cars than die of natural causes.

Many people rent 4WD vehicles so they can get to places not served by buses (such as Volcán Barú), but they underestimate the potential dangers. I once tried to drive a Toyota Land Cruiser to the top of the volcano, only to discover that the road was so rutted that the truck couldn't make it on its own. I happened to luck out; someone with a much stronger engine and better tires chained my truck to his and all but dragged my 4WD up the hill. I could have easily gotten stuck on the little-used road, where nighttime temperatures can drop close to freezing. I was dressed in shorts and a T-shirt, like most people who visit the volcano.

A month later in Darién Province, my truck hit a rut so hard that the spare tire that was chained to the bottom of the vehicle exploded. I immediately turned around and headed back to the city. Had I continued on and lost another tire, I'd have had to hike at least 25km to reach a main road to summon help. The point is, don't lose track of where you are or how far you'd have to hike to get back to where you were just because you're in a 4WD truck. Some Panamanian potholes could be asteroid craters. Some are so deep there are Chinese faces staring back at you from the bottom of them. You get the idea.

If you are involved in an accident, you should not move the vehicles until after the police have arrived and made a report. This is essential for all insurance claims. Injured people should not be taken from the scene except by the paramedics. Try to make a sketch of what happened, and don't make statements except to police. If you're driving a rental, call the rental company to find out what it wants you to do with the vehicle. If the accident results in injury or death, you may be prevented from leaving the country until all legalities are handled. Drive defensively.

If you see oncoming cars with headlights flashing, it often means that there is some kind of road problem or a police speedtrap ahead. Slow down immediately. Also be on the lookout for a pile of branches placed on the road near an edge; this often means that a vehicle is broken down just ahead.

Rental

Due to the low cost and ready availability of buses and taxis, it isn't necessary to rent a vehicle in Panama unless you intend to go to places far off the beaten track. Should you choose to rent, however, you'll find plenty of car-rental agencies in Panama City, but few in other cities. Several agencies also have offices at Tocumen International Airport in the capital. It's also possible to rent vehicles from rental counters at several of Panama City's top hotels, including the Hotel Caesar

Park and the Hotel El Panamá. See the Panama City chapter for rental companies' contact information in the capital city.

Many of the major car-rental companies in Panama, such as Avis, Budget, Dollar, Hertz and National, have offices worldwide, so you can reserve a car in advance from home, which is a very good idea. Normally you need to book a car at least 14 days in advance, and the rate when you book one at home is often lower than the rate you'd receive in Panama.

Car rental in Panama is not cheap. Expect to pay US$45 per day for a car or US$100 per day for a 4WD vehicle; in Panama such a vehicle is called a '4-by-4' or a *'cuatro por cuatro.'* Rates include mandatory insurance and unlimited mileage *(kilometraje)*. From October to April – the high tourist season for rental-car companies – discounts are often available, as the agencies compete for your business.

To rent a vehicle in Panama, you must be 25 years of age or older and present a passport and driver's license (if you rent the vehicle using an American Express card, you need be only 23). In most cases you need to have a credit card; however, some companies, including Hertz, will allow people without credit cards to rent cars if they put down a big deposit. You must have a credit card to rent a 4WD vehicle.

If you rent a car, carefully inspect it for minor dents and scratches, missing radio antennae or hubcaps and anything else that makes the car look less than brand-new. These damages *must* be noted on your rental agreement; otherwise you may be charged for them when you return the car.

There have been many reports of theft from rental cars. You should never leave valuables in an unattended car, and you should remove all your luggage from the trunk when you're checking into a hotel overnight. Many hotels provide parking areas for cars. It is safer to park a car in a guarded parking lot than on the street.

Bringing Your Own

There is some paperwork involved in bringing a car into the country, but not so much

that it should dissuade you (see Land in the Getting There & Away chapter for details). However, unless you plan to be in the country a good while, consider using buses and taxis instead. They are plentiful and cheap. Alternately, if you're traveling far afield, rent a vehicle in Panama.

Remember that if you want to take a vehicle between Central and South America, you will have to ship it around the Darién Gap, as the Interamericana stops short of the Colombian border.

Motorcycle

There are no businesses renting motorcycles in Panama, and bringing in your own isn't a prudent idea due to the number of animals on Panamanian roads, the country's inclement weather and its aggressive motorists.

TAXI

It may come as a surprise to most people that taxis are considered a form of public transportation outside urban areas. Taxis can be hired by the hour, the half-day or the day. Taxi meters are not used in Panama, although there are fixed prices for certain destinations. On long trips you'll want to arrange fares with drivers beforehand.

Set fares for one passenger on standard routes from Tocumen International Airport, as determined by the government, include the following:

destination	fare
Amador, Corozal, Diablo, Los Ríos or Aeropuerto Albrook	US$24
Balboa	US$22
Colón	US$60
La Chorrera or Gamboa	US$40
Paraíso	US$30

The price for each additional passenger ranges from US$8 to US$15.

Additionally, taxi drivers are supposed to adhere to set fares for the following trips: Panama City to the Canal Area, with a two-hour stay and return (US$20 for one or two people); two hours of sightseeing within

Panama City (US$20 for one or two people); a combination of sightseeing in the Canal Area and touring in the city (US$30 for one or two people); a coast-to-coast trip from Panama City to Colón and back, leaving at 8 am and returning at 6 pm (US$100 for one to four people).

Outside these set routes, the price of a ride is negotiable. Usually, if you're not leaving the city limits – even Panama City's wide limits – you'll never pay more than US$5 for a ride during daylight hours. You're expected to pay more at night because the driver is supposedly working after hours; a ride that costs US$2 during the day might cost US$4 at night.

Be advised that sedan taxis parked out front of some of Panama City's best hotels are viewed by the government as luxury taxis for visiting executives. Their drivers are allowed to charge no less than twice the standard taxi fare – and they always do.

BICYCLE

You can bicycle through Panama easily enough, but using a bicycle to travel within larger Panamanian cities – particularly Panama City – is not wise. The roads tend to be narrow, there are no bike lanes, the motorists drive aggressively and it rains a lot, reducing motorists' visibility and your tires' ability to grip the road.

Outside the cities, a bicycle permits you to soak up the lovely countryside while getting good exercise. Roads outside cities tend to be in fine shape, and there are few places where lodging is more than a day's bike ride away. If you have enough time in the country to sit out rainy days and if you're in good health, seeing Panama by bike might be worth considering.

In Panama City bicycles are available for long and short-term rental; see the Panama City chapter for details. Shops selling bicycles can be found in most Panamanian cities. A good mountain bike will cost between US$200 and US$400. Bike repair shops can be found in the country, but you should arrive prepared to do your own repairs.

See Activities in the Facts for the Visitor chapter for more advice about cycling in the country. See Bicycle under Getting Around in the Panama City chapter for information on cycling events.

HITCHHIKING

Hitchhiking is not as widespread in Panama as elsewhere in Central America; most people travel by bus, and visitors would do best to follow suit. The exception is holiday weekends, when buses are full to overflowing and hitchhiking may be the only way out of a place. If you get a ride, offer to pay for it when you arrive; '*¿Cuánto le debo?*' ('How much do I owe you?') is the standard way of doing this.

Hitchhiking is never entirely safe in any country, and Lonely Planet doesn't recommend it. Travelers who decide to hitchhike should understand that they are taking a small but serious risk. If you do choose to hitchhike, try to talk to the occupants of the car to get an idea about them before getting in; if you get bad vibes from them, don't get in. Always try to hitchhike from somewhere (a gas station or store, for example) that you can retreat to if you don't like the look of your prospective ride. And of course, hitchhiking with a companion is safer than hitchhiking alone.

BOAT

Boats are the chief means of transportation in several areas of Panama, particularly in Darién Province, the Archipiélago de las Perlas, and the San Blás and Bocas del Toro island chains. Some of Panama's most fascinating destinations, such as Isla de Coiba, are only reachable by boat. And while at least one eccentric soul has swum the entire length of the Panama Canal, most people find that a boat simplifies the transit enormously.

There aren't many roads in eastern Darién Province, and especially during the rainy season boat travel is often the most feasible way to get from one town to another. The boat of choice here is a long canoe, or *piragua*, carved from the trunk of a giant ceba tree. Piraguas' shallow hulls allow them to ride the many rivers that comprise the traditional transport network of eastern Panama. Many such boats – including the ones travelers usually hire – are motorized. See the Darién Province chapter for more information.

Piraguas are also widely used on the open sea on both sides of Panama. About the only people not using them are sport and commercial fishermen, tour operators serving divers and snorkelers, and vessels used to ferry goods and people.

Colombian merchant boats carry cargo and passengers all along the Caribbean coast between Colón and Puerto Obaldía, stopping at up to 48 of the San Blás islands to load and unload people and goods. Occasionally these boats are used to traffic narcotics. Travel by these often dangerously overloaded boats is neither comfortable nor safe. Hiring a local boatman is a safer option for getting around these islands; see the Comarca de San Blás chapter for further details.

The popular town of Bocas del Toro, on Isla Colón, is accessible from Almirante by speedy and inexpensive water taxis. If pain is your pleasure, you can take the all-day ferry that moves cars and other big items between the mainland and the island. See the Bocas del Toro Province chapter for details.

Many boat trips are offered from Panama City, including ferry trips to offshore Isla Taboga and full and partial transits of the Panama Canal. Trips are also offered to Isla Barro Colorado in the canal's Lago Gatún. See the Panamá Province chapter for details. *Bon oyage!*

LOCAL TRANSPORTATION
Bus

Local buses serve the urban and suburban areas, but services can be difficult to figure out. There are few roadside signs indicating local buses' destinations. Panamanians are usually friendly, and this includes bus drivers; they'll often be able to tell you where to wait for a particular bus, provided you speak Spanish (few bus drivers speak English).

In general, unless you've come to Panama specifically for its urban-bus experience, leave that for another lifetime and take taxis. They're cheap, and you've got better things to do with your time than ride a slow, crowded, frequently stopping bus.

Taxi

As mentioned earlier in this chapter, Panamanian taxis don't have meters, but there are some set fares. Taxis are cheap and, most of the time, they are plentiful. However, they can be difficult to hail late at night and just before and during holidays. At times like these, it's best to call for a radio taxi. Listings for reliable radio taxis can be found in the yellow pages of phone directories throughout Panama, under the heading *Taxis*.

In Panama City several companies offer 24-hour radio taxi service (see Getting Around in the Panama City chapter for a list). Just call and give your location (preferably mentioning cross streets, a landmark or a well-known building or business), and you can expect your taxi to arrive in 10 minutes or sooner. Radio taxi fares are no higher than any other taxi's fares. They're a real bargain!

There is one group of taxis that do charge more than others. These 'sedan' taxis operate from particular upscale hotels (including the Hotel Caesar Park and the El Ejecutivo Hotel in Panama City). Taxi drivers generally mill about the front doors of the hotels and ask every exiting individual if he or she would like a cab. The drivers have a minimum rate that is usually twice what you'd pay a hailed cab. If you're staying at one of these hotels and don't want to pay more than you have to for a taxi, simply leave the hotel's premises and hail a cab.

Walking

Panama has several options for adventurous walks in the mountains and rainforests (see Hiking in the Facts for the Visitor chapter). Walking around cities is generally safe, even at night if you stick to the well-lit areas. As always, there are parts of towns that can be dangerous; these are mentioned where appropriate throughout the book.

If you intend to do a lot of walking, bring comfortable walking shoes with you. A mistake many people make is buying these shoes just before they leave; they don't allow time to break them in. Then while they are on vacation, they get terrible blisters because the shoes haven't had enough time to conform to their feet. The experienced traveler never takes brand-new walking or hiking shoes on a trip.

ORGANIZED TOURS

Although Panama has much to offer the tourist, the country's tourism industry is young and the number of local tour operators quite small. In fact, Panama's tourism industry is so small that there's a list of the country's top guides further on in this section.

Most Panamanian tour companies specialize in nature tours, offering visits to the national parks and wilderness lodges. They can provide entire guided itineraries (with English-speaking guides) and private transportation to any part of the country. Most of these companies also specialize in adventure tourism, such as river running or jungle trekking. Almost all of them also provide services such as day trips to the Panama Canal, Panama City tours, hotel reservations and airport transfers.

Prices vary depending on the services you require. Two people wishing to travel with a private English-speaking guide and a private vehicle will obviously pay more than two people who are prepared to join a group or who can understand a Spanish-speaking guide. If you can afford it, consider hiring a guide for at least a portion of your travels. In my opinion, good guides are like flying first class; they make the trip so much more enjoyable.

Tour Companies in Panama

All of the tour operators in Panama have their headquarters in Panama City. They offer the easiest way to explore Panama's natural wonders and all are reasonably priced. If you can afford it and want to get the most out of your time in Panama, I recommend that you use the services of one of the outfits mentioned below.

The best tour operator in Panama is Ancon Expeditions of Panama (☎ 269-

9414/9415, fax 264-3713, info@anconexpeditions.com), in the El Dorado Building on Calle 49 A Este near Avenida 3 Sur. Created by Panama's top private conservation organization, Ancon Expeditions employs most of the country's best nature guides, offers a variety of exciting tours, and the level of service the company provides is superlative. The majority of Ancon Expeditions' guides are avid birders, and all speak flawless English and are enthusiastic about their work. At one time or another I've employed every one of AEP's guides, and I can't say anything bad about any of them. In Panama, the standard for nature guides and tours is set by Ancon Expeditions.
Website: www.anconexpeditions.com

In 2000, Ecocircuitos and Margo Tours merged to become EcoMargo Tours (☎ 264-4001/8888, fax 264-5355, ecocircuito@ cwp.net.pa), located on Avenida 3 Sur next to Restaurante-Bar Tinajas. The new company offers a wide variety of tours and/ or activities, such as waterfall rappelling, rock climbing and a four-day San Blás trek. Readers are encouraged to contact Eco-Margo for a brochure and price list. See Organized Tours in the Panama City chapter for a sampling of the company's day trips from Panama City (as well as those of Ancon Expeditions).
Website: www.ecocircuitos.com

Panama's Top Guides

Many people in Panama refer to themselves as guides, but most couldn't distinguish a heron from an ibis or tell you which famous pirate's body lies at the bottom of the Bahía de Portobelo. Although the following list is not all-inclusive, those whose names appear on it are true guides.

Hernán 'Howler' Araúz A master naturalist, Hernán specializes in bird watching, natural history, Panamanian history and jungle expeditions. He has vast experience in all of Panama's life zones and historical areas. He's also the foremost guide for the Darién region and the Panama Canal area, with 10 trans-Darién expeditions to his credit, as well as 350-plus tours to the Monumento Natural

Barro Colorado and countless tours around the rest of Panama. Hernán is the official guide for several top US birding and natural history tour operators. He is widely regarded as the best overall guide in Panama, a bit of a wild man who really knows his stuff. There's never a dull moment when this guy's around. He speaks English and Spanish with dramatic precision and works for Ancon Expeditions. Contact him at home ☎ 268-0438, cellular ☎ 625-5755, office ☎ 269-9414, fax 264-3713, birder@sinfo.net, PO Box 3180, Panama 3, República de Panamá.

Guido Berguido Guido is one of the country's most patient, qualified and enthusiastic all-around guides. Guiding seems to come naturally to him; indeed, you can't say his name without nearly saying 'guide' twice. A graduate of the University of Panama with a degree in biology, Guido is one of Panama's truly successful freelance nature guides in a country teeming with wannabes, working regularly for the Smithsonian Tropical Research Institute, Panama's top tour operators and numerous cruise lines. This very pleasant young man speaks English and Spanish and his areas of expertise include the Panama Canal watershed, tropical ecology and bird watching. Some people will also be pleased to know that Guido is very prompt; there's never any waiting for him. Contact him at cellular ☎ 676-2466, fax 228-6535 or gcberguido@hotmail.com.

Vladimir Berrío-Lemm A brilliant man who knows much about Panama's history, Vladimir makes his living as a university professor and head of philately for Panama; among his duties, he decides on the art that appears on Panama's highly respected postage stamps. A perfectionist at heart, Vladimir, whose formal education is in law and history, specializes in historical tours of colonial areas and excels in historical data and interpretation. Anyone interested in stamp collecting and/or Panama City's history is in excellent hands with this newly married man. Vladimir speaks English and Spanish. Contact him at ☎ 225-2803, fax 225-2812, panahistoria@yahoo.es, or write to

him at Apartado 0835-348, Panamá, República de Panamá. You can leave a voice mail for him at ☎ 222-2962. Be advised that due to his duties at the Universidad Interamericana de Panama and the Panamanian Philatelic Service, persons seeking his guiding services should contact him at least a month in advance. In the event he cannot assist you, Vladimir will likely recommend Professor Jesús Prestán, a native of the Comarca de San Blás who speaks English, Spanish and Kuna.

Richard John 'Chicharron' Cahill One of Panama's top nature and expedition guides, Richard specializes in the former Panama Canal Zone, the Monumento Natural Barro Colorado, Isla de Coiba and trans-Darién expeditions (which he has led numerous times). He also has a lot of experience leading expeditions for yachts and small cruise ships. I've called upon Richard's expertise on many occasions – in the Darién, on the Península de Azuero, throughout the Archipiélago de las Perlas and the Archipiélago de San Blás, even into Colombia by small boat – and I've always found him to be extremely hard-working, thoughtful and patient. Richard has a can-do spirit and, as you might have guessed from his nickname, which means 'pork rinds' in English, he has a sense of humor. Educated in Panama and the United States, Richard speaks English and Spanish and works for Ancon Expeditions. Contact him at home ☎ 264-8086, office ☎ 269-9414, cellular ☎ 630-3204, fax 264-3713, cahill2000@hotmail.com.

Maria 'Marisin' Granados Born in Puerto Armuelles in Chiriquí Province and educated in the USA and Panama, Marisin was a nature guide at the prestigious Smithsonian Tropical Research Institute for seven years prior to joining the staff of Ancon Expeditions of Panama in late 2000. Her formal education includes instruction in bird watching and natural history from the American Training Institute in Panama. When not leading nature tours for AEP, Marisin devotes her time to teaching ecology at the Universidad Latina de

Panama, where she holds the title of professor. Marisin, who is fluent in English and Spanish, is a fine nature guide and can speak intelligently about historical, cultural, ecological and social issues in Panama today. And she's as pleasant as she is knowledgeable. She may be reached at ☎ 269-9414, fax 264-3713, or info@anconexpeditions.com.

Ivan Hoyos An extremely enthusiastic, well-traveled and well-educated individual, Ivan specializes in Panama's natural history and bird watching. Born and raised on the Azuero Peninsula, he spent much of the mid-1990s living in Changuinola and becoming the foremost wildlife expert of western Panama before moving to Panama City to work for Ancon Expeditions. Today, he is a freelance guide, working for himself when not on contract with AEP, Wildland Adventures or another leading tour operator. His experience also includes many tours to Barro Colorado Nature Monument and the national parks protecting the Panama Canal watershed. Ivan attended college in the United States and Germany and is fluent in English, Spanish and German. The best way to reach him is via his personal email address (migratorio@hotmail.com).

Wilberto 'Willy' Martinez Willy is one of Panama's best birding guides, on an equal plane with Hernan Araúz in terms of his ability to spot and recognize birds, with many years of experience in this field. He leads tours for several US birding operators in all of Panama's life zones, and his talents are frequently sought after by private individuals as well. His areas of expertise include the Panama Canal watershed, and the Darién and the Chiriquí highlands. Willy's entertaining personality and natural ability to spot birds like few others make him an extremely popular guide. He owns and manages the Rancho Ecológico, on the Chiriquí Grande-David road, but birding tours generally prevent him from being there; see the Bocas del Toro Province chapter for details. Willy speaks English and Spanish. Contact him at ☎ 225-7325, panabird@sinfo.net.

Richard 'Rick' Morales Ask this young, well-mannered Panamanian to tell you the highlight of his life and you'll get a breathless story about the time he saw a mountain lion in Cana Valley near the jungly heart of Parque Nacional Darién. This Chiriquí Highlands native is the kind of nature guide that'll finish leading a group of birders on a long bird-watching expedition only to return to the jungle to admire more birds and add new ones to his bird list. His enthusiasm for his country's wildlife is as addictive as it is appealing. You're more likely to find him without his wallet than without his binoculars. A linguist by training, Rick speaks English and Spanish flawlessly and was a great addition to Ancon Expeditions' staff when he joined the company in early 1999. Contact him at ☎ 269-9415, fax 264-3713, or rick@backpacker.com.

Hector Sanchez Hector is Panama's most experienced white-water guide and outfitter. He owns and manages Chiriquí River Rafting, which runs the Río Chiriquí and the Río Chiriquí Viejo (see the Chiriquí Province chapter for details). For many years Hector was the head tour coordinator for the US Armed Forces recreational activities department in the Canal Area. He emphasizes safety like no one I've ever met. Although the rivers he runs contain lots of rapids, you always feel safe when accompanied by Hector. His team of river guides are equally safety-conscious. Hector speaks English and Spanish and can best be reached at Chiriquí River Rafting (☎ 720-1505, fax 720-1506, cellular ☎ 618-0846, rafting@panama-rafting.com), with its office on Avenida Central in downtown Boquete. Website: www.panama-rafting.com

Iann Sanchez A native of the former Panama Canal Zone, Iann left Panama for a university degree in geology in the United States. His love of nature then led him to work for the US Forest Service as a ranger at several national parks. Thereafter, Iann worked as a rafting guide in Texas before returning to Panama to serve as a guide and operations manager for Chiriquí River

Rafting, which is owned by his father. Most recently, Iann was a guide for a company that ran rafting trips down the Río Chagres near the Panama Canal, and as recently as 2001 he was the top nature guide at the Gamboa Rainforest Lodge on the northern bank of the Río Chagres. Today, he's cutting a trail all his own as a freelance nature guide specializing in leading bird watchers in the Canal area. A fluent English and Spanish speaker, Iann can be reached at ☎ 720-1505, cellular ☎ 617-0449, czbirder@hotmail.com.

Panama City

pop 416,000

Panama's capital is a modern, thriving center of international banking and trade, with a very diverse population, soaring skyscrapers and a cosmopolitan flair. The variety of restaurants in this city rivals that in Sydney, and the nightlife doesn't rest before sunrise. As for shopping, most anything that you can buy in Frankfurt or Montreal you can find in Panama City – and here you can also find an assortment of high-quality handicrafts made by Panama's indigenous peoples. Because the taxis are inexpensive, it's easy to get around on the cheap, and decent accommodations cost as little as US$8 a night.

HISTORY

The city was founded on the site of an Indian fishing village by the Spanish governor Pedro Arias de Ávila (or Pedrarias, as his Spanish contemporaries called him) in 1519, not long after explorer Vasco Núñez de Balboa first looked upon the Pacific and claimed it and everything it touched as the property of Spain.

The Spanish settlement, known as Panamá, quickly became an important center of government and church authority. It was from Panamá, too, that gold and other plunder from the Pacific Spanish colonies were taken along the Camino Real (King's Highway) and the Sendero Las Cruces (Las Cruces Trail) across the isthmus to the Caribbean.

This treasure made Panamá the target of many attacks over the years. In 1671 Welsh buccaneer Sir Henry Morgan and 1200 of his men ransacked the city. A terrible fire ensued – no one knows for certain whether it was set by the pirates or by fleeing landowners – leaving only stone ruins. Now known as Panamá La Vieja (Old Panama), these ruins can still be seen today.

Three years after Morgan's assault, the city was reestablished 8km to the southwest, down the coast at what is now the San Felipe district (or Casco Viejo, as it is popularly

known). The Spaniards believed that the new site, on a small peninsula, would be easier to defend; a shallow sea flanked the city on three sides and a moat was constructed on the fourth side, separating the city from the mainland. The new city was named Nueva Panamá (New Panama).

Unlike Panamá La Vieja, Nueva Panamá was protected by a massive stone-and-brick wall 7m to 14m high and more than 3m wide, with watchtowers every 75m. Access was gained through three massive gateways. So expensive were the fortifications of Nueva Panamá that the council of Spain, auditing the accounts, wrote to inquire whether the wall was constructed of silver or gold. Perhaps the defenses were excessive, but Nueva Panamá was never sacked.

Highlights

- Bustling Casco Viejo, perfect grounds for a stroll through history
- Parque Natural Metropolitano, 265 hectares of jungle close to downtown
- The capital's myriad restaurants, offering everything from haute cuisine French to down-home Panamanian
- The all-night club and bar scene, featuring rock, jazz, salsa and merengue
- Shops selling traditional Panamanian handicrafts – colorful molas, golden huaca replicas and ornate polleras

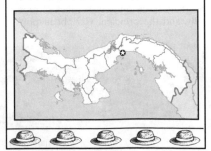

Sir Henry Morgan, 17th-century buccaneer and fashion plate

The streets of the new city were laid out at right angles about a central plaza. A cathedral, governor's house and bishop's palace would eventually face the plaza, and many churches and convents were gradually constructed throughout the town. The famous Arco Chato (Flat Arch) of the ruined church of Santo Domingo was built in the 1670s and is one of the wonders of architecture, as it continues to stand in apparent defiance of the laws of gravity. The cathedral, with its two imposing towers, was completed in 1760. The presidential palace, leading businesses, and municipal offices and those of foreign legations were constructed within a short distance of Parque Catedral.

Unlike Nueva Panamá, the Camino Real overland trade route was attacked repeatedly, and the principal Caribbean port at

Portobelo was destroyed. In 1746 the Spaniards stopped using the route altogether, and Panama City gradually declined in importance. It was not until the 1850s that the city returned to prominence. It was then that the Panama Railroad was completed. The railroad was popular with gold rushers from the US East Coast who made their way to the US West Coast via Panama to avoid hostile Indians in the central USA.

Panama was declared independent of Colombia on November 3, 1903, in Panama City's Parque Catedral; the city then became the capital of the new nation. Since the Panama Canal was completed in 1914, the city has grown in importance as a center for international business and trade. Indeed, today it's by far the wealthiest capital in Central America, and many visitors express shock when they see its many skyscrapers and the plethora of luxury cars that ply its streets.

The city's only major setback in recent times occurred in 1989, when it was invaded by the USA in a successful attempt to oust dictator Manuel Antonio Noriega from power and bring him to America to stand trial for drug trafficking. The capital suffered damage both from the invasion itself and from looting. Many residential blocks of the Chorrillo district were also lost to combat-ignited fire.

But by the start of this century, Panama City had never looked better, thanks in large part to a sweeping beautification program undertaken by its mayor. Visitors will be pleased to learn that the city entered the millennium with a new domestic airport, a new central bus terminal, an expanded international airport and a new seaport – all of which are easy to maneuver and make it

Panama City's Parque Catedral

that much simpler to visit the impressive capital city and points beyond.

ORIENTATION

Panama City stretches about 20km along the Pacific coast, with the Bahía de Panamá to the south, the Panama Canal to the west, protected forest to the north and the stone ruins of Panamá La Vieja (the city's original site) to the east. Buses from Panama City to most other parts of the country arrive at and depart from the Terminal Nacional de Transporte, in the Albrook district about 3km from downtown. The city's domestic airport is conveniently located a short distance from the bus terminal.

In the southwest part of town is the increasingly gentrified neighborhood of Casco Viejo. Situated at the foot of Cerro Ancón (Ancón Hill), it was the site of Nueva Panamá, built after Henry Morgan sacked the original settlement of Panamá.

From Casco Viejo, two major roads head east through the city. The main road, Avenida Central, runs past the cathedral in Casco Viejo to Parque Santa Ana and Plaza Cinco de Mayo; between these two plazas, traffic is diverted and the avenue is a pedestrian-only shopping street. At a fork farther east, the avenue becomes Avenida Central España; the section that traverses El Cangrejo, the financial district, and heads eastward toward Tocumen International Airport is called Vía España. The other part of the fork becomes Avenida 1 Norte (also called Avenida José D Espinar), Avenida Simón Bolívar and finally Vía Transístmica (Transisthmian Hwy) as it heads out of town and across the isthmus toward Colón.

Avenida 6 Sur branches off Avenida Central not far out of Casco Viejo and undergoes several name changes. It is called Avenida Balboa as it curves around the edge of the bay to Punta Paitilla, the bay's eastern point, opposite Casco Viejo; it then continues under various names past the Centro Atlapa (Atlapa Convention Center) to the ruins of Panamá La Vieja. Comprising the remains of the original settlement, Panamá La Vieja was established by the Spanish governor Pedrarias in 1519 and abandoned in favor of the Casco Viejo site in 1674 – three years after Morgan looted the original city. At the time it was set aflame, Panamá La Vieja consisted of about 5200 homes, a cathedral, a government building and eight convents and churches.

In 2000, two expressways opened in Panama City, facilitating travel to the domestic airport, the central bus terminal and the country's main international airport. Corredor Norte links the Curundu district of town to the Autopista Panama-Colón, a partially completed toll road to Colón, and to Avenida Martin Sosa, which extends southeast toward downtown. (Efforts to link Panama City and Colón entirely by highspeed highway were cut short in 2000, when the government stopped funding the project after only a third of it was completed.)

Corredor Sur, the other major expressway that opened in Panama City in 2000, links the Punta Paitilla district southeast of downtown to the town of Tocumen, which is home to Tocumen International Airport.

To the north of the city is forest that has been designated for conservation because it is part of the watershed for the Panama Canal. Protecting the watershed is critical to the canal's survival. If the forest were felled, the water needed to fill the locks that raise and lower transiting ships into and out of Lago Gatún (Gatún Lake) would have to be pumped from the ocean at enormous expense. Moreover, soil erosion as a result of felling the forest would fill much of the canal with silt.

Maps

For highly detailed maps, go to the Instituto Geográfico Nacional 'Tommy Guardia' (☎ 236-2444, 236-1844), just off Avenida Simón Bolívar opposite the Universidad de Panamá; it is open 8 am to 4 pm weekdays. It has an excellent map collection for sale, including topographical maps, city maps, tourist maps and more.

Several free publications available at tourist offices and hotels contain small foldout country and city maps. The maps appearing in this book were made from more than 60 large maps provided by

PANAMA CITY

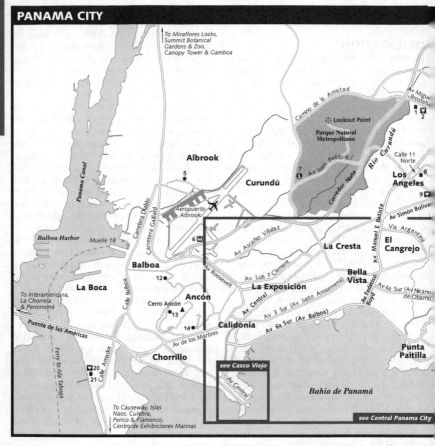

To Miraflores Locks,
Summit Botanical
Gardens & Zoo,
Canopy Tower & Gamboa

Panama's census bureau, which produces the most accurate maps available of Panama. These highly detailed maps are not available to the general public, however.

INFORMATION
Tourist Offices

Panama's tourism bureau, the Instituto Panameño de Turismo (IPAT; ☎ 226-7000, fax 226-4849) has its headquarters in the Centro Atlapa on Vía Israel in the San Francisco neighborhood. IPAT's business hours are from 8 am to 6 pm daily. The

agency also maintains information counters in the Panamá La Vieja area and at Tocumen International Airport. However, few tourists have found IPAT to be all that helpful.

Panama's national environmental agency, the Autoridad Nacional de Ambiente (ANAM; ☎ 315-0855 or 315-0903), is located inside Building 804 of the Albrook district; it's best reached by taxi. ANAM can occasionally provide maps and information on the national parks. It's open 8 am to 4 pm weekdays. Spanish and some English are spoken.

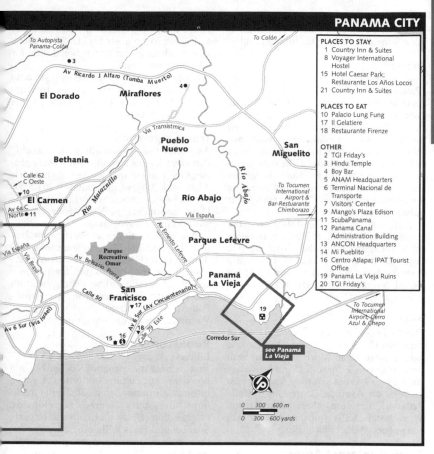

PANAMA CITY

PLACES TO STAY
1 Country Inn & Suites
8 Voyager International Hostel
15 Hotel Caesar Park; Restaurante Los Años Locos
21 Country Inn & Suites

PLACES TO EAT
10 Palacio Lung Fung
17 Il Gelatiere
18 Restaurante Firenze

OTHER
2 TGI Friday's
3 Hindu Temple
4 Boy Bar
5 ANAM Headquarters
6 Terminal Nacional de Transporte
7 Visitors' Center
9 Mango's Plaza Edison
11 ScubaPanama
12 Panama Canal Administration Building
13 ANCON Headquarters
14 Mi Pueblito
16 Centro Atlapa; IPAT Tourist Office
19 Panamá La Vieja Ruins
20 TGI Friday's

Embassies & Consulates

More than 50 countries have embassies or consulates in Panama City. Their addresses and telephone numbers can be found in the Panama white pages, listed under 'Embajada de' followed by the country name in Spanish. Many embassies appear in the 'Embajadas' section of the yellow pages. Following are the embassies of interest to most Lonely Planet readers:

Canada (☎ 264-9731/7115, fax 263-8083) Edificio Banco Central, Avenida Samuel Lewis at Calle Gerardo Ortega

France (☎ 228-7824, fax 228-7852) Plaza de Francia

Germany (☎ 263-7733, fax 223-6664) Bancomer Building, Calle 50 at Calle 53 Este, 6th floor

Great Britain (☎ 213-9518, 213-9515) Swiss Tower, Calle 53 Este, 4th floor

USA (☎ 207-7000, fax 227-1964) Avenida Balboa at Calle 37 Este

Immigration

The Migración y Naturalización (Immigration and Naturalization) office in Panama City (☎ 225-1373, 227-1077, fax 227-1227) is on Avenida Cuba at Calle 29 Este in La

PANAMA CITY

Exposición neighborhood. Visas and tourist cards can be extended here. The office is open 8 am to 3 pm Monday through Friday.

Money

Changing foreign currency into US dollars (Panama's currency of choice) can be a tricky business. There is a Banco Nacional de Panamá at Tocumen International Airport that will change major currencies, and foreign banks will occasionally exchange their native currencies for US dollars. None of the hotels change money. The only places you can count on are the *casas de cambio* (currency exchange houses), and there are few of these in Panama City and even fewer outside the capital.

Panacambios (☎ 223-1800), on the ground floor of the Plaza Regency Building on Vía España near the Hotel Riande Granada, is centrally located. Hours are 9 am to 6 pm Monday to Saturday; it's closed Sunday. There are no casas de cambio in Casco Viejo.

Post

There's a post office on the ground floor of the Plaza Concordia, opposite Vía España from a large Gran Morrison department store. It's open 7 am to 5:45 pm weekdays and 7 am to 4:45 pm Saturday. Another post office is on Avenida Central near Calle Ecuador. There are others around town. Many hotels sell stamps, and some will accept guests' letters for mailing.

Email & Internet Access

Internet-access businesses were springing up like crazy in 2001. Inside the McDonald's at the corner of Vía España and Calle 49 B Oeste, customers who purchase a 'combo plate' for US$3.50 can surf the Web or check email for 30 minutes at no extra charge. McInternet is open 6:30 am to 11 pm Monday through Saturday and 7 am to 11 pm Sunday.

I'm Internet, an air-con Internet-access business on Calle 49 B Oeste at Calle D, is open from 8 am to 11 pm daily (US$1.50 per hour). Inside the Plaza Concordia in Vía España, across from the Gran Morrison, is

the Transfernet Café, which is open from 10 am to 10 pm Monday through Saturday and 11 am to 9 pm Sunday (US$2 an hour). Inquire about cheap international rates for telephone calls here.

Some hotels in Panama have caught onto the wisdom of offering guests Internet access. See Places to Stay later in this chapter for details.

Travel Agencies

As befits the 'crossroads of the world,' Panama City has a great many travel agencies. One that enjoys a sterling reputation is Agencia de Viajes Continental (☎ 263-5531, fax 263-6493, geocar52@orbi.net), at the Hotel Continental on Vía España. English and Spanish are spoken.

Ancon Expeditions of Panama (☎ 269-9414/9415, fax 264-3713, info@anconexpeditions.com), on Calle 49 A Este near Avenida 3 Sur, is a great place to turn for help purchasing domestic airline tickets, whether you're contacting the company from within Panama or from abroad.

Website: www.anconexpeditions.com

Bookstores

Librería Argosy (☎ 223-5344), on Vía Argentina near the corner of Vía España, is a bookstore and cultural institution. Argosy's owner, the interesting and ebullient Greek-born Gerasimos 'Gerry' Kanelopulos, offers a fine selection of books in English, Spanish and French. Be advised, however, that many of his prices are steeply marked up.

Other good places to look for books are Legends (☎ 270-0096), on Calle 50 near Calle 71 Este, and Librería El Campus (☎ 223-6598), on Avenida José de Fábrega in front of the Universidad de Panamá. Also try the Librería Universitaria, located on the university's campus, and Allegro, on Calle 73 Este near Calle 50, which is a good place for books in English (as well as CDs). Librería Cultural Panameña (☎ 223-6267), near the western end of Vía España, has a good literature selection.

There are several Gran Morrison department stores around town (see the Central

Panama City map for two locations); they carry a fairly good selection of books, magazines and postcards in English and Spanish. Farmacia Arrocha, which also has branches around the city, stocks some books and many magazines, also in English and Spanish.

Laundry

Laundromats *(la amáticos)* are easy to find in Panama City. They're also inexpensive: The usual cost per laundry load is 75¢ to wash, 75¢ to dry and 25¢ for detergent unless you bring your own. Normally you drop off laundry, the laundromat washes and dries it, and you pick it up in a few hours. In Casco Viejo, try the Lavamático Tanita, beside Parque Herrera; it's open 7 am to 9 pm daily.

You'll also find plenty of dry cleaners *(la anderías)* in the capital, but these are significantly more expensive. Many of them won't wash undergarments. Luxury hotels usually offer laundry service, but check the prices before you use it. Hotel-furnished laundry service is generally very expensive.

Medical Services

In Panama, as in most countries, there are some excellent doctors and some mediocre ones. Centro Medico Paitilla (☎ 263-8800, 269-0333), Calle 53 Este at Avenida Balboa, has the lion's share of well-trained doctors. Centro Medico Paitilla is widely regarded as the best hospital in Panama, and many of its physicians received their medical training in the USA and speak perfect English. The cost of a consultation with a physician in Panama rarely exceeds US$50. For a referral to a specialist, consult your embassy.

Emergency

The emergency phone numbers in Panama City are as follows:

Ambulance	☎ 227-4142
Drug overdose	☎ 226-0000
Fire	☎ 103
Police	☎ 104

Dangers & Annoyances

Casco Viejo is a very interesting place, but if you enter it looking like a million bucks, there's a fair chance that you'll leave it without any. Muggers look for wealthy, easy prey: an elderly man with a thick bulge in a rear pocket where the wallet belongs; a slightly built person sporting a Rolex watch or flashy jewelry; a single *gringa* with a fancy purse dangling from an arm. Rule of the Road No 64: Look like slim pickings and the predators will leave you alone.

The bar scene in Casco Viejo at night also needs to be approached with caution. These streets contain many people who are down on their luck. When I go bar-hopping in this neighborhood, I never dress better than I have to (a T-shirt, blue jeans and sneakers are fine), and I always wear my cheap watch instead of my Seiko. I take only my passport and enough cash to get me through the night, plus a folded US$20 in each shoe.

Use common sense when you're in a poor neighborhood such as Casco Viejo, Calidonia or La Exposición: Never leave your vehicle unlocked; avoid empty or dimly lit streets; never leave valuables in your vehicle in plain sight; don't use big bills in places where a thug is likely to be watching you.

As for annoyances, there's nothing more annoying than settling into a hotel only to discover at bedtime that your room is above a noisy bar, that the bed sags horribly or that your hotel is a true fleabag. Always ask to see at least two rooms before you check in, as the quality of a room and its contents (including TV, bed and air con) can vary drastically from room to room. And bring earplugs, just in case your neighbors are wild humping monkeys.

There are few antismoking laws in Panama City, but many hotels and restaurants here accommodate nonsmokers. If cigarette smoke bothers you, request a nonsmoking room.

CASCO VIEJO WALKING TOUR

One of the more interesting parts of the city is **Casco Viejo**, with its mix of colonial architecture, cobblestone streets and ethnic

CENTRAL PANAMA CITY

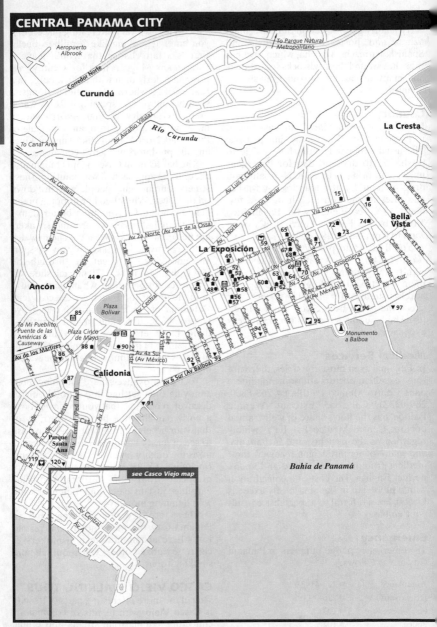

To Parque Natural Metropolitano

Aeropuerto Albrook

Corredor Norte

Curundú

La Cresta

Av Ascanio Villalaz

Río Curundu

To Canal Area

Av Gaillard

Av Luis F Clement

La Cresta

Calle 4a Este

Av Manzanillo

Calle Frangipani

Av 2a Norte (Av José de la Ossa)

Via Simón Bolívar

Via España

15

16

Bella Vista

Av 1 Norte

72   74

73

Calle 24 Oeste

Calle 26 Oeste

La Exposición

65   66

59   Perú (Av 1a Sur

67

68

71

Calle 43 Este

Calle 41 Este

Calle 39 Este

Av 5a Sur

Ancón

44

49

50   52

46   47   53   54

45   48   51   55   58   60   61   62   63   64   69   70

Av 2a Sur (Av

56

57

Av 3a Sur (Av Justo Arosemena)

Calle 37 Este

Calle 35 Este

Calle 33 Este

Av 4a Sur (Av México)

96   97

95

Monumento a Balboa

Plaza Bolívar

Av Central

85

To Mi Pueblito, Puente de las Américas & Causeway

Plaza Cinco de Mayo

89

88   90

Av 4a Sur (Av México)

94

92   93

Calle 30 Este

Calle 29 Este

Calle 27 Este

Calle 25 Este

Av de los Mártires

86

Calle H

Av B

Av Central (Ped Mall)

Calidonia

87

Av 6 Sur (Av Balboa)

91

Calle 17 Oeste

Calle 1a Oeste

Calle 3 Este

Av A

Parque Santa Ana

Calle C

Calle B

119   120

Bahía de Panamá

see Casco Viejo map

Av Central

Av A

● 1

Via Simón Bolívar

To Via Transistmica & Colón

Via Argentina

Via Manuel Batista

Av 2a B Norte

Via España

Universidad de Panamá

Via Brasil

▼ 2
3
(Eusebio A. Morales) ▼ 9
6 7 8
4 5 ▼ 10
▼ 4
Av 2a Norte
Av 1a A Norte
28

El Cangrejo

▼ 11
12 ●
13 ●

14 ▼

Av 1a Sur ▼ 31
30 ▼ 32 ▼
▼ 33
Av 1a D Sur

20 ⓐ
21 ●
22 ⓐ
19 ▲
24 27
23 ⓢ
25 ● ▼ 29
26 ▼

Calle 43 Este
Calle 45 Este
Calle Ricardo Arias
Calle 51 Este

▲ 17
18 ▮

34
▼ 35
36 ▮
38 ▼
39
40 ▼ 41

42 43

Av 2a Sur (Av Samuel Lewis)

To Panamá La Vieja

Av Federico Boyd

Av 3a A Sur
78
77
80 ▼
81 ▼

75 ▲
76

Av 3a B Sur

Calle 52 Este
Calle 54 Este
Calle 55 Este
Calle 56 Este
Calle 57 Este
Calle 58 Este
Calle 59 Este
Calle 60 Este
Calle 61 Este

Av 3a Sur

99 ▼ 100
101 ● ▼ 35
Av 4a A Sur 104
102 ▼ 105
Av 5a A Sur 103
108
106 ▼ 109 113
110 112
▲ 98   107 ▮   111

82
83

Av 4a Sur (Av Nicanor de Obarrio)

Calle 50

84 ▼

Río Matasnillo

Calle 50 B Este

114
▼ 115
▮ 116
▮ 117

Av 6 Sur (Via Israel)

118 ✚

Corredor Sur

Calle 56 Este

Via Italia

122 ✚ 124
▼ 123
121 ▮

Via Italia

Punta Paitilla

⊗

0   250   500 m
0   250   500 yards

CENTRAL PANAMA CITY

PANAMA

PLACES TO STAY
3 Las Vegas Suites Hotel; The Wine Bar
5 Sevilla Suites
6 Coral Suites Aparthotel
7 Hotel Marbella
8 Suites Ambassador
15 Hotel Europa
16 Hotel California
17 Hotel Montreal
19 Hotel El Panamá
28 Hotel Riande Granada
34 Hotel Costa del Sol
37 Hotel Continental; Agencia de Viajes Continental; Joyeria La Huaca
39 Hotel Suites Alfa
45 Hotel Río de Janeiro
46 Hotel Caribe
47 Hotel Benidorm
49 Hotel Veracruz; Comedor Las Palmas
50 Gran Hotel Soloy
52 Hotel 2 Mares
53 Hotel Acapulco
55 Hotel Lisboa
56 Residencial Alemeda
57 Residencial Turistico El Eden
58 Hotel Arenteiro
60 Hotel Villa del Mar
61 Hotel Roma
62 Pensión América
63 Hotel Discovery
64 Hotel Centroamericano
65 Hotel Venecia
66 Pensión Las Torres
67 Residencial Turistico Chorrera
68 Hotel Latino
70 Hotel Marparaíso
71 Residencial Turístico El Dorado
72 Hotel Costa Inn
73 Pensión Las Palmeras; Residencial Jamaica
74 Residencial Primavera
77 The Executive Hotel
78 The Bristol
81 DeVille Hotel
87 Hotel Ideal
88 Hotel Internacional
98 Miramar Inter-Continental

114 Radisson Royal Panama Hotel
121 Hotel Plaza Paitilla Inn

PLACES TO EAT
2 Caffé Pomodoro
4 Cafeteria Manolo
9 Martín Fierro
10 Ginza Teppanyaki
11 Restaurante Matsuei
26 Supermercado Rey
29 Niko's Cafe No 1
30 Athen's
31 Restaurante de las Americas Takeout
32 Restaurante de las Americas
33 Restaurante y Pizzeria Napoli No 2
35 Tre Scalini
38 Costa Azul
40 Restaurante y Pizzeria Sorrento
41 Restaurante Vegetariano Mireya
43 Sushi Itto
54 Restaurante Rincón Tableño
75 Restaurante-Bar Tinajas
80 El Pavo Real
82 Restaurante Casco Viejo
84 Niko's Café
86 Restaurante y Pizzeria Napoli No 1
91 Restaurant Mercado del Marisco
92 La Cascada
93 El Rincón Tableño
94 Restaurante Boulevard Balboa
97 Panama Yacht Club; La Marina
99 La Mexicanita No 1
100 La Toja
101 Nobu
102 Ozone
103 Athen's
104 Gaucho's Steak House
105 Pizzeria Solemio
106 Mango's
107 La Cocotte
109 Madame Chang
111 Crepes & Waffles
115 Le Bistrot
116 La Mexicanita No 2

120 Café Coca-Cola
123 Os Segredor de Carne

OTHER
1 Instituto Geográfico Nacional 'Tommy Guardia'
12 Librería Argosy
13 Aleph Café (night club)
14 El Hidalgo (dance club)
18 Iglesia del Carmen
20 I'm Internet (Internet access)
21 Flory Saltzman Molas
22 McInternet (Internet access)
23 Edificio Banco Nacional de Panamá; Banco del Istmo
24 Post Office; Transfernet Café (Internet access)
25 Gran Morrison
27 Panacambios (money exchange)
36 Bacchus (dance club)
42 Reprosa
44 Smithsonian Tropical Research Institute
48 Immigration Office
51 Museo de Ciencias Naturales
59 Post Office; Stamp Museum
69 Casa-Museo del Banco Nacional
76 EcoMargo Tours
79 Ancon Expeditions of Panama (tours)
83 Plaza Edison
85 Museo de Arte Contemporáneo
89 Museo Antropológico Reina Torres de Araúz
90 Mercado de Buhonerías y Artesanías
95 British Embassy
96 US Embassy
108 Skap (dance club)
110 Café Dalí (dance club)
112 Señor Frog's (dance club); Carlos 'n Charlies
113 TGI Friday's
117 Rock Café (dance club)
118 Centro Medico Paitilla
119 Boite La Cosmopolita
122 Colecciones
124 Gran Morrison; Plaza Paitilla Shopping Center

diversity. Some, though only a few, of the buildings have been pridefully restored, and in those buildings you can sense how magnificent the area must have looked in past years. Sadly, nowadays it isn't one of the more affluent districts and, as mentioned earlier, it's risky to walk here at night. Even in daylight, take care when walking down side streets. But if you stick to the main streets and don't flaunt your wealth, you should be fine.

The capture and plunder of Panamá (the original Panama City) by the pirate Sir Henry Morgan in 1671 convinced the king of Spain that the city was unsafe from buccaneers, and he ordered that it be rebuilt on another site. Three years later, efforts to create a new city began on a rocky peninsula at the foot of Cerro Ancón, 8km southwest of the original city. The new location was easier to defend, and reefs prevented ships from coming up to the city except at high tide. Casco Viejo was surrounded by a massive wall, which is how it got its name (Casco Viejo means 'Old Compound'). Some of the old stone-and-brick wall and original Spanish cannons can still be seen today.

In 1904, at the time construction began on the Panama Canal, all of Panama City existed where Casco Viejo stands today. The city's population was around 30,000 (about the same population as the original city of Panamá when Morgan sacked it). Since that time, the population of Panama City has increased more than twentyfold, and the city has spread so far to the east that Casco Viejo is now merely a district in the southwestern corner of the modern capital city.

You could start a walking tour in Casco Viejo at the **Paseo de las Bóvedas** (Promenade of Vaults), on the southern tip of the peninsula. A walkway runs along the top of the sea wall built by the Spaniards to protect the city. From here you can see ships lining up to enter the canal and the Puente de las Américas (Bridge of the Americas), which arches over the southern entrance of the so-called path between the seas.

Below the wall, on the tip of the peninsula, is **Plaza de Francia**, where large stone tablets tell the story (in Spanish) of the canal's construction and the role of the French in building it. The plaza is dedicated to the memory of the 22,000 workers, most of them from France, Guadeloupe and Martinique, who died trying to create a canal.

Most were killed by yellow fever and malaria, and among the busts of the Frenchmen involved is a monument to Carlos J Finlay, who discovered how mosquitoes transmit yellow fever. His work led to the eradication of the disease in Panama.

On one side of the plaza are nine restored **dungeons** that were used by the Spaniards and, later, by the Colombians. Although they now contain an art gallery and a classy restaurant/piano bar (Restaurante Las Bóvedas), you can still see the dungeons' original stonework. Also on the plaza are the Instituto Nacional de Cultura (INAC, Panama's National Institute of Culture, responsible for maintaining the country's museums and other cultural institutions) and the French Embassy.

Leaving the plaza to walk up Avenida A, you'll soon come to the **Museo de Arte Religioso Colonial**, alongside the ruins of the **Iglesia y Convento de Santo Domingo** on the corner of Calle 3. Just inside the doorway of the ruins is the Arco Chato, a long, flat arch that has stood, with no internal supports, for centuries. It reportedly played a part in the selection of Panama over Nicaragua as the site for the canal; its survival was taken as proof that the area was not subject to earthquakes.

Turning north along Calle 3, you'll pass the **Ministerio de Gobierno y Justicia**, and behind it the **Teatro Nacional**, built in 1907. The ornate interior has been restored, and it boasts red and gold decorations, a once-magnificent ceiling mural by Roberto Lewis (one of Panama's finest painters) that's been allowed to collapse in recent years, an impressive crystal chandelier and several tiers of seats. Performances are still held here; to find out about them or just to have a look at the theater, go around to the office door at the side of the building.

Opposite the theater is the **Iglesia de San Francisco**, facing onto **Parque Bolívar**. In 1826 in a schoolroom opposite this park, Simón Bolívar held a meeting urging the union of the Latin American countries. After many struggles against Spanish domination, Bolívar succeeded in liberating Bolivia, Colombia, Ecuador, Peru and Venezuela, and

CASCO VIEJO

To Parque Santa Ana

Muelle Fiscal

Bahía de Panamá

PLACES TO STAY
2 Hotel Colón
9 Pensión Panamericana
11 Hotel y Restaurante Herrera
15 Pensión Tropical
19 Hotel Central
23 Hotel Foyo

PLACES TO EAT
7 Bar Morales
8 Café du Líban
20 Café de Asís
28 Restaurante Las Bóvedas

OTHER
1 Salon Madrid (dance club)
3 Bar Tropical (dance club)
4 Market
5 Casa de la Municipalidad
6 Iglesia de La Merced
10 Lavamático Tanita
12 Café La Plaza
13 Palacio de las Garzas
14 Iglesia de San José; Altar de Oro
16 Iglesia y Convento de la Compañía de Jesús (ruins)
17 Palacio Municipal; Museo de Historia de Panamá
18 Museo del Canal Interoceánico
21 Iglesia de San Francisco
22 Teatro Nacional
24 Museo de Arte Religioso Colonial; Iglesia y Convento de Santo Domingo; Arco Chato
25 Ministerio de Gobierno y Justicia
26 French Embassy
27 Instituto Nacional de Cultura

Plaza de Francia

0   50   100 m
0   50   100 yards

he created Gran Colombia, which encompassed all these states. Although Bolívar was unable to keep Gran Colombia together, he is nonetheless venerated as a hero throughout Latin America.

On Avenida Alfaro around the block from this park is the presidential palace, called the **Palacio de las Garzas** (Palace of the Herons) for the great white herons that strut about here. The president of Panama lives on the upper floor. A few blocks farther west are the **Muelle Fiscal** (the port) and the **market** – major activity centers that make for strong photographs.

Two blocks south of the palace, at the center of Casco Viejo, is Parque Catedral – later renamed **Plaza de la Independencia** – the central plaza where Panamanian independence was declared on November 3, 1903. In addition to the cathedral, the plaza is fringed by several other historic buildings. On the southern side of the plaza, the Museo de Historia de Panamá is on the top floor of the **Palacio Municipal** (City Hall). Next door is the building that was once the headquarters of the French company that first worked on the canal; in 1997 it became the site of the excellent **Museo del Canal Interoceánico**

(Interoceanic Canal Museum). Many years ago canal officials and other dignitaries stayed at the nearby and still functioning (though rundown) **Hotel Central**, which was a very luxurious place back in those days.

A half-block south of the plaza on Calle 7 are the ruins of another church, the **Iglesia y Convento de la Compañía de Jesús**. Walk to the end of the block to rejoin Avenida A, and then walk a block west to arrive at the **Iglesia de San José**. Its famous Altar de Oro (Golden Altar) is the only thing of value salvaged after Henry Morgan sacked Panamá in 1671. When word came of the pirate's impending attack, according to local tales, a priest painted the altar black to disguise it. The priest told Morgan that the famous altar had been stolen by another pirate and even convinced Morgan to donate handsomely for its replacement. Morgan is said to have told the priest, 'I don't know why, but I think you are more of a pirate than I am.' Regardless of the accuracy of this story, the baroque-style altar, made of carved mahogany painted and veneered with gold, escaped the pirates' attention and was eventually moved to its present site.

A block farther west is another park, **Parque Herrera**, which is vivacious and picturesque with plenty of shoeshines, shade trees, benches and bustling people. A block north of that, on Avenida Central two blocks west of the cathedral, is the **Iglesia de La Merced**.

Walk out of Casco Viejo along Avenida Central, past the Casa de la Municipalidad, and after a couple of blocks you'll come to **Parque Santa Ana**, with its Iglesia de Santa Ana. Parque Santa Ana marks the beginning of the Avenida Central shopping district; it is surrounded by restaurants and there are buses to the financial district.

About five blocks farther north along Avenida Central, past all the big air-conditioned stores with hawkers outside, is the small **Plaza Cinco de Mayo**. Avenida Central between Parque Santa Ana and Plaza Cinco de Mayo is a pedestrian-only shopping street. On Avenida Central opposite Plaza Cinco de Mayo is the excellent **Museo Antropológico Reina Torres de Araúz**,

which focuses on the anthropology and archaeology of Panama; behind it is the handicrafts market, the **Mercado de Buhonerías y Artesanías**.

In El Cangrejo, the white French-Gothic style **Iglesia del Carmen**, on the corner of Vía España and Avenida Federico Boyd, is one of the city's most distinctive buildings. The church is a good 30 blocks away from the handicrafts market, but only US$2 away by taxi.

PANAMÁ LA VIEJA

At the eastern edge of the city are the ruins of Panamá La Vieja. Founded on August 15, 1519, by Spanish conquistador Pedro Arias de Ávila, the city of Panamá was the first European settlement along the Pacific. For the next 150 years it profited mainly from Spain's famed bullion pipeline, which ran from Peru's gold and silver mines to Europe via Panamá. Because of the amount of wealth that passed through the city, the Spaniards kept many soldiers here, and their presence kept the buccaneers away.

For many years Panamá was the metropolis of the Pacific. In addition to being a gateway for the bullion of Peru, it was the entrepôt for the silks and spices of the Orient. From Panamá, these riches were carried across the isthmus to be loaded onto the Spanish galleons at Nombre de Dios or Portobelo. The towns of Venta de Cruces and then Chagres, where the road crossed the Río Chagres, were halfway stations on the road to the northern coast. The Spaniards used to pack bars of silver and gold over this road, which came to be called Sendero Las Cruces, like cordwood. Also used to transport goods was El Camino Real, a land route running from Panamá to Portobelo. It was near Venta de Cruces that the English pirate Sir Francis Drake held up a train of 190 pack mules on the night of February 14, 1573, and made off with tons of gold and silver.

Nearly a century later, in 1671, 1200 pirates led by Henry Morgan ascended the Río Chagres as far as Venta de Cruces and then proceeded overland to Panamá. The city was not fortified, but it was protected

PANAMÁ LA VIEJA

0   150   300 m
0   150   300 yards
Approximate Scale
& Orientation

To Vía España

Río Abajo

Av 6 Sur (Av Cincuentenario)

Mangroves

Av 6 Sur (Av Cincuentenario)

To Panama City

Mudflats

1   Puente del Rey (Bridge of the King)
2   Possible Bread Oven
3   Iglesia de San José (Church of St Joseph)
4   Ermita de San Cristóbal (Hermitage of St Christopher)
5   Antigua Casa del Obispo (Old Bishop's House)
6   Iglesia y Convento de Santo Domingo (Church and Convent of St Dominic)
7   Casa Alarcón
8   Casa de los Genoveses (Slave Market)
9   Iglesia y Convento de La Merced
10 Mal Llamada Piedra del Sacrificio (so-called sacrificial stone)
11 Iglesia y Convento de San Francisco
12 Hospital de San Juan de Dios (Hospital of St John of God)
13 Iglesia y Convento de la Concepción
14 Iglesia y Convento de la Compañía de Jesús
15 Casas de Terrín
16 Catedral de Nuestra Señora de la Asunción (Our Lady of the Assumption Cathedral)
17 Plaza Mayor (Grand Plaza)
18 Cabildo de la Ciudad (City Hall)
19 El Camino Real (King's Highway)
20 Puente del Matadero (Bridge of the Slaughterhouse)
21 Fortín de la Natividad (Nativity Fort)
22 Aguadero Salubre (Public Water Receptacle)
23 Market
24 Museo de Sitio Panamá Viejo
25 Hostal (Inn)
26 El Trapiche; Mercado Nacional de Artesanías
27 Wall Protecting the Casas Reales
28 Casas Reales (Royal Houses)

on three sides by the sea and marshes. On the land side was a causeway, and a bridge in its middle permitted tidal water to pass underneath. But to the bewilderment of historians, when Morgan and his men neared the city, the Spanish soldiers left this natural stronghold and confronted the buccaneers in a hilly area outside town.

It was the first of their many mistakes. When the two forces met in battle, the Spanish infantry left their ranks after mistaking a repositioning of some of Morgan's men for a retreat. The Spanish soldiers ran after the pirates, leaving a high position for

a gully. French sharpshooters within Morgan's band were delighted by the development and opened fire on the Spaniards from nearby knolls. The first volley of musket fire dropped about 100 soldiers, and the Spanish force fell to pieces.

'Hardly did our men see some fall dead and others wounded,' reported the Spanish president at the time, Don Juan Perez, 'but they turned their backs and fled and it was not possible to stop them.' Morgan had control of the town within hours.

At the time Panamá fell, the city contained a magnificent cathedral, several beautiful churches and eight convents. There were more than 200 warehouses stocked with foreign goods, 200 residences of European elegance and 5000 houses of the common sort. The city also possessed a mint, a large hospital, the king's stables and a slave market. When Morgan left, little more than building material remained. Nearly everything of value was plundered by the pirates and divvied up later or was destroyed by a fire set by the pirates or by defiant townspeople.

For the next three centuries, what remained of the abandoned city – mostly beams and stone blocks – served as a convenient source of building materials. Yet most of the remnants of the one-time metropolis were still intact as recently as 1950, when the limits of modern Panama City reached the ruins in the form of a squatter settlement. But by the time the government declared the ruins a protected historic site, 26 years later, most of the old city had been dismantled and overrun.

Today much of Panamá La Vieja lies buried under a poor residential neighborhood. So little of the original city remains that its size, layout and appearance are the subjects of much conjecture. What follows are details agreed upon by experts.

The city was founded on a coastal bar alongside a shallow cove. The primary government buildings were at the mouth of the cove, which was rather spacious at the time and could be used as a port; today it is largely mangroves. The cathedral was erected nearby. The major Catholic religious orders – the Franciscans, Dominicans, Jesuits and Augustines – had churches and convents in town. The best houses and most of the convents were built on the narrow strip of land along the beachfront.

The colonial city seems to have followed a grid plan, with blocks of various sizes and a main square; the visible remains of Panamá La Vieja are certainly laid out that way. The lots tended to be narrow, and the houses often consisted of two or three stories. The suburbs that developed to the north and northwest lacked planning; common houses and hovels were scattered along crooked lanes.

It requires a good imagination to visualize the city before the arrival of Captain Morgan and his men. The churches, some of which faced the sea, were the most outstanding buildings. All were rectangular, with stone outer walls, timber roofs and internal wooden supports. Few had towers. The adjoining convents had inner courts surrounded by wooden galleries. It appears that the larger ones had enclosed gardens and orchards.

Most of the better houses were built of timber and placed wall to wall, with small inner courts, open-air kitchens and separate wings for the servants. Some had ground-floor galleries and balconies; most had plain exterior walls. A few of the fancier homes were built of stone, and their ruins remain. The poor had far simpler dwellings, usually thatched huts built with inexpensive materials like reeds.

The center of power resided at the **Casas Reales** (Royal Houses), a complex ringed by timber ramparts and separated from the city proper by a moat. Within the complex were the customs house, the royal treasury, a prison and the governor's house. Despite the obvious historical importance of the site, past governments have allowed sections of the property to be used as a landfill and for horse stables. Only scattered walls remain of the once-impressive structures.

The **Catedral de Nuestra Señora de la Asunción**, built between 1619 and 1626, is the best-preserved building of them all. In traditional fashion, it was designed so that its two side chapels gave the cathedral a crosslike shape as viewed from the heavens. The bell tower was at the back of the church and may have served double duty as a watchtower for the Casas Reales. The main façade, which faced the Plaza Mayor (Grand Plaza), is gone. Only the walls remain.

Also facing the Plaza Mayor were the **Cabildo de la Ciudad** (City Hall) and the **Casas de Terrín**, houses built by one of the city's wealthiest citizens, Francisco Terrín.

Immediately north of the cathedral are the massive ruins of **Casa Alarcón**, the town's best-preserved and largest known private residence. It dates from the 1640s. Just north of the former residence is the **Iglesia y Convento de Santo Domingo** (Church and Convent of St Dominic), the best-preserved church. The convent dates from the 1570s and the church was built 20 or more years later.

Arriving a decade or so after the Dominican friars were the Jesuits, and they built a stone church, the **Iglesia y Convento de la Compañía de Jesús**, whose ruins are likewise visible today. Just west of the Jesuits' facilities are the spacious ruins of a church and convent, the **Iglesia y Convento de la Concepción**, which were erected by the nuns of Nuestra Señora de la Concepción (Our Lady of the Conception). Most of the ruins, which cover the better part of two blocks, were part of the church; little remains of the convent.

Between the nuns' church and the sea was the city's sole hospital, the **Hospital de San Juan de Dios**. Unfortunately, much of the hospital's remains were scattered when Avenida Cincuentenario and a side road were put in not long ago. Also bordering the avenue, two blocks west of the hospital's ruins, are the remains of the **Iglesia y Convento de San Francisco**, the facilities erected by the Franciscans. The church faced the sea and stood on a massive base.

Continuing two blocks west along Avenida Cincuentenario, you'll arrive at the ruins of the **Iglesia y Convento de La Merced**. Erected by the Mercedarian friars in the early 17th century, the buildings actually survived the fire that swept the city following Morgan's assault. The church's façade is missing because the friars dismantled it and moved it to Casco Viejo, where it can be seen today.

Farther west (beyond the Bohío Turístico Restaurant) and paralleling the modern bridge is the **Puente del Matadero** (Bridge of the Slaughterhouse), a horribly overrestored stone bridge that took its name from a nearby slaughterhouse. It marked the beginning of the Camino Real to Portobelo. A much more significant bridge is visible from Avenida Cincuentenario near the northern edge of town. It is called **Puente del Rey** (Bridge of the King); built in 1617, it may be the oldest bridge in the Americas.

About halfway between that bridge and the Iglesia y Convento de Santo Domingo lies the **Iglesia de San José**, which belonged to the Augustine order. Marking this building as special were its vaulted side chapels – an architectural feature seldom seen in Panama. The ruins of the separate adjacent chapel are gone today.

The city's ruins are not fenced and you can visit them any time. There's the fine **Mercado Nacional de Artesanías** (National Artisans Market) beside the ruins; it is open 9 am to 6 pm daily. Sharing a building with the market is the restaurant El Trapiche (see Places to Eat later in this chapter for details).

Adjacent to the artisans market is the **Museo de Sitio Panamá Viejo**, which contains a rather impressive scale model of Panamá La Vieja prior to 1671. As you gaze upon it, a tape recording in Spanish or English recounts the history of the site. The museum also contains many colonial artifacts, most of which were brought from Spain. Unfortunately, all the signs are in Spanish and all the guides (every tour is guided for security reasons) speak only Spanish. It is customary to tip the guides US$1 or US$2. Hours are 9 am to 4 pm Monday to Saturday, 9 am to 1 pm Sunday. Museum admission is a bargain at US$1.

CAUSEWAY

At the Pacific entrance to the Panama Canal, a 2km *calzada* (causeway) connects the four small islands of Naos, Culebra, Perico and Flamenco to the southern tip of La Boca district. Solidaridad, the beach on Naos, is one of the most popular in the area; it costs US$5 a day to use, and there's a simple, open-sided restaurant serving typical Panamanian food beside the beach. The **Centro de Exhibiciones Marinas** (Marine Exhibitions Center, ☎ 212-8000, ext 2366) is on Culebra, and it includes a museum housed in a building that Noriega often used for entertaining. Nearby are two lovely aquariums, and near the aquariums is a patch of forest containing sloths and iguanas. The causeway, the islands and the Centro de Exhibiciones Marinas make for some fascinating touring.

The causeway, which was constructed from rock that was removed to make the Panama Canal, is a very enjoyable place. Many people arrive in the early morning and the late afternoon to walk, jog, skate, bicycle or drive along it. There's generally a pleasant breeze on the causeway, and it always offers sweeping views of the financial district, some 8km away. Bicycles Moses operates a booth at the causeway entrance where you can rent a bicycle or in-line skates; see the Bicycle section, later in this chapter, for details.

If you don't have a vehicle, it's most convenient to take a taxi to the causeway (US$3) and to hail another when you're ready to return to town (or ask a waitress at Mi Ranchito, mentioned later, or a worker at the marine exhibit to call a taxi for you).

All four of the causeway islands used to comprise Fort Grant, which was established in 1913 to guard the southern entrance to the canal. Between 1913 and WWII, the USA made Fort Grant into the most powerful defense complex in the world.

In 1928 two 14-inch guns with ranges up to 44km were brought to Panama. Mounted on railway carriages, they could be moved across the isthmus via the Panama Railroad to defend either entrance to the canal. The Pacific-side emplacement for the railroad guns was on Culebra. You can still see the tracks today on the driveway leading up to the Centro de Exhibiciones Marinas. The concrete rooms nearby, now used by marine-center staff, once housed the guns' ammunition. In 1941 the Japanese assault on Pearl Harbor showed that carrier-based aircraft could attack successfully far beyond the range of artillery. Suddenly obsolete, many of the big guns were retired from service even before the end of WWII.

The Centro de Exhibiciones Marinas is run by the Smithsonian Tropical Research Institute. There are many exhibits at the center, including a small six-sided building with sweeping views of the Bahía de Panamá that was built by Noriega for intimate gatherings. Today it houses a museum containing exhibits with signs in Spanish and English that mention how Panama's first peoples gradually developed a variety of strategies to harvest fish from the sea.

At the museum you can also learn about the role that Panama's marine resources play in the country's economy, and the destructive and wasteful effects of harvesting fish and shrimp by net. All of the text is beautifully illustrated with high-quality photos.

Outside the museum is something that will thrill ship enthusiasts: large, intelligent illustrations of vessels that allow visitors to glance out at the ocean and identify the types of ships waiting to transit the canal. It's a lot of fun. And there's a telescope here that you can use free of charge. Ever wonder if the crews aboard tankers fish from the bridges of their ships? For me, a person who has spent little time at the ocean, studying the anchored ships with the telescope was like looking upon another world.

Two large aquariums, also part of the marine center, are 50m from the museum. One contains fish from the Pacific, the other fish from the Caribbean, allowing you to compare the two sets. You'll be struck by how much more colorful, and how much smaller, are the fish from the Caribbean. Staff on hand can tell you why that is so. The Centro de Exhibiciones Marinas is open 1 to 5 pm Tuesday through Friday and 10 am to 5 pm Saturday and Sunday; admission costs US$1.

Dry forests once lined Central America's Pacific coast. Relatively easy to clear and burn for agriculture, these forests have now all but disappeared. The forest that you can see from the center, which lines the shore just south of the Puente de las Américas, is one of the largest remaining dry forests in Central America. There's even some dry forest near the aquariums. Be sure to take a stroll into it. I once saw a three-toed sloth asleep in the crook of a tree, two huge green iguanas soaking up the sun and a brown pelican that seemed deep in bird thought.

Just beyond the turnoff for Islas Naos and Culebra, the Causeway winds to Isla

Perico, a mostly undeveloped island which has at its base **Mi Ranchito**, a charming, breezy restaurant under palapas. A variety of seafood items are served at this popular spot, including ceviche (US$3.25) and filet of fish (US$6.25). Red meat is also available (generally US$6.25). There's a full bar and lots of colorful cocktails from which to choose. Mi Ranchito is open 10 am to midnight daily. This place is a very good find.

The most distant of the four islands linked by the Causeway is Isla Flamingo. At the time this book went to press, a resort, marina and shopping center called **Fuerte Amador Resort & Marina** was being built on top of, at the base of and *inside* of the solid-rock island. The portion of the complex that's inside the island occupies a former US military command post completed in January 1942 at the then-enormous cost of US$400,000.

Website: www.fuerteamador.com

The US general who issued orders to build the bombproof structure said it was needed 'for use in case of emergency and vital to the security of important data.' Even today, a full six decades after the command post was completed, the US military will not disclose what data was so important that it needed to be stored at the center of a rock island.

The Causeway, its four islands and a chunk of the peninsula leading the causeway – all part of Fort Amador – was turned over to Panama in October 1979 in compliance with the Panama Canal Treaty of 1977.

PANAMA CANAL MURALS

The story of the monumental effort to build the Panama Canal is powerfully depicted in murals mounted in the rotunda of the Panama Canal Administration Building in Balboa Heights.

The murals tell the story of the canal's construction through four main scenes: the digging of Gaillard Cut at Gold Hill, where the canal passes through the Continental Divide; the building of the spillway of the Gatún Dam, which dammed the Río Chagres and created Lago Gatún; construction of one of the giant lock gates (the canal uses some 80 of these gates); and the construction of the Miraflores Locks near the Pacific entrance to the canal. A frieze located immediately below the murals presents a panorama of the excavation of Gaillard Cut.

The murals were created by William B Van Ingen of New York, an outstanding artist who had achieved considerable fame for his murals in the Library of Congress in Washington, DC, and those in the US Mint in Philadelphia. Van Ingen agreed to produce the murals for US$25 per square foot; the finished murals cover about 1000 sq feet.

According to a leaflet at the administration building, Van Ingen and two assistants first made charcoal sketches of canal construction activities during two visits to Panama in 1914. Van Ingen then painted the murals on separate panels in his New York studio. The panels were shipped to Panama and installed during a three-day period in January 1915 under the artist's personal supervision. The paintings have the distinction of being the largest group of murals by an American artist on display outside the USA.

The administration building is open from 7:30 am to 4:15 pm weekdays. It's closed weekends, but guards will usually let you in between 10 am and 2:30 pm if you ask them politely.

MI PUEBLITO

At the foot of Cerro Ancón, on the western side of town near the intersection of Avenida de los Mártires and Calle Jeronimo de la Ossa, is a life-size replica of a rural village like those found on the Península de Azuero. There's a central square, a colonial church, a grocery store, a barber shop and a fine little restaurant that serves Panamanian specialties.

Created in 1994, Mi Pueblito (My Little Village) is quite a lovely place, even if it isn't authentic. One of its strengths is its numerous craft shops, where you'll find handicrafts from throughout the country. The quality is usually very good to excellent, but the prices are much higher than you'd find in the crafts' cities of origin.

Mi Pueblito is open from 11:30 am to 11:30 pm Tuesday to Saturday and 10 am to 10 pm Sunday.

MUSEUMS

Sadly, the establishment and preservation of museums is not a governmental priority in Panama City. Those that do exist are mostly the products of extraordinary efforts by individuals who took it upon themselves to move a bureaucratic mountain and create institutions in which Panama's human and natural histories could be preserved.

Foremost among this select group of individuals was the late Reina Torres de Araúz, the country's most distinguished anthropologists. Before she passed away in 1982 at age 49, she successfully battled for the creation of seven museums – including the country's finest museum, the anthropology museum that bears her name.

The strength of Panama City's museums lies not in a single institution or two but in their variety. In the capital city there are museums devoted to religious colonial art, natural science, Panamanian history, contemporary art, the Panama Railroad and the canal. Unfortunately, signs at all the museums are in Spanish only, and literature in other languages generally is not available. However, English-speaking guides are available at the anthropology and canal museums and are strongly recommended; a tip of US$3 to US$5 is greatly appreciated.

Following is a list of city museums:

Casa-Museo del Banco Nacional This bank museum displays coins and bills circulated in Panama from the 16th century to the present, as well as stamps and other objects related to the history of the Panamanian postal service. Hours are 8 am to 12:30 pm and 1:30 to 4 pm Tuesday to Friday, 7:30 am to noon Saturday. Admission is free. Calle 34 Este at Avenida Cuba (☎ 225-0640).

Museo Antropológico Reina Torres de Araúz Housed in the imposing former main railway station, built in 1913 and closed in the 1940s, this fascinating must-see museum conveys the rich cultural heritage of Panama. It emphasizes, naturally, pre-Columbian artifacts and culture to give the visitor an appreciation for life on the isthmus before the arrival of the Spaniards. However, a number of exhibits also show how people live in different parts of Panama today, with the various ethnic groups well represented. Hours are 9:30 am to 4 pm Tuesday to Sunday. Admission costs US$2. Be sure to request a brochure. On Avenida Central, near Plaza Cinco de Mayo (☎ 212-3089).

Museo de Arte Contemporáneo This privately owned museum has an excellent collection of works on paper by Latin American artists. The rest is usually not so hot, except for an occasional temporary exhibition by a national or foreign artist and the monthlong Bienal de Arte, the country's largest art exhibition. Hours are 9 am to 4 pm weekdays and 9 am to noon Saturday. Admission is free. Avenida San Blás at Avenida de los Mártires in the Ancón district (☎ 262-8012/3380).

Museo de Arte Religioso Colonial This museum is in a chapel of the Iglesia y Convento de Santo Domingo, which was built in 1756. With the exception of the museum, the church and convent now stand in ruins. This museum contains sacred artifacts from the colonial era, including sacred paintings and sculptures from various parts of the country, dating from the 16th, 17th and 18th centuries. Among the exhibits is a golden altar from the former chapel of the monastery that dates from the 18th century. Within the adjacent ruins is the famous Arco Chato (see the Walking Tour section). Hours are 9 am to 4:15 pm Tuesday to Saturday; admission costs US$1. Avenida A at Calle 3 in Casco Viejo (☎ 228-2897).

Museo de Ciencias Naturales This museum has sections on geology, paleontology, entomology and marine biology. What I found most impressive were the quantity of stuffed animals and the quality of the taxidermy. Numerous examples of Panama's wildlife can be found here, as well as stuffed lions, tigers, rhinos and buffalo. Its hours are 9 am to 4 pm Tuesday to Saturday and 9 am to 1 pm Sunday; US$1/25¢ adults/kids. Avenida Cuba between Calles 29 Este and 30 Este (☎ 225-0645).

Museo de Historia de Panamá This not terribly impressive museum contains exhibits on the history of Panama from Spanish colonial times until 1977, the year the USA agreed to turn over control of the canal to Panama. Hours are 8:30 am to 3:30 pm weekdays; US$1. Palacio Municipal, 3rd floor, beside Plaza de la Independencia in Casco Viejo (☎ 228-6231).

Museo del Canal Interoceánico Widely known only as the Panama Canal Museum, this museum is a must-see and is housed in an elegant building built by the French in French colonial style in the mid-1870s. It opened as a hotel and later became the headquarters of the French and, later still, US canal commissions. The museum, which opened in 1997, contains such varied displays as Spanish armor and weapons, rifles from California's gold-rush days (many US prospectors passed through the city on their way to California), the desk at which Panama's declaration of independence was signed in 1903 and many Panama Railroad and Canal exhibits. The museum presents a detailed history of the railroad and canal through the use of panels covered with well-presented text (in Spanish only), paintings and photos. There are many artifacts as well. English-speaking guides are available when given a six-hour notice; be sure to call ahead and request one. Hours are 9:30 am to 5:30 pm Tuesday to Sunday; US$2. Beside Plaza de la Independencia in Casco Viejo (☎ 211-1650).

PARQUE NATURAL METROPOLITANO

Upon a hill to the north of downtown, this 265-hectare park protects a wild area of tropical forest within the city limits. It has two main walking trails – the Nature Trail and the Tití Monkey Trail – that join to form one long loop, and a 150m high *mirador* (lookout point) offering a view over Panama City, the bay and the canal all the way to the Miraflores Locks. It is the only city park in Latin America that contains tropical semideciduous forest.

Mammals in the park include marmosets, anteaters, sloths and white-tailed deer; reptiles are represented by iguanas, turtles and tortoises. There are more than 250 known species of bird here, including the lance-tailed manakin. Fish, shrimp and turtles live in the Río Curundu, which runs along the eastern side of the park.

An international team of scientists from the Smithsonian Tropical Research Institute (☎ 212-8000, Tupper Building, Avenida Roosevelt, Ancon, Balboa) has set up a crane in the park to study the forest canopy; there is a complete ecosystem 30m to 50m up, including many animals that could never be studied from the ground. Unfortunately, the crane is off-limits to the general public. Website: www.stri.org

The park is bordered on the west and north by Camino de la Amistad and on the south and east by Corredor Norte; Avenida Juan Pablo II runs right through the park.

Admission costs US$1. There's a visitors' center (☎ 232-5516/5552) on Avenida Juan Pablo II, 40m north of the park entrance; it's open 8 am to 4 pm daily. A pamphlet for a self-guided tour is available in Spanish and English. Rangers offer one-hour tours with a slide show for groups of five or more; the cost is US$5.

Additionally, the Panama Audubon Society (☎ 224-9371, fax 224-4740, audupan@pananet.com) holds its monthly meeting at the visitors' center from 7:30 to 9:30 pm on the second Thursday of every month. The meetings are open to the public and often feature interesting speakers. Both English and Spanish are spoken here, and the group's website (www.pananet.com/audobon) is bilingual as well. These meetings provide an excellent opportunity to get to know some Panamanians, to meet other birders and to learn more about birds.

The park was the supposed site of an important battle during the US invasion to oust Noriega (see 'The 'Battle' in the Park'). Also of historical significance are the concrete structures just past the park entrance. They were used by the US military during WWII as a testing and assembly plant for aircraft engines. Today one of the buildings is an environmental education center. The other structure is vacant.

LANGUAGE COURSES

There are two major Spanish-language schools in Panama City. The Language & International Relations Institute (ILERI; ☎/fax 260-4424; in the USA ☎ 800-765-0025; ilery@sinfo.net), at Avenida Amistad, No 42-G, El Dorado, enjoys the stronger reputation. ILERI offers four hours of instruction daily, five days a week, with class sizes limited to four persons. The cost for the first week is US$300 with in-home lodging, two meals daily, laundry service and more, with the weekly rate falling for each subsequent week. The weekly rate starts at US$200 without lodging. More information is on their website at www.isls.com/home/schools/ileri.html.

The US Embassy sends members of its staff to Centro PanUSA (☎ 232-6718, fax

Iglesia del Carmen, Panama City

View of Casco Viejo, Panama City

Detail of colonial architecture, Panama City

Financial district giant, Panama City

A little magical light on the ruins of Iglesia de la Merced in Panama la Vieja, Panama City

Ruins of Portobelo, Colón Province

The 'Battle' in the Park

A key battle was supposedly fought in Parque Natural Metropolitano during the US invasion of Panama in 1989. Here, the US military reported, an American service-woman led troops into battle for the first time in US military history.

According to the report, which was widely circulated during the invasion, Army Captain Linda Bray led a force of 30 military police in a fierce three-hour firefight at a Panama Defense Forces guard-dog kennel that left three Panamanian soldiers dead.

The US Army later acknowledged that the gunfire lasted only 10 minutes and was 'sporadic,' that no one was killed and that 29-year-old Captain Bray was not at the kennel at the time of the shooting but was in fact 1km away at a command post.

Although the initial report was shown to be largely inaccurate, it led to heated debate in the USA about the role of US service-women in combat and eventually led to groundbreaking legislation that allowed them access to various combat jobs previously denied them.

232-7292, panusa@sinfo.net), alongside Avenida Roosevelt, Building 635, Balboa district, next door to the old train station, which periodically offers four-week courses for US$205, with two hours of instruction per day, four days a week.
Website: www.panusa.com

See the Bocas del Toro Province chapter for information on a third Spanish-language school.

ORGANIZED TOURS

There are numerous tours available in and around the city, offered by companies of widely varying standards. The two companies mentioned here enjoy solid reputations in Panama. All of the tours described below commence in Panama City. See Organized Tours in the Getting Around chapter for additional information.

Ancon Expeditions of Panama (☎ 269-9414/9415, fax 264-3713, info@anconexpeditions.com), in the El Dorado Building on Calle 49 A Este near Avenida 3 Sur, hires top-notch guides and offers only well-tested tours, some of which appear below. Contact Ancon Expeditions or visit its website (www.anconexpeditions.com) for a complete rundown of the company's offerings. Prices shown are for one person.

Barro Colorado Nature Monument The tour includes car transport to Gamboa, then boat transport up the Panama Canal to Barro Colorado Island, at the heart of the oldest nature in the Western Hemisphere, where Smithsonian Tropical Research Institute guides take visitors on a tour of the jungle island and discuss the research being done there; lunch included (US$99).

Panama Canal Jungle Boat Tour Cruise in a low-profile expedition boat among the jungle-shrouded islands of Gatun Lake near the belly of the Panama Canal in search of white-fronted capuchins; howler, spider and night monkeys; and scores of exotic birds. Lunch is served on a private island as transoceanic ships pass by (US$89).

Panama Canal Transit The canal's three sets of locks can be viewed from the land, but for those of you who absolutely must pass through a set of locks Ancon Expeditions offers once-monthly full transits of the canal (US$145) and weekly partial transits of the canal (US$99).

Panama City Tour & Miraflores Locks Includes a visit to Panamá La Vieja, Casco Viejo, the excellent Panama Canal Museum and, after lunch, a visit to the Miraflores Locks; a very fine way to take in a lot of Panama City conveniently and efficiently (US$50).

Pipeline Road in Soberanía National Park Birders the world over have at least heard of the legendary Pipeline Road, a 17km jungle-flanked road/trail that repeatedly leads Central American sites for the greatest number of bird species recorded annually; includes a visit to the harpy eagle exhibit at Summit Botanical Gardens & Zoo (US$65).

EcoMargo Tours (☎ 264-4001, 264-8888, fax 264-5355, ecocircuito@cwp.net.pa), located on Avenida 3 Sur next to the large Restaurante-Bar Tinajas, offers more than two dozen day tours from Panama City. Check their website (www.ecocircuitos.com) for details on their tours, which include the following:

Camino de Cruces Trail This trail, originally used by conquistadors to haul gold seized in Peru across the isthmus and later used by Americans heading to California during the gold rush of 1849, takes visitors 13 km through 4000 hectares of primarily dry tropical forest within the Metropolitan and Soberania nature preserves (US$65).

El Valle Indian Market Offered Sundays only, this tour goes to the enchanting alpine hamlet of El Valle de Anton in Coclé province, where members of at least three indigenous peoples gather to sell crafts and other goods; also included are lunch and visits to nearby petroglyphs, El Chorro Macho waterfall and the local zoo (US$95).

Historic Portobelo Tour Tour includes a visit to the Spanish forts at Portobelo, the new museum there and a boat trip to Drake's Island, where some say the remains of the famous pirate Sir Francis Drake are buried; lunch included (US$80, minimum four people).

Panamanian Night Tour Available Tuesday, Thursday, Friday and Saturday, this tour consists of hotel shuttle to and from Restaurante-Bar Tinajas, where visitors dine on fine Panamanian food and watch a good folkloric show; all costs are included in the tour price (US$30).

The Pirate Trail Tour includes travel across the isthmus to Gatun Dam, lunch at the Tarpon Club facing the impressive spillway, followed by a tour of Fuerte San Lorenzo, which was captured by buccaneer Henry Morgan en route to sacking Old Panama (US$90, minimum four people).

SPECIAL EVENTS

Although not as famous as the celebrations in Rio de Janeiro or New Orleans, Carnaval in Panama City is celebrated with the same level of unrestrained merriment and wild abandon during the four days preceding Ash Wednesday. From Saturday until the following Tuesday, work is put away and masks, costumes and confetti are brought to the fore. For 96 hours, almost anything goes.

The festivities formally begin with a coronation ceremony on Friday, during which a Carnaval queen and her attendants are chosen from candidates representing a variety of social clubs, volunteer organizations, neighborhoods and private groups. Throughout her reign, the queen presides at all official receptions and is the center of attention in the daily parades scheduled each afternoon.

Officially, the craziness starts slowly, with a small parade on Saturday that consists of little more than the queen and her court. Unofficially, the cork is way out of the bottle by then. Vía España fills with people, and everyone is in high spirits and partying in an atmosphere that is sexually charged and free of class distinctions. Music pours from all directions and spontaneous dancing breaks out everywhere. Masquerade characters cavort among the crowd. Colorful street vendors wander through the throngs of people, and improvised entertainment abounds. The party moves indoors at night – into cantinas, private clubs and hotels – where combos play Afro-Cuban and typical Panamanian music and the dancing and drinking continue till dawn.

The celebration, the origins of which have been obscured with the passage of time, kicks into a higher gear on Sunday, when folk dance groups decked out in Panama's national costumes join the queen and her attendants in the afternoon parade down Vía España, traveling from near Vía Brasil to near Avenida Federico Boyd (the exact beginning and ending points vary from year to year). To cool the sunbaked masses, fire and garden hoses are turned on the crowd at every opportunity. Fact: The amount of water sprayed on party-goers during Carnaval in Panama City during these four festive days equals the amount the city uses during the previous four *months*.

The madness peaks on Shrove Tuesday with the biggest parade of all. Floats of all sizes rule the avenue, separated by bands of gaily dressed people walking slowly in themed formations – not the least conspicuous of which is the traditional formation of transvestites. Most of them carry a razor in each hand as a warning to macho types that a punch thrown at them will not go unanswered.

Carnaval officially closes with the first rays of sunlight on Wednesday morning, when the hardiest celebrants appear on the beach of the Bahía de Panamá to bury a sardine in the sand – a symbolic gesture intended to convey the end of worldly pleasures for the Lenten season.

PLACES TO STAY

There are dozens of hotels in Panama City, and guestrooms range from cell-like (small, dirty and hot, with shared bathrooms, cold water, etc) to opulent (tastefully appointed with to-die-for views, acres of space, a butler, computer, executive desk, minibar, satellite TV, Jacuzzi tub with separate shower, etc). Prices for a standard room in this town range from US$6 to US$250.

Budget accommodations run up to US$20, mid-range lodgings from US$21 to US$50 and top-end places from US$51 to small house payment. Prices cited here do not include Panama's 10% hotel tax. There's one so-called youth hostel (your youth hostel association card is meaningless here), and there are no campgrounds or RV centers in Panama City.

The hotels appear in order of room rates, beginning with the least expensive. Generally, the longer the write-up, the more attention the hotel deserves from readers like you – prospective patrons with discerning tastes.

While conducting research for this book, I inspected at least two rooms at every hotel. Most of Panama City's hotels appear on the following pages. Those not included opened after January 2001; were rat-plagued, roach-ridden or flea-infested; were in really bad areas; were unpleasant to a kind soul who asked to see two rooms; or, were simply overlooked by the author (as likely as your finding a US$1000 bill inside this book).

Places to Stay – Budget

Casco Viejo The Casco Viejo area is home to most of the city's low-priced lodgings; in fact, only low-priced lodgings are found here. The places mentioned below are, in my opinion, acceptable to streetwise people on a tight budget who find great satisfaction in savings and who generally prefer risky

and adventurous to safe and predictable. (See Dangers & Annoyances earlier in this chapter for safety tips.) None of these hotels has hot water.

The architecturally attractive **Hotel y Restaurante Herrera** (☎/fax 228-8994), beside Parque Herrera, has rooms with fan for US$6/8 single/double with shared bathroom, or US$11 with private bathroom. A room with two beds and private bathroom, fan, fridge and TV goes for US$13. A room with private bathroom, air con, fridge and TV costs US$16. This place needs a fresh coat of paint and a good cleaning but is otherwise OK. There's a laundromat just around the corner. Despite its name, the restaurant no longer exists.

Hotel Foyo (☎ 262-8023), at Calle 6, No 8-25, is basic but clean, with rooms for US$6/9 with shared/private bathroom; a few smaller rooms adequate for one person and equipped with a washbasin cost US$7. Some of the rooms of the same price are better than others; ask to see several.

The **Pensión Tropical** (☎ 228-8889), on Calle 8 near Avenida A, is for hurtin' individuals. There's only a bed and a fan in each room. Sometimes there doesn't even seem to be oxygen. Rooms go for US$7/9 with shared/private bathroom.

The **Pensión Panamericana** (☎ 228-8759), at Avenida A and Calle 10, offers worn rooms for one or two people for US$7/10 with shared/private bathroom. There's a ceiling fan, a dresser and a decent bed in each room.

Hotel Central (☎ 262-8044), on Calle 5 facing Plaza de la Independencia, was grand at the start of the 20th century; illustrious figures from the canal's history lodged here in its early days. The hotel has been allowed to deteriorate, but the bare-essentials rooms still have high ceilings and arched French doors opening onto private balconies overlooking the plaza; overall, it's in an excellent location, and prices are good: Singles/doubles cost US$7.50/8.50 with shared bathroom, US$8.50/10.50 with private bathroom.

Though technically a half block outside the Casco Viejo district, **Hotel Colón** (☎ 228-8506 or 228-8510), at the corner of Calle 12

Oeste and Avenida B, is the best hotel in the neighborhood. Like the Hotel Central, it was built to house Panama Canal workers and was once grand but has fallen on hard times. In the lobby, one can still see the handsome, original-tile floor and walls. The elevator is also original and a real beauty, though cramped and requiring operator assistance. Most of the 46 rooms are naturally cool. Some rooms and beds are much better than others, so ask to see at least three before deciding on one. Also, the roof of the three-story hotel affords a nice view of the canal; be sure to check it out. This building was originally called Hotel Corcó after José Corcó, a Spanish immigrant who built the hotel once the Americans announced plans to construct a canal across the isthmus. Rates range from US$8/9 for a fan-cooled room with shared bathroom to US$13.50 for a room with air con.

La Exposición This bustling neighborhood contains quite a few budget hotels and many mid-range ones. It's a good area for people who value inexpensive but decent lodgings, but it isn't particularly safe (especially at night) and I don't recommend it to women traveling alone. For security, most travelers are better off staying in the safer El Cangrejo district.

Residencial Primavera (☎ 225-1195), simple but clean and well kept, is in a good location on Avenida Cuba near Calle 43 Este, in a residential neighborhood just a block from Avenida Central España. All the rooms have private bathrooms and ceiling fans, and this place is a good value at US$10 a night.

Pensión Las Palmeras (☎ 225-0811), Avenida Cuba, No 38-29, near Calle 38 Este, is also simple but clean, with rooms for US$10 with a shower in the room and toilet down the hall, or US$12 with private bathroom.

Residencial Turístico El Dorado (☎ 227-5767), on Calle 37 Este between Avenidas Cuba and Perú, has basic rooms with private bathrooms for US$8 with fan, US$10 with air con or US$13 with air con and color TV.

The *Pensión América* (☎ 225-1140), on Avenida 3 Sur near Calle 33 Este, offers rooms with fan/air con for US$12/20. None of the rooms has more than one bed. Overall, this place is not very pretty, but some of its rooms are OK.

Pensión Las Torres (☎ 225-0172), on the corner of Calle 35 Este and Avenida Perú, offers rooms with private bathrooms for US$12/15 with fan/air con. This place has lots of character and is popular with college students. I'd be extremely high on Las Torres if it were not for the fact that none of its bathrooms have doors. Also, there are lots of stairs from the ground floor to the second-floor lobby.

The four-story *Residencial Turístico Chorrera* (☎ 225-4813), on Calle 34 Este, opened in 1998 with 40 small rooms, each containing a tiny TV, dresser, closet and phone. The place is newer but not very nice. Rates are US$13/15.

Hotel Ideal (☎ 262-2400, fax 262-0137), Calle 17 Oeste, No 15-55, a block from the Avenida Central pedestrian street, is a large hotel where all the rooms have air con and color cable TV. Singles/doubles with shared bathrooms cost US$18/20; those with private bathrooms cost US$20/22. Downstairs is a 24-hour restaurant.

The *Residencial Jamaica* (☎ 225-9870), on Avenida Cuba, has clean and pleasant rooms with private bathrooms, hot water, private phones, air con and color TV for US$14/23 apiece – an excellent value. There's also secure parking.

Hotel Villa del Mar (☎ 225-8111), at Calle 33 Este near Avenida 3 Sur, has rooms with air con, cable TV, phones and private bathrooms, but it's a bit rundown and has no hot water. It's the kind of place that couples might use for an hour. Rates are US$15 one or two people. The *Hotel Discovery* (☎ 225-1140), on Calle 34 Este near Avenida 3 Sur, is the same kind of place.

Hotel 2 Mares (☎ 227-6149, fax 227-3906), on Calle 30 Este between Avenidas Perú and Cuba, has so-so rooms with air con for a very reasonable US$15/20. A room with a view and a king-size bed costs

US$25. Many rooms have small Jacuzzi tubs. This place offers a very good value.

Hotel Río de Janeiro (☎ 227-2145), on Avenida Perú near Calle 28 Este, has more security bars than the US Mint and more red lights than Disneyland. Its clientele consists mainly of prostitutes and their johns. I mention the Río only because its clerks had noticed that many guests carried with them the last edition of this guidebook. Rates are US$15 with air con, US$13 without.

Hotel Venecia (☎ 227-7881, fax 227-5642), on Avenida Perú near Calle 35 Este, is a new, small but pleasant place offering mediocre rooms with good beds, cable TV, air con and private bathrooms. At US$17/24, this is a good value. There's a restaurant/bar on premises.

The *Residencial Turistico El Eden* (☎ 225-2946, fax 227-5881), at Calle 29 No 474-11, offers 20 clean and simple rooms with air con, a small cable TV, and hot-water private bathrooms. The signs at the front desk indicating the clerk sells condoms and that the hotel is open 24 hours give you an indication of the clientele (yes, all rooms have only one bed). It's a very good value at US$18 per room. Consider bringing earplugs.

Hotel Arenteiro (☎ 227-5883, fax 225-2971), on Calle 30 Este near Avenida Cuba, is a newer place with rooms with cable TV, air con, hot water and phones. Rates are very competitive at US$18/22 single/double.

Hotel Centroamericano (☎ 227-4555, fax 225-2505), at Calle 33 Este and Avenida 3 Sur, is an excellent value, with very clean rooms with air con, TV, private bathrooms, hot water and firm mattresses for US$18/20. There's a pleasant restaurant/bar open 7 am to 10 pm daily except Sunday.

A very good value can be found at the *Hotel Acapulco* (☎ 225-3832, fax 227-2033), at Avenida Cuba and Calle 30 Este. There's a writing desk in each room, as well as air con, TV and a telephone. The rooms (US$20/22) are spacious and some have small balconies.

Residencial Alemeda (☎ 225-1758, fax 225-7806), on Calle 30 Este near Avenida Cuba, offers tiny cubicles that its staff generously calls guestrooms. Rates are US$20/22. Rooms have air con and TV, and parking and fax service are available.

The *Hotel Benidorm* (☎/fax 225-3035), on Calle 29 Este near Avenida Perú, offers air-con rooms with cable TV and telephones for US$20/25. Some rooms smell of cigarette smoke.

Los Angeles Although a bit out of the way, the *Voyager International Hostel* (☎ 260-5913, fax 260-5913, hotelpm@orbi.net), on Calle 11 Norte at Calle 62 C Oeste, is very popular with backpackers. Not affiliated with any hostel associations, the Voyager is a converted house in a residential neighborhood offering dormitory-style accommodations with four to six beds per room, 34 beds in total. Rooms are fan-cooled with shared bathrooms only. The guest rate is US$8.50 per person. There's a self-serve kitchen and laundry, a TV and free Internet access (limited to 30 minutes per guest per day). Price includes Continental breakfast.

Places to Stay – Mid-Range

The *Hotel Latino* (☎ 227-3395, fax 227-3092), on Avenida Cuba near Calle 35 Este, was built in the '90s but allowed to wear badly. Its gloomy rooms come with air con and TV and cost US$17/27. The hotel has a very decent restaurant on the ground floor.

Hotel Montreal (☎ 263-4422, fax 263-7951), on Vía España at Avenida Justo Arosemena, has the usual amenities, plus a rooftop swimming pool and secure parking. Rates are extremely competitive at US$18/20. Be sure to see several rooms, as they vary in quality from one to another.

Of the hotels in this price range, perhaps the best is the *Hotel Marparaíso* (☎/fax 227-6767), on Calle 34 Este between Avenidas 2 & 3 Sur. New in 1999, this Spanish-run hotel offers 72 spacious, clean, tastefully appointed, air-con rooms with cable TV and telephones for US$20/25 for one person/two. There are six floors in all, and those on the sixth floor seem larger than the rest. With secure parking as well, this place is a very good value.

The **Hotel California** (☎ 263-7736, fax 264-6144), on Avenida Central España near Calle 43 Este, has 58 good, clean rooms with private bathrooms, phones and color TV for US$21/33. There's a restaurant/bar downstairs and free coffee in the lobby.

Hotel Internacional (☎ 262-4933, fax 262-7806, hint@latin1.net), facing Plaza Cinco de Mayo, also opened during the '90s and appeared to be well maintained. It offers 80 rooms with air con and cable TV for US$22/27. There's a bar, restaurant and casino on the premises, and free shuttle service to La Playita on the Causeway (leaves at 9 am, returns at 6 pm).

Hotel Covadonga (☎ 225-3998, fax 225-4011, marit@sinfo.net), on Calle 29 Este between Avenidas Perú and Cuba, offers comfortable rooms with air con, cable TV, phones, room service and generally good beds for US$22/27 single/double. There's a 24-hour swimming pool on the hotel's roof and a restaurant on the ground floor.

The **Hotel Lisboa** (☎ 227-5916, fax 227-5919), on Avenida Cuba between Calles 30 Este and 31 Este, offers rooms for US$22/24 for one/two people. It's a newer place, with spacious rooms with air con, writing table, TV and phones. It's quite nice for the price.

The 11-story **Hotel Caribe** (☎ 225-0404, fax 227-2525, caribehotel@hotmail.com), on Calle 28 Este at Avenida Perú, offers spacious rooms, each with air con, phone and cable TV (and a refrigerator, if you request one). There's a pool on the roof and an ice machine on every floor. There's even laundry service. A very good value with rates at US$27/34.

Well situated and totally renovated in 2000, the **Las Vegas Suites Hotel** (☎ 269-0722, fax 223-0047, hotel@las egaspanama .com), at Calle 49 B Oeste and Avenida 2 A Norte in El Cangrejo, offers an excellent value. All rooms have kitchenettes with refrigerators, plus cable TV, new air-con units and phones. The hotel's courtyard restaurant, Caffé Pomodoro, is the highlight of the hotel, and its Wine Bar is very popular as well (see Places to Eat). And even if your travel isn't business-related, you can

request the hotel's corporate rate, which is US$35/40 (US$48 for two beds).
Website: www.lasvegaspanama.com

The **Hotel Veracruz** (☎ 227-3022, fax 227-3789), on Avenida Perú near Calle 31 Este, offers clean rooms with TV and air con for US$35/38. All of the rooms ending with the numbers '08' have balconies. There's a very good restaurant ,on the premises, and laundry service is available.

A fine value and a popular, well-located place, the **Hotel Marbella** (☎ 263-2220, fax 263-3622) is on Calle D between Calles 49 B Oeste and Eusebio A Morales. Every one of its 84 rooms has writing/dining tables, air con, cable TV and good beds. Laundry service is available. Rates are a very reasonable US$39/44 (ask for the corporate rate or you'll pay more!).

Gran Hotel Soloy (☎ 227-1133, fax 227-3948, hgsoloy@pan.gbm.net), on Avenida Perú at Calle 30 Este, has fairly cheerful rooms with air con and cable TV. There's a casino on the ground floor and a bar and dance club on the 12th floor (open Thursday, Friday and Saturday after 5 pm). Rates are US$39/43.

On Avenida Central España is the **Hotel Europa** (☎ 263-6911, fax 263-6749, heuropa@sinfo.net), across the street from the Hotel California, which offers appealing rooms with desks and cable TV for US$45/50.

Taking a large step up in quality and service, we arrive at the **Hotel Costa Inn** (☎ 227-1522, fax 225-1281, costainn@ panama.c-com.net), on Avenida Perú near Calle 39 Este. The 130 rooms come with air con and satellite TV, and there's a gym, a pool, a good restaurant, secure parking, and Internet access for 10¢ a minute. Airport shuttle and city tours are available, and there's a travel agency on the premises (Viajes Florencia, ☎ 225-6083). The hotel's sales manager, Carlos Ledo Vázquez, enjoys an excellent reputation for the personal attention he provides his guests. Rates are US$44/50, with discounts available beginning with the fourth night.

Hotel Roma (☎ 227-3844, fax 227-3711, hroma@pananet.com), on Calle 33 Este at

Avenida 3 Sur, has a pool on its roof and cheerful rooms with air con, TV, phones, good beds and free Internet access for guests Monday through Saturday (unavailable Sunday). However, it's not quite the value of the Hotel Costa Inn. Rooms start at US$50 for one or two persons and go to US$94 for junior suite containing a fax machine and computer with Internet access.

Places to Stay – Top End

There's no shortage of top-end accommodations in Panama City. The room rates shown here are 'rack rates' – the amounts you would be asked to pay if you walked in without a reservation during low tourist season. If you use a local tour operator to reserve a room, or if you request the hotel's corporate rate, you can often get a better nightly rate.

The *Hotel Suites Alfa* (☎ 263-4022, fax 223-0724, suitesalpha@pty.com), on Calle Ricardo Arias at Vía España, is nothing special, but its excellent location and reasonable prices of US$50/60 make it a fairly popular choice. Each room is spacious and equipped with a kitchenette.

Hotel Costa del Sol (☎ 206-3333, fax 202-3336), on Avenida 3 Sur at Avenida Federico Boyd, has some pleasant surprises. For one thing, each room has a kitchenette. The roof of the multistory hotel is home to a swimming pool, restaurant and bar, and has sweeping views of the city; it's a good place to enjoy a drink even if you're not a guest. The food isn't exceptional. There's also a tennis court and spa. It's a very good value at US$56/60.

Website: www.costadelsol-pma.com

The *Crystal Suites Hotel* (☎ 263-2644, fax 264-8125, atencion@crystalsuites.com), on the corner of Avenida 2 Sur and Vía Brasil, is a lovely, newly opened hotel with bright and attractive executive suites with integrated kitchen and dining area for an extremely competitive price of US$65 (junior and grand suites are also available). Services at this service-minded hotel include laundry, room and free Internet service; car and cellular-phone rental; and dry cleaning and airport shuttle. The only

thing not to like about this place is its somewhat isolated location.

Website: www.crystalsuites.com

Sevilla Suites (☎ 213-0016, fax 223-6344, se illasuites@se illasuites.com), on Avenida 2 A Norte, is a six-floor, all-suites hotel that opened in 2000 and immediately put other hotels in its price range on notice. All rooms feature a large cable TV, VCR, fully-equipped kitchenettes, optional sofa bed, and much more. Facilities include a gym, a 24-hour rooftop pool, coin-operated laundry and covered parking. Junior suites (with one queen-size bed) go for US$65, executive suites (two queen beds and balcony) for US$85. Some junior suites have balconies as well. Breakfast is included in the rates.

Website: www.sevillasuites.com

Coral Suites Aparthotel (☎ 269-3898, fax 269-0083, coralsuites@coralsuites.net), on Calle D near Calle 49 B Oeste, is, as its name suggests, an all-suites hotel with a gym, a rooftop pool, laundry room, secure parking and a business center with Internet access (5¢ a minute). It's very similar to the Sevilla Suites in that both are very comfortable, mid-size and built to high standards; the Sevilla is perhaps the nicer of the two. A suite with one queen-size bed or two twin beds goes for US$65, a suite with two queen beds for US$70, and a suite with two twin beds with terrace for US$95.

Website: www.coralsuites.net

A former Holiday Inn, the *Hotel Plaza Paitilla Inn* (☎ 269-1122, fax 223-1470), on Vía Italia at Avenida Churchill, is very well maintained, with tasteful if cheap furniture in its guestrooms. All of its rooms have bathtubs and balconies, and the hotel is on the water. There's a handsome pool and a very popular bar. The rack rate is US$120 for a single or double; the corporate rate is US$78, so don't forget to request it.

Website: www.plazapaitillainn.com

The 20-floor *Panama Marriott Hotel* (☎ 210-9100, fax 210-9110; in the USA ☎ 800-228-9290), located on Avenida 3 Sur, has 296 guestrooms, eight suites, nine meeting rooms, a full business center, a 24-hour room service, a restaurant and a bar, and it offers child-care, concierge and secretarial services. There's also a swimming pool and a health club on the premises. Rates generally start at US$89 and include buffet breakfast for two. Website: www.marriotthotels.com

The **Country Inn & Suites** (☎ 236-6444, fax 264-6082; in the USA ☎ 800-456-4000) is on Avenida Miguel Brostella west of Avenida Ricardo J Alfaro. The lodge has a country-inn feel to it, and it also has a swimming pool, meeting rooms, a business center with Internet access, free self-serve laundry, free local calls and breakfast, and a TGI Friday's restaurant next door. Rates are US$90/100; ask for promotional rates, as they're often available. A second Country Inn & Suites was under construction in 2001 near the entrance of the Causeway. Website: www.countryinns.com

The **Radisson Royal Panama Hotel** (☎ 265-3636, fax 265-3550; in the USA ☎ 800-333-3333), on Calle 53 Este at Avenida 5 B Sur, is an elegant hotel with lovely rooms and a pool, coffee shop, specialty restaurant, piano bar, exercise room and tennis court. Rates for rooms start at US$99 if reserved via the hotel's website (www.radisson.com); otherwise expect to pay at least US$25 more. However, there's a US$90 senior citizen rate available to anyone 50 years of age or older *or* anyone traveling with a person over 50 who is staying at the hotel. Be sure if you call to inquire about promotional prices.

The new, well-located **Holiday Inn** (☎ 206-5556, fax 206-5557, holidayinn@holidayinnpanama.com), on Avenida Manuel E Batista near Avenida 2 A Norte, features 112 deluxe guestrooms and 38 suites with all the usual amenities plus an iron and ironing board, hair dryer and make-up mirror. Services and facilities include an Internet café, a business center, a fine restaurant, a pool, gym, shopping arcade, a sports bar and four meeting rooms. Rates start at US$99. Website: www.holidayinnpanama.com

The **Miramar Inter-Continental** (☎ 214-1000, fax 223-4891, panama@interconti.com), on Avenida Balboa near Avenida Federico Boyd, is competing successfully with the Caesar Park for top honors as Panama's finest convention-capable hotel. The Miramar's gorgeous guestrooms contain all the creature comforts and face either the Bahía de Panamá or the gleaming financial district. The 25-story, 206-room seaside hotel features an informal marina-side restaurant as well as a fine dining restaurant on the 5th floor, a piano lounge, a bar and dance club, a private dining salon, a business center, an inviting pool with an island in the middle, a fully-equipped spa with aerobics and beauty salon, ballrooms, even tennis courts. The hotel posts a corporate rate of US$185 with weekend packages starting at $99, depending on available specials. Prospective guests should contact the hotel and request the lowest prevailing rate. Past guests have included Hillary Clinton, Mick Jagger, Jimmy Carter, Alberto Fujimori, Sting, Ernesto Zedillo, Andres Pastrana and Def Leppard. No, they were not all traveling together. Website: www.interconti.com

Centrally located and offering large, handsome rooms, the **Suites Ambassador** (☎ 263-7274, fax 264-7872, ambassad@sinfo.net) is on Calle D between Calle Eusebio A Morales and Calle 49 B Oeste in El Cangrejo. The smallest room at this very smart hotel would be a junior suite anywhere else. Each room comes with a true sitting area and an attractive kitchenette. Use of a conference room is offered at no extra charge. Service here is the best in town. A state-of-the-art security system monitors every floor, and the rooftop pool is quite inviting. Rooms cost US$100, less if you say you're here on business. Weekly and monthly discounts are available. Website: www.suitesambassador.com

The Executive Hotel (☎ 264-3333, fax 269-1944, hotelger@pty.com), at Avenida 3 Sur and Calle Aquilino de la Guardia, is a longtime favorite with the business crowd because of its central location, modern rooms and nightly open bar for guests. There's also a pool, restaurant and business center. The rates of US$100/110 single/ double are competitive, as the hotel's long-time popularity attests.

The landmark **Hotel El Panamá** (☎ 269-5000, fax 223-6080, reser as@elpanama.com), on Calle 49 B Oeste near Vía España, is a fine hotel with older, spacious poolside rooms that are much more desirable than the newer rooms (so request an older poolside room). In addition to the pool with swim-up bar, there's a casino, a bar and restaurants. Be advised that most of the hotel is not air conditioned, and that's discomforting to many guests. For the money – US$105/120 – you're better off elsewhere.
Website: www.elpanama.com

The **Hotel Continental** (☎ 263-9999, fax 269-4559, riande@sinfo.net), at Calle Ricardo Arias and Vía España, has come down in price in recent years but at US$105 per room (US$140/150 single/double if you fail to ask for the corporate rate!), it's still overpriced. Each guestroom is furnished with a handsome four-poster bed and a bathtub that has handrails – rare features in Panama. Ask for a room in the newer wing.

The **Hotel Riande Granada** (☎ 264-4900, fax 263-7179, granada@hotelesriande.com), on Calle Eusebio A Morales near Vía España, has elegant, very comfortable and fully equipped rooms – every one a junior suite – a pool, casino, bar and restaurant. If the pool and casino are important to you, then at US$130 for a junior suite and US$150 for an executive suite (20% less if you request the corporate rate) the Riande Granada is reasonably priced. If you're really only looking for a safe and appealing room in the desirable El Cangrejo district, stay at the Hotel Marbella, Sevilla Suites or the Coral Suites Aparthotel and save some money.

New in year 2000, the **DeVille Hotel** (☎ 206-3100, fax 206-3111), on Calle 50 Este-near Avenida 4 Sur, is an elegant addition to Panama City's hotel scene. All 33 rooms are suites, ranging from US$145 for a junior suite to US$325 for a grand suite. Expect to find in your beautifully appointed room an antique dresser from Thailand glistening with inlaid mother of pearl, a marble-topped antique table set with Louis XV chairs, custom bed linen made of Egyptian cotton at 300 knots per square inch, goose-feather pillows, finest-quality US-made mattresses, business desk with fax machine and Internet port, a spacious bathroom lined floor to ceiling with white marble imported from Italy, etc, etc. The facilities include a business center, meeting rooms and a terrific French restaurant. This is a wonderful find.
Website: www.devillehotel.com.pa

The elegant, 361-room **Hotel Caesar Park** (☎ 270-0477, fax 226-4262; in the USA ☎ 800-228-3000; info@caesarpark.com), is opposite the Centro Atlapa on Calle 77 Este near Vía Israel. Part of the Westin Hotels & Resorts chain, this is where heads of state usually stay when they visit Panama. Facilities include an athletic club and spa, three floodlit tennis courts, a swimming pool, three executive floors, a casino, a business center, a dance club, upscale stores, a casino and sports bar, and six restaurants (ranging from a pizzeria to a very popular all-you-can-eat buffet to an elegant, 15th-floor dining room with spectacular city views and prime rib to die for). Rates usually range from US$145 for a fully equipped 'standard' room to US$800 for a knock-out, drop-dead suite with awesome views. That said, weekend and promotional rates starting at US$99 are common, and even lower rates are often available to members of Westin's Starwood Preferred Guest program (www.starwood.com), which takes little time to join and membership is free.
Website: www.caesarpark.com

A member of the Rosewood Hotels & Resorts chain, **The Bristol** (☎ 265-7844, fax 265-7829 in the USA ☎ 888-767-3966), on Calle Aquilino de la Guardia, is an elegant hotel with marble and mahogany at every turn. The Rosewood group prides itself on personal service, and The Bristol is overflowing with it: Each guest is attended by a 24-hour butler. Personalized business cards are produced for the guest upon arrival. The guest can have a suit or dress pressed upon arrival. There's laundry service, shoeshine service, newspaper delivery; the list goes on and on. The lovely rooms are equipped with fax machines and separate Internet and telephone lines in addition to all the usual amenities. See the website (www.thebristol .com) for a virtual tour of the hotel. Rates start at US$175 per room.

Man of the People

Presidents from 13 Latin American countries attended a summit in Panama City during December 2000. All of the leaders stayed at the Hotel Caesar Park, in front of which were parked 13 brand-new silver Cadillacs, which Mireya Moscoso's administration purchased solely for the presidents' use while in country.

Due to the vehicles' cost at a time when many Panamanians struggle to make ends meet, Moscoso was widely criticized for ordering the purchase. By comparison, the government spent more money on the luxury cars than it spent promoting Panamanian tourism for the entire year.

As the so-called woman of the people took stabs at putting the Cadillac scandal behind her, a veteran politician scored points with Panama's poor. That person was Cuban President Fidel Castro, who, immediately after checking into the Caesar Park, rode a service elevator to the laundry level and one by one introduced himself to dozens of hotel workers.

'It was very impressive,' recalled executive chef Heiner Gellenberg, 'you know, having a living legend right next to you, shaking your hand.' He said that except for Castro's arrival, when the 76-year-old revolutionary used the hotel's main entrance and gave the hotel's general manager a warm embrace, Castro always came and left by the personnel entrance at the rear of the hotel.

'When he'd walk from the back of the house, these ladies from the housekeeping department would scream like groupies at a concert. He'd stop there and shake their hands and they were, like, all crazy,' Gellenberg said. 'He made a very, very good impression on people here.'

As Panama's press carried reports about what should be done with the 13 silver Cadillacs after the summit (they were eventually given to charities), the stories about Castro's kindness toward the workers at Caesar Park made the rounds among Panama City's poor.

PLACES TO EAT

There's no shortage of restaurants in Panama City. You won't have trouble finding cuisine from Italy, Spain, Mexico, Japan, Argentina, China, France, Lebanon, Britain and Greece. Of course, Panamanian specialties and seafood abound.

The international fast-food giants – *McDonald's*, *Burger King* and *KFC*, to name a few – are well represented. At the other end of the cholesterol spectrum, there are also a couple of vegetarian restaurants. The sections that follow lead with the best restaurant in each category in terms of quality of food, and (unless otherwise stated) I can recommend all the businesses mentioned here.

Panamanian

Restaurante-Bar Tinajas (☎ 263-7890, fax 264-4858), on Avenida 3 A Sur near Avenida Federico Boyd, is a large, multilevel restaurant decorated to resemble a traditional Península de Azuero village. Typical dishes include *pastel de yuca* (country pie made with yucca, chicken, corn, capers and raisins; US$7.50), *chuletas ahumadas* (smoked pork chops with honey-pineapple sauce; US$8.50) and *gaucho de mariscos* (fresh seafood stew, served with coconut rice; US$8.50). Tinajas is well known for its popular folkloric dance shows, offered at 9 pm on Tuesday, Thursday, and Friday nights; there's a US$5 entertainment fee on those nights. Tinajas is open 11:30 am to 11 pm Monday to Saturday.

Less costly than Tinajas but popular with both the working class and the pinstriped crowd is *Restaurante Boulevard Balboa*, on Avenida Balboa at Calle 31 Este. This place specializes in grilled sandwiches, few of which are over US$3, and burgers, which are US$1.50. Very popular is the *milanesa a caballo*, which consists of a breaded steak topped with two eggs served sunny-side up (US$4.50). If you're traveling on a tight budget and looking for a cheap but filling meal, this is a good place to visit. It's open 7 am to midnight daily.

The menu changes daily at *El Rincón Tableño*, on the corner of Calle 27 Este and Avenida Balboa. The items rotate at this open-air eatery, but the type of food never does: it's always 100% working-class Panamanian. Typical items include *sopa de carne* (meat soup; 90¢), *camarones guisados* (shrimp in tomato sauce; US$2.50), and *ropa ieja* (literally, 'old clothes'; marinated shredded beef with a mild red sauce; US$2.10). There are a half-dozen or so natural fruit juices to choose among, each priced less than US$1.

There are many inexpensive restaurants specializing mostly in chicken in the vicinity of Parque Santa Ana. The best of the bunch and a real neighborhood institution is the *Café Coca-Cola*, a very popular air-con diner that's open from 7:30 am to 11:30 pm daily. No breakfast items are over US$2. The long menu for lunch and dinner contains many beef, chicken and seafood plates, most under US$4. The most expensive item is the jumbo shrimp (US$6).

Next to the Hotel Lisboa is the *Restaurante Rincón Tableño*, which serves high-quality typical Panamanian food in a fan-cooled and clean environment. The waitresses here wear the traditional attire of the women of the Península de Azuero. In addition to lots of inexpensive food, you have lots of natural juices to choose from. If you select a bowl of *sancocho* (chicken and vegetable stew) and a glass of ice-cold papaya juice, you'll be styling!

If you're in the vicinity of the Hotel Veracruz and looking for a decent place to eat, look no farther. The hotel's *Comedor Las Palmas* is a popular diner with air con and a surprisingly long wine list. Daily specials are usually under US$4, with the best standard dish being the restaurant's *sancocho de gallina grande* (large bowl of chicken stew, US$3). The seafood soup (US$3.50) is also good. It's open 6 am to midnight daily.

Between the Panamá La Vieja ruins and the ocean is *El Trapiche.* It's known for *tamal de olla* (tamale casserole; US$3.75), corvina Capitán Morgan (sea bass with white sauce containing chunks of jumbo shrimp and lobster; US$12.50) and *cazuela de mariscos Panamá Viejo*, which contains lots of seafood (US$11.50). The restaurant, in the Mercado Nacional de Artesanías building, is open 8 am to 11 pm daily.

Seafood

The *Restaurant Mercado del Marisco*, on Avenida Balboa at Calle 15 Este, is, as its name says, the 'seafood market restaurant.' On the 2nd floor of Panama's two-story seafood market, this very casual place boasts 'the best and freshest fish and seafood in Panama' – and it delivers. The open-sided, fan-cooled diner has been popular since the day it opened in 1997, offering shrimp (US$4.95), squid (US$5.95), mussels (US$6.25), octopus (US$6.95), jumbo shrimp (US$7.95), lobster (from US$10 to US$19) and tropical king crab (US$19.95). Sea bass, guabina and red snapper all cost around US$6. It's open 6 am to 10 pm daily except Sunday.

Elegant and dressy *La Toja*, at Calle Uruguay and Avenida 4 A Sur, excels at *cor ina gratinada en salsa de cangrejo* (sea bass au gratin in crab sauce; US$14), *parrillada de mariscos* (grilled seafood, specifically lobster, shrimp, jumbo shrimp, octopus, squid and mussels; US$14.50) and *paella a la Valenciana* (Valencian-style paella; US$18 for two people). Its hours are noon to 11 pm daily.

The Panama Yacht Club, on Avenida Balboa near Calle 40 Este, has an excellent bar/restaurant called **La Marina**. This cozy 2nd-floor landmark is popular with the business crowd during lunch hours and with yuppies at night. Appetizers include soups (from US$2.75 to US$4), ceviche (US$4.50), clams in red sauce (US$4.50) and shrimp cocktail (US$6.75). Main dishes include sea bass (from US$8.50 to US$12), jumbo shrimp (US$15), paella (US$18) and lobster (US$25). It's open noon to 1 am daily.

The **Costa Azul**, on Calle Ricardo Arias about 100m south of Vía España, serves sea bass a dozen different ways (US$5.50 to US$9.50) and the light white fish guabina. The air-con restaurant's long menu also includes more than three dozen sandwiches (US$1.50 to US$4) and a wide variety of pasta, chicken and beef dishes. It's open 24 hours.

Although occasionally recommended by people who likely haven't eaten there, **La Casa del Marisco**, on Avenida Balboa, is very expensive and has a stuffy ambiance.

Spanish

There have been some nice additions to Casco Viejo in recent years and one such place is the **Café La Plaza**, next to the cathedral. Open from 6 pm 'til early the next morning, Café La Plaza is mostly a place to drink. There are no fewer than five varieties of sangria here, and many coffee drinks, including El Apostal, made with marshmallows, chocolate, chocolate ice cream and cashew nuts. Foodwise, Spanish *topas* are the establishment's strength. They consist of a potato tortilla, which is cooked with eggs, peppers, onions and a host of other ingredients; most of those ingredients are removed from the tortilla before it's served, but the tortilla captures their flavors.

Sandwiches and ceviche are also available. Few items are over US$5. There's often live jazz performed here weekend nights; there's never a cover charge.

Steaks

For beef, the name is **Martín Fierro**, on Calle Eusebio A Morales. The quality of meat here has no equal in the country. The top selections are US-imported 16oz New York rib steak (US$16), US-imported rib eye (US$22) and *bife chorizo* (US$9.50). Bife chorizo is the same cut as the New York steak, but it's local and grass fed. It's chewier but also tastier. Prices include salad bar and a choice of French fries, baked potato or rice. It's open noon to 3 pm and 6 to 11 pm Monday to Saturday and noon to 9:30 pm Sunday.

Gaucho's Steak House, at the corner of Calle Uruguay and Avenida 5 A Sur, is very popular and nicely decorated, but in my opinion the meat isn't quite as good as the meat at Martín Fierro. Selections include bife chorizo (US$11.50), *colita de cuadril* (beef tri tip; US$11.50) and *asado de tira* (beef short ribs; US$12.75). All the meat is imported from the USA. Hours are noon to 3 pm and 6 to 10:30 pm daily.

Brazilian

Os Segredos da Carne, on Vía Italia near the Hotel Plaza Paitilla Inn, is a Brazilian *churrasquería* (steak house), and this one is quite authentic and formal. The name of the game at any churrasquería is beef, and Os Segredos da Carne doesn't stray the course. Here, there's a salad bar (and some seafood to accommodate sensible people) – and no fewer than 21 cuts of meat, most beef cooked rotisserie-style on huge skewers (the way it's done in Brazil). The restaurant is open from noon 'til 12:30 am daily. Cost is US$25.

Argentinean

Restaurante Los Años Locos, on Calle 76 Este behind the Hotel Caesar Park, specializes in grilled Argentinean food. Its most popular dish is the *parrillada Los Años Locos* (mixed grilled meats; US$24 for two people). Its sea bass dishes (all are US$9.50) are also often ordered. People looking for traditional Argentinean dishes order *milanesa Napolitana* (breaded tenderloin with red sauce and mozzarella au gratin; US$12) or the *milanesa Los Años Locos* (breaded tenderloin with two eggs on top and a side of fries; US$12). A typical portion of meat served at this upscale and intimate restaurant weighs 1lb. There's a salad bar, too. Come with an appetite. Los Años Locos' hours are noon to 3 pm and 6 to 11 pm weekdays, noon to 9:30 pm weekends.

Café de Asís, facing Parque Bolívar in Casco Viejo, is a terrific place to go for an intimate evening conversation, and that's due to no accident. Owner Pablo Lo Giudice is from Buenas Aires, and he noticed that in Panama City there are few cafés there like there are in Buenas Aires – with just the right ambiance to inspire relaxed dialogue. With Café de Asís, Pablo opened the first café in Casco Viejo – and almost instantly it was a success. Located on the ground floor of a four-floor beautifully restored, century-old building, Café de Asís opens daily at 6 pm and stays open until 1 or 2 am. The house sangria is very good; food offerings include ceviche (US$5.50), nachos (US$6), and *pulpo endiablo* (deviled octopus, US$8.50).

Peruvian

The *Bar-Restaurante Chimborazo*, on Vía Jose Agustin Arango east of downtown, is both a lively bar on weekend nights and a traditional Peruvian restaurant with dozens of tables out back, each with its own thatched roof. There are 110 items on the menu of this family business. Among the more popular items are the *sopa de le antamuertos* (literally, 'soup to wake you from the dead,' figuratively a solution to male sexual dysfunction; a green soup of seafood, rice and cilantro for US$2.50), *sopa parihuela* (a spicy soup with chunks of seafood, crayfish and root; US$5.50), *filete de cor ina a lo macho* (sea bass served with shrimp, octopus and garlic; US$7) and *langostinos* (jumbo shrimp, prepared in 10 different ways; US$8). It's open 10 am to midnight daily.

French

La Cocotte, on Calle Urug from Avenida Balboa, h Parisian cuisine to Panama. Its chef Migny, studied at the Ecole Hotelliére Belliard from 1984 to 1987 and simultaneously underwent his training at the renowned Restaurant Jamin de Joel Robouchon of Paris. Appetizers include pâté de canard and sautéed mushrooms. Entrées include confit de canard and fresh salmon in a red wine sauce. Desserts include chocolate truffles, apple tarts and crêpes soufflées au chocolat. Dinners average US$30 to US$40. It's open for lunch and dinner weekdays, dinner only on Saturday; it's closed Sunday.

The *Restaurante Las Bóvedas*, on Plaza de Francia in Casco Viejo, is a lovely but overpriced French restaurant situated in the vaults of a 300-year-old fort. The dining rooms were used to house political prisoners for most of the 19th century. The menu varies daily, subject to the catch of the day, but typical prices are US$15 for filet of fish, US$17 for mixed meats and US$18 for a New York steak. This place is particularly well known for its *mero* (grouper). A guitarist performs in the last vault nightly except Friday and Saturday, when there's jazz (the music usually starts around 9 pm).

Another fine French restaurant is the *Restaurante Casco Viejo*, on Calle 53 Este at Calle 50. Some of the better offerings include French onion soup (US$6), escargots au gratin (US$8), veal tongue with passion-fruit sauce (US$16.50) and sea bass filet stuffed with lobster (US$19). Every Friday the popular bar swings into life with live bands, typically playing salsa or merengue. Hours are noon to 3 pm and 7 pm until the last patron decides to move on, Monday to Friday. There's no lunch on Saturday, when the Restaurante Casco Viejo opens at 7 pm.

Crêpes & Waffles, on Avenida 5 B Sur just west of Calle Aquilino de la Guardia, has been a hit since it opened in 1997. The most popular of the restaurant's many crêpes are *espinaca, queso ricotta y tomate Napolitano* (spinach, ricotta cheese and tomatoes; US$3.75); *mozzarella y tomate* (mozzarella

PANAMA

d tomatoes; US$3.75); and *lomito a la pimienta* (strips of roast beef with pepper sauce; US$5.75). There's also a fine selection of sandwiches and desserts. Crêpes & Waffles is open noon to 11 pm daily.

Japanese

Modern and stylish without being fancy, **Sushi Itto**, on Avenida 2 Sur just east of Calle 54 Este, offers traditional sushi and some combinations you'd never find in Japan (such as a maki roll with chicken inside). The combination plates are the best deals here, with an eight-piece plate going for US$9 and a 13-piece plate going for US$13.50. Some of the fish is purchased locally, but most comes from the USA and Chile. Hours are noon to 10 pm weekdays and 12:30 pm to midnight weekends.

All right, with the name **Bar Morales** you have good reason to wonder why it's listed under 'Japanese.' But this pleasant, seaside, air-con bar on Avenida Alfaro at Calle B in the Casco Viejo district offers some delicious sushi, as well as items from the grill and a good selection of sandwiches. Most prices are under US$8. Open 12:30 pm 'til midnight every day. Incidentally, the handsome building in which Bar Morales is located was once owned by Eusébio Morales, a well-known writer during the time of Panama's independence from Colombia.

At all teppan-style Japanese restaurants, including **Ginza Teppanyaki**, on Calle D at Calle Eusebio A Morales, a chef prepares your food on a scalding skillet directly in front of you. These places always tend to be expensive, and this one is no exception: the special dinner combination, which includes fish, prawns, chicken, steak, vegetables and rice, costs US$22. Most items, such as squid (US$6) and scallops (US$8), are cheaper, but you wouldn't order only one. Ginza Teppanyaki's hours are noon to 3 pm and 6 to 10:30 pm daily.

Across the street from Ginza Teppanyaki is **Restaurante Matsuei**, which is known for its sukiyaki (US$12) and tempura (US$13 for a filling combination plate), and for its long sushi bar, Panama's finest. Sushi here ranges from US$15 for eight local pieces

plus four rolls to US$30 for a seven-piece, four-roll combination with fish imported from Miami. Matsuei is open from noon to 11:30 pm Monday to Saturday and 6 to 11:30 pm Sunday.

Chinese

For Chinese food, **Madame Chang**, on Avenida 5 A Sur just west of Calle Aquilino de la Guardia, is hard to top. This elegant and dressy restaurant is known for its *pato al estilo Pekin* (Peking duck), priced at US$20/40 for a half/whole duck; its *filete 'tit pang'* (sizzling sliced beef with oyster sauce; US$10.75) and its *pichón en pétalos de lechuga* (a combination of duck, chicken and pigeon, served on a bed of crispy rice noodles; US$15). Hours are noon to 3 pm and 6 to 11 pm Monday to Saturday and noon to 11 pm Sunday.

Palacio Lung Fung, a huge restaurant on Calle 62 C Oeste at the entrance to the Los Angeles neighborhood, is less expensive than the Madame Chang and is very good. One popular combination, for example, consists of soup, pork with almonds and vegetables, beef chop suey, shrimp rolls, chicken fried rice, and jasmine tea or coffee; cost is US$9. This restaurant serves dim sum until 11 am every day. It's open 6:30 am to 11 pm daily.

Nobu, at Calles Uruguay and 4 A Sur, which is owned by a Chinese man and his Japanese wife, specializes in Chinese food but also has a sushi bar. This fairly elegant and popular restaurant with a lovely full bar is known for its *arroz frito Nobu* (fried rice, vegetables, pork and shrimp; US$6.75 for two people or US$8.75 for four), tempura (US$2 to US$12), *filete Nobu* (chopped filet of beef served with oyster sauce; US$12.75) and its combination sushi plate that consists of 10 pieces (US$20). Hours are noon to 3 pm and 6 to 11 pm Tuesday to Sunday; closed Monday.

Italian

Established in 1963 and today one of the country's top restaurants, **Restaurante de las Americas** is on Calle 57 Este just south of Avenida 1 Sur. The specialty of the house is *ra iolis erdes rellenos de salmón ahumado con salsa de puré* (green raviolis stuffed with smoked salmon, covered with a heavy sauce of tomato and cream; US$13.75). The *capellini importados a la marichelle* (imported capellini with cream, tomato and prosciutto; US$13) is also excellent. Some people say the *sopa de pata* (hoof soup; US$5) is the best in Panama. It's open noon to 10 pm Tuesday to Sunday.

The same award-winning food that's available at Restaurante de las Americas for big money can be had for a fraction of the cost at the restaurant's takeout kiosk around the corner, on Avenida 1 Sur near Calle 56 Este, and you don't need to get dressed up for the kiosk. What a deal!

Not quite up to par with Restaurante de las Americas but still very good, *Tre Scalini*, on Avenida 3 Sur, is most noted for its *pasta prima era especial* (eggplant in white wine sauce, served with spaghetti or fettuccine; US$8.75), *filete Tre Scalini* (filet of beef in red wine, onions, peppers and mushrooms; US$12.75) and *spaguettini o fetuccini a la pepperonccino con langostinos o langosta* (spaghetti or fettuccine prepared with peppers and butter, with jumbo shrimp or lobster; US$15). This casual-to-dressy business is open noon to 3 pm and 6 to 11 pm daily.

Much less expensive and quite popular is *Caffé Pomodoro*, at Calle 49 B Oeste and Avenida 2 A Norte. There's seating inside and outside in this casual but classy restaurant. The antipasti run from US$2 for grilled Italian bread topped with fresh tomato and basil up to US$9 for smoked salmon. The main course consists of a noodle and sauce selection, with no combination over US$9 (and most nearly half that). There's a takeout service next door. Remember this place for breakfasts, too: yogurt with fruit (US$2.75), pancakes (US$3) or a plate of fresh fruit (US$4). It's open 7 am to midnight daily.

A very popular and pleasant restaurant with a varied menu and a specialty in pasta and seafood is *Cafeteria Manolo*, on the corner of Calle 49 B Oeste and Calle D. Gut-busting dinners here will run you about US$8. If you don't want to spend that much, there are 25 sandwiches to choose among, none over US$4. Breakfasts run about US$3.50 and include numerous egg, pancake and omelet offerings. Manolo features a full bar and indoor and outdoor seating. Hours are 6 am to 2 am daily. A very pleasant place.

The Wine Bar, located on the ground floor of the Las Vegas Suites Hotel, opened in 2000 and soon after was the hippest restaurant in Panama City. Open from 5 pm to 1 am daily, The Wine Bar does indeed have a large selection of fermented grape juices, with per-bottle prices ranging from US$11 to US$398. Most of the intoxicating beverage is also available by the *copa*. For food, The Wine Bar offers a long menu of cheese plates, appetizers, and entrées, all plucked from Italy. Daily pasta specials generally cost about US$8 and are delicious. Budget travelers will appreciate the many individual-size pizzas (most under US$5) and low-cost dishes such as the chicken lasagna for US$6. There's live jazz here most nights starting at 9 pm.

Pizza

Panama's oldest pizzeria, *Restaurante y Pizzeria Napoli No 1*, on Calle Estudiante at Lado del Instituto Nacional, just south of Avenida de los Mártires, serves tasty and cheap pizzas fast. A 10-inch combo costs only US$3 and a 15-incher only US$7.50; most small pizzas cost less than US$3, and most large ones about US$6.50. Its clam pizza (US$3.50/7.50 small/large) is quite popular. Also popular are the pastas, particularly the raviolis (US$2.50 to US$4) and the fettuccines (US$2.50 to US$5). The same man who opened this Napoli in 1962 has opened several others around town (there's another on Calle 56 Este south of Avenida 1 Sur). Hours are 11 am to 11 pm daily except Tuesday.

Restaurante y Pizzeria Sorrento, on Calle Ricardo Arias near Avenida 3 Sur, is known throughout the city for serving a large plate of clams in a delicious tomato or garlic sauce for only US$3. Its lasagna cardinale (US$3.50) and fettuccine carbonara

(US$4) are also divine. Its pizzas are cooked in a wood-burning oven and are greaseless, except for the ones with pepperoni or sausage. Still going strong since it opened in 1968, Sorrento charges US$2.50 to US$5 for its 10-inch pizzas. This is an excellent find. Hours are 11:30 am to 11:30 pm Tuesday to Saturday; it's closed Monday.

Restaurante Firenze, at Avenida 4 C Sur and Calle 79 Este, offers 20 pasta, seafood and meat dishes, but it's best known for its pizzas, which range from US$2.75 for a small cheese to US$13 for a large with the works. Pasta dishes go for US$6.50 to US$9.59, meat US$5 to US$12 and seafood US$8.50 to US$17.50. There's indoor and outdoor seating at the popular, very casual diner.

Pizzeria Solemio, on Calle Uruguay, is an Italian-owned and -run air-con restaurant with checkerboard tablecloths and an amiable owner everyone knows as Felice 'El Italiano.' The eatery excels at thin-crust pizzas cooked in a wood-fired oven and priced at US$7 or less for a medium size. Also on the menu are a generous portion of pasta and fish and meat dishes. By the way, the wine is imported from Italy, and the bread that's served is baked at the restaurant every morning. Open 11 am to 3 pm, and 6 to 11 pm Tuesday through Sunday, closed Monday.

Greek

One of the best values in town is *Niko's Cafe*. The original Niko's opened years ago, the dream of a Greek immigrant who initially sold food from a cart, then from a stand and then at the Niko's Cafe No 1 on Calle 51 Este near Vía España. Today there are five Niko's, each owned and managed by a son. The four newer ones are very 'in' these days, and all offer burgers (US$1), breakfasts (US$2), excellent gyros (US$3), pasta (from US$1.25 to US$3.50) and filet mignon (US$3.50). OK, so the food's not very Greek, but it sure is a bargain. And all five restaurants are open 24 hours a day. (You'll find one inside Panama City's bus terminal.)

Athen's, on the corner of Calle Uruguay and Avenida 4 Sur, serves excellent Greek food and pizza, including a delicious roast-beef pizza. Prices are very reasonable, and there are tables inside (where there's air con) or outside on the covered verandah. It's open 11 am to 10 pm daily except Tuesday. There's a second Athen's on Calle 56 Este.

Mexican

Carlos 'N Charlie's, located on the ground floor of the same building that houses Señor Frog's dance club, features *lots* of Mexican fare at tourist prices: taco salad (US$8), beef tips Mexican style (with chilis, onions and garlic; US$10), and a variety of tasty burgers (all around US$6). Open for lunch and dinner, from 11:30 am to midnight daily.

The very casual and low-priced *La Mexicanita* has two locations: on Avenida 4 Sur near Calle Uruguay and on Calle 53 Este close to Calle Anastacio Ruíz Noriega. Typical and tasty items on the long menu include an order of three tacos of your choice (from US$2.75 to US$3), a burrito especial (US$3.60) and an enchilada con salsa roja (US$4.85).

British

El Pavo Real, on Avenida 3 B Sur near Calle Ricardo Arias, attracts yuppies on the prowl for business and social partners. It also attracts quite a few gringos who read about the place in John le Carré's thriller *The Tailor of Panama*. (The British Foreign Service employee turned best-selling novelist spent a lot of time here while conducting research for his book. The pub/restaurant's owner, Sarah Simpson, is also an ex-BFS employee. Coincidence?) The food here is delicious and filling. The offerings include a burger with fries (US$3.50), chicken breast sandwich served on a French roll (US$4.75) and fish 'n' chips (US$6.50). Popular local rock bands play here most Wednesday, Thursday and weekend nights after 9:30 pm; there's never a cover charge. There are dart boards and pool tables to boot. It's open from noon to midnight daily except Sunday.

Lebanese

Café du Líban, on Avenida Alfaro, is not a café at all, but rather a full-blown Lebanese restaurant with tables on two floors as well as outside facing the Bahía de Panamá and downtown Panama City. The decor, down to the attire of the waiters who were imported from Lebanon, is very Middle Eastern, as you'd hope, and the chef/owner is himself from Beirut. Indeed, Giorgio Cheaitelly prepares all of the dishes himself, and they are delicious. This restaurant caters to Panama's elite class, with prices to match. If you arrive and there's a wait, ask to smoke from the hookah, and the pipe will soon come your way. Most appetizers run around US$6, main plates US$12 to $15. Open noon until 11 pm daily.

Vegetarian

Restaurante Vegetariano Mireya, at Calle Ricardo Arias and Avenida 3 Sur, is a budget traveler's delight, with scarcely any item over US$1.25. Typical offerings at this very low-key establishment include eggplant with vegetables (US$1.25), a soy burger (US$1.25), cauliflower and potatoes (US$1.25), yogurt (75¢) and many juices to choose among (US$1). Hours are 6 am to 8 pm daily except Sunday.

International

Mango's, on Calle Uruguay one block north of Avenida Balboa, is popular with Panamanian yuppies. While the crowd is often dressed for success, the decor is informal and cozy. Large works of illuminated stained glass, many tables angled for visibility and yet allowing privacy, and a long, handsome bar create an intimate setting even when the place is packed. And there's not a weakness on the menu. Among my favorites are the house burger (US$4.25), the Greek salad (US$5.50) and the fettuccine carbonara (US$6.75). It's open daily from noon until the last customer decides to leave. Live bands play on Thursday, Friday and Saturday nights (US$5 cover).

The semiformal **Le Bistrot**, on Calle 53 Este near Calle Anastacio Ruíz Noriega, is well known for its appetizer *calamar relleno de cangrejo* (squid stuffed with crabmeat and cooked in its own ink), which goes for US$12 for a half order and US$4 more for a

full order. Other house spe *callos con garbanzos* (tripe US$10.50) and *langostin* (jumbo shrimp and crabme mushroom sauce; US$18). Le Bistrot is open 11:30 am to 11:30 pm daily.

La Cascada, on the corner of Avenida Balboa and Calle 25 Este, is a good place for a pleasant evening out. It has a large garden dining patio and a bilingual menu with many choices. The meals are gigantic and very reasonably priced; for US$5.25 you can get an excellent steak or sea bass filet, or try the giant seafood platter (US$9.25). It's open 3 to 11 pm Monday to Saturday.

Ozone, on trendy Calle Uruguay near Avenida 5 A Sur, is a terrific find. This comfortable, stylish restaurant is renowned for its excellent salads (most US$6.50, US$8.75 with chicken), but it also serves a tasty chicken curry (US$9.50), a delicious linguini salmón (US$9.75) and a good Jamaican jerked chicken sandwich (US$7). There are also several well-prepared Middle Eastern appetizers on the menu, including hummus and baba ghanoush (both US$4.50). Open noon to 3:30 pm and 6 to 10:30 pm daily.

Ice Cream

The best ice cream in town is sold at **Il Gelatiere**, on Avenida Belisario Porras at Avenida 3 L Sur, a six-block walk from the Hotel Caesar Park. As you may have guessed, Il Gelatiere specializes in Italian ice cream. This cheerful little ice cream parlor and restaurant also offers tasty but cheap pizzas, a dozen sandwiches, delicious cookies and many desserts. It's open from 11 am to 11 pm daily.

ENTERTAINMENT

Panama City has *mucho* to offer in this area, especially to party animals. The club scene ignites about 11 pm and its embers are still glowing at sunrise. The cinemas throughout town show the latest Hollywood releases, usually in English, with or without Spanish subtitles. There's plenty of casinos in town for you gamblers, and there are numerous strip clubs and brothels for you horn dogs.

For information about cultural events in the capital city, check *Talingo*, a supplement that appears in the newspaper *La Prensa* every Sunday and lists happenings for the coming week.

Clubs

The club scene in Panama City is quite vivacious, but don't bother arriving at any of the clubs mentioned here before 11 pm; the nightlife doesn't start to heat up before then. Also, keep in mind that Panamanians are dressy people. At clubs, local men wear office-appropriate attire, and local women generally deck out in black dresses and black heels. Male travelers will want to bring with them at least one dress shirt, one pair of slacks and one pair of leather shoes. Female travelers will want to bring at least one dress and appropriate footwear.

Due to a severe parking shortage, even if you're renting a vehicle in Panama, you'll want to take a taxi if you'll be clubbing in the Calle Uruguay area. Also, remember to bring identification with you, as you might be asked for it.

Rock A *Señor Frog's* opened in Panama City in 2000 and quickly leaped to the forefront of the city's dance-club scene. Located on the second floor of a building on Avenida 5 A Sur, Señor Frog's consists chiefly of one large room done up in cheesy Mexican-American decor with a bandstand against one wall and bars against two others. Tables and chairs fill most of the floor, which, oddly, makes dancing a bit awkward (it is a dance club, after all). There's live music most Wednesday, Thursday, Friday and Saturday nights, with a typical cover charge of US$7.

Another hot dance club is *Bacchus*, on Calle 49 A Este south of Vía España. Decorated in an elaborate Roman theme, this place has state-of-the-art sound and light systems, a big-screen TV and strategically placed monitors for rock videos, occasional live bands and the requisite liquid-smoke machine. All that's missing is Travolta. Cover charge is typically US$10; the club is closed Monday.

Café Dalí, on Calle 5 B Sur, is yet another hip, beautiful-people dance club, which features a long, wooden bar, lots of couples tables and a substantial dance floor. This upscale club wouldn't be out of place in New York or Toronto, and indeed the music that booms out of the club's big black speakers when a band isn't performing is usually American rock 'n' roll. There's live music Fridays only. There's a US$10 cover charge most days; the cost of admission includes two drinks.

Down the street from Señor Frog's is *Skap*. What it lacks in smart decor (the walls are painted orange and are otherwise bare), it makes up for in noise. This is a very popular dance club, but really not one of the better ones. There's live music weekend nights, and generally a cover charge of US$8 or US$10.

'Meat market' accurately describes *TGI Friday's*, on Calle Aquilino de la Guardia, just about the witching hour on its namesake night. Since there's no live music, just canned rock 'n' roll, most people who saunter in have something other than dancing on their minds. Unlike the loud dance clubs, you can actually converse here. There's never a cover charge. A second TGI Friday's was under construction in 2001 near the entrance of the Causeway.

Mango's is a beautiful-people restaurant by day and a rock scene with live bands on Thursday, Friday and Saturday nights. It's on Calle Uruguay. (If you're standing in the bay, you really meant to go one block the *other* way.) There's a second, even pulpier Mango's at Plaza Edison on Vía Brasil. It also features live music on Thursday, Friday and Saturday nights, and the cover charge is usually around US$8.

Without the same level of zaniness of some of the above clubs, but also never charging an entrance fee, is *El Pavo Real*, on Avenida 3 B Sur. Home to strong rock 'n' roll bands on Friday and Saturday nights, the Peacock (its English name) is very popular with locals and visitors alike. It's an easy place to meet people because its two pool tables lend themselves nicely to newcomers asking to join in. It's open until midnight every night but Sunday.

At all the aforementioned places, you can enter with a receding hairline or support stockings and not feel out of place. But *Rock Café*, on the corner of Calles 53 Este and Anastacio Ruíz Noriega, isn't that kind of place. You practically have to be under 25 to get in, and once you're inside it's wall-to-wall youth, very dark and best enjoyed by people who love secondhand smoke. The music's live most nights and, despite the club's name, it's usually salsa, not rock. The cover is usually US$10.

Aleph Café, on Vía Argentina at Vía España, features one rock 'n' roll band every Tuesday night. This is the place where new Panamanian bands usually get their start. The cover charge varies with the popularity of the band, but is normally no more than US$5.

Jazz A lovely place to listen to live jazz is *Restaurante Las Bóvedas*, on Plaza de Francia in Casco Viejo. The bands set up at one end of this former dungeon with 4m-thick brick walls and play to a fairly small audience tucked into intimate cushioned niches along the walls. The acoustics are perfect and the atmosphere is something special. Jazz is offered on Friday and Saturday nights only, from 9 pm to 1 am. There usually isn't a cover charge. Las Bóvedas is known for its *caipirinhas*, Brazilian drinks made from cachaça, lemon juice, sugar and ice.

Another place to hear jazz is the lobby-level *Mi Rincón* lounge of the Hotel Caesar Park, on Calle 77 Este one block from the bay. Jazz is featured every Wednesday night with the Jimmy Maxwell Quartet. There's no cover.

Salsa & Merengue The elegant French *Restaurante Casco Viejo*, on the corner of Calle 53 Este and Calle 50, has a very popular bar that features live music, usually salsa or merengue, every Friday night. The cover charge is typically US$10 but can be more.

Salsa can also be heard at Rock Café. See the preceding Rock section for details.

Cuban Five nights a week at the Hotel Plaza Paitilla Inn, on Vía Italia at Avenida Churchill, you can enjoy a group of talented Cuban musicians and dancers who go by the name of *Cole-Cole*. The singing and dancing is thrilling, really worthwhile. The price of the show is a bargain at US$10. Shows are held Tuesday and Saturday, starting at 10 pm. For reservations, call ☎ 263-6759, cellular ☎ 697-0942 or send an email to aparicio@hotmail.com.

Folk/Traditional Music The *Restaurante-Bar Tinajas* (☎ 263-7890, fax 264-4858, rest_tinajas@cwp.net.pa), on Avenida 3 A Sur near Avenida Federico Boyd, presents Panamanian folkloric dancing at 9 pm on Tuesday, Thursday, Friday and Saturday nights. There's a US$5 charge. Most guests have dinner during the show; meals run about US$15 per person including drink, tip and tax. These shows are very popular – reservations are recommended.

Gay & Lesbian As mentioned in the Gay & Lesbian Travelers section of the Facts for the Visitor chapter, gay clubs aren't easy to find. They're never advertised, their façades are never suggestive and even their names aren't always posted, so eager are the establishments' owners to avoid problems with gay-bashers and other intolerant people.

That said, the country's largest and wildest gay dance club, *Boy Bar*, is in Panama City next to an ice factory on an unnamed street in an industrial area north of downtown. There is no sign in front of the club, which occupies a former auto-painting shop and looks like every other structure in the neighborhood, but its entire façade is painted black. There's no cover charge on Thursday, when all drinks are US$1.25 apiece. On Friday and Saturday you pay US$7 at the door and drinks are free. On Sunday there's no cover and all drinks are US$1 each. The music is mostly recorded. There's a show with live music monthly, usually for charity; the date varies. Call ☎ 230-3128 for further details (English-speakers should ask to speak with Minerva, Spanish-speakers with Irving). Boy Bar, open 10 pm to 7 am Thursday to Sunday, is best reached by taxi; drivers often know the place as Le Garage.

A little closer to downtown is another popular dance club, **El Hidalgo**, on Vía Brasil near Vía España (it's a low-profile place, so you might have to ask someone to point it out). Also known to taxi drivers as Pasos (its name for many years), El Hidalgo is very popular late on weekend nights, when it usually features a male strip show (and a US$10 cover charge). But unlike Boy Bar, there's never live music here.

Most of Panama City's gay and lesbian clubs, however, are at the fringes of the Casco Viejo district. Typically the clubs consist of one long, narrow room with a dozen or so couples' tables scattered about, a bar to one side and a jukebox in the back. What they lack in decor they make up for in atmosphere.

Among the most popular of the bunch near Casco Viejo are **Boite La Cosmopolita**, at Calles C and 13 Oeste; **Salon Madrid**, on Calle 12 Oeste between Calles B and C; and **Bar Tropical**, on Calle B near Calle 12 Oeste (be advised there's no signage out front of the Bar Tropical, which is two doors down from the Hotel Colón, and its doors only open after dark). There are a good many other gay bars in the area.

Cinemas
There's no shortage of movie theaters in town; many are on the main boulevard, Vía España. Check the yellow pages under *Cines* for a list of cinemas, with addresses. Check the daily entertainment pages of *La Prensa* for listings and show times.

Casinos
None of the casinos are on the verge of stealing business away from the megacasinos of Las Vegas, but there are three attractive and popular houses of chance in the capital city and three others that simply serve their purpose. All are located inside top hotels.

The three most attractive casinos can be found in the **Hotel Caesar Park**, the **Miramar Inter-Continental** and the **Hotel El Panamá**. The three others are in the **Hotel Plaza Paitilla Inn**, the **Gran Hotel Soloy** and the **Hotel Riande Granada**. See Places to Stay for telephone numbers and addresses.

Theater
Performances by the experimental theater troupe Oveja Negra (Black Sheep) are periodically held at the **Alianza Francesa Panameña** (☎ 223-5792), on Calle 43 Este. Productions are also held at the **Teatro En Circulo** (☎ 261-5375) on Avenida 6 C Norte near Vía Transístmica, and the **Teatro Nacional** (☎ 262-3525) on Avenida B at Calle 3. Check *Talingo* for upcoming performances.

Strip Clubs & Brothels
Prostitution in Panama is legal and, despite the moral issues and sexual diseases at play, business is booming on the isthmus. If you're a young man far from home, you may be tempted to enter one of these places. The information given here is intended only to inform, not to promote.

In Panama City there are two kinds of sex parlors, both geared for men: There are fancy strip clubs, and there are rooms-in-the-back brothels. The strip parlors have fancy names: **Josephine's Gold**, **Elite**, **Le Palace** and so on. They open in the evening on most days, and they close around 4 am. There's no cover charge, but what they don't get out of you at the door they'll get out of you in drinks; a beer usually costs US$3, and well drinks US$4 and up.

These places are swarming with young women in lingerie, and about every 30 minutes one of them appears on stage and removes her clothes, usually to French music. All the women are available for lap dances (usually US$15 per dance), and all are available for 'servicing,' as they call it here; typically, you pay the establishment US$50 and negotiate a price with the woman. The servicing that's provided by these women is expected to take place at a hotel.

The brothels – **La Gruta Azul**, **La Gloria**, **Club Fenix**, **Club Costa Brava** – follow the same basic design: a large room, well-stocked bar, lots of little tables and dim lighting. Some have strip stages. Most have a half-dozen rooms in the back; the price charged varies with the services that the women perform.

Regardless of the club, these women are justly terrified of AIDS and insist on using condoms. If you're considering a visit to any of these places, you ought to read the Sexually Transmitted Diseases section in the Facts for the Visitor chapter first.

SHOPPING

Most anything that you can buy in other modern capital cities you can find in Panama City. This is so because many of the stores in Colón's Zona Libre have outlets in the capital. Often these outlets can arrange to have an item from a Colón store – a particular Rolex watch or Nikon camera, for example – sent from Colón to Tocumen airport, where you can pick it up just prior to leaving the country; you can avoid the sales tax by doing business this way.

Because of their proximity to mineral-rich Colombia and Brazil, the jewelry stores here often have high-quality gems at excellent prices. Beware: There are many fake gems on the world market, as well as many flawed gems that have been altered to appear more valuable than they really are. The only jewelry store here with which I have done business is the very reputable **Joyeria La Huaca**, in front of the Hotel Continental at Calle Ricardo Arias and Vía España. A high-quality sapphire ring made for me there cost one-third less than I would have paid for it in Los Angeles or New York.

The most authentically Panamanian items to take home are described below. The handicrafts mentioned here can often be found at the **Mercado de Buhonerías y Artesanías**, behind the Reina Torres de Araúz anthropological museum; at **Mi Pueblito**, a life-size replica of a rural village at the foot of Cerro Ancón near the intersection of Avenida de los Mártires and Calle Jeronimo de la Ossa; and at the **Mercado Nacional de Artesanías**, beside the ruins of Panamá La Vieja.

Additionally, **Colecciones**, a well-priced, high-quality crafts and furniture store facing the Hotel Plaza Paitilla Inn on Vía Italia,

The National Hat

The classic woven-straw hat that many people associate with Panama was made internationally famous in the late 19th century by Ferdinand de Lesseps, builder of the Suez Canal and the brains behind the failed French attempt to build a canal in Panama.

The much-photographed Lesseps was balding when he arrived in Panama, and he found that the light but durable hat provided excellent protection against the sun. Most newspaper photographs taken of him here showed the larger-than-life figure looking even more worldly in his exotic headgear. Soon men around the globe began placing orders for the 'Panama hat.'

Oddly, most Panama hats are made in Ecuador, just as they always have been. Some hats of this style are made in Panama, however, and the best-quality ones can be found in the towns of Ocú (Herrera Province) and Penonomé (Coclé Province). The Ocú hats are always white; the hats from everywhere else are black-and-white. The finest Panama hats are so tightly woven that they can hold water.

Ferdinand de Lesseps

often has tagua carvings and baskets made by the Emberá and Wounaan peoples. The store's owner, Irene De Vengoechea, also stocks top-quality ceramics and serving trays from Mexico, hammocks from Colombia, Filipino handicrafts of a quality one rarely sees, and much more.

Huacas

It's possible to purchase high-quality replicas of *huacas* – golden objects made on the isthmus centuries before the Spanish conquest and placed with Indians at the time of burial. The Indians believed in an afterlife, and the huacas were intended to accompany and protect their souls on the voyage to the other world.

The huacas were mainly items of adornment, the most fascinating being three-dimensional figure pendants. Most took the form of a warrior, crocodile, jaguar, frog or condor. Little else is known about the exact purpose of these golden figures, but probably each held mystical, spiritual or religious meaning.

You can purchase exact (solid gold) and near-exact (gold-plated) reproductions of these palm-size objects. They are available at reasonable cost at *Reprosa* (☎ 269-0457, fax 269-3902, sales1@reprosa.com), at Avenida 2 Sur and Calle 54 Este. Also available here are well-priced necklaces made of black onyx and other gemstones. If you're looking for something special to bring back for a loved one, this is the place to come. Open 9 am to 7 pm Monday through Saturday.

Baskets

The Wounaan and Emberá in Darién Province produce some beautiful woven baskets, most of which are exported to the USA and Europe, although many can be found in Panama. The Guaymís in Chiriquí and Veraguas Provinces also produce baskets, but they are of an inferior quality and in little demand.

The baskets of the Wounaan and Emberá are of two types: the utilitarian and the decorative. The utilitarian baskets are made primarily from the chunga palm but can contain bits of other plants, vines, bark and leaves. They are usually woven, using various plaiting techniques, from single plant strips of coarse texture and great strength. They are rarely dyed. These baskets are often used for carrying seeds or harvesting crops.

The decorative baskets are much more refined, usually feature many different colors and are created from palm materials of the nahuala bush and the chunga tree. The dyes are 100% natural and are extracted from fruits, leaves, roots and bark. Typical motifs are of butterflies, frogs, toucans, trees and parrots. The baskets are similar in quality to the renowned early 20th-century Chemehuevi Indian baskets of California.

You can often buy baskets at Colecciones (see above) and at Gran Morrison stores (see the Central Panama City map for two locations).

Wood & Tagua Carvings

In addition to producing fine baskets, the Wounaan and Emberá also carve animal figures from the wood of the cocobolo tree and the ivory-colored tagua nut (variously known as the palm seed, ivory nut and vegetable ivory). The figures made from the tropical hardwood are often near-life-size; popular subjects are boas, toucans and parrots. From the egg-size tagua nut come miniature iguanas, crocodiles and birds.

The quality of both the cocobolo and tagua carvings can be very fine. A superior cocobolo boa, for example, is a meter or more in length, with its back polished shiny-smooth and its underside a field of perfectly carved scales. Its eyes and mouth are delicately formed and its head perfectly proportioned. The highly honed skills of a true craftsperson are readily apparent in the finest of these carvings.

A high-quality tagua carving is also finely carved, well proportioned and realistic, if miniature. While the natural color of cocobolo figures is left unchanged, the tagua nut – after it is carved with hand tools and polished with fine abrasives – is beautifully painted with vibrant colors, using India inks and natural plant extracts.

The best place to shop for tagua carvings is *Galería Bernheim*, in the Tronlap Building on Avenida 4 Sur near Calle Aquilino de la Guardia. Cocobolo carvings can be found at Gran Morrison department stores.

Molas

A popular handicraft souvenir from Panama is the *mola*, a colorful, intricate, multilayered appliqué textile sewn by Kuna women. Small, simple souvenir molas are widely available in Panama City and can be bought for as little as US$5, but the best ones are sold on the San Blás islands and can fetch several hundred dollars.

Flory Salzman Molas, on Calle 49 B Oeste, has a large selection. Molas are also on sale in stores inside the Hotel El Panamá, the Hotel Caesar Park and other upscale hotels. Gran Morrison stores also stock molas.

Artwork

The works of some of Panama's best contemporary painters and sculptors can be viewed and purchased at a number of galleries around the city. Try *Galería y Enmarcado Habitante*, on Calle Uruguay; *Mvsevm*, on Vía Italia near the Hotel Plaza Paitilla Inn; *Galería Bernheim* (see Wood & Tagua Carvings, earlier); *Legacy Fine Art*, in the Centro Comercial Balboa on Avenida Balboa near Calle Aquilino de la Guardia; and *Galería Arteconsult*, on Avenida 2 Sur between Calles 55 Este and 56 Este.

GETTING THERE & AWAY
Air

International flights arrive at and depart from Tocumen International Airport, 35km northeast of the city center. See the Getting There & Away chapter for more information about the airport and services to Panama.

International airlines serving Panama City from the USA include the following:

airline	in Panama
American Airlines	☎ 269-6022
Continental Airlines	☎ 263-9177
COPA	☎ 227-5000
Delta Air Lines	☎ 214-8118
EVA Air	☎ 270-2222
Mexicana	☎ 264-9855
United Airlines	☎ 213-9824

Airlines serving Panama City from Europe include Iberia from Spain and LTU International Airways charters from Germany. Numerous Central and South American airlines serve the city from Latin America and the Caribbean; see the Getting There & Away chapter for details.

Five airlines provide service between Panama City and other parts of the country. Flight information follows, in order of destination, airline, one-way airfare, departure time(s) and day(s) of departure. The phone numbers given are the airlines' reservation numbers at Aeropuerto Albrook. Note: Aerotaxi and Ansa have identical flight schedules and fares.

Achutupo – Aereotaxi (☎ 315-0300) & Ansa (☎ 315-7520), US$34, 6 am Monday through Saturday (via Playón Chico); Aviatur (☎ 315-0307), US$34, 6 and 9 am Monday through Saturday; 12:30 and 1 pm Tuesday, Thursday and Sunday

Ailigandí – Aereotaxi (☎ 315-0300) & Ansa (☎ 315-7520), US$34, 6 am Monday through Saturday; Aviatur (☎ 315-0307), US$34, 6 and 9 am Monday through Saturday; 12:30 pm Tuesday, Thursday and Sunday

Bahía Piña – Aeroperlas (☎ 315-7500), US$44, 9:30 am Tuesday, Thursday, Saturday; Aviatur (☎ 315-0307), US$44, 9:30 am Monday, Wednesday and Friday

Bocas del Toro town – Aeroperlas (☎ 315-7500), US$50, 8:30 am and 1:30 pm Monday through Friday; 7 am Saturday; 2 pm Sunday; Aero Mapiex (☎ 315-0888), US$50, 9:15 am Monday through Friday; 6:30 am Saturday; 12:30 pm Sunday

Caledonia – Aviatur (☎ 315-0307), US$36, 9 am Monday through Saturday; 12:30 pm Tuesday, Thursday and Sunday

Cartí – Aereotaxi (☎ 315-0300) & Ansa (☎ 315-7520), US$29, 6 am Monday through Saturday (via Corazón de Jesús); 7 am Sunday (via Corazón de Jesús); Aviatur (☎ 315-0307), US$29, 6 and 9 am Monday through Saturday; 7 and 8 am Sunday

Changuinola – Aeroperlas (☎ 315-7500), US$53, 8:30 am and 1:30 pm Monday through Friday (via Bocas del Toro town); 7 am and 3 pm Saturday (via Bocas del Toro town); 8 am Sunday (via Bocas del Toro town); 3 pm Sunday (nonstop); Aero Mapiex (☎ 315-0888), US$53, 9:15 am Monday through Friday; 6:30 am Saturday; 12:30 pm Sunday

Chitré – Aeroperlas (☎ 315-7500), US$32, 7:40 am and 4:15 pm Monday through Saturday; 4:15 pm Sunday

Colón – Aeroperlas (☎ 315-7500), US$36, 7:15, 8:15 and 9:15 am and 3:55, 4:55 and 5:40 pm Monday through Friday

Corazón de Jesús – Aereotaxi (☎ 315-0300) & Ansa (☎ 315-7520), US$30, 6 am Monday through Saturday; 7 am Sunday; Aviatur (☎ 315-0307), US$30, 6 and 9 am Monday through Saturday; 7 and 8 am Sunday

David – Aeroperlas (☎ 315-7500), US$57, 6:30 and 10:30 am and 2 pm Monday through Friday; 7 and 10:30 am and 2 pm Saturday; 8 am and 4 pm Sunday; Aero Mapiex (☎ 315-0888), US$57, 6:25 am Monday through Thursday; 6:25 am and 12 and 4 pm Friday; 10:30 am and 4 pm Saturday; 9 am and 3:30 pm Sunday

El Porvenir – Aereotaxi (☎ 315-0300) & Ansa (☎ 315-7520), US$30, 6 am Monday through Saturday; 7 am Sunday; Aviatur (☎ 315-0307), US$30, 6 and 9 am Monday through Saturday; 7 and 8 am Sunday

El Real – Aeroperlas (☎ 315-7500), US$39, 9 am Monday, Wednesday and Friday; 9:10 am Saturday

Garachiné – Aeroperlas (☎ 315-7500), US$36, 9:10 am Tuesday and Friday (via La Palma); Aviatur (☎ 315-0307), US$36, 8 am Monday through Friday; 9:30 am Saturday

Isla Contadora – Aeroperlas (☎ 315-7500), US$27, 8 am and 5 pm Monday through Friday; 8, 8:50 and 9:45 am and 5 pm Saturday; 8:50 am and 3:50 and 4:40 pm Sunday; Aviatur (☎ 315-0307), US$24, 8 am Monday through Friday; 8:30 am and 4:30 and 5 pm Monday through Saturday; 9:30 am Monday, Wednesday, Friday and Saturday; 7 and 8 am and 4 and 5 pm Sunday

Isla Tigre – Aviatur (☎ 315-0307), US$30, 6 and 9 am Monday through Saturday; 7 and 8 am Sunday

Isla Tupile – Aereotaxi (☎ 315-0300) & Ansa (☎ 315-7520), US$33, 6 am Monday through Saturday; Aviatur (☎ 315-0307), US$33, 6 and 9 am, Monday through Saturday; 12:30 pm Tuesday, Thursday and Sunday

Jaqué – Aeroperlas (☎ 315-7500), US$44, 9:30 am Tuesday, Thursday and Saturday; Aviatur (☎ 315-0307), US$44, 9:30 am Monday, Wednesday and Friday

La Palma – Aeroperlas (☎ 315-7500), US$36, 9:10 am Monday through Saturday; Aviatur (☎ 315-0307), US$36, 8 am Monday through Saturday

Mamitupu – Aviatur (☎ 315-0307), US$34, 6 and 9 am Monday through Saturday; 12:30 pm Tuesday, Thursday and Sunday

Mansucum – Aviatur (☎ 315-0307), US$36, 9 am Monday through Saturday; 12:30 pm Tuesday, Thursday and Sunday

Mulatupo Sasardí – Aereotaxi (☎ 315-0300) & Ansa (☎ 315-7520), US$36, Monday through Saturday (via Achutupo); Aviatur (☎ 315-0307), US$36, 6 and 9 am Monday through Saturday; 1 pm Tuesday, Thursday and Sunday

Ogobsucum – Aereotaxi (☎ 315-0300) & Ansa (☎ 315-7520), US$35, 6 am Monday through Saturday (via Tikantiki); Aviatur (☎ 315-0307), US$35, 6 am Monday through Saturday; noon Sunday

Playón Chico – Aereotaxi (☎ 315-0300) & Ansa (☎ 315-7520), US$32, 6 am Monday through Saturday; Aviatur (☎ 315-0307), US$32, 6 and 9 am Monday through Saturday; 12:30 pm Tuesday, Thursday and Sunday

Puerto Obaldía – Aereotaxi (☎ 315-0300) & Ansa (☎ 315-7520), US$47, 11:30 am Wednesday and Sunday; Aviatur (☎ 315-0307), US$47, 9 am Monday through Saturday; 12:30 pm Tuesday, Thursday and Sunday

Río Azucar – Aviatur (☎ 315-0307), US$30, 6 and 9 am Monday through Saturday; 7 and 8 am Sunday

Río Sidra – Aereotaxi (☎ 315-0300) & Ansa (☎ 315-7520), US$30, 6 am Monday through Saturday (via El Porvenir); 7 am Sunday (via El Porvenir)

Sambú – Aeroperlas (☎ 315-7500), US$36, 9:10 am Monday, Wednesday and Friday; Aviatur (☎ 315-0307), US$36, 8 am Monday through Friday; 9:30 am Saturday

San Miguel – Aviatur (☎ 315-0307), US$24, 4:30 pm Monday through Saturday; 4 pm Sunday

Ustupo – Aereotaxi (☎ 315-0300) & Ansa (☎ 315-7520), US$35, 6 am Monday through Saturday (via Ailigandí); Aviatur (☎ 315-0307), US$35, 6 and 9 am Monday through Saturday; 12:30 and 1 pm Tuesday, Thursday and Sunday

Tikantiki – Aviatur (☎ 315-0307), US$30, 6 and 9 am, Monday through Saturday; 7 and 8 am Sunday

Tubualá – Aviatur (☎ 315-0307), US$36, 9 am Monday through Saturday; 12:30 pm Tuesday, Thursday and Sunday

Bus

Buses to most other parts of the country arrive at and depart from the Terminal Nacional de Transporte (☎ 314-6171) in the Albrook district.

Below is a listing of most of the major bus routes and schedules. Fares cited are one-way; a roundtrip ticket costs double.

Aguadulce US$4.70; 3 hours; 185km; 33 buses daily; 5:50 am to 8:20 pm

Antón US$3.35; 2 hours; 126km; every 20 minutes; 6 am to 6 pm

Cañita US$2.50; 2½ hours; 80km; 11 buses daily; 6:40 am to 5:10 pm

Chame US$2; 75 minutes; 77km; 37 buses daily; 5:10 am to 10 pm

Chitré US$6; 4 hours; 241km; 18 buses daily; 6 am to 11 pm

David (Expreso) US$15; 6 hours; 438km; 14 buses daily; 5:30 am to midnight

David (Padafront) US$12; 7 hours; 438km; 11 buses daily; 7 am to 12 midnight

El Copé US$5.25; 4 hours; 188km; 9 buses daily; 6 am to 6 pm

El Valle US$3.50; 2½ hours; 123km; 23 buses daily; 7 am to 6:40 pm

Las Minas US$6.50; 4½ hours; 126km; 6 buses daily; 8:15 am to 3:45 pm

Las Tablas US$6.50; 4½ hours; 282km; 11 buses daily; 6 am to 6:30 pm

Macaracas US$7; 5 hours; 244km; 5 buses daily; 7 am to 3:30 pm

Ocú US$6; 4 hours; 228km; 8 buses daily; 7 am to 5 pm

Penonomé US$3.70; 2½ hours; 144km; 48 buses daily; 4:45 am to 11 pm

Pesé US$6; 4½ hours; 272km; 6 buses daily; 8:15 am to 3:45 pm

San Carlos US$6; 1½ hours; 92km; 25 buses daily; 5:10 am to 10 pm

Santiago US$6; 4 hours; 250km; 16 buses daily; 1 am to 11 pm

Soná US$7; 6 hours; 288km; 6 buses daily; 8:30 am to 6 pm

Villa de Los Santos US$6; 4 hours; 245km; 18 buses daily; 6 am to 11 pm

Yaviza US$14; 6 hours; 266km; 5 buses daily; 4:15 am to 2 pm

Additionally, one bus leaves the terminal at 8 am daily to Chiriquí Grande (US$18, 8 hours), proceeds to Almirante (US$20, 9½ hours) and continues on to Changuinola (US$23,12 hours).

Buses to the Canal area (Miraflores and Pedro Miguel Locks, Paraíso and Gamboa) depart from Plaza Cinco de Mayo on Avenida Central. A ride usually costs no more than US$2.

Bus service from Panama City to San José, Costa Rica, is offered by Panaline and Tica Bus. See the Land section in the Getting There & Away chapter for details.

Train

The historic train that used to take the famously scenic route alongside the Panama Canal and through the canal's lush watershed from Panama City to Colón was allowed to fall into disrepair during the 1980s. It was being repaired in 2001. To learn its current status, check with IPAT (see Information) or, better yet, with any of the local tour operators mentioned in the Organized Tours section.

Boat

Passenger ferries between Panama City and Isla Taboga depart from Muelle (Pier) 18 in the Balboa district, west of downtown. Tour boats go along the Panama Canal. See the Panamá Province chapter for details.

Cargo boats to Colombia depart from the docks near Casco Viejo. See Dangers & Annoyances in the Facts for the Visitor chapter for a warning about cargo boats plying between Panama and Colombia.

GETTING AROUND
To/From the Airport

Tocumen International Airport is 35km northeast of the city center. Buses to Tocumen depart every 30 minutes from Terminal Nacional de Transporte; the ones that reach the airport via Calle 50 and Vía España cost 25¢ and take about two hours, while the ones that reach the airport via Corredor Sur cost 75¢ and take about one hour. A taxi ride from downtown to the airport costs US$20.

When you arrive at Tocumen from abroad, look for the *'Transportes Turísticos'* desk at the airport exit. Beside it is a taxi stand, with posted prices. Taxi drivers will assail you, offering rides into town for US$20, but the staff at the desk will inform you that you can take a *colecti o*, or shuttle van, for US$8 per person (for three or more passengers) or US$12 per person (for two passengers). For two or more people traveling together, a taxi can be cheaper.

Aeropuerto Albrook handles domestic flights. A taxi ride to the airport rarely costs more than US$5 or US$6 from any part of the city, unless you hit some bad traffic.

Bus

Panama City has a good network of local buses, which run from 5 am to 10 pm daily and charge just 15¢ a ride. However, they are always crowded and take forever to get from one side of the city to the other due to frequent stops. A taxi, for a little more money, is the only sensible way to get around town if you value your time and don't have your own wheels.

Car

For details on renting a car or truck in Panama, see Car & Motorcycle in the Getting Around chapter. Rental-car companies in Panama City include the following (airport numbers listed are at Aeropuerto Albrook and Tocumen International Airport):

Avis	☎ 213-0555
	☎ 315-0434 (Albrook)
	☎ 238-4056 (Tocumen)
Budget	☎ 263-8777
	☎ 315-0201 (Albrook)
	☎ 238-4069 (Tocumen)
Hertz	☎ 264-1111
	☎ 315-0418 (Albrook)
	☎ 238-4081 (Tocumen)
National	☎ 265-2222
	☎ 315-0416 (Albrook)
	☎ 238-4144 (Tocumen)
Thrifty	☎ 264-2613
	☎ 315-0144 (Albrook)
	☎ 238-4955 (Tocumen)

As always, it pays to shop around to compare rates and special promotions. At the time of writing, rates ranged from US$30 to US$45 per day for the most economical cars, with insurance and unlimited mileage *(kilometraje)* included.

It is also possible to rent vehicles from rental counters at the Hotel Caesar Park and the Hotel El Panamá.

Taxi

Taxis in Panama City are plentiful and cheap. They are not metered, but there is a list of standard fares that drivers are supposed to charge, measured by zones. The fare for one zone is a minimum of 75¢; the maximum fare within the city is US$4. An average ride, crossing a couple of zones, costs US$1 or US$2, plus 25¢ for each additional passenger.

Watch out for unmarked, large-model US cars serving hotels as cabs. Their prices are up to four times that of regular street taxis. If it's late at night, if you're in a hurry or if you're in an area not frequented by cabs, call for a radio taxi. These taxis are dispatched moments after you call and usually arrive within minutes. Larger radio-taxi companies include the following:

Ama	☎ 221-1865
America	☎ 223-7694
Atlantic	☎ 224-6700
El Parador	☎ 220-5322
Libertad	☎ 267-7515
Paitilla	☎ 226-1446
Union Servicio Unico	☎ 221-4074
Villa Lucre	☎ 277-4687

Bicycle

Cycling within the capital city is not a great idea, due to narrow roads and aggressive drivers. Cycling outside the city, however, is safer and can be quite enjoyable.

There's only one place in town to rent a bicycle: Bicycles Moses (☎ 228-0116), out at the entrance to the causeway, operates a booth where you can rent a mountain bike for US$2.25 per hour (more around the

Christmas and Easter holidays) or in-line skates for US$1 per hour. It also has economical daily and weekly rates. The booth is open 10 am to 7 pm weekdays, 7 am to 7 pm weekends. The owner speaks English.

Panamá Province

pop 1,388,400

Panamá Province has a little bit of everything and most of the canal. It's got *two* island groups that have been great escapes since the days of the pirates. It's got more history than any one place has a right to. It offers lots of wild jungle for exploring, scores of lovely beaches and road trips that'll knock your socks off. And this province has an ample array of cultural attractions and nocturnal distractions in its capital, Panama City.

Statistically, the province contains the largest population of Panama's nine provinces. It also has a population density of 90 people per square kilometer – three times the national average. There are slightly more women than men here, but the figure of four women to every man often heard in Panama City bars is only wishful thinking on the part of some men. The province has a surface area of 11,887 sq km, making it the second largest behind Darién Province (16,671 sq km).

As might be expected, Panamá Province also boasts the highest ratio of urbanites to rural folk – 79.6% to 20.4%, respectively. Yet the province also claims highly developed agriculture in Chepo and La Chorrera, shrimp farming in Chame and large fruit farms in Capira. Perhaps its success in those fields has something to do with the fact that the province also contains the country's best-educated people: Its illiteracy rate of 4.3% is by far the lowest in the country, which has an overall rate of 10.7%.

Highlights

- The awesome Panama Canal, a must-see for Panama visitors
- Pipeline Road in Parque Nacional Soberanía, one of the world's premier birdwatching sites
- Isla Barra Colorado, a world-famous jungle research center at the heart of Lago Gatún
- Archipiélago de las Perlas, the islands named for their pearls and known for their pirate past
- Surfing beaches and romantic hideaways on the Pacific coast southwest of the capital

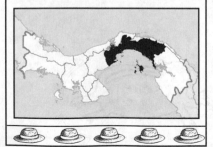

Around Panama City

PANAMA CANAL

The USA's construction of the Panama Canal during the early 20th century is a true story of adventure, ordeal and accomplishment. It followed the catastrophic French attempt to cut a path between the seas, which claimed 22,000 lives. Despite all the technological advances that have taken place since the completion of the canal almost 90 years ago, the lock-and-lake waterway remains one of the great engineering marvels of all time.

The canal extends 80km from Colón on the Caribbean side to Panama City on the Pacific. Each year more than 12,000 ocean-going vessels transit it – well over 30 a day. So significant is the canal to international shipping that ships the world over are built to fit within the dimensions of its locks: 305m long and 33.5m wide. At times a huge

PANAMÁ PROVINCE

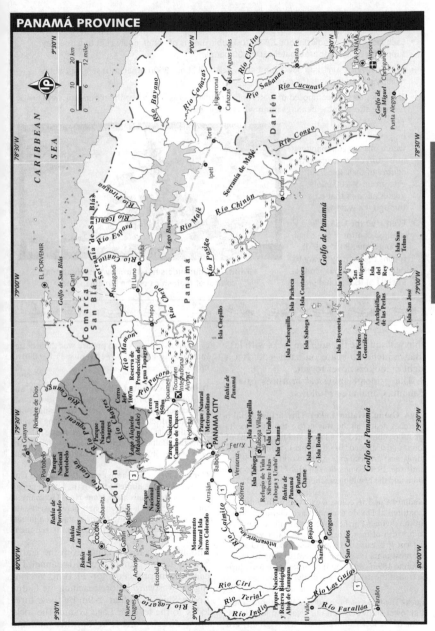

PANAMÁ PROVINCE

Canal Facts

- Each lock chamber holds about 2,675,200 cubic meters of water, equivalent to a one-day supply for a city of approximately 100,000 people.

- During WWII, more than 5300 combat vessels and about 8500 other craft serving the US military passed through the canal.

- The lock gates are composed of watertight compartments that make them buoyant, largely relieving stress on the bearings upon which they rest.

- The Panama Canal is the only place in the world where military commanders must turn over navigational control of their ships. An elite group of 200 pilots guides all ships that pass through the waterway.

- Even after the USA relinquished control of the canal on December 31, 1999, it retains the right by treaty to defend the waterway in the interest of its national security.

Military commanders must turn over navigational control of their ships on the Panama Canal.

ship will squeeze through the locks with less than a meter to spare on each side. It's a sight onlookers never forget.

The principal physical features of the Panama Canal are as follows:

Lago Gatún (Gatún Lake) This artificial lake stretches nearly all the way across the isthmus. Its creation submerged 29 villages and huge swaths of forest and displaced 50,000 people. Gatún remained the largest artificial lake in the world for 22 years, until the 1936 completion of the USA's Hoover Dam and the resulting creation of Lake Mead.

Gaillard Cut This colossal excavation through the Continental Divide extends Lago Gatún to locks on the divide's Pacific slope. Originally excavated to a width of more than 90m and later widened, the cut was carved through solid rock and shale for most of its 14km. It is currently being widened again to 189m (219m on the curves) to allow ships to transit the canal more quickly.

Locks The locks on both sides of the isthmus raise and lower ships between sea level and lake level; some of the locks' enormous doors weigh upward

of 800 tons apiece, yet so precise was their design that only a 40-horsepower motor is needed to move them.

Balboa & Cristóbal The ports of Balboa and Cristóbal are on the Pacific and Caribbean coasts, respectively. It is at these ports that canal pilots board and disembark from vessels passing through the canal. The port of Balboa borders the safe and attractive Balboa suburb of Panama City, and the port of Cristóbal borders the unsafe city of Colón.

Gamboa At the northern end of the Gaillard Cut, this small port is home to two of the largest cranes in the world, confiscated from Nazi Germany at the end of WWII. Resembling giant insects, the cranes are so intriguing to mechanical engineers the world over that many travel here to see them.

The approach to the canal from the Caribbean is along 7.2km of dredged channel. The canal then proceeds for 11.1km, veering slightly westward before reaching the Gatún Locks. Ships are lifted 25.9m by these three locks, to the level of Lago Gatún. The locks open directly into one another and are

PANAMA CANAL

80°00'W

79°30'W

Parque Nacional Portobelo

Isla Grande
La Guayra

Playa Palenque

Nombre de Dios

Palenque

CARIBBEAN SEA

9°30'N

Portobelo

Bahía de Portobelo

Playa Langosta

Colón

Río Gatún

Río Pequení

Río Cuango

9°30'N

Playa María Chiquita

Bahía Las Minas

Cristóbal

Sherman

Bahía Limón

COLÓN
Airfield

Área Recreativa Lago Gatún

Puerto Pilón

Sabanita

Parque Nacional Chagres

Río Chagres

Fuerte San Lorenzo

Meliá Panama Canal

Gatún
Gatún Locks

Panamá

Gatún Dam

Limón

Vía Transístmica

Cerro Jefe 1007m

Río Agua Salud

Lago Gatún

Lago Alajuela (Madden Lake)

Escobal

Isla Barra Colorado

Madden Dam

Parque Nacional Soberanía

Río Chagres

Cerro Azul 950m

To Yaviza

Bahía Trinidad

Monumento Natural Isla Barro Colorado

Gamboa
Gamboa Rainforest Resort
Canopy Tower

Pedregal

Summit Botanical Gardens & Zoo

Parque Nacional Soberanía Headquarters

Tocumen
Tocumen International Airport

Gaillard Cut

Contractors Hill

Parque Nacional Camino de Cruces

Pedro Miguel Locks
Paraíso
Pedro Miguel

Interamericana

Corredor Sur

9°00'N

Lago Miraflores
Miraflores Locks

Parque Natural Metropolitano

9°00'N

Arraiján

PANAMA CITY
Balboa
Amador
Playa Kobbe

Panamá

Río Caimito

Autopista Arraiján-Chorrera

Fort Kobbe

Playa Far Fan

La Chorrera

Veracruz

Playa Veracruz

Bahía de Panamá

Interamericana

Ferry

Isla El Morro

Isla Taboga
Taboga Village

Isla Taboguilla

Parque Nacional y Reserva Biológica Altos de Campana

Capira

Refugio de Vida Silvestre Islas Taboga y Urabú

Isla Urabú

To Punta Chame, Beaches & Penonomé

Isla Chamá

80°00'W

79°30'W

0   5   10 km
0   3   6 miles

paired, as are the other locks, so that one ship can be raised while another is lowered. All the lock chambers have the same dimensions.

From the Gatún Locks, the canal passes through Lago Gatún in a southern and then southeastern direction to the mouth of the Gaillard Cut. At the end of the cut are the Pedro Miguel Locks, which have a drop of 9.4m. The locks border Lago Miraflores, which is 16.8m above the level of the Pacific. The canal continues 2.1km through Lago Miraflores and reaches the two Miraflores Locks, which lower ships to Pacific tidewater level. From the locks, the canal runs 4km to Balboa, and from there a dredged channel extends 8km out into the Bahía de Panamá.

In 2001, the Panama Canal Authority was considering a US$4.5 billion proposal to widen Lago Gatún and create additional locks to handle ships which existing locks can't accommodate.

Auxiliary facilities include the Madden Dam on the Río Chagres, which provides a reservoir to maintain the level of Lago Gatún during the dry season; breakwaters that protect channels at both ends of the canal; hydroelectric plants at the Gatún and Madden Dams; and the presently incapacitated Panama Railroad, which extends 76.6km from Colón to Panama City.

To lessen the risk of a mishap, ships are cabled to locomotives at the approach to each series of locks and are pulled through them. There are 80 such locomotives in use, all made by Mitsubishi. Their cost? A mere US$1 million apiece! In 1998 another 100 locomotives were ordered from Mitsubishi at a cost of US$2 million each; they were still being delivered, a few at a time, in 2001. The locomotives are pricey, but then transit fees earn Panama hundreds of millions of dollars every year.

Ships pay according to their weights; the average fee for commercial ships is around US$30,000. The largest passenger ships passing through the canal are assessed in excess of US$150,000 per transit. The lowest fee ever assessed was 36¢, paid by Richard Halliburton, who swam through the canal in 1928.

Miraflores Locks

The easiest and best way to see the canal is to go to the Miraflores Locks, the set closest to Panama City, where a viewing platform gives you a good look at canal locks in operation. A bilingual guide and bilingual illustrated pamphlets offer information on the canal, and there's a museum with a model and film about the famous waterway.

Hours are 9 am to 5 pm daily; admission is free. To get to the locks, you can take any Paraíso or Gamboa bus from the Plaza Cinco de Mayo bus stop in Panama City. These buses, which pass along the canalside highway that runs from the capital to Gamboa, will let you off at the 'Miraflores Locks' sign on the highway, about 8km from the city center. It's a 15-minute walk to the locks from the sign. Or, you can take a taxi. Even with a 30-minute visit expect to pay no more than US$15 for the round trip (agree on a price beforehand to avoid a surprise).

Other Locks

Farther north, past the Miraflores Locks, are the **Pedro Miguel Locks**, which can be seen from the highway to Gamboa. One hundred meters beyond the locks there's a parking area and a strip of grass where onlookers are encouraged to park and watch ships transit the canal. Unfortunately, you can't get a very good look at the locks from here and only authorized personnel are allowed any closer.

On the Caribbean side, the **Gatún Locks** have a viewing stand for visitors and a small replica of the entire canal that lets you place the locks in context. You can also get a good look at the locks if you cross the canal to visit Fuerte San Lorenzo. See the Colón Province chapter for more details on these locks and the nearby Gatún Dam.

Canal Tours

Argo Tours (☎ 228-6069, fax 228-1234), the leader in canal tours for many years, operates partial canal transits every Saturday morning. These boat tours depart from Pier 18 in Balboa, a western suburb of Panama City, travel through the Miraflores Locks to Lago Miraflores and back, and then cruise

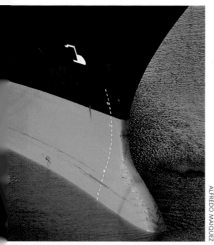

Cargo ship in Miraflores Locks, Panama Canal

Construction at Gaillard Cut, Panama Canal

Pedro Miguel Locks in action, Panama Canal

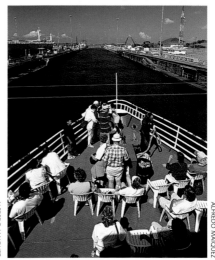

Cruising through the Gatun Locks, Panamá Canal

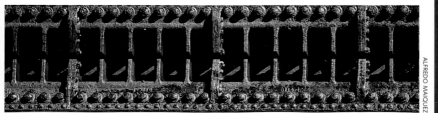

Detail of door lock on the Panama Canal, Panamá Province

The busy Muelle Fiscal, Panama City

The charming coastline of Isla Taboga, Panamá Province

Waterfront homes in La Palma, Darién Province

out into the bay for scenic views of the city and the Pacific approach to the canal. These fine tours last about 4½ hours and cost US$90/45 for adults/children 12 and younger. It's a good idea to make a reservation at least a day ahead.

One Saturday a month, Argo Tours offers a full transit of the canal, from Balboa to Cristóbal, passing through all three sets of locks. The transit takes all day, from about 7:30 am to 5:30 pm; the cost is US$135/55 adults/children. Check the company's website (www.big-ditch.com) for dates of upcoming transits. Be advised that many people find the full transit a bit much due to the heat.

Most taxi drivers know where to take you if you say 'pier 18 Balboa' or 'muelle dieciocho Balboa'; the one-way fare is usually US$10.

If you take a trip to the Isla Barro Colorado area, you will travel by boat along part of the canal, from Gamboa to Isla Barro Colorado, but you won't go through any locks. (See Isla Barro Colorado later in this chapter for details on these trips.)

CANAL AREA

On a day trip from Panama City, you could first visit the Miraflores Locks, then the Summit Botanical Gardens & Zoo, and finish by crossing into Colón Province to visit the Sendero El Charco nature trail in Parque Nacional Soberanía. The last stop is 25km from the center of Panama City but seems like a different world.

All these places are along the highway that runs from Panama City to Gamboa, the small tropical town where the Río Chagres meets the canal. Buses passing by the Miraflores and Pedro Miguel Locks, Paraíso and Gamboa depart every 30 minutes from Plaza Cinco de Mayo in Panama City. The first bus leaves at 4:45 am, the last at 10 pm. The cost is less than a dollar each way. In addition, there are two buses that go directly to Miraflores Locks, leaving at 2:30 and 3 pm daily.

Summit Botanical Gardens & Zoo

On the highway to Gamboa, 10km past the Miraflores Locks, are the Summit Botanical Gardens & Zoo (☎ 232-4854). The botanical gardens were founded in 1923 to introduce, propagate and disseminate tropical plants from around the world into Panama. They contain more than 15,000 plant species, and many of these are marked along a trail.

Also at the park is an expanding zoo that contains animals native to Central America. Its greatest attraction is its harpy eagle compound, which opened in 1998 in hopes that conditions would prove conducive to breeding; at the time of writing, there were no baby harpies to report. The harpy eagle is the national bird, and many ornithologists consider it the most powerful bird of prey. Also at the zoo is a roomy jaguar compound and a remarkably spacious cage containing lots of seemingly content macaws and other loud and large colorful birds.

The park is open 8 am to 4 pm daily. Admission is a great bargain at 25¢/10¢ for adults/children; the fee includes information and a trail map of the park. The same buses that pass by Gamboa will stop here if you ask the driver.

Parque Nacional Soberanía

A few kilometers past Summit, across the border into Colón Province, 22,104-hectare Parque Nacional Soberanía is one of the most accessible tropical rain forest areas in Panama. It extends much of the way across the isthmus, from Limón on Lago Gatún to just north of Paraíso. It features hiking trails, the Río Chagres, part of Lago Gatún and a remarkable variety of wildlife – its known residents include 105 species of mammal, 525 species of bird, 55 species of amphibian, 79 species of reptile and 36 species of freshwater fish.

Warning

There have been recent reports of several armed attacks against tourists in the Parque Nacional Soberanía. If you decide to visit the park, be sure to leave your valuables, passport and credit cards back at your hotel.

Hiking trails in the park include a section of the old **Sendero Las Cruces** (Las Cruces Trail), used by the Spaniards to transport gold and minerals by mule train between Panama City and Nombre de Dios, and the 17km **Pipeline Road**, providing access (by driving or hiking) to Río Agua Salud, where you can walk upriver for a swim under a waterfall.

Pipeline Road is a favorite with bird watchers. A healthy cluster of golden-collared manakins, colorful birds that produce a variety of sounds – including a firecrackerlike snap – is usually readily found at the end of the first 100m of the road, on the left side. Other typical sounds on the first 2km of the road come from white-bellied antbirds, black-bellied wrens, collared aracaris, keel-billed toucans and buff-throated woodcreepers. You'll likely hear a few howler monkeys as well. In addition, you may be treated to such rarities as the tiny hawk, the hook-billed kite, the great jacamar and the black-tailed trogon. And that's only the beginning. The jungle and wildlife on both sides of the road get increasingly thick as you proceed.

Unless you have a keen eye and are well versed in Panama's avifauna, I strongly recommend that you hire a guide to fully appreciate Pipeline Road. This is one of the world's premier birding sites; it would be a minor tragedy to give it short shrift. See Guides in the Getting Around chapter for a list of the country's top naturalist guides. Most of the guides listed there charge about US$35 to guide a group of four for an entire morning on Pipeline Road, if you provide the transportation; they charge more if you don't.

A shorter, very easy nature trail is the **Sendero El Charco**. The trail is signposted from the highway, about 3km past the Summit Botanical Gardens & Zoo.

Fishing is permitted on the Río Chagres and Lago Gatún. Leaflets and information about the park, including a brochure for self-guided walks along the nature trail, are available from Parque Nacional Soberanía headquarters (☎ 276-6370) in Gamboa.

Canopy Tower

In the 1960s the US Air Force built a radar installation atop a hill in what is now Parque Nacional Soberanía as an essential part of the USA's intercontinental defense. The site was later taken over by the US Federal Aviation Administration to control air traffic in the area. Most recently, it was used by the Panama Canal Commission as a communications tower.

The installation – its major feature is a three-story, cylindrical, enclosed tower with a viewing platform on top – was transferred to Panama in November 1996 in compliance with the Carter-Torrijos Treaties. Raúl Arias de Para, a friendly, forward-thinking man with a love of nature, saw its tourism potential and obtained a 20-year concession to develop the site.

Today, Canopy Tower (☎ 264-5720, 800-854-2597 in the USA, fax 263-2784, stay@canopytower.com) contains a small ground-floor museum devoted to the history of the former military site and the local wildlife, and guest quarters with a private hot-water bathrooms on the 2nd floor. Most of the rooms are attractive and comfortable, with desks, tables and chairs, firm beds and even hammocks. Two 'guide rooms' contain only a bed; guests share a bathroom with the staff. A communal room with library, cozy sitting areas and dining tables is on the 3rd floor. A built-in steel ladder leads to the rooftop viewing deck.

What's really fun about this place, besides the childlike thrill of staying in a building that feels like an enormous backyard fort, is the surrounding forest. From the 3rd and rooftop levels, you have a 360° view over some magnificent rain forest – and you can even see ships passing through the canal, a mere 2km away. The bird watching in the area is excellent. And a study conducted by Ancon has found that the hill upon which the tower was built hosts the greatest variety of mammals and reptiles along the eastern bank of the Panama Canal.

The per-person, double-occupancy rates vary with season and room, from US$75 to US$185, and are likely to rise annually. The rates include breakfast, lunch and dinner, hotel tax, and two guided walks daily. Additional guided tours are available, most for

US$55. Please note, the Canopy Tower is not open to nonguests who just want to admire the view from the 3rd floor or viewing deck, so don't simply drop in. Also, the tours are available to guests only. Website: www.canopytower.com

Gamboa Rainforest Resort

Near the junction of the Panama Canal and the Río Chagres, 9km past the turnoff for Canopy Tower on the road to Colón and about 40km from Panama City, is the new, US$30-million Gamboa Rainforest Resort (☎ 314-9000, fax 314-9020, 877-8000-1690 in the USA, reser ation@gamboaresort.com). The main building's attraction is its sweeping vistas of the jungle-flanked Río Chagres – an awesome panorama of river and rain forest seen through windows three stories high. All 110 luxurious guestrooms, housed in wings on both sides of the main building, offer slices of the same view. Flanking the driveway to the main building and lacking the gorgeous view are 65 'villas' (spiffed-up concrete duplexes really) that once housed the administrators who managed canal dredging operations nearly a century ago. Website: www.gamboaresort.com

The accommodations are nice enough – the guestrooms are spacious with all the amenities, an oversized bathroom and a hammock-strung balcony – but it's the resort's activities that really make this place shine. If you purchase one of its tour-inclusive packages, the steep room rate is reduced. For example, the 'nature/wildlife tour' (US$675 per person for double-occupancy) is a four-night package that includes a morning boat tour of Lago Gatún, a sunrise birding tour on Pipeline Road, and a slow ride through rain forest canopy aboard the resort's aerial tram. All packages include roundtrip airport shuttle, unlimited use of kayaks, pedal boats, bicycles, gym and tennis courts, unlimited access to all resort exhibits (which include a snake house, a butterfly farm and a small aquarium), and the 10% hotel tax and buffet breakfast are included. If you don't purchase a package, you're looking at US$200 a night plus tax for a guestroom April 16 through December 14 and US$235 plus tax December 15 through April 15.

Regardless, you have the option of taking advantage of many individual tours the resort offers, most of which run US$50. At that price, some of the tours offered are unreasonable (the Aerial Tram Canopy tour is too short and you won't likely see any wildlife, the Summit Gardens tour should cost a third of the price, and the Canopy Tower tour – really just a short visit – is grossly overpriced at US$50). But a guided tour on Pipeline Road with a professional birder and the nocturnal wildlife boat tour in crocodile- and caiman-stirred waters offer better value. Other offerings include: sportfishing on Lago Gatún for peacock bass, snook and tarpon (US$175) and, in case you forgot to make a reservation for Isla Barro Colorado (see below), the resort can likely squeeze you into STRI's schedule (Gamboa charges US$95 per person). There's also a full-service spa and a tacky 'model Emberá Indian village' at the resort. Unfortunately, helicopters rides are available; their noise drives away wildlife and spoils many a tranquil moment.

In short, Gamboa is an impressive resort in a spectacular setting with mediocre service and pricey but spotty-quality meals.

Isla Barro Colorado

This lush island in the middle of Lago Gatún was formed by the damming of the Río Chagres and the creation of the lake. It is managed by the Smithsonian Tropical Research Institute (STRI), which administers a world-renowned research facility here. Although the 1500-hectare island was once restricted only to scientists, a limited number of guided tourists are now allowed, and a visit to the island makes a fascinating day trip from Panama City. The trip includes an STRI boat ride down an attractive part of the canal, from Gamboa across the lake to the island.

The institute traces its 75-year history in Panama from the construction of the Panama Canal, when scientific surveys of the area's flora and fauna were undertaken with the goal of controlling insect-borne diseases such as yellow fever and malaria. After the canal opened, entomologists and biologists involved in these studies sought to establish a permanent biological reserve on an island created by the canal's construction. In 1923, Isla Barro Colorado (BCI) became one of the first biological reserves in the New World. Since that time, the island has become one of the most intensively studied areas in the Tropics.

Home to 1316 recorded plant species, 381 bird species and 102 mammal species, the island also contains a 59km network of marked and protected trails. Visitors are only allowed on one designated nature trail to prevent them from inadvertently damaging anyone's valuable research. This 2.5km trail winds through some spectacular rain forest and ends at one of STRI's earliest structures, a headquarters-turned-visitors center. It has a jungly and time-forgotten look and contains a gift shop and a small museum with vintage photos of researchers at work, a case containing tools used by the researchers and lots of other neat stuff. The laboratories on BCI are off-limits to the public.

Tour reservations are essential; the further in advance you inquire, the better chance the date will be available for your visit. Reservations can be made through STRI's visitor services office (☎ 212-8026, fax 212-8148, visitstri@tivoli.si.edu), located in the Tupper Building, Avenida Roosevelt, Ancon, Balboa. Foreign non-students pay US$70, foreign students with ID pay US$35, and foreign nationals half as much; children under 10 are not allowed on BCI. The visitor services office is open 8 am to 4:30 pm weekdays.
Website: www.stri.org

The boat to BCI leaves the Gamboa pier at 7:15 am on Tuesday, Wednesday and Friday, and at 8 am on Saturday and Sunday. There are no public visits on Monday, Thursday and on certain holidays. The entire trip lasts four to six hours, depending on the size of the group and on the weather. Lunch is included.

CERROS AZUL & JEFE

About an hour's drive northeast of Panama City is Cerro Azul, a 950m peak just south of Parque Nacional Chagres, a mountainous area of natural forest and streams. Several kilometers northeast of Cerro Azul is Cerro Jefe, a windy, cool ridge with rare elfin forest. Both peaks are popular with birders, who come looking for foothill species, including some from the Darién. Because of the difficulty of the terrain, particularly in the vicinity of Cerro Jefe, a 4WD vehicle is highly recommended. Buses do not go to this rugged area.

To reach the hills from Panama City, take Corredor Sur toward Tocumen. Corredor Sur will become Interamericana where it crosses the Tocumen Highway. From this point, proceed 6.8km and look for an Xtra supermarket on the left side of the road. Just beyond the market is a police station and a turnoff, which you should take. After 1.9km, you'll see a large Chinese pavilion on the left side of the road. Turn left onto another paved road. This road ascends Cerro Azul. After 9km, you will see the Las Vistas residential development; continue along the same road for 3km and you'll come to the La Posada de Ferhisse, an inn with a red-roofed, opened-sided restaurant that's very visible from the road. In this area there's some good birding, but the bird watching is superior on Cerro Jefe. To get there, continue on the same road another 6km, until you're into the elfin forest. You'll know you're in this rare forest when you find yourself surrounded by trees that looked twisted, dwarfed and windswept; it's a very unusual forest indeed. Also, Cerro Jefe is easily identified by the huge microwave tower at its summit.

Unfortunately, no signs mark the way from Panama City to the mountains, and the razing of the Chinese pavilion could render these directions useless. Don't hesitate to ask for directions if you feel lost. If you don't speak Spanish, don't despair. Simply ask, '¿Cerro Azul (or Jefe), derecho?' (day-RAY-cho; straight ahead?); '¿derecha?' (day-RAY-cha; to the right?); '¿izquierda?' (eez-key-AIR-da; to the left?) For clarity's sake, point in the relevant direction, and your listener will probably provide some helpful finger-pointing in return. If you hear the word *regreso* in the reply, it means you missed a turnoff and need to double back some distance.

Places to Stay & Eat

La Posada de Ferhisse (☎/fax 297-0197), is an inn with six comfortable rooms with private phone, hot-water private bathroom, local-channel TV and a firm double bed. The cost is US$40 per room with up to four people. There's a pool and a restaurant on the premises serving *tipico* (typical) food at reasonable prices. The restaurant is open 9 am to 10 pm daily. Another inn was under construction next door at the time of writing.

If you take the road toward Cerro Jefe, 5.6km from La Posada de Ferhisse you'll see a ranger station on the left side of the road. At this point it's 7.4km to *Cabañas 4X4* (☎ 297-0098, 680-3076), which you'll find by following a series of road signs with the cabins' name. Be advised Cabañas 4X4 can only be reached by a high-clearance 4WD truck and only if the road is dry. You'll come to a small wooded valley dotted with comfortable cabins (US$20 per person Monday through Thursday; US$30 per person Friday through Sunday) and some rustic hutlike *bohios* for budget travelers (US$10 per person). There's also a superior, romantic cabin for US$60 weekdays, US$80 weekends. There are picnic areas, a pool and lots of trails that lend themselves well to birding. Website: www.cabanas4x4.com

BAHA'I & HINDU TEMPLES

On the crest of a hill on the outskirts of Panama City, 11km from the city center on the Vía Transístmica, is the white-domed Baha'i Temple (☎ 231-1137, 231-1191). It looks egglike from the outside, but inside it is surprisingly beautiful, with a breeze always blowing through. This is the Baha'i House of Worship for all of Latin America. Information about the faith is available in English and Spanish at the temple; readings from the Baha'i writings (in English and

Spanish) are held at 10 am Sunday. The temple is open 10 am to 6 pm daily. Any bus from Panama City to Colón can let you off on the highway, but it's a long walk up the hill. A taxi ride from Panama City costs around US$15.

An attractive Hindu Temple, which is also atop a hill, is on the way to the Baha'i Temple. It's open 7:30 to 11 am and 4:30 to 7:30 pm daily. Admission is free at both temples.

Islas Tabogas

pop 1400

This group consists of 10 main islands and dozens of smaller ones 20km south of Panama City. The largest – **Isla Taboga** – is a mere 571 hectares, yet the size of the small island belies its rich history.

Taboga was inhabited until 1515 by indigenous people who resided in thatch huts and made their living from the sea. In that year Spanish soldiers reached the island, killed or enslaved the Indians and took their substantial pieces of gold. This occurred just two years after Balboa first sighted the Pacific and before the city of Panamá was constructed. A small Spanish colony was developed on the island, and the Spaniards had the place to themselves until 1549, when Panama freed its Indian slaves and a good number chose to make Taboga their home.

Peace did not reign. Pirates, including the infamous Henry Morgan and Francis Drake, frequented the island, using it as a base from which to attack Spanish ships and towns – or simply as a place to catch their breath between raids. On August 22, 1686, the ship of Captain Townley, who was in command of English and French buccaneers, was lying in front of Taboga when it was attacked by three Spanish ships armed with cannons. During the ensuing battle, one of the Spanish ships blew up, and Townley's men were able to take the other two vessels as well as a fourth ship that had arrived as reinforcement.

The pirates' loss was only one man killed and 22 wounded, including Townley himself. The buccaneer commander sent a messenger to the president of Panama demanding supplies, the release of five pirates being held prisoner and ransom for Townley's many captives. When the president instead sent only some medicine, Townley said that heads would roll if his demands weren't met. When the president ignored that threat, Townley sent him a canoe that contained the heads of 20 Spaniards.

The severed heads got the president's attention, and he released the five prisoners and paid a ransom. Townley had won another battle, but he died of his wounds on September 9. For years afterward peace continued to escape the little island. As late as 1819, the pirate Captain Illingsworth and his party of Chileans landed on Taboga and sacked and burnt its village.

Around 1840, tiny Isla El Morro, which can be reached from Taboga by a sandbar at low tide, became the headquarters of the Pacific Steamship Navigation Company. The PSNC consisted of a fleet of 12 vessels used to transport passengers and cargo between Valparaíso, Chile, and Taboga. The completion of the Panama Railroad in the mid-1850s put the PSNC out of business. Today you can still see remnants of the PSNC building and pier, and handblown bottles bearing the company's crest can be found among the islet's vegetation. Also on Isla El Morro is a tiny cemetery containing the remains of some PSNC workers.

During the 1880s, when the French took a stab at digging a canal across the isthmus, Taboga became the site of an enormous sanitarium for workers who had contracted malaria or yellow fever. The 'Island of Flowers,' as it is sometimes called, might well have earned its name from all the flowers placed on graves here. Sadly, Taboga's centuries-old cemetery has been looted so many times that it looks like it was hit by artillery fire.

Real artillery fire also took a toll on Taboga. The US Navy used the broad hill facing the town for artillery practice during WWII. At that time the US military also installed searchlights, antiaircraft guns and

bunkers atop the island. The bunkers, abandoned in 1960, can be visited.

Today, peace has finally come to Taboga. Now the island is only assailed by weekend vacationers from Panama City and the occasional foreign tourist. There are two hotels, a few restaurants and bars on Taboga, but people primarily come just to stroll the town's quaint streets and to hike about the island. More adventurous types come to scuba dive in waters once rich with plunder. Taboga also offers its visitors a chance to take it easy, to maybe do a little bird watching, exploring and snorkeling, and to watch ships lining up in the Bahía de Panamá and storm fronts moving in from the south.

Orientation

A ferry serves Isla Taboga from Muelle (Pier) 18 in the Balboa district of Panama City twice daily, tying up at a pier near the north end of the sole town on the island. As you exit the pier, you'll see the entrance of the Hotel Taboga to your right. To your left, you'll see a narrow street that is the island's main road. From this point, the street meanders 5.2km before ending at the old US military installation atop the island's highest hill, Cerro El Vigía.

Information

There's no tourist office, no bank, no post office and no store of any kind on Taboga, but there are scattered public phones.

ANAM has an office (☎ 250-2082) on Taboga east of the ferry dock; it's supposedly open 8 am to 4 pm weekdays, but the posted hours seem to be a suggestions rather than rules. It has some information on the island's natural features and snorkeling spots.

Casco Viejo Walking Tour

One of the pleasant ways to pass time on Taboga is to walk to the top of the island. Walk left from the pier and you will first pass a beach (unless the tide's in) on a road that's barely wide enough for a car and is mainly used by pedestrians. The road forks after 75m or so; you will want to take the high way. After a few more paces you will come to a modest **church**, in front of which is a simple square. This unassuming church was founded in 1550 and is the second-oldest church in the Western Hemisphere. Inside is a handsome altar and lovely artwork.

Farther along you'll come to a beautiful public garden filled with flowers. At its center is a statue of the island's patroness, **Nuestra Señora del Carmen** (Our Lady of Carmel). Every July 16 she is honored with a procession: The statue is carried upon the shoulders of followers to the oceanside, placed on a boat and ferried around the island. Upon her return she is carried around the island, while crowds follow and everyone else watches at their windows. The Virgin is returned to her garden shrine and the rest of the day is one of rejoicing. Seemingly everyone partakes then in games, fire-breathing or dancing.

Continuing along the same road, you'll pass the Hotel Chu and, 400m farther, a **cemetery** that dates from the 16th century but is so overgrown with weeds and so picked over by looters that there's hardly anything worth seeing. Nearly all the mausoleums have been broken into and there are open graves everywhere. It seems that all the old headstones are gone; I could not find any dating from before 1900.

Continuing on, you'll note a cross upon Cerro de la Cruz, the large hill just ahead of you. It was placed here by the Spaniards in the 16th century. The US Navy used the hillside just below it for target practice during WWII. The road leaves the residential area and the incline increases as it passes some of the plants that earned Taboga the nickname 'Island of Flowers.' The wild hibiscus, bougainvillea, oleander and jasmine on the island explode in a riot of colors in April and May. During a morning stroll, you can hear and see the many birds that nest and feed among the flowers.

After 2km of this now-strenuous and woodsy walk, the road forks one last time. To the left are abandoned **bunkers** used by US troops during WWII. The bunkers are large and you can enter them. When you stand amid the thick concrete walls, it doesn't seem like the war was so long ago. Climb

atop the bunkers for grand views: of ships in the bay, each awaiting its turn to enter the canal; of the skyscrapers of Panama City; of the nearby islands, forested coastline and wide-open sea. The view out over the ocean recalls the time of the great explorers, when mariners hugged the coasts, the Atlantic was called the 'Sea of Darkness,' and most Europeans believed that if you sailed out upon it, you would never return.

If you look below and to the right of the old cross, you'll see a white-and-brown pile of rubble amid thickening vegetation. It's the ruins of a Spanish cannon emplacement put there 300 years ago to protect the island from pirates. The green-blue water below the ruins offers decent diving. Not visible from land but tucked into the cliff below the bunkers are two caves where Indian artifacts have been found. Up the road from the bunkers, on the road's less-traveled branch, are a radar installation and the island's secondary electrical plant; they are off-limits to the public.

Beaches

Many people come to Taboga to go to the beach. There are fine beaches in either direction from the ferry dock. You can visit any of them for free.

Many visitors head straight for the Hotel Taboga, to your right as you walk off the ferry dock; the hotel faces onto the island's most popular beach, arcing between Taboga and tiny Isla El Morro. A day entrance fee of US$5 gives you access to dressing rooms and showers and use of the large garden grounds; the hotel also rents paddle boats, beach umbrellas, hammocks, mats, snorkel and dive gear and the like. There's no need to pay the hotel simply to use the beach, however; there's an easily overlooked walkway to the beach, beside the gate entrance to the hotel.

Forest

On the trip back from the island, look to the west of the Puente de las Américas and you will see one of the last tracts of Pacific dry forest remaining in Central America. Such forests used to line much of the Pacific coast

PANAMÁ PROVINCE

of Central America. Because they are easy to clear for agriculture, however, these forests have now all but disappeared.

Along the edge and near the center of the otherwise forested stretch of coastline are several large structures. They comprised Panama's last leper colony, which closed during the late 1970s. Today the facilities serve as a retirement home.

Snorkeling
On the weekends, when most people visit Taboga, you can find fishermen at the island's pier who will take you around the island in their small boats, so that you can see it from all sides and reach some of its good snorkeling spots. There are some caves on the island's western side that are rumored (of course) to hold golden treasure left there by pirates. During the week, when the small boats are nowhere to be found, you can still snorkel around Isla El Morro, which hasn't any coral but attracts some large fish.

Diving
Taboga offers typical Pacific-style diving, with rocky formations and a wide variety of marine life. The beauty of the Pacific lies in the schools of fish that roam about: On a good dive you can expect to see jack, snapper, jewfish, eels, corvina, rays, lobsters and octopuses. With a little luck, you may also come across old bottles, spent WWII-era shells and artifacts from pirate days.

Scubapanama (☎ 261-3841, fax 261-9586, renegomez@scubapanama), at the intersection of Av 6a C Norte and Calle 62 C Oeste in the El Carmen district of Panama City, offers dive trips to Isla Taboga that include pick-up from a Panama City hotel, a speedboat ride to the island, a divemaster, two tanks, weights, lunch and sodas. Per-person rates are US$100 (for five or more people), US$125 (four people), US$160 (three people), US$220 (two people) and US$320 (one person).
Website: www.scubapanama.com

Bird Watching
The islands of Taboga and nearby Urabá are home to one of the largest breeding colonies of brown pelicans in the world. The colony has contained up to 100,000 individual birds, or about half of the world population of this species. A wildlife refuge, the **Refugio de Vida Silvestre Islas Taboga y Urabá**, was established to protect their habitat. The refuge covers about a third of Taboga as well as the entire island of Urabá, just off Taboga's southeast coast. May is the height of nesting season, but pelicans can be seen from January to June.

Whale Watching
On your way to and from the island, keep an eye on the ocean. On rare occasions during August, September and October, migrating humpback and sei whales can be seen leaping from the water near Taboga in spectacular displays.

Places to Stay & Eat
There are only two places to stay on Isla Taboga, and the better value is *Hotel Chu* (☎ 250-2035 on Taboga, ☎ 227-4442 and 635-0310 in Panama City). This two-story wooden structure, built on the beach in the early 20th century, has 15 basic but comfortable and breezy rooms upstairs, each with its own private balcony. Guests share a clean bathroom. Rates are US$18/22 for one/two people. This is a fine place to return to at day's end. At night guests sleep to the soothing sound of surf. There's a public phone out front. Downstairs there's an open-air restaurant with good and inexpensive food (seafood, pizzas, chow mein, chop suey, burgers, a delicious shrimp omelet and tipico fare) and a sweeping view of the bay.

Hotel Taboga (☎ 264-6096, fax 223-5739) is an example of the disparity that sometimes exists between price and value. Rates range from US$55 to US$70 plus tax, and though the 54 rooms have air con, cable TV and hot water, they often smell mildewy, they don't have private phones and you can't hear the ocean from them. Still, the rooms are located amid a pleasant setting of gardens beside the beach, and there's a pool. The food at the Hotel Taboga is nothing special and it's more expensive than the food at Hotel Chu.

Entertainment

There isn't much nightlife on Taboga. It's pretty much limited to the bar/restaurant at Hotel Taboga and to *Bar El Galeon*, which serves the cheapest drinks in town and is located beneath Hotel Chu. This place is easy to miss, but it's right on the ocean and very unpretentious, and there are two pool tables on the premises.

Getting There & Away

The one-hour boat trip to Taboga is part of the island's attraction. The **Calypso Queen** ferry (☎ 232-5736, 264-6096) departs from Muelle 18 in the Balboa district of Panama City, and it passes along the Balboa port, under the Puente de las Américas and along the last part of the Panama Canal channel on its journey out to sea. It also passes the Causeway that links La Boca district to four small offshore islands.

From Tuesday to Friday, the ferry leaves Balboa at 8:30 am and departs Taboga on the return trip at 4 pm. On weekends and holidays, the ferry departs Balboa at 7:45 and 10:30 am and at 4:30 pm; the return trip leaves Taboga at 9 am and at 3 and 5:45 pm. The roundtrip fare is US$7.50. A taxi ride from most parts of Panama City to Muelle 18 rarely exceeds US$10 per party. Because Taboga is a popular retreat, you'd be wise to reserve a seat on the Calypso Queen a few days in advance.

Archipiélago de las Perlas

In January 1979, after the followers of the Ayatollah Ruholla Khomeini had forced Shah Mohammed Reza Pahlavi to pack up his hundreds of millions of dollars and flee Iran, the shah looked the world over and moved to Isla Contadora. It's one of 90 named islands in the Archipiélago de las Perlas, or Pearl Islands, any one of which is fit for a king – or a shah.

These islands, plus 130 unnamed islets in the Pearl chain, lie between 64km and 113km southeast of Panama City and are the stuff of travel magazines: tan-sand beaches, turquoise waters, swaying palms, colorful fish and sea turtles sharing lagoons with snorkelers. And out of the oysters that abound here have come some of the world's finest pearls, including the 31-carat 'Peregrina' pearl, which has been worn by a Spanish king, an English queen and a French emperor and today belongs to actress Elizabeth Taylor. (When the pearl was found, more than 400 years ago, it was considered so magnificent that the slave who discovered it was given his freedom.)

In fact, it was pearls that initially brought the islands to the Old World's attention. Vasco Núñez de Balboa, within days of his discovery of the Pacific Ocean, learned of nearby islands rich with pearls from an Indian guide. Balboa was anxious to visit the islands, but he was told that a hostile chief ruled them, and the explorer decided to postpone the visit. He nonetheless named the archipelago 'Islas de las Perlas' and declared it Spanish property. The year was 1513, and Balboa vowed to return one day to kill the chief and claim his pearls for the king of Spain.

But before he could fulfill his vow, Spanish governor Pedro Arias de Ávila, who loathed the great explorer for his popularity with the king, dispatched his cousin Gaspar de Morales to the islands to secure the pearls spoken of by Balboa. Once on the islands, Morales captured 20 chieftains and gave them to his dogs to tear to pieces. The purportedly hostile chief, a man named Dites, initially resisted Morales and his men, but after a battle in which many Indians died, the chief saw the futility of warring with the Spaniards, and he presented Morales with a basket of large and lustrous pearls. Despite the gift, all the Pearl Indians were dead within two years.

History books do not record the circumstances of Dites' death, but they do record Balboa's. In 1517, the same year that Morales raided Las Perlas, Pedrarias (as the governor was often called) falsely charged Balboa with treason and had the loyal public servant and four of his closest friends beheaded in the Caribbean coastal town of

ARCHIPIÉLAGO DE LAS PERLAS

Isla Pachequilla
Isla Pacheca
Isla Contadora
Isla Saboga
Isla Chitre
Isla Chepra
Golfo de Panamá
Isla Mogo Mogo o Pájaro
Isla Bolaños
Isla Casayeta
Golfo de Panamá
Isla Gibraleón
Isla Lampón
8°30'N
Isla Casaya
Isla Bayoneta
Isla La Mina
Isla Viveros
Punta Hueca
Isleta Señora
San Miguel
Isla del Espíritu Santo
Isla Trapiche
Punta Casa Sola
Isla Caña
Isla Pedro González
Isla del Rey
Isla de Puerco
Punta Gallinazo
Bahía del Rey
Punta Gorda
Punta Trapiche
Punta Platanal   Punta Cabezón
Punta Paraquito
Punta Chivo
Punta Encanto
Bahía San Telmo
Isla San Telmo
Punta Cocal
Punta Bonga
Punta Timón
8°15'N
Punta Níspero
Punta Cabo   Hacienda del Mar   **Isla San José**
Punta de Pedregal
Punta Coco
Punta de Cruz
Isla Marin
Isla de Hicaco
Isla Galera

Aclá. (See the Comarca de San Blás chapter for details.)

In the years that followed Morales' arrival in the archipelago, the Spaniards harvested the islands' oyster beds like the greedy businessmen they were. Because they had slain all the Indians, they found it necessary to import slaves from Africa to collect oysters. The island that was used for counting the pearls before they were shipped to Panama City – and thence to Spain – was named Contadora, which is Spanish for 'counting house.' The island has retained its name, and descendants of the first slaves who came to the Archipiélago de las Perlas presently live on the island.

Today, people inhabit no more than a dozen of the 220 islands and islets that comprise the Archipiélago de las Perlas. The largest of the group is Isla del Rey at 240 sq km, followed by Isla San José (45.3 sq km), Isla Pedro González (14.9 sq km), Isla Viveros (6.6 sq km) and Isla Caña (3.2 sq km).

With few exceptions, tourists visit only five of Las Perlas: Isla Contadora (at 1.2 sq km), Isla Saboga (2.96 sq km), Isla Casaya (2.75 sq km), Isla Casayeta (0.46 sq km) and Isla San José. Of these, Contadora is the

Pirates in the Bay

From the late 17th century, the Bahía de Panamá, home to the Pearl and Taboga island groups, was the scene of pirate exploits unsurpassed anywhere in the New World. Henry Morgan's successful 1671 sacking of the city of Panamá enticed other buccaneers to enter the area and try their hands at plundering and pillaging Spanish territory and ships along the Pacific coast. Many are the stories of pirates using the Archipiélago de las Perlas as a hideout and springboard for attacks.

One of the era's most significant escapades occurred in May 1685 near Las Perlas, when the largest number of trained seamen and fighters ever assembled under a buccaneer flag in the Pacific played cat-and-mouse with a Spanish armada of 18 ships. The pirate fleet consisted of 10 French and English vessels united under the English captain Edward Blake. Because his fleet was deficient in cannons but sufficient in muskets, it was Blake's policy to avoid long-range fighting. Despite his fleet's inferior numbers, he itched for a close encounter with the Spaniards.

When the two great forces came within sight of each other on May 28, Blake ordered two of his principal ships (one led by a Frenchman, the second by an Englishman) to initiate an attack on the Spanish fleet. Fearing the Spaniards' cannons, both men refused to obey. Blake's crew exchanged shots with the Spanish vice admiral, but Blake – seeing the imprudence of continuing battle with the odds stacked against him and with some of his officers bowing out – ordered his slower ships to flee while his and another fast vessel delayed the conquistadors.

The Spaniards opened fire with their big guns, but the pirates managed some nifty and risky evasive maneuvers between rocky islets at the northern end of the archipelago, and their pursuers gave up the chase. Blake's ships anchored off the archipelago's Isla Pacheca that night, fully expecting the Spanish armada to engage them the next day. Instead, for reasons that mystify historians, the Spanish admiral ordered his fleet to return to Panamá. In the days that followed, dissent arose among the buccaneers, and the short-lived French-English pirate confederacy dissolved.

Today, little evidence of the pirates and Spaniards remains in the Archipiélago de las Perlas besides the distant descendants of the Spaniards and their slaves. Forests once felled to make ships have grown back. Storms, termites and wood worms have destroyed the old Spanish structures. Only a church and a stone dam on Isla Saboga and wells on Islas Pacheca and Chapera testify to the Spaniards' presence.

most accessible, developed and visited; Isla San José is the site of a new resort; Saboga attracts the occasional explorer who must check out the colonial church, but it is pillaged, unattractive and poorly maintained. Casaya and neighboring Casayeta are frequented by pearl shoppers.

Unfortunately, coral fields throughout the archipelago were severely damaged during the 1982–83 El Niño. (El Niño is a change in ocean temperatures that, among a great many other horrible things, starves marine life along the entire eastern Pacific coast.) The coral, which is mostly of the mushroom and elkhorn variety, was making a strong comeback when the 1997–98 El Niño struck. In 2001, the coral was doing fairly well. Regardless of the state of the coral, these waters contain many lovely creatures, including leatherback, carey and

PANAMÁ PROVINCE

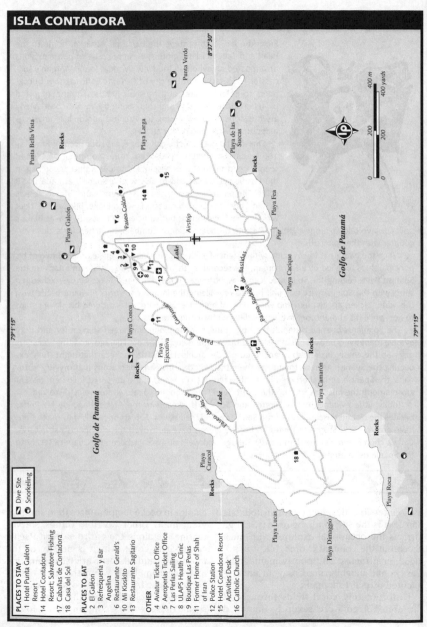

ISLA CONTADORA

8°37'30"

79°1'15"

79°1'15"

Punta Verde

Punta Bella Vista

Rocks

Playa Larga

Playa Galeón

Paseo Colón

Airstrip

Lake

Playa Conca

Paseo de las Guabas

Playa Ejecutiva

Rocks

Golfo de Panamá

Paseo de las Cañas

Lake

Playa Caracol

Rocks

Playa Lucas

Playa Dimaggio

Playa de las Suecas

Rocks

Playa Fea

Pier

Paseo Rodeo de Bastidas

Playa Cacique

Golfo de Panamá

Playa Camarón

Rocks

Playa Roca

Dive Site
Snorkeling

PLACES TO STAY
1 Hotel Punta Galeón
    Resort
14 Hotel Contadora
    Resort; Salvatore Fishing
17 Cabañas de Contadora
18 Casa del Sol

PLACES TO EAT
2 El Galeón
3 Refresquería y Bar
    Angelina
6 Restaurante Gerald's
10 Mi Kioskito
13 Restaurante Sagitario

OTHER
4 Aviatur Ticket Office
5 Aeroperlas Ticket Office
7 Las Perlas Sailing
8 ULAPS Health Clinic
9 Boutique Las Perlas
11 Former Home of Shah
    of Iran
12 Police Station
15 Hotel Contadora Resort
    Activities Desk
16 Catholic Church

hawksbill turtles; bull, nurse and white-tip reef sharks; shovelnose guitarfish; and a wide variety of rays.

There is no tourist office, bank or post office on any of the islands in the Archipiélago de las Perlas, and accommodations are limited to the islands of Contadora and San José.

ISLA CONTADORA
pop 350

This small island is one of the closest of Las Perlas to Panama City and is by far the most visited. There are convenient daily flights to and from the capital, several options for lodging, good snorkeling and beaches, and a variety of restaurants.

Nearly all the tourist facilities are on the northern side of the island, within walking distance of the airstrip. The other side consists primarily of forest, beautiful homes and secluded beaches. Contadora is also home to the country's only official nude beach, Playa de las Suecas (Swedish Women Beach).

There's a ULAPS Health Clinic (☎ 250-4209) a short walk from the airstrip that offers 24-hour service. If no one answers the door, walk around to the back of the facility to the house there. That's the doctor's home and he doesn't mind being disturbed if someone's in need.

Beaches

There are 12 beaches on this 1.2-sq-km island, all covered with tan sand and most unoccupied except during major holidays. Five beaches are particularly lovely: Playa Larga, Playa de las Suecas, Playa Cacique, Playa Ejecutiva and Playa Galeón. Although spread around three sides of the island, all can be visited in as little as 20 minutes on a rented four-wheeler.

Playa Larga is always the most crowded of the beaches, as it is in front of the expansive Hotel Contadora Resort, but it's also perhaps the best for spotting marine life. Around the corner to the south is Playa de las Suecas, where you can sunbathe in the buff legally. Continuing west 400m, you'll find Playa Cacique, a fairly large and un-visited beach. On the northern side of the island, Playa Ejecutiva is intimate except during holidays; the large house on the bluff to the east is where the shah of Iran once lived. Playa Galeón, to the northeast, is good for snorkeling.

Snorkeling

The snorkeling around Contadora can be fantastic. There are five coral fields near the island, and within them you can expect to see schools of angelfish, damselfish, moray eels, parrotfish, puffer fish, butterflyfish, white-tip reef sharks and a whole lot more. Even in the waters off Playa Larga, the most popular of Isla Contadora's beaches, you can often see sea turtles, manta rays and amberjack; if you have time for only one dip, do it here.

The coral fields are found offshore from the following places: the eastern end of Playa de las Suecas; Punta Verde, near the southern end of Playa Larga; both ends of Playa Galeón; and the western end of Playa Ejecutiva. Also, although there is little coral at the southwestern end of the island, there is a lot of marine life among the rocks in front and east of Playa Roca.

Snorkeling trips can be arranged at Hotel Contadora Resort (see Places to Stay, later in this section). Salvatore Fishing (see Fishing, following) offers an attractive snorkeling package: three hours, three islands, for US$30 per person. It also offers a seven-island, whole-day snorkeling tour that costs a very reasonable US$25 per person (minimum eight people).

Diving

Hotel Contadora Resort was the only place offering scuba diving in the Pearl chain in 2001, but because none of its divemasters had received formal training in scuba diving, I do not recommend diving here. Also, because the snorkeling is so good and accessible, there's little reason to scuba dive here.

Fishing

Salvatore Fishing (☎/fax 250-4109, cellular ☎ 686-0413, morello@cwp.net.pa), which operates out of Hotel Contadora Resort, offers half and full-day fishing trips for US$50 and US$100, respectively, with a four-fisherman minimum. You can rent a boat for US$200 per half-day. The business is run by a married couple, Salvatore Morello and Josefina Mejia, both of whom speak English and Spanish. Their boats include two 32-foot cabin cruisers and one 26-foot open fisherman.

Four-Wheeling

Contadora lends itself very well to tooting around on a four-wheeler, which is a small vehicle like a golf cart but a lot more sturdy. There are few other vehicles on the island to collide with, and four-wheelers are pretty easy to operate. If you're short on time and tight with your money, you can rent a four-wheeler first thing in the morning for an hour, scout out your favorite beaches or other sites, return the vehicle and have pretty much the whole day in front of you to walk back to your selected spots. **Las Perlas Sailing** (☎/fax 250-4214, hcorrand@usa.net), on the road to Hotel Contadora Resort, rents four-wheelers for US$20 an hour. It's open 8 am to 6 pm daily.

Jet Skis & Sailing

If it's in your nature to destroy the peace and quiet of other vacationers while chasing innocent marine life out into a dangerous sea, by all means you should rent a Jet Ski from Las Perlas Sailing (US$15 for 15 minutes).

However, Las Perlas Sailing offers a 'Jet Ski safari' that's a whole lot of fun and doesn't disturb many people. For US$75 per person, a guide leads you and other Jet Skiers to various nearby islands (see Four-Wheeling for information).

Las Perlas Sailing also offers a sailing tour from 9 am to 5 pm. Lunch included, the per person cost is US$75. You can also rent a parasail from the company. The cost is US$30 for the flyer and US$10 for the rider. Owners Henri Corrand and wife Valerie Lamour speak French, Spanish and English, and they're very friendly.

Glass-Bottom Boat

Owned and operated by the very amusing Jayson Young, *Glass Bottom* is a 28-foot boat with eight glass panels you know where. The Jamaican boatman takes tourists all the way around Isla Contadora, giving a detailed history of the island and a rundown of the area's marine life during the 90-minute tour.

Expect to see parrot fish, sergeant majors, puffer fish; occasionally you'll pass over sea turtles, dolphins, manta rays, sharks, even humpback whales. The boat is partially shaded, so there's relief if you start catching too many rays. At US$15 per person, this is the best-value tour on the island and highly recommended.

The boat departs from Playa Larga, but the departure time changes with varying tides. To find out when Jayson will be making his next departure, inquire at the reception desk of Hotel Contadora Resort or Hotel Punta Galeón Resort. Or, try the activities desk of Hotel Contadora Resort mid-beach on Playa Larga.

Places to Stay

Isla Contadora offers a fine variety of housing options.

A great addition to the island's hotel scene is the centrally located **Hotel Punta Galeón Resort** (☎ 250-4134, fax 250-4135, hpgaleon@sinfo.net). The hotel offers 48 lovely air-con rooms with cable TV, hot-water bathrooms, private phones, minibars, good beds and a sea-facing terrace. Facilities at this Colombian-owned hotel include a sauna, swimming pool, kid's pool, an open-sided restaurant and an air-con restaurant, and several viewing platforms with tables and chairs. Singles/doubles run US$96/120, including breakfast.

Hotel Contadora Resort (☎ 250-4033, fax 250-4000) is a 354-room monstrosity of French Colonial design, built in 1975. It had been allowed to deteriorate pretty badly until 2000, when its owners put a smart manager in charge and gave him a budget he could do something with. Facilities include a large swimming pool, three tennis courts (two lighted) and a nine-hole golf course, all of which are free for guests. Meals are included and always buffet style. The hotel's greatest asset is the beach in front, which is kissed by the gentle waves of a protected bay. The rack rate is US$76 per person double occupancy, but most people arrive on package deals and pay less. Golf clubs, tennis rackets, snorkeling equipment and board games are available for guests' use free of charge. Guests can rent mountain bikes for US$5 an hour, golf carts for US$20 an hour and four-wheelers for US$25 hour. At the bar, guests pay nothing for national drinks most of the time.

A young German couple named Kirsten and Tolsten Loeffler who prefer to be called by their nicknames (Kitty and Spoon) have made one room of their lovely home available to rent. Called **Casa del Sol** (☎ 250-4212, skytoxin@bigfoot.com), the home is located in a residential neighborhood where silence is mostly broken by birdsong and hummingbirds outnumber people. It's a great find; guests have a hot-water bathroom with hair dryer, and their room in the modest but beautifully detailed house is separated from the owners' by an office for added privacy. The friendly owners, who speak English, German and Spanish and carry on intelligent conversation, prepare a delicious breakfast for guests at no extra cost. The rate of US$30 for one person and US$40 for two is an excellent value, and lower weekly rates are available. It's a 20-minute walk from the B&B to the airstrip and five minutes by bike (the couple has two bikes available to guests for US$5 a day). The Loefflers offer massage and intimate, four-tourist trips to unoccupied islands and snorkeling sites aboard their fine boat. Custom trips, such as overnighting on a lovely unoccupied island, are also available. Website: www.panama-isla-contadora.com

About a 10-minute walk from the airstrip through a lush, upscale residential neighborhood is **Cabañas de Contadora** (☎/fax 250-4214), which is owned by the same French couple that owns and manages Las Perlas Sailing and who live next door to the cabins. The cabañas are actually four side-by-side fan-cooled apartments with cool-water showers. Each apartment has a refrigerator and a microwave, and rents for US$50 single or double, including breakfast.

Places to Eat

Refresquería y Bar Angelina near the Aeroperlas office, was until recently owned by singer-songwriter Michael Bolton and named Michael's Gelatiere-Pizzeria. It offers pizzas, sandwiches, ceviche, pork chops, a daily Panamanian plate, Italian ice cream, sodas, coffees and juices. Everything here is reasonably priced, and this is a good place to hook up with other travelers. Don't overlook the four seaside tables behind the kitchen. It's open 8 am to 10 pm daily.

The small shop **Mi Kioskito**, just uphill from the Aeroperlas office, houses a sandwich-and-beverage counter where it's possible to purchase a glass of the finest drink on Earth: sangria, containing fruit steeped in Burgundy a night before serving. Mi Kioskito also sells ceviche, sandwiches, ice cream and cake. The captivating Spanish owner, Carmen Andrés, speaks Spanish and English.

For truly fine food, you should try **Restaurante Gerald's**, which overlooks a pretty golf course. Gerald's offers salads (US$3), shrimp cocktails (US$9), fish plates (US$9 to US$12), meat dishes (US$9.50 to US$12.50), shrimp dishes (US$14) and lobster (US$12 to US$25). Gerald's offers several German dishes as well, ranging in price from US$12 to US$15. It's open noon to 3 pm and 6 to 10 pm daily. There's also a full bar.

For typical Panamanian food at a low, low cost, head for **Restaurante Sagitario**. Everything here is under US$5. It's open 6:30 am to 8 pm daily.

Shopping

Pearls Oysters are still caught, and pearls are still found, around the Archipiélago de las Perlas. Although pearls are sometimes offered for sale on other islands, the best places to shop for them are Isla Casaya and neighboring Isla Casayeta, about 12km to the south of Contadora; contact Salvatore Fishing for transportation. Prices are generally very reasonable, and there's always room for bargaining.

When you're looking at pearls, it's good to keep two things in mind. First, pearl sellers tend to keep their goods in oil, so that they'll have a lovely shine when presented; always dry the pearl that intrigues you and then see how it looks. Second, you can't add luster to a pearl; if the dry pearl in your hand looks dull, that's the way it's going to stay.

Clothing On Contadora, **Mi Kioskito** is *the* place to look for islandwear. The shop offers many all-cotton dresses of Balinese design made by owner Carmen Andrés. The women's sun hats, also made by Carmen, are light, brightly colored and unique. There are lots of T-shirts, purses, dark glasses and knickknacks as well.

Boutique Las Perlas, a short walk uphill from Mi Kioskito, sells sun dresses, souvenirs, beverages, sunglasses, lotions and so on. It's open 8 am to 9 pm daily.

Getting There & Away

Aeroperlas (☎ 250-4026 on Contadora, ☎ 315-7500 in Panama City) flies direct from Isla Contadora to Panama City at 8:25 am and 5:25 pm from Monday to Saturday, at 9:15 am on Saturday and Sunday, and at 4:15 pm on Sunday. The roundtrip fare is US$54. Flying time is 15 minutes each way. Flights from Panama City to Isla Contadora leave at 8 am and 5 pm from Monday to Friday; at 8, 8:50 and 9:45 am and 5 pm Saturday; and at 8:50 am and 3:50 and 4:40 pm Sunday. See the Panama City chapter for flights to Isla Contadora.

Aviatur (☎ 250-4192 on Contadora, ☎ 315-0307 in Panama City) flies from Isla Contadora to Panama City and back a minimum of four times daily. The roundtrip fare is US$54.

Getting Around

Because the island is so small, there are no taxis on it. Hotel Contadora Resort has a van that shuttles guests to and from the airstrip. There are four-wheelers for rent (see Four-Wheeling earlier in this chapter).

ISLA SAN JOSÉ
pop 350

Most of this 45.3 sq km island is covered in a bank of rain forest that's networked by 100km of all-weather roads installed by the US military decades ago. With the exception of roads, the only development on the island is *Hacienda del Mar* (☎ 269-6634, 269-6613 in Panama City, fax 264-7214, hdelmar@ quik.com.pa), a gorgeous resort at cliff's edge that presently has the island and its 37 tan-sand beaches, its nine year-round rivers and its seven accessible waterfalls all to itself. Website: www.haciendadelmar.com

The Hacienda del Mar is the creation of Aeroperlas President George Novey, who spared no expense in the construction of his resort. Facilities include 12 luxurious cabins, each fully equipped and overlooking either the open sea or a picture-perfect sweep of beach. The main building is home to a sports bar with pool table and big-screen DirecTV, and a second-story dining room with a menu that includes mostly seafood but also pork chops, filet of beef and chicken cordon bleu. Dinner here with appetizer and dessert will set you back about US$20, and the food is delicious. Between the main building and the cabins is a very inviting swimming pool.

Service here is terrific, led by a charming manager who speaks English, Spanish, Italian, German and French. She leads new arrivals on a tour of the resort, which includes showing guests a sea turtle hatchery that's helping to stave off the animals' extinction. She also introduces guests to the resort's many tours, which include four hours of deep-sea fishing (US$60 per person), a boat tour around the island, stopping at secluded beaches and other places of interest (US$60), a three-hour four-wheeler safari through the rain forest to at least one long beach (US$60), and various night and day excursions by truck. On the roads it's common to see large iguanas, wild pigs, dwarf anteaters and white-brocket deer.

The nightly rate for one cabin with two queen-size beds is US$250, while the rate for a larger cabin with one king-size bed, a sofa bed and up to two portable beds if needed (at US$3 each) is US$350. The cost includes breakfast. Air transportation between Panama City and Isla San José is arranged by the Hacienda del Mar.

Eastern Panamá Province

Beyond the capital city, the Interamericana heads eastward through several small towns before arriving at the Darién Gap, that last defiant stretch of wilderness separating the continents of North and South America. The Darién Gap is the sole barrier in the way of an otherwise unbroken 30,600km highway winding from Circle, Alaska, to Puerto Montt, Chile.

Since the first Pan-American Highway Congress met in Buenos Aires in 1925, the nations of the Americas have devoted considerable money and engineering skills to the completion of a great hemispheric road system. Today, only 150km of unfinished business prevent that system from being realized. Until recently, the governments of Panama and Colombia stood poised to construct this missing bit of pavement.

But with civil war raging in Colombia, it appears that the hemispheric highway won't be completed any time soon. Until it is, the highway on the Panamanian side of the divide will continue to end at the sweaty, ramshackle town of Yaviza, in Darién Province. Separating Yaviza and Panama City are 266km of mostly bad road and cattle country. Efforts to pave the road all the way to Yaviza, perhaps a two-year project, were begun in 2001.

The drive from the capital to Yaviza takes about six hours during the dry season, longer during the rainy season, and less once the road is completely paved. For information on towns along the way beyond the Panamá-Darién border, see the Darién Province chapter.

CHEPO
pop 12,700
Beyond the urban sprawl east of Panama City, the landscape becomes increasingly barren on both sides of the Interamericana. Gas stations and accommodations become somewhat scarce and the views monotonous.

Not 40 years ago the highway ended at Chepo and a sign announced the start of the Darién Gap. (Today, most Panamanians still consider all the country east of Chepo as the Darién, although much of it is actually within Panamá Province.) From Chepo to beyond the Colombian border, there was only roadless jungle. To go any farther by vehicle, one resorted to *piraguas* – needle-like canoes hollowed from logs. These were placed in the Río Mamoní and pushed deep into the Darién rain forest by outboard motors. The 'roads' from there on out were creeks, streams and rivers.

Today, a main road swings out from the Interamericana and into Chepo. The town, 32km past the turnoff for Cerro Azul, continues to exist mainly as a launching point into the Darién: there are two gas stations, a place to buy ice and general stores with lots of canned goods. There's not a single *pensión* or hotel in town.

There's a checkpoint 1km east of town where people coming from the Darién are stopped, asked to show their IDs and are sometimes searched. It's less than an hour's drive from Panama City, but it seems like another country and another time.

Buses leave the Terminal Nacional de Transporte, in the Albrook district of Panama City, for Chepo (US$1.20 one way, 75 minutes) almost hourly from 6:40 am to 5:10 pm. The bus continues on to Cañita.

NUSAGANDI
pop 30
Just before you reach the town of El Llano and 16.2km from Chepo, you'll see the turnoff for Nusagandi, an area inside the Área Silvestre de Narganá wildlife reserve. The reserve was created by the Kuna, primarily to try to keep squatters from settling on their land. But it consists mostly of species-rich primary forest and was a perfect choice for conservation.

If you're a bird watcher driving a 4WD vehicle with a strong engine and plenty of clearance, I highly recommend working this

20km detour into your road trip to the Darién Gap. The road is really bad and rarely traveled, but this is the best spot in Panama to look for the speckled antshrike, the black-headed antthrush and the black-crowned antpitta. Various tanagers, including the rufous-winged, are numerous. There are some gorgeous waterfalls in this jungle as well.

There's the very basic and rarely visited *Nusagandi Nature Lodge* at about the 20km mark. However, you can't just show up there. Contact Ancon Expeditions of Panama (☎ 269-9414/9415, fax 264-3713, info@anconexpeditions.com), in Panama City, and ask them to make the arrangements with the lodge's Kuna owners.

EL LLANO
pop 2800

Eighteen kilometers separate Chepo and El Llano, a small community with a couple of simple restaurants, plus a tire repair service and a public phone. The town is surrounded by rice fields and, beyond these, rolling hills covered with cattle and teak trees. Teak farms now abound in Panama. Teak projects reduce the pressure to log the remaining natural forests, but local birds don't know what to do with them. The trees were introduced to Panama from Asia and the local wildlife hasn't adapted to them. If you stroll deep inside a teak farm, you won't hear a single bird chirp.

CAÑITA
pop 2100

This small town, also bisected by the Interamericana, is 8.7km beyond El Llano. It has a gas station and a public phone in town, as well as three restaurants. At one of them, thatch-roofed, open-sided *El Descanso*, the nailed-up skins of jaguars, ocelots and other animals attest to the health of the rain forest that once blanketed the area. It was felled within the last 20 years, mainly to make room for cattle ranches (see 'Logging the Darién' for more information).

El Descanso is decent and cheap, with few meals over US$2. It's typical of the restaurants between Chepo and Yaviza: It doesn't have menus, but a waitress will tell you what's available. Meals typically consist of chicken or beef or pork with rice and beans. The selection is usually dependent upon which trucks have stopped by recently. There's a bar next door. Nearby are the *Flor de Cañita* and the *Interiorano* restaurants, which aren't so good.

Buses leave Panama City's Terminal Nacional de Transporte for Cañita almost every hour from 6:40 am to 5:10 pm. The trip takes 2½ hours; the one-way fare is US$2.50.

LAGO BAYANO

Fourteen kilometers from Cañita you'll come to Puente Bayano (Bayano Bridge), which crosses Lago Bayano. The paved road stopped here at the bridge at the time of writing. East of the bridge, the Interamericana was either bone dry and bumpy or muddy and deeply rutted.

Around the lake and near the highway here you'll see some healthy secondary forest. It exists to protect Lago Bayano's

---

Logging the Darién

Trees are still being felled in Darién Province, and many are transported by truck along the Interamericana to two huge mills: One is in Chepo, and the other is in 24 de Diciembre, a village near Tocumen. On a single day in the dry season, you can count dozens of lumber trucks passing by.

An even greater number of Darién trees, which are clear-cut, are moved to the mills by barge. Still others are sprayed with a chemical that prevents rot and floated down rivers to the mills. The chemical has killed most of the fish in the rivers used by loggers.

The deforestation has also resulted in severe water shortages from Chepo to Yaviza during the dry season and other environmental problems. Regardless, Panamanian politicians agreed in 2000 to pave the Interamericana to Yaviza, which will permit logging trucks to work the Darién year-round and accelerate the region's destruction. In Panama, loggers have a lot of influence.

watershed. Lago Bayano, which supports a hydroelectric project, was created by the damming of the Río Bayano. Because the forest is owned by a utility company, it will likely remain intact.

IPETÍ
pop 530

This town, 45km east of Lago Bayano, offers the visitor a couple of restaurants, a provisions store and a public phone. Between here and Las Aguas Frías, on the Darién Province-Panamá Province border, the Serranía de Majé (Majé Range) runs along the southern side of the highway. The range contains some lovely forest, at a distance from the highway; you can see this forest best as you approach the town of Tortí. It's disappearing rapidly but should still be visible through the shelf life of this book.

TORTÍ
pop 8000

In Tortí, 12km from Ipetí, you'll come across the first pensión east of Panama City – the *Hospedaje Tortí*. It has 20 rooms, each with a firm mattress, a portable fan, towels and soap. The four shared showers and two shared toilets are clean, and there's electricity 24 hours. For US$5 a night, it's a great value. Be advised: There's no better hotel between here and Yaviza.

Also in town are three public phones, a health clinic, police and gas stations and several restaurants. The best restaurant is *Parrillada Ñata*, which specializes in *tasajo* (smoked beef, with side dishes, US$2.25) and *sancocho de gallina* (free-range chicken soup, US$1). It's open 6 am to 10 pm every day.

Next door to the Parrillada Ñata and at the road's edge you'll see a leather-goods store named *Echao Pa-lante* ('Going Forward'). Inside, hard at work, you'll find Pedro Guerra. Pedro was age 28 at the time of writing and he'd handmade more than 5000 saddles (it takes him a day to make one) and countless belts and sandals. And his prices are low. It's open 10 am to 8 pm daily.

HIGUERONAL
pop 190

Higueronal is 10.2km from Tortí. There's a gas station, two restaurants and a public phone here. Down the road a little, the town of Cañazas offers tourists only a pay phone. There's also a military checkpoint at Cañazas. Foreigners should expect to be asked for their passports, which a soldier will disappear with for a few minutes, note in his ledger your name and nationality and the day's date, and then return your passport to you. That way, if something happens to you and someone is looking for you, this checkpoint will be able to inform the search party that you passed by here.

TO THE DARIÉN GAP

Crossing the border from Panamá Province into Darién Province, you'll pass the towns of Las Aguas Frías, Santa Fé and Metetí before you arrive in Yaviza. See the Darién Province chapter for details on these towns.

Western Panamá Province

There are many communities in the western section of Panamá Province, but the area is known primarily for its many lovely beaches. Every weekend thousands of stressed-out Panama City residents hop into their cars or board buses and head west on the Interamericana, determined to have some fun in the sun beside the lapping Pacific.

LA CHORRERA
pop 55,900

Despite being home to so many people, La Chorrera has relatively little to offer visitors. It is bisected by the Interamericana and located in a fairly prosperous agricultural area, but as one tourism official put it: 'It's a city people pass by.' Still, La Chorrera is a place with a past, a culture, a waterfall and a unique local drink: the *chicheme* (see Places to Eat later in this section).

Orientation

The Interamericana runs from east to west through La Chorrera, slowing to one sluggish lane in each direction as vehicles enter and exit the highway from side streets. It was mainly to reduce the traffic on the highway, which becomes Avenida de las Américas as it passes through town, that a parallel, four-lane highway was built just south of town in the 1980s. This young stretch of highway – the Autopista Arraiján-Chorrera, which is only 28km long – diverges from the Interamericana just west of La Chorrera and at Arraiján, a town northeast of La Chorrera. The new road enables motorists to bypass La Chorrera altogether, saving 30 minutes of driving time. There's one catch, however: The Autopista Arraiján-Chorrera exacts a US$2 toll.

Information

There is no tourist office in La Chorrera, but people who want to know more about the city and surrounding area can obtain reliable information from the office of the Instituto Nacional de Cultura (INAC; ☎/fax 253-2306) on Calle Maria Leticia 75m north of the Interamericana, at the east end of town (the turnoff is 100m before the Super 99 supermarket). The office, located in an art school, is open 8 am to 5 pm weekdays and 10 am to 2 pm Saturday. Only Spanish is spoken. Here you can learn about the town's culture and festivals (see Special Events, following, for details).

There is no shortage of banks in La Chorrera, and most of them are conveniently located on the Interamericana halfway through town. Among them are the Banco Nacional de Panamá and the Banco del Istmo, with normal business hours.

The post office is on Calle San Francisco two blocks south of the Interamericana. It's open 8 am to 5 pm weekdays and 8 am to noon Saturday. There are many pay phones in town.

Waterfalls

La Chorrera has only one true tourist attraction and, sadly, it isn't what it once was. It's a series of cascades on the Río Caimito called El Chorro, the last of which takes a 30m plunge into a broad swimming hole. Years ago the Caimito was a raging river, and both of its banks were swathed in pristine jungle. Today, much of the river has been siphoned off upstream and dozens of plastic bottles bob in the natural pool below the falls. Some of the jungle still remains, and with a little effort by ANAM, Panama's public environmental agency, the site's beauty could be restored. But until then only blind romantics can ignore the pollution.

To get here from the Interamericana, turn north onto Calle Larga at the Banco del Istmo and drive 1km until you reach an intersection with a Super La Fortuna market on one side and a Mini Super Pacifico market on the other. Turn right just before the minimarket and then stay to the left on the road. The falls are at the end of this road, 1km from the intersection. If you do not have a vehicle, you can hire a taxi (US$1.50 each way) or hail a bus with 'Calle Larga' scrawled on its windshield; they run all day and charge 25¢ a ride.

Lago Gatún

Adventurous souls might want to venture to Lago Gatún (Gatún Lake), which is easily reached from La Chorrera. To get to the lake by car, turn off the Interamericana onto the unmarked road beside the Caja de Ahorros, which is 100m west of the Banco del Istmo and turn off for El Chorro. Proceed north 800m to the Plaza de 28 de Noviembre, on the right side of the road. Just beyond the plaza, on a corner on the left side of the street, you'll see a butcher shop called Carniceria Victor Loo. Turn left onto the street in front of Victor Loo. (The street's unmarked and no one seems to know the name, hence all these landmarks instead of street names. However, most people know this as the road to Mendoza, or 'calle a Mendoza.')

To reach Lago Gatún from here, stay on the road to Mendoza for the 16.9km to Mendoza and there continue on another 5km; this will put you at lake's edge. There's a pier there and at it you can always find a boatman who will take you fishing for US$25 for two hours. When you've returned with your catch, walk from the pier up the road a little way to the Club Campetre Arco Iris, where there are some bohios. There, for a couple of dollars, someone will gladly cook your fish for you. Be prepared: Bring at least a plate and a fork with you.

If you're relying on public transportation, back at the Caja de Ahorres store, catch a bus with 'Mendoza' or 'Mendoza/Represa' on the windshield and tell the driver that you want to go to Lago Gatún. If you don't speak Spanish, just say 'Lago Gatún, por favor' and smile sincerely. The one-way fare is US$1.50.

Special Events

The region is known for its beautiful folkloric dances, which can best be seen during its popular fair. La Feria de La Chorrera lasts 10 days and is held in late January or early February; dates vary from year to year. The festivities also include parades, a rodeo and cockfights. La Chorrera is also known for drum dances that have their origin in African music brought by slaves. You can see these dances during the fair.

Places to Stay

Hospedaje Lamas (☎ 253-7887), on Avenida de las Américas near the west end of town, has 10 rooms with air con for US$18 apiece and 12 rooms with fans only for US$14 apiece. All of the rooms have private bathrooms, somewhat firm beds, TVs, tiled floors and cold water only.

Places to Eat

Across the avenida from Hospedaje Lamas is *Pandería Lupita*, a bakery that's been around since the dinosaurs. The breads here are so-so, but the danishes and cakes are yummy. It opens very early and closes very late.

Broster Pollo, on Avenida Libertador one block east of Calle 31 Sur, serves tasty and filling red meat soup (US$1), a very decent bistec picado (US$3) and several chicken dishes (US$3.50). For Chinese

food, locals recommend *Shangri La*, which is on the Interamericana near the eastern end of town.

A popular activity in La Chorrera is drinking *chicheme*, a nonalcoholic beverage made of milk, mashed sweet corn, cinnamon and vanilla. People come from as far away as Panama City just to drink the stuff, which many view as a life-extending concoction. An excellent place to try chicheme is the takeout restaurant *El Chichemito*, on the corner of Calles L Oeste and 26 Norte. As you're driving west on the Interamericana, turn right onto Calle 26 Norte (just beyond the 'bbb' shoe store sign) and look for the restaurant, 30m farther on the left.

While you're at El Chichemito, try another local specialty, the *boyo chorrenano*. It's a sweet-corn tamale filled with marinated chicken, bell pepper, garlic, celery, onion and raisins. The women who make it and other boyos (fillings vary; five kinds are made) insist that they're the best in town, and the number of people who flock to this corner food stand evidently agree. El Chichemito is open 7:30 am to 10:30 pm daily.

Entertainment

About 3km east of La Chorrera on the Interamericana is **Club La Herradura**, offering three popular public swimming pools and picnic facilities, which are open Sunday only from 10 am to 5 pm; the cost for adimision is US$3 for women and children, US$5 for men.

The club is also a hopping bar/dance club late on Thursday, Friday and weekend nights. Admission is free for women and usually costs US$5 for men.

Getting There & Away

East- and westbound buses stop at the Delta station, opposite the Pribanco bank and Matrox pharmacy on the Interamericana. Buses for Panama City leave every eight minutes and cost US$1. The ride lasts one hour. Ask for the express bus or you'll be making frequent stops. There are plenty of taxis in town.

PARQUE NACIONAL Y RESERVA BIOLÓGICA ALTOS DE CAMPANA

The easy-to-miss turnoff for this national park is 25km southwest of La Chorrera, on the western side of the Interamericana. More specifically, it's at the top of a steep and windy section of the Interamericana known locally as the Loma Capana. From the turnoff, a rocky road winds 4.6km to an ANAM ranger station at the entrance to the park, which is located on Cerro Campana. At the station you must pay a US$1 entry fee. Camping is allowed (US$5 per night); there are no facilities.

About 200m beyond the station, there's a lookout point from which you have a fantastic view of mostly deforested but completely uninhabited mountains and the Pacific Ocean. Here you're at 1007m and the breeze is very refreshing.

This park requires at least several hours to be appreciated because it's best viewed on foot. Starting at the road's end, beyond the microwave tower, trails will take you into some lovely forest, which is on the much greener Atlantic slope. The difference between the deforested Pacific and the lush Atlantic slopes is nowhere more evident.

Birders are almost certain to see scale-crested pygmy-tyrant, orange-bellied trogon and chestnut-capped brush-finch. The list of rare possibilities includes the slaty antwren, the white-tipped sicklebill and the purplish-backed quail-dove.

No buses go up the road leading to the park. You pretty much need to have your own vehicle, rely on the services of a guide company or do some rather serious hiking to get in. However, getting to the turnoff for the park is easy. Virtually any bus using that section of the Interamericana will drop you there; indeed, there's a bus stop beside the turnoff. Getting picked up isn't a problem during the day, either, as there are many buses that pass by the turnoff during daylight hours.

PUNTA CHAME
pop 390

The turnoff from the Interamericana for Punta Chame is immediately east of the tiny hamlet of Bejuco, 13.6km west of the turnoff for Parque Nacional Altos de Campana. The paved road that links the Interamericana to the point first winds past rolling hills, then passes flat land that consists mainly of shrimp farms and red and white mangroves, and then passes dry forest. Few people live along this 25km road because very little rain falls in the area and brackish water makes farming difficult.

Punta Chame is a one-road town on a long, 300m wide peninsula, with residences and vacant lots lining both sides. To the north is a muddy bay; to the east is the Pacific. The bay is popular with windsurfers, but there's no windsurfing equipment available for rent here. The beach on the Pacific side (Playa Chame) has lovely sand, but almost no one comes here due to its inconvenient location and its lack of facilities. Also, due to the number of stingrays that nestle in the sand 50m to 100m shore, locals don't swim on the bay side during low tide.

What's intriguing about Punta Chame is that it's slowly being developed, but not in the way that one might expect. The entire point consists of a very clean sand, which is very desirable for use in concrete. So desirable, in fact, that when the Americans began building the locks for the Panama Canal, they used barges to bring sand from the point. Today barges are still taking chunks of Punta Chame away for use in building Panama City skyscrapers. Unless the barges stop arriving, there won't be a Punta Chame in another 100 years.

Places to Stay & Eat

Decent food is available at **Hotel Punta Chame** (☎ 240-5498, fax 263-6590), the only accommodation on the point, but I can't think of any reason that anyone would want to overnight here. The beds form a U-shape when you sit on them and the rates are excessive. It has two concrete-walled cabins (US$55 per cabin), three rooms in a four-unit trailer home (US$44 per unit), and two stand-alone trailer homes for rent (US$120).

As you enter Punta Chame, on the right side of the street you'll see a sign for

Fundacion Amigos de las Tortugas Marinas *(☎ 227-5091 in Panama City, cellular ☎ 630-1347 and 630-3612).* The Friends of Sea Turtles Foundation was founded by brother and sister Ramon and Vilma Morales in 1998 to reverse the declining numbers of sea turtles returning to nest on Punta Chame-area beaches every year. Here, there are several hatcheries, where a turtle hunter-turned savior hatches sea turtles and releases them when they are of a good size. To help finance their project, the Moraleses had several cabins built next to the hatcheries. These looked to be comfortable, but you'd be wise to bring mosquito netting. The rates were US$30 per person.

Getting There & Away
To get to Punta Chame from the Interamericana, catch a bus at the stop at the Punta Chame turnoff (at Bejuco). A bus to the point leaves hourly from 6:30 am to 5:30 pm daily. The fare is US$1.

BEACHES
Starting just south of the town of Chame and continuing along the Pacific coast for the next 40km are dozens of beautiful beaches that are very popular weekend retreats for Panama City residents. About half of these beaches are in Panamá Province, while the remainder are in Coclé Province; those in Coclé are discussed in that chapter.

The beaches are quite similar to one another: All are wide, covered with salt-and-pepper sand and fairly free of litter. The waves in the vicinity of five of the beaches (Playa Malibú, Playa Serena, Playa Teta, Playa El Palmar and Playa Río Mar) attract surfers. See Surfing in the Facts for the Visitor chapter for details.

The most popular of these beaches can be reached by local bus or taxi from the Interamericana. Taxis can be hailed at the turnoffs for the beaches and are inexpensive.

Gorgona
Six kilometers southwest of the turnoff for Punta Chame is the turnoff for Gorgona, a small oceanside community with a choice of accommodations. The long, curving beach is mostly black sand – lots of iron and very hot. However, the surf is free of riptides and relatively safe for swimming.

There are two places to stay in Gorgona which, except for the beach, has little to offer the tourist. The better of the two is ***Cabañas de Playa Gorgona*** *(☎ 269-2241/2433, fax 223-1218),* which offers 43 concrete cabins, and some rooms are able to accommodate big families. All have kitchenettes and air con, and there's a pool. Prices for one room with one bed are US$34/45 per night on weekdays/weekends. The largest cabañas cost US$70/100, respectively. This place is a good value, especially if you are in a group. Credit cards are accepted. The hotel also has beach property, which is open to all its guests and contains two pools, lots of simple thatch-roofed shelters known locally as *palapas* and a bar. You can hang out there during the day and retire to the hotel in the evening.

BEACHES

El Canadian (☎ 240-6066) offers seven concrete cabins, all with air con, firm beds, kitchenette and private cold-water bathroom. There's an adults' pool, a kids' pool and a full bar. It's a minute's walk from the beach. It's a bit pricey at US$50/60 per cabin weekdays/weekends. Some cabins might be better than others; ask to see at least two. The owner is from Canada and speaks English and Spanish.

A few kilometers west along the highway is *Restaurante Bar Mi Posada* in Las Lajas, 200m east of the turnoff for Playa Coronado. This place is very popular and has air con and lots of cheap but tasty food.

Playa Coronado

The turnoff from the Interamericana for Playa Coronado, an affluent beachside community, is 4km southwest of the turnoff for Gorgona. The sand is salt-and-pepper with black patches, very hot to the touch on a sunny day. There are far better beaches to the west.

Places to Stay & Eat *Club Gaviota* (☎ 224-9053, 224-9136, fax 224-9042, turista@ sinfo.net), adjacent to the beach, offers extremely good value. There are five cabañas here, each with air con, hot water, firm bed and TV. There's an inviting adults' pool and kids' pool, bohios on the beach for shade, and a restaurant. Be advised that the staff leave at 5 pm. Reservations are recommended.

Coronado Hotel & Resort (☎ 240-4444, fax 240-4380), is a true resort: 75 standard rooms, all gorgeous and spacious with every amenity; 12 grand suites and six with kitchenettes; the best beachside golf course in Central America; a good restaurant and another more elegant one; tennis courts; a weekend casino; and other luxuries such as Jacuzzis, saunas, pools, an exercise room, bars and so on. The resort also shuttles guests to and from its beachside property, which features a lovely pool and bar, and guests can rent kayaks, Jet Skis and other water toys. Room rates range from US$165 to US$350.
Website: www.coronadoresort.com

There are two very good restaurants in the area. Beside the turnoff for Playa Coronado is *Restaurante Los Che's*, an attractive place with excellent but not inexpensive food, such as sandwiches (US$4), pasta (US$5), grilled sea bass (US$8), filet mignon (US$9.50) and lobster thermidor (US$18). Los Che's is well known for its rotisserie-cooked meats and fish, its lobster and clams. *Mi Posada* is 1km east on the highway, and here you can get a tasty and gut-busting meal for as little as US$4.

To get to Club Gaviota and the Coronado Hotel & Resort from the highway, take one of the van buses that park from 6 am to 7:30 pm daily under the mango tree beside the Texaco station at the Playa Coronado turnoff; one departs every 20 minutes. They charge 25¢ to take you to the Coronado Hotel & Resort, and US$4.50 to take you to Club Gaviota. Taxis with longer hours are available in Bejuco, 9km northeast on the Interamericana. If you have your own vehicle, just head into Playa Coronado and ask the guard at the gate to point toward the hotel you want. To get a taxi back to the highway, ask your hotel to call one for you.

San Carlos

This mostly-white-sand beach, 10km west of the Playa Coronado turnoff and 1.8km from the Interamericana, fronts a fishing community. Unfortunately for sunbathers, the fishermen park their boats on the best sand on the beach. Regardless, on the weekend this beach is often packed with Panamanians having a good time. There are no lodging options near the beach, but there are a couple of unappealing, inexpensive places on the Interamericana.

Also on the Interamericana in San Carlos is *El Cevichito*, which sells pretty good ceviche cheap: US$2 for a mix of shrimp, sea bass, octopus, onion, red pepper and lime juice, packed in a plastic container to go.

Playa Río Mar

Two kilometers west of San Carlos along the Interamericana is the turnoff for this small community, which has a nice surprise for the tourist: *Hotel Playa Río Mar*

(☎ 240-8027, 223-0192, fax 264-2272), 800m from the highway on a bluff overlooking the ocean. Located 95km from Panama City, this place is a popular weekend retreat for residents of the capital. The hotel has an inviting pool, a bar and a restaurant. Below it is a favorite surfers' beach (see Surfing in the Facts for the Visitor chapter). There are 20 rooms, and each comes with a little table, a dresser, air con and small TV. Five of the rooms have only one large bed; the rest have one big bed and two small beds. The couples' rooms cost US$60 on the weekends, half that during the week. Add US$5 for the larger rooms. Rooms numbered 15, 16 and 17 – all couples' rooms – are best. As with many of the hotels along this stretch of coast, there's a chance that you'll have the place to yourself on weekdays.

The restaurant here spe   cializes in corvina: the *cor ina apanada* (breaded sea bass; US$10) is particularly good. The serving is generous, but if you're very hungry, you're better off with one of the rice dishes, such as the fried rice with chicken (US$6). The lobster thermidor (US$20) is excellent. The restaurant also serves four meat dishes (US$7 to US$11). It's open 8 am to 11 pm.

Playa Corona

Five kilometers west along the Interamericana from the Playa Río Mar turnoff is a small sign announcing the turnoff for *Hotel Playa Corona* (☎ *240-8037, fax 264-0872*), out the front of which is a beautiful beach and a shallow surf. In fact, the beach is perhaps the safest in the area, because silt from a nearby river has tapered an otherwise quick drop-off. Unfortunately, the rooms of this hotel have been neglected and Lonely Planet can no longer recommend it.

Bocas del Toro Province

pop 89,300

Bocas del Toro Province is bordered by the Caribbean Sea to the north, Veraguas Province to the east, Chiriquí Province to the south and Costa Rica to the west. Most of the province is on the slopes of the Talamanca and Central mountain ranges, but the majority of its inhabitants live in low-lying areas along the coast and on islands.

The province contains the large Archipiélago de Bocas del Toro at the mouth of the Laguna de Chiriquí, beginning 35km from the Costa Rican border. The chain consists of 68 islands and numerous mangrove keys. Around them are fields of coral, a titanic variety of marine life and emerald green waters.

Highlights

- The glorious Archipiélago de Bocas del Toro, a prime snorkeling and diving spot
- San-San Pond Sak Wetlands, a swampy home to monkeys, sloths and iguanas
- Isla Bastimentos' lovely, seldom-visited beaches, nesting grounds for sea turtles
- Parque Internacional La Amistad, home to jaguars, Indian villages and spectacular jungle rivers
- Península Valiente, where forested slopes and postcard-perfect beaches meet a hammering surf

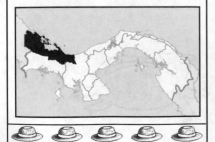

When Christopher Columbus visited the territory in 1502, on his fourth and final New World voyage, it was inhabited by many nomadic tribes. He was so taken by the beauty of the area that he affixed his name to many sites: Isla Colón (Columbus Island), Isla Cristóbal (Christopher Island), Bahía de Almirante (Admiral's Bay), the major port of Almirante and other locations. Because little gold was found in Bocas del Toro, the Spaniards did not colonize the region, and the Indians were spared their wrath for a while.

During the 17th century, the archipelago became a haven for pirates, mainly because the Spaniards didn't have a presence here. The buccaneers repaired their ships on the islands, built others with wood from their forests and fed upon the many sea turtles that nested on the beaches. Even today most of the archipelago is flush with virgin rain forest, and four species of sea turtle continue to lay their eggs on its beaches, just as they have for thousands of years. The pirates are said to have buried treasure on a number of the islands, but to date none of this loot has been found (or at least reported).

During the 17th and 18th centuries, most of the Indians were killed in battles among themselves, by Old World diseases brought by the Spaniards and by Spanish swords. Some Indians intermarried with French Huguenot settlers who arrived on the coast of Bocas del Toro around the end of the 17th century. By 1725 many of the Indians and Huguenots had been killed in fights with Spanish militiamen sent to dislodge the French settlers.

In the early 19th century, blacks from the USA and Colombia's San Andrés and Providencia Islands arrived as slaves of wealthy landowners looking to reestablish themselves in the province. When slavery was abolished, in 1850, the former slaves stayed and eked out a living as fishermen and subsistence farmers. Jamaican blacks joined them toward the end of the 19th century, as

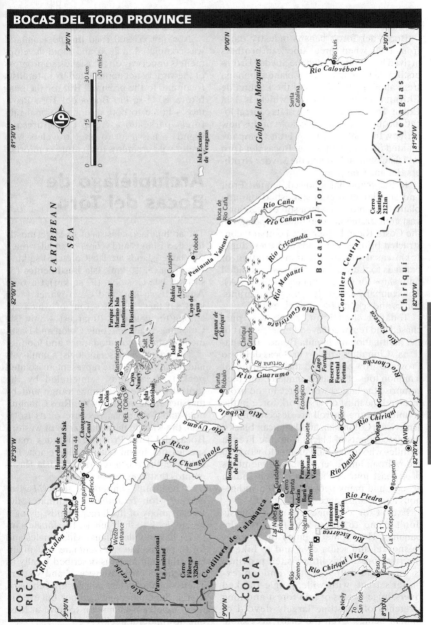

the province's banana industry began to develop.

Bocas del Toro's banana industry dates from 1890, when three American brothers arrived here and founded the Snyder Brothers Banana Company. They planted banana trees all along the shores of the Laguna de Chiriquí, at the mouth of which is Isla Colón. That island, because of its central location, quickly became the heart of this new activity. In 1899 the United Fruit Company planted itself in the town of Bocas del Toro on Isla Colón and bought the Snyder Brothers Banana Company.

In the years that followed, United Fruit and smaller growers established banana plantations, most of which still exist, over a vast area stretching from the archipelago to the Costa Rican border. The company constructed bridges and roads and even dug a 15km canal to ease the transportation of bananas to the sea, where they were loaded onto ships for export (mainly to the USA). The company also built houses, restaurants, clinics and schools for its workers.

Today, United Fruit, which was purchased and renamed several times, is part of the multinational Chiquita Brands International. Chiquita's workers in Bocas del Toro Province grow and export three-quarters of a million tons of bananas annually, and they comprise the largest work force in the province and the most diverse work force in the country. On the payroll are descendants of American, Colombian and Jamaican blacks; the descendants of blacks from the French Antilles who arrived in Panama to work on the railroad and, later, the canal; members of at least four of Panama's seven Indian groups; and many people of mixed indigenous and Spanish ancestry.

Except for a strange few, most tourists don't come to Bocas del Toro for the bananas. They come to enjoy the islands, to snorkel and scuba dive, and to hike in the rain forest. This little-visited province is an island-buff's delight and an explorer's treat, with wide, jungle-flanked rivers, huge swaths of rain forest and long stretches of coastline largely devoid of human beings. Even the easily accessible islands remain relatively tourist-free and only sparsely inhabited.

A major coastal road on the mainland was completed in 2000, and rapid development is underway on the islands, so progress of the variety not appreciated by naturalists *is* coming to the province. But for the near future, 8745-sq-km Bocas del Toro Province – home to both an international rain forest park and a group of picturesque islands – has a lot to offer travelers who prefer wild creatures to creature comforts.

Archipiélago de Bocas del Toro

The archipelago consists of six large, mostly forested islands and scores of smaller ones. The large islands are Isla Colón (61 sq km), Isla Popa (53 sq km), Isla Bastimentos (51 sq km), Isla Cristóbal (37 sq km), Cayo de Agua (16 sq km) and Cayo Nancy (8 sq km). Of these islands – four of which are among the country's 10 largest – only Isla Colón has roads, and only Colón and Bastimentos offer accommodations and food.

The archipelago is a biologist's fantasy. It and the adjacent shore represent an isolated pocket of lowlands, semicircled by the foothills of the Talamanca range and by marshes at the mouths of the Ríos Changuinola and Cricamola. Because of its isolation, the wildlife in the lowlands of western Bocas del Toro Province includes many species not found outside the region. For example, there is a red frog on Isla Bastimentos that lives nowhere else.

A beautiful, conifer-like tree *(Myristicaceae:* prob *Iryanthera)* dominates the forest canopy of the larger islands, giving a unique look to their jungle. The jungle's interior has abundant lianas, vine tangles and forest palms. The rainy climate that maintains this rain forest is described locally as consisting of two seasons: 'wet' and 'wetter.' There's generally less rain during February, March, September and October, but even in these months it's common to have at least one downpour a week.

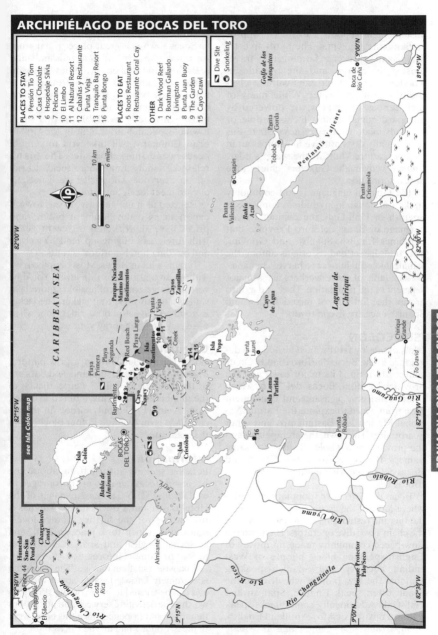

ARCHIPIÉLAGO DE BOCAS DEL TORO

PLACES TO STAY
3 Pensión Tío Tom
4 Casa Chocolate
6 Hospedaje Silvia
7 Pelícano
10 El Limbo
11 Al Natural Resort
12 Cabañas y Restaurante
    Punta Vieja
13 Tranquilo Bay Resort
16 Punta Bongo

PLACES TO EAT
5 Roots Restaurant
14 Restuarante Coral Cay

OTHER
1 Dark Wood Reef
2 Boatman Gallardo
    Livingston
8 Punta Juan Buoy
9 The Garden
15 Cayo Crawl

Dive Site
Snorkeling

Golfo de los
Mosquitos

Boca de
Río Caña

9°00'N

81°45'W

Punta
Gorda

Tobobé

Península Valiente

Cusapín

Punta
Cricamola

Punta
Valiente

Bahía
Azul

82°00'W

CARIBBEAN SEA

82°15'W

Parque Nacional
Marino Isla
Bastimentos

Cayos
Zapatillas

Cayo
de Agua

Laguna de
Chiriquí

Punta
Vieja

Playa Larga

Red Beach

Playa
Segunda

Isla
Bastimentos

Salt
Creek

Isla
Popa

Punta
Laurel

Chiriquí
Grande

To David

82°00'W

Playa
Primera

Bastimentos

Cayo
Nancy

Isla Loma
Partida

Punta
Robalo

82°15'W

Río Guarumo

see Isla Colón map

Isla
Colón

BOCAS
DEL TORO

Isla
Cristóbal

Bahía de
Almirante

Ferry

82°30'W

Humedal
San-San
Pond Sak

Changuinola
Canal

Finca 44

Río Changuinola

To
Costa
Rica

Changuinola

El Silencio

Río Changuinola

Almirante

Río Risco

Río Uyama

Río Robalo

Bosque Protector
Palo Seco

9°00'N

9°15'N

82°30'W

82°15'W

82°00'W

0   5   10 km
0   3   6 miles

Culturally, the islands and the lowlands around them support a distinct group of Indians, the Guaymís. They still live by fishing and subsistence farming, they travel mostly by canoes and they reside in wooden, thatch-roofed huts without electricity or running water. While many of their canoes, or *cayucos*, are powered by outboard engines, most locals paddle or use sails made from rice sacks. Since this tribe usually does not live in groups but in widely scattered huts at the water's edge, cayucos remain the Guaymís' chief mode of transportation.

The Guaymí language is still commonly spoken, although many Indians converse in Spanish or Gali-Gali, the distinct Creole language of Bocas del Toro Province that combines English, Spanish and Guaymí. This odd dialect had its origins among the Jamaicans brought over to harvest bananas. Descendants of these workers are a major segment of the population. They and a third group, the 'Latinos' of mixed Indian and Spanish ancestry, live in towns.

ISLA COLÓN

Isla Colón is by far the most visited and developed of the Bocas del Toro islands. On its southeastern tip is its major town and the provincial capital, **Bocas del Toro**, which offers tourists a pleasant and convenient base from which to explore the Parque Nacional Marino Isla Bastimentos and other nearby sites. The town, the archipelago and the province as a whole all share the same name – Bocas del Toro. Isla Colón and Bocas del Toro town are often referred to as 'Bocas Isla.'

Bocas del Toro town (population 4020) is where most of the archipelago's accommodations and restaurants are found, as well as the chain's two dive operators. The town is a slow-paced community made up mostly of English-speaking black people of West Indian ancestry and Spanish-speaking Latinos. The few Indians who live on the island often speak English, Spanish and Gali-Gali. Additionally, some blacks speak Patois, a mixture of Afro-Antillean English, Spanish and Gali-Gali which is widely

spoken on Isla Bastimentos, a 10-minute boat ride southeast of Isla Colón.

Bocas town is a great place to hang out for a few days. On the nearby islands and reefs are wonderful opportunities for swimming, snorkeling and diving, or lounging on white sandy beaches fringed by reeds and coconut palms. Water taxis (or *taxis marinos*), readily available in this small town of wooden houses built by the United Fruit Company, will take you to remote beaches and snorkeling sites. The town's relaxed, friendly atmosphere seems to rub off on everyone who visits; it's especially easy to meet locals and travelers here.

Relaxed as it is right now, Bocas town is experiencing a development boom; land prices have skyrocketed in recent years, with foreigners buying up land like crazy and building hotels and restaurants.

It rains a lot in Bocas. Most people arrive without an umbrella or rain attire. You'd be wise to bring a small, collapsible umbrella as well as a light waterproof jacket. The jacket is good to have for boat rides, too, when wind can blow sea spray your way.

Orientation

Bocas town is laid out in a grid pattern. Most of the hotels, restaurants and bars are on the main street, Calle 3. Perpendicular to the numbered streets are lettered avenues, from 'A' to 'H.' The only airport in the archipelago is on Avenida E, four blocks from the main street.

Information

Persons seeking information about the history of Bocas del Toro are encouraged to contact José 'Tito' Thomas, manager of the Hotel Bahía and a Bocas native. Thomas is responsible for the historic hotel's lovely renovation, which took place in 2001, and he speaks English and Spanish. See Places to Stay for contact information.

Likewise, Jonathan Parris at The Bocas Inn is extremely knowledgeable about the area and can be trusted to give you the skinny on worthwhile activities, services and attractions that might have opened since this book went to press. Contact him at The Bocas Inn.

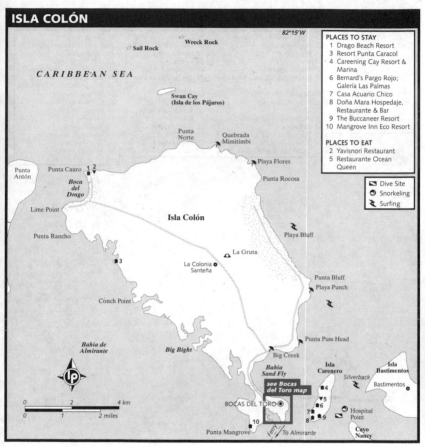

ISLA COLÓN

82°15'W

CARIBBEAN SEA

Sail Rock
Wreck Rock
Swan Cay
(Isla de los Pájaros)
Punta Norte
Quebrada Mimitimbi
Playa Flores
Punta Cauro
Punta Antón
Punta Rocosa
Boca del Drago
Lime Point
Isla Colón
Punta Rancho
Playa Bluff
La Gruta
La Colonia Santeña
Punta Bluff
Playa Punch
Conch Point
Punta Puss Head
Bahía de Almirante
Big Bight
Big Creek
Isla Carenero
Isla Bastimentos
Bahía Sand Fly
Silverback
Bastimentos
see Bocas del Toro map
BOCAS DEL TORO
Hospital Point
Cayo Nancy
Punta Mangrove
To Almirante
Ferry

0   2   4 km
0   1   2 miles

PLACES TO STAY
1 Drago Beach Resort
3 Resort Punta Caracol
4 Careening Cay Resort & Marina
6 Bernard's Pargo Rojo; Galería Las Palmas
7 Casa Acuario Chico
8 Doña Mara Hospedaje, Restaurante & Bar
9 The Buccaneer Resort
10 Mangrove Inn Eco Resort

PLACES TO EAT
2 Yavisnori Restaurant
5 Restaurante Ocean Queen

Dive Site
Snorkeling
Surfing

BOCAS DEL TORO PROVINCE

The IPAT tourist office (☎/fax 757-9642), at water's edge on Calle 1, occupies one of the finest buildings on the island, but has little of value to offer the tourist. The office is open 8:30 am to 4:30 pm weekdays.

Panama's public environmental agency, ANAM (☎ 757-9244), maintains an office a few doors down from IPAT and may answer questions regarding the area's wildlife. The office is open 8 am to noon and 1 to 4 pm weekdays.

The Banco Nacional de Panamá, on Avenida E, is the only bank in town. It has

an ATM, changes traveler's checks and is open 8 am to 3 pm weekdays, 9 am to noon Saturday.

There's a post office in the large government building on Calle 3, beside Parque Simón Bolívar.

International telephone calls can be made from any of the pay phones around town and from the Cable & Wireless office on Calle 1.

The Internet Café, midway down Calle 3, has five deathly slow computers available for public use (US$1.50 per half hour) from 8 am to 9 pm Monday to Saturday, and 9 am to 4 pm Sunday.

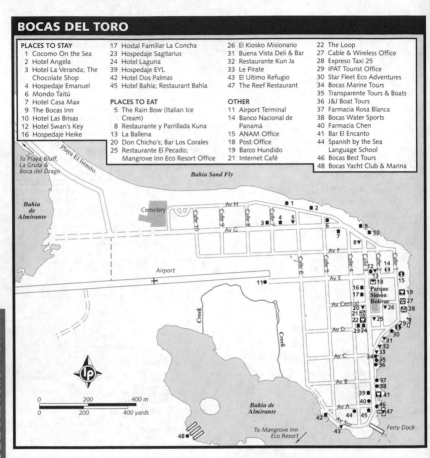

BOCAS DEL TORO

PLACES TO STAY
1 Cocomo On the Sea
2 Hotel Angela
3 Hotel La Veranda; The Chocolate Shop
4 Hospedaje Emanuel
6 Mondo Taitú
7 Hotel Casa Max
9 The Bocas Inn
10 Hotel Las Brisas
12 Hotel Swan's Key
16 Hospedaje Heike
17 Hostal Familiar La Concha
23 Hospedaje Sagitarius
24 Hotel Laguna
39 Hospedaje EYL
42 Hotel Dos Palmas
45 Hotel Bahía; Restaurant Bahía

PLACES TO EAT
5 The Rain Bow (Italian Ice Cream)
8 Restaurante y Parrillada Kuna
13 La Ballena
20 Don Chicho's; Bar Los Corales
25 Restaurante El Pecado; Mangrove Inn Eco Resort Office
26 El Kiosko Misionario
31 Buena Vista Deli & Bar
32 Restaurante Kun Ja
33 Le Pirate
43 El Ultimo Refugio
47 The Reef Restaurant

OTHER
11 Airport Terminal
14 Banco Nacional de Panamá
15 ANAM Office
18 Post Office
19 Barco Hundido
21 Internet Café
22 The Loop
27 Cable & Wireless Office
28 Expreso Taxi 25
29 IPAT Tourist Office
30 Star Fleet Eco Adventures
34 Bocas Marine Tours
35 Transparente Tours & Boats
36 J&J Boat Tours
37 Farmacia Rosa Blanca
38 Bocas Water Sports
40 Farmacia Chen
41 Bar El Encanto
44 Spanish by the Sea Language School
46 Bocas Best Tours
48 Bocas Yacht Club & Marina

There are two pharmacies and a health clinic in Bocas town.

Dangers & Annoyances Bocas town has a water treatment plant, but locals say the tap water isn't to be trusted. The water is certainly fine for brushing your teeth, but you're probably best off siding with caution and purchasing bottled water for drinking.

The Bar El Encanto occasionally cranks up its music and keeps it there until very late. If you're planning on staying at the nearby Hospedaje EYL or the Hotel Bahía, you might consider bringing ear plugs just in case.

Beaches

Boca del Drago Located on the western side of Isla Colón, Boca del Drago is one of the best beaches on the island, though the surf can be rough at times. Just offshore from the beach is a patchy coral-and-sand sea bottom that offers good snorkeling when the sea is calm and the water clear.

Boca del Drago isn't nearly as nice as Red Frog Beach or Playa Larga on Isla Bastimentos, where there's a good chance of seeing sea turtles if you camp out or make a night hike from one of the island's hotels.

BOCAS DEL TORO PROVINCE

However, the surf at those beaches makes swimming unsafe.

A bus operates from Boca del Drago to Bocas town, ferrying workers who live at the beach to and from town. It leaves Boca del Drago around 7:30 am and returns in the late afternoon. In Bocas town the bus parks in front of the market between Hotel Las Brisas and the fire station; at about 8:30 or 9 am, you can ask the driver if he'll take you out to the beach. The trip to Boca del Drago takes about 45 minutes; the roundtrip fare is about US$2.50. Or hire a pickup taxi and have it return at a specified time. The roundtrip ride is about US$20.

Other Beaches There are plenty of other beaches around Isla Colón, reached by a road that skirts up the eastern coast from town. There's no public transportation to them, but a taxi will take you there, and you can arrange for the driver to come back for you at an appointed time.

Playa El Istmito, also called Playa La Cabaña, is the closest to town. It's on Bahía Sand Fly, and the *chitras* (sand flies) that live here have an itchy bite. Repellent is available in town. This is not the most attractive beach; better ones are farther north.

Farther up the coast are **Big Creek**, **Punta Puss Head** and **Playa Punch**, which is dangerous for swimming but good for surfing. After you round Punta Bluff, the road takes you along **Playa Bluff**, which stretches all the way to Punta Rocosa. Endangered sea turtles nest on Playa Bluff from around May to September.

La Gruta (The Cave)

Halfway to Boca del Drago, 8km from town, is a cave ingeniously named La Gruta (The Cave). It's also called the 'Santuario Natural de Nuestra Señora de la Gruta' for the statue of the Virgen del Carmen at its entrance. It could also be called 'Bat Crap Cave,' because if you walk through it (there's an exit after 100m), you'll be ankle-deep in bat poop and be doused with it, too; and the smell – the smell! Besides the bats (and the fact that local villagers wash their clothes in the stream leaving the cave), there's nothing remarkable about La Gruta.

There's an interesting story about those bats, though. In 1974 a small village was born near the cave. The villagers had pigs, and soon the villagers noticed that the pigs' nipples were red and sore. One night a villager heard a pig squeal and came out to find a bat biting the pig's nipples. The villagers were so upset with the nipple-biting bats that they went to the police. The police, being police, tear-gassed the Santuario Natural de Nuestra Señora de la Gruta, sending thousands of furious bats out of the cave in broad daylight, but the bats were back as soon as the smoke cleared.

In time the villagers learned that if they applied a substance similar to hot sauce to their pigs' nipples, the bats left them alone.

Diving & Snorkeling

Beware that although the Cayos Zapatillas are within the boundaries of a national marine park, they don't make for particularly good dive/snorkel trips due to strong currents. Better sites include Cayo Crawl (also called Coral Cay and Coral Key, a lovely reef in shallow water with lots of fish, coral and lobster), south of Isla Bastimentos; Dark Wood Reef (with many nurse sharks and occasional hammerheads), north of Bastimentos; Hospital Point, a 50-foot wall off Cayo Nancy (also called Isla Solarte); and the base of the buoy near Punta Juan (with some beautiful coral), north of Isla Cristóbal. Of these, only the Punta Juan buoy and Hospital Point are also good for snorkeling. Another superior spot for snorkeling is The Garden, near Cayo Nancy; there's lots of coral there.

Be forewarned that the archipelago's waters are notorious for poor visibility. Sometimes you go under and find the visibility is very good; sometimes your visibility is limited to 3m. More than 40 rivers expire at bayside around the islands, and they unload a lot of silt into the sea after heavy rains in the mountains. If it's rained a lot in recent days, don't expect good visibility.

A variety of diving and snorkeling trips at comparable prices, generally US$15 to

US$20 per daylong outing, gear included, are offered by Star Fleet Eco Adventures (☎ 757-9630, scuba@vacationmail.com), on Calle 1, and Bocas Water Sports (☎/fax 757-9541, magicbay@cwp.net.pa), on Calle 3. Their respective websites are at www.explorepanama.com/starfleet.htm and www.bocasdeltoro.net. See Organized Tours, later in this section, for information on other operators who offer snorkel and dive tours.

Both Star Fleet and Bocas Water Sports offer two-tank dives for about US$50 per person (two person minimum; includes all equipment), and both offer PADI open-water-diver certification for around US$195. Star Fleet offers instruction in English, German and Spanish. Be advised that while Star Fleet enjoys a sterling reputation, Bocas Water Sports does not.

Readers have reported that IPAT employee Hernan Cortéz, who leads snorkeling tours on the side, is an excellent snorkeling guide and charges reasonable fees for his services.

Bird Watching

While the birding on the islands isn't as good as that on the mainland, it can nonetheless be rewarding. Particularly rare birds, or at least those poorly known to Panama, have been recorded on the islands in recent years, including the semiplumbeous hawk, white-tailed kite, zone-tailed hawk, uniform crake, olive-throated parakeet, red-fronted parrotlet, lesser nighthawk, green-breasted mango, chestnut-colored woodpecker, snowy cotinga, brown-capped tyrannulet, yellow-bellied elaenia, stub-tailed spadebill, purple martin, tree swallow and black-cowled oriole.

In early March and October many thousands of turkey vultures can often be seen gliding just above the forest canopy on the large islands. These are big black birds with featherless heads and reddish necks, and they are masterful fliers, often soaring for long periods without a flap, tilting from side to side to take advantage of every favorable air current. These birds range from Canada to Chile. Many of the northern birds winter in Central America and northwestern South America.

Language Courses

On Calle 4 the *Spanish by the Sea Language School* (☎/fax 757-9518, spanishbythesea@ hotmail.com) offers affordable Spanish classes in a casual setting. Five-day-a-week rates for group/private lessons are US$70/100 for two hours a day, US$100/145 for three hours a day and US$130/190 for four hours a day.

Other rates include US$9 per hour for one-on-one lessons, US$7 per hour for two students, and US$6 per hour for three or more students. Want to learn just enough Spanish to get by? There's a 'traveler's survival Spanish course' for US$40 that includes six hours of instruction over two or three days, phrasebook included.

Owner-instructor Ingrid 'Ins' Lommers speaks English, Spanish, Dutch, French and German. The school offers two **rooms for rent** – see Places to Stay for more information.

Website: www.spanishbythesea.com

Organized Tours

If you'll be in Panama City and you're tinkering with the idea of spending a few days in Bocas, you might want to consider Ancon Expeditions' 'Bocas del Toro Adventure.' It's a three-day, two-night package tour that includes air transportation to and from Bocas, two nights at The Bocas Inn, all meals, and tours to Isla de los Pájaros (Island of the Birds), Cayos Zapatillas (within a marine national park), and a protected frog sanctuary on Isla Bastimentos. The all-inclusive price of US$295 is reasonable.

In addition to Star Fleet Eco Adventures and Bocas Water Sports (see Diving & Snorkeling, earlier), J&J Boat Tours (☎/fax 757-9915) and Transparente Tours & Boats (☎ 757-9600, cellular ☎ 687-3913), both on Calle 3, offer a variety of boat tours, all of which leave from their oceanside offices at 9 am and include some amount of snorkeling. Rates range from US$10 to US$20 per person, depending on the proximity of the destination. Most tours include three stops, usually a beach and two snorkeling sites.

The two companies also offer fishing trips. J&J even rents a 40-foot sportfishing boat with fresh-water shower (for family tours of the islands and for sportfishing), for US$400 a day; price includes captain and mate and the use of fishing gear. This is a excellent value, much less than you'd pay in neighboring Costa Rica, for example.

J&J and Transparente enjoy strong reputations. But at the time of writing, all of J&J's boats had shade covers, while Transparente Tours' boats did not. If you're concerned about being exposed to too much direct sunlight, be sure to ask whether the boat you'll be on has a cover.

If you're just looking for a boat ride and can do without a guide, turn to Taxi Marítimo Galapagos Tours (☎ 757-9073), which despite its name is a straight boat taxi service. Need a ride to Red Frog Beach? Galapagos will take you there for US$7. Isla Bastimentos? US$4. Boca del Drago? US$20. If you've got a destination that requires a boat, who do you call? Galapagos. Located on Calle 3.

Bocas Best Tours (☎ 620-5130 and 689-2680), on Calle 3, might provide superlative service but has not been tested by the author.

Special Events

Bocas town observes all of Panama's holidays and a few enjoyable local ones besides. Annual events celebrated in Bocas town and on Isla Bastimentos include the following:

May

May Day (May 1) – While the rest of Panama is celebrating the Día del Trabajador (Worker's Day), the Palo de Mayo (a Maypole dance) is done by young girls in Bocas town and on Isla Bastimentos.

July

Día de la Virgen del Carmen (3rd Sunday) – Everyone in Bocas town makes a pilgrimage to La Gruta, the cave in the middle of the island, for a mass in honor of the Virgen del Carmen.

September

Feria del Mar (28th) – The 'fair of the sea' is a four-day festival held on Playa El Istmito, north of Bocas town; from September 28 through October 2.

November

Fundación de la Pro incia de Bocas del Toro (16th) – Celebrating the founding of the province in 1904, this day is celebrated with parades and other events; it's a big affair, attracting people from all over the province, and the Panamanian president also attends.

Día de Bastimentos (23rd) – Bastimentos Day is celebrated with a parade and drumming on Isla Bastimentos.

Places to Stay

Isla Colón has many places to stay and more under construction. Still, you'd be wise to make a reservation. If Bocas town becomes a wildly popular tourist destination, as I suspect it one day will, it might be difficult finding a room at a price you like, particularly from December to April.

In Town On Calle 3 near the center of town, *Hospedaje Heike* (☎ 757-9708) was completely rebuilt in 2001. It offers superlative value in seven charming, 2nd-floor rooms with fans, mosquito nets, furniture and two shared hot-water bathrooms for US$5 (single bed), US$12 (two single beds or one big bed) or US$15 (the latter plus private balcony). The restaurant downstairs is managed by the very friendly owners, who speak German, English and Spanish.

Hostal Familiar La Concha (☎ 757-9609, ☎/fax 758-5037 in Changuinola), on Calle 3, consists of five attractive, clean rooms above a friendly family's residence at excellent value. Those with fan go for only US$6/11 single/double, and those with air con for US$13/17. Because every room is unique, ask to see several.

Mondo Taitú (☎/fax 757-9425), on Avenida H, offers nine basic guestrooms on two floors, each with a good bed, fan and light (US$7 or US$8 per person, depending on room) and a dormitory with seven beds for US$6 per person. The hot-water bathrooms are shared but very clean. Guests receive a fresh towel and sheets every three days. This place has a peaceful, woodsy cabin feel with a communal kitchen and hammocks hung on a porch, and some food is available. The friendly German owner Rike Waldschmitt speaks English, Spanish, Italian, German and French. Reservations are not accepted.

ANDREW MARSHALL & LEANNE WALKER

Bocas del Toro's main street

BOCAS DEL TORO PROVINCE

Hospedaje Emanuel (☎ 757-9958), on Avenida G, offers four clean rooms with fan and private cold-water bathroom for US$7 per person – a good value. Most rooms contain a double bed and a single above it, bunk-bed style. There's also a room with air con (US$15).

The *Spanish by the Sea Language School* (☎/fax 757-9518, spanishbythesea@ hotmail.com), on Calle 4, has basic but comfortable rooms with ceiling fans, good beds, shared bathrooms and a communal kitchen for US$6 per person. The rooms are also available to non-students.

Hospedaje EYL (☎ 757-9206), on Calle 3, offers seven basic rooms in a poorly constructed, concrete-walled, metal-roofed building. Most guestrooms have good beds, fans, and private cold-water bathrooms. The cost is US$6 to US$22 per person.

Hotel Las Brisas (☎/fax 757-9248), on the northern end of Calle 3, is a recently renovated old place. Rooms with private hot water bathrooms and fan/air con cost US$14/24. Despite the renovation, readers have reported bed bugs at Las Brisas.

The Dutch owned and operated *Hotel Casa Max* (☎/fax 757-9102, casamax1@ hotmail.com), on Avenida G, is a beautiful, wooden two-story building containing 10 cheerful and spotless guestrooms, each tastefully done and offering a terrific value. All rooms have private hot-water bathrooms, and several have balconies and cost US$15 for one person, US$20 for two. Morning coffee and fresh fruit are available free of charge to guests.
Website: casamax.netfirms.com

The seaside *Hotel Angela* (☎/fax 757-9813, claudio@hotmail.com), on Avenida H, offers 10 simple but comfortable rooms with fan and good beds for US$15 per room (half have two beds). Only shared hot-water bathrooms were available at the time of writing, but guestrooms with private bathroom were planned. A communal kitchen, pleasant sitting areas, free Internet access and the very amiable owner (English- and

Spanish-speaking Claudio Talley) add to this hotel's popularity.
Website: www.hotelangela.com

Hotel Dos Palmas (☎ 757-9906), on Avenida Sur, sits entirely over the water and offers eight rooms with private hot-water bathrooms, good beds and ceiling fans. Six with air con for US$27 for one or two people and two with fan only for US$22 all offer an excellent value. There's a seaside porch with hammocks, tables and chairs, and free coffee is served.

Hospedaje Sagitarius (☎/fax 757-9578), at the intersection of Calle 4 and Avenida D, offers 16 rooms with private hot-water bathrooms, color TVs, fans and air con for US$16 for one or two people – another very good value.

Hotel La Veranda (☎/fax 757-9211), at the intersection of Avenida G and Calle 7, is a lovely residence-turned-inn built in 1910 and pridefully maintained by its Canadian owner, Heather Guidi, down to its gleaming hardwood floors and pretty antique windows and doors. None of the six guestrooms are alike, except that all contain regional furniture dating from the early 20th century as well as firm new mattresses, and all are equipped with private hot-water bathrooms. There's a communal kitchen and a cozy corner sitting area. Rates are very reasonable at US$25 and US$35 per room (price varies with room size).
Website: www.laverandahotel.com

The stately **Hotel Bahía** (☎/fax 757-9626, cellular ☎ 676-4669, hotelbahia@cwp.net.pa), at the southern end of Calle 3, was built in 1905 by the United Fruit Company and originally served as its local headquarters. Today, the huge safe that held workers' pay can still be seen, and in 2001 most of the structure was returned to its original splendor. The American pine lining the halls of the two-story structure is original, as are the oak floors. During the renovation, the 18 guestrooms were modernized, though the new fixtures conform to the originals in design. Every room has air con and a private hot-water bathroom, and some have balconies with oceanviews.

Rates are US$35 per room with beds, and US$40 per room cor singles. Internet access is avail for US$2 an hour.
Website: www.panamainfo.com/hotelbahia

Ancon Expeditions manages **The Bocas Inn** (☎/fax 757-9226 in Bocas; ☎ 269-9414, fax 264-3713 in Panama City, info@anconexpeditions.com), which offers 12 spacious and appealing guestrooms with air con, firm mattresses, dressers, night stands and private hot-water bathrooms. Some of the rooms have seaviews, and there are communal seaside porches as well as a restaurant and bar. Rates range from US$40 to US$60 per room, breakfast included. Full packages including lodging, all meals and day tours start at US$90 per person.
Website: www.anconexpeditions.com

Cocomo On the Sea (☎ /fax 757-9259, cocomoonsea@cwp.net.pa), on Calle H, is an attractive seaside inn. Two of its four breezy rooms have oceanviews, and all have access to seaside terraces strung with hammocks. These rooms were built with attention to detail, from the soundproof roofs that squelch the noise of driving rains to matching decor to orthopedic mattresses (for bad backs) and slightly elevated beds (for bad knees). Rates for one or two people are US$45, breakfast included. No pets or children under eight are allowed. English is spoken.
Website: www.panamainfo.com/cocomo

Hotel Laguna (☎ 757-9091, fax 757-9092, hlaguna@cwp.net.pa), on Calle 3, is a two-story hotel offering 16 attractive rooms with lots of pretty wood, good beds, air con and hot-water private bathrooms at US$58 for one or two people, US$68 for three. There's also one suite with a kitchen for US$91.
Website: www.bocas.com

Hotel Swan's Key may look to be one of the better-built hotels in town, but readers can find better value elsewhere.

Around the Island The **Mangrove Inn Eco Resort** (☎/fax 757-9594, manginn@usa.net), a 10-minute boat ride from town, consists of four wooden cabins and a

BOCAS DEL TORO PROVINCE

.estaurant/bar, all built on stilts over the water and connected by walkways. One room has a double bed, air con and a hot-water private bathroom. The others have a mixture of double beds and bunk beds and can hold four to six people each, but they have cold-water private bathrooms and fans only (air con isn't needed much of the time). All of the rooms have oceanfront porches, and the reef right out front offers quality snorkeling. This place has occasional trouble with gnats, particularly at sundown. The rate of US$42 per person includes three meals, water taxi from Bocas town, and the 10% hotel tax.
Website: www.bocas.com

Continuing another 10 minutes by boat past the Mangrove Inn and toward Boca del Drago is the **Resort Punta Caracol** (☎ 676-7186, 690-8468), which consists of five pleasing two-story cabañas built entirely over the water of wood and *penca* (palm tree leaves) in conformity with traditional Caribbean architecture. Unlike the Mangrove Inn, these cabañas were built far enough away from the nearby mangroves so that they aren't visited by biting gnats. The upper room in each cabaña is the bedroom, with a king-size bed and mosquito netting (mostly for decor). There's a comfortable living room on the ground floor with two sofabeds and an adjacent terrace facing the open sea and distant jungled hills. A sea breeze keeps the rooms pleasant most of the time. Solar panels power this low-key resort, and a septic tank handles waste. The price of US$100 per couple (and US$25 per extra person) includes breakfast. The restaurant is a beautiful building on the water, and the menu consists mostly of seafood prepared Spanish or Caribbean style. With meals ranging from US$6 to US$17, the food isn't cheap, but it sure is delicious! If you're in the mood to splurge, take a water taxi here around 5 pm and pig out on lobster. Open mornings 'til the last customer leaves.'
Website: www.resortpuntacaracol.com

Under construction at the time of writing, **Drago Beach Resort**, located on Punta Cauro, promises to be an upscale, gorgeous facility. Its position gives guests immediate access to both a long, sweeping beach facing calm Boca del Drago bay, and to a straight run of beach facing a choppier open sea. There's decent snorkeling to be found in both locations, and there's a terrific restaurant next door. The accommodations were slated to consist of 15 modern, fully equipped cabañas, most built over the water. One was nearly completed at the time of review and it was very appealing, with a living area and terrace on the ground floor and sleeping quarters above. Unlike Punta Caracol, these cabins are equipped with air con (a good thing on still nights). Also, unlike Punta Caracol, which is an island unto itself basically, Drago Beach Resort is walking distance from attractions such as the beaches and a terrific 19th-century cemetery filled with early European settlers (tombstones indicate several lived to be more than 100 years old). Check with the resort for rates. Next door is the **Yavisnori Restaurant**, a fine open-sided, thatch-roofed, sandy floored restaurant open from 7:30 am to 7:30 pm daily and serving tasty seafood meals at reasonable prices (US$2.25 to US$12). Check with tour operators in Bocas town for day trips out here, as taxi rides are too pricey at US$25 one way.
Website: www.dragobeachresort.com

Places to Eat

Bocas town is small but has several fine places to eat and plenty that are easy on your wallet.

It doesn't look like much, but **El Kiosko Misionario**, next to Parque Simón Bolívar, fires up a grill at sundown and soon-after sells barbecued chicken in brown paper bags. Don't let the presentation fool you; you'll ravage your bird like a starving hyena. A football-size breast costs just US$1.50.

From sunrise to late, **Don Chicho's** serves thoroughly mediocre Panamanian food that rarely exceeds a few bucks; lots of people like the place.

For a filling breakfast, try **Restaurante y Parrillada Kuna**, on Calle 3, where a Kuna family serves omelets for US$2 and other inexpensive items. Lunch and dinner offerings include mixed seafood (US$8), squid (US$5.50), and seafood and rice (US$4).

For a delicious breakfast at slightly higher prices, try the restaurant at **Hotel Laguna**. Breakfast options include German pancakes with chocolate and banana (US$3.50), and yogurt and fruit (US$2.50). Lunch and dinner options (pizza, pasta, seafood, *tipico*) generally run from US$5 to US$8.

Breakfast and sandwiches at **La Ballena**, on Avenida E, are good and cheap. Indeed, La Ballena and the restaurant at the Laguna Inn may well offer the best breakfasts in town. However, the dinners are hit and miss. I had a spaghetti dish that was very salty and not any tastier canned spaghetti you buy at a supermarket – and with soup, two juices and a so-so tip my bill came to US$20.

El Ultimo Refugio, on Avenida Sur, is a great find. This rustic, mellow place, resting on the edge of the sea specializes in seafood (fish filet US$6, octopus US$8, lobster US$12) but also offers gazpacho (US$2.75), pizza (around US$6) and *pollo agri-dulce* (seasoned chicken topped with salsa flavored with lemon, orange and pineapple, US$5.50). It's open 11:30 'til 10 pm.

Le Pirate, on Calle 3, serves seafood in large quantities, but at very affordable prices. This seaside restaurant also offers a fine selection of fruit drinks, and there's a full bar (happy hour is from 4 to 6 pm).

Restaurante El Pecado, on Calle 3, has excellent food. Open for dinner only (4:30 to 10 pm), El Pecado specializes in Thai-Panamanian combinations, such as filet of fish smothered in coconut milk-based curry (US$7), but you'll find some hearty burgers and sandwiches here for around US$4.

A **Restaurant Bahiá** was slated to open on the porch of the Hotel Bahía in early 2002, offering Caribbean dishes similar to that which might have been served in Bocas a century ago. The hotel owner is a meticulous fellow; the food will likely be delicious.

Buena Vista Deli & Bar, on Calle 1, serves good food at reasonable prices. A filling breakfast or sandwich here costs under US$5 (the teriyaki chicken breast sandwich is outstanding). There's a full bar

and DirecTV; if there's a major sporting event, the American owners will have it on. This place is popular with the yatching crowd and with ex-patriot Americans. Beware: The margaritas here are powerful concoctions. Closed Tuesday.

Restaurante Kun Ja, on Calle 1, serves very good and very cheap Chinese food. A big plate of chop suey with chicken costs only US$3.

The restaurant at **Hospedaje Heike** is open only for supper and only from 6 to 11 pm Monday through Friday, and that's a pity, because the Heike serves big portions of curried chicken, roast beef and fresh fish for little pieces of silver. There's a bar here, too, where beer costs just 75¢ and the best rum & Cokes in Panama sell for US$1.50.

The Reef Restaurant, on a dock that juts from Calle 3, offers mostly seafood at reasonable prices. There's nothing special about the food or the décor, but the tables beside the sea provide soothing views.

If you're hot or possibly bothered, **The Rain Bow** on Avenida G will cool you down. It sells Italian ice cream. By the way, all you chocolate lovers will want to take a look at the Shopping section, later in this chapter.

Entertainment

The hippest place in Bocas is **Barco Hundido** (that's the name on the sign, but most people know this open-sided, thatch-roofed bar as The Wreck Deck). Partially built over the sea, the bar takes its name from a submerged banana boat that rests in the clear Caribbean water a cork's flight from the farthest bar stool. A short boardwalk extends from the main portion of the bar over the vessel to an island seating area that's perfect for intimate conversations. The American owners usually spin rock 'n' roll, and that's just fine with the patrons, most of whom are twentysomethings from the USA, Europe or Down Under. Happy hour's from 4 to 6 pm. There are a couple of rooms for rent at backpacker prices on the premises.

The Loop, on Calle 3, was supposed to be The Pool Bar, but due to a little problem with the sign maker…Well, now you needn't ask owners Marcell Schmitt from Germany and Mathilde Grand from France to explain the bar's name. The, uh, Pool Bar takes its name from the four pool tables inside. From 8 am to 5 pm, M&M serve breakfast, sandwiches and fruit juice. At 5 pm, the booze appears, the party crowd shuffles in, and the fun runs 'all night, until we decide it's enough, or until everybody's gone,' as Mathilde puts it. There's DirecTV, and when it's raining the set is tuned to a movie. Happy hour is from 5 to 7 pm.

Bar Los Corales is a locals bar, where mature regulars generally hunch over a wrap-around bar and recall events of the day. It's a very low-key place with low drink prices. *Bar El Encanto*, farther down Calle 3, is ruled by a younger crowd and is much more lively. Thursday through Saturday night, you might hear live music (usually a local band that belts out popular Panamanian songs).

Shopping
Cacao is a traditional crop in Bocas. The Guaymís have been using it in wedding celebrations for generations. The chocolate sold at *The Chocolate Shop*, inside the Hotel La Veranda, is made from Bocas cacao using age-old methods. If you visit Heather Guidi's shop, she will gladly give you an information sheet telling you all about the local theobromine-rich chocolate. Theobromine is a natural stimulant. If jet lag or the tropical sun has sapped your mental batteries, recharge them with a bar of Heather's dark chocolate.

Getting There & Away
There are two practical ways to get to Isla Colón: by boat or by plane.

Air Bocas del Toro has a fine little airport. Aeroperlas (☎ 757-9341 at the airport) offers daily flights from Panama City to Bocas (see the Panama City chapter for flight information). From Bocas, Aeroperlas flies to the capital at 9 am and 1:30 pm Monday through Friday, and 8:10 am Saturday and 5 pm Sunday (US$50, one hour).

Aero Mapiex (☎ 757-9841 at the airport) also has flights between Panama City and Bocas departing at 10:15 am Monday through Friday, 8 am Saturday and 2 pm Sunday (US$50, one hour).

Boat Two companies – Expreso Taxi 25 and Bocas Marine Tours – operate water taxis between Bocas town and Almirante (US$3, 35 minutes). Both companies' taxis leave more or less hourly from 6:30 am to 6:30 pm. Be advised that although these are covered boats, their roofs leak. Dress expecting to be hit with sea spray.

The Ferry Turistico Palanga, which carries passengers and vehicles, runs between Almirante and Bocas Wednesday, Friday, Saturday and Sunday. The ferry leaves Almirante at 9 am and Bocas at 5 pm (US$15 per vehicle, US$1 per person; 1 hour and 20 minutes each direction). Just prior to departure, you can purchase tickets from the ferry dock at the southern end of Calle 3.

A short dinghy trip from town is the **Bocas Yacht Club & Marina** (☎ 757-9800, fax 757-9801), which was under construction in 2001. It's slated to feature world-class floating concrete docks capable of holding 100 boats up to 100 feet in length (rental cost is US$8/foot/month). Showers, laundromat, water, electricity, security, maintenance, parts, full-service haul-out facilities, a fuel dock, a restaurant and a swimming pool were also planned. Website: www.bocasmarina.com

Getting Around
Taxis prowl Calle 3 from dawn to dusk and will take you to the airport for a couple of bucks and all the way across the island and back for US$20. When going to La Colonia Santeña or points north, hail a pickup-truck taxi because the interior road is usually badly potholed and slippery.

Bicycles can be rented from Galapagos Tours on Calle 3 for US$5/8 for a half/full day.

At the time of writing, the local government had plans to build a tour-guide center near the ferry dock. These guides would be Bocas natives trained to assist tourists.

ISLA CARENERO

A few hundred meters from Isla Colón is the small and sparsely populated island of Isla Carenero, which in recent years has become popular with business folk hoping to lure tourists off Isla Colón and into their establishments.

The island takes it name from *careening*, which in nautical talk means to lean a ship on one side for cleaning or repairing. It was on Careening Cay in October 1502 that ships under the command of Christopher Columbus were careened and cleaned while the admiral recovered from a bellyache.

Places to Stay & Eat

Located almost within swimming distance of the Barco Hundido on Isla Colón, **Bernard's Pargo Rojo** (☎ *757-9649, bbahary@hotmail.com*) is the kind of place that attracts people who'd try it just to see if they could make it. At Bernard's Red Snapper (its English name), you can indeed catch red snapper with a line from the bar. There are six rustic rooms here, with plank floors and walls and thatch roofs. *Very* reasonable rates are usually US$25 per room with private hot-water bathroom, a downstairs bed and a loft with another bed. It's a very casual, mellow place, frequented by surfers. Want a soda? Just help yourself and jot it down on the drinks notepad. Owner Bernard Bahary, originally from Iran and a total character, is an excellent cook. Meals vary with the catch of the day, but a variety of delicious sauces are always offered. Bernard serves a traditional Iranian meal upon request. Meal prices range from US$5 to US$12. If you're coming from Almirante, get the water taxi driver to drop you here and you'll save yourself the minor trouble of hiring a boat to bring you here from Isla Colón.

Doña Maria Restaurante Hospedaje & Bar (☎/fax 757-9551) offers six guestrooms, all with air con, hot-water bathrooms and local TV. The rooms have the feel of a city hotel, and they are arranged in a U layout with only the two end rooms having a seaview. The reasonable single/double rates of US$35/45 include a shuttle service to and from Isla Colón. There's a restaurant open 8 am to 11 pm daily.

Casa Acuario Chico (☎/fax 757-9565, *joberg1301@cwp.net.pa*) is a handsome house built on the water with four gorgeous guestrooms, air con, DirecTV, awesome seaviews, snorkeling off the porch, a beach next door and friendly American owners. It's a fantastic place! The cost is a very reasonable US$65 per room (includes breakfast for two), and guests are welcome to use the kitchen.

Website: www.boattoursofbocas.com

The American-owned and -run *Careening Cay Resort & Marina* (☎/fax 757-9242, *marcar@cwp.net.pa*) features four large, attractive stand-alone cabins, each with a divided hot-water private bathroom, a porch, a divider separating a parents' room (with queen bed) from a children's room (with two sets of bunk beds), and a table and chairs. Rates are US$65 per cabin for up to four people. There is also a couple's cabin for US$45. The marina features 26 berths to 55 feet (20-foot maximum width) with 120/240 volt, 60Hz power, pressurized water, showers, dinghy dock, garbage disposal, shaded work areas, and access to laundry, fax and email services. The dockage rate of 25¢/foot/night (US$7.50/foot/month) includes normal power and water usage; rates improve with longer stays. *The Sunset Grill* restaurant is worthy of the trip over from Isla Colón, especially on Tuesday night for Texas barbecue (US$9.50) and Wednesday night for Mexican (US$8). Regular fare includes Philly steak sandwich or cheeseburger (US$5), a variety of seafood plates (US$8), grilled pork tenderloin (US$9) as well as USDA Select steaks. It also serves hearty American breakfasts and is open 7 to 9 am, 11 am to 2 pm and 4 to 10 pm daily except Sunday (breakfast only).

Website: www.careeningcay.com

The Buccaneer Resort (☎ *757-9042, tiothom@cwp.net.pa*) offers four suites cabañas and eight smaller cabañas on a lovely strip of beach. All of the cabañas are elevated and feature polished hardwood floors and walls, a romantic thatch roof, a screened porch, a ceiling fan, a sitting area, and a modern tiled bathroom with air con.

The four suites cabañas, which are special for their living rooms, are honeymoon material – very romantic and private. The suites rent for US$85 for one or two persons and the standard cabañas for US$65. There's a restaurant and a bar on the premises. Sea kayaks are available to rent (US$20 per day), as are Sunfish sailing skiffs (US$50 per day). Website: www.buccaneer-resort.com

Restaurante Ocean Queen is a locally owned, open-sided over-the-water place with lots of unrealized potential. The food here is reasonably priced, but often an absence of ambience turns prospective patrons away. Meals include chicken (US$3.50), crab (US$7) and lobster tail (US$10). It's open noon to 9 pm daily.

Shopping

Laurie Bjorklund had been selling molas made by Kuna Indians and textiles made by Guatemala's Mayan Indians at her store in Key West, Florida, for years when she and her husband Dan Lahey decided to move to Bocas to open **Galería Las Palmas** on Isla Carenero. Located on the beach between Bernard's Pargo Rojo and Casa Acuario Chico, Galería Las Palmas sells artesania made by most of Panama's indigenous peoples plus handicrafts produced by the native peoples of Colombia, Guatemala and Nicaragua, including Guatemalan textiles, Nicaraguan hammocks and baskets made by the Emberá Indians of Darién. There's also a small museum containing an intriguing collection of Indian artifacts, costumes and clothing. It's open 10 am to 5 pm daily.

Getting There & Away

A shuttle service between Isla Carenero and Isla Colón is provided by J&J Tours (with the same owners as Casa Acuario Chico) in Bocas town. J&J water taxis are available sunrise to 10 pm Sunday through Thursday, and to midnight on Friday and Saturday (US$1).

ISLA BASTIMENTOS
pop 1400
Isla Bastimentos is a 10-minute boat ride from Bocas town. There are two communi-

ties on the island, the larger being the village of Bastimentos, which has no roads, only a concrete footpath lined on both sides with rustic wooden houses. Though near Isla Colón, the language here is very different.

Until the 1990s, most of Bastimentos' adults were hard-working people who traveled to Almirante daily to tend to banana fields. By 2001, only 17 residents of the island were still working the fields. Most of the men had taken to fishing, farming small plots or just hanging out while their spouses sell little cakes and things.

On the southeastern side of the island is the Guaymí village of Salt Creek. Between Salt Creek and Bastimentos a wide swatch of rain forest falls within the Parque Nacional Marino Isla Bastimentos, which is the terra firma section of a mostly marine park. You can explore the park, but go only with a local guide (children who know the area often offer their services), as it's possible to get lost.

The island has several beautiful beaches. You can walk from Bastimentos to **Playa Primera** in 20 minutes or so. Other fine beaches along the northern side of the island include **Playa Segunda** and the lengthy **Playa Larga**, where sea turtles nest from April to August. Playa Larga is inside the national marine park, but some locals continue to kill turtles there for their meat and shells and rob their nests of eggs.

Salt Creek
pop 500
On the southeastern edge of Isla Bastimentos is the Guaymí village of Salt Creek, at the end of a long canal cut through mangrove forest. The community consists of 60 thatch-and-bamboo houses, an elementary school, a handicrafts store, a general store and a soccer field.

Most of the people here eke out a living by fishing and subsistence farming. Their main 'cash crop' is the sale of lobsters to restaurants in Bocas town. In 2001 Salt Creek was suffering because, while its members won't take lobsters until they have reached a certain size, thus protecting the local stock, non-members who live elsewhere had been coming in and leaving with all the lobsters they could find.

If you wander around Salt Creek, you'll likely notice a pole sticking straight out of the ground. Several times a year, during a celebration, a bottle of rum is placed on top of the pole, which is then greased. Whoever is able to climb the pole and take the bottle gets to drink the rum.

Places to Stay & Eat

The author's favorite place in all of Panama is the *Al Natural Resort* (☎ 623-2217, 640-6935, ☎/fax 757-9004, alnaturalbocas@cwp.net.pa). This intimate all-inclusive resort contains five elegant-yet-rustic elevated cabañas on the beach, each featuring gorgeous seaviews from bed. Each thatch-roofed cabaña has only a half wall (that being the half of the cabaña facing the jungle), while the half of the cabaña facing the sea has no wall at all. A draping mosquito net keeps bugs off you at night. Don't let the sound of white-faced monkeys rustling in nearby branches concern you. Every cabaña has a private bathroom and two have toilets a dozen or so steps from the cabañas for added privacy. There's a communal dining and hang-out area and an inviting sunbathing platform at the end of a dock. Just in front of the dock is a coral reef, which cries out to snorkelers. There's no extra cost to use the resort's kayaks or it windsurfing or snorkeling equipment, nor is there a fee to use its archery range. The daily price of US$60 to US$75 per person (two-day minimum, double occupancy) includes three delicious meals daily, wine with dinner and roundtrip transportation from Isla Colón. While all of the cabañas are appealing, the nicest ones account for the higher rates, and they are worth the additional cost. For single occupants, add 50% to the per person rate. The 7th night is free. The friendly Belgian owners/managers speak French, English and Spanish.

Website: www.bocas.com

El Limbo (☎ 620-5555, 624-1965, ellimbo@hotmail.com) offers eight rustic but attractive rooms in a two-story wooden lodge with electricity, good cross ventilation and private bathrooms. Every room is different, with lots of unique touches such as headboards made of driftwood and seashells arranged in room corners for artistic effect. There's a fine beach and reef out front. This place appeals to the hippie in us all. The rate of US$40 per person includes breakfast, dinner and the use of snorkeling equipment. Tours to Salt Creek and Cayos Zapatillas are available for US$15 per person.

Website: www.ellimbo.com

Cabañas y Restaurante Punta Vieja consists of several very basic and small raised cabañas, with one light bulb each, and a shared rustic shower and bathroom. There's a simple and inexpensive restaurant built on stilts over the water 25m from shore. It serves dishes such as grilled fish (US$5), whole lobster (US$9) and octopus (US$7). The three most appealing things about this place, in addition to its rate (US$5 per person), are its owner, Alberto Livingston (who goes by the name Ñato, which means man with little nose); the seaview, with mesmerizing, non-stop breakers; and the waves, which surfers would appreciate most of all. Ñato, who's about the friendliest man you'll ever meet, speaks Gali-Gali and a little Spanish.

Plans for *Tranquilo Bay Resort* (☎ 757-9967, fax 757-9541), under construction at the time of writing, called for 10 air-con, concrete-walled, zinc-roofed cabañas with all the amenities, an elevated swimming pool, and a restaurant for guests. Contact the resort for further information or see its website (www.tranquilobay.com).

Casa Chocolate (☎ 690-8648, hs_pri ate@yahoo.com) is a good-value Austrian-run guesthouse and cabañas that offers basic accommodations for US$5 per person or US$10 per room. You can sleep in a hammock in the garden if you wish (US$3, hammock provided). If you have your own tent, you pay US$3 per night to camp out. Jungle, snorkeling and fishing trips can be arranged here. English, German and Spanish are spoken.

Hospedaje Silvia (☎ 757-9442) offers five simple rooms with stand fans attached to a home for US$10 per room. The beds are of varying comfort and there's a small porch with seaview.

Pensión Tio Tom (☎/fax 757-9831, tomina2000@hotmail.com) is a pleasant bar/restaurant/inn on stilts over the water owned and managed by a friendly German couple. The rooms are rustic and the plumbing non-existent; yes, what you *do* goes right into the sea. One of the four rooms has a private hot-water bathroom (US$20 per couple) and the others share a bathroom (US$10 per room). The food here is delicious, and offerings include rabbit in a red wine cream sauce served with vegetables (most dinners are US$5). German, English and Spanish are spoken here.

Owned and run by an Italian-Panamanian couple, **Pelicano** (☎ 757-9830) is a bar, restaurant and hotel. There are two basic but comfortable rooms with fans and shared bathrooms; three more rooms with private bathrooms are located on shore. Singles/doubles cost US$10/14. The bar and restaurant are built over the water, and (tasty!) pizza is the specialty of the house and only US$5.50. Also available is a filling meal of spaghetti with lobster (US$9); many less expensive dishes are also available. It's open 8 to 10 am for breakfast, and noon to 9 pm. Kayaks are available for rent at US$2 per hour and snorkel gear is US$5 per day.

Roots Restaurant is a fine, locally owned and managed, open-sided and thatch-roofed restaurant built on stilts over the water and has an exceptional seaview. The relaxing atmosphere is made all the more enjoyable when its owners spin reggae. It serves Creole dishes like rice and beans with coconut milk and chicken for US$3, seafood starting at US$2.50, and strong rum & Cokes for 60¢. Co-owner Oscar Powell is one of the 17 people on Isla Bastimentos who still works for the banana company; if he's around, sit down with him and talk banana. Oscar's a friendly English and Spanish speaking man with an interesting perspective on life. Roots is open 9 am to late.

Restaurante Coral Cay is an island unto itself – a cluster of thatch-roofed *bohios* on stilts beside a clump of mangrove and a field of coral reef. This is a terrific place to relax, lay in the sun, snorkel and eat, and the boat ride out is an adventure. Dishes include filet of fish in either a Jamaican curry or a tomato sauce (US$6), octopus in coconut milk with side dishes (US$10), lobster with butter and garlic (US$12) and shrimp in white salsa (US$6). When you're meeting fellow travelers, talk a few into making the trip out here – that way you can split the cost of the water taxi. Beer and some booze is available. It's open 8 am to 5 pm daily.

Getting There & Away

At the time of writing, there was no reliable shuttle service between Isla Bastimentos and Bocas del Toro town. Your best bet is to go to J&J Boat Tours and ask to be taken to Isla Bastimentos. The secretary there will hail a local boatman for the trip (around US$3 per person).

For your return trip, either make arrangements with the boatman who brought you over *(if* the boatman seems reliable), ask how you get to Isla Colón at Tio Tom or one of the other businesses mentioned here, or go to the home of boatman Gallardo Livingston and ask him to take you to Isla Colón (expect to pay US$10 per party).

OTHER ISLANDS

The archipelago has many other beautiful islands, all with good snorkeling spots.

Cayo Nancy, also called Isla Solarte, is distinguished by Hospital Point, named for the United Fruit Company hospital that was built here in 1900, when the company had its headquarters in Bocas town. The hospital was established to isolate victims of yellow fever and malaria; at the time it was not yet known that these diseases, then rampant in the area, were transmitted by mosquitoes. The hospital complex eventually included 16 buildings. It was here for only two decades, however; when a fungus killed United Fruit's banana trees, the company moved its banana operations to the mainland and abandoned the hospital.

Swan Cay, also called Isla de los Pájaros, is home to a great many birds and, not surprisingly, is popular with bird watchers.

Turtles' Tragic Troubles

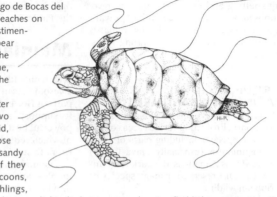

Four of the world's eight sea turtle species nest on the beaches of the Archipiélago de Bocas del Toro, particularly the long beaches on the northern side of Isla Bastimentos. The loggerheads appear from April to September, the leatherbacks in May and June, the hawksbills in July and the greens in July and August.

Sea turtles leave the water only to lay their eggs. Two months after the eggs are laid, the hatchlings break loose from their shells, leave their sandy nests and enter the sea – if they are not first eaten by raccoons, birds or dogs. Many hatchlings, which are guided to the sea by moonlight, die because people using flashlights unintentionally steer the tiny turtles into the rain forest, where they are preyed upon or get lost and die from starvation or the heat.

However, it's not so much people's unintentional behavior that is threatening the turtles' survival in Bocas del Toro Province: Although the local Guaymís are aware of the turtles' precarious grip on life, many of the Indians still kill nesting mothers to eat their meat and eggs. Sea turtles are now threatened with regional extinction, following in the sad path of other animals such as the tapir and the jaguar.

It's not just in Bocas del Toro Province that turtles are threatened, but all along both coasts of Panama. In the Archipiélago de San Blás, the Kuna Indians kill sea turtles that aren't even a year old. Fishermen in the Golfo de Chiriquí hack off the flippers of large sea turtles for meat and then throw the animals back into the water, where they drown because they cannot swim to the surface to breathe.

Most hope to see red-billed tropic birds and white-crowned pigeons. Nearby are **Wreck Rock** and **Sail Rock**, which are responsible for the premature retirement of more than a few boats whose skippers mistakenly chose to sail at night in unfamiliar waters.

The **Cayos Zapatillas** are touted by tour operators for snorkeling, despite strong currents in the area. The two keys, Cayo Zapatilla Norte and Cayo Zapatilla Sur, have beautiful white-sand beaches surrounded by pristine reefs. Nearly every meter of the south key, incidentally, was dug up in the early 20th century on the rumor that Captain Henry Morgan had

buried treasure here. None was found. There is an ANAM station on the south key and it's often possible to stay at it. Check with ANAM in Bocas town.

Punta Bongo

At the time this book went to press, ***Punta Bongo Lodge*** (☎ 626-1988) was under construction on a point facing the Laguna de Chiriquí. Although not on an island at all, the planned resort was then only reachable by boat and had more in common with the archipelago than it did with the mainland. Plans called for six adobe-style bungalows, each with ocean and mountain views, a

solar-powered ceiling fan and lighting, oversized bathrooms with open-air shower, a king bed or two queen beds draped in mosquito netting, and a roof-top garden terrace. Proposed activities included hiking, kayaking, canoeing, sailing, snorkeling, billiards and tours to local sites and surfing spots. Contact the lodge for prices.
Website: www.puntabongo.com

PARQUE NACIONAL MARINO ISLA BASTIMENTOS

Established in 1988, this was Panama's first marine park. Protecting various areas of the Bocas archipelago, including parts of large Isla Bastimentos (especially Playa Larga) and the Cayos Zapatillas, the park is an important nature reserve for many species of Caribbean wildlife.

Its beaches are used as a nesting ground by four species of sea turtle. The abundant coral reefs, great for snorkeling and diving, support countless species of fish, lobster and other forms of sea life. The lagoons are home to other wildlife, including freshwater turtles and caimans, and there is still more wildlife in the forests. Unfortunately, poaching also occurs in the park.

The park entrance fee is US$10. If you want to camp out anywhere in the park, you are required to first obtain a permit from ANAM.

CHANGUINOLA CANAL

In 1903 a 15km canal connecting the Río Changuinola and Bahía de Almirante was dug parallel to the Caribbean shoreline, running within several hundred meters of it for most of its length. The work was begun six years earlier by the Snyder Brothers Banana Company to facilitate the barging of bananas from the fields to ships. The 30m-wide channel allowed transfer of the heavy fruit without interference from the open sea.

The canal, which sliced through dense rain forest, was abandoned years ago, and until the mid-1990s it was a bird watcher's dream. Today, sadly, this is no longer true; nearly all of the jungle on both sides of the waterway has been cleared for cattle pasture. In 2001, there was talk of a tour operator offering Jet Ski safaris and a water-taxi service up and down the canal. A water taxi to Changuinola from Bocas, or vice versa, would be a nice alternative to the land route.

Mainland

The mainland of Bocas del Toro Province is awesome. As in the Darién, there is forest in parts of Bocas del Toro Province that is able to support jaguars and the world's most powerful bird of prey, the harpy eagle, both of which require enormous amounts of territory to survive.

The mainland is an explorer's dream. Its jungles are the stuff of Indiana Jones movies, complete with isolated Indians, snakes the size of fire hoses and insects that make your skin crawl. Its swamps, with their jet-black, anything-can-be-in-there waters, are as alluring as they are creepy. Some months of the year, in the dead of night, sea turtles lumber out of the choppy surf and onto the beaches north of Changuinola to lay eggs and then head back to the water until the same time next year.

In Parque Internacional La Amistad, half of which is in Panama and half in Costa Rica, are 407,000 hectares of rain forest that contain seven of the 12 classified life zones. It's possible to ride some of its rivers for hours and only see a handful of human beings – Bribri or Teribe Indians floating downstream on rafts made of balsa wood held together by vines. These crude one-trip rafts have been used by the Indians for generations.

CHIRIQUÍ GRANDE
pop 2100
This backwater town is dying. Until 2000, it was on the route from the Interamericana to eastern Costa Rica and its population exceeded 7600 people. To make this journey you'd reach Chiriquí Grande from the Interamericana by bus or car, then take a water taxi to Almirante, and continue by bus or car to Changuinola and the border or vice versa. Since then, a highway connecting

the Interamericana-Chiriquí Grande road to the Almirante-Changuinola road has been completed. The former connection occurs 8km outside of Chiriquí Grande, while the latter connection occurs 1km outside Almirante. With the highway's completion, travelers making the trip from the Interamericana to eastern Costa Rica can bypass Almirante and Chiriquí Grande – and that's exactly what they are doing.

While Almirante remains an important banana town, Chiriquí Grande is in an economic coma. Still, it's not inconsequential: Chiriquí Grande is the Caribbean terminus of the Trans-Panama Oil Pipeline, which has its Pacific terminus at Puerto Armuelles. The oil is brought by tankers from Valdez, Alaska, to Puerto Armuelles, and then pumped over the Continental Divide. The oil is initially stored in containers on a hill above Chiriquí Grande and then loaded onto tankers that dock in front of the town. The pipeline alleviates the need for many tankers to transit the Panama Canal and pay steep passage fees.

RANCHO ECOLÓGICO

Located 29km south of Chiriquí Grande on the road to David (also called the 'Fortuna Road' because the road passes by the Lago Fortuna reservoir), Rancho Ecológico (☎ 225-7325, panabird@ sinfo.net) is a cloud forest-level campground. In a lush gorge high in the Talamanca range, it consists mainly of a large, thatch-roof structure under which four four-person tents are pitched (bring your own sleeping bag and mat) and hammocks slung. Rates are charges US$26 per person per night, or US$48 with three meals. The price with food, lodging and guide service is US$90 a day. There are toilets and showers, hot and cold water, and a kitchen and dining area.

In the immediate vicinity is a crystal-clear stream that feels great after a hike. There are several trails, one of which leads to a lovely set of waterfalls and bathing pools. You can bring your own food or ask the staff to prepare your meals. There's a stand about 100m farther up the road that

sells cucumbers and bananas and other delicious fruit.

Rancho Ecológico is only 16km from Lago Fortuna, a picturesque reservoir that serves a power plant. All around the reservoir is some of the finest forest in Panama, which is strictly protected because it serves as the watershed for the Fortuna Dam. The bird watching near the campground is excellent due to Rancho Ecológico's proximity to this large forest and to the Bosque Protector Palo Seco, a forest reserve. Birders will want to keep an eye out for ashy-throated bush-tanagers; this is Panama's only known site for them.

Getting There & Away

Almost any bus that travels Fortuna Road can drop you at Rancho Ecológico. Ask the driver to let you out before you pass it; the campground is on the southern side of the road, where it makes a tight curve. Don't try to reach the campground at night, because it is set back from the road and easy to miss.

Getting a ride out of the area basically requires catching one of the buses heading in the direction you wish to go. Any of the Toyota buses will stop. As a courtesy to the bus driver and for safety reasons, walk a little way up the road so that the driver doesn't have to pull over on a corner.

ALMIRANTE
pop 12,500

From the traveler's perspective, this port town is the jumping-off point for a boat ride to Bocas del Toro town or a bus or taxi ride to Changuinola. From the resident's perspective, Almirante means bananas – Chiquita bananas. Most Almirante residents are in the banana business, the vast majority are poor folk who toil in the fields. These people inhabit the board-and-tin hovels you'll see throughout town.

Train tracks are seemingly everywhere in Almirante, because it's here that the banana trains from the huge plantations to the west bring their green, crescent-shaped fruit (the bananas turn yellow later). It's also in Almirante that the trains are repaired and housed when not in use. The rusting hulks and most of the town are owned by the Chiriquí Land Company, a subsidiary of the multinational banana giant Chiquita Brands International, which exports the fruit to more than 40 countries.

The most important train tracks lead to the Muelle de Almirante (Admiral's Pier), which is used almost exclusively by banana ships. For more information than you could possibly want to know about the company – including 'The Story of Miss Chiquita' (no, she's not a transvestite) – see Chiquita's bright-yellow website at www.chiquita.com.

Be advised that accommodations in Almirante are limited to three lousy hotels, and the few restaurants seem to specialize in grease.

Getting There & Away

Bus Buses to Changuinola (US$1, 35 minutes, hourly from 6 am to 10:30 pm) run from near the canal used by Almirante's water-taxi companies. The bus terminal is located on the other side of the train yard if you're coming from Bocas and heading north; when exiting the water taxi, turn left on the canalside road and follow the sidewalk around the train yard.

Buses to David (US$10, every 45 minutes from 5:30 am to 7:30 pm) leave from a bus stop at the edge of the new highway. To find the bus stop, find the bus terminal and walk 1km north on the paved street heading out of town. Or take a taxi to the bus stop; there's unusually one at the terminal, and the cost to the bus stop shouldn't exceed US$1.50.

Taxi In this city, taxis arrive in bunches to accommodate the hordes headed for Changuinola (US$12, 35 minutes). A taxi ride from the Costa Rican border to Almirante, or vice versa, officially costs US$17; it takes about 45 minutes.

Boat Two companies operate water taxis between Almirante and Bocas town (US$3, 35 minutes). In Almirante, you can easily walk from one to the others. The water taxis leave when they're at least half full, so avoid the company that has an empty waiting

area. Taxis more or less leave Almirante hourly, from 6:30 am to 6:30 pm.

The Ferry Turistico Palanga operates between Almirante and Bocas, carrying passengers as well as motor vehicles and other objects that are too heavy or large for water taxis. The ferry runs between Almirante and Bocas Wednesday, Friday, Saturday and Sunday, leaving Almirante at 9 am and Bocas at 5 pm (US$15 per vehicle, US$1 per person, 1 hour 20 minutes).

CHANGUINOLA
pop 39,900

Halfway between the Costa Rican border and the Archipiélago de Bocas del Toro, this city has been transited by many tourists, but few ever overnight here – and for good reason: This city is usually humid and variously dusty or muddy.

But from Changuinola it's easy to get to the Río Teribe, from which you can make a dramatic entrance into the Parque Internacional La Amistad. If you head in the opposite direction (north, toward the coast), you can visit an extremely memorable boardwalk that passes through a swamp and ends at a Caribbean beach where four species of sea turtle lay their eggs.

Orientation

The city can be described as very tall and slim; it runs considerably farther north-south than it does east-west. Its main street is Avenida 17 de Abril (also commonly called Avenida Central), which runs north to south. Most of the hotels and restaurants are along this long, two-lane avenue, from which the rest of the city stems. There's an airport near the northern end of town, and the bus station is near the city center – close to restaurants, bars, markets and hotels.

Vast banana plantations flank the city. Most of the in-city sites of interest to the traveler are easily reached on foot. Taxis are cheap and it's a good idea to use them after dark.

Information

There's no tourist office, but the police are helpful and friendly; they speak only

Spanish, however. The ANAM office No 2 (☎ 758-8967), near the center of town, can provide information on transportation to Parque Internacional La Amistad. Its open 8 am to 4 pm weekdays. Some English is spoken here.

The town has a Banco Nacional de Panamá, a Banco del Istmo, a post office and an immigration office. The best pharmacy in the city is in the Atlantic Plaza, on Avenida 17 de Abril. Laly Tours (☎ 758-5037) is open 8 am to noon and 1 to 5 pm weekdays and 8 am to 1 pm Saturday.

Places to Stay

Hotel Changuinola (☎ 758-8678, fax 758-8681), near the airport, offers 32 shoddy singles/doubles/triples with air-con and private hot-water bathrooms for US$17/21/23.

Hotel Ejecutivo Taliali (☎ 758-6010, fax 758-8636, taliali@cwp.net), on Avenida 17 de Abril, has 15 very well maintained single/ double guestrooms with good beds and all the amenities for US$17/22, which is an excellent value.

Hotel Carol (☎/fax 758-8731), on Avenida 17 de Abril, was recently rebuilt and offers bargain single or double rooms with all the amenities for US$18.

Hotel Chalet Suizo (☎ 758-8242, fax 758-8165, raulda i@cwp.net.pa), also on Avenida 17 de Abril, offers 12 worn, overpriced rooms with all the amenities for US$25/30. Tours of the area are offered here in English and German.

El Gran Hong Kong Hotel (☎ 758-5044), on Avenida 17 de Abril, offers six worn, basic rooms with private bathrooms for US$28 for one or two people.

Hotel Golden Sahara (☎/fax 758-7908), has 27 attractive rooms with air con, hot water, cable TV and fridges. It's a good deal at US$22/24.

Hotel Semiramis (☎ 758-6006, fax 758-6016) is a nice, competitively priced place with 20 fully equipped guestrooms for US$24/28. There's a restaurant on the premises as well.

Atlantic Suites (☎ 758-9999, fax 758-9064) has 15 spacious rooms each with a

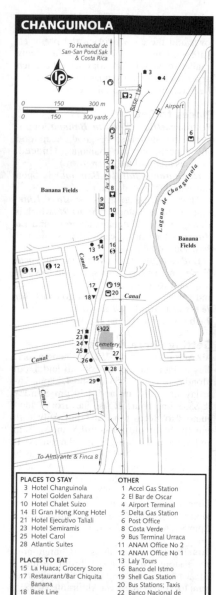

CHANGUINOLA

PLACES TO STAY	OTHER
3 Hotel Changuinola	1 Accel Gas Station
7 Hotel Golden Sahara	2 El Bar de Oscar
10 Hotel Chalet Suizo	4 Airport Terminal
14 El Gran Hong Kong Hotel	5 Delta Gas Station
21 Hotel Ejecutivo Taliali	6 Post Office
23 Hotel Semiramis	8 Costa Verde
25 Hotel Carol	9 Bus Terminal Urraca
28 Atlantic Suites	11 ANAM Office No 2
	12 ANAM Office No 1
PLACES TO EAT	13 Laly Tours
15 La Huaca; Grocery Store	16 Banco del Istmo
17 Restaurant/Bar Chiquita	19 Shell Gas Station
Banana	20 Bus Stations; Taxis
18 Base Line	22 Banco Nacional de
24 Restaurante Julio10 Bon	Panamá
Jour	26 Atlantic Plaza; Pharmacy
27 Super 96	29 Immigration Office

BOCAS DEL TORO PROVINCE

sofa, desk, large cable TV and lots of pretty wood. These are the finest guestrooms in town and there's a pool on the premises. Rates range from US$34 for a lovely smaller room to US$80 for one of the much larger rooms with two queen-size beds. Website: www.atlantic-suites.com

Places to Eat

Restaurant/Bar Chiquita Banana, opposite the bus station, serves good, cheap food but surprisingly no bananas. (Indeed, bananas are hard to find in town.)

Restaurante Julio10 Bon Jour is open late, which is its strong suit.

There are three markets: *Base Line*, which is the best stocked; *Super 96*, which is a hangout for old banana laborers; and *La Huaca*, which has a café. Beer is cheaper than soda at all three.

If it's a liquid supper you want, hit *Costa Verde*, one of the cheapest bars in town. If you want to accomplish two things at once and you've got a car with you, go to *El Bar de Oscar* to drink *and* get your car cleaned; the bar's adjacent to a car wash.

Getting There & Away

Air Aeroperlas (☎ 758-7521 in Changuinola) flies to Panama City at 8:50 am and 1 pm Monday to Friday, 8:55 am and 4:40 pm Saturday, and 9:30 am and 4:30 pm Sunday (US$53, one hour). It also flies from Changuinola to Bocas town at 1 pm daily with extra flights at 4:40 pm Saturday, and 9:30 am and 4:30 pm Sunday (US$10, 10 minutes). It also has flights to David leaving at 1 pm daily and an extra flight at 10:10 am Monday through Friday (US$26, 30 minutes).

Aero Mapiex (☎ 758-9841) flies from Changuinola to Panama City at 10:15 am Monday through Friday, 8 am Saturday and 2 pm Sunday (US$53, one hour).

Bus The two bus stations in Changuinola are a stone's throw apart. From Terminal Urraca, buses to David depart hourly from 5 am to 6 pm (US$8); via Almirante (US$1). There are two buses daily to Panama City, one at 7 am arriving at 6 pm and the other at 7 pm arriving at 9 am (US$24).

At Transporte Sincotavecop, there are buses to Guabito (70¢, every 20 minutes, from 6 am to 7:30 pm), El Silencio (50¢, every 20 minutes, from 5 am to 8:30 pm), Almirante (US$1, every 20 minutes, from 6 am to 10 pm), David (US$8, every 40 minutes, from 5:15 am to 7 pm), and San José in Costa Rica (US$8, one bus daily, departing at 10 am and arriving 3:30 pm).

Taxi Taxis can be found at the city bus station. A taxi ride from Changuinola to Almirante takes about 20 minutes and costs US$12; if you're arriving in Changuinola by bus or plane, you can often find a few other passengers to share the ride and the cost. A taxi ride from Changuinola to the Costa Rican border at Guabito takes about 15 minutes and costs US$5.

AROUND CHANGUINOLA
Finca 8

If you feel a little stressed out or enjoy a good walk, I encourage you to take an afternoon stroll through Finca 8 (Farm 8), a neighborhood southwest of central Changuinola. Here you'll wander among older two-story wooden houses, plenty of trees and lots of tranquillity. There are no fewer than 50 bird species in the area.

Between 5 and 6:30 pm, the silence of Finca 8 is shattered by the screeching *keerr keerr* calls of hundreds of crimson-fronted parakeets. These birds, with their noticeable bare white eye-rings, range from Nicaragua to western Panama. You won't likely find these noisy creatures south of Changuinola.

San-San Pond Sak Wetlands

These wetlands, also called Humedal de San-San Pond Sak, 5km north of central Changuinola, are fantastic, but they must be approached with a sense of humor and a spirit of adventure. Some luck is required as well, and jungle boots or other shoes that can get soaked are advisable. Sandals with straps will suffice.

Administered by ANAM, the wetlands are on the edge of Finca 44, a huge banana farm reached by a road extending from the northern end of town. The best way to get here is to hire one of the 4WD taxis that hang out at the Changuinola bus station, have it take you as close to the wetlands as it can and arrange for the driver to pick you up two hours later. The ride will cost US$15 per person for the round trip.

Between Finca 44 and the designated wetlands is an undesignated wetlands that you must cross. Fortunately, the mud is only ankle-deep. If your driver only takes you to the edge of the banana fields, you'll have a 200m mud walk. To your right you will see a barbwire fence. Follow it to its end and then proceed straight another 20m to a gate; the trail is directly out front. Welcome to the start of the San-San Pond Sak Wetlands boardwalk.

Almost immediately you'll enter rain forest rising from jet-black water. The boardwalk, which is less than a third of a meter wide in some places, is barely raised above the water and sometimes disappears into it. With the naked eye it's impossible to tell how deep the water is, but your instincts will encourage you to avoid it at all costs.

The crazy boardwalk is a treat. It weaves through beautiful vegetation that's rich with howler and white-face monkeys, iguanas, sloths and toucans. Snakes are a sure bet, though it's best not to think about them. You can spot a variety of wrens, warblers and woodpeckers. And, 1.2km later, you'll arrive at the Caribbean.

The beach is strewn with driftwood and other stuff, but it's also a place where loggerhead, leatherback, green and hawksbill turtles lay their eggs. If you're in the area between April and August, I encourage you to spend the night out at the beach and watch the turtles do their thing. And you'll never see so many stars.

There's a basic shelter right at the northern end of the boardwalk, always occupied by an ANAM ranger, and for US$5 he'll give you a roof over your head and use of a bathroom there. ANAM also rents a very rustic house with two beds with no sheets or blanket. Regardless of the house, bring your own food and drink, a light sleeping bag or blanket, a mosquito net, and lots of bug

spray. Dress warmly; it does cool off at night.

PARQUE INTERNACIONAL LA AMISTAD

This 407,000-hectare park, established jointly by Panama and Costa Rica in 1988, has territory in both countries – hence its name, La Amistad (Friendship). In Panama the park covers portions of Chiriquí and Bocas del Toro Provinces and is home to members of three Indian tribes: the Teribe, the Bribri and the Guaymís.

The park, slightly more than half of which is in Panama, contains some gorgeous rain forest that remains home to a recorded 90 mammal species (including jaguars and pumas) and more than 300 bird species (including resplendent quetzals and harpy eagles). Most of the park's area is rather remote, high up in the Talamanca mountain range, where rapid settlement is occurring illegally and unabated.

It's possible to enter the park from Changuinola, although it's much easier to enter it from Chiriquí Province. The two main Panamanian entrances to the park are Las Nubes (in Chiriquí Province) and Wetzo (in Bocas del Toro Province). Only the Wetzo entrance is discussed here; see the Parque Internacional La Amistad section in the Chiriquí Province chapter for details on the Las Nubes entrance and nearby facilities.

The Wetzo entrance is a 45-minute boat ride up the Río Teribe from the hamlet of El Silencio, which is reached via a 30-minute drive or bus ride from Changuinola. In El Silencio, there should be Indians willing to take you up river. If you go to the ANAM Office No 2 and tell the people there you want to go to Wetzo, ANAM will radio ahead and make sure there is someone at river's edge. Due to the high price of gasoline, river trips are expensive: about US$40 roundtrip per party.

Once on the river, you'll pass hills blanketed with rain forest and intermittent waterfalls, and the backdrop is always the glorious Talamanca range. The jungle comes all the way down to the river water. There are a few sandbars, but the current's too swift for crocodiles. You're likely to see iguanas lounging in trees (though you'll have to look hard for them) and lots of birds; waterproof binoculars help a lot.

After about 45 minutes on the river, you'll come to a sign on the right bank that announces your arrival at Wetzo, which is actually a protected area but still some ways from the park (hence, you do not have to pay an ANAM park entrance fee to be here).

Before the US invasion in 1989, Wetzo was named Pana-Jungla and was *the* jungle-survival training facility for Panamanian soldiers. As of 2001, many of the old structures (barracks, mess hall, chapel, armory, serpentarium etc) were still there, though dilapidated. Lovingly painted on many of the walls were poems (in Spanish, of course) such as this one:

> Faithful Pana-Jungla, your life will always be immortal as long as there's a horizon and you always know how to reach the end.
>
> While the jungle puts your mind in a stupor and your feet swell as you walk, there will be no jungle in the present that a Pana-Jungla cannot dominate.

> My life will always be the green gold and the mountains of my heart. I am a Pana-Jungla that never gets lost in your trails of pure illusion.
>
> When I look to the infinity and the green leaves of the immensity, the Pana-Junglas yell to God asking for your freedom.

There are some inexpensive and very rustic bamboo bungalows here for hard-core back-packers. You're best off getting to Wetzo early and heading back before nightfall.

There's a 3.5km loop trail at Wetzo that cuts through recently disturbed, secondary and virgin rain forest. It's interesting to compare the three types, and the bird watching is excellent. You can also take a dip in the river, but be careful not to wade out very far into the water, or the current will carry you downstream. Keep in mind that the guides at Wetzo, all of whom are Indians raised in the area, speak only Spanish and Naso, their first language. At least that was the case in 2001.

GUABITO

For information on entry requirements at the border crossing at Guabito (Sixaola on the Costa Rica side), see Costa Rican Border Crossings in the Getting There & Away chapter.

Chiriquí Province

Chiricanos claim to have it all, and there's an element of truth in what they say: Panama's tallest mountains are in Chiriquí Province, as are some of its longest rivers. The province is home to spectacular rain forest, and yet it is also the country's top agricultural and cattle-ranching region. Two of the country's largest islands and one of the world's biggest copper mines are in Chiriquí Province as well.

But it is the pleasant climate and beauty of several mountain towns that make the province a favorite vacation spot of Panamanians. Mention Boquete, Cerro Punta or Guadalupe to Panama City residents, and they'll tell you how cool and lovely these towns are. It brightens their day just to hear *Boquete*. Nestled in a valley at the foot of Volcán Barú, the country's tallest mountain, Boquete is also famous for its delicious oranges and coffee.

So proud are Chiricanos of their home province that talk of creating an independent República de Chiriquí is popular. Indeed, the inhabitants of the region have been fiercely independent in spirit for a long time.

When the Spaniards first visited the area in the 1520s, they were astonished by what they found. Instead of one or two Indian tribes, they found many small groups living in relative isolation. Although often separated by only a few kilometers, these groups had distinct languages and religions. They fought among themselves and later against the conquistadors.

In the early 17th century, Spanish missionaries led by Padre Cristóbal Cacho Santillana decided to make Christians out of the Indians and had 626 natives rounded up and placed in two towns he had founded. Santillana identified six distinct languages among this group, and he had started to record a vocabulary of the most common when measles brought by the colonists swept through the towns and killed half the Indians.

The survivors, having had enough of the Spaniards, took to the hills. The cleric was not discouraged, however. Santillana was determined to save the Indians' souls even if he had to kill all of them in the process. Of the many tribes that lived in the region at the time of the cleric's arrival – the Cotho, Borisque, Dorasque, Utelae, Bugabae, Zune, Dolega, Zariba, Dure and others – only the Guaymís survived. Today they are the most populous of Panama's seven Indian groups.

During the 17th century and into the 18th century, pirates attacked Chiriquí. It was

Highlights

- Boquete, a cool mountain town in a picturesque valley

- The awesome scenery of the rapids-packed Ríos Chiriquí and Chiriquí Viejo, ideal for white-water rafting

- The Sendero Los Quetzales, one of Central America's loveliest nature trails, on the slopes of Volcán Barú

- Isle-studded Parque Nacional Marino Golfo de Chiriquí, with magnificent reefs and beaches

- The mysterious carved boulders of El Nancito

- Finca La Suiza, a Swiss-run lodge set amid pristine cloud forest that's a hiker's paradise

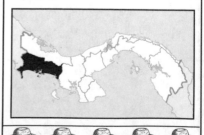

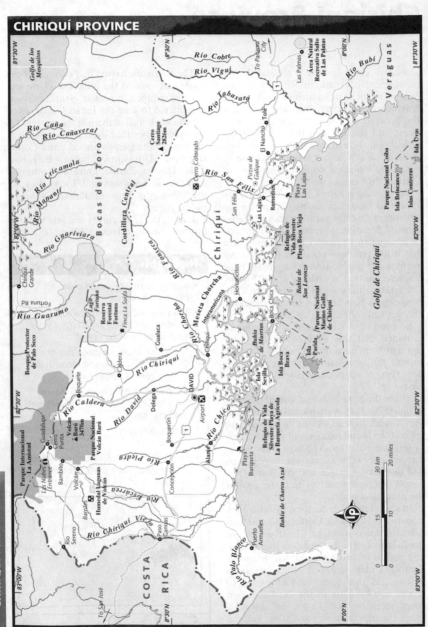

just outside Remedios in 1680 that English buccaneer Richard Sawkins, attempting to lead an assault against the well-defended city, was fatally wounded. Six years later, pirates coming down from Honduras sacked the towns of Alanje and San Lorenzo. And Miskito Indians behaving like pirates invaded the region in 1732, plundering and burning the city of David.

In the 19th century, another sort of foreigner moved in – farmers from the USA, Italy, Germany, England and Switzerland who viewed the climate and slopes of the Chiriquí highlands as prime for coffee, timber and other crops. Today their descendants are being joined by a new group of immigrants – *gringos* – who look on the verdant hills and meadows and see a need for B&Bs.

And the Guaymís? They're living on a large reservation in the Chiriquí highlands and are seeking statehood. Their lives revolve around subsistence agriculture, just as they did when white people first arrived nearly 500 years ago. But these days the Indians have political clout, and their future is in their own hands.

Lowlands

DAVID
pop 77,800

Panama's third most populous city, David is the capital of Chiriquí Province and the center of a rich farming region. It has plenty of places to stay and eat, but few tourist attractions – and David is hot and sticky all year. Travelers stop here mainly on their way to or from the Costa Rican border at Paso Canoas, 54km away. David is also used as a springboard for visits to Boquete and Volcán, Parque Nacional Volcán Barú and islands in the Golfo de Chiriquí.

Orientation

David is about halfway between Panama City and San José, Costa Rica – it's about six hours by road from either place. The Carretera Interamericana does not enter the town but instead skirts around its northern and western sides. The city's heart is its fine central plaza, the Parque de Cervantes, about 1.5km southwest of the highway.

Information

David, being a provincial capital, has the usual services you'd expect, such as the 24-hour Chiriquí Hospital on Calle Central. The main church is at the center of things, across from Parque de Cervantes.

Tourist Offices There's an IPAT tourist office (☎/fax 775-4120) on the second floor of the Edificio Galherna, the building beside the church on the central plaza. The office is open 8:30 am to 4:30 pm weekdays and has information on the whole of Chiriquí Province. English and Spanish are spoken.

The environmental agency ANAM (☎ 775-7840/3163) has an office near the airport. Here you can get information on national parks and permits to camp in them. It's open 8 am to 4 pm weekdays.

Consulate The Costa Rican consulate (☎/fax 774-1923, cosurica@chiriqui.com) is in the center of the city, opposite the Restaurante El Fogon. It is open 8 am to 3 pm weekdays.

Immigration The Migración y Naturalización office (☎ 775-4515), on Calle C Sur near Avenida Central, is one of three offices in Panama where visas and tourist cards may be extended. The office is open 8 am to 4:30 pm weekdays. (See the Facts for the Visitor chapter for details).

Money There's an ATM at the Banco del Istmo, on Calle H Norte at Avenida Belisario Porras, and it's possible to cash American Express traveler's checks here. The same is true regarding the Banco del Istmo on Avenida 3 de Noviembre. There's also a Bancomer on Avenida Bolívar, across the street from the Parque de Cervantes. All three banks are open normal business hours weekdays and Saturday morning, closed Sunday.

CHIRIQUÍ PROVINCE

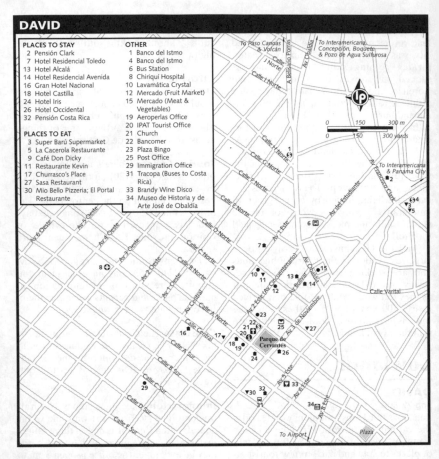

DAVID

PLACES TO STAY
2 Pensión Clark
7 Hotel Residencial Toledo
13 Hotel Alcalá
14 Hotel Residencial Avenida
16 Gran Hotel Nacional
18 Hotel Castilla
24 Hotel Iris
26 Hotel Occidental
32 Pensión Costa Rica

PLACES TO EAT
3 Super Barú Supermarket
5 La Cacerola Restaurante
9 Café Don Dicky
11 Restaurante Kevin
17 Churrasco's Place
27 Sasa Restaurant
30 Mio Bello Pizzeria; El Portal
    Restaurante

OTHER
1 Banco del Istmo
4 Banco del Istmo
6 Bus Station
8 Chiriquí Hospital
10 Lavamática Crystal
12 Mercado (Fruit Market)
15 Mercado (Meat &
    Vegetables)
19 Aeroperlas Office
20 IPAT Tourist Office
21 Church
22 Bancomer
23 Plaza Bingo
25 Post Office
29 Immigration Office
31 Tracopa (Buses to Costa
    Rica)
33 Brandy Wine Disco
34 Museo de Historia y de
    Arte José de Obaldía

Post & Communications The post office is on Calle C Norte, northeast of the Parque de Cervantes. It's open 7 am to 5:30 pm weekdays and 7 am to 4:30 pm Saturday.

Domestic and international calls can be placed from any of the many pay phones around town.

Laundry The Lavamática Crystal, on Calle D Norte between Avenidas 1 and 2 Este, will wash, dry and fold your laundry in a few hours (75¢ to wash, 75¢ to dry). It's open 7 am to 7 pm Monday through Saturday and 8 am to 1 pm Sunday.

Things to See & Do
Despite its size and role as a provincial capital, David has few attractions. However, within an hour's drive are many good places to visit, including Boquete, Volcán, Cerro Punta and Playa Las Lajas.

David's small **Museo de Historia y de Arte José de Obaldía** is in a two-story house on Avenida 8 Este, near Calle A Norte. The museum contains many fine examples of colonial-era religious art, a wing devoted to Indian artifacts found in the vicinity of Volcán Barú, lots of photos from Chiriquí's past and many impressive photographs of the Panama Canal under construction.

The museum is in the former home of José de Obaldía Orejuela, founder of Chiriquí Province. The residence was built in 1880, and it is worth the admission price (US$1) just to get a good look at it. All the furniture on the 2nd floor is original. A garden behind the museum is quite lovely, and beside it you'll find a representation of a traditional rural kitchen. The museum is open from 8:30 am to 4:30 pm except Sunday.

Incidentally, the museum is in the old section of town, which is known locally as Barrio del Peligro (Danger Zone) because the cemetery, the jail and the slaughter-house are all located here. However, the neighborhood isn't as dangerous as its nickname suggests. Just don't stroll around it on a night when there's a full moon out!

There are two **markets** in David that are worth a look if you've never seen a traditional Latin American market. The larger of the two faces the junction of Avenidas Bolívar and Obaldía, and the other is at the corner of Avenida 2 Este and Calle D Norte. Both sell produce for far less than you'd pay at a supermarket.

Special Events

The Feria de San José de David, held for 10 days each March, is a big international fair; contact the IPAT tourist office for exact dates, as they vary from year to year.

Concepción, half an hour's drive west of David, celebrates its patron saint's day on February 2 (or the following Saturday if the 2nd lands on a weekday).

Places to Stay – Budget

Pensión Costa Rica (☎ 775-1241), on Avenida 5 Este between Calles Central and A Sur, offers singles/doubles with fans for US$4/9 with shared bathrooms or US$6/11 with private bathrooms. The 48 guestrooms tend to be clean, but some rooms are uncomfortably warm.

Pensión Clark (☎ 774-3452) is on Avenida Francisco Clark about 1km northeast of the Parque de Cervantes, the fourth house from the corner of Avenida del Estudiante. It's a pleasant little family-run place, clean, quiet and respectable, with six rooms (four with private bathrooms), all priced at US$8.

Hotel Residencial Toledo (☎ 774-6732, fax 774-6733), on Avenida 1 Este, an upstairs hotel built in 1995, has 28 clean rooms with air con, private hot-water bathrooms, color TVs, firm mattresses and telephones for US$16.50 for one or two people. Ask for a room with windows.

Three-story *Hotel Iris* (☎ 775-2251, fax 775-7233), on Calle A Norte across from the Parque de Cervantes, has 69 rooms with good beds and private bathrooms. Rates are US$15/18 single/double for a room with air con and one bed, US$20 for air con and two beds. A single with fan goes for only US$12. This place is OK, as is its restaurant.

Hotel Residencial Avenida (☎ 774-0451, fax 775-7279), opposite the Hotel Alcalá on Avenida Bolívar, features 20 rooms, 15 with only fans for US$13 per person and five with air con for US$15 per person. All had firm beds and private cold-water bathrooms. The owner had plans to remodel, so these rates and features are likely to change.

Hotel Occidental (☎ 775-4695, fax 775-7424), on Avenida 3 de Noviembre beside the Parque de Cervantes, has 40 rooms with air con and private bathrooms for US$17/21/25 single/double/triple. The rooms are a bit worn, but this place offers excellent value and is quite popular. There's a casino and laundry service on the premises. The restaurant is cheap and popular.

Hotel Alcalá (☎ 774-9018, fax 774-9021, halcala@chiriqui.com) is a newcomer on Avenida Bolívar. The hotel's 54 guestrooms each feature air con, good beds, a desk, a 32-channel TV, a phone and a private hot-water bathroom. There's a restaurant and bar on the premises. Rates are extremely competitive at US$18/22 single/double.

Places to Stay – Mid-Range

Hotel Castilla (☎ 774-5260, fax 774-5246), on Calle A Norte near the Parque de Cervantes, is an excellent, centrally located hotel offering one of the best values in David. Every room in this three-story, 70-room hotel is cheerful and equipped with air con, phone, private hot-water bathroom and 50-channel TV. Castilla's rates are US$25/30 single/double, and US$55 for suites.

Gran Hotel Nacional (☎ 775-2222), on Calle Central near Avenida Central, is a large hotel with a restaurant, pizzeria, casino, safe parking and a large swimming pool with a diving board and slide. The 75 rooms, all with air con, phones, good beds, 50-channel TV and private hot-water bathrooms, cost US$48/56 single/double.

Places to Eat
There are plenty of restaurants in town, as you can see from this section. If you're looking for just a healthy snack, drop by the Esso station opposite the Gran Nacional Hotel and purchase a tub of Frank Marth Yogurt from the station's snack stand. The tubs contain chunks of fresh tropical fruit in vanilla yogurt with an inch of Jell-O at the bottom. They are an absolute steal at US$1 apiece.

Central David The restaurant at the **Hotel Occidental** is the best value in town. Typical items include scrambled eggs and toast (75¢), ham and eggs (US$1), sandwiches (under US$2) and even a banana split (US$1.50). A chocolate sundae costs 60¢. The restaurant is open daily from 7 am to 10 pm.

Mio Bello Pizzeria and the adjacent **El Portal Restaurante**, on Calle A Sur near Avenida 3 de Noviembre, share a menu and a kitchen but retain distinct names. The biggest difference between them is that the pizzeria has air con, while El Portal doesn't. These places are popular with the college crowd on weekend nights, mainly because El Portal has a cozy, cavelike, subterranean dining room that's quite hip. Pasta and seafood are the specialties of the house. A family-size pizza will set you back US$8. Fish and meat dishes run US$4 to US$7.

Churrasco's Place, on Avenida 2 Este near Calle Central, is popular with locals for its good, inexpensive food. Its specialty is grilled meats. Downstairs is a covered, open-air restaurant; a slightly more expensive air-conditioned bar/restaurant section

is upstairs in the rear. Churrasco's Place is open 24 hours a day, every day.

Café Don Dicky, on Calle C Norte, is also open 24 hours a day. From the front it looks like a cheap open-air diner, but it makes good food; there's a more attractive dining area in the rear. Most dishes cost about US$3.

The **Sasa Restaurant**, on Calle C Norte near Avenida 3 de Noviembre, is open-sided (and therefore hot), but it offers an excellent seafood soup (US$3.50 for a large portion). Sasa also serves up a tasty *guacho*, a thick soup consisting mainly of rice, peas and clams. Guacho is not found outside Chiriquí Province.

A pleasant little place for an inexpensive breakfast or lunch is the small open-air **Restaurante Kevin**, in the front of the Hotel Saval. Service is friendly here, and meals go for US$2.

Eastern David The **Super Barú** supermarket, near the corner of Avenidas Francisco Clark and 3 de Noviembre, has large deli and produce sections and a well-stocked pharmacy. There's even a small area where you can enjoy a dessert or cold beverage.

Among stores on the southern side of the Super Barú supermarket/shopping complex is **La Cacerola Restaurante**, a popular buffet-style diner with plenty of air con. Most dishes cost about US$2; seafood soup is US$2.50. The restaurant is open 7:30 am to 9 pm daily.

Entertainment
Half a block northwest of the Parque de Cervantes is **Plaza Bingo**, a casino that's open from 10 am to 4 am daily.

There are many dance clubs in town, most with the longevity of a gnat. **Brandy Wine Disco**, a couple of blocks south of the central plaza, is a popular place that has been around at least several years. It features pool tables and dancing.

Getting There & Away
Air David's airport, the Aeropuerto Enrique Malek, is about 5km from town. There are no buses to the airport; take a taxi.

Aeroperlas (☎ 721-1195 at the airport; 315-7500 in Panama City) has flights from David to Panama City at 7 and 11:30 am and 5 pm Monday through Friday, 8:30 am and 5 pm Saturday, and 9:30 am and 5:15 pm Sunday (US$57). The airline also flies from David to Bocas del Toro town on Isla Colón with a stop in Changuinola at 8:10 am and 2:10 pm weekdays, and 2:10 pm weekends (US$26).

There's an Aeroperlas office (☎ 775-7779, fax 774-2916) on Calle A Norte, next to the Hotel Castilla. It's open 8 am to 5 pm weekdays and 8 am to 3:30 pm Saturday.

Bus The bus station is on Avenida del Estudiante, about 600m northeast of the central plaza. It has a small office where you can leave luggage for 50¢ per day and a restaurant that's open 5 am to midnight.

David is the hub of bus transportation in western Panama and has buses to many places. Below is a listing of most of the major bus routes and schedules. Fares cited are one-way.

Almirante – US$3; three hours; 150km; every 45 minutes; 5 am to 7 pm

Boquete – US$1.20; one hour; 38km; every 25 minutes; 5 am to 7 pm

Caldera – US$1.50; 45 minutes; 20km; eight buses daily; 8:15 am to 7 pm

Cerro Punta – US$2.65; 2¼ hours; 79km; take the Volcán bus; departing hourly; 5 am to 5 pm; bus continues from Volcán to Bambito (10 minutes from Volcán) and Cerro Punta (30 minutes more)

Chiriquí Grande – US$6; 2¼ hours; 106km; every 45 minutes; 5 am to 7 pm Monday to Saturday; every two hours on Sunday

Horconcitos – US$1.50; 45 minutes; 45km; two buses daily; 11:30 am and 5 pm

Las Lajas (town) – US$2; 80 minutes; 100km; hourly; 11:45 am to 5:20 pm

Panama City – 438km; regular bus every 45 minutes (US$12; seven hours; 7 am to 8 pm); four express buses (US$15; six hours; 10 am, 2 pm, 10 pm and midnight)

Paso Canoas (Costa Rican border) – US$2.65; 70 minutes; 54km; every 15 minutes; 4:15 am to 9:45 pm

Puerto Armuelles – US$2.65; 2½ hours; 88km; every 15 minutes; 4:15 am to 9:45 pm

Río Sereno (Costa Rican border) – US$4; 2½ hours; 104km; hourly; 5 am to 5 pm; via Volcán

Volcán – US$2.30; 1 ¾ hours; 57km; hourly; 5 am to 5 pm

In addition to operating buses between David and the border crossings at Paso Canoas and Río Sereno, Tracopa (☎ 775-0585) also provides bus service between David and San José, Costa Rica. There's only one direct bus each day, and it departs at 8:30 am from the Tracopa office at the corner of Avenida 5 Este and Calle A Sur, beside the Pensión Costa Rica; it arrives in San José about eight hours later. From San José, buses depart on the return trip to David at 7:30 am. The one-way fare is US$12.50.

You can buy your ticket when you show up for the bus or up to two days before your trip. The Tracopa office is open from 7 am to noon and 1 to 4 pm Monday to Saturday and from 7 to 11 am Sunday.

Getting Around

David has local buses and plenty of taxis. Taxi fares within the city are 65¢ to US$1; the fare to the airport is US$2.

Rental-car companies with offices in David include the following:

Avis	☎ 774-7075
Budget	☎ 775-1667
Chiriquí	☎ 774-3464
Hertz	☎ 775-6828
Hilary	☎ 775-5459
Mike's	☎ 775-3524

If you want a 4WD vehicle, request a *cuatro por cuatro*.

AROUND DAVID

Within an hour's drive of David are two rivers that, at the time of writing, were the only rivers used by a reputable **white-water rafting** outfit in Panama. The Río Chiriquí and the Río Chiriquí Viejo both flow from the fertile hills of Volcán Barú and are flanked by forest for much of their lengths. At some places waterfalls can be seen at the edges of the rivers, and both pass through narrow canyons with awesome sheer rock walls.

CHIRIQUÍ PROVINCE

The Río Chiriquí is most often run from May to December, and the Chiriquí Viejo is run the rest of the year; the rides tend to last four and five hours, respectively. Bring along plenty of sunscreen. (See 'Chiriquí Is for Kayakers' later in this chapter for further information about the rivers.)

The country's most reputable white-water rafting outfit, Chiriquí River Rafting (☎ 720-1505, fax 720-1506, rafting@panama-rafting.com), in downtown Boquete, switches between the rivers, depending on rainfall, the age and experience levels of its clients and other factors. The company's owner, Hector Sanchez, speaks English and Spanish and is very safety conscious (see Guides in the Getting Around chapter for a profile of Hector).
Website: www.panama-rafting.com

Chiriquí River Rafting offers a variety of options, including those listed below. All prices include a hearty lunch. The former prices include roundtrip transportation from Boquete; the latter prices include roundtrip transportation from Panama City, six meals, two nights' lodging on a secluded coffee plantation, and a day hike. These packages offer excellent value.

• The Palon section of the Chiriquí Viejo; December through April only; US$100/225; four hours; minimum age 14

• The Bajo Mendez section of the Río Chiriquí; known for big water and long wave trains; US$92/215; 3½ hours; minimum age 12

• The Sabo section of the Chiriquí Viejo; less emphasis on rapids, more on nature; US$90/210; 2½ hours; minimum age 10

• The Barrigona section of the Río Chiriquí; perfect for beginners and families; US$75/200; 2½ hours; minimum age 8

PASO CANOAS
See Costa Rican Border Crossings in the Getting There & Away chapter for information on this major border town.

PUERTO ARMUELLES
pop 22,700
Located 34km south of the Paso Canoas border crossing, Puerto Armuelles is a city

of souls who lived for bananas and (economically) died with them. In January 2001, after more than 70 years in Puerto Armuelles, Chiquita Brands International shut down its operations there.

The reason: The plantation workers of Puerto Armuelles bruised too many bananas.

Banana workers the world over are all paid about the same, but while banana workers generally adopted picking and transporting methods that minimized bruising (ie, waste), the workers in Puerto Armuelles did not. The banana workers' union leaders in Puerto Armuelles refused to tell the workers that they had to change their harvesting methods; doing so would have cost the elected leaders their positions. This, coupled with the fact that during the 1990s the world's supply of bananas exceeded demand, causing the price of bananas to fall, led Chiquita, which was losing money in Puerto Armuelles, to cut its losses.

As for the city of Puerto Armuelles, 60% of its population is now unemployed. Those residents who can are leaving the city. By the time you read this, the population of Puerto Armuelles might well be under 10,000 – down from 46,100 in 1990 and 22,700 in 2000.

Only the old wooden homes built for workers by the banana company decades ago warrant a trip to Puerto Armuelles. But when weighed against the sad scenes of depressed people moping about, there's no reason for a tourist to go there anymore.

PLAYA BARQUETA
Unfortunately, most of the land bordering this long and lovely beach southwest of David had been subdivided into small lots that were selling quickly in 2001. By the time you read this, there likely will be dozens of homes lining this shoreline, spoiling what until recently was a gorgeous stretch of undeveloped coast.

Capping the eastern end of this sad development is the **Las Olas Resort** (☎/fax 772-3000, lasolasresort@aol.com), which was under construction when I passed through in late 2000. Plans called for

31 standard guestrooms, six standard suites, two double suites and a penthouse, all with ocean views, air con and color TVs with a movie channel. Room rates were expected to range from US$90 to US$1350 for the penthouse. Facilities were to include a gourmet restaurant, a bar-discotheque, a poolside restaurant-bar, a weight room, a beauty salon and spa, a gift shop and a convention center. Laundry service and a variety of guided tours were to be offered. Be advised that the surf in front of the resort is dangerous due to riptides, and the resort's planned helicopter tours will undoubtedly scare off much of the wildlife in the area. The resort was being built next to the Refugio de Vida Silvestre Playa de La Barqueta Agrícola, a wildlife refuge created to protect nesting birds.

Website: www.lasolasresort.com

GOLFO DE CHIRIQUÍ

South of David, the Golfo de Chiriquí is home to the **Parque Nacional Marino Golfo de Chiriquí**, the 14,740-hectare national marine park that protects 25 islands, plus 19 coral reefs and abundant wildlife. Attractions include beaches, snorkeling, diving, surfing, bird watching and big-game fishing.

The 3000-hectare **Isla Boca Brava** is the only place near the park with accommodations. On Boca Brava, married couple Frank Köhler and Yadira Pinzon operate the *Restaurante y Cabañas Boca Brava* (☎ 676-3244; no reser ations accepted). The lodgings consist of four modern and comfortable rooms with private bathrooms for US$12/15 to US$17/20 for singles/doubles and four rustic rooms with shared bathroom for US$10. If you want to sleep in a hammock, the cost is US$3. The seventh night is free. There's an open-sided restaurant that features seafood at budget prices. Before making the trip to Boca Brava, call a few hours ahead of time to make sure there's room for you.

From the restaurant, you're but a stone's throw from the boundary of the national marine park. And sharing the island, which has no less than 12km of trails, are hundreds of howler monkeys, four species of sea turtle and 280 recorded species of bird. From here it's possible to hire water taxis to take you to some excellent snorkeling sites in the park. There are many coral reefs and picturesque beaches in the area; Frank and Yadira can tell you all about them in English, German or Spanish.

Getting There & Away

To reach Boca Brava, you must first drive or take a bus to the Horconcitos turnoff, which is 39km east of David; two buses daily run to Horconcitos from David (US$1.50 one-way, 45 minutes, 45km, departures at 11:30 am and 5 pm). Note that you don't need to take either of these specific buses; any bus going by this turnoff will do, as long as you tell the driver to drop you at the Horconcitos turnoff. From the turnoff you must take a pickup-truck taxi to Horconcitos (5km) and then to the fishing village of Boca Chica (US$15, 40 minutes by 4WD or one hour by 2WD truck, 21km). If you drive, you can safely leave your vehicle near the dock as long as there's nothing in it. At the dock you can hire a water taxi (US$4) to take you 200m to the island.

EAST TO VERAGUAS PROVINCE
Meseta Chorcha

On the northern side of the Interamericana, 24km east of David, is the enormous Meseta Chorcha (Chorcha Plateau), which photographers won't want to miss. As you approach the plateau from the west, you'll see a white streak running down its glistening granite face. As you come closer, you'll see that the streak is an extremely tall waterfall.

Unfortunately, the highway's as close to the falls as you can get without trespassing. The land between the highway and the foot of the falls belongs to a rancher who doesn't like strangers on his property.

Playa Las Lajas

Playa Las Lajas, 62km east of David and 13km south of the Interamericana via a paved road, is one of several lengthy, palm-lined beaches along this stretch of the Pacific coast. With its broad expanse of white sand, Playa Las Lajas is quite popular on the weekends but often empty during the week. The waves are perfect for body surfing without much undertow, and the sand is cool and ideal for sunbathing.

There's one place to stay at this lovely beach, and it's **Las Lajas Beach Cabins** (☎ *775-4171 and 690-7275, argonx@ yahoo.com)*. The cabins consist of nine rustic but appealing cabañas right on the beach, a clam's toss from sizzling surf. The cabins have concrete floors, which is good because it means you'll take less sand with you to your sleeping quarters – the loft above. The walls are made of bamboo and the roof of thatch, neither of which retain heat. There are windows on all sides, which offer plenty of cross ventilation. Each cabaña contains a double bamboo bed (a two-inch foam mat and sheets are provided), a night table, a shelf, a laundry line and a solar-powered light. The bathrooms are communal in a nearby concrete structure. The cabañas rent for a very reasonable US$7.50/12 single/double.

The owner was building an additional concrete structure 50m back from the beach in which he was planning several rooms (US$15/22) and two dormitory rooms (one for women, one for men; US$6.50 per bed). If you've got a tent and want to camp, you can do so here and use the facilities for US$4 per tent. There's a restaurant serving three meals a day for nothing more than US$6.

To get here, take any bus except a nonstop that travels by the Las Lajas turnoff on the Interamericana, and ask the driver to drop you at the Las Lajas turnoff (from David, expect the ride to cost several dollars and take about 90 minutes). At the dropoff, take a taxi the 13km to where the road reaches the sea. Turn right and proceed 1.5km until you arrive at the cabins. The taxi ride should cost no more than US$5 per party.

At the turnoff to Las Lajas, there's **Restaurante El Cruce** that's open 'early til late' every night. Buses stop here every 30 minutes from 5 am to 4:30 pm, so heading out won't be a problem, and because of the restaurant, you've got a place to rest in

comfort until the next bus heading in the direction you want to go shows up.

Be advised that 500m northwest of the restaurant and about 50m south of the Interamericana is a wooden-walled structure where Guaymí Indians sell **Guaymí handicrafts**. Most of the residents of San Félix 3km north of the Restaurante Le Cruce, are Guaymí.

While you're at Las Lajas Beach Cabins consider taking a **reforestation tour** offered by Futuro Forestal (☎ *727-0010*, fax *727-0100*, *keegan@co2ol-usa.com* in English, *ae@futuroforestal.com* in Spanish, *simonmews@aol.com* in German), a tree farm that's growing mostly native Panamanian trees on 200 hectares of former pasture. The goal of the company is to make money in a socially and ecologically responsible manner, by eventually felling and selling the trees they grow while temporarily improving the biodiversity of the area and lessening the pressure to harvest natural forest.

The tour begins every Saturday at 8 am at Las Lajas Beach Cabins with a pickup truck ride to the reforested area. During the ride to the re-forest and once inside it, an English-speaking guide will drive you through newly reforested area as well as 50-year-old forest and describe the ecological benefits of the project. There's some walking involved, though not a lot. The tour lasts roughly three hours and costs US$5 per person, less if the group is larger than five persons. In the works was a forest cabin beside a creek with hammocks for beds and a lantern for light. You'd be left and picked up by truck the following day. The price is US$20 for one person, and US$5 for each additional person.

Website: www.futuroforestal.com

Cerro Colorado

One of the world's largest copper mines is an hour's drive north of the Interamericana via a private road that begins nearly opposite the Playa Las Lajas turnoff. Mineralogists estimate that there's approximately 1.4 million tons of copper in Cerro Colorado. The open-face mine is not open to tours, but some readers might be interested to know it's here.

Pozos de Galique

The Pozos de Galique (Springs of Galique) are three no-frills hot springs, each of which can accommodate several people, at the end of a 3.8km badly rutted dirt road that winds north from the Interamericana. If you usually enjoy hot springs, you'll likely enjoy these – especially if you reach them in the early morning (before the day heats up) and bring lots of cold drinks. These hot springs have 'day trip' written all over them.

The easy-to-miss turnoff for the road to the springs, which requires a 4WD vehicle, is 27km east of the Interamericana turnoff for Horconcitos and 4km east of the turnoff for Playa Las Lajas. The turnoff is 30m west of a small bridge with 'Galique' written on it.

Rock Carvings

About 5km west of the town of Tolé is a turnoff for El Nancito, a small community known for its carved boulders. Local people say the carvings were made more than 1000 years ago, but no one really knows; the rocks have yet to be studied. Few people even know about them.

From the Interamericana, turn north onto the road to El Nancito, and when you reach the 'Cantina Oriente' sign, turn west and drive 75m. You'll come across some rather large boulders with figures carved into them. The largest of the boulders is on the far side of a barbed-wire fence, behind a cattle chute. There are many other carved boulders in the area.

No buses stop in El Nancito. If you are relying on public transportation and your legs are in good shape, the best thing to do is to take any bus that passes by El Nancito, ask the driver to drop you at the turnoff on the Interamericana, and then hike the 1.5km to the boulders. Afterward, walk back to the highway and catch any bus heading in the direction you want to go. Be careful doing this in the late afternoon; you'll have difficulty catching a bus after sunset.

Highlands

BOQUETE
pop 3900

This small town is only 38km north of the hot, bustling provincial capital of David, but it feels like it's in another country. Nestled in a craggy mountain valley at 1060m, with the sparkling Río Caldera running through it, Boquete is known throughout Panama for its cool, fresh climate and pristine natural environment. It's a fine place for walking, bird watching and enjoying a respite from the heat of the lowlands. *Bajareque*, which roughly translates as 'slow drizzle', is the name locals give to the light rainfall that visits this pleasant town almost every afternoon.

Flowers, coffee, vegetables and citrus fruits are grown in and around Boquete. The navel-orange season, from November to February, is a popular time to visit. Boquete oranges, originally brought from Riverside, CA, are known for their sweetness, and the coffee is widely regarded as the country's finest.

Some nights can get very chilly. Visitors should pack some warm clothes if you plan to do any camping in the area.

Orientation

Boquete's central area consists of only a few square blocks. The main road, Avenida Central, comes north from David, passes along the western side of the central plaza and continues up the hill past the church.

Information

There's an IPAT tourist office on Avenida Central atop a bluff overlooking town, but the staff at the Chiriquí River Rafting office, on Avenida Central in central Boquete, are more helpful (see Around David earlier in this chapter).

There's a Banco Nacional de Panamá on Calle 5a Sur Avenida Central, and there's a post office on the eastern side of the plaza, open 7 am to 6 pm weekdays and 7 am to 5 pm Saturday. International calls can be made from any of the pay phones around town.

BOQUETE

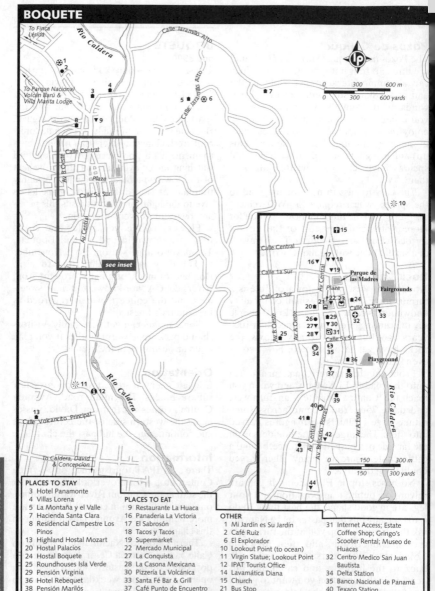

PLACES TO STAY
3   Hotel Panamonte
4   Villas Lorena
5   La Montaña y el Valle
7   Hacienda Santa Clara
8   Residencial Campestre Los Pinos
13 Highland Hostal Mozart
20 Hostal Palacios
24 Hostal Boquete
25 Roundhouses Isla Verde
29 Pensión Virginia
36 Hotel Rebequet
38 Pensión Marilós
39 Pensión Topaz
41 Hotel Fundadores

PLACES TO EAT
9   Restaurante La Huaca
16 Panadería La Victoria
17 El Sabrosón
18 Tacos y Tacos
19 Supermarket
22 Mercado Municipal
27 La Conquista
28 La Casona Mexicana
30 Pizzería La Volcánica
33 Santa Fé Bar & Grill
37 Café Punto de Encuentro
42 Restaurant Chinese Food
44 Ristorante Salvatore

OTHER
1   Mi Jardín es Su Jardín
2   Café Ruíz
6   El Explorador
10 Lookout Point (to ocean)
11 Virgin Statue; Lookout Point
12 IPAT Tourist Office
14 Lavamática Diana
15 Church
21 Bus Stop
23 Post Office
26 Chiriquí River Rafting Office
31 Internet Access; Estate Coffee Shop; Gringo's Scooter Rental; Museo de Huacas
32 Centro Medico San Juan Bautista
34 Delta Station
35 Banco Nacional de Panamá
40 Texaco Station
43 Eduardo Cano (Horse Rental)

There's a laundry (Lavamática Diana) on Avenida Central, opposite and a little downhill from the church. Its staff will wash, dry and fold your clothes for US$1.50 a load, and it's open from 7 am to 6 pm Monday to Saturday.

Two gas stations and a supermarket are on Avenida Central as well. On Calle 4a Sur, you'll find a medical center, **Centro Medico San Juan Bautista**, and if the prognosis is unfavorable there's a **church** four blocks north.

Internet Resources

The **Estate Coffee Shop**, on Avenida Central, is an Internet café offering cappuccinos, other coffee drinks, snacks, pastries, and email access (US$2.50 an hour). It's open 7 am to 8 pm daily. Also here are satellite TV, souvenirs, a tour desk and paperbacks.

Scooters & Bicycles

Next door to The Estate Coffee is **Gringo's Scooter Rental**, which rents out motorized scooters for US$6.50 an hour and US$25 for eight hours. They also have bicycles for US$2.50 an hour and US$10 for eight hours.

Things to See & Do

Boquete, with its flower-lined streets and nearby forest, is ideal for walking, hiking and birding. The town lends itself well to picturesque strolls. The more ambitious might fancy climbing 3478m **Volcán Barú** in the nearby national park; there are several entrances to the park, but the easiest access is from Boquete (see Parque Nacional Volcán Barú later in this chapter for details).

A stroll around town will allow you to see the **Parque de las Madres**, with its flowers, fountain and children's playground; the fairgrounds; and the river. You'll also come across an old railway and an exhibition wagon – leftovers from the days when a train linked Boquete with the coastal town of Puerto Armuelles.

The **Kotowa Coffee Estate** (☎/fax 720-1430, kotowa@myroaster.com) offers the best coffee-estate tour in the area. The hour-long tour features a description of the estate's history (beginning with a Canadian's

arrival in 1918), emphasis on the estate's environmentally friendly methods of coffee production, a full tour of the production facilities, a fascinating tour of the estate's original processing mill with all the original machinery, and a cupping session, during which guests learn what to look for in high-quality coffee. It's a very worthwhile tour that's well priced at US$10 per person. The estate requests 24 hours' notice prior to your visit.
Website: www.myroaster.com

The **Café Ruíz** (☎ 720-1392, fax 720-1292, info@caferuiz.com), on the main road about 600m north of the town center, offers two tours: a free tour of the roasting and packaging plant, and a three-hour tour (US$10 per person) that features transportation to a nearby coffee plantation, a presentation of the history of coffee in Boquete, and a description at the processing plant of how fresh-picked coffee beans are prepared for roasting. Next, you're led to the roasting facility where tourists learn the process involved in the final processing of the beans for consumer use. The tour rounds out with a cupping session. The tour hours weren't defined at the time of writing; contact the company for tour times.
Website: www.casaruiz.com

Mi Jardín es Su Jardín, just uphill from Café Ruíz, is a magnificent garden surrounding a luxurious private estate. The residence is off-limits to the public, but you are free to stroll about the garden as long as you like during daylight hours. There's no entrance fee, and the grounds are open every day of the year.

Museo de Huacas, located in the same complex as Gringo's Scooter Rental and the Estate Coffee Shop, is a small museum that contains a mixture of real huacas and replicas. For information about huacas, see Shopping in the Panama City chapter.

In a hilly area 45-minutes' walk from the town center, **El Explorador** is a cafeteria and gardens. The cafeteria serves breads, hot chocolate, coffee drinks, chicken and fried bananas. Reached by a path behind the cafeteria, the gardens are like a page ripped from *Alice in Wonderland*. The path passes

Chiriquí Is for Kayakers

John Miller has made more first descents of Panama's white-water rivers than anyone else. The teacher of instructors for US-based Nantahala Outdoor Center, the largest kayaking school in the world, John's an expert kayaker – especially when it comes to Panama's rivers. He prepared the following report for Lonely Planet's readers:

There are other rivers in Panama, but nothing compares to Chiriquí. And if someone wants to paddle in Panama, this is where they should go.

The Chiriquí province of Panama has three elements that make it a paddler's paradise: terrain, rainfall and accessibility. During the rainy season, the area around Boquete has over 20 different runs within a two-hour drive of this small mountain town, varying from easy Class 1/2 to scary Class 5. The Continental Divide ranges from over 10,000 feet near the Costa Rican border in the west to around 6000 feet at the border with the Veraguas Province in the east. The river gradient is steep and consistent almost to the Pacific Ocean, resulting in long continuous stretches of white water. In addition, Volcán Barú towers over Boquete at 12,500 feet on the Pacific side of the Continental Divide. This dormant volcano tends to attract rainfall and has six runnable rivers draining its flanks.

Most of the watersheds in this area are small, but thanks to the bountiful precipitation in the rainy season (May through early December), they are usually runnable every day during the rainy season. During the dry season, only the two biggest watersheds, the Río Chiriquí and the Río Chiriquí Viejo, have enough water to be runnable, and most of the paddling in Panama is found in these two watersheds. By far, the best time of year to paddle is from September through November.

Finally, the Pacific slope of Panama has a network of roads and bridges that make most of the runs easily accessible for day runs. Few of the runs require 4WD vehicles or overnight trips.

Almost all of the rivers in this area follow a very predictable pattern. They are very steep and continuous at the higher elevations, tending to be small, steep streams. As the rivers flow down the mountains, the gradient gradually levels off, and the rivers pick up tributaries and grow in volume and width. As you approach sea level, the rivers are high volume but also drop/pool. You can generally gauge how difficult the run will be by the elevation. The hardest runs start as high as 5000 feet while anything below 1000 feet tends to be no harder than Class 3.

The Rio Chiriquí drains to the east of Boquete and has the largest dam (Fortuna) in Panama. Over 50% of the nation's electricity comes from this hydroelectric project, and while the dam is upstream of all the sections described here, the water from the power plant only returns to the river in the lowest section.

The Río Chiriquí has four distinct sections: the Frijole section, the Witches section, the Bajo Mendez section and the Barrigona section. The 8-mile-long Frijole section is steep, Class 5 creeking. The gradient is often in excess of 300 feet per mile. At medium water levels, this section is drop/pool, but often the drops are close together and quite vertical (the tallest being about 15-20 feet). At higher water levels, eddies and opportunities to stop are few and far between.

The next section, the Witches, is a continuous Class 3/4 run depending on the water level and is about 6 miles long. There are good stopping places at the bottom of the big rapids, many long boulder gardens to play through, but no big vertical drops.

Chiriquí Is for Kayakers

The Bajo Mendez section is about 10 miles long; it's Class 4 for the first mile and generally Class 2/3 after that with the exception of three or four long, large rapids. Because a power plant (from the Río Caldera and the Río Los Valles) dumps water into the river at the put in, the volume in this section is generally double that of the Witches section.

The final section, the Barrigona, starts on a small feeder stream that is raging because of the dam water from Lago Fortuna (above the Frijole section) that dumps back into the river. This section is generally Class 2 with several large Class 3 rapids on it and is about 10 miles long. And this is where the play-boating takes off! There are several world-class play spots on this section, including a big, hungry retentive hole called the Three Wise Men, and a breaking-wave hole called the Christmas Hole that can hold four boaters at one time.

Flowing into the Río Chiriquí are a number of incredible rivers: Río Los Valles, Río Caldera, Río Cochea, Río Majagua and the Río Esti. The Río Los Valles is a difficult Class 5 run with long, steep rapids through complicated boulder gardens. The Río Caldera has five distinct sections, three of which are Class 5 (one of which may be considered unrunnable) and two that are fun Class 4 runs. The Río Cochea is a long, continuous Class 4 run but without any large drops. The Río Majagua has two different sections, the Upper and the Lower. The Upper is Class 3/4 at the top and gradually lets up to be Class 2. The Lower is mostly Class 2 with a few easy Class 3 rapids. The Río Esti is probably the easiest run in the area, Class 1/2 and a perfect run for beginners.

Except for the Frijole section of the Río Chiriquí, all of the above runs are accessible by two-wheel drive vehicles on paved roads. All the put-ins and take-outs are easy walks, and except for some of the Class 5 sections of the Río Caldera, paddlers can portage all the big rapids.

The Río Chiriquí Viejo is the other major watershed in the province; draining from the north side of Volcán Barú toward Costa Rica, it can be considered the jewel of Panamanian white water. Although the river generally has easy access points and travels through populated areas of the country, once on the river you are remote, often feeling as if you are hundreds of miles from civilization as you pass through gorge after gorge and are surrounded by forest and cascading waterfalls.

The Viejo has five sections: Cerro Punta, Sereno, Caison, Palon and Sal Si Puedes (which means 'get out if you can'). Generally, the access is more difficult, the runs are long and walking out could be very difficult.

continued on page 228

CHIRIQUÍ PROVINCE

Chiriquí Is for Kayakers

continued from page 227

The top section, Cerro Punta, is the only easily accessible section on the river, with over half the run being road side. It starts around 5000 feet, is about 15 miles of Class 4+ and is steep, continuous and narrow (average gradient over 200 feet per mile). On this section, you can often go over a mile before finding a good stopping point to gather up the group.

The Sereno section is the longest on the river. From the put-in bridge to the take-out bridge is over 20 miles, and there are no other access points. This section passes through miles of vertical gorges. Most of the run is continuous Class 4, but it often lets up to be continuous Class 3.

The Caison section is about 8 miles of Class 4 water, except for one distinct gorge with several Class 5 rapids at high water. These rapids are walkable but only with great effort.

The Palon section marks the beginning of the uppermost raft run, one of the most exciting raft runs in Central America. The Palon is about 10 miles long, the first three or four containing numerous Class 4 rapids, some of which are very difficult Class 4. The bottom half of the run is generally Class 3.

The final section of the Viejo, Sal Si Puedes, is generally big volume Class 3 rapids and is about seven miles long and ends at the Interamericana.

Except for the Cerro Punta section, access to this river often requires a 4WD vehicle. The entire run can be done as a three-day trip, if you are willing to paddle 20+ miles of continuous white water each day.

In addition to these two watersheds, there are a number of other rivers in the Chiriquí Province. Starting to the west of Boquete, the Río Macho de Monte is over 20 miles of continuous, Class 4 white water. It flows into the Río Piedra, which is also continuous Class 4 but only about 12 miles long. As you travel east from Boquete, the mountains begin to lose elevation, and the character of the rivers becomes more drop/pool. As you go east, the Río Fonseca, Río Tabasará, and the Río Vigui are all Class 2/3 runs and require 4WD vehicles, especially if it has been raining.

One word of warning: During the rainy season, it rains nearly every day, and thus the rivers tend to rise and fall every day. The watersheds are often small and steep, and the rivers often flash. The higher up the river you go, the earlier you should start. When paddling Class 5 runs in Panama, I prefer to be off the river by 1 pm (with beer in hand, of course).

between tiny terraced gardens and over an itty-bitty bridge. On a small grassy slope beneath tall trees, big bunnies hop about freely. El Explorador is open only on weekends and holidays, from 9 am to 6 pm (US$1).

Finca Lérida, located above town, is a coffee farm owned by the Collins family. Bordering the farm is prime habitat for the quetzal, the national bird of Guatemala that's nearly extinct there but has found refuge in Chiriquí Province. In all, nearly 900 bird species have been identified in these woods. The Hotel Panamonte, also owned by the Collins, offers tours of Finca Lérida, leaving the hotel at 7 am daily. The per person cost of US$150 (party of one), US$75 (party of two) or US$65 (party of four to six people) includes lunch and transportation. The quetzals are most likely to be seen January though August. See the Hotel Panamonte listing in Places to Stay later in this chapter for contact information.

Every Saturday, hundreds of Guaymí Indians from outlying areas descend upon the central plaza to buy bolts of material, rubber boots, etc, at the **Mercado Municipal**.

Hiking Tours Due to its lovely natural scenery and cool climate, Boquete lends itself well to hiking. Danny Poirier, a Canadian who has been hiking in Boquete for years, offers numerous hiking tours. Danny is very personable, and his guiding services are highly recommended. Following are some of the tours he offers:

A Place Called Paraíso This hiking tour lasts five to six hours and involves one hour of arduous walking. The effort is rewarded by an afternoon laze in a steep canyon with weeping walls and splendid waterfalls. Bring a lunch and a bathing suit. US$35 per group.

Cuernos del Chivo This difficult hiking tour lasts six to eight hours, five to seven of which are spent walking. It features a hike through pristine cloud forest and prime quetzal habitat in Parque Internacional La Amistad to the top of the Continental Divide and (clouds permitting) a view of the Pacific and Atlantic oceans.

Exploring Boquete This hiking tour lasts three to four hours and involves one hour of easy walking. It features intriguing basalt formations, waterfalls, country drives and views. US$35 per group.

Hot Springs of Caldera This five- to six-hour tour involves one hour of moderately difficult walking and features a therapeutic dip in hot springs near the town of Caldera, followed by a refreshing plunge .into the gorgeous Río Chiriquí. US$35 per group.

Sendero Los Quetzales This difficult hiking tour lasts seven to eight hours, five to seven of which are spent walking one of the country's premier hiking trails and a trail renowned for quetzals. Cost is US$40 per group.

Danny is best reached via email (poirierdanny2000@yahoo.com), but he can also sometimes be reached at El Montaña y El Valle – The Coffee Estate Inn (see Places to Stay later in this chapter for contact information). Danny speaks English and Spanish.

Another local guide with an excellent reputation is Santiago Chago, known around town simply as Chago. Though his English isn't particularly good, Chago is one of the few guides in Panama who can call birds, and he knows the English names of all the bird species in the area. His specialty is leading bird watchers 3km up the road to Volcán Barú to places where he's had success calling quetzals and other birds. He charges US$50 per group for this service, which last four to six hours. Chago is best reached by calling his cellular phone (☎ 626-2200).

Horseback Tours Don't care to exert yourself on your vacation? That's understandable. Consider having a horse do the legwork for you. Eduardo Cano (☎ 720-1750) offers guided horseback tours for US$8 an hour (US$5 for the horse and US$3 for himself, as he likes to say). Friendly Eduardo, whose home is located beside Avenida Central, speaks Spanish only, but that doesn't matter. If you're a party of one and don't speak Spanish, as many of his parties are, you'll just have to make do with tranquility and beauty and a relaxed state of mind. Poor you.

Special Events
The town's annual festival, the Feria de las Flores y del Café (Fair of Flowers and Coffee), held for 10 days each January, draws people from near and far. Contact IPAT for exact dates, as they vary.

Places to Stay
Because of the cool climate, all the accommodations in Boquete have hot showers.

Camping The *Pensión Topaz* (☎ 720-1005, schoeb@chiriqui.com), on Avenida Belisario Porras, is mostly an inn, but it also offers camping on its premises (US$5 per couple who have tent; and US$7 per couple, tent provided). Hot-water shared bathrooms are provided.

The couple who owns the Pensión Topaz also owns the *Highland Hostal Mozart* (☎/fax 720-3764, coyaldps@chiriqui.com), on Calle Volcancito Principal near the IPAT tourist office, where camping is available for the same price. Hot-water shared bathrooms are provided.

Website: www.panamareservations.com

La Montaña y el Valle – The Coffee Estate Inn (*☎/fax 720-2211, montana@ chiriqui.com*), on Calle Jaramillo Alto, offers camping (for adults only) on a weather-permitting basis (usually January through March). The cost is US$7 per couple. Features include electricity, a library and a concrete platform for protection from dampness. English and Spanish are spoken. Campers *must* call ahead, and those who show up after 4 pm will not be admitted.

Website: www.coffeeestateinn.com

See the following section for additional details on all three of these sites.

Hotels The charming **Highland Hostal Mozart** (see Camping, above, for contact information and location) is a terrific new place offering two guestrooms with a shared bathroom for US$9/12 single/double and three with private bathrooms for US$25/35. Most or all of the rooms have views to the Pacific. There's a lovely garden restaurant where Peruvian food is often served (owner Lorenza Diaz Phillip Schoeb is German-Peruvian). German, English and Spanish are spoken. A taxi ride to here from downtown Boquete costs US$1.

The centrally located **Roundhouses Isla Verde** (*☎/fax 720-2533, isla erde@ chiriqui.com*) were under construction at the time of writing, but the beginnings were impressive. German owners Eddie Seeling and Eva Kipp were building six modern, two-story cabañas, each with a kitchen and roomy bathroom (three of the cabañas are fully wheelchair friendly). The three largest cabañas can accommodate up to six people and go for US$65; the others can accommodate four people and rent for US$50. There's a beautiful garden on the grounds, and breakfast and afternoon cocktails are offered.

The new **Hostal Palacios** (*☎ 720-1653*), on Avenida Central, features two guestrooms with private bathrooms and four guestrooms with shared bathrooms for US$6.50 per person. There's a kitchen for guests' use. Some rooms are better than others, but this centrally located place offers a good value.

Also new, **Hostal Boquete** (*☎ 720-2573*), near the beautiful Río Caldera, offers five clean and quiet rooms with decent beds and private bathrooms for US$10/16 single/double.

Hacienda Santa Clara was under construction at the time of writing, but enough of it was complete to discern that this was going to be a terrific hotel. Located on a hillside with splendid valley views, the Hacienda will contain five standard guestrooms and two suites with all the amenities, a large salon with a pool table, and a hot tub. All this inside a Spanish-colonial-style lodge with actual 100-year-old Spanish tiles! Outside was a putting green and riding ring (horse rental available). Rates were expected to be about US$100 per room, more for suites, of course.

Website: www.cometoboquete.com

The new **Residencial Campestre Los Pinos** (*☎ 775-1521, fax 774-6536, acaemoac@ chiriqui.com*) offers five spacious two-story apartments with views for US$40 for one or two people – an excellent value.

Website: http://lospinos.tripod.com

Villas Lorena (*☎/fax 720-1848, jrshydro@ sinfo.net*) is a large, two-story apartment building beside the Río Caldera offering very spacious and fully equipped two-level guest quarters with living rooms and two bathrooms apiece. This is a terrific find and bargain priced at US$40 for one or two people from May 2 to October 31 and US$50 from November 1 to May 1. There's a 30% discount for seniors Friday through Sunday and a 50% discount for them Monday through Thursday.

Villa Marita Lodge (*☎ 720-2165, illamarita@cwpanama.net*) offers seven stand-alone cabins on the edge of a plateau that overlooks three coffee farms and offers a striking view of Volcán Barú. Each of these lovely cabins is pridefully maintained and contains a cozy sitting area. There's a restaurant that's open to guests and a large common room. It's very reasonably priced at US$50 for one person or two. English and Spanish are spoken.

Website: www.panamainfo.com/marita

Pensión Marilós (☎ 720-1380), on Avenida A Este at Calle 6 Sur, is family-run, clean and comfortable. You can cook in the kitchen, and morning coffee is complimentary. Single/doubles go for US$7/10 with shared bathrooms, US$10/16 with private bathrooms. Owner Frank Glavas speaks English and Spanish.

Pensión Virginia (☎ 720-1260), on the central plaza, is an older hotel with worn but clean singles/doubles for US$8/16 with shared bathrooms or US$12/22 with private bathrooms. There's an inexpensive restaurant downstairs and a piano and color TV in the upstairs sitting room.

The *Pensión Topaz* (see Camping, above, for contact information and location) offers eight lovely rooms, a swimming pool and an organic garden (help yourself). Six of the rooms have private bathrooms and cost US$15/20 single/double from mid-May to November and US$20/26 from December to mid-May. Two rooms, with an outdoor solar-heated bathroom, are substantially less. Breakfast is available to guests and nonguests for US$4. Children under 10 stay free. The gracious host, Axel Schoeb, speaks English, Spanish and German.

The centrally located *Hotel Rebequet* (☎ 720-1365) has nine appealing rooms with private bathrooms for US$20/30 single/double. Each room also has a TV and fridge; guests are welcome to cook in the kitchen or use the TV room.

The *Hotel Fundadores* (☎ 720-1298, fax 720-1034, hotfundland@cwp.net.pa), on Avenida Central, was completely renovated in 2000 and charges US$22 to US$60 (single or double) for its 40 attractive guestrooms and suites. Highlights include a pleasant creek that runs through the property, massage service and aerobics classes. Its Sunday brunch (US$7.50; 11:30 am to 3:30 pm) is very popular.

The *Hotel Panamonte* (☎ 720-1327, fax 720-2055, panamont@chiriqui.com), at the northern end of town, is a beautiful old hotel with dollhouse-like charm that's in perfect harmony with its surroundings. The hotel is renowned for its gourmet cooking and for the guided tours it offers for quetzal viewing (see the Finca Lérida listing under Things to See & Do, earlier in this chapter). A variety of other nature tours and a coffee farm/processing tour are also offered here. The owners, the Collins family, have hosted many visiting naturalists over the years. Rooms cost US$54 to US$138. Bicycle rentals are available.

La Montaña y el Valle – The Coffee Estate Inn (see Camping, above, for contact information and location) is a terrific find, offering three luxury bungalows, each with a well-equipped kitchen, spacious living room/dining area, separate bedroom, hot-water bathroom and private terrace with valley views. Two of the bungalows have DirecTV. Each bungalow, on a working coffee estate with trails into a lovely patch of forest, holds three to five people; the price of US$90 per couple includes estate coffee roasted daily and nature tours. Gourmet dinners prepared by owners Barry Robbins and Jane Walker, two very likable expatriate Canadians, are available to guests only. No children younger than nine years are allowed.

Places to Eat

Boquete has many inexpensive restaurants to choose from. The *Café Punto de Encuentro* is a little purple house on Calle 6 Este whose owner serves the best breakfasts in town (mostly omelets and pancakes) in a casual garden setting. Nothing on the menu is over US$3, and the coffee is good and bottomless. Open 7 am to noon daily.

The *Santa Fé Bar & Grill*, beside the Río Caldera, is an excellent find. Here you can order a variety of delicious foods (sandwiches, burgers, burritos, chili, etc) with Southwestern USA flavors; few items cost over US$5. It offers indoor and outdoor seating, and music and satellite TV.

La Conquista, on Avenida Central near the plaza, has typical food including *trucha* (local rainbow trout); no dishes are over US$5. Across the road, the *Pizzería La Volcánica* offers pizza and Italian dishes for around US$5. *El Sabrosón*, a bit farther up Avenida Central, is a simple place that offers standard regional food at incredibly low prices.

Ristorante Salvatore, two blocks south and one block east of the plaza, has tables inside and out. It's slightly more expensive than the Volcánica, but the pizza's better. Other items include ceviche (US$3) and meat dishes (US$5 to US$8).

La Casona Mexicana, on Avenida Central near the center of town, serves good, cheap Mexican food. The restaurant is divided into a number of small, semiprivate rooms, and thus it's popular with couples. Readers report a new place, *Tacos y Tacos*, located behind the larger El Sabrosón restaurant on Avenida A Este, also offers good Mexican food at great prices. Other readers have said that a new place called *Restaurant Chinese Food*, near the Pensión Topaz, serves good meals.

The *Restaurante La Huaca*, north of the plaza on Avenida Central, is an Argentine grill situated in a beautifully restored and modernized colonial-style building with river and mountain views and the best wine cellar in town. Most meals are priced between US$6 and US$12. There's a popular bar on the premises.

The area's fresh produce is sold at the weekly *Mercado Municipal*, on the northeastern corner of the plaza. Among the several bakeries in town, the *Panadería La Victoria*, on Avenida Central, is tops; it's worth a visit just to inhale the divine smells. The *Café Alemana* on Avenida Central also has delicious pastries.

Getting There & Away

Buses to David, and local buses that will take you around the Boquete area, depart from the northern side of the central plaza. Buses run between Boquete and David every 30 minutes. From David, the first bus leaves at 6 am; the last leaves at 9 pm. From Boquete, the first bus leaves at 5 am; the last leaves at 6:30 pm. The 38km trip on a well paved road takes an hour and costs US$1.20 each way.

Getting Around

Boquete is a small town, and you can easily walk around the center in a short time. If you're not in a rush, walking is a great way to see the environs, as well. The local *urbano* buses, winding through the hills among coffee plantations, farms and forest, cost just 50¢ and are a good way to get oriented. There are also taxis; US$2 fares are the norm.

Getting around on horseback is another option; the Pensión Marilós, the Pensión Topaz and the Hotel Panamonte can all arrange for you to hire a horse (see Places to Stay earlier in this chapter for contact information).

PARQUE NACIONAL VOLCÁN BARÚ

Volcán Barú is Panama's only volcano and the dominant geographical feature of western Panama. Its fertile volcanic soil and the temperate climate of its mid-altitude slopes support some of Panama's most productive agriculture, especially in the areas around Cerro Punta and Boquete. Large trees dominate the volcano's lower slopes, giving way on the upper slopes to smaller plants, bushes, scrub and alpine wildflowers.

Volcán Barú is no longer active; its last eruption was about 500 years ago. It has not one but seven craters. Its summit, at 3478m, is the highest point in Panama, and on a clear day it affords views of both the Pacific and Caribbean coasts.

The 14,300-hectare Parque Nacional Volcán Barú contains walking trails and provides ample possibilities for hiking, mountain climbing and camping. The park is home to abundant wildlife, including pumas and the *conejo pintado*, a raccoonlike animal. The resplendent quetzal is often seen here, especially from January to May.

There are entrances to the park on the eastern and western sides of the volcano. The eastern access to the summit, from Boquete, is easiest. The road from town to this entrance is paved, but if you plan on driving the unpaved road from the entrance to the summit, you'll need a 4WD vehicle and a winch.

To reach this entrance from central Boquete, turn west on Calle 2 Norte (see the Boquete map) and continue along this paved road for 7.5km, until it forks. Take the left fork, which forks again in 600m; here you'll want to take the gravel road to the right.

It takes most hikers six hours to summit Barú and five hours to make it back down. It is a strenuous hike best accomplished early in the morning, initially by the light of the moon. Within an hour after sunrise, the summit's usually socked in with clouds, and hopes of seeing both oceans are dashed. There is no water en route, so bring plenty (no fewer than four liters), and bring warm clothes and a windbreaker, as it is cold as well as lonely at the top.

AROUND PARQUE NACIONAL VOLCÁN BARÚ

A road branches off the Interamericana at Concepción (1200m) and climbs steadily through the towns of Volcán (1500m), Bambito (1600m) and Cerro Punta (1800m) until it stops at Guadalupe (2130m), on the western side of Volcán Barú. It's a good, paved road the entire way, frequently traversed by buses from David.

As in Boquete, the climate up here is cool and the air is brisk. The farmland around Cerro Punta has rich, black volcanic soil and is a great area for walking. As you near Cerro Punta, everything starts to look European, with meticulously tended agricultural plots and European-style houses with steep-pitched tin roofs. A Swiss colony was founded here many decades ago. Later immigrants included Croatians, and you can still hear their language spoken in the area.

This area produces not only abundant cool-climate crops, including vegetables, fruits, strawberries and flowers, but also livestock and thoroughbred racehorses. You'll pass several *haras* (stables) where racehorses are bred along the Cerro Punta road. There are also dairies along the road where you can watch cows being mechanically milked.

As on the Boquete side of Volcán Barú, there are accommodations that range from budget to expensive. And you can camp in the national park, or in the more remote Parque Internacional La Amistad. Another option is to visit this area on a day trip from David; buses run frequently between David and Cerro Punta via Volcán and Bambito.

BUENA VISTA

In this small community, 16km north of Concepción near the road to Volcán, is one of the nicest couples you'd ever meet. Canadians Dorothy and Claus Claassen (☎ 697-5024, claassendc@email.com) built and later sold Cocomo On the Sea, a gorgeous B&B in Bocas del Toro town. They relocated to Buena Vista to a house with engrossing views of the Pacific Ocean and Volcán Barú. In 2001, they began renting a charming suite adjacent to their home. It contains a hot-water bathroom, a stocked kitchenette, a sofa and other furnishings, and a queen-size bed with orthopedic mattress. There's a brand-new swimming pool. At US$45 a night, this suite is an excellent value. It is available for rent November 15 through May 15. Buena Vista makes a good base for forays into other Chiriquí highlands communities.

VOLCÁN
pop 6900

As you head north from Concepción, this is the first town you'll encounter, 32km uphill from the Interamericana turnoff. Clinging to the flanks of the giant Volcán Barú, the town is dwarfed by its namesake. There isn't a lot to do in Volcán itself, but the town has a pleasant feel and makes a good base for excursions.

Orientation & Information

The road that links Concepción and Volcán forks in the center of town: one arrow points left toward Río Sereno, on the Costa Rican border (47km); the other points right toward Cerro Punta (16km).

There's no IPAT tourist office in Volcán, but there is a **Highland Adventures** office (☎ 771-4413, 685-1682, jcaceres@ chiriqui.com) on Volcán's Avenida Central (look for a 'Turismo Ecologico' sign). This tour company offers a host of fun guided tours and activities, including rappelling beside a river, bicycle rides, a photo safari, kayaking, water tubing and climbing Volcán Barú. Most of the tours run about US$30 per person and are a bargain at that. The guides speak English and Spanish.

There is a pharmacy and a health clinic on Avenida Central. Also on Avenida Central, there's Internet access offered to guests and nonguests alike at the Hotel y Restaurante Don Tavo (US$1.50 an hour).

Things to See & Do
On the western side of the Concepción-Volcán road, 3km south of Volcán, you'll see **Arte Cruz Volcán – Artesania en Madera**, where artist José de la Cruz González (☎ 623-0313) makes fine-quality etchings, signs, sculptures and furniture out of wood, and etchings on crystal and glass. José was trained in fine arts in Italy and Honduras, and his work has been commissioned by buyers worldwide. Visitors are welcome, and José is happy to demonstrate and explain his art. Small items are for sale, and he can make you a personal souvenir in just a few minutes. Open 8 am to noon and 1 to 5:30 pm daily.

The ruins of the pre-Columbian culture at **Barriles** are about a five-minute drive from the center of town. The ruins are on private land, but the family who lives on the land allows visitors to see the ruins. Major artifacts from the archaeological site, including statues, *metates* (flat stone platforms used for grinding corn), pottery and jewelry are displayed in the Museo Antropológico Reina Torres de Araúz in Panama City.

Just past Volcán, on the way to Bambito, is one of the entrances to Parque Nacional Volcán Barú; see that section, earlier in this chapter, for details.

Other attractions around Volcán include springs, rivers, trout fishing, a botanical garden, coffee plantations (Cafetales Durán, with a million coffee bushes!), racehorse ranches and habitats of the quetzal and other exotic birds. Hiking trails in the area include one to the top of Cerro Punta; the Sendero Los Quetzales (the Quetzals Trail), which crosses the national park to Boquete (see the Guadalupe section, later in this chapter, for trail details); the Sendero del Tapir (Tapir Trail), which leads to a place where many tapirs live; and a number of others. Also nearby are the Lagunas de Volcán (see that section, later in this chapter).

On weekends, a **market** is held at the San Benito school in town; handicrafts are sold, as well as ordinary items at good prices. All proceeds benefit the school.

Places to Stay
As you drive along the road to Río Sereno, the first place you'll see is the ***Motel California*** (☎ 771-4272), which is run by Zdravko Zizic, a friendly man who speaks English, Spanish and Yugoslavian. His 23 clean, basic cabins with private hot-water bathrooms and good beds cost US$22, and there's a pleasant bar.

A little closer to Río Sereno, ***Oasis Place*** (☎/fax 771-4644) has 27 basic rooms with inconsistent beds and charges US$10/15 a single/double. Some of the rooms are new; ask to see several. For the young and the restless, the dance club at the Oasis is *the* place to be on Friday and Saturday nights.

Continuing, the ***Hotel y Restaurante Don Tavo*** (☎/fax 771-4258), built in 1996, has 16 pleasing singles/doubles with good beds beside a charming garden for US$25/33. Every room has a private hot-water bathroom.

The next recommendable place you'll come to is the ***Cabañas Las Huacas*** (☎ 771-4363), where five worn but rustically romantic two-story A-frame cottages, each with a kitchen, six beds and hot-water bathroom, are set around attractive grounds that include a goose pond and gorgeous mountain vistas. Prices start at a very reasonable US$25 for two people. There's a restaurant on the premises.

Farthest from central Volcán, the ***Hotel Dos Ríos*** (☎ 771-4271, fax 771-5794) has the look and feel of a hunting lodge. The entire hotel is made of teak, and all 24 guestrooms face a creek and the mountains. Rates at this attractive though thin-walled place are US$50 single or double. The hotel was built in 1967 to replace the original Hotel Dos Ríos, which was built beside the

Río Caldera in Boquete in 1961 and washed away during a storm five years later.

Places to Eat

New in 2000 and a strong addition to Volcán is the *Restaurante y Pizzeria Biga* on Avenida Central, which offers spaghetti for US$4 to US$6, many pizzas for US$6.25, and a variety of salads (most US$3 or less). Open noon to 9 pm, closed Monday.

The restaurant at the *Hotel Dos Ríos* serves very good food that's reasonably priced. It's open for breakfast, lunch and dinner, and items include sandwiches (US$1.50 to US$3), chicken (US$4.50) and fish or meat dishes (US$4.50 to US$7.50).

The food at the *Hotel y Restaurante Don Tavo* on Avenida Central is reasonably priced and includes pizza, spaghetti, soups, sandwiches, chicken and beef dishes.

Getting Away

Buses from Volcán to David depart from the Shell station on Avenida Central every 15 minutes from 5 am to 7:30 pm (US$2.30, 57km, 1¼ hours).

LAGUNAS DE VOLCÁN

At 1240m, the Area Silvestre Protegida Lagunas de Volcán, 4.5km from Volcán, is the highest lake system in Panama. The two lakes here swell after a big rain and are quite picturesque, with lush, virgin forest at their edges and Volcán Barú rising majestically in the background.

The lakes and the woodland around them are excellent sites for bird watching. On the lakes, the birds of special interest are the masked duck and the northern jacana. At water's edge, keep an eye out for the rose-throated becard (rare), pale-billed woodpecker, and mixed flocks of tanagers, flycatchers and antbirds.

To get to the lakes from the Concepción-Volcán road, turn west onto Calle El Valle (near central Volcán) and follow the signs. No buses go to the lakes, but you can hire a taxi in Volcán to bring you here. If you take your own vehicle, be advised that there have been reports of thefts of belongings from vehicles here.

BAMBITO

Seven kilometers past Volcán on the road to Cerro Punta, Bambito is barely a town at all. Its only noticeable feature is the large Hotel Bambito. Opposite it, worth a look is the **Truchas de Bambito** rainbow trout farm, where thousands of trout are raised in outdoor ponds with frigid water from the nearby river. You can buy fresh trout here.

The four-star *Hotel Bambito* (☎ 771-4265, fax 771-4207, bambito@chiriqui.com) offers singles/doubles for US$125/140 and numerous suites. It features a swimming pool, sauna, hot tub, tennis courts, business center, massage, horseback riding, mountain bikes, a restaurant, Internet access, a lounge and more.

Past the trout farm, *Cabañas Kucikas* (☎/fax 771-4245) has 18 spacious A-frame cottages that are set around 36 hectares of parklike grounds with children's play areas, barbecue sites and a river that offers trout fishing. Cottages of various sizes, sleeping two to 10 people, have kitchens and hot-water bathrooms. Rates range from US$60 to US$165.
Website: www.cabanaskucikas.com

Located in the hamlet of Nueva Suiza, 3.3km past the Hotel Bambito on the road to Cerro Punta, is the *Hostal Cielito Sur B&B* (☎/fax 771-2038, glee@cielitosur). New in 2001 and not yet open as of writing, this B&B appeared to be a terrific find. Four spacious

What's That in the River?

Rainbow trout are not native to Panama, but the rivers in Chiriquí Province are filled with them. That's because in 1925, at the suggestion of a US official living in Panama, the Panamanian Bureau of Fisheries cast a few of the cold-water fish into the Río Chiriquí Viejo. The trout didn't flounder in their new home, and the delicious fish made such a splash with area residents that they began introducing trout into other rivers. Today, no matter where you are in Chiriquí Province, you aren't far from a trout stream.

CHIRIQUÍ PROVINCE

guestrooms featuring private hot-water bathrooms with bathtubs, living rooms with fireplaces, and riverside patios rent for US$50 and US$65 (price varies with room size). There's also a *bohio* (rustic hut) with hammocks and a bathhouse with a Jacuzzi spa for guests' use. The prices include a country-style breakfast. This B&B is owned by Janet and Glen Lee, a friendly Panamanian-American couple who worked for the US Army in Panama until the Carter-Torrijos Treaty of 1977 shut down US military operations in Panama. They speak English and Spanish. Website: www.cielitosur.com

CERRO PUNTA

At an altitude of 1800m, this small town is surrounded by beautiful, rich agricultural lands. About 7km north of Bambito, it offers spectacular views across a fertile valley to the peaks of Parque Internacional La Amistad, a few kilometers away. This is a great place for taking in natural scenery.

Visitors come here primarily during the dry season (January to April) to visit the two nearby parks (Volcán Barú and La Amistad) and to enjoy the beauty of the surroundings. During this time, quetzals are often seen right on the road; though they can be seen here year-round, they tend to live farther down in the mountains during the rainy season.

Other attractions in Cerro Punta include **Fresa de Cerro Punta** and **Fresas Manolo**, where strawberries are grown, and **Panaflores** and **Plantas y Flores**, where flowers are raised for commercial sale; you can visit all of these places. Racehorse and prize cattle farms are also here and welcome visitors free of charge.

The main road continues through Cerro Punta and ends at Guadalupe, 3km farther. Another road takes off to the west, heading for the Las Nubes entrance to Parque Internacional La Amistad, 6.8km away; the turnoff is marked by a large wooden sign (see Parque Internacional La Amistad, later in this chapter, for details on the park).

...es to Stay & Eat

...lotel Cerro Punta (☎/fax 771-2020, *...@hotmail.com*), on the main road,

has 10 rooms, all with private bathrooms and hot water and slated for renovation, for US$22/27 single/double. Internet access for guests was planned. Also at the hotel is an excellent restaurant that offers several meals daily. Whether you stay here or not, drop by for a blended fruit drink. The local strawberries are the best you'll ever taste, and the strawberry drink is divine, as are the carrot, orange and rhubarb drinks. The pies and jams are homemade and quite good.

Pensión Eterna Primavera (☎ 775-3860) is 500m down the road to Las Nubes, opposite the Delca store. This is a much more basic place, with just five rooms; the two with cold water cost US$12.50 apiece, and the three with hot water cost US$15. With the dormitory at Los Quetzales Lodge & Spa (see below), there's no need to stay here.

Getting There & Away

A bus runs from David to Cerro Punta en route to Guadalupe (US$2.75 one-way, 2¼ hours, 79km, every 15 minutes from 5:30 am to 6 pm daily), stopping at Volcán and Bambito along the way. If you're coming from Costa Rica, you could catch this bus at the turnoff from the Interamericana at Concepción. If you're in Volcán, catch one of these buses at the parking lot opposite the Shell station.

GUADALUPE

Guadalupe is at the end of the road, 3km past Cerro Punta. It's a glorious area where you can walk among meticulously tended farms and gardens and enjoy the climate. The little community is full of flowers, and the agricultural plots curling up the steep hillsides are dreamy. Please do respect the signs that read: 'Esteemed Visitor: We are making all Guadalupe a garden – please don't pick the flowers.'

Sendero Los Quetzales

Two kilometers past Cerro Punta on the road to Guadalupe, a sign points the way to the Sendero Los Quetzales. Keep following the 'Los Quetzales' signs all the way through Guadalupe to reach the trail. One of the most beautiful in Panama, this trail goes at least 10km to Boquete, crossing back and forth over the Río Caldera. A guide is not necessary as long as you stay on the well-trodden path. Bear right at most forks.

See the Getting There & Away section for Cerro Punta for transport information.

Places to Stay & Eat

In the center of town, the *Los Quetzales Lodge & Spa* (☎ 771-2182 and 771-2291, fax 771-2226, stay@losquetzales.com) is a 10-room lodge with a lovely restaurant, bar/lounge, cafeteria, bakery and pizzeria. Every room features a tall ceiling, cheerful decor and detailed woodwork. The rooms, all with private hot-water bathrooms, cost US$50/60 without/with a bathtub. Additionally, there are five cedar-walled suites, all containing a romantic fireplace, a kitchenette, a bathtub, sofas, satellite TV, a bar, a telephone and a rain forest-facing balcony. These are an ex-

---

Orchids A-Bloom

About 600m above the Hotel Los Quetzales (see Places to Stay) lies the Finca Dracula Orchid Sanctuary, one of Latin America's finest and most varied orchid collections, with more than 2000 species. Comprehensive tours are available by appointment (☎ 771-2070). A fee of US$7 is requested.

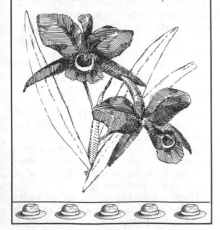

---

cellent value at US$70 or US$80, price varying with suite size. For travelers on a tight budget, Los Quetzales offers an elegant 10-bed dormitory with a hot-water bathroom for US$11 per person. Lodge facilities include a full-service spa with massage, mud therapy, aromatherapy, facials, sauna, bust and shoulders treatment, vegetal peeling, hair care, etc. Also on the premises are three riverside whirlpool spas. Website: www.losquetzales.com

PARQUE INTERNACIONAL LA AMISTAD

This 407,000-hectare park, half of which is in Panama and half in Costa Rica, has three Panamanian entrances: one at Las Nubes (near Cerro Punta on the Chiriquí side), one near Wetzo (near Changuinola; see the Bocas del Toro Province chapter), and a third at the upper Guadalupe area (a 10-minute walk from Cabañas Los Quetzales (see below).

There's a ranger station at Las Nubes where tourists can stay (see below). Permits are required to camp in the park; they're available for US$5 at the ranger station. Entrance to the park costs US$3. Parking costs an additional US$1.

There are three main trails that originate at the Las Nubes ranger station. One is a 1.4km trail that winds up to the **Mirador la Nevera**, a lookout point at 2500m. A second trail winds 1.7km to **La Cascada**, a 45m high waterfall with a lovely bathing pool. A third trail, named Sendero El Retoño (Rebirth Trail), loops 2.1km through secondary forest.

If you plan to spend much time at Las Nubes, be sure to bring a jacket. This side of the park, at 2280m, has a cool climate. Temperatures are usually around 75°F in the daytime and drop to about 38°F at night.

Places to Stay

A *ranger station* at Las Nubes has a dormitory room with bunk beds where tourists can stay for US$5 per night. Due to the popularity of these beds among school groups from Canada and the USA, reservations are well advised. To make them, call the ANAM office in David (☎ 775-7840/3163). Guests must bring their own bedding.

Carlos Alfaro, the same fellow who owns Los Quetzales Lodge & Spa in Guadalupe, also owns four chalets inside the international park, the **Cabañas Los Quetzales** (see the contact information for the Lodge & Spa). Each chalet features a fully equipped kitchen, separate bedrooms, a hot-water bathroom, a fireplace, kerosene lanterns and canopy-level terraces. Best of all, they're deep in the rain forest. Here you can stroll the jungle and take in all the sights – or just enjoy complete relaxation. Built in 1996, these chalets are famous all over Panama for their loveliness. Rates range from US$75 to US$132. More adventurous types might inquire about a planned waterproof-cloth dome with beds at canopy level; hot-water shower and flush toilet nearby (US$44 per dome, four-person limit).

Getting There & Away

Cabañas Los Quetzales is about 20 minutes' drive north of Guadalupe in a 4WD vehicle. You can get a ride to the chalets from the Lodge & Spa. Two 4WD taxis make the trip (US$5).

RÍO SERENO
pop 18,300

At Volcán, a paved road turns off and heads west 47km to Río Sereno, on the Costa Rican border. The road winds through lush valleys sprinkled with coffee fields, teak plantations and stands of virgin forest. A sparkling river occasionally appears at roadside, and just as quickly it disappears back into the foliage. Travelers coming from the border crossing at Río Sereno usually have a very favorable first impression of Panama.

See Costa Rican Border Crossings in the Getting There & Away chapter for further information on this border town.

FINCA LA SUIZA

Located high in the Talamanca range to the [south] of Boquete, amid cool, fresh air, is one [of tho]se easily overlooked places that [bo]ok writers, hikers and birders just love to find. Finca La Suiza (☎ 615-3774, afinis@chiriqui.com) consists of 200 hectares of mostly mountain rain forest, accessed by hiking trails that originate at a lodge. Inside the lodge are three lovely rooms with two single beds each, rocking chairs, reading lamps, private hot-water bathrooms, and (on cloudless days) views to the Pacific Ocean, Costa Rica and Volcán Barú! Adding a cherry to this cake is a woodsy community room with a fireplace.

The setting alone would make Finca La Suiza a terrific find, but Swiss owner-managers Monika Kohler and Herbert Brullmann have cut four trails through their pristine property, presenting hikers and birders alike with easy access to some spectacular rain forest. The trailside sights include waterfalls, dipping ponds and superb vantage points across the forest canopy. All the while you hike, you pass through virgin mountain and cloud rain forest. Outstanding!

Rates are a bargain at US$28/36 single/double, and US$8 per spare bed. Use of the trail system is US$8 for guests their entire stay. Non-guests pay US$8 per day. Payment is in cash only. English, German, French and Spanish are spoken fluently, some Italian. A bird list is available to guests, as are breakfasts and dinners.

Emails sent to the finca are checked only once a week, and you must put 'Finca La Suiza' on the subject line for your email to reach Herbert and Monika. Also, for phone calls, the best time to reach this friendly fifty-something couple is 7 to 9 pm.

The lodge and trails are closed June, September and October – the area's wettest months.

Getting There & Away

The lodge is located 1km from the Chiriquí-Chiriquí Grande road, atop a steep driveway. If you're driving, call ahead and you'll be met at the end of the driveway, where you can park within the property and be taken by 4WD to the lodge.

If you're traveling by bus, just tell the bus driver to drop you at Finca La Suiza. If you arrive unannounced, leave your luggage with the workers beside the finca's entrance and walk up. Your luggage will be brought to you.

The lodge is 40km from Chiriquí and 60km from Chiriquí Grande. The roadside gate to the property is open from 7 to 10 am (later if Herbert and Monika are expecting you). Honk several times in the event a worker is not at the driveway to attend to you when you arrive.

Veraguas Province

pop 209,100

Panama's third-largest province, near the center of the country, is the only province that has both Caribbean and Pacific coastlines. Veraguas was also the site of the Spaniards' first attempt to obtain a footing on the continental New World; it was here that Christopher Columbus tried to establish a colony, but he abandoned his attempt in the face of an imminent Indian attack. Two later attempts to settle the area were also thwarted, both ending in death by starvation and cannibalism. But Veraguas was then and remains today a land of tremendous natural beauty, with robust rivers and stunning peaks. Nearly 500 years after Columbus' arrival, the area is still

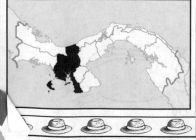

one of the least-developed regions on the isthmus.

Most of Veraguas Province's population make their living through farming or ranching. From an airplane, the Caribbean and Pacific slopes of Veraguas look as different from each other as Canada's Rocky Mountains do from Australia's Great Sandy Desert. Heavy rainfall, virgin forest and little evidence of people characterize the Caribbean slope. Most of the Mosquito Coast of Veraguas can be reached only by boat, although there are plans to extend roads from the Carretera Interamericana over the Cordillera Central and into the lush forests that still remain here.

The Pacific slope of Veraguas – from the summit of the cordillera to the Pacific Ocean – is an environmentalist's nightmare. Perhaps 5% of the original forest remains. Where vast forests filled with tropical animals and plants once stood, today there are only barren rocks and grassy hills on which graze the livestock for tomorrow's cheeseburgers. Farther south, the land gives way to farm after farm. Longtime residents say they used to get a lot of rain, but much less falls since the forests were cut down, and water shortages and pesticide pollution are recurring problems. Parque Nacional Cerro Hoya was established in 1984 to save what little remains of the original forest.

Off the Pacific coast but still within the province is Panama's largest island, Isla de Coiba, which is both part of a national park and home to residents of a federal penal colony who live on beaches in huts and eat lots of coconuts. The diving around Coiba and neighboring islands is excellent, and the fishing is world class. Also world class are some of the waves that curl up to nearby Playa Santa Catalina, which is more of a lava field than a beach, at the end of a bad road near the western edge of the mouth of the Golfo de Montijo. Waves that have 5m faces and 150m rides are not uncommon here in April, July and August.

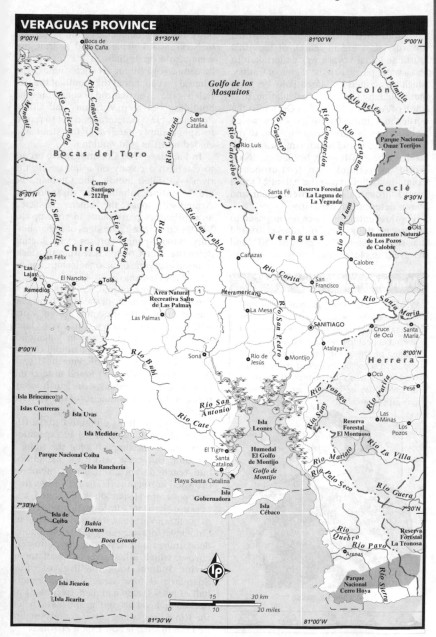

VERAGUAS PROVINCE

9°00'N · 81°30'W · 81°00'W · 9°00'N

Boca de
Río Caña

Río Mananti

Río Cricamola

Río Cañaveral

**Golfo de los
Mosquitos**

Santa
Catalina

Río Chucará

Río Caloyebora

Río Guazaro

Río Concepción

Río Belén

Río Veraguas

Río Palmilla

Colón

Parque Nacional
Omar Torrijos

Bocas del Toro

Río Luis

Coclé

▲ Cerro
Santiago
2121m

Santa Fé

Reserva Forestal
La Laguna de
La Yeguada

8°30'N

Río San Félix

Río Tabasará

Río Cobre

Río San Pablo

Veraguas

Río San Juan

Olá

Monumento Natural
de Los Pozos
de Calobre

Chiriquí

San Félix

Cañazas

Río Corita

Calobre

Las
Lajas

El Nancito

Tolé

Área Natural
Recreativa Salto
de Las Palmas

Interamericana

San
Francisco

Río Santa María

Remedios

Las Palmas

1

La Mesa

Río San Pedro

SANITIAGO

Cruce
de Ocú

Santa
María

8°00'N

Soná

Río de
Jesús

Montijo

Atalaya

Herrera

Río Bubí

Ocú

Pesé

Isla Brincanco

Islas Contreras

Isla Uvas

Río San
Antonio

Río Ponuga

Río Parita

Isla Medidor

Río Cate

Isla
Leones

Río Suay

Reserva
Forestal
El Montuoso

Las
Minas

Los
Pozos

Parque Nacional Coiba

Isla Ranchería

El Tigre
Santa
Catalina

Humedal
El Golfo
de Montijo

Río Mariato

Río La Villa

Playa Santa Catalina

**Golfo de
Montijo**

Río Palo Seco

7°30'N

Isla
Gobernadora

Isla de
Coiba

**Bahía
Damas**

Isla
Cébaco

Río Guera

Boca Grande

Río
Quebro

Reserva
Forestal
La Tronosa

Río Pavo

Arenas

Isla Jicarón

Río Sierra

Isla Jicarita

**Parque
Nacional
Cerro Hoya**

N
LP

0 · 15 · 30 km
0 · 10 · 20 miles

81°30'W · 81°00'W

History

Columbus' first three voyages westward toward Asia were in search of land; his fourth and final voyage was undertaken to find a water passage to the region of Cathay, which was visited by Marco Polo – a strait that would, by Columbus' calculation, pass south of Asia into the Indian Ocean. To the north the admiral had found Cuba, which he believed was part of eastern Asia. To the south he had found South America, which he described in his log book as a 'New World' as yet unknown to Europeans. Columbus believed that the Atlantic Ocean flowed through a strait between them, and he was determined to find it.

For this venture, in which he proposed to sail around the world, Columbus chartered four small vessels. The year was 1502, and the great explorer spent most of it com-

manding his little worm-eaten fleet up and down the Caribbean coast from Venezuela to Nicaragua. Unable to find a strait, but seeing gold on Indians in the region and hearing from them of rich mines, the admiral cast anchor at the mouth of the Río Belén – the river that today constitutes the boundary between Veraguas and Colón Provinces. He was determined not to return to Spain empty-handed: If the strait had eluded him, the gold wouldn't.

In February 1503 Columbus gave orders to establish a colony on a hill beside the river's silt-filled mouth. The Quibian, the area's native inhabitants, disapproved. Armed with spears, the Indians massacred an exploratory party that had gone up the Río Belén to investigate signs of Indian hostility. When Spanish corpses came floating down the river, Columbus, fearing an attack, ordered everyone back to their ships, and he set sail for Hispaniola.

Writing in his journal, Columbus said: 'I departed, in the name of the Holy Trinity, on Easter night, with the ships rotten, worn out, and eaten with holes.' Three years later the admiral died in an inn in Valladolid, Spain, of diseases he had acquired during his voyages. He died believing he'd seen Asia, unaware that he'd found instead the second-largest landmass on Earth, composed of the two continents of the Western Hemisphere.

A few years after Columbus fled the Río Belén, Diego de Nicuesa led an expedition to the site to accomplish what the admiral couldn't. But even before the expedition had reached shore, four of its members drowned in rough surf. The provisions they brought from Hispaniola had spoiled, and because there was little recognizable food in northern Veraguas, starvation soon set in. One day a foraging party of 30 came upon a dead Indian and devoured the putrescent corpse, which killed every one of them. Living Indians took the lives of other Spaniards. Before Nicuesa called it quits, half of his 400 men had died. Eventually he packed up his ships, and he and his men fled the Río Belén, sailing east to found Nombre de Dios in what is now Colón Province.

Man Without a Face

What did Christopher Columbus look like? No one really knows. If a portrait of the admiral was painted during his lifetime, it doesn't appear to have survived. Instead, the images of the great Italian explorer that appear in schoolbooks around the world are merely later artists' renditions of the man, all of which may be far from accurate. Here's one artist's rendition.

A good likeness?

In 1535 a third attempt was made to found a colony on the Caribbean coast of Veraguas, along the shore of the aptly named Golfo de los Mosquitos. This time the Spaniards, led by Felipe Gutierrez, landed beside the mouth of the Río Concepción, about 10km west of the Río Belén. As is usual on this coast, it rained almost continuously, damaging their supplies and interfering with planting. Floods came and swept away some settlers and most of their houses. The disasters that had plagued earlier New World colonists also assailed the Gutierrez party: Provisions became scarce, the men became sick and death paid frequent visits.

In little time 400 healthy men were reduced to 280 sickly wretches. Journals from the time report that many of the men dug their own graves. To add to the party's distress, some of the settlers were poisoned by drinking from a certain spring, which caused their lips to swell and their gums to soften, and sometimes killed them. At one point the settlers caught, killed and ate several Indians. One day nine settlers killed and devoured a fellow settler; the two who were considered the most culpable were later burned to death for their crime, while the other seven merely had a 'C' branded into their faces for eating a Christian.

The conquistadors, not ones to forget the reports of gold in Veraguas, returned to the area two decades later and eventually overcame the Indians and the torrential rains of northern Veraguas. They found gold, established mines and, in 1560, at the town of Concepción, 10km west of the Río Belén, they set up a headquarters and a smelter for the mines. African slaves were brought in to extract the gold (most of the blacks who live in Veraguas Province today are their descendants).

Because the heavy rains prevented cultivation of the land, supplies were brought from Hispaniola, Cuba, Jamaica and Nicaragua. From Concepción, it was 40km to the mountain town of Santa Fé, by a road passable only on foot; that same road still exists today, and it is still passable only on foot. Fifty kilometers beyond Santa Fé was Natá

in what is now Coclé Province, from whence cattle were brought to furnish the miners with meat. The towns of La Filipina, Los Santos and Parita were created to provide food for the miners.

By 1590 the mines were spent. Many miners left for newfound gold deposits in Colombia. Others escaped or were set free and took to farming throughout Pacific Veraguas and the Península de Azuero. Today, the people on the peninsula fall into three main groups: black-skinned descendants of the slaves, fair-skinned descendants of the conquistadors, and people of mixed ancestry. Many of the Indians who had lived on the peninsula died by Spanish swords and from Old World diseases. The rest retreated to the slopes of the Cordillera Central, where their descendants live today.

SANTIAGO
pop 32,500

Santiago, 250km from Panama City, is bisected by the Interamericana, and its central location – just north of the Península de Azuero and about halfway between Panama City and Costa Rica – has made it a hub of rural commercial activity.

This town is a good place to break up a long drive from the Costa Rican border to the capital or to get your vehicle serviced if you encounter mechanical problems. Other than that, Santiago offers little to the tourist. Most of the town's commerce and services – including stores, banks, gas stations, restaurants and hotels – are along the Interamericana and Avenida Central, which splits off from the highway.

Information

The Instituto Panameño de Turismo (☎ 998-3929) has an office on the northern side of Avenida Central, 500m west of its junction with the Interamericana. The office is staffed with three people, one of whom speaks some English. Maps and brochures are available. The office is closed on weekends.

There's a Migración y Naturalización (Immigration and Naturalization) office and an ANAM office in Santiago as well.

VERAGUAS PROVINCE

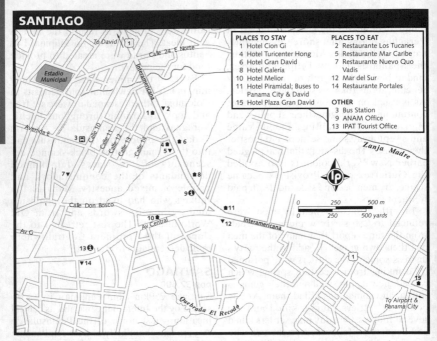

SANTIAGO

PLACES TO STAY
1 Hotel Cion Gi
4 Hotel Turicenter Hong
6 Hotel Gran David
8 Hotel Galeria
10 Hotel Melior
11 Hotel Piramidal; Buses to Panama City & David
15 Hotel Plaza Gran David

PLACES TO EAT
2 Restaurante Los Tucanes
5 Restaurante Mar Caribe
7 Restaurante Nuevo Quo Vadis
12 Mar del Sur
14 Restaurante Portales

OTHER
3 Bus Station
9 ANAM Office
13 IPAT Tourist Office

Places to Stay

The *Hotel Gran David* (☎ *998-4510, fax 998-1866*), on the Interamericana about 500m north of the Avenida Central intersection, is a good value, with clean though dark singles/doubles with decent beds and private hot-water bathrooms for US$10/13, or US$15.50/19 with air con and TV.

Hotel Melior (☎ *998-4158*), on Avenida Central just west of its intersection with the Interamericana, has 23 worn rooms with cold-water private bathrooms and four-channel TV. Rates are US$10/16 per person with fan/air con.

Hotel Cion Gi (☎ *998-2756, fax 998-7272*), on the highway close to the center of town, has 72 dirty and gloomy rooms ranging from US$15 for one person without air con to US$26 for one or two people with air con. The rooms' only strength is their size; if you're traveling with a large pet – an elephant, for instance – it could stay in your room without cramping your style.

Hotel Plaza Gran David (☎ *998-3433, fax 998-2553*), on the Interamericana on the eastern side of town, offers a great better value. It is one of the nicer places around, with 33 singles/doubles with air con, good beds and private hot-water bathrooms for US$18/27. There's also a swimming pool and a Chinese restaurant on the grounds.

Hotel Turicenter Hong (☎ *998-0671, fax 998-4059*), on the Interamericana opposite the Hotel Gran David, is a good find, offering 45 clean rooms with one double bed each, TVs, phones and private hot-water bathrooms for US$13/16 without/with air con. The rooms that have windows are much more cheerful than those without.

If you're in a pinch, *Hotel Piramidal* (☎ *998-3132, fax 998-5411*), at the junction of the Interamericana and Avenida Central, has 62 boxy rooms lined up row after row; the rooms do have air con and 39-channel cable TV, though. Rates are US$24/33 for one double bed/two double beds. There's a restaurant and a bar here.

The best rooms in town are at *Hotel Galería* (☎ 958-7950, fax 958-7954), on the Interamericana north of the Avenida Central intersection. Each room has air con, a large TV, firm mattresses and a private bathroom with hot water. There's a restaurant and gym, but no swimming pool. Rates are US$33/38.

Places to Eat

Restaurante Los Tucanes, on the Interamericana just north of the Hotel Gran David, has excellent food at reasonable prices. The chef salad (US$3), *pollo asado con salsa especial* (US$4), *filete a la parmesana* (US$6) and *langostinos a la criolla* (US$6.50) are delicious. It's open late every day.

For superb Peruvian-style seafood, try *Mar del Sur*, on Avenida Central at the intersection of Interamericana. Main dishes range from US$7 to US$14. The *ce iche* is particularly good and served the Peruvian way – very spicy. It's open for lunch and dinner daily.

At *Restaurante Nuevo Quo Vadis*, on Calle 10, you can enjoy an excellent filet mignon (US$5.50), a tasty shrimp with curry sauce (US$7.50) and the fantasía marinera, an orgy of seafood (US$8.50). Nuevo Quo Vadis' paella, served only on Sunday, is very popular.

Restaurante Portales, on Avenida Central close to the IPAT office, offers mediocre food for about US$7 per meal. What's more, its margaritas are made from an awful mix and arrive in teeny-tiny glasses.

Restaurante Mar Caribe, across the street from Hotel Gran David, is popular with IPAT officials.

Getting There & Away

Aeroperlas, which had provided daily flights between Santiago and Panama City, cancelled the service indefinitely in 2000.

From the bus terminal (☎ 998-4006) in front of the Hotel Piramidal, buses depart for Panama City (US$6, hourly, from 3:15 am to 9:15 pm) and David (US$6,

hourly, from 9 am to 2 am). Buses to nearby communities depart from Santiago's bus station on Calle 10 near Avenida E.

Getting Around

Taxis are *the* way to travel in Santiago. They are easy to hail and they go anywhere in town for US$2 or less.

IGLESIA SAN FRANCISCO DE VERAGUAS

In the small town of San Francisco, 16km north of the Interamericana on the road from Santiago to Santa Fé, is one of the best and oldest examples of Baroque art and architecture in the Americas that was created by Indians using native materials. Unlike most Baroque churches, in which seemingly everything is covered in gold leaf, the altar and interior of this church are colorfully painted.

The highly ornate altar is made of ash and bitter cedar. Carved into the altar and elsewhere around the church are the usual Old Testament scenes – the crucifixion, the Virgin looking divine, the saints ever so saintly – but also throughout the church are finely carved and well-preserved images of the artisans and prominent Indians. Their faces are cleverly inserted into the religious scenes; some appear atop the bodies of cherubs.

One large carving includes items that had special meaning for the Indians or otherwise impressed them – an eagle piercing its own heart with its beak, three large dice, a Spanish sword, a lantern and a human skull.

The captivating altar (most colonial altars in the Americas were brought over from Europe) and the church were constructed within a few years of each other; the date of completion is estimated to be 1727, but no one is exactly sure of the date because the Spaniards kept tight control over church record books, and when they left they took the books with them.

The steeple, incidentally, is not original. The original bell tower survived until 1942, when it suddenly collapsed without warning. Unfortunately, the new one doesn't even resemble the old one. The original served two purposes, one good, one evil – it was, of course, used for religious purposes, but the Spaniards also used it as a lookout tower to monitor the movements of the Indians and slaves in the community.

The church was in the midst of a major renovation in 2001 and should look spectacular by the time of your visit.

Near the church in San Francisco is **El Chorro del Spiritu Santo** (Holy Ghost Waterfall), which has a fine swimming hole. To get to it, follow the road as it winds around the church, and then take the road just behind the church. After a few hundred meters, take the first right; after another several hundred meters the road will bring you to the small cascades.

Getting There & Away

To reach the church, drive 16km north on the San Francisco turnoff from the Interamericana, until you reach the police substation (you'll see a stop sign there, and the station is conspicuously located on the main road). Veer right, proceed 400m, and then turn right again at the Supermercado Juan XXIII de San Francisco. Drive 100m farther; the church is on the left.

A bus leaves the Santiago station for San Francisco (US$1, 25 minutes, every 30 minutes, from 7 am to 6 pm).

If you're short on time, an alternative is to hire a taxi in Santiago to take you to the church and, if you wish, to Santa Fé. Expect to pay US$12 roundtrip to and from San Francisco, and another US$28 if you hire the taxi to take you all the way to Santa Fé.

SANTA FÉ
pop 2800

This pleasant little town lies in the shadow of the Continental Divide, 52km north of Santiago and 36km from San Francisco. Because it's at an altitude of about 1000m, the town is cooler than the lowlands, and it's still very green. Much of the forest remains as it did when the Spaniards founded the town in 1557. This is a great place for hikers and birders.

Orientation & Information

City planning is not a characteristic of Santa Fé. If you look long enough at a map of the town, you can see spaghetti in octopus sauce. The road that heads north to town from Santiago and the Interamericana, winding through lovely valleys along the way, branches out in three directions at the southern edge of town. The middle 'branch' forks yet again after a few more blocks.

None of the streets in town have names, and that's just fine with Santa Fé's residents; everybody here seems to know where everybody else lives. And the structures in town that aren't homes – the mayor's office, the cooperative, the church and so on – can be counted on two hands.

There's no tourist office, bank, laundry or gas station in town, but there is a post office and an orchid lady whose pet parrot can whistle the Panamanian national anthem – and frequently does.

Orquideario y Cultivos

Santa Fé is known throughout Panama for its orchids, and in Santa Fé the person to see about these flowers is Bertha de Castrellón (☎ 954-0910), who has an impressive collection of them (no fewer than 265 species) in her backyard and enjoys showing them to enthusiasts. Among her orchids are some of the largest and the smallest varieties in the world.

Most of the orchids are handsomely displayed in hanging coconut shells. They include a lovely lavender orchid found only in the hills around Santa Fé. Bertha, who speaks a little English, can tell you a great many things about her plants if you can communicate with her in Spanish.

To get to Bertha's house, take the right 'branch' at the point where the Santiago–Santa Fé road forks at the southern edge of town. Then take the second right and proceed 100m or so farther, until you see a driveway flanked by a sign that reads: 'Orquideario y Cultivos Las Fragacias de Santa Fé.' You have arrived.

There are two other things you should know about Bertha: She's the area's top birding guide, offering tours of nearby Cerro Tute, where there's a lovely set of waterfalls, a cliff with wind currents that seemingly prevent anyone from falling off, and fine bird watching; and, when Bertha claps,

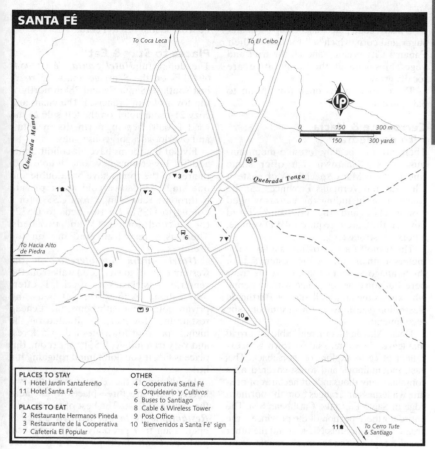

SANTA FÉ

To Coca Leca

To El Ceibo

Quebrada Mamey

Quebrada Tonga

To Hacia Alto
de Piedra

To Cerro Tute
& Santiago

PLACES TO STAY
1 Hotel Jardín Santafereño
11 Hotel Santa Fé

PLACES TO EAT
2 Restaurante Hermanos Pineda
3 Restaurante de la Cooperativa
7 Cafetería El Popular

OTHER
4 Cooperativa Santa Fé
5 Orquideario y Cultivos
6 Buses to Santiago
8 Cable & Wireless Tower
9 Post Office
10 'Bienvenidos a Santa Fé' sign

her green parrot bobs up and down and whistles US and Panamanian popular songs.

Although Bertha does not charge a fee for showing her orchids, feel free to leave a donation. Please remember you are visiting a home, so be considerate: Don't show up before 9 am or after 5 pm, and if you call out to her from her gate and there's no answer, assume she's not home. *Don't* open the gate unless she instructs you to do so.

Cooperativa Santa Fé

The Santa Fé Cooperative and the cooperative's store above the Restaurante de la Co-

operativa sell hats made of mountain palm (called *palmilla*) that are much more durable than hats found elsewhere in Panama – and they cost much less (generally from US$16 to US$25). They are not as refined as the hats available in Ocú and Penonomé, but if you're looking for a rugged hat in classic Panama-hat style, you can't do better.

While in the cooperative, you might want to pick up some Café El Tute, the locally grown coffee; it comes in US$1 half-pound bags and convenient 15¢ 28g pouches (you can get four cups of coffee out of one pouch). The Cooperativa Santa Fé is also a good place to stock up on beans, sugar and corn, which sell for half of their Panama City prices – and all the fruit and vegetables sold at the cooperative are locally grown.

The cooperative is open from 6 am to 8:30 pm daily.

Cerro Tute & Hacia Alto de Piedra

There are two heavily forested mountainous areas near town that offer some fine birding. Many specialties of eastern Chiriquí and Veraguas Provinces can be found here, including the rufous-winged woodpecker and the crimson-collared tanager. Both areas require a 4WD vehicle, a horse or strong legs.

The turnoff for Cerro Tute is a few kilometers south of town, on the western side of the Santiago-Santa Fé road. There are trails here, but you'd be wise to go with someone who knows the area well, such as Bertha de Castrellón (see above) or with someone she recommends.

Hacia Alto de Piedra, reachable by a road that leaves the western side of town, is an excellent place to explore on horseback. This vast, mountainous and forest-covered area contains many thousands of hectares of pristine wilderness and ranges from the northern edge of Santa Fé to the Caribbean Sea. The entire northern portion of the province – the area where Columbus, Nicuesa and the other Spanish explorers had so much trouble – contains not a single road and is sparsely inhabited. The edge of the awesome forest is only a couple of kilometers from town, and the forest becomes a jungle once you clear the ridge and proceed down the Caribbean slope.

Special Events

There's an orchid exposition in Santa Fé every August (the exact date varies). Collectors from all over Panama display their finest orchids at this popular event. The IPAT office in Santiago (☎ 998-3929, fax 998-0928) can provide you with the precise date of the exposition, as can Bertha, the orchid lady.

There is also an agricultural fair in Santa Fé from January 28 to February 2.

Places to Stay & Eat

The delightful *Hotel Santa Fé* (☎ 954-0941) is on the Santiago-Santa Fé road, just south of Santa Fé and 38km north of the town of San Francisco. The clean and cozy 21-room hotel, on the left side of the road if you're heading north, sits on a bluff and overlooks a gorgeous valley.

Five of the rooms have air-conditioning and TV. Five rooms have one double bed; the rest of the rooms have one double and one single. All have cold-water private bathrooms. Rates range from US$13 for a double to US$15 for two beds to US$25 for air-conditioning, TV and two beds. There is a restaurant and bar on the premises.

Hotel Jardín Santafereño, on the western edge of town a good walk from the center, is a backpacker's special. It offers four cabañas with worn, soft beds and private cold-water bathrooms, and a cheap restaurant. However, it's situated on the highest point in town, nestled in a forest and very tranquil. At US$10 per room, this place is OK if you don't mind roughing it a little.

In addition to the restaurants at the two hotels, there are three places to eat near the center of town. The best of the three is *Restaurante de la Cooperativa*, which is open 6 am to 7 pm daily and serves fish, pork, beef and chicken with a side of rice and vegetables for around US$5.

Neither *Restaurante Hermanos Pineda* nor *Cafetería El Popular* will be winning culinary awards anytime soon, but their prices are painless; at either place, expect to pay US$2.50 for a plate of chicken, rice and beans, and a soft drink.

Getting There & Away

Buses leave the Santiago station for Santa Fé (US$1.50, 1½ hours, hourly, from 7 am to 4 pm). A taxi ride from Santiago costs US$40.

Buses from Santa Fé to Santiago (US$2, every 45 minutes) leave from 6 am to 6 pm.

CERAMICA LA PEÑA

This artisans' market is on the Interamericana, 8km west of Santiago. Here you can find wood carvings and baskets made by the Emberá and Wounaan peoples of the Darién and woven purses and soapstone figurines made by Guaymís living in the area, as well as ceramics from the town of La Arena in Herrera Province and masks from the town of Parita, also in Herrera Province. There's also a workshop on the premises where you can occasionally see ceramics being made. The market is open 9 am to 4:30 pm weekdays and is closed weekends.

LAS PALMAS

There's nothing of special interest in sleepy Las Palmas, a town 10km south of the Interamericana and 32km northwest of the town of Soná. But if you love waterfalls and have your own wheels, you'll want to know about the nearby cataract and its enticing swimming hole. The scene is set amid light forest, and you'll likely have the place to yourself.

To get to the falls from the Interamericana, take the Las Palmas turnoff and drive 10km. Bypass the first road into town, but turn left at the second road just before the town's cemetery. Follow this dirt road for 1km and then take the fork to the right. This last kilometer to the falls, along a much rougher road, requires a 4WD vehicle. If you aren't driving one, it's best to play it safe and walk the last kilometer to the falls. Be sure to lock up and take your valuables with you.

If you are coming from Soná, drive 32km along the road that leads toward the Interamericana and turn right just beyond the cemetery. Then follow the directions in the preceding paragraph.

Keep in mind that there is no place to stay in Las Palmas, and the few restaurants in town are mediocre at best.

SONÁ

pop 10,100

Soná, 45km from Santiago, is set in a farming region bisected by the road that links the Interamericana to El Tigre and a host of other small communities on the peninsula that comprises the western shore of the Golfo de Montijo. Soná's chief feature is its bars – about one in every five businesses here is a cantina.

If that sounds good to you, you might like to know that there are two places to stay in Soná. *Pensión Min* (☎ 998-8331), on the main road, has 10 basic, fan-on-a-stand twin rooms with shared cold-water bathroom for US$7. *Hotel Águila*, near the center of town on a side street a stone's throw from the main road, has slightly better rooms with fan/air con for US$11/14.

Buses from Soná to Panama City (US$7) depart the bus terminal on the main road in the middle of town at 5, 8:30 and 10 am, and 1:30 and 4:30 pm daily. Buses to Santiago leave the terminal every 20 minutes from 4:30 am to 6:30 pm (US$1.50).

SANTA CATALINA

Sixty-six km south of Soná is Santa Catalina, where several hundred people lead simple lives in simple homes near a beach that attracts surfers from around the globe. **Playa Santa Catalina** is a major break, where you can nearly always find a decent wave to ride. At its best it's comparable to Oahu's Sunset Beach on a good day. For more information on the surfing here, see Surfing in the Facts for the Visitor chapter.

Orientation

To get to the three oceanside surf hotels from the bus station, take the dirt road that's 20m past a large raised sign for the Casablanca Surf Resort on the left side of the road into Santa Catalina just before the road ends. Walk or drive 1km until you come to another sign for Casablanca. Here, the road forks. If you take the right fork, you'll be at Casablanca in another 50m.

If you take the left fork and proceed 200m, you'll come to Kiki O'Brien's place and the driveway to Surfers' Paradise Camp.

Places to Stay & Eat

All four places to stay in the area are designed for surfer dudes and dudettes who have their own boards (there are no rentals) and offer easy access to the waves.

A budget place that's popular with hardcore surfers is **Cabañas Rolo** (☎ 998-8600, ask for Rolo Ortega), which has seven cabins, each with one to three good beds, a fan, and a shared cold-water bathroom for US$7 per person. It's the easiest of the four places to find, near the end of the only road into town. Rolo offers breakfast (typically US$2) and lunch and dinner (typically US$3). He can also arrange fishing trips and gear rental. He speaks English and Spanish and is very friendly.

Surfers' Paradise Camp (☎ 220-9615 in Panama City), sits on a breezy bluff overlooking the ocean and offers five rustic and basic wooden rooms (US$10 per person) and a loft (US$5 per person). Breakfast and dinner are available. The rooms at Rolo's place are more comfortable, but the seaviews at Surfers' Paradise Camp are awesome.

Casablanca Surf Resort (☎/fax 226-3786) contains eight housing options in a park-like setting bordering the beach: one house with five beds, air con, and fans (US$30 per person); one duplex with three beds in each unit, fan only (US$20 per person); and five stand-alone cabins with fan only (US$10 per person). The house and duplex feature tiled roofs and concrete floors and walls, cold-water bathrooms, and are comfortable and clean. The cabins are similar except they have thatch roofs. Camping is available for US$3 per person, tents provided. There's a restaurant (breakfast around US$4, lunch and dinner around US$8).

El Rancho de Kiki (☎ 316-4022/4030, fax 316-4031, offshore@cwpanama.net and cosa_mia@hotmail.com) is a comfortable two-story house with natural finishes, seaviews, a fully-equipped kitchen and a dining room that can seat six. Upstairs are two guestrooms with air con; one has a double bed and an excellent seaview, while the other contains six single beds. The rate is US$25 per person. There's no restaurant, but guests can use the one at Casablanca's. Kiki O'Brien is one of Panama's top surfboard makers (he makes the Cosa Mia boards).

Getting There & Away

To reach Santa Catalina from Panama City, first take a bus to Soná (see Soná, above, for details). From Soná, three buses serve Santa Catalina daily, leaving at 5 am, noon and 4 pm (US$3). Unless the driver is pushed for time, he will take you to any one of the hotels that are mentioned above for an additional US$1.

From Santa Catalina, three buses serve Soná daily. They leave at 7 and 8 am and 2 pm. In Santa Catalina the bus stops at the Jorón Brisas de Mar – a conch-shell's throw from Cabañas Rolo. If you're staying at one of the other hotels, it's a 1km walk to them on mostly flat terrain. There are no taxis in town.

PARQUE NACIONAL COIBA

In the Golfo de Chiriquí is Panama's largest island, 493-sq-km Isla de Coiba. The island is part of a protected scenic area and it's a Devil's Island: In 1991 Coiba, which for decades has been the site of a federal penal colony, became the centerpiece of a 270,000-hectare national park, over 80% of which is oceanic. Today hundreds of murderers, rapists and other convicts live in a large, ominous-looking cellblock known as 'Central' and in huts at 10 beachside prison camps that are scattered around the densely forested island. Also on Isla de Coiba are crocodiles, snakes and the country's last cluster of scarlet macaws.

Due to the presence of the prisoners, tourists cannot simply show up on the island, and their movement and numbers are very restricted. Anyone entering the park's boundaries must first have permission from the ANAM office in Santiago (☎ 998-4271) and must also check in at the ANAM ranger station at the northern end of Coiba before engaging in fishing, snorkeling and/or diving.

Because the island is quite far from the mainland (two hours by fast boat), unless you've got your own boat you usually must go through a tour operator to visit this park – and that means money, a rather large amount of it (see Diving, Snorkeling & Fishing, later, for prices). But if you're looking for something completely different,

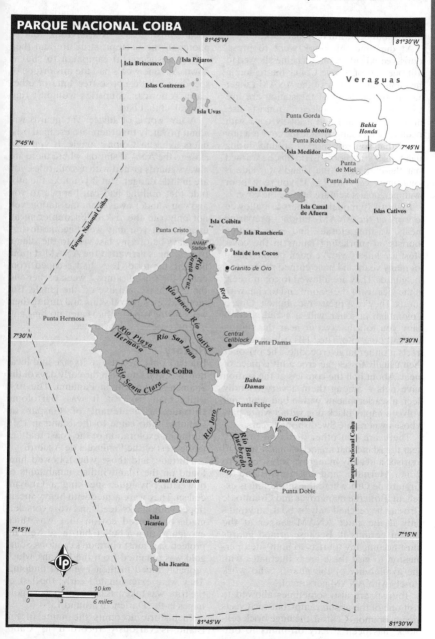

PARQUE NACIONAL COIBA

Isla Brincanco
Isla Pájaros
Islas Contreras
Isla Uvas

Veraguas

Punta Gorda
Ensenada Monita
Punta Roble
Isla Medidor
Bahía
Honda
Punta
de Miel
Punta Jabalí

Isla Afuerita

Isla Canal
de Afuera

Islas Cativos

Isla Coibita
Punta Cristo
Isla Ranchería
ANAM
Station
Isla de los Cocos
Granito de Oro

Parque Nacional Coiba

Reef

Río Santa Cruz
Río Juncal
Río Catívá

Punta Hermosa

Río Playa
Hermosa
Río San Juan

Central
Cellblock
Punta Damas

Isla de Coiba

Río Santa Clara

Bahía
Damas

Punta Felipe

Río Joto
Boca Grande

Río Barco
Quebrado

Parque Nacional Coiba

Reef

Canal de Jicarón

Punta Doble

Isla
Jicarón

Isla Jicarita

0   5   10 km
0   3   6 miles

81°45'W
81°30'W
7°45'N
7°30'N
7°15'N
81°45'W
81°30'W

chances are you'll find it in this highly unusual but beautiful national park.

At the time this book went to press, tourists could only count on being allowed to visit one part of Isla de Coiba: the region in the immediate vicinity of the ANAM ranger station. Within 100m of the station are five cabins with four beds apiece for tourists' use, an attractive beach and a lovely cove with mediocre snorkeling. Beside the cove is a tiny island that you can snorkel around during high tide; if you choose to do this, be warned that the current on the island's far side is sometimes very strong. If you're a poor swimmer, do not venture outside the cove.

Eight to 10 model prisoners are allowed to work at the ANAM station – preparing meals, washing clothes, and even leading tourists on snorkeling jaunts in the cove. Most are killers who've been on the island for many years and have earned the trust of the guards. They are allowed to roam freely in the vicinity of the station and to chat with guests. They're a pretty nice bunch. One, a Colombian prisoner, will, if asked, accompany you to a backwater near the station and call out, 'Tito, Tito.' His call always attracts a rather large crocodile. The prisoner then usually tosses the croc a little piece of meat. About half the convicts at the station have pets – among them a very friendly deer, a scarlet macaw with a bad wing, and Volvo, a happy black dog with a white paw whose owner stole Swedish-made cars.

There are two other areas on or very near the island that are occasionally open to tourists: a healthy mangrove forest close to Punta Hermosa and the tiny island of Granito de Oro, where the snorkeling is excellent. Both the mangroves and Granito de Oro can be reached only by boat, and that's only if the chief ANAM ranger at the station permits it. Because armed guards must accompany tourists to both sites, permission to visit these areas fluctuates with the availability of the guards, who work closely with ANAM personnel.

Tourists are also sometimes allowed to visit one of the prison camps, but such visits are uncommon. Central, the huge brick cellblock, has been strictly off-limits to outsiders since 1990, when a human-rights advocate posing as a tourist took lots of photos of the decrepit structure and then led an unsuccessful campaign to shut it down. Anyone who's had the misfortune of spending a little not-so-free time in other Latin American countries wouldn't find Central all that bad.

A few words of advice: The guards will admit privately that there are escaped prisoners living in Coiba's jungle. If you stay close to the ANAM station, where there are always guards armed with assault rifles, you are in little danger. But if you take the attitude that nothing bad can happen to you and you wander away from the station, you not only run the risk of encountering an escapee, but you may well become lost. A few days before my last visit to the island, two escapees arrived at the ANAM station, begging for food. They had escaped from one of the prison camps a week earlier and thought they could live off the jungle. But they had few survival skills, and during their week on the run they had eaten nothing and had become very dehydrated.

History

Isla de Coiba, because of its size and location, was well known in the early days of the Spanish settlement in Panama. The first white man to visit it was Bartolomé Hurtado, a lieutenant of Gaspar de Espinosa, who came to the island in 1516 during an exploration of the coast that lies to the west of the Península de Azuero.

Hurtado, and those who followed him, found on the island Indian inhabitants of powerful physique, speaking a Guaymí dialect. They were armed with heavy spears tipped with sharks' teeth and wore corselets made of layered cotton that was thick enough to turn a bullet, but these were no protection against Hurtado's cannons. Some gold was obtained from the Indians, which probably aided in their eventual undoing. They were exterminated early; the last of the tribe was taken as laborers to work gold mines in the Darién, in around 1550.

In historic accounts the name of the island is variously recorded as Cabo,

Cobaya, Quibo, and Coiba, apparently all variations of the name of the Indian chief in control during the time of the Spanish discovery. There is no record of Spanish settlement of Coiba.

Captain George Shelvocke of the British navy, in his account of his voyage around the world, recorded that he came to Coiba on January 13, 1720. He anchored off the northern point and found three deserted huts that he supposed were used by pearl fishermen, as there were heaps of oyster shells strewn around them. Shelvocke returned to Coiba 15 months later and then recorded a considerable description of it, in which he mentions 'the great variety of birds, which the woods would not permit us to follow,' and the abundance of black monkeys and iguanas.

In time, some coconut plantations were established on Coiba, but it seems that there was never any extensive settlement of the island until the 20th century. At the start of that century a pearl fishery was in operation, and a store, a bar and other buildings were present.

The depletion of the oyster beds led the government of Panama to acquire the private holdings, and (according to a plaque on the main guardhouse) the island was set aside as a penal colony in November 1919. A number of work camps were created on the eastern side of the island, and land was cleared for pasture and the planting of food crops adjacent to the camps. Some cattle were later brought to Coiba to add protein to the residents' diet. Today there are more than 2000 head of cattle on the island, providing beef for the convicts and the prison personnel.

The Park

A preliminary study of the marine life in the national park during 1996-97 identified 69 species of fish, although many more are likely to exist here. Additionally, humpback whales are often seen in the park, as are spotted and bottle-nosed dolphins. Killer, sperm and Cuvier's beaked whales are also present in park waters, but in fewer numbers.

Seventeen species of crocodile, turtle and lizard, as well as 15 species of snake (including the very dangerous fer-de-lance and the coral snake), are found in the park. Although the list is far from complete, to date 147 species of bird (including the Coiba spinetail, a little brown-and-white bird found only on Coiba) have been identified on the island. Scarlet macaws are among the species that nest on Coiba.

Coiba is home to the second-largest eastern Pacific coral reef and arguably the finest diving and snorkeling to be found along the Pacific coast from Colombia to Mexico. The entire island is covered with a heavy virgin forest, except for the prison camps and along the lower courses of the larger streams, where there are swampy woodlands. Rocky headlands project along the coast, and there are sandy beaches broken by mangroves at river mouths.

In addition to Coiba (50,314 hectares), islands within the park include Isla Jicarón (2002 hectares), Isla Brincanco (330 hectares), Isla Uvas (257 hectares), Isla Coibita (242 hectares), Isla Canal de Afuera (240 hectares), Isla Jicarita (125 hectares), Isla Pájaros (45 hectares) and Isla Afuerita (27 hectares).

The Prison

In 2001 there were more than 800 prisoners on Coiba. At that time ANAM officials hoped the penal colony would be shut down and all the prisoners removed from the island. They said that the national park could not be fully enjoyed by tourists as long as the prisoners are there. However, overcrowding at all Panamanian prisons and the reluctance of Panama's legislature to allocate funds to build more prisons make it unlikely the penal colony will be closed any time soon.

As previously mentioned, some prisoners are held in Central, the cellblock on the eastern side of the island, but most live in beachside camps. At night the camp guards lock themselves inside their rooms with their guns while the much larger population of prisoners roams freely. Each morning roll is taken, and all prisoners who fail to respond are considered escapees. First-time escapees face two to three years added to their sentences if caught, while second-time escapees face life sentences if apprehended.

About 10% of Coiba's prisoners attempt an escape. Nearly all escapees try to get away on homemade rafts made of balsa wood (the trees grow all over the island), but nearly all of them are captured, according to guards. Prisoners, however, say that many escapees are never seen again, and it is their belief that some escapees are today living in freedom, while many others were caught and shot by guards and their bodies dumped at sea.

The stories abound: Once, a five-log raft holding seven men caught a current that carried the raft all the way to the Galapagos Islands. Only two men were aboard when the raft reached the Galapagos; the others apparently had been forced off the craft or died along the way. Another time, two men shoved off at night, got confused and landed back on Coiba thinking that they'd made it to the mainland; they were captured and their sentences were promptly elongated. Yet another time, a drug kingpin used a prison phone and the next day swam straight out from shore, was met by a yacht, boarded it and was never seen again.

Certainly one of the big attractions on the island *is* the penal colony; if you ask a lot of questions, you'll hear some incredible stories – from prisoners and guards alike, in Spanish and in English. Once the stories start, everyone's a captive audience. According to prisoners who were on the island during the 1980s, the penal colony was once a great place to serve time. Manuel Noriega ran it like a pet project and paid it frequent visits. For a time he and his men vacationed in the cabins that are now used by tourists. During the 1980s, prisoners were allowed to make things to sell, such as wood carvings and jewelry made from the shells of sea turtles. Noriega allowed tourists to visit the cellblock and prison camps and buy souvenirs directly from the convicts. 'Man, that was a great time,' one twice-convicted car thief said. 'But now we can't make nothing and no tourists can come to visit us. All day long we just sit around doing nothing.'

Diving, Snorkeling & Fishing

Ancon Expeditions (☎ 269-9414/9415, fax 264-3713, info@anconexpeditions.com), in the El Dorado Building on Calle 49 A Este near Avenida 3 Sur, provides guided tours to Coiba upon request. Prices vary depending on group size, length of stay and other factors. Contact the company for prices.
Website: www.anconexpeditions.com

Readers have raved about the M/V Coral Star (in the USA ☎ 307-733-3127, 800-215-5169, fax 307-739-9137, info@coralstar.com), a 115-foot luxury live-aboard ship that cruises the islands in and around Parque Nacional Coiba, carrying its passengers to some great dive spots in the Western Hemisphere. Between scuba diving, guests have the option of sea kayaking, fishing, snorkeling or exploring the beaches and rain forests on uninhabited islands. Accommodations consist of two master staterooms with queen-size beds and full bathroom on the main deck, two deluxe and four standard cabins on the lower deck with portholes, sink and vanity, private and semiprivate shower and toilet. Weekly rates – which include in-country flights and transfers, rum punch party, most meals, lodging, scuba tanks and weight belts, airfills, nature tours and more – run at a very reasonable US$1650 to US$1850, depending on choice of stateroom.
Website: www.coralstar.com

Coiba Adventure (☎ 999-8108, 628-0810; in the USA ☎ 800-800-0907; coibadvent@cwpanama.net) is a sportfishing operation run by Tom Yust, and nobody knows the area better than he does. Widely regarded as Panama's top sportfishing captain, Tom runs a very personalized operation. Rates vary depending on time of year, boat used and the size of the party, but in general expect to pay between US$2600 and US$5000 per week. Cost includes domestic flights, transfers, lodging, meals, park fees, tackle, English-speaking and professionally licensed crew – the works.
Website: www.coibadventure.com

The Coiba Explorer (in the USA ☎ 504-871-7181, 800-733-4742, fax 504-871-7150, info@coibaexplorer.com) offers separate diving and fishing adventures from a 115-foot live-aboard mothership, with diversions such as jungle exploration. The company's dive season runs from June through mid-September and the first two weeks of December. Most divers get in between 20 and 25 dives a week. The weekly rate is US$2500 per diver. The company's fishing season runs from November into May, with weekly rates ranging from US$3000 to US$4000 per person. The prices include lodging, in-country transportation and most meals – just about everything except transportation to and from Panama.

Website: www.coibaexplorer.com

PARQUE NACIONAL CERRO HOYA

On the southwestern side of the Península de Azuero, this 32,577-hectare park protects the headwaters of the Ríos Tonosí, Portobelo and Pavo, 30 endemic plant species and fauna that includes the carato parakeet. It contains some of the last remaining forest on a huge peninsula that is one of the most agriculturally devastated regions of Panama. Although the park was created in 1984, much of the forest had been chopped down prior to that time, and it will be a long time before the park really looks like a park.

Anyone thinking of visiting the park should be advised that there are no accommodations for visitors in or near the park (the ranger station is officially open to tourists, but there's nowhere for them to sleep) and that the trails into it are ill defined.

The best way to get to the park is by boat from Playa Cambutal. There, it's always possible to find a boatman to make the two-hour trip; the cost is generally US$60 to US$80 per party one way. If you happen to come upon a boat going from Playa Cambutal to the park or to Punta Ventana nearby, the ride could cost as little as US$5 per person.

It's also possible to reach the park by a road that winds along the western edge of the Península de Azuero. However, even with a 4WD vehicle and only during the dry season, visitors are only able to get as far as Restigue, a hamlet south of Arenas, at the edge of the park. Unfortunately, two of the park's main attractions are its waterfalls and rivers, which are reduced to trickles during the dry season.

In short, until the park is more accessible and facilities are developed for tourists, the attractions don't warrant the special effort needed to see them.

Herrera Province

pop 102,700

The Península de Azuero, long overshadowed by the canal and the cities at its ends, is looked upon by Panamanians as their country's heart and soul. It is here, on plains that more closely resemble rural USA than the American Tropics, that the Spanish legacy is strongest, in festivals and in faces. On the Azuero, fair complexions, hazel eyes and aquiline features prevail. The people have little Indian ancestry; their descent is nearly pure Spanish.

But culture on this semiarid peninsula didn't arrive with the Spaniards; it was here centuries before a teenage Italian named Cristóbal Colón got his first sailing lesson. What we know of this culture has been gleaned mainly from archaeology, and perhaps no excavation sites have told us more about the people the conquistadors encountered in Panama than the digs near Parita, in Herrera Province, and those at nearby Sitio Conte, in Coclé Province.

An excavation during the 1940s of tombs within 10km of Parita uncovered some of the most artistic pottery that was ever produced by pre-Columbian Indians. Brightly colored, fanciful bird and reptile designs adorn the ancient pottery. The bowls were often shaped to resemble king vultures, with finger-long wings flaring from their sides and bulbous heads and stubby tails at their ends.

The remains of a young child with a necklace of hollow gold beads were found in one large painted bowl. In another tomb scientists found long-necked bottles and 40 painted pots in the form of bird effigies. Also found in this tomb were exquisitely carved batons shaped like stylized alligators, made from manatee ribs.

Perhaps the most amazing find was an urn that contained the remains of a single man and a necklace made of 800 human teeth. Nearly all the teeth were front incisors, which means that the teeth of at least 200 people were required to make the jewelry. The circumstances under which the necklace was made remain a mystery.

Other sites near Parita have yielded large quantities of ceremonial pottery. These are mostly vessels mounted on tall pedestal bases of two types: painted globular bowls and other bowls in the form of king vulture effigies, brightly painted with outstretched wings. More than 100 nearly identical red-painted globular jars with short necks were found in one mound.

Tantalizing but far from adequate descriptions of the people who created these objects have been left to us by Gaspar de Espinosa and Gonzalo de Badajoz, who led looting expeditions on the peninsula between 1515 and 1525. According to their writings, at that time the area was controlled

Highlights

- La Playa El Aguillito, the Grand Central Station of migratory seabirds and bird watchers
- Pottery factories in La Arena, where artisans produce ceramics that mimic pre-Columbian designs
- Historic Parita, with pridefully maintained buildings dating back to the 16th and 17th centuries
- Ocú, where women braid some of the world's finest Panama hats

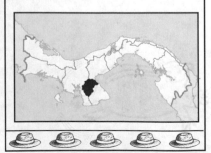

HERRERA PROVINCE

by a powerful chief named Parita, of the Guaymí tribe.

Parita's warriors were able to prevent the Spaniards from settling on the Azuero for several years, but when Espinosa led a later raid on the peninsula, he found to his pleasant surprise that Parita had recently died. Instead of confronting the chief in combat, the raiders found him lying in state in a room containing 355lbs of gold ornaments. Also found near the dead leader were 20 Indian captives who were lashed to house posts by cords around their necks; these poor souls had been destined to be buried alive with the great chieftain. Also expected to be buried with Parita were his wives and household attendants.

Today, very few Indians live near the Parita site. Those Guaymís who could flee went to the jungled mountains in what is now Chiriquí Province. They lived primarily by hunting and by cultivating corn, beans, manioc and bananas. So fearful were they of white people that until only a few decades ago they placed deadly traps along trails to kill or maim outsiders.

Herrera Province, which is in the center of the Península de Azuero, was lush and only sparsely inhabited during the 16th century; today the country's smallest province not only contains little forest but also has the third-highest population density of Panama's nine provinces, with 44 residents per square kilometer. Its inhabitants are mostly farmers. The province's chief industries are Panama rum, shoes and detergents, as well as leather products.

Herrera has maintained its Spanish legacy mainly through Spanish festivals. The town of Ocú holds a popular patron saint festival, which begins with religious services and includes the joyous parading of a just-married couple through the streets. Las Minas and Parita are known for their feasts of Corpus Christi (Body of Christ), festivals celebrated 40 days after Easter in honor of the Eucharist. Pesé hosts dramatic public reenactments of the Last Supper, Judas' betrayal and Jesus' imprisonment during the week preceding Easter. And during Carnaval Chitré becomes a city of 80,000 fun-loving souls.

Anyone looking for the soul of Panama would do well to visit Herrera Province.

CHITRÉ
pop 42,500

Chitré, the capital of Herrera Province, is the largest city on the Península de Azuero and a convenient base for exploration. It is the site of some of the area's best-known festivals. If you plan to attend any festivals in Chitré, be warned that you will have difficulty finding a place to stay if you arrive without a reservation. This is particularly true during Carnaval, when most of the city's rooms are spoken for months in advance.

In the vicinity of Chitré are the Parque Nacional Sarigua; the Humboldt Ecological Station at Playa El Aguillito; and, a fair walk or short bus ride away, the village of La Arena, 3km west of Chitré, where you can see ceramics being made. All of these sites are covered in this chapter.

Villa de Los Santos, where some of the peninsula's most important festivals take place, is 4km southeast of Chitré, just inside Los Santos Province (see that chapter for details).

Orientation

The Interamericana connects with the Carretera Nacional (the National Hwy, also known as the Carretera Central) at the town of Divisa, atop the Península de Azuero, and from there the Carretera Nacional runs southeast 37km to Chitré. From Chitré it runs 31km farther to Las Tablas, in Los Santos Province, and there the highway becomes a loop road that links the coastal and inland towns near the southern edge of the peninsula. Buses travel this circular road in clockwise and counterclockwise directions, with Las Tablas at the noon position.

As the Carretera Nacional winds southeast from Divisa, the first major town it encounters is Chitré. When the highway reaches Chitré, it becomes Paseo Enrique Geenzier; the road changes name again a dozen blocks farther east, becoming Calle Manuel Maria Correa. The Carretera Nacional reemerges at the southern end of town. The Carretera Nacional changes names quite frequently along its length.

The town's cathedral and the adjacent central square, Parque Union, are one block south of Calle Manuel Maria Correa, between Avenida Obaldía and Avenida Herrera. There are numerous places to stay and eat within a short walk of the square.

One Name, Many Highways

When you see signs for the Carretera Nacional in Herrera Province, keep in mind that this is also the name given to the loop road that links Chitré, Pesé, Las Minas, Ocú and other Herrera towns that lie at the center and top of the Península de Azuero. Basically, 'Carretera Nacional' doesn't refer to one highway on the peninsula but to several. This can be a little confusing at times, but if you realize at the outset that there are several highways known as the Carretera Nacional, you'll have a better idea of what's going on when you notice mentions of the seemingly omnipresent National Hwy.

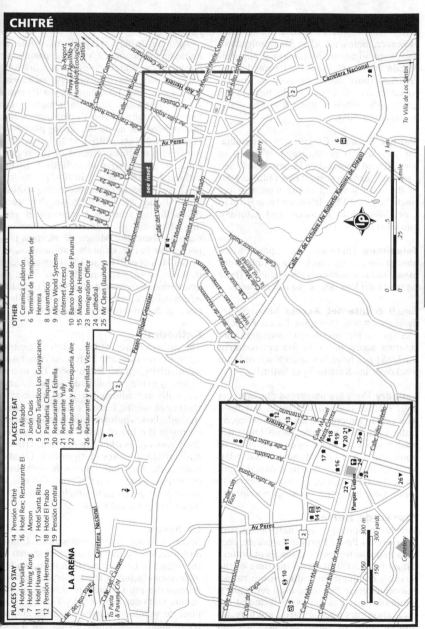

CHITRÉ

PLACES TO STAY
4 Hotel Versalles
7 Hotel Hong Kong
11 Hotel Hawaii
12 Pensión Herrerana
14 Pensión Chitré
16 Hotel Rex; Restaurante El Meson
17 Hotel Santa Rita
18 Hotel El Prado
19 Pensión Central

PLACES TO EAT
2 El Mirador
5 Jorón Oasis
13 Panadería Chiquita
20 Restaurante La Estrella
21 Restaurante Yully
22 Restaurante y Refresquería Aire Libre
26 Restaurante y Parrillada Vicente

OTHER
1 Cerámica Calderón
6 Terminal de Transportes de Herrera
8 Lavamatico
9 Micro World Systems (Internet Access)
10 Banco Nacional de Panamá
15 Museo de Herrera
23 Immigration Office
24 Cathedral
25 Mr Clean (laundry)

Centro Turístico Los Guayacanes

LA ARENA

Information

There is no tourist office in Chitré. However, there's an office for Immigration and Naturalization (Migración y Naturalización; ☎ 996-3092) south of Parque Union. Officials there might be able to answer whatever questions you might have about Chitré. The office is open 8 am to 4 pm Monday to Friday.

Money Because Chitré is a provincial capital, there is no shortage of banks in town. Banco Nacional de Panamá, on Paseo Enrique Geenzier several short blocks west of the town square, has the most services (including an ATM). It's open from 9 am to 1 pm Monday to Thursday and Saturday, and 9 am to 3 pm Friday.

Telephone There are many pay phones around town from which you can place domestic and international calls, including those on the Hotel Rex side of the town square.

Email & Internet Access Micro World Systems (☎ 996-1596), on Paseo Enrique Geenzier, offers two dozen computers with Internet access in an air-con environment for US$1 per hour. It's open 8 am to 9 pm weekdays and 8 am to 7 pm Saturday.

Laundry There are numerous places to get your clothes cleaned in Chitré, but most won't clean undergarments. Lavamatico, on Calle Luis Ríos at Calle Fabio Díaz, will wash underwear and is open from 9 am to noon and 1:30 to 4 pm Monday to Saturday. Mr Clean, at Calle Meliton Martin and Avenida Centenario, is more centrally located, but it won't wash *ropas interiores*.

Museo de Herrera

This anthropology and natural history museum, on Paseo Enrique Geenzier, contains many well-preserved pieces of pottery dating from 5000 BC until the time of the Spanish conquest, including some rather elaborate pieces that were used for trading. Some of the pieces that were found at the excavation sites outside Parita are here, although most of those artifacts are on display at the anthropology museum in Panama City.

Also on display are replicas of *huacas* found on the peninsula, as well as numerous photographs of archaeologists at work and maps showing where the pottery and huacas were found (see Shopping in the Panama City chapter for more information on huacas). Be sure to visit the museum's 2nd floor, where you'll find interesting photos of Azuero residents, authentic folkloric costumes and religious artifacts of the region (including the original bell of Chitré's cathedral, which was cast in 1767).

There is a lot of other interesting stuff in this museum, including photos that were taken during Chitré's Carnavals; if you don't have the good fortune of attending Carnaval here, the Museo de Herrera is a good place to check out the zaniness you've missed. It's open 9 am to 12:30 pm and 1:30 to 4 pm Tuesday to Saturday and 9 am to noon Sunday. Admission costs US$1/25¢ for adults/children. All of the signage and literature at the museum is in Spanish only.

Cathedral

The cathedral, adjacent to Chitré's central square, dates from the 18th century but was substantially remodeled in 1988. The entire ceiling is made of polished mahogany and the walls are adorned with near-life-size figures of saints. Large, beautifully vivid stained-glass windows depict momentous events in the life of Jesus. The Stations of the Cross are marked by 4m teak crosses and intricately carved figurines. Unlike many cathedrals that impress through their ornateness and overuse of gold, this one is striking for its elegant simplicity and fine balance of gold and wood.

La Arena

Several kilometers west of downtown Chitré and bisected by the Carretera Nacional is the village of La Arena, which is known for its ceramics factories. The pottery made here mimics the pre-Columbian designs of the culture that once lived nearby. This is a good place to watch pottery being made, and to try to make some yourself (just ask if you can take a spin at the potter's wheel; if you don't speak Spanish, simply point at yourself and then at the clay and the wheel, and be sure to smile). It's only after you've taken a turn at the wheel – your hands shaping a freaky tornado-resemblant thing instead of a lovely vase – that you are able to appreciate the skill involved in this seemingly simple craft.

The best of the several pottery factories is **Ceramica Calderón**, near the intersection of Calle del Río Parita and Carretera Nacional, where you can buy traditional painted ceramics at low cost. These pieces are made on the premises in a workshop directly behind the roadside showroom. All the pottery here is made by hand with the help of a foot-powered potter's wheel. The trick is to make a piece that is not only pleasing to look at, but also has no bubbles (otherwise it will break while firing).

The artisan who makes most of the ceramics sold here is Angel Calderón. In 1997 he told the author that he had been making ceramics professionally for 41 of his 52 years. After several minutes of calculation, he estimated that he had made no fewer than 500,000 pieces. Although he owns the factory and has several capable workers, Angel said he works every day except Christmas and Easter. He said that he works so hard to set a good example for his workers. In 2001, he told the author he that was now taking his birthday off, in addition to Christmas and Easter. That slacker!

If you visit Angel's shop, be sure to take a look at the ovens out back. They are quite impressive.

Other than shopping for pottery and trying your hand at making some, there isn't much to do in La Arena – except eat (see Places to Eat) and enjoy the views. There are no hotels in La Arena, but the village makes an excellent day trip from Chitré.

A taxi ride from Parque Union costs US$2, but be sure to agree on the price beforehand to avoid a squabble with your driver when you arrive. There's also bus service from Chitré (see Getting There & Away, following).

Special Events
Chitré's Carnaval festivities, held each year on the four days before Ash Wednesday (in February or March), feature parades, folkloric dancing, water fights and lots of drinking. On June 24 Chitré's patron saint festival, the Fiesta de San Juan Bautista, starts with a religious service followed by bullfights (the animals are merely teased), cockfights and other popular activities. And on October 19, festivities that celebrate the Founding of the District of Chitré (1848) include parades, historical costumes and much merriment.

Places to Stay
The selection of lodging options in Chitré ranges from hot and rundown cubicles to spacious, tastefully appointed guestrooms with all of the creature comforts. Room reservations for Carnaval must be made six months or more in advance. At the upscale Hotel Hong Kong, reservations must be made three years in advance.

Pensión Herrerana (☎ 996-4356), on Avenida Herrera 2½ blocks north of the cathedral, is a fairly clean but basic, worn place with some of the cheapest rooms in town at US$8 per person. Three rooms have private cold-water bathrooms; the rest have shared facilities.

Pensión Chitré (☎ 996-1856), on Calle Manuel Maria Correa near Avenida Perez, offers six clean singles/doubles with ceiling fans and private cold-water bathrooms for US$8/10. Some beds are better than others; ask to see several rooms.

Pensión Central (☎ 996-0059), on Avenida Herrera just a few dozen paces north of the cathedral, offers 15 rooms with air con (US$15 per room) and 10 without (US$10/12) – an excellent value. All the rooms have private hot-water bathrooms, good beds and 40-channel TV.

Hotel El Prado (☎ 996-4620), on Avenida Herrera just south of Calle Manuel Maria Correa, is a clean, well-kept hotel with a 2nd-floor restaurant, sitting area and balcony overlooking the street. The fairly worn rooms are set back from the street, so they're not too noisy; each has a private hot-water bathroom, TV and phone. Singles/doubles with fan cost US$12/18, or US$17/26 with air con.

Hotel Santa Rita (☎ 996-4610, fax 996-2404), on the corner of Calle Manuel Maria Correa and Avenida Herrera, is also a good deal. One of the city's first hotels, Santa Rita has 20 rooms, a restaurant/bar and phone and fax service. Rates for the hotel's well-maintained rooms range from US$14 for one person without air con to US$16/24 for singles/doubles with air-conditioning. All rooms have private hot-water bathrooms.

Hotel Rex (☎ 996-6660, fax 996-4310), beside the town square on Calle Meliton Martín, offers 32 air-con rooms with cable TV, phone and private hot-water bathrooms for US$17 to US$20 for an individual, and US$25 for two people. For space, ask for room Nos 104 or 106. Rooms 114, 116, 118 and 120 are the next best. There's a dance club, bar and restaurant.

Hotel Hawaii (☎ 996-3534, fax 996-5330), on Calle San Pedro near Paseo Enrique Geenzier, has 33 cheerful air-con singles/doubles with cable TV, phone and private hot-water bathrooms for US$18/33.

As you enter the city from the west, you may notice the appealing *Hotel Versalles* (☎ 996-4422, fax 996-2090, ersalles@ cwp.net.pa) on Paseo Enrique Geenzier. The hotel was remodeled in 1999, with a swimming pool and a restaurant/bar. Guestrooms with air con, cable TV, hot-water private bathrooms, phone and desks cost US$23/34. There are suites as well for US$29/40.

Hotel Hong Kong (☎ 996-4483, fax 996-5229), on Carretera Nacional, is the best hotel in Chitré, offering well-maintained guestrooms with all the amenities and suites with Jacuzzi tubs and kitchenettes. Some of the rooms are wheelchair accessible. There are two swimming pools (one for kids) and a fine restaurant and bar. The rate of US$27 for a single or double applies most of the year. A suite rents for US$80. Check out their website at http:// welcome.to/hotelhongkong.com.

Places to Eat

Chitré's fishermen fish from 2 to 6 am and sell their haul soon after their return from the sea. As a result, most of the seafood served in Chitré is caught the same day. For this reason, Chitré is known throughout the peninsula as having fresh seafood – and it's surprisingly cheap.

In Town At Hotel Rex, *Restaurante El Meson* has good, reasonably priced food. Chicken and beef dishes cost US$4 to US$9. The paella (US$5), served only on Sunday, is quite good. The *lomo relleno al horn* (baked roast beef, US$5) is excellent, but the seafood soup is surprisingly disappointing. The chef will prepare paella for groups of five or more any time, if he's given at least two hours' notice. El Mason is open for breakfast, lunch and dinner.

There are several Chinese restaurants in town, the best of which is inside *Hotel Hong Kong*. Breakfasts range from US$2 to US$4. Lunch and dinner items include shrimp chow mein (US$4), Creole-style shrimp (US$4.50), smoked pork chops (US$5) and chicken with cashew nuts (US$5.50). It's open 7 am to 10 pm daily.

Another very good Chinese restaurant is *Restaurante y Parrillada Vicente*, on Avenida Herrera two blocks south of the cathedral. The chow mein, the chicken with sweet and sour sauce and the roast pork (US$3.75 each) are all recommendable. The grilled octopus (US$6.25) is delicious. Budget travelers might want to look closely at the *menu familiar* on the last page of the menu, which lists three set dinners for US$5.50 per person, with a two-person minimum.

Restaurante La Estrella, across from the cathedral, serves typical Panamanian food buffet style and very cheap (nothing over US$3.25). It's open from 5 am to 11 pm daily.

Restaurante Yully, on Calle Meliton Martín a block east of the cathedral, is good for cheap food. Offered buffet-style are rice (30¢), roast beef (75¢), chicken (US$1.50), ham (US$1.50), steak (US$2), chow mein (US$2) and so on. Food generally seems higher quality here than at La Estrella. It's open 5 am to 6 pm daily.

Facing the western end of Parque Union is *Restaurante y Refresqueria Aire Libre*, an open-air cafe that features lots of beverages. Also available here at low cost (nothing's over US$3.50) are a variety of rice, chow mein and chicken dishes. You can also find ice cream here. The most popular dish here is the *camarones al ajillo* (shrimp with garlic, US$3.50). This pleasant cafe is open 6:30 am to 10 pm daily.

Centro Turistico Los Guayacanes, up Calle 19 de Octubre (Av Roberto Ramirez de Diego) from the Hotel Hong Kong, contains the finest restaurant in town. Situated on a bluff overlooking downtown Chitré, the restaurant offers a host of seafood dishes for around US$9, grilled meats from US$4.50 to US$12.50, and many specials such as octopus salad for US$8. Hardwood buffs go bonkers at the sight of the materials used at this spacious indoor-outdoor restaurant, which includes a ceiling made of spiny cedar supported by pillars of 1m-thick guayacan trunks. The owner of this impressive facility, which also has a bar and a large swimming pool available for tourists' use, is one of Panama's major loggers.

La Arena The highest point within 5km of downtown Chitré is the restaurant *El Mirador* (The Lookout), atop a hill in La Arena. This open-sided restaurant is very casual, with Formica tables, leather-backed chairs and an obnoxious TV. The Mirador is popular for its panoramic views and atmosphere (the food is mediocre). All items range from US$3 up to US$7. It's open from 4 pm to midnight daily.

To find the Mirador from downtown Chitré, head westward on the Carretera Nacional about 2.5km and turn left onto the road that begins just past the large 'Chino Bar' sign. Keep to the right for 400m until you reach the top of the hill. If you don't have wheels, a taxi ride will cost US$2 each way. The restaurant will call a radio taxi for you when you want to leave.

Also in La Arena and quite popular with locals is *Jorón Oasis*, on the southern side

of the Carretera Nacional opposite the Accel gas station. The *sopa de carne* (meat soup) at this typical roadside open-air restaurant is very good and should be ordered with rice. The local way to eat this combination is to fill your spoon with rice and dip it into the soup. When you're nearly finished with the soup, you'll find a chunk of steer rib in it. Pick up the bone and chew the beef off it. The entire price for this typical regional meal: US$1. Add 75¢ if you want a beer with it.

Getting There & Away

Air Chitré's airport is northeast of town; follow Avenida Herrera north from the town square to reach it. A taxi ride there costs US$2.50.

Aeroperlas (☎ 996-4021 at the airport) flies from Chitré to Panama City at 8:25 am and 5 pm Monday to Saturday, and at 5 pm Sunday (US$32).

Bus Chitré is a center for regional bus transportation. Buses arrive at and depart from Terminal de Transportes de Herrera, 1km south of the center of town. To get from downtown to the station, take a taxi (US$2) or catch a 'Terminal' bus (25¢) at the intersection of Calle Aminta Burgos de Amado and Avenida Herrera. The station has a restaurant that's open 24 hours a day.

Tuasa (☎ 996-5619) buses depart Chitré for Panama City at 1:30, 2:30, 4, 5 and 6 am, and then leave every 45 minutes until the last bus departs at about 6 pm. Transportes Inazun (☎ 996-4177) also has buses to the capital, departing hourly from 6 am to 3 pm. Both companies charge US$6 (3½ hours, 255km).

Other service from Chitré includes the following (fares are for one way travel):

Divisa – US$1, 30 minutes, 37km, frequent departures

La Arena – 25¢, five minutes, 3km, frequent departures

Las Minas – US$1.50, one hour, 51km, hourly

Las Tablas – US$1, 30 minutes, 31km, every 10 minutes

Ocú – US$2, one hour, 46km, hourly from sunrise to sunset

Parita – 50¢, five minutes, 10km, every 45 minutes from sunrise to sunset

Pedasí – US$2, one hour, 73km, every 30 minutes

Pesé – US$1, 20 minutes, 24km, every 20 minutes

Playa El Aguillito – 50¢, 12 minutes, 7km, frequent departures

Playas Monagre and El Rompío – US$1, 30 minutes, 20km, leaves when full

Santiago – US$2, 1¼ hours, 71km, every 30 minutes

Tonosí – US$4, two hours, 103km, at noon, 1, 2, 3, and 4 pm

Villa de Los Santos – 35¢, 10 minutes, 4km, every 10 minutes

To get to David or Panama City, take a bus to Divisa and then catch a *directo* (direct bus) to either city; they leave from the Delta station at the intersection of the Interamericana and the Carretera Nacional. You likely won't have to wait more than 30 minutes. The bus fare will set you back US$7 or US$8. If you're trying to get to Chitré from the Interamericana, ask the bus driver to stop in Divisa. He'll know to stop near the Delta station. At the station, catch any bus heading toward Chitré. There are plenty of them.

Getting Around
If you need to travel by vehicle, a taxi is the best way to go. They're so cheap – US$2 is the most you would pay in town, and most fares are US$1 – that it doesn't make any sense to bother with the hot, slow and crowded local buses.

PLAYA EL AGUILLITO
Seven km from Chitré's Parque Unión is Playa El Aguillito, which is not so much a sandy beach as it is a mudflat created by silt deposited by two nearby rivers, the Río Parita and the Río La Villa. At low tide the mudflat stretches more than 2km from the high-water mark to the surf, and thousands of birds descend on the mud in search of plankton and small shrimp.

Most of the birds are migratory, flying between Alaska and various South American countries. For reasons that escape scientists – including Francisco Delgado, who heads the **Humboldt Ecological Station** near

the northwest end of the beach (look for an 'Estacion Ecologica Alejandro Humboldt' sign) – these birds return year after year to exactly the same beach and to no others in the area. A roseate spoonbill that lands on this beach will never land on Playa El Retén, even though it's only 2km away, and vice versa.

This is rather amazing when you consider how many thousands of kilometers the birds fly during a single season and how many feeding grounds they must fly over. In addition to the spoonbills, other Playa El Aguillito regulars include black-necked stilts, white-winged doves, yellow-crowned Amazons (which are frequently seen here) and also common ground-doves (which in Panama are found only on this beach).

When the tide is high, these birds congregate around salt ponds to the immediate east of Playa El Aguillito. Few birders know about the beach or the salt ponds, but the bird watching at the ponds during high tide is terrific.

Another reason for birders to visit the beach and ponds is the ecological station. It was established by a group of local environmentalists in 1983. Since then, Francisco and others have banded more than 15,000 birds and monitored them with the help of scientists in other countries. Among the items on display at the station is a map showing the migratory routes of all the bird species that pass through the area.

Francisco, who speaks English and Spanish, knows as much about the birds on the Península de Azuero as anyone. If you have questions about the birds or his work, Francisco usually can be reached at his home (☎ 996-1725) and through the restaurant/bar (☎ 996-1820) beside the beach. The bartender's name is Frederico, and he will pass along messages to Francisco as long as you speak the one language he understands: Spanish.

Getting There & Away
Playa El Aguillito is reached from Chitré via Avenida Herrera (see the Chitré map); it's just past the airport. A bus leaves the Chitré station for the beach every

30 minutes or so from sunrise to sunset. The one-way fare is 50¢. A taxi ride from town costs US$3.

PARQUE NACIONAL SARIGUA

Ten kilometers north of downtown Chitré, this national park consists of 8000 hectares of wasteland that ANAM, Panama's environmental agency, would have you believe is *tropical desert*. The park is not without attractions. The area may be the most important pre-Columbian site in Panama. The Sarigua site has been dated back 11,000 years based on shell mounds and pottery fragments and offers some rich archaeological opportunities. It's a pity that the government isn't allocating money for excavation of the area. Today, all you'll find in the way of artifacts from the site are some arrowheads and a few pieces of pottery on display at the ANAM station here.

Part of the park actually serves as the waste disposal site for Chitré, Parita and other cities. As a matter of fact, directly behind the ANAM station (where you pay the US$3 entrance fee), you can see garbage poking up out of the ground – because until recently the very land upon which the station is now located was a garbage dump.

The wasteland to which I refer goes far beyond the pockets of actual urban waste buried in this national park, which was created in 1984. Where deciduous forest once stood, the landscape now resembles a desert. Where animals once frolicked amid trees and meadows and creeks, a movie crew could now film a reenactment of man landing on the Moon. And yet the area receives more than 1m of rain each year!

Sarigua is the end product of slash-and-burn agriculture. People moved into the area, cut down all the trees, set fire to the debris, planted crops for a few harvests and then left. Because the forest that had held the thin topsoil in place was removed, the heavy rain that falls here every year carried the topsoil into creeks and thence into rivers and out into the sea. What you see in Sarigua today is the nutrient-deficient rock that had been underneath the topsoil.

Shamefully, despite the example of Sarigua, the Panamanian government wants to open Darién Province and northern Veraguas Province to the same variety of wasteful and unsustainable agriculture.

Getting There & Away

To get here from the Carretera Nacional, take the Puerto Limon turnoff, a couple of kilometers northwest of Parita. After 1km you'll notice a foul smell. It's coming from a pig farm with more than 5000 animals. After another 1km you'll come to the park turnoff. Follow the signs for 2km, until you come to a structure on the left. This is the ANAM station.

Buses do not go to the park. A roundtrip taxi ride to the ANAM station from Chitré costs about US$20. The ANAM station is open 8 am to 4 pm daily, but you can arrive earlier or later; the ranger lives in a house next to the station, and will come out and collect the three bucks regardless of when you arrive.

PARITA
pop 3600

This beautiful and historic town is 10km northwest of downtown Chitré, just off the Carretera Nacional. It's known to few people outside the Península de Azuero, and there are no hotels here, but the town does offer several pleasant surprises.

Things to See

Parita follows a grid pattern. As you come to intersections near the town's center, which is about 500m from the Carretera Nacional, and glance both ways, you'll see building after building that look much the way they have for centuries. This town was founded in 1558, and most of the structures near its center date from at least the 18th century. They're real beauties, looking very much like Spanish imports. The walls are thick and the beams are as solid as railroad ties. The roofs are made of red convex tiles and the fancier structures have arcades on the side facing the street.

The **church** in Parita is the only one in Panama that has its steeple located directly over its entrance rather than over a corner of the structure. This is very unusual, because bell towers are always extremely heavy and therefore are generally built on pillars that rest upon a massive foundation. It is a major curiosity to the old people of Parita that the steeple hasn't collapsed upon the entryway. Although the church was completed in 1723, you'll never see an old Parita resident loitering near the entrance.

Beside the church is a grassy square in which cattle-roping demonstrations are held from August 3-7, during the town's patron saint festivities.

Two doors down from the southeastern corner of Parita's church is a **workshop** (☎ 974-2242/2036) that specializes in the restoration of altars. It is the only such workshop in the country. The artisans working here – Macario José Rodriguez and the twin brothers José Sergio Lopez and Sergio José Lopez – have been restoring the altars of Panama's colonial churches since the 1970s.

Because at least 15 colonial churches in the republic are in varying states of repair, there's no shortage of work for these three. But don't hesitate to stop by and say hello. All three men speak some English and they are very friendly. Chances are they'll let you take a look around. Here, it takes little effort to imagine that you're in a colonial-era workshop that's producing altars for the new churches of the New World.

To find the home of one of the country's top **mask makers**, Darido Lopez, return to the Carretera Nacional and find the Shell station near the turnoff. Across the street from the gas station and 100m northwest of it you'll be in front of Darido's house. In 2000 he began hanging masks beside his front door so visitors could identify his home.

Darido has been making colorful masks for folkloric dancers since the 1960s. While he continues to make masks and satin costumes worn by dirty-devil dancers, these days most of his masks are exported to the USA and to Europe. Darido can make a mask in a single day, and he usually asks between US$20 and US$80 for each one. When asked what he likes most about his

work, Darido says that he lives for the Corpus Christi celebrations, because it is only then that he can see his work in its best light.

(For information on one of Panama's other top mask makers, see the Villa de Los Santos section of the Los Santos Province chapter.)

Getting There & Away

Parita makes an excellent day trip from Chitré. Buses for Parita leave the Chitré station every 45 minutes from sunrise to sunset and cost 50¢ each way. A faster way to get here is to take a taxi, which costs about US$4.

REFUGIO DE VIDA SILVESTRE CENEGÓN DEL MANGLE

This wildlife refuge near Parita protects a mangrove forest at the mouth of the Río Santa María, an important wildlife area and nesting ground for herons. Its primary attraction is the birds.

However, there are a half-dozen bucket-size pools here containing water that is said to have health-giving properties. Some people lift the water out with cups and pour it over their skin. The water is cold and doesn't have the sulfuric odor characteristic of thermal water; it's more like rainwater or regular ground water.

The refuge is not reachable by bus; it's a 45-minute drive north of Chitré via the Carretera Nacional. Take the turnoff to **Los Pozos** ('The Wells'; there's a sign on the road). After 1km the road forks at a church in the village of Paris; take the right branch and it becomes a dirt road. Proceed 3.8km on this road, after which you'll come to a sign with an arrow showing you where to go and indicating you're 1.88km from the wells. There's a viewing tower there as well as a bathroom and a couple of picnic tables.

PESÉ
pop 2600

The town of Pesé, 22km from La Arena, is ringed by sugar-cane plantations and becomes extremely popular on Holy Friday during its annual live representation of the

Birds can be seen in abundance at the Refugio de Vida Silvestre Cenegón del Mangle.

Golgotha drama, a reenactment of Christ's crucifixion.

Pesé is home to the country's largest seco factory, **Seco Herrerano** (☎ 974-9621, fax 974-9593), established in 1936. It's a rather small factory, with only 45 workers, but its output is impressive: 36,000 one-liter bottles every business day (Monday to Saturday). The distillery and mill are open for tours.

The part of the process that seems to impress most people is the bottling of the liquor and the labeling of the bottles. There is something peaceful and spellbinding about all the machinery working in unison, and the air in the bottling room is practically intoxicating. Alas, there is no free sampling.

The mill operates only during the harvest season, which lasts from mid-January to mid-March. During this time, you can see tons of sugar cane fed into huge presses, which extract sweet juice. The juice is pumped into huge containers, where it ferments. What's neat about this operation is the speed of the pressing and the power of the machinery.

If you wish to take a tour, you must fax your request at least a week in advance. Address your request to Carlos Cedeño. Carlos speaks so-so English, so keep your request simple – along these lines: 'Dear Sir, I would like to tour Seco Herrerano on (month) (date). I will arrive at (hour). I would be grateful if you would tend to me then. Sincerely, (your name).' If Carlos can't tend to you that day, someone else will. Don't expect a reply. Most Panamanian hotels will let a guest send a one-page fax for US$1.

Getting There & Away

Pesé is 19km southwest of the Carretera Nacional. It can be reached by bus from the Terminal de Transportes de Herrera in Chitré (US$1, 20 minutes, every 20 minutes). Allow for delays.

LAS MINAS
pop 2200

Las Minas (The Mines) was founded in 1668 and takes its name from the gold mines in its hills that were worked under Spanish control during the 17th century. Today, you can spend hours roaming the cool hills and coffee plantations asking locals to point you in the direction of the mines, but no one will admit knowing anything about the mines. Perhaps they really don't know anything about them. Regardless, this country town with no tourist services is pleasant to tour. Just don't expect to see any gold mines.

Buses leave Chitré for Las Minas hourly (US$1.50, one hour). To leave Las Minas, catch any bus heading toward your next destination and make transfers as warranted. For example, if your destination is Santiago, take a northbound bus to the Interamericana; if the driver heads east (away from Santiago) upon reaching the highway, hop off and catch a westbound bus.

OCÚ
pop 8200

This sleepy town, 49km by road southeast of bustling Santiago, is distinguished by its hat makers. Not long ago, Ocú – which straddles a loop road that links it and the major Herrera Province towns of Chitré, Pesé, Los Pozos and Las Minas – used to be where Panamanians went to buy the finest Panama-style hats made in their country; now people often go to Penonomé, in Coclé Province.

Be advised that there are no hotels in Ocú. However, there is a Banco Nacional de Panamá, a post office and a couple of decent restaurants.

Hat Makers

Until the 1990s, Ocú's many hat makers took their intricately braided merchandise to the town square every morning and sold all they had by noon. Truckers, who were major hat buyers, used to make special trips to Ocú for their headgear. But once good-quality hats became available in Penonomé, which is conveniently located on the Interamericana, the truckers stopped making the special trip, and the hat makers began selling to vendors who resell the hats in Penonomé.

Today, there are still 20 to 25 hat makers in Ocú, and if you wish, you can visit some of them and see how a genuine Panama hat is made – with great patience and attention to detail. The finest are so tightly braided that you can turn them over and fill them with water, and they won't leak. Of course, don't expect to leave a hat maker's home (they all work out of their homes) without a little soft sell. The time needed to make a hat varies from one week to one month. The cost ranges from US$25 to US$150.

The hat makers are always women. If you ask one why, you'll get the same answer every time: Men's fingers are too large and clumsy for the intricate work involved in making superior hats!

If you decide to visit a hat maker, go see Elena Montilla and/or Ezequela Maure. They live only two houses apart at the northern end of town on the main street, Avenida Central. To find their houses, drive or walk about 1km on Avenida Central from the town plaza until you reach a fork in the road (a dirt road splits to the left, while the main paved road sweeps right; if

you pass the Jorón El Tijera, in the fork of the road, you've gone too far). Ezequela's house is on the left side of the street, about four houses south of the fork. Elena's house is two doors down. None of Ocú's hat makers speaks English.

Special Events

The Festival del Manito, one of the country's best folklore programs, is held in Ocú, usually during the third week in August (check with IPAT for dates). The three-day festival was established to maintain the region's traditional culture, and during it folklore groups from throughout Herrera Province present their dances in traditional dress. The fiesta's climax is a Sunday-morning church wedding, after which the couple is paraded through the streets on horseback by friends and family.

Ocú is also famous for its patron saint festival, usually held January 20 to 23 (check with IPAT, as the dates are flexible). During this festival, an effigy of St Sebastian is paraded through the streets at night, and devotees walk behind the statue carrying lighted candles. The festival includes folklore programs and an agricultural fair.

CRUCE DE OCÚ

At the intersection of the Ocú highway and the Interamericana, there's an Accel station and a Texaco station. Between the two is a small field that borders the Interamericana. Most buses traveling this section of the Interamericana, including the David-Panama City buses, stop beside the field to pick up and drop off passengers. There's no identifiable bus stop. If you're in Ocú and trying to get back to the Interamericana and from there go elsewhere, catch any bus leaving the main square in Ocú that's heading north, and at Cruce de Ocú transfer to a bus going in the direction you want to be going.

Be advised that *Café Daytona* beside the Accel station has terrific food, including a 'mega Texas hamburger with cheese' for US$2.70. Every item here is made to order – nothing is premade, not even the meat patties. The burger tastes especially good with the 'Turtle Love,' a milkshake flavored with lemon, grapefruit and orange juice and fresh milk (US$1.75 for 11 delicious ounces!). The restaurant's Greek owner and chef, Antonio Joannou, takes great pride in his inexpensive and tasty food – and it shows. It's open 7 am to 11 pm daily.

Los Santos Province

pop 83,500

This province, covering the southeastern third of the Península de Azuero, is home to cowboys, statuesque people and gorgeous beaches. It was here that Panama's cry for independence from Spain was first uttered. And yet the residents of The Saints Province take great pride in its Spanish history, and they show it in folkloric festivals that date back to the first settlers.

The Fiesta de Corpus Christi, in Villa de Los Santos, and the Fiesta de Santa Librada, in the provincial capital of Las Tablas, are marked by exuberant displays of traditional clothing and dances born in Spain during the Middle Ages. The most intricate *polleras* –

Highlights

- The people of Los Santos Province – some of the friendliest and most animated on earth
- Celebrations such as Las Tablas' Carnaval and Villa de Los Santos' Corpus Christi bash
- Isla Caña, whose beaches are visited each year by thousands of sea turtles
- Dressmakers who create *polleras*, the beautiful national costume, in La Enea and Santo Domingo
- Playa Venao, one of Panama's finest surfing beaches and also one of its most beautiful

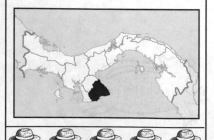

the national costume that is an elaboration on the dresses worn by Spanish peasants during the 17th and 18th centuries – are made in the village of La Enea and in villages around Las Tablas.

As in Herrera Province, in Los Santos Province many locals look distinctly European. The people are taller, their skin fairer, their features more chiseled than those of people elsewhere on the isthmus. Their eyes are often hazel or blue. Some people have red or blond hair. In Los Santos more than in any other province of Panama, the European bloodline is apparent and the whites want to keep it that way.

Yet for at least the past 100 years, the residents of Los Santos Province have known only racial harmony, and their sense of community pride is so strong that one wonders if it's hereditary. If you meet a black, Indian or white Los Santos native in another part of the country you'll surely know it, as he or she will tell you in short order.

If you speak Spanish, you'll notice a few things about the people of Los Santos Province: They often end their sentences with an 'eh' (it rhymes with *hey* and *say*). They also say 'chi' a lot (it rhymes with *lie* and *cry*, and it's short for a common local euphemism). They also tell stories with great flair.

VILLA DE LOS SANTOS
pop 7200

The Río La Villa, 4km south of downtown Chitré, marks the boundary between the provinces of Herrera and Los Santos, and it is just south of that river that one comes to Villa de Los Santos (often called simply 'Los Santos'), on the Carretera Nacional.

This picturesque town, replete with many colonial structures, is where Panama's first cry for independence from Spain was heard, on November 10, 1821. The event is honored with a museum and an annual celebration. Also worth a look is the old church. There's a good hotel and a wild bar/ dance club in town too.

LOS SANTOS PROVINCE

LOS SANTOS PROVINCE

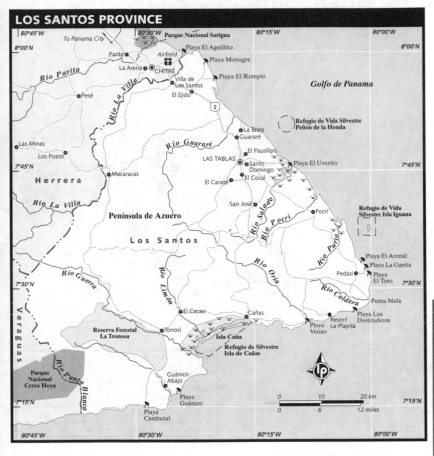

Information

There's an IPAT tourist office (% 966-8013, fax 996-8040) on Calle José Vallarino beside the Parque Simón Bolívar. The brochures here are in Spanish, and the staff of three speaks Spanish only. The best reason to contact these people is to ask if they know of any upcoming celebrations in the area.

There's also a Banco Nacional de Panamá, a police station and a pharmacy in town, as well as a laundry (Lavamatico Chele; open 8 am to 6 pm Monday to Saturday, 9 am to noon Sunday).

Museo de la Nacionalidad

This unimpressive museum, opposite Parque Simón Bolívar, occupies the former house where Panama's Declaration of Independence was signed in 1821. In the years that followed, the handsome brick-and-tile residence served as a jail, a school and a legislature. It predates the town's church, but no one knows exactly when it was built. Inaugurated as a museum in 1974, it was one of the first specialized museums in the country.

The museum contains artifacts related to Panama's independence, which was declared

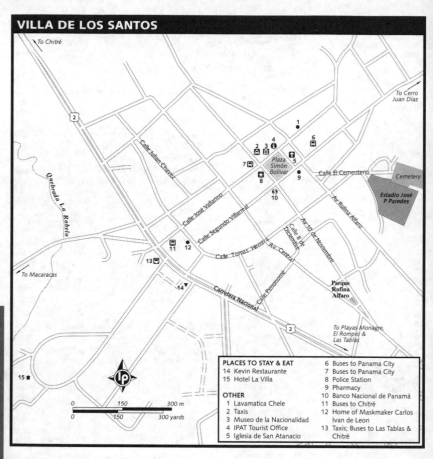

VILLA DE LOS SANTOS

To Chitré

To Cerro Juan Díaz

Calle Julian Chaves

Quebrada La Robela

Plaza Simón Bolívar

Calle El Cementerio

Cemetery

Estadio José P Paredes

To Macaracas

Calle José Vallarino

Calle Segundo Villarreal

Av Rufina Alfaro

Av 10 de Noviembre

Calle 8 de Diciembre

Calle Tomás Herrera Av Central

Carretera Nacional

Calle Pentonomir

Parque Rufina Alfaro

To Playas Monagre, El Rompio & Las Tablas

PLACES TO STAY & EAT
14   Kevin Restaurante
15   Hotel La Villa

OTHER
1   Lavamatica Chele
2   Taxis
3   Museo de la Nacionalidad
4   IPAT Tourist Office
5   Iglesia de San Atanacio

6   Buses to Panama City
7   Buses to Panama City
8   Police Station
9   Pharmacy
10   Banco Nacional de Panamá
11   Buses to Chitré
12   Home of Maskmaker Carlos Ivan de Leon
13   Taxis; Buses to Las Tablas & Chitré

0   150   300 m
0   150   300 yards

in Los Santos 18 days before it was declared by the government, as well as objects from the era of the Spanish conquest. Pre-Columbian ceramics and colonial-era religious art comprise most of the exhibits. There's a lovely garden courtyard in back. It's open 9 am to 4:30 pm Tuesday to Saturday and 9 am to 1 pm Sunday; admission costs US$1/25¢ for adults/children.

Iglesia de San Atanacio

Villa de Los Santos' church, alongside Parque Simón Bolívar, opened its doors to the public in 1782, after nine years of con-

struction. It is a fine example of the Baroque style – lots of intricately carved wood depicting cherubs, saints, Jesus and the Virgin. Almost everything in the church is original, and some of the objects even predate the structure itself. The 12m arch in front of the altar, for example, bears its date of manufacture (1733) and the names of its two creators.

The altar is made of mahogany and rosewood and covered nearly from base to top in gold leaf. Figurines of the Virgin, angels and Jesus adorn it. In a glass sepulcher in front of the altar is a near-life-size wooden statue of Christ that is carried through the streets of Villa de Los Santos on Good Friday, behind a candlelit procession.

In the interior walls of the church are headstones, and behind them are the remains of the church's ministers. Note the black Christ in the altar against the southeastern wall. While inside the church, look above the entrance, where you'll see a balcony; the choir sang from it in years past.

The original church bells have been moved to the Museo de Arte Religioso Colonial in Panama City; those that are in the steeple today were cast in 1907. This church was granted national monument status by the government in 1938 and is truly a national treasure.

Masks

Carlos Ivan de Leon makes the most elaborate and frightening masks in Panama. He specializes in one kind of mask, that of the devil for the famous *baile de los diablos sucios* (dance of the dirty devils). Most of Carlos' masks are sold to professional dancers, but increasingly they are being bought by European and American collectors. Several are on display at the IPAT office here in Los Santos, while others appear in the lobby of the Hotel Versalles in Chitré.

Carlos charges a minimum of US$150 for his two-foot-wide masks, each of which takes him on average 15 days to make. Unfortunately, the demand for his masks prevents him from keeping more than one or two on hand at any time. Before making a special trip to his home just to see a mask, you'd be wise to call to see if he's got any available to show or sell. The best time to reach Carlos (☎ 966-9149) is noon to 1 pm and 6 to 10 pm. Carlos speaks only Spanish; if you don't speak the language, ask someone who does to place the call for you.

Oddly, when Carlos isn't making devil masks, he's making concrete angels for churches; that's the source of most of his income. Carlos' home is located on Calle Tomas Herrera near Calle Segundo Villareal. Look for the house with a black front door and a sign with his family name (De Leon) nearby.

(For information on one of Panama's other top mask makers, see the Parita section of the Herrera Province chapter.)

Special Events

The anniversary of the cry for independence is celebrated in Los Santos each November 10, or the nearest Saturday to it. Other notable festivals include Carnaval (celebrated four days before Ash Wednesday, February/March), Semana Santa (Holy Week, April), the Feria de Azuero (the Azuero Fair, late April/early May) and the Fiesta de Corpus Christi (Thursday to Sunday, 40 days after Easter, May/June).

The Feria de Azuero features folkloric dancing, agricultural attractions and competition among local singers performing regional songs. The Corpus Christi festival, one of the most animated in the country, draws masked and costumed dancers who represent angels, devils, imps and other figures while enacting dramas.

The exact dates of all these events vary from year to year. Contact IPAT or a tour operator for precise dates.

Places to Stay & Eat

The *Hotel La Villa* (☎ 966-9321, fax 966-8201), 500m from the Carretera Nacional in the southwestern section of town, is a bit on the pricey side; if you're on a tight budget, you'll get more value for your money in nearby Chitré. There are 38 rooms at the Villa, including small singles/doubles with air con and private bathrooms for US$20/27 Monday to Thursday and US$26/33 the rest of the week. There are standard rooms (the hotel generously calls them 'suites') with air con, private bathrooms and firm beds for US$31/38 Monday to Thursday and US$40/47 the rest of the week. The hotel has a swimming pool, a bar and a good restaurant.

Kevin's Hotel (☎ 966-8276, fax 966-9000), set back a little way from the Carretera Nacional, features 20 new-in-2000 guestrooms, each with air con, DirecTV, two double beds and private hot-water bathrooms. This is a much better option than the Hotel La Villa, though more expensive for lone travelers at

US$33 per room. The hotel's restaurant, which is open 8 am to 9 pm, is also very good and reasonably priced. Specials include *chuleta a la barbecue* (barbecue pork chops, US$4.50) and *cacerola de mariscos* (seafood casserole, US$8).

Getting There & Away
Chitré-Las Tablas buses stop on the Carretera Nacional. Chitré-Villa de Los Santos buses stop on Calle José Vallarino half a block from the Carretera Nacional. Fares to these destinations or anywhere in the province are usually between 50¢ and US$2.

Buses to Panama City depart from two stops: one is on Calle José Vallarino at Avenida 10 de Noviembre, and the other is on Calle Segundo Villarreal a block and a half north of Parque Simón Bolívar.

Getting Around
Taxis are the best way to get around Villa de Los Santos and between Villa de Los Santos and Chitré, if you don't feel like walking. The fare won't exceed US$3 if you stay within these cities. Taxis can usually be found near the bus stop on the Carretera Nacional and northwest of Parque Simón Bolívar.

PLAYAS MONAGRE & EL ROMPÍO
Ten kilometers northeast of Villa de Los Santos are the Playas Monagre and El Rompío. Both beaches are popular with fishermen, families and body surfers, but beware of possible rip currents (see Swimming Safety in the Facts for the Visitor chapter for information on rip currents). El Rompío is less frequented than Monagre and has less litter, but both have a lot of driftwood on them and the sand is dark and hot on sunny days. Both have a couple of simple, open-sided restaurants serving shrimp, sea bass and squid. There are a couple of inexpensive inns nearby.

A bus leaves the Chitré station for Playas Monagre and El Rompío hourly from sunrise to sunset. The roughly 20km ride to either destination costs US$1 each way. This bus passes through Villa de Los Santos on the way to the beaches and can be hailed from the Carretera Nacional in town. Look for a bus with 'Monagre' on its windshield. The fare from Villa de Los Santos to either beach is 50¢. A taxi ride from Chitré to either beach costs about US$5; a taxi from Villa de Los Santos costs half that.

ROAD TO LAS TABLAS
The Carretera Nacional from Villa de Los Santos to Las Tablas runs mostly past small farms and cattle ranches. There's no forest in sight. The men of this province are so proud of their ability to fell trees that they've denuded most of the province. Many have since relocated to Darién Province, where they work for lumber companies.

About 3km southeast of Los Santos along the Carretera Nacional is **Kiosco El Ciruelo**, a rustic trucker stop where everything is cooked on a wood-fire grill. The most popular item sold here is a traditional specialty of Los Santos Province: tamales made with old corn, salt, onions, chilis, pepper, tomato, garlic, soy sauce, Worcestershire sauce and a chunk of pork all wrapped up in a plantain leaf (40¢). This institution, which opened for business in 1970, sells 500 of them a day. It's open 6 am to 10 pm Friday, Saturday and Sunday; closed the rest of the week.

From Kiosco El Ciruelo, travel 5.6km southeast, and on the eastern side of the road you'll see a bright blue public phone and just beyond it a small hut beside a large pile of coconut husks. The hut is named **La Casa de la Pipa** (The House of Coconut Juice), and here owner Nelson Robles reaches into an oversize fridge, pulls out a cold coconut, hacks a hole into it with a machete, and serves it to a customer with a straw. On a good day, he goes through the drill 600 times. The coconuts cost him 15¢ each and he sells them for 25¢.

The coconut is still in its thick green husk when it's handed to you, so the fruit is quite large – about the size of a human head. The proper way to drink the semisweet yet raw-tasting juice is to raise the coconut to your lips, tilt your head back and guzzle. Even though the juice is clear, try not to spill any on your clothes; it stains terribly. Coconut juice (or 'milk,' as they call it here) is said to be very good for your kidneys.

As you travel the two-lane Carretera Nacional toward Las Tablas, you'll occasionally see stands with sausages dangling in front of them. The **pork sausages** made on the Península de Azuero are nationally famous for their delicious taste, but avoid the ones sold at these stands – you don't know how long they've been around. If you like sausages, you might want to get some at one of the grocery stores on the peninsula.

If you're traveling the highway around Carnaval time, you'll also see dozens of smashed-up cars on the roadside. These cars belonged to motorists killed by drunk drivers during Carnaval. The police realize that most of the people on the road during Carnaval are intoxicated. Instead of trying to arrest all the drunk motorists, the police display the old wrecks, hoping the sight will encourage drunks to drive slowly. Try to avoid highway travel during Carnaval.

GUARARÉ
pop 3900

The tiny town of Guararé, on the Carretera Nacional between Villa de Los Santos and Las Tablas, offers little of interest to tourists, but it does have some attractions, including a museum, nearby pollera makers and a large annual festival.

Museo Manuel F Zárate

Zárate was a folklorist who was devoted to conserving the traditions and folklore of the Azuero region. The museum, in Zárate's former home, contains polleras, masks, *diablito* (little devil) costumes and other exhibits. It's two blocks behind the not-so-impressive church, about six short blocks from the main road (turn off at the Delta fuel station). It's open 8 am to noon and 12:45 to 4 pm Tuesday to Saturday and 8 am to noon Sunday. Admission costs 75¢/25¢ for adults/children.

La Enea

Some of the finest **polleras** are made in this small village northeast of Guararé. The

pollera, once nothing more than the daily attire of the lower classes of 17th- and 18th-century Spain, has become today an entire national costume of stirring beauty and elegance. Almost every part of the costume is made by hand, from the attractive embroidery on the blouse and skirt to the delicate filigree ornaments tucked around the gold combs in the hair.

The traditional assortment of jewelry worn with a pollera consists of three to seven gold neck chains, two to five combs trimmed with gold and pearls, a dagger-shaped ornament once used to relieve the itching caused by the combs, a bracelet, earrings, four gold buttons on the waistband, buckles on the shoes, small ornaments worn over the temples and 12 pairs of delicate hair ornaments. The jewelry alone can cost US$50,000, and often does.

One of the best-known makers of the national costume lives beside Parque de La Enea, in the green-tiled house next door to the small market with 'Roxana' painted over its door. The dressmaker's name is Ildama Saavedra de Espino (☎ 994-5527), and she made her first pollera in 1946 at the age of 16. She's been making them ever since, averaging one pollera every six months. Ildama sold her first dress for US$300. Today, she charges US$1800 per dress.

By convention, the pollera consists of two basic pieces: a blouse that rests upon the tops of the shoulders and a long skirt divided into two fully gathered tiers. Each dress requires no less than 10m of fine white linen or cotton cloth. Elaborate needlework in a single color enriches the white background. Flowers, leaves, vines and fruits are the common motifs.

Anyone with a keen interest in needlecraft is welcome to visit Ildama, who speaks Spanish only. She is accustomed to strangers stopping by her home to marvel at her handiwork. If you're lucky, Ildama will show you her scrapbook, containing photos of many of the dresses she's made. Be advised that every dress is made to order. She does not have a rack of polleras on hand, but rather just sections of the one she's working on.

Special Events

Like most towns in Los Santos Province, Guararé is not without at least one festival, in this case the Feria de la Mejorana, a combined patron saint and folkloric festival held September 23 to 27. As in all patron saint festivals, a statue of a saint is paraded through the streets.

The folkloric festival, however, is very different from others in Panama. It is the country's largest. Begun by Manuel Zárate in 1950 to stimulate interest and participation in traditional practices, the Feria de la Mejorana has become the best place to see Panama's folklore in all its manifestations. Dance groups from all over the country – and even some from other Latin American countries – attend this annual event. There is even a colorful parade in which participants are hauled through the streets in oxcarts.

Folkloric dances that were once part of other celebrations in other places are today sometimes seen only at this event. For example, this is the only festival in which a dance known as La Pajarita (Paper Bird) is performed. The dance was once part of the Corpus Christi celebration in Villa de Los Santos, but is no longer. In contrast to the various exuberant devil dances, a calm, religious quality pervades La Pajarita, and the dancers' costumes are simple and unique.

Over dark trousers and a short-sleeved shirt, each dancer wears two tiers of yellow streamers made from palm leaves, one around the neck and the other around the waist. Dancers wear tall hats shaped like bishop's miters, usually made of leather and covered with patches of brightly colored paper. Each dancer carries a maraca (a hollow-gourd rattle containing pebbles or beans) wrapped in a white handkerchief. A single guitar accompanies the Pajarita, which may involve as many as 10 male dancers. Rhythmic patterns and chord progressions indicate when the dancers should change positions. The men shake their maracas in unison throughout the dance, following the underlying beat of the guitar. Taking their instructions from the music of the guitar, the dancers form two parallel lines and kneel before a cross. The dance is simple and complicated, peculiar and logical. It's one of many performed at this most interesting fair.

Getting There & Away

Guararé is beside the Carretera Nacional, 20km south of Villa de Los Santos. La Enea is to its northeast. You can hop on any bus that travels the highway in the direction of Guararé; you'll be dropped off at the town.

To get to La Enea, take a taxi (US$2).

LAS TABLAS
pop 8000

Las Tablas is the capital city of Los Santos Province and has a fine church and a small museum devoted to former Las Tablas statesman and three-time president Belisario Porras. The city is famous for its Carnaval, widely regarded as Panama's most authentic. This city is also famous for its combined patron saint/pollera festival – a fun brew of religious ceremony and beauty contest.

Orientation

Las Tablas is 31km southeast of Chitré via the Carretera Nacional and 282km southwest of Panama City via the Carretera Interamericana and the Carretera Nacional. The Carretera Nacional becomes Avenida Laureano Lopez at the northern edge of town and reemerges as the road to Santo Domingo on the southeastern side of town. Avenida Laureano Lopez runs for nine blocks before ending at the Museo Belisario Porras, beside the central plaza.

Almost everything of interest to the tourist is within five blocks of the plaza. This includes remnants of one of the finest colonial churches on the peninsula, two banks, a post office, two decent hotels and several restaurants. Out a little farther is a bus station, as well as two taxi stands for the newly arrived.

Information

There is no tourist office in town. However, there's a Mercado de Artesanias on the

LAS TABLAS

To Guararé,
Villa de Los Santos
& Chitré

To El
Pausílipo

To Playa
El Uverito

To Santo Domingo,
Pedasí & Tonosí

PLACES TO STAY & EAT
5 Hotel Las Tablas;
   Supermercado Las Tablas
8 Jorón Moravel
11 Hotel Hospedaje Zafiro
14 Hotel Piamonte
15 Restaurante El Caserón

OTHER
1 Mercado de Artesanías
2 Bus Station
3 Lavandería Popular
4 Post Office
6 Banco Nacional de Panamá
7 Taxis
9 Iglesia Santa Librada
10 Museo Belisario Porras
12 Banco del Istmo
13 Café Internet
16 Taxis

Carretera Nacional coming into town; it's not well stocked but the staff might be able to answer your questions. It's open 8 am to 4 pm Monday to Saturday.

There's a Café Internet (☎ 994-0184) on the corner of Calles Belisario Porras and Los Santos, which charges US$1.50 an hour. It's open 9 am to 8 pm Monday to Saturday, and 9 am to noon Sunday.

There's a Banco Nacional de Panamá on Avenida Laureano Lopez near Calle 2 and a Banco del Istmo on Calle Belisario Porras. The post office is on Calle 2. A laundry (Lavandería Popular; open 8 am to noon and

1 to 5 Monday to Saturday) is on Calle Doctor Emilio Castro.

Museo Belisario Porras

This museum is in the mud-walled former home of three-time president Belisario Porras, during whose administration the Panama Canal opened. Porras, who is regarded as a national hero, was president for all but two years from 1912 to 1924. He is credited with establishing Panama's network of public hospitals, creating a national registry for land titles, and constructing scores of bridges and aqueducts.

Among the many artifacts on display are Porras' law school diploma, a post from his canopy bed and his presidential sash. Note that the sash has only seven stars, one for each of Panama's provinces at the time Porras entered office; the country has nine provinces today because Porras divided two of the original seven to create Herrera and Los Santos.

Incidentally, the huge tomb inside the museum, which bears Porras' name, is empty. Plans to move his remains here from a cemetery in Panama City were never carried out. Interestingly, all of Porras' male descendants wear their whiskers in his unusual style – a thick, prideful mustache resembling the horns of a Texas longhorn steer.

The museum, opposite Central Plaza, is open 9 am to 12:30 pm and 1:30 to 4 pm Tuesday to Saturday and 9 am to noon Sunday. Admission costs 50¢/25¢ for adults/children.

Iglesia Santa Librada

This Baroque-style church near the central plaza opened its doors on March 9, 1789, but sustained major damage in 1950 in a fire set off by faulty wiring. Of the structure, only the walls are original. The base of the pulpit is original as well. The painted faces on the ornate 23-karat gold-leaf altar are original, but the figurines of Christ, the Virgin and the saints were added after the blaze. Cedar wood was used in the construction of the altar, which was being renovated in 2001.

Special Events

Las Tablas is perhaps the best place in Panama to spend Carnaval, which is held during the four days that precede Ash Wednesday. By tradition, the town is divided into two groups, *calle arriba* (high street) and *calle abajo* (low street), which compete intensely with each other in every aspect of the fiesta. Each calle has its own queen, floats and songs. Each day begins with members parading in street clothes, singing songs that poke fun at the rival group. During the parade, jokesters from both sides toss tinted water, blue dye and

shaving cream at the other side. No one, onlookers included, is spared; dress expecting to get creamed.

Both sides take a rest during the heat of the day and don costumes or put finishing touches on their floats in the late afternoon. Then at dusk, the groups' parades begin on parallel streets, led by floats that are followed by musicians seated in the back of flatbed trucks, who are followed in turn by calle members. Every night, each calle has a different float and different costumes. Crowds pack the sidewalks and fireworks light up the night. The queens make their appearances on Saturday night, dressed at first in gaudily decorated costumes and later in exquisite evening gowns. Their coronation is held on Sunday. Monday is masquerade day, and Tuesday all the women in town who have polleras don them and fill the streets with color and beauty.

Another excellent time to be in Las Tablas is July 21, when the provincial capital hosts two big events: the Fiesta de Santa Librada and the Festival de La Pollera. The highlight of the patron saint festival is the procession through the streets. The sacred event and services inside the church are accompanied by street celebrations that recall a medieval fair – gambling, dancing, singing, bullfights, and excessive eating and drinking. It's a strange juxtaposition of the sacred and the profane. The pollera festival is a photographer's delight. Beautiful young women model the national costume as they pass through the streets, all the while being judged on their grace as well as on the artisanship, design and the authenticity of their costumes. The scene is like a slice of Spain dropped into Panama, which is the intention.

Places to Stay

A handful of budget lodgings in town are unabashed whorehouses or 'push buttons,' places where married people conduct affairs. The hotels mentioned here are neither.

Hotel Piamonte (☎ 994-6372), on Calle Belisario Porras, was rebuilt in 2001 and offers an excellent value in its 15 guestrooms (all on the second floor, above a restaurant-bar). Singles/doubles with air con, private hot-water bathrooms, telephone and TV cost US$14/18. The owner speaks English.

Hotel Hospedaje Zafiro (☎/fax 994-8200), on Calle Belisario Porras, offers nine second-story rooms. Clean and cheerful singles/doubles with air con, color TV and private cold-water bathrooms are a good value at US$15/18. There's an upstairs balcony where guests can look out over the central plaza.

The new *Hotel Las Tablas* (☎ 994-6366, ☎/fax 994-7422), located above the Supermercado Las Tablas on the corner of Calle 2 and Avenida Laureano Lopez, is very nice and offers 15 air-con rooms with TV and private hot-water bathrooms for US$25.

Places to Eat
On Calle 1, *Jorón Moravel*, a very pleasant and attractive, open-sided restaurant under a thatch roof, specializes in pizzas, the most expensive of which is the family-size *especial* with shrimp for US$9. Most pizzas are under US$5. Sandwiches, fresh fish and many grilled items are also available. It's open 7 am to midnight daily.

Perhaps the best restaurant in town is the fan-cooled *Restaurante El Caserón*, on the corner of Calles Augustin Batista and Moises Espino. Breakfast items include the popular *especial ranchero* (steak and eggs, US$3.75), lunch and dinner items include chow mein (US$4), beef steaks (US$3 to US$5.57) and fish (US$6.50).

Getting There & Away
Las Tablas' bus station is on Avenida Laureano Lopez at Avenida Doctor Emilio Castro. Hourly buses connect Las Tablas with Santo Domingo (30¢, 10 minutes, 5km), Chitré (US$1, 30 minutes, 31km), Tonosí (US$3, 1½ hours, 79km) and other places. There's also a daily service to Pedasí (US$2, one hour, 41km) and Playa Venao (US$3, two hours, 68km).

There are 10 daily departures to Panama City (US$6.50), more during holidays and festivals.

Getting Around
Las Tablas is a small town and is very easily walked. However, taxis are available for hire. You can find a taxi stand on Calle 1, two blocks north of the central plaza, and another is on Calle Belisario Porras at Calle Estudiante. Fares within town never exceed US$2.

AROUND LAS TABLAS
El Pausílipo
In the countryside a few kilometers from town is El Pausílipo, the former country estate of Belisario Porras. His surname means 'tranquillity' in Greek; it's easy to see how the Las Tablas statesman would have treasured the tranquillity here.

The humble residence is located in a park-like setting. The small home has adobe walls covered with a cement sheet that is painted white with a sky-blue trim, just as it was during Porras' lifetime. Most of the rooms are empty today, but one contains handsome leather chairs and a fine table.

The tiny separate structure beside the residence is the original kitchen; kitchens in Porras' day were usually set apart from the living quarters to lessen the likelihood that a kitchen fire would destroy the entire house. A well with a pump was sunk on the property in 1917, and with 60 or 70 vigorous pumps water still reaches the surface.

El Pausílipo and the grounds around it are open 9 am to 4 pm Tuesday to Saturday and 8 am to noon Sunday. Admission is free. The easiest way to get there is to take a taxi from Las Tablas. For US$5, a taxi driver will take you to the former estate, wait while you take a look around and then return you to the city.

Santo Domingo
If you're in the market for Panama's **polleras**, the beautiful national costume, you'll want to know that there are several places besides Guararé where the colorfully embroidered dresses are made. Keep in mind that the polleras may cost US$2000 apiece.

The small town of Santo Domingo, about 10 minutes from Las Tablas by car, is known for its fine polleras, as are the nearby hamlets of **La Tiza**, **El Cocal**, **El Carate** and **San José**. If you haven't got wheels, your best bet is to hire a taxi. San José, the most remote of the bunch, will set you back US$40 for the roundtrip. Rides to the other communities won't cost you half as much. San José is also known for its guitars, although they are not particularly good by international standards.

Playa El Uverito

The best beach in the vicinity of Las Tablas is Playa El Uverito, 11km away. Still, this is a dark-sand, driftwood-strewn beach – nothing special. There are kiosks selling sodas, but there are no places to stay. It is not reachable by bus – a taxi will take you there from Las Tablas for US$5.

PEDASÍ
pop 1900

This pleasant coastal town of friendly souls, 41km southeast of Las Tablas, makes a good base for exploration of the area's beaches. It is also from Pedasí that many people make forays to the Refugio de Vida Silvestre Isla Iguana, a wildlife refuge that offers some fine snorkeling and diving.

Orientation & Information

The Carretera Nacional passes down the western part of Pedasí; it is a low-speed, two-lane road with little traffic as it slices through town. There are some fine beaches (see following) a few kilometers to the east. There are a couple of very comfortable places to stay in town, and there's good food to be had. But there are no banks in Pedasí, nor is there a tourist office or post office; if you have postage you can leave your letters with your hotel to be picked up by the postal agent. There are pay phones around town.

Playas El Toro & La Garita

The surf at these beaches (Bull Beach and Gatekeeper's Box Beach, respectively) is usually safe for swimming; this is particularly true at La Garita, but El Toro is the more accessible of the two. At El Toro you can actually drive onto the beach if you have a vehicle, but La Garita is flanked by a

rocky slope, and a hike of about 100m through light scrub and dirt (mud if there's been any recent rain) is required to reach the beach. Despite their proximity to Pedasí, both beaches are quite isolated and private. However, neither offers an opportunity for snorkeling – the water is simply too murky.

Unfortunately, neither beach is served by buses, and because Pedasí is so small, it isn't served by taxis. To reach these beaches, you'll need to have your own vehicle, plan on doing some walking, or stand by the road that goes to the beaches and try to coax a lift out of someone heading toward the ocean. To drive to the sand from central Pedasí, turn east off the Carretera Nacional onto the paved street beside the Pensión Moscoso, and drive about 250m to the Cantina Hermanos Cedeño bar. Then take the dirt road just past the bar for 1km until the road forks. Follow the signs to the beaches, which are 2km farther along.

Special Events

Pedasí holds patron saint festivals on June 29 and November 25, or the nearest Saturday. These are fun affairs, with long parades and lots of merriment. On July 16, there's a

---

Rescuing the Tuna

Thirty kilometers southwest of Pedasí, on the southern side of the road, is the entrance to the Laboratorio Achotines, where a group of US marine biologists studies the early life of yellowfin tuna. Their research has played a key role in the implementation of fishing quotas to protect the tuna stock in Pacific Ocean waters from California to Ecuador. Their recommendations to an international regulatory commission on the use of certain types of fishing nets have also played a direct role in reducing the number of dolphins that are killed by tuna fishing in the eastern Pacific, from 500,000 annually to 3000. The research center is not open to the general public.

celebration for fishermen held at Playa Arenal, a beach 3km northwest of town.

Places to Stay

There are three places to stay in Pedasí, all of which offer good values and are located on the Carretera Nacional.

Pensión Moscoso (☎ 995-2303) offers 19 double rooms, 16 of which have air con and all of which have local TV and private cold-water bathrooms. The rooms with no air con rent for US$11, the others from US$16.50 to US$22. The owner is related to Panama's president, Mireya Moscoso, who is from Pedasí.

Hotel Residencial Pedasí (☎/fax 995-2322), near the northern end of town, has 17 comfortable singles/doubles, all with air con and cold-water private bathrooms, for US$17/22. There is a restaurant on the premises.

Dim's Hostal (☎/fax 995-2303) is a bed and breakfast in a lovely family home attended to by the amiable Mirna Batista. Each of the five rooms features one double bed and two singles, and a private cold-water bathroom (Dim's only drawback). The cost is US$20 per room, up to three people per room. Breakfast is served in the backyard under a grand mango tree. There are hammocks to relax in and bicycles to rent (US$3 an hour). This is the best hotel in Pedasí.

Places to Eat

A good French restaurant, *Restaurante JR*, is 100m south of the Hotel Residencial Pedasí, on the opposite side of the street. The owner-cook-server was a chef in France and Canada before he 'retired' to Pedasí. The menu varies daily but often includes flaming pepper steak, chicken curry with seafood, and garlic lobster (all priced around US$12). It's open noon to 1 pm and 6 to 8 pm.

If you have a sweet tooth, be sure to try a slice of cake at *Dulceria Yely*, opposite and 50m down a side street from the Pensión Moscoso. Slices of Mrs Dalila Vera de Quintero's delicious cakes sell for 25¢, and they are divine. Her rum cake is glorious, as is her *manjar* cake (manjar resembles caramel in taste and appearance and is a specialty of the region). Also sold here is *chicheme*, a wonderful drink made from milk, mashed sweet corn, cinnamon and vanilla (25¢). The desserts served to Panama's president are purchased here. It'll interest some readers to know that Mrs Dalila's fanciest piece of cooking equipment is a small Hamilton Beach mixer.

Two blocks south of the Dulceria Yely is the colorfully painted *Restaurante Las Delicias*, which is a fine place to have a cheap, hearty breakfast. Three eggs with shredded beef and two cups of coffee cost less than US$3. The same can be said of the Restaurante Angela, at the northern end of town.

Getting There & Away

At least one bus an hour passes through this town. To proceed south, simply hail any southbound bus on the Carretera Nacional. Vice versa if you're heading north.

REFUGIO DE VIDA SILVESTRE ISLA IGUANA

The Iguana Island Wildlife Refuge is a 55-hectare protected island ringed by coral fields, much of which died in the 1982-83 El Niño (a change in weather patterns that shifts ocean currents and starves marine life along the eastern Pacific coast). However, the surviving coral is pretty spectacular and is shallow enough to be snorkeled.

Humpback whales inhabit the waters around Isla Iguana from June to November. These large sea mammals, 15m to 20m long, mate and bear their young here and then teach them to dive. The humpbacks are the famous 'singing whales'; occasionally you can hear their underwater sounds when you're diving here.

The island is supposed to be maintained by Panama's environmental agency, but the main beach is often strewn with litter. Also, the island was used for target practice by the US Navy during WWII, and unexploded ordnance is occasionally discovered here; you really don't want to stray off the island's beaten paths.

Isla Iguana is reachable by boat from Playa El Arenal, a beach 3km northwest of the Accel station in Pedasí. At the beach, boatman Lionel Ureña takes parties of up to eight people to the island for US$20 each way. Be sure to tell him when to return for you. Lionel speaks Spanish only.

In 2001, there was talk of a bus service to Playa El Arenal from Pedasí, but there was nothing definite. Mirna Batista at Dim's Hostal will likely know if the service now exists.

RESORT LA PLAYITA

This 'resort' (☎ 996-2225 in Chitré, ask for Guillermo Calderón), 31km southwest of Pedasí, consists of two lovely cabins, with private hot-water bathrooms and a caretaker's house. At this so-called resort, guests are expected to bring their own food, which the caretakers will gladly prepare. What's special about this place is its beach: La Playita is located beside a beautiful, long beach with (generally) no one on it.

At US$50 a night for a cabin *and* a beautiful beach to oneself, some people would view La Playita as a terrific find. But be advised that the driveway to the resort from the Carretera Nacional is 1.3km of road that requires a 4WD vehicle most of the time. If you've got your own wheels and are cruising the Azuero, you might want to drop by and see if La Playita appeals to you.

PLAYA VENAO

Playa Venao is a long, curving protected beach (no riptides) that's very popular with surfers because it almost always has waves to surf, and because the waves break both ways. (See Surfing in the Facts for the Visitor section for further information.)

The Playa Venao turnoff is 33km by road southwest of Pedasí, or 2km past the Resort La Playita turnoff. Facilities here are limited to an open-sided restaurant/bar and very rustic cabañas for US$16 a night. They'll do if you don't mind roughing it. An option is to bring a tent and camp beside the beach for free. There's a public phone beside the restaurant (☎ 995-8107).

Six northbound and six southbound buses pass the turnoff to Playa Venao daily. These buses are two-toned and have 'Tonosí-Chitré' on their windshields. If you want to catch one, just hail it. The cost to either city is US$4.

ISLA CAÑA

At the end of August and all through November, thousands of Olive Ridley sea turtles come ashore at night to lay eggs in the sand on the broad beach of Cane Island. This is one of five places that these endangered turtles nest in such numbers. The others: two beaches on the Pacific side of Costa Rica, and two beaches in Orissa, India, on the Bay of Bengal.

The turnoff for Isla Caña is easy to miss. It's beside a bus stop on the south side of the Carretera Nacional, 6.5km west of the turnoff for the town of Cañas; next to the bus stop, there's a brown-and-yellow sign that reads 'Bienvenidos Isla Caña via Puerto 2.5km.' The bus stop is served by Toyota Coaster buses that travel between Chitré and Tonosí hourly from 7 am to 4 pm.

From the turnoff, a 5km drive or hike on a dirt road takes you to the edge of a mangrove forest. There's usually a boatman there who will shuttle you to and from the island for US$5 per party. If there's no boatman to greet you, find the truck wheel hanging from a tree at the mangrove's edge

and hit it hard five times with the rusty wrench atop it. If the sun's out and the tide's up – if there's water in the mangrove – a boatman will fetch you.

Because one boatman was robbed of his boat motor at gunpoint when he responded to the clanging truck wheel at night, you either have to arrive during daylight hours or call ahead (☎ 995-8002) and, in Spanish, ask for boatman Pedro Perez and tell him when you'll be arriving.

Once you reach the island, you will be approached by a guide. As a rule every foreign visitor must be accompanied by an island guide. That's because these people would sell all the turtle eggs they could find on the black market if they couldn't make money from the turtles another way. As it is, about half of the turtle eggs that are laid on the beach are dug up and sold illegally in Panama City. The other half are placed in hatcheries.

The turtles arrive late at night, so there's no point in hiring the guide during daylight hours. Instead, agree on a meeting place and an hour when the guide can take you. When that time arrives, the guide will walk you across the island to the beach, and if you're lucky you'll arrive when many expectant mothers are arriving. Sea turtles are easily frightened, particularly by bright lights such as flashlights. Don't bring one. Instead, just let your eyes adjust to the moonlight and you'll be able to see just fine.

The guides speak Spanish only, so be prepared to state a time and a place to meet in Spanish; the guide will likely charge US$10 per party an hour when working (that was the price in early 2001, but there was talk of lowering it). At the time of writing, a restaurant and some cabañas had just opened. If you don't know Spanish, you might want to simply point at your watch and state a time ('once pm,' *own-SAY pay-emmay*, for example, for 11 pm), followed by 'Las cabañas' *(loss caban-YAS)*.

The three cabañas, which had neither a phone nor a name in early 2001, are fancooled with concrete floors, bamboo sides, thatched roofs and shared bathrooms. One cabin has two single beds (US$8) while the others have two double beds (US$10). Better built, air con cabins were planned for 2002. Bring a mosquito net and *lots* of insect repellent, long pants, a windbreaker or bug jacket and mosquito coils if you have them. Even if you have your own car and are not spending the night, you'll want protection from the mosquitoes the entire time you're on the island. Be sure to put some repellent on your ankles to keep the sand fleas at bay.

TONOSÍ
pop 2300
This cowboy town, 57km southwest of Pedasí, offers little of interest to the tourist. Its chief attractions are its scenery – the town is in a green valley ringed by tan hills – and its proximity to many isolated surfing beaches.

Tonosí's streets roughly follow a grid pattern. If you arrive from the north as most people do, you'll be on the Carretera a El Cacao from the town of El Cacao until you reach the center of Tonosí, where the highway intersects with Avenida Central, Tonosí's main street, which is flanked on both sides by homes.

There is a bank, a bar, a pool hall, a couple of restaurants and three hotels near the intersection of the Carretera a El Cacao and Avenida Central.

Places to Stay & Eat
The *Residencial Mar y Selva (☎ 995-8153/8003)* is on the Carretera a El Cacao as you enter town from the north. Located above the Restaurante Lindy, the hotel features 10 air-con guestrooms with private hot-water bathroom and four-channel TV. Most of the rooms contain a double bed with a single above it, bunk-bed style. Singles/doubles/triples cost US$18/20/24 – an excellent value.

The next-best housing option is *Hospedaje Irtha (☎/fax 995-8316)*, which offers 13 air-con singles/doubles with private cold-water showers for US$10/12. To get to it from the Carretera a El Cacao, take Calle Antonio Degracia one block. The Irtha will be on your right. Calle Antonio Degracia is one street north of Avenida Centra; one end of Calle Antonio Degracia is straight out front of the easily found Restaurante Lindy.

Near the intersection of Carretera a El Cacao and Avenida Central are **Pensión Boamy**, which is satisfactory, and **Pensión Rosyini**, which is mostly used by drunks to sleep off hangovers. Neither place has a phone; both are around US$10 per person.

The best place to chow down is **Restaurante Lindy**, which specializes in – surprise! – rural Panamanian food. There's nothing fancy about this open-sided diner, but after a long day of surfing or exploring or just lying on a beach, the food and the ice-cold sodas and beer taste great – and they're cheap. A dockworker's helping of beef stew and two beers will set you back only US$4.

AROUND TONOSÍ

Tonosí offers visitors a few services but no real attractions. There are a few natural attractions in the area, among them a feed-a-croc river activity near the restaurant of El Charcón and Playas Cambutal and Guánico.

El Charcón

This open-sided thatch-roofed restaurant/bar is 1km from the Restaurante Lindy on the road to Playa Guánico. It specializes in smoked and grilled meat, mostly beef and pork. The *carne de res humada* (smoked beef, US$2.75) tastes a lot like jerky and comes with side dishes, including a salad. The *pollo humado* (smoked chicken, US$2.50) is good, and it's also possible to order saltwater and freshwater shrimp. For breakfast, the owner recommends *egalo* (liver, onions and boiled potatoes, US$2.50). The food is very authentic for the region and good to try and good to eat. This is also a very pleasant place, made all the more so because of all the lovely hardwood (mostly corotú, found in Panama) used in its construction. It's open 7 am to 11 pm daily.

One hundred meters south of the restaurant and just below the road you'll see a slow-moving river that's home to cattle egrets, American caimen and yellow-eared

turtles. Check it out, but before you do ask the owner of El Charcón for a bag of fat to take with you to toss to the caimen. He'll gladly oblige for 25¢. Because the caimen (and the turtles) are accustomed to being fed by people, they'll move toward you the moment they see you. There's something intriguing about watching these reptiles feed, but be careful not to fall into the river – or they'll feed on you.

PLAYAS CAMBUTAL & GUÁNICO

Playas Cambutal and Guánico are two of the numerous beaches along the southern coast of the Península de Azuero that thrill most surfers. Both are reachable by dirt road from Tonosí, but neither is served by bus. If you don't have your own wheels, go to Restaurante Lindy and ask its owner to give you a ride and to pick you up at a certain time. Guánico is about 16km away from Tonosí, and Cambutal is about 22km away.

Taxi driver Ricuarte Dominguez (☎ 995-8491, cellular 696-6414), in Tonosí, can take you anywhere you want to go and be relied upon to pick you up. Try his cell phone first. He can sometimes be found at the Restaurante Lindy.

Give some thought to camping on the beaches if you're planning to be in the area during September or thereabouts. There aren't any stores near the beaches, but you can take some food with you from Restaurante Lindy or from a store. You'll likely see some nesting sea turtles if you're on the beaches in late August, September or early October.

MACARACAS

pop 2700

Little Macaracas, 57km northwest of Tonosí and 40km southwest of Chitré, is another small town bisected by a highway. It has nothing to offer the tourist in year-round attractions, but its annual folkloric festival, featuring the drama *The Three Wise Men,* is very popular. The festival is held January 5 to 10.

There are two banks in town, a couple of mediocre restaurants and one hotel, **Pensión Lorena** (☎ 995-4181), which consists of 11 rooms above a pharmacy. The hotel is on the main road and charges US$12/14 for singles/doubles with air con or US$8/12 without it.

Buses run between Macaracas and Chitré and Macaracas and Tonosí (US$2, one hour, hourly, from 7 am to 4 pm).

Coclé Province

Coclé – land of sugar, salt and presidents. More sugar has been refined in this province, more salt has been produced here, and more Panamanian presidents have been born in Coclé than in any other province in the country. These are facts in which the people of Coclé take great pride, but the province isn't without a lion's share of tourist attractions as well.

From the traveler's perspective, there are two Coclés: the mountainous and the coastal. The beautiful mountain town of El Valle (officially El Valle de Antón) is home to a popular Indian arts and crafts market, lovely nature scenes, some interesting petroglyphs from long ago and a rain forest–canopy ride that uses the suspen-

Highlights

- El Valle, home to an exotic Sunday handicrafts market and a wild rain forest–canopy ride
- The artisans' market and fine cigar factory in the foothill town of La Pintada
- The Iglesia de Natá, completed in 1522, with an intricate colonial façade and interior carvings
- Aguadulce's Las Piscinas, four tideland swimming pools that offer an unusual escape from the heat
- The Ingenio de Azúcar Santa Rosa, where you can watch sugar being made

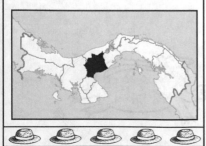

sion equipment of spelunkers and canyon rappelers.

Farther west along the Cordillera Central is an area named Chiguiri Arriba, where the landscape is defined by peaks jutting out of the ground, resembling the famous karst formations of southern China much more than anything else in Panama. Perched atop one such prominence is a lodge from which one can view and explore the dramatic landscape.

Farther west along the mountain range yet still within the province is Parque Nacional Omar Torrijos, which has some of the most beautiful forests in Panama. The road leading up to the park requires a four-wheel-drive vehicle with a winch, and it rains seemingly every day, but the bird watching can be tremendous. The park is known for its many species of hummingbird, but birders can expect to see a variety of tanagers, too.

Coastal Coclé is a wonderful area as well. The beach at Santa Clara is idyllic, and there's a variety of lodging in this community, including the nation's only motor-home park. Down the road a little is the village of Farallón, where Manuel Noriega once kept a vacation home. Today, a Colombian company is building the country's largest resort complex on land once occupied by a major Panamanian military base.

A bit back from the coast but not quite into the foothills are Penonomé and Natá. Penonomé, Coclé's bustling provincial capital, is famous for its hats and its Carnaval and its patron saint festival. Natá is one of the oldest cities in the country, and it is also home to one of the oldest churches in the Americas (a real beauty).

Up the road from Penonomé, toward the mountains, is La Pintada. Few Panamanians have heard of this town, but it's a must-visit for cigar aficionados. Owned and run by a savvy Latina, the Panabanos Cigar Factory here uses only the finest Cuban

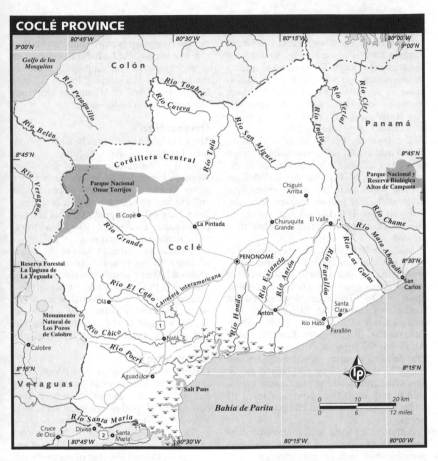

COCLÉ PROVINCE

Golfo de los Mosquitos

Colón

Cordillera Central

Parque Nacional Omar Torríjos

Panamá

Parque Nacional y Reserva Biológica Altos de Campana

El Copé

La Pintada

Chiguiri Arriba

Churuquita Grande

El Valle

Reserva Forestal La Laguna de La Yeguada

Coclé

PENONOMÉ

Río Grande

Río El Caño   Carretera Interamericana

Olá

Monumento Natural de Los Pozos de Calobre

Calobre

Río Chico

Nata

Río Pocri

Aguadulce

Salt Pans

Bahía de Parita

Veraguas

Río Santa María

Cruce de Ocú   Divisa   Santa María

Río Hondo

Anton

Río Hato

Santa Clara

Farallón

Río Las Guías

San Carlos

Río Chame

Río Mata Ahogado

Río Estancia   Río Antón   Río Farallón

0   10   20 km
0   6   12 miles

seeds in the production of its *habanos* (Havana cigars). If you've never visited a cigar factory, you'll find a trip to Panabanos educational and fun.

Moving farther southwest on the Carretera Interamericana, you'll come to the coastal town of Aguadulce (Sweet Water), which is not without surprises. Among them are four elevated swimming pools built in tideland. When the tide's out, you can walk to them and take a dip; when the tide's in, the pools refill with water. They are glorious on a sunny day. And not to disappoint those of you whose breath quickened at the earlier mention of salt and sugar, it *is* possible to tour a huge sugar refinery here, and you *can* look out upon salt flats all day, and no one will bother you. After a long day of watching salt crystallize and sugar being refined, you can swim in the pools.

Putting an accent on Coclé are its many festivals. In this province there are no fewer than eight major celebrations, ranging from an aquatic parade on a river in Penonomé to a tomato festival in Natá to patron saint and folkloric festivals in the farming town of Antón.

EL VALLE
pop 6200

This picturesque town, 123km west of Panama City, is nestled in the crater of a giant extinct volcano. The volcano erupted 3 million years ago with such force that it blew its top off, creating a crater 5km across – one of the largest in the Americas. The crater gradually filled with rainwater, and a rather large lake resulted.

The lake level fell markedly between 25,000 and 10,000 BC. Eventually, through erosion or collapse, a breach opened at the present site of Chorro de Las Mozas (Young Women's Falls) and the entire lake drained. Later, Indians moved into the valley to farm its fertile soil, but to date no one has attempted to determine when they arrived.

Much more recently, a road suitable for 4WD vehicles was carved from the Interamericana to the valley. That horribly rutted 28km road was greatly improved upon in 1997. Today an elevated, paved road allows motorists to reach El Valle (formally known as El Valle de Antón) from Panama City in little more than two hours. And what the urbanites find as they enter the volcano's crater is a tranquil town ringed by verdant forest and jagged peaks. Sparkling creeks add to the beauty of the valley, and at 1000m above sea level El Valle is much cooler than Panama's coastal towns.

Although El Valle is best known for its handicrafts market – a popular weekend event at which Indians trade vegetables and sell lovely baskets, painted clay figurines and carved serving trays – the town is also a superb place for walking. Many trails lead into the hills around the valley and, because they are often used by Indians, they are well defined.

Nature lovers, and birders in particular, won't be disappointed. The valley's forests offer very good bird watching (various hummingbirds abound, such as the green hermit, the violet-headed hummingbird and the white-tailed emerald), and El Valle is home to an impressive set of waterfalls and some rare golden frogs.

People who stand to gain from increased tourism to the area like to mention El Valle's *arboles cuadrados* (square-trunk trees). They also like to point out La India Dormida, a set of nearby peaks that supposedly resemble the silhouette of a sleeping Indian princess. Square-trunk trees? Mountains that look like people? You be the judge.

Orientation

The road that heads north to El Valle from the Interamericana becomes Avenida Central at the eastern edge of the valley. Avenida Central is El Valle's main street, along which are numerous places to stay and eat and most of the town's businesses. Branching off of Avenida Central are two dozen roads, a number of which lead to yet more hotels and restaurants.

Avenida Central ends west of the center of town. Here you can turn right and proceed 100m or so until the road forks. The branch to the left – Calle La Reforma – reaches the Cabañas Potosi after about 800m. The branch to the right – Calle del Macho – leads to the rain forest–canopy ride, a lovely waterfall and the petroglyphs.

Information

Despite the popularity of El Valle with tourists, the Panamanian tourism agency has yet to open a tourist office here. Your best source of local information while in El Valle is likely to be your hotel manager.

For your health needs, turn to the pharmacy or the 24-hour health clinic near the east end of Avenida Central. For your postal needs, visit the post office behind the handicrafts market (open 8 am to 4 pm weekdays only).

Handicrafts Market

More than anything else, El Valle is known for its weekend handicrafts market to which Indians – mostly Guaymís, but also some Emberá, Kuna and Wounaan – bring vegetables, fruit and flowers to sell and trade, and a variety of handicrafts to sell to tourists (most of whom are Panamanians from Panama City).

One of the most traditional items for sale here is the *batea,* a large tray carved from a

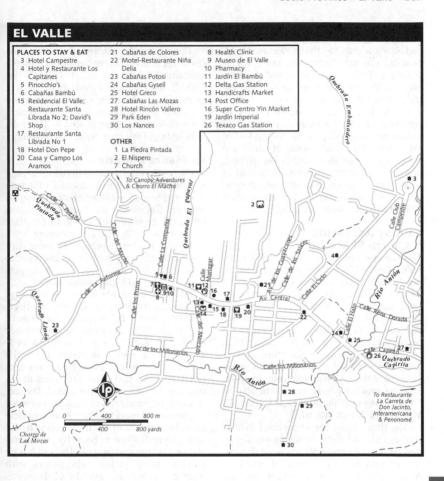

EL VALLE

PLACES TO STAY & EAT
3   Hotel Campestre
4   Hotel y Restaurante Los Capitanes
5   Pinocchio's
6   Cabañas Bambú
15 Residencial El Valle;
    Restaurante Santa
    Librada No 2; David's
    Shop
17 Restaurante Santa
    Librada No 1
18 Hotel Don Pepe
20 Casa y Campo Los
    Aramos
21 Cabañas de Colores
22 Motel-Restaurante Niña
    Delia
23 Cabañas Potosi
24 Cabañas Gysell
25 Hotel Greco
27 Cabañas Las Mozas
28 Hotel Rincón Vallero
29 Park Eden
30 Los Nances

OTHER
1   La Piedra Pintada
2   El Nispero
7   Church
8   Health Clinic
9   Museo de El Valle
10 Pharmacy
11 Jardín El Bambú
12 Delta Gas Station
13 Handicrafts Market
14 Post Office
16 Super Centro Yin Market
19 Jardín Imperial
26 Texaco Gas Station

local hardwood that's heavy as rock when newly cut but surprisingly light once dried. The wood is generally blonde, tan or light brown, and most trays possess two of these colors side by side. The trays may be polished or unpolished, depending on the maker. Most sell for less than US$10. The Guaymís use them for tossing rice and corn.

Other popular items here, also made by the local Guaymí community, are figurines, typically owls or frogs carved from soapstone and palm-size clay statuettes of Panamanians in common rural settings (such as a

campesino in a Panama hat seated at a little table with a tiny *seco* bottle and a glass).

Other items for sale include colorful baskets made from palms by the Emberá and Wounaan; gourds painted in brilliant colors, most often depicting animal faces or typical country scenes; *molas* painstakingly stitched by Kuna women; clay flowerpots; Panama hats; and birdcages made of sticks. Few items at the market cost more than US$20, and the posted prices are always negotiable.

The covered handicrafts market is open 8 am to 6 pm every Saturday and Sunday, rain or shine. There's usually more of a selection on Sunday, which until recent years had been the only day the market was held. Monday through Friday, the same site is mostly a fruit, vegetables and flowers market, though there are usually a few Indians on hand selling *artesenia*.

If you like shopping, be sure to visit **David's Shop** a brief walk away. Here, and at a shop next door, it's possible to find lots of high-quality handicrafts, some of which are made in a shop on the premises. Be advised, however, that many of the T-shirts sold at these shops contain dyes that bleed onto your skin and material that sometimes doesn't survive a single washing.

Canopy Adventure & Chorro El Macho

The Canopy Adventure (☎ 983-6547 in El Valle; ☎ 612-9176 in Panama City) is a suspended ride that uses cables, pulleys and a harness to allow you to view a rain forest from dozens of meters above the jungle floor. The ride is kind of like a ski lift, except that you are in a harness rather than on a bench, and you are descending rather than ascending. And you're dangling among jungle trees instead of snow-covered pines. Suspended this way, you ride from one platform to another (there are six in all), at times gliding over the 85m-high Chorro El Macho (The Manly Waterfall).

Are these rides for everyone? No. If you're afraid of heights or have a weak grip, pass on this adventure. Riders need to have at least a normal grip to brake themselves. Also, you must be at least 10 years old and not a day over 80. Anyone weighing more than 200lbs is prohibited. Unless you like to expose your private parts to strangers, don't do this in a dress or short shorts.

You don't have to do the ride to admire Chorro El Macho or to take a dip in the bathing hole at its base. A large swimming pool made of rocks, surrounded by rain forest and fed by river water was recently constructed below the falls. Naturalists will find the pool and the accompanying birdsong and frog calls very appealing. The cost to take a dip in the pool is US$2, same as the cost to see the falls. Don't forget your bathing suit.

The cost of the canopy adventure is excessive at US$40. This writer would enthusiastically recommend it at US$10, but US$40, as one reader delicately put it, is 'a gross rip-off.' Another reader questioned the knots used in the rope that keep riders from descending straight down. The ride, falls and pool are open 8 am to 4 pm daily.

La Piedra Pintada

In the northwestern corner of the valley, in a neighborhood known as La Pintada (Colored Stone), is a huge boulder adorned with pre-Columbian carvings. Locals often fill in the grooves with chalk, to facilitate their viewing, but their meaning isn't clearer. That doesn't prevent Guaymí children who offer themselves as interpreters from giving their interpretation of the petroglyphs for US$2 (in Spanish only).

Interpreter Seneida Milena Rivera says she learned the 'story of the rock' in school. In 2001, amid a 10-minute explanation of the graffiti-like carvings, she took her bamboo pointing stick and identified an X carved into the rock. It represents the burial site of a powerful chief who died many centuries ago, she said. 'The site moos like a cow every time it rains,' she added. The lectures are definitely worth a couple of bucks.

Due to one report of theft from a vehicle near the entrance of the trail leading to the petroglyphs, it's best to come by bus even if you've got your own wheels. The site can be reached by a yellow school bus with 'Pintada' above the windshield. It passes along Avenida Central every 30 minutes, from 6 am to 7 pm (15¢ one way).

Museo de El Valle

On the eastern side of El Valle's conspicuous church is the easily overlooked Museum of El Valle. If you don't have time to visit the museum while you're in town, don't cancel your upcoming trip to Mykonos to return for it.

However, it does contain some interesting exhibits, including petroglyphs and ceramics left by Indians who lived in the area hundreds of years ago. There is also some religious art (the museum is owned by the church next door), mostly statues of Christ and the Virgin, and some information on El Valle's volcano. The museum is only open on Sunday from 10 am to 2 pm. A donation of 25¢ is requested.

The **church** was constructed about 200 years ago, but neither the priest nor any of the nuns knew what year – that despite the fact that the town's largest celebration (replete with a grand parade) takes place on or about March 17 to honor the founding of the church. Most of the church, incidentally, is modern. The altar is original.

Square Trees & a Princess

Directly behind the Hotel Campestre is a thicket that supposedly contains square-trunked trees. Well, they aren't round, but they're not exactly square, either. You might want to see them for yourself and then ponder, 'What's the big deal even if they are square?'

Ask any resident of El Valle to point out **La India Dormida** (The Sleeping Indian, also known as The Sleeping Indian Princess). The local will point to a mountain ridge that will resemble whatever you want it to if you look hard enough.

There's a disturbing local story about a betrayed warrior named Yaravi, a horny Spaniard soldier, and a two-timing, indecisive and successfully suicidal Indian maiden aptly named Air Flower associated with La India Dormida that the author will spare you.

Zoo & Gardens

About 1km north of Avenida Central is a zoo and gardens named **El Níspero** (☎ 983-6142). Most Latin American zoos are sad, cruel places. This is such a zoo. Here, for example, there are numerous eagles and hawks in a cage smaller than a walk-in closet.

The zoo is open from 7 am to 5 pm daily. Admission to the zoo costs US$2 for adults and US$1 for kids ages three to 12. A taxi ride to the zoo will cost you about US$1.50 each way.

Places to Stay

Budget travelers who can tolerate soft mattresses will want to check out the four guestrooms at the **Restaurante Santa Librada No 1** (☎ 983-6376), on Avenida Central. Rates are US$15 to US$20 per room with a private hot-water bathroom.

The **Motel-Restaurante Niña Delia** (☎ 983-6110), on Avenida Central, has six worn rooms, two with private cold-water bathrooms. They cost US$18/23 a single/double on Friday, Saturday and Sunday nights, and US$5 less the rest of the week.

The **Hotel Greco** (☎ 983-6149), near the entrance of town, has 14 wearing cabins with decent beds, private cold-water bathrooms and nice grounds. There are eight rooms with a twin bed in each for US$20, three cabins with a twin bed and a single for US$25, and two cabins with a twin bed and two single beds for US$45.

The **Cabañas Bambú** (☎ 983-6251) have not been maintained and now consist of four very worn cabins with cockroaches. Rates run US$20 to US$60 per room.

The new **Residencial El Valle** (☎ 983-6536 and 636-2619, residencialel alle@ hotmail.com), on Avenida Central, offers 12 appealing stucco-wall, tile-floor guestrooms above a handicrafts shop and the Restaurante Santa Librada No 2. Every room contains a private hot-water bathroom, cable TV and attractive wooden furniture made downstairs. Rates are: US$25 with one double bed, US$40 with two double beds, US$65 with two double beds and one single. Bikes can be rented (US$2 per hour) and guides are available (US$10 per half day per person).

The new **Hotel Don Pepe** (☎ 983-6425, fax 983-6835, hoteldonpepe@hotmail.com) offers 12 spacious rooms, each with a fan, private hot-water bathroom, and one double bed and two single beds for US$35 per room weekdays, US$45 Friday, Saturday and Sunday nights. Single travelers pay US$25. This hotel is owned by the sister of the owner of the Residencial El Valle and is no better and no worse – equally appealing. However, the Don Pepe has a self-operated washer/drier for US$1 per load. There's a communal room with cable TV.

The oldest hotel in town is the **Hotel Campestre** (☎ 983-6146, fax 983-6460), which has 12 rooms in its original 1920s-era two-story lodge, plus 20 rooms in a 1990s addition. It's a fair value at a rate of US$25 per person. There are also three family-size cabins for US$60. There's a restaurant and a bar, and horses for rent.

The **Cabañas Potosi** (☎ 983-6181, fax 264-3713), on Calle La Reforma about 1.5km west of downtown El Valle, are four cabins on park-like grounds. Each cabin has two beds and a hot-water private bathroom and rents for US$30. The views of the craggy ridges ringing the valley seem especially pleasing from here. Meals are available for US$5 apiece. Tent camping, with showers and toilets available, is an option for US$10 (two-person tent provided). The owners speak English and Spanish.

On Avenida Central on the east side of town are the **Cabañas Gysell** (☎ 983-6507), offering five comfortable rooms with private hot-water bathrooms for US$35 to US$45 per room.

The **Hotel y Restaurante Los Capitanes** (☎ 983-6080, fax 983-6505, capitanes@cwp.net.pa) offers 10 very appealing rooms with lots of fine details, firm beds, spacious hot-water bathrooms, TVs and VCRs. Rates: Two rooms with one queen-size bed (US$40/50 weekdays/weekends); four disabled-friendly rooms with two queen beds each (US$50/65); three suites (US$65/85). There's a bar with DirecTV, fine dining, horse rental available, and a children's pool. English, Spanish, German, Italian and French are spoken by the owner-manager, a former captain in the German merchant marine. Website: www.panamainfo.com/loscapitanes

Cabañas de Colores (☎ 983-6613) offers three attractive cabins, each with the feel of a small house, and in fact built in the owner's backyard. Each stucco-walled cabin has a lovely hot-water bathroom, double bed with a firm mattress, and local TV. Rates are US$44 per cabin for the two one-bedroom cabins and US$77 for the two-bedroom cabin with a double bed and a bunk bed.

Los Nances (☎ 983-6126), a very appealing private residence owned by a retired US Army civilian and his wife, is high above the valley floor and offers lovely views. The friendly couple rents four of their bedrooms for US$50 each; the price includes a large breakfast. An inviting indoor spa is available to guests.

The **Hotel Rincón Vallero** (☎ 983-6175, fax 226-6567), in a lovely residential neighborhood, offers 14 comfortable rooms with air con and private hot-water bathrooms in a former residence. Most go for US$65/75 weekday/weekend, but there are also two junior suites (US$75/95) and one suite (US$95/105). Among the standard rooms, Numbers two and seven are tops. There's a restaurant with delicious food, and several very pleasant sitting areas.

Park Eden (☎ 226-8858, 613-5056, fax 226-6392, parkeden@cwpanama.net), consists of park-like grounds and a gorgeous home owned by a retired couple who offer three very tastefully appointed rooms in their home (US$115 to US$125 per room, includes two or three breakfasts), plus a separate two-story house (US$250, includes four breakfasts), a cottage (US$115, includes two breakfasts) and a little room behind the cottage (US$65, includes two breakfasts). The man of the house was an American-trained designer, and it shows (his wife is from Ecuador). Park Eden, overflowing with country charm, is a beautiful retreat. Mountain bike rental, guided hikes, and beach excursions are available here. Website: www.parkeden.com

Places to Eat

There are two **Restaurante Santa Libradas** in El Valle. Both offer good Panamanian food at attractive prices, such as *lomo de arroz* (roast beef with rice, US$3) and *bistec picado* (spicy shredded beef, US$3.50). Most sandwiches and breakfasts are under US$2. The restaurants' *sancocho de gallina* (a stewlike chicken soup; US$2) is excellent. Open early till late.

On the ground floor of the Hotel Don Pepe is **Restaurante Don Pepe**, a clean and inviting place that offers six chicken dishes, five sea bass dishes, four beef dishes and five prawn dishes; they range in price from US$5 to US$8. There's generally a daily special as well for US$5. Open 7 am to 11 pm daily.

Pinocchio's, a pizzeria next to Cabañas Bambú, makes tasty and cheap pizzas. A 12-inch pizza with all the toppings costs US$5.50. Also available here is one-quarter of a rotisserie-cooked chicken (US$3.50), meaty burgers (US$2.75) and tacos (US$3.50). Open 3 to 9 pm Friday, 11 am to 9 pm Saturday, and 11 am to 4 pm Sunday; closed Monday through Thursday.

The restaurant inside the *Hotel Rincón Vallero* offers delicious food in a cozy, covered area beside a lovely pool filled with koi. Meals here include shrimp with salsa or pepper (US$7), beef with mushrooms and pepper steak (both US$7.50), and filet of sea bass (US$9). Open for breakfast, lunch and dinner.

Four kilometers before reaching El Valle, on a hillside overlooking two valleys, is the *Restaurante La Carreta de Don Jacinto,* a charming restaurant with good food, good service and reasonable prices – definitely worth a taxi ride. The house special is the *filete a la Don Jacinto,* an 8oz beef filet on a bed of spinach with a white mushroom sauce (US$12). Not on the menu but highly recommended is the *salsa de la casa,* made with bone marrow from a steer, red pepper, salt, onions, garlic, cilantro and red wine, cooked 12 hours until reduced to a thick chocolate color; you'd order this with a beef filet. Also available are barbecued meats (US$5.50 to US$7) and fish and chicken (US$8 to US$12). Open 11 am to 9 pm Monday through Friday, 8 am to 9 pm Saturday and Sunday.

The restaurant at the *Hotel y Restaurante Los Capitanes* is perhaps the fanciest in town, but readers have complained that the prices of the German, French and Italian cuisine there far exceed the quality of the food. Offerings include sea bass layered with smoked salmon and topped with more sea bass and jumbo shrimp smothered with a honey-pineapple sauce (US$15.75). Open

7:30 am to 8 pm Sunday through Thursday (to 10 pm Friday and Saturday).

Entertainment
The *Jardín El Bambú,* one of the locals' popular watering holes, is 50m to the west of the conspicuous Super Centro Yin Market on Avenida Central. Here standard-size beers go for 50¢; the large bottles cost 85¢. There are pool tables in the back, as well as a very simple restaurant where two tacos cost only 30¢. The *Jardín Imperial* is a similar place.

Getting There & Away
To leave El Valle, you can hop aboard a bus traveling along Avenida Central. The buses' final destinations are painted on their windshields. If your next destination isn't posted, catch a bus going in the same direction and transfer when appropriate.

Getting Around
Despite El Valle's small size, taxis ply Avenida Central all day long. You can go anywhere in town for US$2.

SANTA CLARA
The small community of Santa Clara, on the coast 11km southwest of the Interamericana turnoff for El Valle, offers visitors the loveliest beach along this stretch of coast and several cozy places to stay. The area around Santa Clara is arid and sparsely populated, with patches of thin, dry forest. If you are looking for a place with pleasing scenery where you can relax and/or explore, you'll find it here.

Things to Do
In 2001, the owners of XS Memories (see Places to Stay & Eat) launched **Kayak Panama** (☎ 993-3096, fax 993-3069, kayak-panama@hotmail.com) with canoeing guide Sven Schiffer (☎/fax 993-3620, vsschiffer@cwp.net.pa). At the time this was written, Kayak Panama was only weeks old. It was offering trips on the Río Chame and the Río Santa Maria, as well as salt marsh paddling tours and kayak trips from the top of the Continental Divide to the Caribbean. Tours

started at US$60 per person, with a three-person minimum. Interested parties are encouraged to contact Kayak Panama or visit its website; English and Spanish are spoken. Or, contact Sven Schiffer, who speaks German in addition to English and Spanish. Website: www.panaman.com

Places to Stay & Eat

There are two Santa Clara turnoffs from the Interamericana; one is posted for the town and the other is posted for the beach (Playa Santa Clara). The first turnoff you'll see as you come from the east is the turnoff for town. If you go down this road about 1km, you'll see signs for Restaurante y Cabañas Las Veraneras and Las Sirenas.

A great find, *Las Veraneras* (☎/fax 993-3313, las_eraneras@cwp.net.pa) has seven two-story cabins set upon a knoll 150m from the ocean, and an eighth cabin on the beach. Each of the seven rustic-yet-charming cabins has ocean views from its front porch, a loft with a thatch roof, and four have kitchenettes with fridges. There's a double bed on the ground floor and a double bed with a bunk single and a stand-alone single on the second floor of each cabin. These go for US$55 per cabin (a very good price). The cabin on the beach is a romantic loft containing two single beds and a double, a TV and a fan (US$40); unlike the other cabins, guests use public bathrooms nearby. There's also a ninth cabin for a large family set back from the others that goes for US$110 a night. New at the time of writing were eight air-con rooms with private hot-water bathrooms in a garden setting for US$65 a room; very nice, but no seaviews. The owners accommodate tent campers (US$5 per person; a great deal). There's an inviting beachside restaurant serving delicious food at low prices; open 8 am to 9 pm daily. The owner speaks some English.

Las Sirenas (☎ 993-3235, fax 993-3597, 263-7577 in Panama City) is another great find consisting of 11 modern rooms with all the amenities, set on a lush hillside 150m from the surf. Five rooms are particularly attractive, with very tall ceilings. All have kitchenettes and dining areas; there is no restaurant on the premises. Rooms rent for US$80 apiece.

Just north of the turnoff for Playa Santa Clara, 100m from the Interamericana, is the American owned and run *XS Memories* (☎ 993-3096, fax 993-3069, xsmemories@ hotmail.com). The property contains three spacious guestrooms with air con and private hot-water bathrooms: one with a double bed and kitchenette (US$45), one with two double beds (US$50), and one with three double beds (US$55). Also on the premises: a restaurant serving breakfast, lunch and dinner (big burgers cost just US$2.75) and 12 water, sewer and electrical hookups for motor homes. There's an area to pitch tents (US$4 per tent per night), an inviting swimming pool and a sports bar that has DirecTV. There are 10-, 12- and 18-speed bikes available to guests only (US$5 a day). Website: www.xsmemories.com

Getting There & Away

To get to Santa Clara, just take any bus that would pass through Santa Clara and tell the bus driver to drop you in town. When it's time to leave Santa Clara, just stand at any of the bus stops in town and hail a bus going in the direction you want to go. When you reach a larger city, you can likely catch a bus going to your specific destination.

Getting Around

Except late at night, there are always taxis parked beside the turnoff for Santa Clara (the town, not the beach). You can take one for US$2 to get to any of the places mentioned above. The beach is 1.8km from the Interamericana.

RÍO HATO & FARALLÓN

About 1km past the Playa Santa Clara turnoff, you'll notice an open area where a wide, paved path stretches straight out from both sides of the Interamericana. It looks like an immense road, but there are no lines painted on it, nor are there any signs indicating that it's a road. That's because it's a runway, or rather it once was. In fact, it was a key runway used by Noriega's forces, and it has some interesting history.

During the days of the Panama Defense Forces (PDF), there was a major army base here, known as Río Hato, to which the runway belonged. There were many barracks, an armory, a clinic – all the stuff you'd expect to find at a major base. And near the end of a 3km road that runs from the Interamericana to the coast, paralleling the runway, was Noriega's vacation home, near the hamlet of Farallón.

At 1 am on December 20, 1989, the 'H-hour' of the US invasion of Panama, two F-117A Stealth fighters swooped undetected out of the night sky and dropped two 2000lb bombs near the Río Hato PDF barracks. The bombing marked the first time that the USA's most sophisticated fighter plane was used in combat.

The US secretary of defense said at the time that the sleek, black, triangular planes performed their missions flawlessly, precisely hitting their intended targets after flying all night from their base in Nevada. Later the Pentagon admitted that the pilots had confused their targets, hitting one out of sequence and badly missing the second. The planes, incidentally, cost US$106 million each.

Río Hato was also where the US Army suffered its highest concentration of casualties during the invasion, but most were not the result of combat. Moments after the bombs exploded, an 850-man contingent of Army Rangers parachuted onto the runway. However, because they jumped from an altitude of only 150m and landed on pavement, many of them sustained serious injuries. More than two dozen members of the elite force were incapacitated by broken legs, torn knee ligaments and other injuries.

What interests me about all this is not the Army's errors in planning the jump, but that the US military acted with great humanity in its bombing. Strange as that may sound, the targets the Stealths were ordered to hit were empty fields near barracks filled with young Panamanian soldiers, not the barracks themselves. By dropping bombs near the barracks, the US military hoped to scare the soldiers into surrendering and thus avoid unnecessary bloodshed. In fact, hundreds of Panamanian soldiers at Río Hato did surrender immediately. For all the criticism leveled at the USA during and after the invasion, there were many such instances of restraint that went unmentioned.

Post-invasion, the site of the former PDF base is profoundly creepy. During a past visit, the camouflaged buildings, 11 in all, stood vacant among tall weeds. Their windows were blown out, their walls pock-marked by bullets. Along one long wall was a wobbly line of holes made by heavy machine-gun fire, most likely .50-caliber rounds unleashed by a helicopter gunship. Small trees grew in rooms where PDF soldiers once carried out their orders. Scattered about were the burned hulks of cars and trucks. If ghosts exist, there must certainly be some here.

A kilometer or so south of the scene of the fighting is the hamlet of Farallón, which is home to a small general store and simple homes housing a few hundred people. A little farther down the road, the houses become increasingly fancy and the walls around them increasingly impenetrable. Many were owned by Noriega's top officers during the 1980s. One – the abandoned two-story house on the right side of the road, pocked from top to bottom with bullet holes – was owned by the general himself.

There's an interesting little war story attached to this residence. One of the reasons US President George Bush ordered the invasion was to arrest Noriega and bring him to trial on drug-trafficking charges. A big story on the third day of the invasion was US General Maxwell Thurman's announcement that US soldiers had found more than 50kg of cocaine in Noriega's Farallón house. It wasn't until a month later, under persistent questioning from reporters, that the Pentagon admitted that the suspicious substance was actually a flourlike powder used to make tamales.

But enough war stories. Fact is, the Decameron hotel chain recently opened a 360-room ***Royal Decameron Costa Blanca Beach Resort*** (☎ 214-3535, fax 214-3539) on the beach at Farallón directly in front of the old base. The company has already started construction of an additional 600 rooms, plus tennis courts, restaurants and so on, where those old shot-up buildings stood. The rate for the new rooms starts at US$67 per person and includes meals.

Website: www.decameron.com

Back out on the Interamericana and 1km west of the turnoff for Farallón is Río Hato, which is home to a *Hospedaje Las Delicias* (☎ 993-3718), a very good value located on the north side of the highway. There are 10 comfortable rooms here, five with fans only (US$12) and five with air-con (US$15).

Also in Río Hato is the Bar-Discotec Don Tuly. A holdover from the days of the military base, Don Tuly is a nothing-special bar Sunday through Wednesday, but on Thursday, Friday and Saturday nights starting at 9, there are naked-except-for-high-heels strip shows in a second-floor room accessed from the bar.

ANTÓN
pop 8400
Antón, 15km west of Farallón, is in the center of a lush valley that's sprinkled with rice fields and cattle ranches. It has little to offer the tourist in the way of attractions, except for its natural beauty, its annual patron saint festival (from January 13-16) and its folkloric festival, Toro Guapo (October 13-15). The people of Antón seemingly live for these events. There's a bank, several restaurants and a couple of gas stations in town.

Places to Stay & Eat
There are two hotels in Antón that are good values. The *Pensión Panama* (☎ 239-3163), beside the Interamericana, consists of 16 fairly clean guestrooms with private cold-water bathrooms (US$10, add US$2 for TV).

Directly across the street is the *Hotel Rivera* (☎/fax 987-2245), which has 30 rooms with good beds, air-con and TV, and private bathrooms. There's a pool on the premises. Rates are US$20 for one bed, US$30 for two.

PENONOMÉ
pop 15,800
This provincial capital 144km west of Panama City and 16km northwest of Antón is a bustling city with a history. The town was founded in 1581; by 1671 it had become so prominent that it served as the isthmus' capital after the destruction of the first Panama City (now known as Panamá La Vieja), until Nueva Panamá (New Panama) was founded a few years later.

Today, the city offers the tourist two principal attractions: its annual festivals and its traditional Panama hats.

Orientation
The city straddles the Interamericana. On the eastern side of town, the highway forks around an Esso gas station. One branch, Avenida Juan Demostenes Arosemena, goes to the right, and the other, the Interamericana, goes to the left.

Avenida Juan Demostenes Arosemena is the city's main street. Along it are two banks, a tourism office, a post office and the town church. The avenue actually ends at the church, which faces the central plaza. During Carnaval, the plaza and every street for three blocks around it are packed with people.

The best place to stay, however, isn't near the plaza but at the Hotel Dos Continentes (see Places to Stay), back near the Esso station. Here you're within 100m of three restaurants, a supermarket, a laundry, a bakery, a pharmacy, a bank and the main bus stop. You're also in the area where the best Panama hats are sold.

Information
There is no tourist office in town. For banking services, try the Banco del Istmo on Avenida Juan Demostenes Arosemena, and the Banco Nacional de Panamá on the same avenue. Both have ATMs and are open 8:30 am to 1 pm Monday through Thursday, 8:30 am to 3 pm Friday and 9 am to noon Saturday.

The post office is in the Palacio Municipal on Avenida Juan Demostenes Arosemena, behind the church. It's open 8 am to

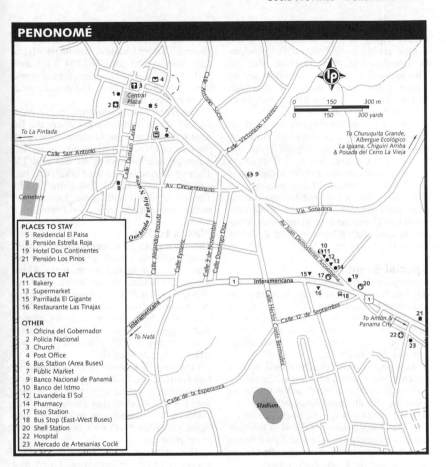

PENONOMÉ

0   150   300 m
0   150   300 yards

To La Pintada

Calle San Antonio

Cemetery

Central Plaza

Calle Antonio Sucre

Calle Victoriano Lorenzo

To Churuquita Grande,
Albergue Ecológico
La Iguana, Chiguirí Arriba
& Posada del Cerro La Vieja

Av Cincuentenario

Quebrada Pueblo Nuevo

Calle Damián Carles

Vía Sonadora

Av Juan Demóstenes Arosemena

Calle Alejandro Posada

Calle Egocelt

Calle 3 de Noviembre

Calle Domingo Díaz

Interamericana

Interamericana

To Natá

Calle Héctor Conte Bermúdez

Calle 12 de Septiembre

To Antón &
Panama City

Calle de la Esperanza

Stadium

PLACES TO STAY
5 Residencial El Paisa
8 Pensión Estrella Roja
19 Hotel Dos Continentes
21 Pensión Los Pinos

PLACES TO EAT
11 Bakery
13 Supermarket
15 Parrillada El Gigante
16 Restaurante Las Tinajas

OTHER
1 Oficina del Gobernador
2 Policia Nacional
3 Church
4 Post Office
6 Bus Station (Area Buses)
7 Public Market
9 Banco Nacional de Panamá
10 Banco del Istmo
12 Lavandería El Sol
14 Pharmacy
17 Esso Station
18 Bus Stop (East-West Buses)
20 Shell Station
22 Hospital
23 Mercado de Artesanias Coclé

5 pm Monday through Saturday. The city's principal hospital is located beside the Interamericana at the eastern end of town. There's a public market (mercado publico; open 4:30 am to 3:30 pm) near the Central Plaza that's fun to browse.

Laundry The Lavandería El Sol is on Avenida Juan Demostenes Arosemena, across the street from the Esso gas station. Getting one T-shirt or a pair of blue jeans washed and dried costs 50¢. Having a pair of trousers or a dress shirt cleaned and pressed costs US$1.25. Turnaround time is usually three hours. It's open 8 am to 6 pm Monday to Saturday.

Panama Hats

Penonomé is known throughout Panama as the place to buy the hats that bear the country's name. Unlike the better-known *panamas* from Ecuador, which are woven from crown to brim in one piece, this kind is made by a braiding process, using a half-inch braid of palm fiber, usually of alternating or mixed white and black.

The finished braid is wound around and around a wooden form and sewn together

COCLÉ PROVINCE

at the edges, producing a round-crowned, black-striped hat. It's as common in the central provinces of Panama as the wide-brimmed sombrero is in rural Mexico. The highest-quality Penonomé hats are so tightly put together that they can hold water. The price of these hats ranges from US$10 up to US$150.

There's no one place to buy these hats in Penonomé. They are made in outlying towns, such as Ocú, and brought to the city for sale. Many are sold by hat vendors standing outside stores and restaurants near the Esso gas station by the entrance to town. For starters, try the Shell gas station near the Esso station, in front of Restaurante Las Tinajas, and the Mercado de Artesanias Coclé (open 8 am to 4 pm daily) at the east end of town.

Special Events

Carnaval, held during the four days preceding Ash Wednesday, is a huge happening in Penonomé. In addition to the traditional festivities (the dancing, the masks, the costumes, the queen's coronation and so on), here floats are literally *floated* – down a tributary of the Río Zaratí.

Less popular but still a big crowd pleaser is Penonomé's patron saint festival, generally held on December 8 and 9 (or the following Saturday if both these dates fall on weekdays). Following a special Mass, the city's Catholics carry a statue of the saint through the city's streets. The Mass and procession seem incidental to the celebration that takes place outside the church for two days.

Places to Stay

Several blocks from the central plaza is the *Pensión Estrella Roja (no phone)*. Features: good beds; fans; thin, plywood walls; one exposed light bulb per room. There are four showers and four toilets for 20 rooms, but rooms cost only US$6.

The *Residencial El Paisa* (☎ 997-9242), a half-block from the central plaza, has seven rooms for US$7.50 per person. Each has two soft beds, a fan on a stand, and a cold-water private bathroom, but there is little ventilation.

The *Pensión Los Pinos (no phone)*, on the Interamericana at the entrance to town, several hundred meters southeast of the Esso station, charges US$12/14 for rooms with fans/air con. These rooms are clean and have decent-to-soft beds and private cold-water bathrooms.

The *Hotel Dos Continentes* (☎ 997-9326, fax 997-9390), near the point where the Interamericana forks, has 61 guestrooms and a popular cafeteria. All the rooms have hot-water private bathrooms, air con and TV. Those with one bed go for US$25; one bed and air con, US$27.50; two beds, US$30. There are rooms with three, four or five beds as well. This hotel is a good value.

Places to Eat

The *Parrillada El Gigante,* on the Interamericana a short walk to the west of the Esso station, is known for its pizza, which comes in an individual size and costs about US$4. Its *sancocho de gallina* (chicken soup, the national dish) is delicious and cheap (US$1.75). The owner-chef is from Lebanon and makes some delicious Lebanese dishes as well (US$1 to US$3). Best food in town, followed by Las Tinajas.

Opposite El Gigante is the *Restaurante Las Tinajas,* which offers typical Panamanian food in a buffet style. Few items cost over US$2; full meals cost a little more. For US$2.75, for example, you get *bistec picado* (spicy shredded beef) with rice, beans and sweet plantains.

The restaurant at the *Hotel Dos Continentes* is open for breakfast, lunch and dinner, and it is usually crowded. Sandwiches cost US$4 or less, steaks cost US$5 or less, seafood from US$5 to US$12. The club sandwich (US$3.50) arrives with a fried egg in it.

The town's top bakery and a supermarket has been placed on the Penonomé map for you do-it-yourselfers.

Getting There & Away

Buses traveling to and from Penonomé via the Interamericana use a small parking lot opposite the Hotel Dos Continentes as a passenger pick-up and drop-off point. Area buses, such as those to Churuquita Grande, Aguadulce, La Pintada, San Pedro, Chiguiri Arriba, El Copé and El Encanto use a station two blocks southeast of the central plaza.

Getting Around

Due to its size and importance, Penonomé has no shortage of taxis. The best place to hail one is by the Esso gas station, near the entrance to town. They can also be seen in numbers near the central plaza. The fare for any destination in town is never more than US$3, and usually it's half that.

LA PINTADA

This small foothill town, which boasts an artisans' market and a cigar factory, is 12km northwest of downtown Penonomé. Anyone with a real hankering for handicrafts or a love of cigars would enjoy a visit to La Pintada.

The **Mercado de Artesanias La Pintada** (☎ 983-0313) specializes in Penonomé-style Panama hats. The material used in Panamas occasionally varies from one town to the next. Here the headgear is made of *bellota* and also of *pita*, which is related to cactus. There are several bellota and pita plants growing in front of the market, so you can see what they look like. Also found here are lots of miniature hats, fans, baskets and drums (50¢ each).

Other items of particular interest at this store are dolls wearing handmade folkloric costumes and seco bottle covers made from hat palm. The dolls sell for around US$12. The bottle covers go for US$5.

There are many other items for sale as well. Take a look at the brooms. These are of the classic variety, such as you might find in a witch's closet. But instead of a clump of sticks at the business end, the maker chose to use slices of palm. They sell for US$1 each.

The market is easy to find. As you drive through La Pintada on the main road from Penonomé, you'll come to a very large soccer field on the left side of the road. The market is on the far side of this field. Open 9 am to 4 pm daily.

To get to the **Cigars Joyas de Panama** (☎/fax 983-0304, joyapan@yahoo.com) from the artisans' market, just drive southeast from the artisans' market, straight toward Penonomé (ignore the Pana American Cigar Co, which is en route to Joyas de Panama). You'll come to Cafe Coclé, on your right; take the well-maintained dirt road just beyond it (the road that initially parallels the paved road, not the next right). Follow this road about 1km until you see a simple thatch-roof restaurant on the right side of the road immediately followed by the open-sided cigar factory with a corrugated metal roof. You've arrived!

The factory's owner, Miriam Padilla, began growing tobacco in La Pintada with three Cubans in 1982. They went their separate ways in 1987, when the Cubans emigrated to Honduras to open a cigar factory. Left on her own devices, Miriam sent choice samples of her tobacco to tourists and other people she'd met in Panama over the years, seeking investors for a factory.

Today Miriam and her son, Braulio Zurita, are La Pintada's largest employers, employing 80 workers who make a total of 22,000 cigars a day. The employees work at rows of desks in a long, concrete-sided, aluminum-roofed, one-story building the size of a large home, which is the pride of the neighborhood.

The cigars are made in an assembly process that begins at one end of the building with leaf separation from stem, and ends at the other end of the building with the packaging of the final product. From here, the cigars are shipped primarily to the USA, France and Spain.

A box of 25 of their highest-quality cigars costs US$45 in Panama and twice that outside the country. Joyas de Panama cigars also come flavored – with a hint of vanilla, rum or amaretto.

Miriam speaks English, and cigars are clearly much more than a business to her. If Miriam isn't here when you arrive, ask to see Braulio, who likewise speaks English and knows a great deal about cigars.

ALBERGUE ECOLÓGICO LA IGUANA

This *albergue ecológico* (ecological shelter; ☎/fax 983-8056), 14km northeast of Penonomé, consists of a handsome, open-sided restaurant, a small private zoo and guests' quarters set on 75 hectares that also contain a modest waterfall and various tree-production projects. There's also a substantial patch of forest on the property that contains iguanas, red-nape tamarins and even a few caimans. Among the 75 species of bird that have been identified here are the white-winged dove (known only in Herrera and Coclé Provinces) and the rare black-and-white hawk-eagle.

The emphasis here is on outdoor recreation. Bicycles and horses are available for rent, and there's a volleyball court and swimming pools for adults and children, but mostly visitors are encouraged to wander the trails through the woods and get in touch with nature. There's an attractive restaurant serving good food at reasonable prices (ceviche for US$3, sea bass for US$7 and steak stuffed with shrimp for US$12).

The eight pleasant guestrooms each feature one good double bed and three firm single beds, a private hot-water bathroom and ceiling fan. Room rates are US$35/45 for single/double, and US$60 for a family. Camping is available for US$10 per tent.

I'd be more excited about this retreat if the owner, a friendly fellow who speaks English and Spanish, didn't keep many birds and about a dozen mammals in small cages. The owner insisted in 1997 that he would be enlarging the cages, and when LP revisited the *albergue ecológico* in 2001, some of the cages had indeed been enlarged. Unfortunately, the owner had purchased more animals and these were being kept in torturously small cages. Once again, he promised to improve his animals' living habitats, but this writer isn't hopeful animals kept at the so-called ecological shelter will ever be properly housed or tended.

Getting There & Away

To reach the Albergue Ecológico La Iguana from the center of Penonomé, take the well-marked turnoff for Churuquita Grande, several hundred meters northwest of the Hotel Dos Continentes. Proceed 13km and begin looking for a sign announcing the retreat on the right side of the road. If you take a taxi from Penonomé, the ride will cost US$10 each way (less if you haggle).

You can also go to Penonomé's area bus station, two blocks southeast of the central plaza, and look for a bus with 'Churuquita Grande' or 'Chiguiri Arriba' on its windshield. Buses to both locations pass by the ecological shelter. Be sure to tell the driver to stop at the shelter's entrance, or he won't. The one-way fare is US$1. The buses run every 30 minutes during daylight hours only. To return to Penonomé, flag down any southbound bus.

POSADA DEL CERRO LA VIEJA

Reachable by paved road and located in Chiguiri Arriba, 29km to the northeast of Penonomé, is the Posada del Cerro La Vieja (☎ 983-8900, 317-0098, posada97@hotmail.com). The Inn of the Old Mountain, as the name translates into English, sits atop a summit with sweeping views of green valleys and imposing peaks intermittently shrouded by clouds, looking not so much like a slice of Central America but rather the famous karst formations outside Guilin, China.

The main structure, set amid gardens that attract many species of bird, consists of a one-story lodge with four guestrooms: Two have a double and a single bed with a private bathroom, and the other two have two bathrooms and three bedrooms with two beds in each. There is also an outstanding restaurant and bar, the views from which are simply breathtaking. Also available here, a short walk from the main building, are 10 lovely rooms with sweeping views, the best of which are named El Turega Rooms 1 and 2 and Chichibalí Rooms 1 and 2. Due mostly to their views, these four comfortable rooms with private hot-water bathrooms and firm beds are among the very best in Panama. All of the rooms except Chichibalí No 2 rent for US$60 per person, which includes three delicious meals a day (a great value).

Chichibalí No 2 costs a little more (US$75), because word has slipped that it is one of President Moscoso's favorite rooms and many Panamanian guests now request it.

Activities offered include mud baths (US$15), massage (US$15 for 30 minutes, or US$25 for one hour with herbal oil), and various inexpensive guided hiking tours, ranging from easy nature walks to arduous treks and taking in river, waterfall and forest scenes. Area animals include three-toed sloths, night monkeys, deer and armadillos. Four species of toucan and many species of hummingbird also live here; these can occasionally be seen from the comfort of the inn's creek-fed swimming pool.

Posada del Cerro La Vieja is a great find, well worth the time it takes to get there. Website: www.posadacerrolavieja.com

Getting There & Away
To get to the inn from central Penonomé, take the well-marked turnoff for Churuquita Grande, several hundred meters northwest of the Hotel Dos Continentes. Proceed past Churuquita Grande and follow the signs to Chiguiri Arriba and the inn.

Alternately, go to Penonomé's area bus station and look for a bus with 'Chiguiri Arriba' (US$1.50 one way; one hr and 20 minutes) on its windshield. Buses depart at 6, 10 and 11 am and 12:30, 2, 4:30 and 6 pm.

PARQUE NACIONAL OMAR TORRIJOS
The turnoff for this national park is on the Interamericana, 18km west of Penonomé. From the turnoff, it's another 32.8km to the park's entrance. The road, paved for the first 26km, winds through rolling countryside dotted with farms and small cattle ranches. The paved road ends at the small town of El Copé. The remaining 6.8km of the drive to the park are on a dirt road that's so bad that a 4WD vehicle with a very strong motor and excellent tires is needed. There is no public transportation to the park; visitors must drive.

Partly because the road is so horrible, the forests here are among the most beautiful in Panama and offer superb bird watching.

The park starts in montane forest on the Pacific side of the Continental Divide and continues onto the Caribbean side, where the forest is noticeably more humid. Among the rare birds that have been recorded here are the golden-olive woodpecker, red-fronted parrotlet, immaculate antbird, white-throated shrike-tanager and red-headed barbet.

One of the wonderful surprises that greet visitors here is the condition of the park's trail system, which was recently given a major makeover by US Peace Corps volunteers, ANAM rangers and members of Panama Verde (a Panamanian student ecological group). Another surprise: This park offers the easiest and surest point from which to see both the Pacific and Atlantic Oceans (from the lookout above the cabin).

There is a ranger station just inside the entrance of the park where visitors are charged US$3 for the day and US$5 per night if you come to camp; the station is open from 6 am to 8 pm daily. There's a cabin 200m farther up the road that can sleep 10 people comfortably (you'll need a sleeping bag; it cools off at night in the mountains so bring some warm clothing as well).

Drivers: From the Interamericana turn off as marked and proceed 26km. You will then see a sign directing you to the park (to the right) and another to the park's administrative office ('Sede Administrativa'). There's no reason to go to the administrative office, so stay to the right and continue until you reach the park's entrance. Only a powerful 4WD vehicle can make it to the park; don't even think about going there in an automobile.

PARQUE ARQUEOLÓGICO DEL CAÑO
This park is one of only two archaeological sites in the country that are open to the public (the other is Barriles, in Chiriquí Province). It has a museum that contains a few objects that were found nearby. There's an excavation pit in the park as well, which contains a burial site in which were found five skeletons in the exact same position as visitors see them today.

Nearby there's a field containing dozens of stone columns that were lined up and stood on end in recent years; they aren't much to look at and their significance to the lost culture is unknown.

The site was excavated during the 1920s by an American who allegedly left with most of the objects he came across. The museum contains dozens of pieces of pottery, arrowheads and carved stones. The objects are believed to date from a culture that lived in El Caño about 1500 years ago. The few signs at the museum are in Spanish only, and the site's caretaker/guide can offer no reliable information about El Caño's history.

The park is open from 9 am to noon and 12:30 to 4 pm Tuesday to Saturday and 9 am to 1 pm Sunday. Admission costs US$1/25¢ for adults/children.

The turnoff for the town of El Caño is on the Interamericana, about 8km north of Natá. The park is another 3km from the turnoff, down an occasionally mud-slick road. El Caño is not served by bus, but you can take a taxi here from Natá.

NATÁ
pop 5900

In 1515 an Indian chief named Tataracherubi, whose territory covered much of what would later become northern Coclé Province, informed the Spanish conquistadors Alonso Perez de la Rua and Gonzalo de Badajoz of the wealth of his neighbor to the southwest, a chief named Natá. 'Natá has much gold, but he has few fighting men,' was the gist of that conversation.

Naturally, the conquistadors went after Natá's gold. Perez and his 30 men arrived first; Badajoz and his 130 men were not far behind. Perhaps a bit overanxious, Perez and his party soon found themselves amid a large Indian settlement. Retreat was impossible, but Perez grabbed the Indian chief and threatened to kill him, and thus forced Natá to tell his warriors to back off.

Then Badajoz and his well-armed soldiers showed up, and Natá was forced to surrender a large quantity of gold. The Christians remained for two months in the village named after the chief before they headed south and plundered more villages. Two years later, the Spaniards, led by Gaspar de Espinosa, returned to Natá and established one of the earliest European settlements on the isthmus.

The Indians, meanwhile, were enslaved. As an incentive to settle in Natá, the ruthless Spanish governor Pedro Arias de Ávila divided the village and its Indians among 60 soldiers who agreed to start a pueblo here.

Today, Natá is a quiet town, and most of its inhabitants work at the area's sugar refineries or in the fields around town. Its church, which was completed in 1522 and is one of the oldest in the country, is Natá's main attraction. There are also a number of well-preserved colonial houses in town.

Iglesia de Natá

The church, which has remained close to its original state all these years, is well worth a visit. Indeed, a five-year renovation of the church ended in 2001; the church hasn't looked so good in several hundred years! It has a fine colonial façade and a remarkable interior.

If you look closely at the altar of the Virgin, you'll notice sculpted fruit, leaves and feathered serpents on its two columns – clearly the influence of its Indian artisans. The position of the carved angels at its base signifies the power the artisans felt the angels possessed.

Notice also the Holy Trinity painting to the right of the altar. The painting was made in 1758 by the Ecuadorian artist José Samaniego. For many years it was kept from public view because it represents the Trinity as three people who all look like Christ, which is not in conformity with Church canon.

Under the floor beneath the painting are the remains of three people placed there many years ago. No one knows who they are or how many other skeletons there are beneath the church's floor. Restorers stumbled upon the remains in 1995 while working on the floor.

Father Victor Raul Martinez leads Natá's congregation and he can usually be found inside the church. He speaks English and he'll unlock a door and lead you up a narrow flight of stairs to the belfry if you politely ask him to. Once in the belfry, you'll discover four bells, all dating from the 20th century. The original bells were made of solid gold and were stolen years ago.

The choir platform above the entryway was built in 1996 to the specifications of the original. The original columns (the rough ones) that support the church's roof are made of *nispero*, a hardwood found in Bocas del Toro Province. The smooth columns are new and also made of nispero. The entire ceiling was replaced in 1995 and is made of pine and cedar.

The church does not have regular hours. If it's closed when you arrive, you might consider knocking on the door of the house to the right of the church. This is where Father Martinez lives, and if you look respectable and if he isn't too busy, he just might unlock the church for you. When visiting churches in Panama, never enter one in shorts or other clothing you wouldn't wear to a funeral.

Special Events

Natá holds its Fiesta de Tomate (Tomato Festival) in mid-April. Dates of the three-day agricultural fair vary each year; check with IPAT in Panama City (see 'Tourist Offices' in the Panama City chapter for contact information).

Places to Stay & Eat

There's one place to stay in Natá, the ***Hotel Rey David*** (☎ 993-5149), which is on the main road that leads into town from the Interamericana. An excellent value, it offers 20 comfortable rooms with air con for US$18/22 single/double. Two doors up, the ***Restaurante Vega*** serves good chow mein and decent rice with shrimp (both US$3).

Getting There & Away

Natá can be reached by all the buses that use this stretch of the Interamericana, except for the few nonstop buses that cruise between Panama City and Paso Canoas. Tell the driver to drop you at Natá, and he'll let you off beside the Restaurante Vega. Often there's a taxi parked in front of the café. If not, you'll be able to hail one within 30 minutes.

AGUADULCE
pop 7700

Aguadulce's name is a contraction of *agua* and *dulce* (meaning 'sweet water'), and it is said that this bustling city was named by Spaniards who were pleased to come across a freshwater well amid the arid landscape.

Today, Aguadulce is known for its sugar, its jumbo shrimp and its salt. There are salt flats south of downtown, and until recently there was a sizable saltworks. Unable to compete with the lower prices of Colombian salt, the saltworks here closed their doors in 1999. The flats provide excellent bird-watching opportunities; you can see marsh and shore birds, particularly the roseate spoonbill and wood stork.

Just outside town are fields and fields of sugar cane. From mid-January to mid-March of each year, the cane is cut and then refined at several large refineries in the area. One of these mills, the Ingenio de Azúcar Santa Rosa (Santa Rosa Sugar Refinery) offers tours – a must-do if you're in the area during the grinding season. (See details on the refinery at the end of this chapter.)

The sugar and salt industries date back several centuries, and the city's residents, many of whom until recently made their living from these products, celebrate their history with the Museo de la Sal y Azúcar (Museum of Salt and Sugar). The museum, in the heart of the city, deserves a look.

Generally a place in Latin America that acquires a reputation for its crustaceans quickly overharvests them and then has none to offer. But in Aguadulce, which for years has been nationally famous for its jumbo shrimp, restaurants continue to serve them in generous portions.

One of the best places to enjoy shrimp as well as conch is a very casual beachside diner beyond the salt flats called Restaurante Johnny Tapia. If the tide's out, consider feasting here and then taking a dip in one of

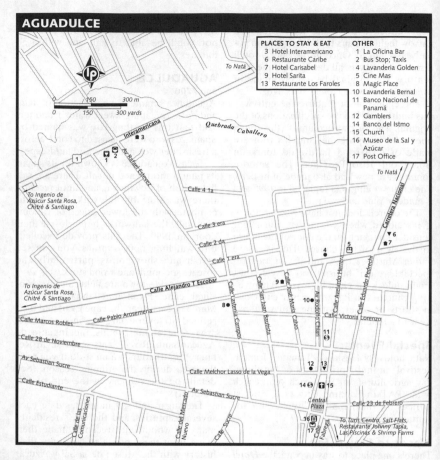

AGUADULCE

PLACES TO STAY & EAT
3 Hotel Interamericano
6 Restaurante Caribe
7 Hotel Carisabel
9 Hotel Sarita
13 Restaurante Los Faroles

OTHER
1 La Oficina Bar
2 Bus Stop; Taxis
4 Lavanderia Golden
5 Cine Mas
8 Magic Place
10 Lavanderia Bernal
11 Banco Nacional de Panamá
12 Gamblers
14 Banco del Istmo
15 Church
16 Museo de la Sal y Azúcar
17 Post Office

To Natá

Quebrada Caballero

Interamericana

To Ingenio de Azúcar Santa Rosa, Chitré & Santiago

Calle 4 1a
Calle 3 era
Calle 2 da
Calle 1 era

To Ingenio de Azúcar Santa Rosa, Chitré & Santiago

Calle Alejandro T Escobar
Calle Marcos Robles
Calle Pablo Arosemena
Calle 28 de Noviembre
Av Sebastian Sucre
Calle Estudiante
Calle Lasteria Campos
Calle San Juan Bautista
Calle José María Calvo
Av Rodolfo C Hari
Av Avelado Herrera
Calle Victoria Lorenzo
Calle Eduardo Pedrecht
Carretera Nacional

To Natá

Calle Melchor Lasso de la Vega
Av Sebastian Sucre
Calle de las Comunicaciones
Calle del Mercado Nuevo
Calle Sucre
Calle Fabrega

Central Plaza
Calle 23 de Febrero

To Turis Centro, Salt Flats, Restaurante Johnny Tapia, Las Piscinas & Shrimp Farms

the nearby pools. There's nothing fancy about either Johnny Tapia or the pools, but they do make for pleasant memories.

There is no tourism office in town, but there are a couple of banks, a post office, a laundry, several hotels and plenty of restaurants.

Orientation

Aguadulce is in hot, dry country, 10km south of Natá, 185km west of Panama City and 251km east of David. Like so many cities and towns in Panama, Aguadulce is beside the Interamericana. Its downtown, however, is a kilometer or two from the highway.

The main road into town from the Interamericana is Avenida Rafael Estevez. La Oficina Bar is on one side of the intersection of the highway and the avenue; the Hotel Interamericano is on the other side. There are always taxis near La Oficina, and the parking lot next to the bar is also the town's principal bus stop.

To get to Aguadulce's central plaza, drive south on Avenida Rafael Estevez several blocks until it ends at its intersection with Calle Alejandro T Escobar. Turn left here, onto Calle Alejandro T Escobar, drive three and a half blocks to Avenida Rodolfo Chiari and then turn right. The central plaza and church will appear on your left, four blocks later.

Information

Money There are two banks in town, the Banco Nacional de Panamá and the Banco del Istmo. Both are on Avenida Rodolfo Chiari near the central plaza, and both are open from 8:30 am to 1:30 pm Monday through Thursday, 8:30 am to 3 pm on Friday and 9 am to noon on Saturday. Both have outside ATMs.

Post & Communications The post office is near the central plaza, just around the corner from the Museo de la Sal y Azúcar. It's open 8:30 am to 4:30 pm Monday to Saturday.

There are many pay phones in town from which you can place domestic and international calls.

Laundry At Lavanderia Bernal, on Avenida Rodolfo Chiari three blocks north of the central plaza, you can drop off your clothes to be washed and tumble-dried for US$3 per load. The turnaround time is usually four hours. Also offering prompt service at a reasonable price is the Lavanderia Golden, on Calle Alejandro T Escobar.

Museo de la Sal y Azúcar

This rather unusual museum faces the central plaza. As its name suggests, the museum contains exhibits that document the history of the Aguadulce area's salt and sugar industries. However, the museum also contains artifacts from the Colombian civil war (1899-1903), in which many Panamanians fought. These include guns, uniforms and swords.

A number of pre-Columbian artifacts are also on display here, mostly ceramics and tools found in the cane fields nearby. But the majority of exhibits tell how the salt flats were developed, detail the role Aguadulce's salt and sugar have played in Panamanian life, and so on. The museum is open 9 am to 4 pm Monday through Friday, and 9 am to noon Saturday. Admission is free. Signage is in Spanish only.

Turis Centro

This place is 4km from downtown Aguadulce, on the road to Restaurante Johnny Tapia. Here, in the middle of salt flats and scrub brush, someone decided what was needed was a roller rink with jumps (skates rent for US$1.50 a day), a BMX track for cross-up bikes (bikes rent for US$1 per hour), paddleboats and kayaks on a small pond (US$6 an hour), a volleyball court and a good, inexpensive restaurant.

If this place sounds OK to you, the cost to check it out is nothing. A bus shuttles patrons between Turis Centro and the Restaurante Los Faroles, opposite the church in downtown Aguadulce, free of charge. The bus leaves at the tourist's request, so there's not a lot of standing around at either end. Call for pickup at the restaurant (☎ 997-3720). Open 11 am to 11 pm daily.

Las Piscinas

Las Piscinas (The Pools) are 9.5km from downtown Aguadulce, just beyond the salt flats and 250m past Restaurante Johnny Tapia. They consist of four 1.5m high swimming pools that were constructed in tideland about 150m from the high-water mark. If the tide is out, you can walk over the muddy sand that separates the pools from the shore and take a dip in them. The water's murky (it's saltwater, after all), but it's not polluted, as the pools are nearly 10km from town. And the pools are very refreshing on a hot day, which is every day in Aguadulce. The view from the pools is mostly one of a big, beautiful sky, with distant foothills on one side and the ocean spreading out before you on the other.

The tideland is quite expansive. When the tide is out, you can walk 2km before reaching the ocean. But be careful; once the tide turns, it rises rather quickly. If you've walked a kilometer or so beyond the pools and you're admiring the shore birds out there and notice the tide rising, head inland immediately. How high does the water rise?

Sea lions have been seen swimming near the pools when the tide's in. And if you decide to take some soft drinks out to the pools, please think about those sea lions and take all your litter with you when you leave.

The best way to get to the pools is by taxi. Tell the driver to take you to Restaurante Johnny Tapia. From Johnny Tapia, walk south (away from town). On the left side of the road are mangroves, beginning a little way from the restaurant. After you've walked about 100m, you'll see a clearing in the mangroves perhaps 50m wide, and through the clearing you'll be able to spot the pools (if the tide is out). Don't let the view from the road fool you; the pools are lovely in a funky way. Initially there's no path connecting the road to the pools, just muddy sand, but it's not at all deep. After 50m you'll reach some concrete steps that will lead you to the pools.

Special Events

Aguadulce parties hearty three times a year: during Carnaval, held the four days before Ash Wednesday; during its patron saint festival, on July 25 (or, if that's a weekday, the following Saturday); and in honor of the city's founding, on October 18, 19 and 20. The Carnaval festivities are predictably lively. But the founding-day festivities are also great fun. Although the city was officially founded on October 19, the celebration begins at least a day in advance and lasts at least a day afterward. A series of parades, a streetful of floats, Miss Aguadulce ceremonies, and lots of music, dancing and drinking characterize the event.

Places to Stay

Hotel Sarita (☎ 997-4437), on the corner of Calles José Maria Calvo and Pablo Arosemena, has 20 rooms with air con, hot-water private bathrooms and TVs for US$16/23 single/double, and eight rooms with fans only, cold-water private bathrooms and no TVs for US$10/12. All the rooms are clean. This is a very good value.

The *Hotel Interamericano* (☎ 997-4363, fax 997-4975), on the Interamericana near Avenida Rafael Estevez, is also a very good value. All 30 rooms have TVs and hot-water private bathrooms. There's also a swimming pool, a restaurant and a popular bar on the premises. The 15 rooms with air con cost US$26 apiece; the 15 rooms with fans only cost US$20.

Near the downtown area is the *Hotel Carisabel* (☎ 997-3800, fax 997-3805), on the corner of Calle Alejandro T Escobar and Carretera Nacional. This newer place offers 21 rooms, all with air con, TVs and hot-water private bathrooms. Nine rooms have double beds; 12 have single beds. The rates are US$24/28/31 for one/two/three people. There's a pool, a bar and a restaurant as well.

Places to Eat

At the *Restaurante Caribe,* beside the Hotel Carisabel, there are four ceviches to choose among (US$3 or less). Other offerings at this popular restaurant include chicken and beef dishes (US$6.50 or less), seafood (US$4.25 to US$9.50) and several chow mein plates (US$3.75 to US$4.50).

The *Restaurante Los Faroles,* opposite the church in downtown Aguadulce, offers many items but specializes in pizza. Its Hawaiian pizza has raisins and maraschino cherries in addition to the regular pineapple and ham toppings. Prices range from US$2 for a small cheese pizza to US$11.50 for a large shrimp one. Seating is indoors with air con, or outdoors – you choose. It's open for breakfast, lunch and dinner.

The restaurant at the *Hotel Interamericano* offers jumbo shrimp prepared four ways, each for US$8. The restaurant is known for its lunches, especially the *ejecuti o* (executive lunch; US$2.50), which includes soup, salad, rice, beans, beef and fried plantains.

Just past the salt flats, 9km from downtown Aguadulce, is a basic place named for its ebullient owner-waiter: *Restaurante Johnny Tapia.* Typical offerings here include ceviche (US$2.50); shrimp salad (US$3), fresh fish (US$3.50) and fish soup (US$3.50). Open 8 am till the last person leaves.

Entertainment

The hot dance club in town is the *Magic Place,* close to the intersection of Calles Lastenia Campos and Pablo Arosemena. There's live music and an open bar on Thursday, Friday and Saturday nights. Admission is free for women, but men pay as much as US$10 at the door; the price varies with the quality and popularity of the band. The club doesn't start hopping before 10 or 11 pm. Closing time is usually around 4 am.

For movies, try the *Cine Mas* (☎ 997-6829), on Calle Alejandro T Escobar. This large movie house, which opened in 2000, shows movies in English and Spanish. The first film usually starts rolling at 5 pm. There are four screens in all, and Hollywood's latest releases are the main fare here.

Gamblers, the casino just a stone's throw from the church and the Banco del Istmo, is beckoning to you. It wants your hard-earned money. Open 10 am to 2 am Monday through Friday, and 2 pm to 2 am Saturday and Sunday.

Two kilometers west of the Pensión Aguadulce (a motel on the Interamericana that's favored by prostitutes and their johns) is the *Mocambo,* possibly the most famous brothel on the international highway between North America and the Darién Gap. This is a great place to catch a sexually transmitted disease, and perhaps even die from it. Dudes: Keep your pants on. The risk just isn't worth the momentary thrill. However, the Mocambo certainly is an interesting place to have a drink.

Getting There & Away

Buses arrive and depart from the small parking lot beside La Oficina Bar on the Interamericana. A taxi from La Oficina Bar into town costs US$1. Just flag one down if there isn't one parked nearby.

Getting Around

Taxis are the best way to get from one part of Aguadulce to another if you don't feel like walking. Fares rarely exceed US$2, although you can expect to pay a little more at night. Always agree on a price before entering a taxi.

INGENIO DE AZÚCAR SANTA ROSA

The Santa Rosa Sugar Refinery, 15km west of Aguadulce, is a must-see if you're in the area when the factory is in operation. That would be from mid-January to mid-March – the grinding season. During these two months, the refinery grinds 6500 tons of sugar cane per day, and the sights at the factory are ones you won't forget. The facility makes for some interesting sightseeing even if you arrive out of season.

Because the land here is hilly and rocky, the cane must be harvested by hand. Four thousand people are hired to help with harvesting and production, and they bring the cane in as fast as they can, 24 hours a day, six days a week (the mill is quiet on Sunday). Most of the cane is harvested on company land, but the mill still buys about 3% of its cane from campesinos who bring it in on carts pulled by tractors and oxen.

I won't detail the refining process, but it may interest you to know that 135kg of cane enter the mill each second via a huge conveyer belt that's continually fed from trucks coming in from the fields. All this cane is sent through grinders that resemble a stack of studded roller pins – except that each one weighs 20 tons and is about the size of a Buick. They spin quickly, and the cane that passes through them is crushed flat. Things happen really fast and furious here.

Because of Aguadulce's hilly terrain, sugar cane must be harvested by hand.

COCLÉ PROVINCE

Occasionally the machine chokes. A 10-second choke results in a pileup of 1350kg of cane, and jackhammers are required to remove the clog. To give you an idea of the grinders' power: When a choke starts to occur, railroad ties are pushed into the grinders. In the fraction of a second it takes for the ties to pass through, they are chewed up as if they were breadsticks, but even as they're pulverized, they act as battering rams, punching bunched-up cane through the machines.

Also on the property is a replica of the original house of the mill's first owner, built in 1911 (the year the refinery opened). This museum is very nicely done and contains many exhibits; all its furniture and other articles are originals.

Tours are available 7 am to 4 pm weekdays and 7 to 11:30 am on Saturday. The refinery would like at least 24 hours' notice to receive visitors; call Gonzalo Peréz (☎ 987-8101/8102) for a tour. He speaks English and Spanish.

Getting There & Away

If you're driving from Aguadulce, the turnoff for the mill will be on the right side of the Interamericana. The mill's turnoff is marked by a sign, and there's an Esso station opposite the turnoff (the station is much easier to see than the sign). Take the road half a kilometer, and you'll come to a white guard station with a tiny chapel in front of it. Give your name to the guard and follow instructions.

If you don't have wheels, you can take a taxi from Aguadulce (which could cost US$25 if the driver waits for you and takes you back to town), or you can catch any bus headed in the direction of the refinery and tell the driver to drop you at the Ingenio de Azúcar Santa Rosa. Be forewarned that the walk from the guard station to the mill is more than 1km, down a paved road lined with mature teak trees (it's not a bad walk at all). If there is more than one of you in your party, you're better off taking a taxi.

Colón Province

pop 204,200

Panama's fourth most populous province has a very rich history. In the colonial era, gold and silver pilfered from indigenous peoples of Panama and Peru were stored at the Caribbean coastal towns of Nombre de Dios and Portobelo, in the northeastern portion of the province, until ships arrived to take the bullion to Spain. For decades these were the wealthiest towns on Earth, veritable treasure troves that attracted scores of pirates.

The earliest known history of the province was recorded by Panama's first Spanish settlers. It was here in 1510 that Diego de Nicuesa, the governor of a vast region that included present-day Panama, fled after a failed attempt to settle the Río Belén in what is now Veraguas Province. Leading a small fleet of sick and starving men, Nicuesa looked upon the seemingly fruitful shore near the northernmost point of the isthmus and exclaimed, *'¡Paremos aquí, en nombre de Dios!'* ('Let us stop here, in the name of God!').

His followers, sensing a lucky augury in his words, decided to call the place Nombre de Dios even before they had landed. But Nombre de Dios' humidity and apparent absence of food took a heavy toll on the settlers. They abandoned the site in just a couple of months. It wouldn't be resettled until 1519 – a full nine years later.

Supplies from Spain were unloaded at the new Nombre de Dios and sent across the isthmus to the city of Panamá. Moving in the opposite direction were gold and silver taken from Indians on the isthmus and in Peru. Both supplies and stolen bullion traveled along the Sendero Las Cruces (Las Cruces Trail), which consisted of a land route from Panamá to the village of Venta de Cruces and a river route on the Río Chagres from Venta de Cruces to the Caribbean. At the river's mouth, cargo was placed in ships and taken by sea to Nombre de Dios. Eventually a land-only route – the Camino Real (King's Highway) – was also used to transport supplies and ore.

During the 200 years in which Nombre de Dios and, later, Portobelo acted as temporary warehouses for pilfered riches, the ports came under repeated attack from English, French, Dutch and Welsh pirates. Many attacks were successful, as were the assaults on galleons that tried to reach Spain after taking on a king's treasure.

The Spaniards built forts to protect their fortunes, but the forts weren't enough. In 1572 the English privateer Francis Drake easily entered Nombre de Dios – 'the treasure house of the world,' as he called it – and was deciding which riches to plunder when a wound forced his retreat. Drake returned to Nombre de Dios in 1596, and this time his men not only emptied the treasure house but also torched the town.

Highlights

- Historic Portobelo, home to the well-preserved ruins of several colonial forts
- Gatún Locks, the largest of the Panama Canal's three sets of locks
- Fuerte San Lorenzo, built of cut coral and still displaying its old cannons
- Isla Grande, a popular weekend getaway ringed by fine snorkeling and dive sites
- Gatún Dam, once the world's largest earthen dam and still an impressive sight

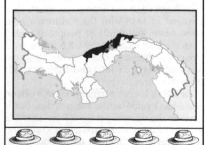

COLÓN PROVINCE

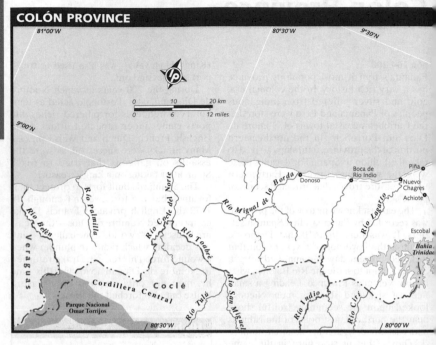

In 1671 the Welsh buccaneer Sir Henry Morgan took Fuerte San Lorenzo, at the mouth of the Río Chagres, then crossed the isthmus and sacked Panamá. In 1739 Portobelo, which was plundered twice during the 17th century, was destroyed by British Admiral Edward Vernon. After this blow, Spain abandoned the Panama crossing in favor of sailing around Cape Horn to the southern coast of the isthmus.

From then until the mid-19th century, the Caribbean coast of Panama was quiet. That changed in 1848 with the California gold rush, when thousands of people traveled from the East Coast of the USA to the West Coast via Panama. The Panama Railroad was built between 1850 and 1855 to profit from these travelers.

In 1881 a French company began work on a sea-level canal across the isthmus, but it gave up the effort eight years later after the monetary costs had proved too great and yellow fever and malaria had killed 22,000 workers. Twenty-five years later, the US effort to build a lock-and-lake canal was successful, and the sleepy backwater town of Colón, at the Caribbean terminus of the canal, was transformed into a vibrant provincial capital.

Colón received another big boost in 1948, when a free-trade zone was created within its borders. Today, the Zona Libre (Free Zone – as in free of import and export taxes) is the largest free-trade zone in the Americas. It links producers in North America, the Far East and Europe with the Latin American market. More than 1600 companies and nearly two dozen banks conduct business in the high-walled, 482-hectare compound in the southeastern corner of town, but not much wealth crosses the walls into the city itself.

And the fortified marketplaces of yesteryear in Portobelo, 43km to the northeast? Several still exist, their rusting cannons facing the Bahía de Portobelo as if still on duty. Where Spanish soldiers once stood

COLÓN PROVINCE

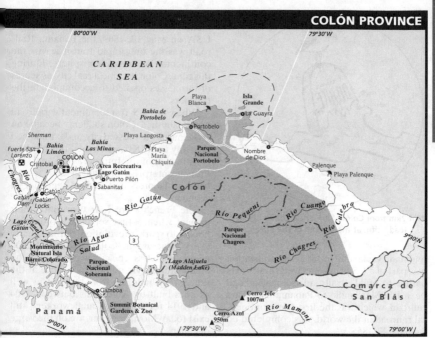

guard beside the cannons, today little boys cast fishing lines. Where Spanish captains once prayed their galleons would slip undetected past the waiting gauntlet of pirate ships, today yachters share gourmet mustards and drone on about anchorages and trade winds and the weather.

And not 2km away, in a leaden coffin at the bottom of the ocean, lies Drake's body. The English pirate led the sacking of Nombre de Dios in January 1596, but later that month he died of dysentery that he'd acquired in the Tropics. The captain was buried at sea within striking distance of the scenes of his earlier exploits, his descent to the ocean floor accompanied by a thunderous salute fired by his fleet.

In Drake's honor, two of his own ships and his share of the Nombre de Dios treasure were sunk near the spot. A nearby point and a small island were named after him, and a sermon was read aboard Drake's ship, the *Defiance,* with all of the

captains of his fleet in attendance. It went like this:

> 'Where Drake first found, there last he lost his name,
> And for a tomb left nothing but his fame.
> His body's buried beneath some great wave,
> The sea that was his glory is his grave.
> On whom an epitaph none can truly make,
> For who can say, "*Here* lies Sir Francis Drake?"'

COLÓN

The capital of Colón Province occupies a square of land that juts northwest into the Bahía Limón (Lemon Bay). It is noteworthy mainly for its Zona Libre, a free-trade zone second only to Hong Kong in sales. It is also the northern terminus of the Panama Canal, and was the northern terminus of the now-defunct Panama Railroad.

The city sits on a former island, which was linked at its southernmost tip to the

Not 2km from Colón, Sir Francis Drake lies in a lead coffin at the bottom of the ocean.

mainland via landfill in 1852. The unification was part of a US plan conceived three years earlier to build a railroad from what had been Isla Manzanillo to Panama City. That railroad, which was the first transcontinental railroad in the world, was completed on January 27, 1855.

The town that sprang up where Colón stands today was initially called Aspinwall, in honor of William Aspinwall, one of the founders of the Panama Railroad. The government of Colombia changed the name to Colón in 1890, and the adjacent area, which was inhabited by Americans and inside the Canal Zone, was named Cristóbal. As a result of the 1977 Carter-Torrijos pact, Cristóbal is now in Panamanian hands.

The discovery of gold in California in January 1848 was the impetus behind the railroad's construction. At that time, most of the US public lived on the East Coast of the USA. Traveling out to California via Panama was cheaper, quicker and less dangerous than traveling through the USA's heartland, which was vast and home to many hostile Indians. Would-be millionaires took steamships from the East Coast to the mouth of the Río Chagres and walked the Sendero Las Cruces to the Pacific coast; then boarded ships bound for California. The Panama Railroad made walking the Sendero Las Cruces unnecessary.

From its 1855 completion until the completion of a transcontinental railroad in the USA on May 10, 1869, the Panama Railroad was the only rapid transit across the continental Western Hemisphere. During this time, Colón became a real city, as scores of businesses opened to accommodate the travelers.

When the US transcontinental railroad was established, Colón suddenly became an economically depressed city, and it remained that way until 1881, when the French began construction of the Interoceanic Canal. The French enterprise brought with it a new batch of laborers and revived the sluggish economy.

The French were four years into their project when a fire, set by a Colombian hoping to spark a revolution, burned nearly every structure in Colón and left 10,000 people homeless. The city was rebuilt in the architectural style popular in France at the time. Many buildings from that era, as well as ones built by Americans between 1904 and 1914 for Panama Canal workers, still exist today. Most, however, are on the verge of collapse.

After the completion of the canal, the city's economy began to reel under the weight of thousands of suddenly unemployed canal workers and their families. The Zona Libre was created in 1948 in an attempt to revive the city, but none of the US$10 billion in annual commercial turnover seems to get beyond the compound's walls. Unfortunately, the Zona Libre is an island of materialism in a sea of unemployment, poverty and crime (Colón's rates in all three areas are the highest in Panama).

Inside the guarded compound, entrepreneurs cut deals involving the latest technologies and fashions, but outside its walls, children run about in rags and the city's largely black population lives in rotting buildings. With the exception of one seaside residential neighborhood where some fine houses are tucked away behind high walls and security systems, the city is a slum. If you walk its streets, even in the middle of the day, expect to get mugged. It really is that bad.

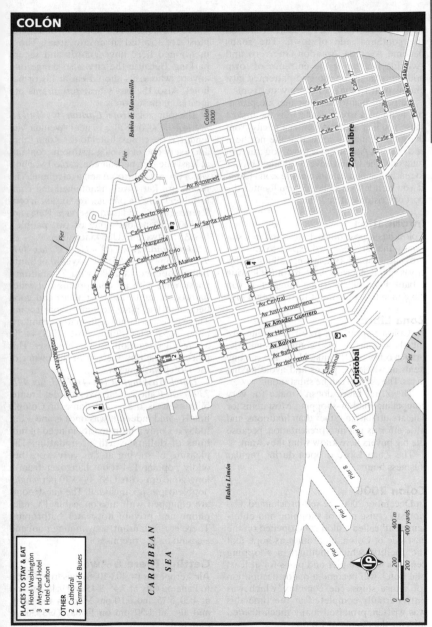

COLÓN

PLACES TO STAY & EAT
1 Hotel Washington
3 Meryland Hotel
4 Hotel Carlton

OTHER
2 Cathedral
5 Terminal de Buses

Bahía de Manzanillo

Colón 2000

Pier

Pier

Paseo Gorgas

Pier

Av Roosevelt

Calle E
Paseo Gorgas
Calle D
Calle C

Zona Libre

Calle 17
Calle 16
Puente Silvio Salazar
Calle 8
Calle 17

Calle Porto Bello
Calle Limón
Av Santa Isabel
Av Margarita
Calle Monte Lirio
Calle Las Marietas
Av Meléndez

Calle de Lesseps
Calle Escobal
Calle Chagres

Av Central
Av Justo Arosemena
Av Amador Guerrero
Av Herrera
Av Bolívar
Av Balboa
Av del Frente

Calle 10
Calle 1
Calle 2
Calle 3
Calle 14
Calle 15
Calle 16

Paseo de Washington
Calle 1
Calle 2
Calle 3
Calle 4
Calle 5
Calle 6
Calle 7
Calle 8
Calle 9

Cristóbal
Calle Terminal

Pier

Bahía Limón

Pier 6
Pier 7
Pier 8
Pier 9

CARIBBEAN
SEA

0   200   400 m
0   200   400 yards

Orientation

The city is reached via two major roads on the southern side of town. The roads become Avenida Amador Guerrero and Avenida Bolívar at the entrance of town and run straight up the grid-patterned city, ending near Colón's northern waterfront.

Perpendicular to these avenues are, primarily, numbered streets. Calle 16 is the first of these you'll cross as you enter the city from the south; Calle 1 is located at the northern end of town. As you enter town, you can turn right on Calle 13 and drive about eight blocks to reach the main entrance of the Zona Libre. If you turn left on Calle 13, you'll enter the port of Cristóbal after 200m.

Information

Colón has a post office, banks and gas stations – the services you'd expect to find in a provincial capital. But, again, walking in this city is very dangerous. A white tourist leaving a bank here will likely be mugged. If you have mail to send, send it from another city.

Zona Libre

In Colón's sprawling free-trade zone are the showrooms of 1650 companies and the branch offices of 21 banks. Here, you can buy items at wholesale prices and avoid paying taxes. The savings can be substantial.

The Zona Libre doesn't make for very compelling window-shopping. Most items for sale are utilitarian rather than luxurious, and little effort is put into presentation, because the big buyers here know what they want.

The Zona Libre is open during regular business hours.

Colón 2000

In December 2000, the self-proclaimed 'Caribbean cruise port of shopping and entertainment' called Colón 2000 opened on the east side of Colón. Its promoters hope that the facility, which includes a shopping center, a modern pier and plans for at least one hotel, will become a major destination for cruise ships. The complex, which was only partially completed at the time this was written, promised many much-needed jobs for the people of Colón.

Places to Stay & Eat

There are quite a few hotels in Colón, but most are located in unsafe areas. Those mentioned here have guards and secure parking. Because the city is so dangerous, anyone who visits should eat at his or her hotel. Also, the city's best restaurants are located in these hotels.

The four-story *Hotel Carlton* (☎ 441-0111, fax 447-0114), on Calle 10 near Avenida Melendez, is the closest hotel to the Zona Libre and every one of its 64 guestrooms contains at least one firm bed, air con, cable TV, a hot-water private bathroom and a telephone. The rooms are fairly well maintained and comfortable. There's a popular restaurant, a conference room and laundry service. Rates are US$30 for one bed (one or two people), US$35 for two and US$45 for three.

Meryland Hotel (☎ 441-7055, fax 441-0705), on Calle 7 at Avenida Santa Isabel, opened in 2000 with 79 standard guestrooms with air con, private hot-water bathrooms, cable TV, telephones and good beds, and had plans to build more rooms. These rooms are unexceptional but comfortable. A single/double costs US$44/50. There's a restaurant on the premises. This place is owned by the son of the owner of the Hotel Washington.

Hotel Washington (☎ 441-7133, fax 441-7397), on Calle 2 near Avenida del Frente, bills itself as the grand dame of Colón's hotels – and indeed it was once grand – but today it's only a monstrosity in need of millions of dollars worth of updating. The pleasure of staying at this very worn but oddly popular 124-room hangover from a long-gone era costs US$50/59/70 per single/double/triple, tax included. The guestrooms are equipped with air con, cable TV, telephone and private hot-water bathrooms. There is a restaurant, a swimming pool and a casino on the premises.

Getting There & Away

Air Aeroperlas (☎ 403-1038) flies from Colón to Panama City at 7:45, 8:45 and 9:45 am, and at 4:20, 5:15 and 6:10 pm Monday to Friday, and also at 1:30 pm on Friday (US$36, 15 minutes).

Bus Colón's Terminal de Buses (☎ 441-4044) is at the intersection of Calle Terminal and Avenida Bolívar. It serves towns throughout Colón Province, including the following:

Escobal/Cuipo – US$1/1.50; hourly; 10 am to 7 pm

La Guayra – US$2.25; hourly; 6:30 am to 6 pm

Nombre de Dios – 66km; US$3; hourly, 6:30 am to 6 pm

Palenque – 66km; US$4; hourly; 6:30 am to 5:30 pm

Portobelo – 43km; US$1.30; hourly, 6:30 am to 9 pm (6 pm on Sunday)

Additionally, there are buses departing this terminal for Panama City's bus terminal, and vice versa, every 20 minutes (US$2, two hours).

Getting Around

If you visit Colón, don't walk any farther than you must. If you arrive by bus, take a taxi from the station to your destination, even if that destination is only three blocks away.

AROUND COLÓN
Gatún Locks

The Gatún Locks, 10km south of Colón, raise southbound ships 25.9m from Caribbean waters to the level of Lago Gatún. From there, ships travel 37km to the Pedro Miguel Locks, which lower southbound ships 9.3m to Lago Miraflores, a small body of water that separates the two sets of Pacific locks. The ships are lowered to sea level at the Miraflores Locks.

The lock chambers all have the same dimensions (305m by 33.5m) and were built in pairs, two chambers running side by side in order to accommodate two lanes of traffic. The Gatún Locks consist of three such pairs. There is one pair at Pedro Miguel and two at Miraflores, making six pairs – or 12 chambers – in all.

Not only are the Gatún Locks the largest of the three sets, but their size is mind-boggling. In his superlative book *The Path Between the Seas,* David McCullough notes that if stood on its end, a single lock would have been the tallest structure on Earth at the time it was built, taller by several meters than even the Eiffel Tower. And each chamber could have accommodated the *Titanic* with plenty of room to spare.

The amount of concrete poured to construct the locks at Gatún – 1,820,000 cubic meters – was record-setting. That amount of concrete is enough to build a wall 2.4m thick, 3.6m high and 213km long. The concrete was brought from a giant mixing plant to the construction site by railroad cars that ran on a circular track. Huge buckets maneuvered by cranes carried the wet concrete from the railroad cars and poured it into enormous steel forms. The forms themselves were moved into place by locomotives.

Concrete is a combination of gravel, sand and cement. The gravel used in the concrete at Gatún came from Portobelo, the sand from the harbor at Nombre de Dios and the cement from New York. It took four years to build the locks. Despite the enormity of the Panama Canal project, they were completed on schedule.

Today you can see the locks in action. From a well-placed viewing stand opposite the control tower, you can watch southbound ships enter the two lower chambers at sea level, rise to the level of Lago Gatún in three steps and then steam onto the lake en route to the Pedro Miguel and Miraflores Locks. While in the chambers, the ships are cabled to locomotives that pull them from one lock to the next.

Just before you reach the viewing stand, you'll see a model of the entire canal and photos of it under construction. Additionally, you will be given a brochure in English or Spanish that provides information about the canal. There is no fee to visit the locks, which are open to the public 9 am to 4 pm daily.

Getting There & Away Buses to the Gatún Locks leave the Terminal de Buses in Colón hourly; the ride costs US$1.25 one way and lasts 20 minutes. It's better to arrive by taxi, however, because you would probably enjoy visiting the Gatún Dam (see below) in addition to the locks; it's only 2km away. A taxi ride from Colón to the locks and dam and back should cost no more than US$15 per party. Agree on a price before leaving.

Gatún Dam

The Gatún Dam, which was constructed to shore up the Río Chagres and to create Lago Gatún, was the world's largest earthen dam until the Fort Peck Dam was built in Montana (USA) in 1940. And until Lake Mead was formed by the 1936 completion of the Hoover Dam on the Nevada-Arizona (USA) border, Lago Gatún was the world's largest artificial body of water. When the Gatún Dam's spillway is open, the sight is quite a rush. The guard at the entrance to the Gatún Locks speaks English and can tell you if the spillway is open.

Power generated by the dam drives all the electrical equipment involved in the operation of the Panama Canal, including the locomotives that tow ships through the locks. Another interesting bit of information: When Lago Gatún was created, it submerged 262 sq km of jungle – an area far greater than that of most capital cities. Also submerged were entire villages and the original tracks of the Panama Railroad.

For directions on how to reach the dam, see the Getting There & Away section under Gatún Locks, above.

Fuerte San Lorenzo

Fuerte (Fort) San Lorenzo is perched at the mouth of the Río Chagres, on a promontory west of the canal. It was via this river that the pirate Henry Morgan gained access to the interior in 1671, enabling him to sack the original Panama City (the ruins of that destroyed settlement, today known as Panamá La Vieja, are still visible).

Like the fortresses at Portobelo, this Spanish fort is built of blocks of cut coral and displays rows of old cannons. A British cannon you notice among the Spanish ones bespeaks the time when British pirates overcame the fort. Much of San Lorenzo is well preserved, including the moat, the cannons and the arched rooms. The fort commands a wide view of the river and bay far below.

There is no fee to enter this or any of Panama's other forts. There's no bus service to the fort, but you can take a taxi there (about US$20 from Colón). If you're driving, go to the Gatún Locks, continue past the stoplight near the northern entrance to the locks and then follow the signs directing you to the dam, 2km away. Drive over the dam and follow the 'Fort San Lorenzo' signs. These will lead you to the entrance of Sherman, a former US military base, where you'll be asked to show ID. Once you've done this, you will be allowed to proceed the remaining 9km to Fuerte San Lorenzo. The fort is open to tourists 8 am to 4 pm daily.

At the time this was typed, the Panamanian government hadn't yet decided what to do with Sherman. However, it was considering making a large part of the former military base a nature habitat, and indeed there is some spectacular rain forest on the grounds that until 1999 had been used for jungle-warfare training by elite US Army units. To check the status of Sherman, call ☎ 433-1676 or visit the website www.sanlorenzo.org.pa.

WEST OF COLÓN

The many small coastal communities west of Colón (Piña, Nuevo Chagres and Boca de Río Indio, to name a few) are relatively

The Gatún Dam

unattractive with little to offer the tourist. The beaches along this stretch of coast are strewn with litter and the surf contains lots of riptides. There are no banks, post offices, hotels or restaurants to speak of.

However, southwest of Colón, along the banks of the Lago Gatún, is the fishing village of Escobal (population 2181), which with the help of the US Peace Corps has put together a homestay program for tourists and a host of activities that will no doubt interest some adventurous readers.

Escobal

Inhabited mostly by the descendants of former canal builders and people who were displaced with the flooding of the Río Chagres to create Lago Gatún, Escobal contains one of the most densely diverse populations in Panama. Here, residents are as likely to be the descendants of Haitians, Jamaicans or Colombians as they are Panamanians. And many of the people living in Escobal today hail from the Península de Azuero and have more in common culturally with Spaniards than they do with the Afro-Antilleans who comprise the majority of the population of nearby Colón.

The friendly Escobolanians are one of the main reasons to visit Escobal. There are no hotels in town, so some of the people have literally opened their homes to visitors. A homestay program created in early 2001 allows for tourists to be placed in private residences, where they are assured of a bed, a fan and a simple local breakfast for the beetle-belly-low price of US$6/10 for a single/double. You also have the option to camp beside a family's home and use their bathroom for US$2 per person (tent not included).

Also available in Escobal through the homestay program are: kayak rental (US$4 per hour), bicycle rental (US$15 a day), guided lake tours in a canoe (US$5 per hour, includes rower/guide), boat rental and guide (US$20/30 half day/full day), guided jungle walks (US$5), and horse rental (US$15 per day, guide included).

Interested readers should contact homestay program coordinators Granville 'Bill' Eversley (☎ 434-6020, English and Spanish spoken) or Saturnino Díaz or Aida Gonzalez (☎ 434-6017/6106, Spanish only). If you show up in Escobal unannounced, go to the Restaurante Doña Nelly (there are only two restaurants in Escobal) and ask for Saturnino or Aida, the restaurant's owners.

Forts Davis & Gulick

Just before reaching Colón, there's a turnoff called Quatro Altos that leads to the former US military bases of Fort Davis and Fort Gulick, which were handed over to Panama as part of the Carter-Torrijos Treaty of 1977. At both, you'll still see former military buildings that the Panamanian government is allowing to deteriorate while it decides what to do with them.

However, at Gulick (renamed Fort Espinar after the handover) a Spanish hotel chain has converted Building 400 into a 310-room hotel, the *Meliáa Panama Canal* (☎ 470-1100, fax 470-1925). The US$30-million hotel, which features guestrooms with all the amenities, a cluster of swimming pools with a swim-up bar, and numerous reasonably priced tours (fishing, kayaking and night safaris among them), occupies a finger of land that juts into Lago Gatún. A rack rate of US$205 per room applies, but substantially discounted packages are usually available.
Website: www.solmelia.com

Building 400 used to be home to the US Army School of the Americas, which was established in 1949 and trained more than 34,000 Latin American soldiers before moving to Fort Benning, Georgia, in 1984. The school was created to keep communism out of Latin America, and quickly that translated into teaching Latin American soldiers how to thwart armed communist insurgencies.

In time, the school graduated some of the worst human rights violators of our time, including former Argentine President Leopoldo Galtieri, who 'disappeared' thousands during Argentina's Dirty War of the 1970s; and El Salvador's Roberto D'Aubuisson, who led death squads that killed Archbishop Oscar Romero and thousands of other Salvadorans during the 1980s. Not too surprisingly, the Meliá's staff has painted over all evidence that the hotel has ever been anything but an upscale fun center.

At former Fort Davis, travelers who have business in Colón but who don't want to stay there or at the Meliá will find a very attractive alternative in the *Davis Suites* (☎ 473-0639, 628-6454). There are 10 spacious suites with two or three beds, a kitchenette and a living room in each. Every suite comes with air con, a private hot-water bathroom and cable TV. The suites are reasonably priced at US$55 per night. To get there, follow the signs from the Quatro Altos turnoff. Be advised that there are few taxis in the area, but the staff can call one for you.

PORTOBELO
pop 3867
This bayside town, 99km from Panama City and 43km from Colón, was given the name 'Puerto Bello' (Beautiful Port) by Christo-

pher Columbus in 1502 on account of the beauty of its natural harbor. As often happened with Spanish names, this one was abbreviated over time.

Portobelo consisted of not more than 10 houses when it was visited, in 1586, by Juan Bautista Antonelli, who designed many fortresses in the Spanish Indies and was sent to examine the Caribbean ports. After the celebrated Italian engineer noted how well Portobelo's bay lent itself to defensive works, King Félipe II ordered that Nombre de Dios be abandoned and Portobelo colonized.

Despite the order, it wasn't until after Drake's 1596 attack on Nombre de Dios that a gradual transfer took place. At the time of the transfer, which occurred from 1597 to 1601, two forts were built beside the bay. These forts were reinforced and others were constructed in the years that followed. But in spite of these defenses, Portobelo suffered numerous invasions at the hands of buccaneers and the English navy.

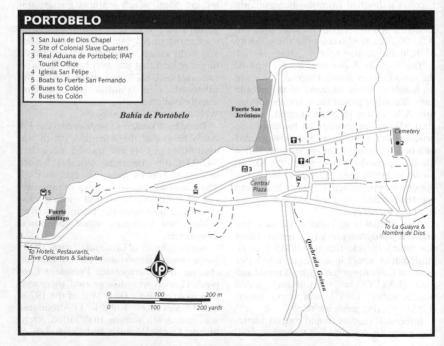

PORTOBELO

1 San Juan de Dios Chapel
2 Site of Colonial Slave Quarters
3 Real Aduana de Portobelo; IPAT Tourist Office
4 Iglesia San Félipe
5 Boats to Fuerte San Fernando
6 Buses to Colón
7 Buses to Colón

Bahía de Portobelo

Fuerte San Jerónimo

Cemetery

Fuerte Santiago

To Hotels, Restaurants, Dive Operators & Sabanitas

Central Plaza

To La Guayra & Nombre de Dios

Quebrada Guinea

0   100   200 m
0   100   200 yards

However, not all of the invasions were the products of superior tactics or numbers. In 1679 the crews of two English ships and one French vessel united in an attack on Portobelo. They landed 200 men at such a distance from the town that it took them three nights of marching to reach it (the pirates hid in the forest during the day). As they neared Portobelo, they were seen by a farmer, who ran ahead to sound the alarm. But the pirates followed so closely behind that the town had no time to prepare. Unaware of how small the buccaneer force was, all the inhabitants fled.

The pirates spent two days and nights in Portobelo, collecting plunder in constant apprehension that the Spaniards would return in great numbers and attack them. However, the buccaneers got back to their ships unmolested and then distributed 160 pieces of eight to each man. At the time, one piece of eight would pay for a night's stay at the best inn in Seville.

Today Portobelo is a sleepy town. Most of its inhabitants make their living from the sea or tending to crops. Their homes and small businesses (mainly food stands) are situated among the ruins of military buildings, half of which retain some of their original form and appear on the accompanying map. The other half are simply small piles of cut stone or coral, and their origins have been obscured by time.

In addition to the ruins in and about the town, Portobelo is popular for its scuba diving. There are eight major dive sites in the area (including a 110-foot cargo ship and a C-45 twin-engine plane), and their

Salvaging Sunken Galleons

During the Spaniards' colonization of the New World in the 16th, 17th and 18th centuries, galleons left Spain carrying goods to the colonies and returned loaded with gold and silver mined in Colombia, Peru and Mexico. Many of these ships sank in the Caribbean Sea, overcome by pirates or hurricanes. During these years, literally thousands of ships – not only Spanish but also English, French, Dutch, pirate and African slave ships – foundered in the green-blue waters of the Caribbean.

The frequency of shipwrecks spurred the Spaniards to organize operations to recover sunken cargo. By the 17th century, Spain maintained salvage flotillas in the ports of Portobelo, Havana and Veracruz. These fleets awaited news of shipwrecks and then proceeded immediately to the wreck sites, where the Spaniards used Caribbean and Bahamian divers, and later African slaves, to scour sunken vessels and the sea floor around them. On many occasions great storms wiped out entire fleets, resulting in a tremendous loss of lives and cargo.

As early as the 1620s, salvagers were using bronze diving bells to increase the time they could spend underwater. The bell was submerged vertically from a ship and held air in its upper part, allowing divers to enter it to breathe, rest and observe. Over time, such divers became very skilled and the salvaging business very lucrative – so lucrative that the English, who were established in Bermuda and the Bahamas, entered the Caribbean salvage business at the end of the 17th century. And pirates, as you'd expect, were always pleased to come upon a salvage operation.

In recent decades advances in diving and underwater-recovery equipment have led to a boom in Caribbean salvaging efforts. In most cases salvagers get to keep a portion of the treasure they recover, but the larger share is turned over to the government in whose waters the recovery took place. Among the items most frequently raised from the depths are silver coins minted in Spain and brought to the New World. Such coins are still found upon occasion at water's edge in Portobelo and Nombre de Dios – pieces of eight that most likely slid through a hole in someone's pocket or were otherwise lost.

quality ranges from fair to good. There is no exceptional diving in the vicinity of Portobelo, but few people leave here unhappy because the diving's relatively cheap and offers very good value.

There are no places to stay in Portobelo, although there are several hotels on the Sabanitas-Portobelo road into town. Likewise, while there are some food stands in town, there are no restaurants; along the Sabanitas-Portobelo road, however, there are several good restaurants.

Orientation

Portobelo consists of about 15 square blocks of mostly rundown homes and businesses beside a well-paved, two-lane road. That road intersects with the Panama City-Colón road at the town of Sabanitas, 33km to the west.

East of Portobelo, the road forks after 9km. The right branch of the road extends 14km farther east to Nombre de Dios; the left branch extends 11km to the hamlet of La Guayra, where visitors can hire boats to take them to Isla Grande, a few minutes' ride away.

Information

There is no tourist office in Portobelo, nor is there a bank. Probably the best place to find answers to area questions in town is the Real Aduana de Portobelo (see following).

Forts

To defend his bullion and galleons from pirates, King Félipe II ordered forts be constructed at Portobelo. By 1601 two had been built, both near the mouth of the bay: Fuerte San Félipe was on the northern side, and on the southern side was Fuerte San Diego. In the years that followed, many more fortresses would be erected, some on the sites of earlier, less substantial forts.

Today the remnants of **Fuerte San Jerónimo** and **Fuerte Santiago** can still be seen near town, and the ruins of **Fuerte San Fernando** occupy a grassy flat across the bay from town. Sadly, most of San Fernando was deconstructed by Americans who used its walls to create the breakwater protecting the northern end of the Panama Canal. Boats can be hired at water's edge near Fuerte Santiago for the trip across the bay to this fort. The roundtrip ride costs US$10 per person.

Santiago is the first fort you'll see as you near town from the west. It was built after British Admiral Edward Vernon's 1739 attack and contains many musket ports. Several of its walls are 3m thick, made entirely of cut coral – or 'reef rock,' as the Spaniards called it. Coral was used because it is as tough as granite and yet as light as pumice and can be shaped with a saw. The ruins at Fuerte Santiago include an officers' quarters, an artillery shed, a sentry box, a barracks and batteries.

On a hill overlooking Santiago and much of the bay is a small but well-preserved watchtower built at the time as Santiago. If you're in good health, hike up the grass-covered slope to it. The hike is only a couple of hundred meters long, but the slope is steep at times and the grass can be slippery. Beautiful views await those who make it to the watchtower, which has a dry moat around it and a well in the center.

Fuerte San Jerónimo, closer to the center of town, was the largest fortress ever built to protect the bay. If you're short on time, San Jerónimo is more complete and makes for a better visit than Santiago. Beyond its impressive gateway are the remains of the officers' quarters, a barracks and a guard room. Facing the mouth of the bay are 18 cannon embrasures. Some of the original cannons remain exactly where the Spanish troops left them when they returned home in 1821 – the year Panama declared its independence from Spain.

Real Aduana de Portobelo

This handsome two-story building, whose name translates to Royal Customs House of Portobelo, was originally built in 1630 to serve as the *contaduría* (counting house) for all the king's gold. It was in this building that the treasure brought across the isthmus was recorded and stored until it could be placed on galleons and sailed to Spain.

A Kuna family, Comarca de San Blás

Chocoé girl, Darién Province

Hunters in the rainforest, Darién Province

Children, Darién Province

Hanging out in Puerto Obaldía, Darién Province

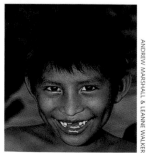

A Bocas del Toro smile

A friendly face in a familiar hat, Colón Province

Pensive boy in Panama City

Dominoes is popular in Chorrillo, Panama City.

Taking a breather in Chorrillo, Panama City

Ruperto Rivera takes in the scene, Panama City

According to early records, the building was originally called the King's House, and no fewer than 253 soldiers were assigned to it. The structure was severely damaged twice – by cannon fire in 1744 and by a strong earthquake in 1882. See the sidebar, 'Restoration or Destruction?,' for details about the building's third and latest restoration.

The Real Aduana consists of two main rooms, which are now used as exhibition halls. At the time of writing, one was used to display dozens of robes donated by believers and placed on the statue of the Black Christ every October, when thousands of followers worship the icon. (See Special Events, following, for details.) Most of the robes are made of purple velvet. Among the donors are boxer Roberto Duran and salsa star Ismael Rivera.

The other room contains replicas of Spanish-colonial rifles, sketches of Portobelo's forts, many photos taken of the *contaduría* during the 20th century, and a couple of dozen rusty cannon balls. Half of the room was taken up by an Instituto Nacional de Cultura office, attended by staff who knew little or nothing about their displays. Signage is in Spanish only.

Don't forget to visit the building's second story, which features an intriguing collection of photos and drawings of the Spanish-colonial fortresses that exist throughout Latin America. Also, don't overlook the bronze cannon recovered from a sunken galleon and bearing a Spanish coat of arms and the date of manufacture: 1617. It's located at the museum's entrance. Hours are 8 am to 4 pm daily. A donation is requested.

Diving & Snorkeling

As mentioned above, the diving around Portobelo isn't spectacular, but offers good value for the money. There are three dive operators, all located on the Sabanitas-Portobelo road, west of town.

Dive rates vary with the distance traveled and the amount of equipment rented. But people who have their own personal gear, a regulator and a buoyancy control device can expect to pay about US$30 for a two-tank dive. People who just want to snorkel

---

Restoration or Destruction?

There's an interesting story behind the restoration of Portobelo's old counting house. The large structure, which was where treasure was recorded before it was loaded onto Spanish galleons, was originally built of solid blocks of coral taken from a nearby reef. In the mid-1990s the Spanish government offered to pay for restoration of the historic building, but because it didn't trust the Panamanian government to do the work properly, it insisted on hiring the workers and overseeing the job.

Over the strong objections of environmentalists and others, the Spaniards destroyed most of a coral reef just north of Drake's Island in the process of rebuilding the former counting house. The reef is in the middle of the 35,929-hectare Parque Nacional Portobelo. Restoration of the reef, which can only be performed by nature, will require at least several hundred years. One Panamanian environmentalist, angry that Spain continues to have a role in Panama's affairs, told the author: 'The Spanish still think they can dictate to us.'

They can, and they do.

---

and have their own equipment can expect to pay US$10 per outing.

Scubaportobelo (☎ 261-3841, fax 261-9586) enjoys a solid reputation. It has a wide variety of rental equipment, and on-site tank refill is available. To rent equipment here, you must possess a scuba certification card and leave a cash deposit or signed Visa or MasterCard slip for the equipment's value.

Nautilus Dive Club (☎ 448-2028, cellular ☎ 613-6557) is very popular. Its owner, Javier Freiburghas, probably knows Panama's dive sites as well as anyone. His company also has 10 complete sets of gear, he is Nitrox certified and he speaks English and Spanish.

Padama (☎/fax 448-2067, 448-2163) offers a slew of PADI certification courses in addition to dive trips, and the staff claims to be trained to respond to any emergency. Only PADI-certified instructors or divemasters are allowed to lead divers here, same as Nautilus Dive Club.

Special Events

The Black Christ Festival in honor of the statue housed in the Iglesia de San Félipe is held every October 21 and is a fascinating event to witness. Pilgrims arrive from all over Panama on this day to dance and celebrate in honor of Jesus, many wearing purple (the color of the robe Christ wore). The exact origins of this festival and the black Christ statue it celebrates are a matter

of speculation: Many fanciful stories exist (see 'The Story of the Black Christ'), but any definitive church records were likely lost in the fire that followed Henry Morgan's sacking of Panamá in 1671. Regardless, on each anniversary of the statue's discovery, it is taken from the Portobelo church and paraded around town. The parade begins promptly at 6 pm, and street festivities follow.

Los Congos, a festivity in which black people assume the role of escaped slaves and run around taking 'captives,' is held in Portobelo and sometimes elsewhere in the province during Carnaval, on New Year's Eve and on patron saint days (March 20 in

The Story of the Black Christ

Many tales have attempted to explain the origins of the black Christ statue in Portobelo's church and the festival that honors it. One story has it that a ship bound for Cartagena, Colombia, from Portobelo tried to leave the port five times, but on each occasion a mighty storm appeared and blew the ship back to the town's edge, nearly sinking it in the process. The terrified crew are said to have lightened their vessel by tossing a heavy box overboard. On their sixth attempt to sail out of the bay, no storm appeared and they were able to go on their way unmolested.

According to this tale, several fishermen found the discarded box floating off Portobelo and were shocked to discover a statue of a black Christ inside it. They are said to have placed it in Portobelo's church out of respect. As word got around about the dark wooden statue, which stands 1.5m high, the figure took on a mythic reputation.

A second story claims that the church on Isla Taboga, clear on the other side of the isthmus, ordered a Jesus of Nazareth (a black Christ) statue from a supplier in Spain at about the same time that the Portobelo church ordered an image of Santo Domingo from the same supplier. It is said that the boxes in which the two statues were shipped to Panama were incorrectly labeled, so the church on Isla Taboga received the Santo Domingo statue while the one in Portobelo received the black Christ.

Many efforts were made to swap the figures, according to this tale, but each time something occurred that prevented the black Christ statue from leaving Portobelo. Today the congregation in Portobelo won't allow further attempts because it is convinced the statue is imbued with divine powers and that the black Christ wishes to remain with the people of Portobelo.

Still another story has it that Portobelo fishermen found a box floating at sea during a cholera epidemic. It contained a black Christ statue that, out of respect, the men placed inside the town church. Almost immediately, so goes this story, the epidemic passed, and people who had been reeling from the terrible disease quickly recovered.

There are other stories. Regardless of the veracity of any of them, the Black Christ Festival on October 21 makes for an interesting time. It begins with the parading of the statue and continues all night, as many people in purple robes – some wearing crowns of thorns and carrying crosses – roam around dancing, gambling and drinking.

Portobelo). 'The Congos' is both the name of the festivity and the name of the people who maintain this intriguing tradition, which is based around a satire of colonial Spaniards.

The tradition dates from the days of Panama's slave trade, when some black slaves escaped into the jungle and formed communities there. The satire consists of taking someone prisoner and demanding a huge ransom, but the prisoner is freed when he or she pays a token ransom, perhaps only 50¢. The celebrants are generally dressed in outlandish outfits that include tattered clothes and hats that resemble crowns. Many of them also carry wooden swords. All are so animated that they look like they've just come from an insane asylum.

Los Congos usually perform before audiences that assemble to watch them 'captivate' people, but sometimes a really crazy-looking group of men wielding wooden swords will descend upon a person who's just walking down the street and demand thousands of dollars (but they'll settle for a few coins). Sound bizarre? It is. If you ever find yourself an innocent 'victim' of this tradition, try not to freak out and kill someone. They're just harmless Congos.

Places to Stay

As you approach Portobelo from Sabanitas, the first place you'll see, on the left side of the road, is *Nautilus Dive Club* (☎ 448-2028, cellular 613-6557), which offers five spacious rooms, each with air con, at least two double beds and a private hot-water bathroom. The rate is US$40 per room. There are also five smaller rooms with all the amenities for US$30. Most of the rooms are over the water. There's a pleasing bar-restaurant here and a pool table.

The next available lodgings can be found at *Scubaportobelo* (☎ 448-2147, 261-3841 in Panama City, fax 261-9586), which charges US$35/50 per cabin weekdays/weekends. Each has air con and private cold-water bathroom. There's also a dormitory on the premises with beds available for US$10.

There are other places in the area, but none cheaper or as nice as these.

Places to Eat

There are several good restaurants along the Sabanitas-Portobelo road. All open for breakfast, lunch and dinner.

As you travel toward Portobelo, the first place you'll come to is *Restaurante Los Cañones,* which is over the water and faces a lovely inlet. The menu includes red snapper, sea bass, squid, clams and baby shrimp – all US$6 each. The dish that this restaurant is really known for is octopus, slowly cooked to perfection in a spicy tomato-based sauce and served on a bed of coconut rice. At US$6, it's a sin.

The next place you'll come to is *Restaurante Grupo Marin*, located at the water's edge. This is a pleasant place that features seafood, with most prices in the US$6 to US$9 range.

Continuing on toward Portobelo, you'll next spot *Restaurante Cabañas del Mar*, which serves all the same food you'll find at Los Cañones at the same prices. It's just not quite as delicious.

Closer to town, on the right side of the road, is *Restaurante La Torre*, which advertises 'cheeseburgers in paradise' and delivers the goods. A tasty cheeseburger with fries goes for US$3. English is spoken at this breezy, Colombian-owned restaurant, which displays the day's winning lottery number beside its posted menu. The seafood here is excellent. Typical dishes, which are served with your choice of side order, include half a roasted chicken (US$4.50) and conch in coconut sauce (US$6). This place also serves wonderful juices; melon, passion fruit and orange are usually available.

Getting There & Away

Buses to Portobelo depart Colón's Terminal de Buses hourly from 4:30 am to 6 pm and cost US$2.30 each way. To go to Panama City from Portobelo, you must first go to Colón.

Getting Around

There are occasional taxis in Portobelo, but not many. The best way to travel the Sabanitas-Portobelo road is to flag down any of the buses headed in the direction you wish to go. No public transportation is available after dark.

ISLA GRANDE
pop 1000

This island, 15km east of Portobelo, is a popular weekend destination for Panama City's party animals. The inhabitants of this island are of African descent and most make a living from fishing and coconut production. Seafood and coconut milk are the principal ingredients of the island's food, which includes seafood soups, ceviche, Caribbean king crab, lobster, shrimp, octopus, sea turtle (tortuga; please don't eat it), shad and sea bass.

There are some lovely beaches on the northern side of the island that can be reached by boat (hire a water taxi at the dock in front of Cabañas Super Jackson) or on foot (there's a water's-edge trail that loops around the 5km long, 1.5km wide island, as well as a slippery trail that crosses the island). There are also some fine snorkeling and dive sites within a 10-minute boat ride of the island. There's one dive operator (Isla Grande Dive Center; no phone), which operates on weekends only. It's located 50m west of Cabañas Super Jackson.

For US$30 (or US$25 if you're a sweet talker), one of the boatmen in front of Cabañas Super Jackson will take you on a half-day adventure. The possibilities are quite appealing: There are mangroves east of Isla Grande that make for fun exploring, and you could also go snorkeling and take a picnic to a beach on the mainland or a small secluded island.

About 200m east of Cabañas Super Jackson is a Club Turqueza – a restaurant-bar from which it's possible to make a sailing excursion with San Blás Sailing (☎ 214-3446, cellular 687-8521) to the San Blás islands aboard a 41-foot sailing yacht or a 42-foot catamaran. Prices range from US$85 to US$180 per person per day and include drinks, meals, lodging, use of snorkeling equipment, kayaks, surfboards and more.

The French built a lighthouse on the island in 1893, which sent red, green and white light over 100km out to sea. The lighthouse still functions today, but its light is now white, and it is visible for only 70km.

Special Events

San Juan Bautista is celebrated here on June 24 with swimming and canoe races. The Virgen del Carmen is honored on July 16 with a land and sea procession, baptisms and Masses. Carnaval is also celebrated here; the locals dance the conga with ribbons and mirrors in their hair, the women wearing traditional pollera dresses and the men in ragged pants tied at the waist with old sea rope. Along with the dancing, there are satirical songs about current events and a lot of joking in the Caribbean calypso tradition.

Places to Stay & Eat

There are many temporary housing options on Isla Grande. Only those that impressed the author in some way are mentioned here.

The closest place to the main pier is *Cabañas Super Jackson* (☎ 448-2311), which has five rooms, each with different features: one bed or two small beds with fan (US$20), two/three/four beds and air con (US$35/45/50). All rooms have private bathrooms and are very clean and cheerful. The hotel is beside a small store selling ice-cold beverages – a major plus on this humid island.

About 200m west of Super Jackson is *Hotel Isla Grande* (☎ 225-6722, fax 225-6721), which mostly consists of several multilevel blocks of rooms, each with a fan, private bathroom and an ocean view (US$45 per night). However, there are also 10 oceanside cabins with air con at US$55 that are quite popular. Among the places to stay that you can easily walk to, this is the only one with a sandy beach.

To the east of Super Jackson and maybe better is *Cabañas Cholita* (☎/fax 448-2962), which offers 14 oceanside rooms, all with air-con, good mattresses and private cold-water bathrooms. Rates are US$39 for one or two people, US$50 for three or four people and

US$66 for five or six people. Lunch and dinner items are mostly around US$6.

Next door is a better deal than Cholita – *Posada Villa Ensueño* (☎ 448-2964) has 16 rooms, all more attractive than those at the places mentioned above. There are four air con rooms with one twin bed in each (US$44 per room), 10 rooms with two beds (US$50) and two rooms with three twin beds (US$60). There's even a large lawn for campers (US$10 per tent per night, use of showers and toilets included).

Banana Village Resort (☎ 263-9766, fax 264-7556), on the northern side of the island, includes an open-sided restaurant, a bar with a pool table, a swimming pool, and a long, clean beach. Accommodations consist of eight two-story houses with three guestrooms apiece (two downstairs and one upstairs). All of the houses are backed by jungle and fronted by the sea. Every room is cheerful, and all have white wicker furniture, French doors and a safe. Single/double rates, which include meals and boat shuttle from the mainland, are reasonable at US$110/150. The resort often lowers its rates April 15 to October 15.
Web site: www.bananasresort.com

The pickings are generally slim at the island's stand-alone restaurants, which seem to specialize in bland, overcooked food. The exception is *Club Turqueza,* east of Posada Villa Ensueño, which offers huevos rancheros served with homemade marmalade and bread (US$7), salad niçoise (US$6.50), and many seafood and crêpe dishes.

Getting There & Away

Buses to La Guayra (the coastal hamlet where visitors can hire boats to get to Isla Grande) depart Colón's Terminal de Buses (US$2.25, hourly) from 6:30 am to 6 pm. These buses can be boarded at Sabanitas, the turnoff for Portobelo, La Guayra and Nombre de Dios, and you can thus avoid Colón.

In La Guayra, there are always skippers hanging about near the water's edge, waiting to take people to the island. The 10-minute boat ride costs US$5 to US$10 per party depending on the skipper and the size of the party.

PLAYA BLANCA

A few kilometers west of Isla Grande is lovely Playa Blanca (☎ 232-4985 in Panama City; cellular ☎ 613-1558,) which consists of a seaside lodge with a breezy common area, and five guestrooms with private hot-water bathrooms. This relaxing retreat is situated on four hectares on a roadless peninsula and faces a small private cove with an inviting white-sand beach.
Website: www.pblodge.com

The retreat's main attraction is the peaceful setting and fine snorkeling that's available in the cove a shell's toss away. There's a pristine coral reef close to shore and another, significantly deeper one about 100m farther out. These may be the least disturbed reefs between Colón and the Archipiélago de San Blás.

The comfortable guestrooms can each accommodate one couple. There are two fully equipped kitchens for you do-it-yourselfers. Mosquito netting accompanies each bed. The lodge's per-night prices of US$150/250 per person without/with meals include boat transportation to and from Portobelo.

If you must use a hairdryer and aren't complete without a morning cappuccino, this casual place isn't for you. The available electricity is limited to 12 volts, supplied by solar panels. That voltage is perfect for charging the portable fans guests can place beside their beds, although the nightly dip in temperature generally makes them unnecessary. The water is solar-heated – warm but not steamy.

Meals are hearty and often consist of barbecued chicken, pasta or beef and local vegetables and fruits. The food's not fancy, but it is delicious and filling. There's plenty of beer and wine to go around.

The retreat, which is owned and run by a couple of retired US military officers, is connected to 'land line,' which is slightly different from your usual telephone line. To place a call directly to the retreat, dial ☎ 441-0672, followed by 7801 after you hear a chime.

NOMBRE DE DIOS

Nombre de Dios, 23km east of Portobelo, has a colorful history but isn't much to look at today. There are no ruins from the Spanish settlement to be found, although people here still occasionally pick up the silver-cross coins used by the Spaniards 400 years ago. There's a salt-and-pepper beach, but it's nothing special.

History

From 1519 to 1598, this settlement was the northern terminus of trade across the isthmus. It was here in 1510 that Nicuesa ordered his small fleet to land after they failed to establish a colony at the mouth of the Río Belén in Veraguas. The little harbor and the beach buttressed by dense vegetation looked promising from the sea, but the area's humid climate and scarcity of food took a heavy toll on the settlers.

About 280 settlers made it to Nombre de Dios (800 men had left Hispaniola with Nicuesa in November 1509), and they used what little strength they had to build a blockhouse and huts. For many weeks the men lived on rotten provisions. On a good day they fed upon an alligator; many lived beside the rivers that drained into the Caribbean, but catching one was never easy. Nicuesa sent a ship to Hispaniola for bacon and other supplies, but the vessel was never heard from again.

One day a scouting party from the Spanish colony at Antigua, in the Darién, stumbled upon Nombre de Dios. By this time only 60 settlers remained; the rest had died of disease or hunger. The survivors told the scouts nasty stories about Nicuesa, who was more concerned about establishing a capital than he was about his men. The scouts returned to Antigua with horror stories about Nombre de Dios and its leader.

Nicuesa and 17 men reached Antigua a few days after the scouts, but they were told not to come ashore. The settlers at Antigua wanted nothing to do with Nicuesa. But the governor was stubborn, and the next day he and his party paddled to shore. The men were seized, placed on the worst vessel in

the harbor and forced to sail. The rotting craft left Antigua on March 1, 1511, and the ship and its passengers were never seen again.

It was rumored that the worm-eaten vessel wrecked on the coast of Veraguas, where these words were found carved into a tree: *'Aqui andu ó perdido el desdichado Diego de Nicuesa'?* ('Here wandered lost the wretched Diego de Nicuesa'). Another version has it that, while landing on the coast for water, Nicuesa and his men were captured by Indians, barbecued and eaten. According to yet a third version, a tree was found in Cuba with the words *'Aqui feneció el desdichado Nicuesa'* ('Here died the wretched Nicuesa') carved into it.

The 43 miserable survivors who were barely clinging to life at Nombre de Dios were soon rescued from their hell and taken to Antigua by that colony's leader, Vasco Núñez de Balboa. Eight years later, in 1519, the city of Panamá was founded, and later that year Nombre de Dios was resettled. Nombre de Dios soon became the Caribbean terminus of trade across the isthmus, and so it remained until the late 1590s, when nearby Portobelo took over that role.

But even in its heyday as a trading center, Nombre de Dios was a dreadful place. During the mid-16th century, there were 200 houses in the town, but most of the owners lived here only when Spanish fleets arrived to trade supplies for gold and silver stolen from various tribes on the isthmus and in Peru. During the rest of the year, only about 50 people remained. It rained most days, and the heat was excessive.

According to a 16th-century historian, the town was so unhealthy that Indian women living there became barren, and even the native fruits refused to grow. Strong men are said to have died before their time, and disease always claimed the lives of Spanish children. The town was known as a graveyard for travelers. So many men attached to fleets shuttling between Spain and Panama perished while in Nombre de Dios that the biannual trade fairs, initially lasting 60 days, were shortened to 40. It is fitting that Drake, who spent so much of his life in the Tropics, died of dysentery within days of sacking Nombre de Dios.

The town was attacked not only by pirates but also by bands of runaway slaves. Hundreds of escaped black slaves, whom the Spaniards referred to as Cimarrones, mingled with the equally abused Indians and formed settlements of their own during the mid-16th century. By 1574 the escaped slaves had become such a nuisance to the settlers that the king of Spain granted the Cimarrones their freedom on the condition that they'd keep to themselves.

Following Francis Drake's attack on Nombre de Dios and the rise of Portobelo at the end of the 16th century, the town was all but abandoned, and it remained a backwater hamlet for the next 300 years. At that point it gradually revived to a community of about 2000 people, most of whom were the descendants of slaves. People still died like flies in Nombre de Dios until the beginning of the 20th century, when Americans arrived to dredge sand from the harbor for use in concrete for the Gatún Locks. The Americans built a public hospital, screened houses, dug wells and improved sanitation.

The Americans even rebuilt all the structures in town, but not by design: In April 1910 a spark from a locomotive used in the sand-dredging operations started a fire that leaped from one wooden, thatch-roofed structure to another until all 73 buildings in Nombre de Dios had gone up in flames. The Americans took it upon themselves to rebuild the town. Some of the wooden buildings from those days still exist, but the material of choice today is cinderblock.

Orientation & Information

As you enter the town, you'll pass some uncomfortably warm and very rustic houses on both sides of the road. After perhaps 100m, a short road curves to the left, toward the ocean, where there are more homes.

If you stay on the main road, 50m or so past the first turnoff you'll reach a second road that turns toward the ocean. In 75m this road reaches the center of town, marked by a small plaza. Facing the plaza is the only place to stay, the Casa de Huespedes.

The one pay phone in town is near the plaza. There is no post office or bank.

Places to Stay & Eat

Casa de Huespedes (☎ 448-2068, ask for *Alejandrina Vega*) has nine rooms, each of which contains a stand fan. This no-frills place is clean and offers good value. Rooms with shared/private cold-water bathrooms cost US$4/5. There is no restaurant here, but there are a couple of simple restaurants nearby.

Getting There & Away

Buses to Nombre de Dios depart Colón's Terminal de Buses (US$3, hourly) from 6:30 am to 6 pm. These same buses can be boarded at Sabanitas, which is the turnoff for Portobelo, La Guayra and Nombre de Dios, so you can avoid Colón. Buses from Nombre de Dios to Sabanitas leave hourly from 6 am till 4 pm.

Getting Around

There are no taxis in Nombre de Dios. The only way to get around is by foot. However, this is a very small town. Walking across it takes 20 minutes, tops.

Comarca de San Blás

The Comarca de San Blás is an autonomous region that comprises the Archipiélago de San Blás and a 226km strip of Caribbean coast from Colón Province to Colombia. The southern boundary of the *comarca* (district) consists of two strings of jungle-clad mountains, the Serranía de San Blás and the Serranía del Darién – the highlands of the San Blás and Darién regions.

The Kuna Indians have governed the 2360-sq-km region since the 1920s, when the Panamanian government granted the tribe the right of self-rule following a Kuna uprising that led to the death of 22 Panamanian policemen and 20 Kuna who had befriended them. Today, the Kuna not only govern themselves but have two representatives in the Panamanian legislature, as well as the right to vote in Panamanian elections.

Highlights

- The islands, mostly uninhabited and fit to appear on the covers of travel magazines
- The Kuna, a fiercely independent people who maintain their traditions in a changing world
- Romantic Needle Island, with its postcard-perfect inviting sand and surf and friendly locals
- Wreck Reef, a snorkeling site that's become a graveyard for many a boat

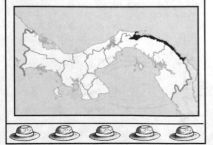

The best time to visit the comarca is May through November, when the winds are stronger and the temperatures are generally lower. When there's no breeze and the mercury rises and the humidity sets in, life on the San Blás islands can be miserable.

Kuna Indians

The Kuna have lived in eastern Panama for at least the last two centuries, but scholars don't agree on their origin. Language similarities with people who once lived several hundred kilometers to the west would indicate that the Kuna migrated eastward. However, oral tradition has it that the tribe emigrated from Colombia after the 16th century, following devastating encounters with other tribes armed with poison-dart blowguns.

Some scholars contend the Kuna were well established in eastern Panama at the time the conquistadors arrived, because the Spanish chroniclers indicated that the Indians they met used the Kuna words *ulu* for 'canoe' and *oba* for 'corn.' These scholars also note that many geographic names in eastern Panama during the colonial epoch were Kuna. Nearly all the rivers in Darién Province have Kuna names, for example, although the Emberá and Wounaan Indians live there now.

No matter where the Kuna came from, scholars agree that life on the islands is relatively new for the Indians. Historians at the end of the 18th century wrote that the only people who used the San Blás islands at that time were pirates, Spaniards and the odd explorer.

Today there are an estimated 70,000 Kuna: 32,000 live on the district's islands, 8,000 live on tribal land along the coast and 30,000 live outside the district. So communal are the island Kuna that they inhabit only 40 of the hundreds of keys; the rest are mostly left to coconut trees, sea turtles and iguanas. On the inhabited islands, so many traditional bamboo-sided, thatch-roof houses are clustered together that there's scarcely room to maneuver between them.

The Kuna like to say that their archipelago consists of 'one island for every day of the year.' In fact, there are nearly 400 islands in the chain, all small creations of sand and palm rising barely far enough above the blue-green Caribbean to escape complete inundation by breakers during storms. Reefs to the north and east prevent destructive waves from striking the islands. From the tourist's perspective, there are two kinds of San Blás islands: the white-sand, palm-sprinkled, magazine-cover beauties, and the overcrowded keys where feces and rubbish are found just a few meters from shore.

Few of the islands are more than 10km from the district's mainland, and all the heavily inhabited islands are very close to the coast because the Kuna's agricultural areas and their vital natural resources – such as water, firewood and construction materials – are there. Also on the mainland are the giant trees from which the Indians make their chief mode of transportation – the *cayuco*, a dugout canoe made from a burned and hollowed-out trunk. There are nine towns on the mainland, all within 100m of the sea; there are no restaurants or hotels in these towns.

The Kuna still adhere to traditions that astonish tourists. For example, a Kuna woman is not given a name until she has had her first menstrual period, at which time a party is held, the young woman's hair is cut short and her parents select a name for her with the help of a medicine man. Until that day the young woman answers to a nickname.

Most Kuna women continue to dress as their ancestors did. Their faces are distinguished by a black line painted from the forehead to the tip of the nose. A gold ring is worn through the nose. A length of colorful printed cloth is wrapped around the waist as a skirt, topped by a short-sleeved blouse covered in brilliantly colored *molas* (traditional Kuna textiles). A printed head scarf and many necklaces, rings and bracelets complete the daily outfit. To make

themselves more attractive, the women also wrap their legs, from ankle to knee, in long strands of colorful beads.

The Kuna sometimes appear unfriendly to tourists, and understandably so, because most visitors view them as oddities that must be photographed. Cruise ships visit several islands, and when the ships arrive, the number of people on an already congested island can triple, leaving barely enough room for anyone to turn around. Nonetheless, virtually two-thirds of the populace (the tourists) are trying like crazy to photograph the other third (the Kuna). It's a pretty ugly scene, and it's repeated time and again.

In addition, the behavior of many tourists is appalling to the Kuna. For example, Kuna women dress conservatively, always keeping their cleavage, bellies and most of their legs covered. In their opinion, to do otherwise would be offensive. Yet many foreign women arrive in Kuna villages in bikini tops and short shorts, not only embarrassing themselves in the eyes of the Indians but also showing disrespect for Kuna sensibilities. Likewise, local men don't go shirtless and travelers who do so risk offending Kuna sensibilities. As a result of repeated violations of their privacy and sensibilities, the Kuna often ask that travelers pay a visitation fee and fees for photographs taken of them (see Visiting the Comarca de San Blás, below).

Until the late 1990s, the district's principal currency was the coconut. (In recent years, the sale of molas replaced the sale of coconuts as the Kuna's number one revenue source.) The Kuna grow coconuts like crazy: In a good year they'll harvest more than 30 million of them. They barter away most of these to Colombians, who make the rounds of Kuna towns in old wooden schooners, each of which can hold 50,000 to 80,000 coconuts. In return for the fruit, the Colombians give the Kuna clothing, jars of Nescafé, vinegar, rice, sunglasses, canned milk, batteries, soups and other goods.

In Colombia the coconuts are used in the production of candy, gelatin capsules, cookies, shampoos and other products. Colombia has

COMARCA DE SAN BLÁS

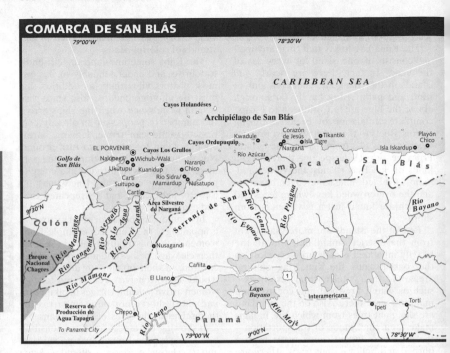

many processing plants for the fruit, but Panama, oddly, has none. The Colombians also sell Kuna coconuts to other South American countries.

The Kuna are shrewd businesspeople. Because, until recently, their economy was based on the sale of coconuts, they protect it by selling the fruit at a predetermined price to prevent their buyers from playing one Kuna off another to bring down the cost. Every year the tribe's chiefs agree on one price for coconuts. If a Kuna is found selling coconuts at another price, the tribe punishes that Indian. By price fixing and enforcement, the chiefs prevent price wars among the Kuna. Price wars would hurt the community by lowering the standard of living, and they could even force some Kuna out of business.

In another protectionist move, the chiefs passed a law a few years ago prohibiting outsiders from owning property in the district. Thus they promptly forced out the handful of foreigners living on the islands without compensation. As a result of that law, there are fewer than a dozen places to stay on the islands, because few Kuna have enough money to construct even a basic hotel. None of the hotels that do exist are fancy.

Visiting the Comarca de San Blás

On most of the heavily inhabited islands, the Kuna require tourists to register and pay a visitation fee upon arrival. That fee ranges from US$3 to US$5 (the price varies from island to island), and the visitor is expected to pay it regardless of whether he or she stays a week or only half an hour. For brevity's sake, this fee isn't mentioned again in this chapter, but remember: If you arrive on a populated San Blás island, you might be expected to present your passport and pay a visitation fee as well.

With few exceptions, visitors must also pay for any photo they take of Kuna. If you

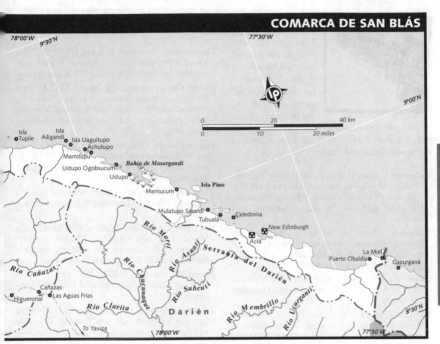

want to take someone's photo, be sure to first ask his or her permission, and be prepared to pay at least US$1 per subject (some Kuna expect to be paid US$1 per photo).

Another thing visitors should know is that all the uninhabited islands are privately owned. It's usually OK to use the island, but be prepared to pay a small fee if the owner shows up. Some largely uninhabited islands have a single family living on them; if you spot such an island and like it, you can usually visit it for a few hours if you pay the family US$2. Unless you speak Kuna, your boatman might have to do the talking for you. Not all Kuna speak Spanish, and very few speak English.

If you want to camp on an uninhabited island, US$5 a night per couple will usually do the trick. But camping on such islands isn't wise, because you run the risk of encountering drug traffickers in the night. The Kuna do not allow the Panamanian coast guard or US antidrug vessels to operate in the archipelago, so the uninhabited islands are occasionally used by Colombian drug traffickers running cocaine up the coast.

There are only a handful of lodgings on the islands, and none on the mainland. Most of these are basic, although a couple are quite comfortable. Most densely populated islands in the district have a store selling basic items, as well as coin telephones from which you can place domestic and international calls. Though the phones are public, there's usually a Kuna standing nearby charging a telephone tax of up to US$1 per call.

Getting There & Away

Air Three airlines fly between Panama City and the Comarca de San Blás: Aereotaxi (☎ 315-0300), Ansa (☎ 315-7520) and Aviatur (☎ 315-0307). See the Panama City chapter for flight information to the islands.

Flight informa-
tion from the
Comarca de San
Blás to the capital
appears below.
The telephone
numbers given on
page 331 are for
the airlines' offices
at Aeropuerto Albrook, which handle reservations. Aereotaxi and Ansa have identical
flight schedules and fares.

Achutupo - Aereotaxi & Ansa, US$34, 7:20 am
Monday through Saturday; Aviatur, US$34,
7:15 and 10:15 am Monday through Saturday,
1:45 and 2:15 pm Tuesday, Thursday and
Sunday

Ailigandí - Aereotaxi & Ansa, US$34, 7 am
Monday through Saturday; Aviatur, US$34, 7
and 10 am Monday through Saturday, 1:30 pm
Tuesday, Thursday and Sunday

Caledonia - Aviatur, US$36, 10:15 am Monday
through Saturday, 1:45 pm Tuesday, Thursday
and Sunday

Cartí - Aereotaxi & Ansa, US$29, 6:55 am
Monday through Saturday, 8 am Sunday;
Aviatur, US$29, 6:30 and 9:30 am Monday
through Saturday, 7:30 and 8:30 am Sunday

Corazón de Jesús - Aereotaxi & Ansa, US$30, 6:40
am Monday through Saturday, 7:40 am Sunday
(via Cartí); Aviatur, US$30, 7:20 and 10:20 am
Monday through Saturday, 8:20 and 9:20 am
Sunday

El Porvenir - Aereotaxi & Ansa, US$30, 6:35 am
Monday through Saturday, 7:35 am Sunday;
Aviatur, US$30, 6:30 and 9:30 am Monday
through Saturday, 7:30 and 8:30 am Sunday

Isla Tigre - Aviatur, US$30, 7:20 and 10:20 am
Monday through Saturday, 8:30 and 9:20 am
Sunday

Isla Tupile - Aereotaxi & Ansa, US$33, 6:50 am
Monday through Saturday (via Achutupo);
Aviatur, US$33, 6:50 and 9:50 am Monday
through Saturday, 1:20 pm Tuesday, Thursday
and Sunday

Mulatupo Sasardí - Aereotaxi & Ansa, US$36,
Monday through Saturday; Aviatur, US$36, 6:50
and 9:50 am Monday through Saturday, 1:50 pm
Tuesday, Thursday and Sunday

Mamitupu - Aviatur, US$34, 7 and 10 am Monday
through Saturday, 1:30 pm Tuesday, Thursday
and Sunday

Mansucum - Aviatur, US$36, 10:30 am Monday
through Saturday, 2 pm Tuesday, Thursday and
Sunday

Ogobsucum - Aereotaxi & Ansa, US$35, 7:35 am
Monday through Saturday; Aviatur, US$35, 6:30
am Monday through Saturday, 12:30 pm Sunday

Playón Chico - Aereotaxi & Ansa, US$32, 6:45 am
Monday through Saturday (via Achutupo);
Aviatur, US$32, 6:40 and 9:40 am Monday
through Saturday, 1:10 pm Tuesday, Thursday
and Sunday

Puerto Obaldía - Aereotaxi & Ansa, US$47, 12:45
pm Wednesday and Sunday; Aviatur, US$47, 10
am Monday through Saturday, 1:30 pm Tuesday,
Thursday and Sunday

Río Azúcar - Aviatur, US$30, 6:30 and 9:30 am
Monday through Saturday, 7:30 and 8:30 am
Sunday

Río Sidra - Aereotaxi & Ansa, US$30, 6:55 am
Monday through Saturday, 7:55 am Sunday;
Aviatur, US$30, 6:30 and 9:30 am Monday
through Saturday, 7:30 and 8:30 am Sunday

Tikantiki - Aviatur, US$30, 6:30 and 9:30 am
Monday through Saturday, 7:30 and 8:30 am
Sunday

Tubualá - Aviatur, US$36, 10:15 am Monday
through Saturday, 1:54 pm Tuesday, Thursday
and Sunday

Ustupo - Aereotaxi & Ansa, US$35, 7:25 am
Monday through Saturday; Aviatur, US$35, 7:45
and 10:45 am Monday through Saturday, 2:15
and 2:45 pm Tuesday, Thursday and Sunday

Reservations are advised, as only small aircraft serve the district, and seats fill up
quickly. An airplane flying from Panama
City to San Blás may stop at several islands
before reaching your destination, so be sure
to ask the name of the island you're on
before you leave the plane. Likewise, it's
probable that the aircraft you board in San
Blás to return to Panama City will make
several stops before it arrives in the capital.

Car Only one road leads into the district,
the rugged El Llano-Cartí road that connects the town of El Llano, on the Carretera Interamericana 70km east of Panama
City, to the San Blás coastal hamlet of
Cartí.
The road begins near El Llano at the
turnoff for Nusagandi, a forest reserve just

Buying a Mola

A mola, a traditional Kuna handicraft, is made of brightly colored squares of cotton fabric laid atop one another. Cuts are made through the layers, forming basic designs. The layers are then sewn together with tiny, evenly spaced stitches to hold the design in place. *Mola* means 'blouse' in Kuna, and Kuna women make molas in thematically matching but never identical pairs. A pair will comprise the front and back of a blouse.

As is true of all art forms, the beauty of a mola is in the eye of the beholder. If you're in the market for a mola, choose one you would like to see on your wall, as a place setting, as part of a dress; don't be swayed by what you think someone else might find attractive. I happen to like molas that feature sea turtles, but then I'm a simple fellow.

Regardless of the design, Kuna believe that the very best molas have the following characteristics:

- Stitches closely match the color of the cloth they are set against.
- Stitches are very fine and neatly spaced.
- Stitches are pulled evenly and with enough tension to be barely visible.
- Curves are cut smoothly and the sewing follows the curves of the cut.
- Outline strips are uniform in width, with no frayed edges.

ALFREDO MAIQUEZ

When you're buying molas, it's a good idea to think about how you intend to use them. If you're thinking of making pillows out of them, consider the piece of furniture you'll place the pillows on. On the other hand, if you see a mola you really like, get it and worry about its use later. You can always add a mola to the back of a denim jacket, which gives you a justification for purchasing yet another article of clothing.

inside the Comarca de San Blás. The reserve begins at the southern boundary of the district, 20km north of the Interamericana. A few kilometers north of the district boundary is the very rustic Nusagandi Nature Lodge. (See the Panamá Province chapter for more details on the reserve and the lodge.)

The lodge is reachable only by a 4WD vehicle with a powerful engine, a winch and good off-road tires. Beyond the lodge, the remaining 20km to Cartí is on a road that even a German assault tank would have difficulty traveling. For all practical purposes, the El Llano-Cartí road ends at the lodge.

Getting Around

The best way to see the islands is with a tour guide. If you can afford one, contact one of the tour operators listed in the Getting Around chapter and see the archipelago with someone who knows the islands and can make all the necessary arrangements for you.

If you don't use a tour operator, be sure to make a hotel reservation. If you do, chances are you'll be met at the airport by someone who will then take you by boat to your hotel. If no one meets you, find a boatman and ask him to take you; if you don't speak Spanish, just say the name of your hotel a few times, look lost and have US$5 or US$10 out.

Colombian merchant boats travel the Caribbean Sea between Colón and Puerto Obaldía, stopping at inhabited San Blás islands to pick up and drop off people and goods. Other Colombian vessels visit the inhabited islands to take on coconuts. Both fleets are occasionally used for drug trafficking. Travel by these often overloaded boats is neither comfortable nor safe, and it's always very slow going.

A much better way to get around is to pick an area of the archipelago you want to visit, fly as close to it as the nearest airstrip will allow and hire a boatman to take you around. If you speak Spanish or Kuna and have some cash in hand, you can usually find someone with a motorized cayuco who

will assume the role of boatman. If you don't speak either language, you could find yourself stranded.

One of the most pleasant sights you'll encounter on a boat trip in the archipelago is the coastline to the south. Behind the generally sandy shore are jagged peaks that run the length of the district. Initially the verdant hills are covered with a mixture of manioc fields and patches of rain forest, but the farther east you travel the fewer fields there are, and at times the mountains are covered with jungle as far as the eye can see.

This is the coast as Christopher Columbus saw it – unspoiled, the very darkest of greens and teeming with wildlife. Always making a welcome appearance just above the mountains are cumulus clouds. They may be pure white or gray with rainwater, but they are never tainted by smog. Sunsets are particularly colorful, displaying generous proportions of reds and oranges, violets and lavenders.

EL PORVENIR

El Porvenir, at the northwest end of the district, is the gateway to the San Blás islands. Visitors to the keys tend to fly here, proceed directly to the island's small dock and take a boat elsewhere. That 'elsewhere' is more often than not the Hotel San Blás, on the nearby island of Nalunega; the Kuna Niskua Hotel, on the island of Wichub-Walá; or the Ukutupu Hotel, on an artificial island known simply as Ukutupu (which in Kuna might mean 'eye of an enigma wrapped inside an enigma looking at itself, wanna buy a mola?').

There's a police station, two public phones and a few homes on El Porvenir, as well as a hotel with a restaurant: *El Porvenir Hotel* (☎ 229-9000, ☎/fax 221-1397; ask for Mrs Bibi). Most of its 13 rooms contain three twin beds, and each has a toilet, a cold-water shower, one light and one power outlet. Electricity is provided from 6 pm 'until all of our guests have gone to bed.' The hotel's walls are concrete and its roof is corrugated tin – nothing fancy – but the place is cool and pleasant. Rates are US$30 per person September to March and US$25 the rest of the year.

NALUNEGA
pop 340

This island, with its many traditional Kuna homes close together, is similar to the inhabited San Blás islands found farther south and east in the archipelago. However, Nalunega is considerably cleaner than the others because the owner of its sole hotel pays several boys to keep the small island free of litter. There was no public phone on this island in 2001.

The *Hotel San Blás* (☎ 290-6528) is the best value and most popular hotel in the district. It has 29 rooms; most are simple but OK bamboo-and-board adjoining rooms with sandy floors, thatch roofs and shared bathrooms. The guestrooms above the open-sided dining area and the adjacent general store are cooler and cleaner than the others because their floors are not sandy; although the sea is a stone's throw away, the views from these rooms are mostly of thatch roofs. Ask to see several rooms, as their appeal and the firmness of the beds varies substantially. The per-person rate for all these rooms is US$35, which includes three meals and a boat tour. The cost to use the beach of a nearby private island is US$1 a day.

The hotel's owner, Luis Burgos, speaks English, and the food he provides is the best in the islands (expect lobster; king crab is occasionally served). If Luis knows you're coming, he'll arrange for a boatman to meet you on El Porvenir. Luis opened his hotel in 1972, at which time it consisted of three Spartan huts, and Luis served triple duty as cook, maid and boatman. Today he is the largest employer on Nalunega, with a staff of four.

WICHUB-WALÁ

This small and unusually clean inhabited island with one public telephone, a five-minute boat ride from El Porvenir, is home to the *Kuna Niskua Lodge* (☎ 225-5200; kunaniskua@hotmail.com). The Niskua has 12 fine rooms in a two-story thatch-and-

---

Moon Children

Few Kuna marry outside their villages. The result is an inbred people – usually short, large-headed and thick-necked – with the world's highest incidence of albinism. Albinos' eyes are dark pink, their hair yellow-white and their skin pale pink. When seen amid their brown-skinned, black-haired relatives, Kuna albinos are quite captivating.

In some societies, albino children are viewed as freaks of nature and are ostracized by their peers. Not so in Kuna society. Kuna children are taught that albinos are special people – children of the moon – and that they are destined to be leaders.

As a result, the moon children of the Comarca de San Blás are not only the most popular kids in the tribe, but they are also the most recalcitrant due to their big egos. Kuna children have a lot of confidence as it is, but when you tell some of them that they are particularly gifted – and they surely do look different – they can become very confident indeed.

Unsurprisingly, an unusually high percentage of moon children put their abundant confidence to work for them and actually become community leaders – a fact that further supports the notion that they really are special people.

---

bamboo structure with shared bathrooms. These rooms are in the middle of the island and do not have ocean views, but they are nicer than the rooms at the Hotel San Blás and there's a very pleasing dining room. The year-round rate of US$35 per person includes meals and a snorkeling tour. Three rooms with private bathrooms go for US$42 per person. Snorkel gear is available for rent at US$5 per day.

Just east of Wichub-Walá, on an unnamed island about the size of two basketball courts, is the very rustic *Cabañas Turisticas Yery* (☎/fax 255-0463 in Panama City). Don't come expecting five-star accommodations. The Yery consists of two leaning thatch-roof-and-bamboo lodges, each containing four tiny bathroomless rooms with swaying beds, and there's no electricity here. The rate of US$27 includes meals and a boat tour.

IKUPTUPU

One hundred meters from Wichub-Walá is the tiny artificial island of Ikuptupu, home to the *Ikuptupu Hotel* (☎/fax 220-9082 in Panama City). The hotel was a research facility used by the Smithsonian Tropical Research Institute from 1974-98. Ikuptupu consists of a basketball court-size island, from which several boardwalks connect to 16 bamboo-sided, tin-roofed and linoleum-floored guestrooms, all built over the water. All bathrooms are shared (and toilets 'flush' directly into the sea, a reality that disturbs some guests). The rate of US$35 per person includes meals and a boat tour. For isolation and seaviews, this beats the three islands mentioned so far. But if you want to mingle with or at least observe the Kuna, you're better off at one of the other places.

CARTÍ SUITUPO

Cartí Suitupo is the island closest to the coastal hamlet of Cartí. The hamlet is distinguished by the fact that it is the only town in the district reachable by road, although that road (the El Llano-Cartí road; see Getting Around earlier in this chapter) is really more of a wide, horribly rutted jungle trail. A mere 100m separates the two Cartís. There's an airstrip near the hamlet, and from it you can travel by boat to Cartí Suitupo and thence to other islands.

Cartí Suitupo is very typical of the inhabited islands from here to the Colombian border; it's the size of three football fields, crowded with bamboo houses and terribly polluted. Cartí Suitupo is also one of the San Blás islands that are visited by exploratory boats from cruise ships. Packed with tourists, these boats visit an average of five times a month.

If you speak Spanish, it's very easy to get from Cartí Suitupo to a pristine, sparsely populated island. Just talk to Tony Adams Harrington, who holds the keys to the Dormitory Cartí Sugdup (see below). To prevent competition and potential animosity, the island's population elected Tony its sole guide. He will find you shortly after your arrival on Cartí; *wagas* (foreigners) don't go unnoticed on the inhabited islands for more than a few nanoseconds.

For US$5 per person, Tony can arrange for a boatman to take you to nearby **Isla Aguja** (Needle Island) and pick you up later. The US$5 pays for the boatman, but it would be wise to give Tony a tip as well, just to ensure he'll remind the boatman to pick you up at the specified time. There are only two families living on Isla Aguja, and the beach and swimming there are lovely. Needle Island is the kind of islette that appears in your most romantic island dreams, with lots of leaning palm trees bursting with coconuts, gentle waves that kiss your toes and ankles then turn back to the sea, surf as inviting as any found on our planet, golden sand that cries out to be rolled wild on, preferably wrapped in the arms of a passionate lover. The few friendly souls who live on Needle make your stay all the more pleasant.

The one hotel on Cartí Suitupo, *Dormitory Cartí Sugdup* (☎ 299-9002), is a 30-by-20m concrete, bamboo-and-thatch structure over the water. The dormitory has five basic rooms with worn beds and a shared bathroom (toilet and shower empty directly into the sea) for US$8 per person. There is one light bulb in the hotel, and each guestroom contains a lantern.

There are three public phones on the island.

NUSATUPO & RÍO SIDRA/MAMARDUP

Nusatupo and Río Sidra/Mamardup (the communities of Río Sidra and Mamardup share an island) are densely populated islands 15km east of Cartí Suitupo. Only a few minutes' boat ride apart, they are served by an airstrip that's a few kilometers away on the mainland. Nusatupo, which has a hotel, is the closer of the islands to the airstrip. Río Sidra/Mamardup has no tourist services at all, but it does have two public phones (in 2001 there were no phones on Nusatupo).

On Nusatupo, the **Hotel Kuna Yala** (☎ *315-7520 in Panama City; ask for Manuel Alfaro*) has three rooms with concrete floors, a tin roof, no fans, and a shared bathroom with an over-the-water toilet. The kitchen service here is excellent, and the portions of fruit and seafood are generous. The US$40-per-person rate includes three meals daily and a boat ride to and from several snorkeling sites. If requested, a guide will take you to a Kuna cemetery and on a jungle tour on the mainland free of charge (tip suggested). Because of its proximity to the keys mentioned below, people who don't mind roughing it a little will find this place to be a good deal.

KUANIDUP

This little island, 30 minutes by motorized cayuco from the airstrip serving Río Sidra/Mamardup, is home to a cluster of seven bamboo-and-thatch cabins, lots of palm trees, a few iguanas, soft white sand and little else. It's a beautiful island with a lovely beach for swimming. Hammocks are hung between some trees, and it's awfully easy to fall asleep in one as your mind drifts from the lapping surf to the arcing sea-sky horizon to the swaying palms above you. This island, and others around it, are the stuff of travel-magazine covers and faraway dreams.

Each of the stand-alone cabins at **Cabañas Kuanidup** (☎ *227-7661, fax 227-1396*) has two firm beds, a lantern, a platform to place your bag on and sandy floors. A short walk away are pairs of showers, sinks and toilets, and beyond those is a small kitchen and dining area. The per-person rate of US$65 includes three meals daily (the food here is usually nothing special) and one snorkeling trip. The friendly owner, who speaks English, also owns a nearby uninhabited island where, he says, it's OK to sunbathe in the buff – and quite a few guests do.

NARANJO CHICO

Three kilometers northwest of Río Sidra/Mamardup is the relatively large, lovely and

While away an afternoon in one of the hammocks on Kuanidup.

sparsely populated island of Naranjo Chico (Little Orange, which is also known as Narascandub Pipi, its Kuna name). Here exist four sand-floored thatch-and-bamboo cabañas that leak during downpours, there is no electricity, and cold-water bathrooms are shared. But the two families here (one owns one cabaña, another owns the other two) couldn't be nicer, which is important because their rate of US$50 per person including meals is steep. If the cost isn't terribly important to you and you don't mind the basic accommodations, you'll surely love the beach, the snorkeling and the sheer beauty of the island and its surroundings.

There's no phone on Naranjo Chico and no established reservations procedure. A family member said that interested parties should call one of the public phones on Río Sidra/Mamardup (☎ 299-9007) and tell whomever answers that you'd like to reserve a cabaña at **Cabañas Narascandub Pipi** that you'd like to speak to someone from Narascandub Pipi and that you will call back in one hour. Callers should be fluent in Spanish – and they shouldn't hold their breath until they speak to someone from Narascandub Pipi.

CAYOS LOS GRULLOS, HOLANDÉSES & ORDUPUQUIP

The dozen or so sparsely inhabited islands known as Cayos Los Grullos are 10km northeast of Río Sidra/Mamardup, at the lower left (southwestern) corner of a triangle of three island groups. Cayos Holandéses (Dutchmen Keys), north of Los Grullos, top the triangle. Cayos Ordupuquip make up the lower right (southeastern) corner of the triangle. These groups, popular with yachters, are 12km from one another, separated by calm blue-green water. There are no tourist facilities on these islands.

All of the islands in these groups are lovely, but the Cayos Holandéses are best because they are the closest to a shallow reef that makes for some interesting snorkeling – not so much for fish and corals as for numerous pieces of wreckage. This ridge of rocks, sand and coral, 100m north of Cayos Holandéses, is called **Wreck Reef**, and it earned its name by snaring all kinds of vessels over the years. The reef's been able to do that because it's pretty far from the closest island, and though the water south of the reef is barely 1m deep, the ocean floor north of the reef plunges 100m in half that distance – or, from a sea captain's perspective, the ocean floor *rises* 100m to a dangerously shallow depth in half that distance. Wreck Reef's distance from the islands and the presence of deep water so close to the reef have fooled many experienced sailors.

Most crafts that smack into the reef these days belong to drug traffickers and contraband smugglers operating at night. These people are alerted to the presence of the reef by the loud, crunching sound of rock and coral taking bites out of their hulls. Over time, the surf that crashes against these wrecks breaks them up, and their cargo is tossed into the surrounding sand.

In 1995 a smugglers' boat filled with TV sets slammed into the reef at night, and the crew abandoned ship. The smugglers had hoped to bring the TVs (bought in Colón's Zona Libre) into port at Cartagena, Colombia, without paying any import taxes. The next morning, scores of Kuna in cayucos helped themselves to the TVs. The smugglers were never caught, and today their rusting, looted boat is perched on the reef like a trophy.

Historically, most of the boats claimed by Wreck Reef were the victims of *chocosanos*

('storms that come from the east,' in Kuna). Chocosanos are ghastly tempests that whip up monstrous waves that can overrun entire islands. Such waves have swept many San Blás Indians and their homes out to sea. The violent storms are always preceded by a purple-black eastern sky and a lack of breeze and birdsong.

As soon as it's evident that a chocosano is approaching, the Kuna – particularly the older ones – combat it by blowing into conch shells. The sound alerts their benevolent god, who tries to disperse the threatening storm. If he fails, as he usually does, the eerie stillness is broken by ground-shaking thunderclaps, howling winds, pounding downpours and a vengeful sea. At the southern end of Wreck Reef is a freighter that lies with its hull fully exposed and its deck flat against the ocean floor – a big vessel that was flipped like a pancake by a mighty chocosano.

RÍO AZÚCAR

This typical, jam-packed island is close to the mainland and has no lodgings or places to eat. But it's known for its festive Carnaval, which is held during the four days preceding Ash Wednesday. It is the only San Blás island that hosts Carnaval festivities, mainly because celebrating in style – and they do celebrate in style here – takes money, and the Kuna have very little of it.

But every year a wealthy and benevolent Panama City lawyer gives generously to the island's Carnaval fund, and the people respond enthusiastically with four days of dancing, singing and costume-wearing. Needless to say, the lawyer never has to pay for his fishing trips when he vacations in the area.

Like most heavily populated islands in the district, Río Azúcar has a public coin-operated telephone from which you can place domestic and international calls. There's also a clinic with a US-trained doctor. There's a very modest store on Río Azúcar, as there is on all the densely populated San Blás islands, that sells batteries, soups and other household products. You can buy sodas at these stores (sorry, no diet drinks), but bottled water is rarely available.

Also on Río Azúcar is a simple church showing its age, built in 1945 by Italian engineers at the direction of a Spanish priest. The priest is long gone, but the islands have no shortage of *Merki* (American) missionaries who want the Kuna to forget their storm-clobbered god and accept Jesus as their lord.

NARGANÁ & CORAZÓN DE JESÚS

The inhabited islands of Narganá and Corazón de Jesús are 5km northeast of Río Azúcar and reachable by a coastal airstrip. The two islands are linked by an arcing wooden foot bridge perhaps 70m long. At the southwestern end of the bridge is Narganá, home to the district's only courthouse, its only jail and its only bank. There are also a few policemen on the island; if any ask for your passport, politely present it. Jotting down tourists' names in little books gives them something to do.

The Banco Nacional de Panamá branch office on Narganá is open 8 am to 3 pm weekdays and 9 am to noon Saturday. It is possible to have money wired to this office, but be aware that the service takes 24 hours. It is also possible to cash American Express traveler's checks here, and there's an ATM out front.

Corazón de Jesús is the most westernized of the San Blás islands – few Kuna practices are observed here, and most of the structures are made of concrete and tin instead of bamboo and thatch. There are no places to stay on Corazón de Jesús, but you can buy bottled water, canned goods, rope and razor blades here.

ISLA TIGRE

This surprisingly clean, traditional Kuna island is 7km east of Narganá. Here, Kuna women can be readily seen in their doorways offering molas to passersby; on other islands women often stay out of sight if they know tourists are moving about. On most inhabited San Blás islands, narrow dirt pathways separate the homes. Here, however, the walkways are unusually wide.

Cabañas Tigre (☎ 229-9006, 299-9092, the island's public phones; ask for Fidel Chiari, say you'll call back in 15 minutes, and do so) features five sand-floored bamboo-and-thatch cabañas on an attractive beach. The cabañas, which are near the northwest end of the island's airstrip, contain two hammocks each and two platforms on which to place your bags. The cost is US$10 per person, or US$50 with three meals – yes, a lot for a place without beds.

At the time of writing, there were plans to shut down the airstrip and turn it into a fairgrounds, with fairs featuring Kuna dances, handicrafts and cayuco races every October 13-16. Indeed, this is a particularly traditional Kuna community. Most of the people on Isla Tigre are from Narganá originally, but they settled this island when some of the people on Narganá began wearing Western clothing.

Keep in mind that on this island, you will be charged US$50 if you brandish a video camera, even if you say that you won't be using it (at least, that was the case in 2001). The Kuna believe that if you have a video camera, you will use it, and thus they require that you pay the fee. Photos of Kuna cost US$1 here, as elsewhere in the district.

ISLA ISKARDUP

This idyllic island, the size of a soccer field and at the center of a cluster of unpopulated islands, is occupied by *Sapibenega 'The Kuna Lodge'* (☎ 299-9116, 299-9117, on nearby Playón Chico; ask for Paliwitur Sapibe, say you'll call back in one hour, and do so). This 'lodge' isn't a lodge at all, but rather a large open-sided restaurant/bar and 13 stand-alone water's-edge cabins. Together, they represent the finest retreat in the archipelago. Here are four plank-floored, bamboo-walled, thatch-roofed cabins with twin beds, seven cabins with two twin beds, and two cabins with two full-size beds. Each cabin is well constructed and raised a foot off the ground to help keep internal temperatures down. Windows, which are rarely found in the comarca, abound in all of the cabins, letting in breezes and gorgeous seaviews. Every cabin has a private bathroom with a flush toilet, tiled shower, overhead lights and 24-hour solar-powered electricity. The rate of US$75 per person includes all meals and a daily boat tour to a snorkeling site and a private beach.

Owner-manager Paliwitur Sapibe speaks English, Spanish and Kuna and offers numerous excursions, including: a daylong hike through mainland jungle to a waterfall and mountain top (US$15); a six-hours-each-way boat trip up a jungle-flanked river to a truly spectacular waterfall, overnight in a hammock under a palapa, meal prepared by an accompanying chef, stops along the river to swing on lianas Tarzan-style (US$25); and a four-hour fishing adventure beyond the reef using the Kuna fishing tools of nylon, hook and stone (US$15). A visit to Playón Chico, a densely inhabited island great for mola-browsing or investigating the Kuna lifestyle, costs a mere US$5. Lobster, octopus, crab, flan and a delicious coconut dessert are typically served at the restaurant.

ISLA TUPILE TO ISLA UAGUITUPO

The ocean can be treacherous along the central part of the archipelago, particularly in the 15km stretch of roiling blue sea from densely populated Isla San Ignacio de Tupile past equally crowded Isla Ailigandí to within 1km of Isla Uaguitupo (Dolphin Island). Here, 3m swells are the norm. If you've been frightened by the sea in the northern part of the archipelago, you can expect to be terrified as you ride these waves. If you plan to travel these waters in a motorized cayuco and have any doubts about your boatman, you may want to consider hiring another one before attempting this trip.

Isla Ailigandí

Ailigandí is a densely populated island that's not accustomed to seeing foreigners. Here visitors find *Hotel Palmera (☎ 299-2969, 299-2968, both public phones; ask to speak with Bolí ar Arango, who speaks Spanish and Kuna)*. The hotel is a two-story building with five rooms with shared bathrooms, two or three decent beds in each,

and much-needed windows. The rate of US$10 per person is fair. Downstairs there's a restaurant that's occasionally open.

Isla Uaguitupo

Uaguitupo is a pleasant, grassy little isle, 100m from the island of Achutupu (which is served by a coastal airstrip). Taking up almost all of Uaguitupo is *Dolphin Island Lodge (☎ 225-8435, fax 225-2521, cdolphin@sinfo.net)*, which consists of nine new and very comfortable concrete-floor stand-alone cabins with private cold-water bathrooms with environmentally friendly flush toilets. There's a pleasant open-sided restaurant that serves good food and faces long sets of breakers. Included in the per-person rates of US$110/95/86 single/double/triple are all meals, plus a tour of Achutupu and one or two snorkeling sites. Dolphin Island Lodge receives a substantial number of repeat foreign visitors. English is spoken here and the owner-managers are very accommodating; for example, if you want them to find a boat and a guide for you for some serious area investigating, they'll gladly hook you up with a boatman.

USTUPO OGOBSUCUM
pop 5000

This island, 15km southeast of Uaguitupo, has the largest population of all of the San Blás islands. Ustupo Ogobsucum, widely known as simply Ustupo (the same name used by a tiny community on the mainland a short distance away), is crowded and unattractive, and it offers little of interest to the visitor.

Should you decide to visit Ustupo Ogobsucum, you must immediately go to the police station, which is in a two-story structure beside two very tall radio antennae. There you must present your passport and your tourist card or visa, whichever pertains to you (see Visas & Documents in Facts for the Visitor), and pay US$5. Next, you must ask permission from the island's chiefs for permission to wander around the island. If you don't speak Spanish or Kuna, you will have a very difficult time explaining yourself, as none of the chiefs speak any English.

If they don't like the way you look, your request will be rejected.

Lodgings on Ustupo Ogobsucum consist of the **Motel Awibe Kuna** *(no phone)*. This is a concrete, two-story structure with six partitioned cubicles in one decent-size but fanless room. There's a worn mattress on a swaying steel frame in each cubicle and bars on all the windows. The shower consists of a bucket of water in a public area outside the motel, and the toilet is a hole in a board over the ocean with just a little privacy. The price: US$7 a night.

ISLA PINO

Isla Pino (Pine Island), named for the lovely forest that covers most of the island, is 25km southeast of Ustupo Ogobsucum (or 1½ hours by 15-horsepower boat). As you approach the 2km-long, 1.5km-wide island, you'll note that it looks astonishingly similar to a whale.

There's a sleepy little town on the western side of Isla Pino, and its 300 inhabitants spend the better part of the day trying to beat the oppressive heat by staying in their hammocks in their thatch houses. When they work, they harvest coconuts and fish.

There are no hotels on the island. In fact, there are no services in town of use to the tourist, except a small provisions stand that also serves some snacks, beer and soda – nothing much, but the beverages go down really nicely in this hot place.

If you haven't gotten enough exercise lately and enjoy the occasional walk on the wild side, you can take a trail that winds around the island. It skirts dense jungle that's home to large boas, wild rabbits and red-naped tamarins, among other creatures you probably don't have at home.

No one on Isla Pino asked me to pay a visitation fee when I visited, but a plain-clothed policeman did ask to see some ID. In general, it's OK to hand over your passport when someone in Panama asks to see it. With few exceptions, the person is a police officer or bouncer who's just doing his or her job.

MULATUPO SASARDÍ

This typical San Blás island, 7km south of Isla Pino, is far removed from the cruise-ship scene, and its 4000 residents actually see very few tourists. The Kuna here are extremely friendly, particularly the children, many of whom will come up to shake your hand and say, 'Hello, mister' or 'Hello, lady' in English (it's about all the English they know).

The place to pay the visitation fee is a two-story building (one of just a few here) facing the island's basketball court. The chiefs usually hang out in this building, and it's important to ask them for permission to see the island. The chiefs, who speak Spanish and Kuna, will give you permission as long as you're not doing something offensive to them, such as going about in a bikini top or shirtless.

There's a place to stay on the island: the very basic **Isla Herrera Hotel** *(☎ 262-5562 in Panama City; ask for the hotel),* which costs US$20 per person. You bathe here by dipping a bucket into a big barrel and pouring water over yourself. The barrel is behind a family's home near the hotel, as is the toilet, an over-the-sea contraption.

Also on the island is the **Restaurante Mi Pueblo,** which is run by a Kuna woman who has a smile that could melt a glacier. A delicious chicken, a plate of French fries and a soda will set you back US$3 here.

PUERTO OBALDÍA

Information on Puerto Obaldía, the last significant town in the district before one reaches Colombia, appears in the Getting There & Away chapter.

Aclá & New Edinburgh

In the eastern portion of the Comarca de San Blás are the sites of Aclá and New Edinburgh, which were the settings for dramatic and bloody events in Panama's colonial history. Although jungle has swallowed the ruins of both sites and they are now inaccessible to visitors, the stories of what happened in these settlements still fascinate travelers.

On the coast 40km west of the Colombian border is the historic site of Aclá, long reclaimed by the jungle and all but forgotten. It was here in 1517 that Vasco Núñez de Balboa – the first European to set eyes on the Pacific, a man who was a legend in his time and much adored by the king and queen of Spain he so honorably served – was put to death by the envious and spiteful Spanish governor Pedro Arias de Ávila.

Vasco Núñez de Balboa met with a violent end in Panama.

For years Pedrarias, as the governor was widely known, had sought a hero's recognition from the Spanish royalty – recognition he felt was fully deserved. But the spotlight always seemed to be on Balboa, who, among numerous famous deeds, claimed the Pacific Ocean and all the territories that bordered it for King Ferdinand and Queen Isabella.

It might be said that Balboa's violent end had its origin in romance – the desire he and another man, Andrés Garabito, felt for a woman. The woman was none other than the beautiful daughter of Careta, chief of the largest Darién tribe. Balboa was smitten with the Indian maiden, and his fondness for her brought about a peaceful alliance between the explorer and the chief. Careta pledged his daughter to Balboa, an action that didn't sit well with Garabito. Garabito and Balboa had been friends, but the men had some fiery words over the Darién beauty, and Garabito slunk away and awaited his opportunity for revenge.

He didn't wait long. Garabito was a crafty fellow and knew of Pedrarias' hatred for Balboa. He also knew that Balboa had been intimate with Pedrarias' daughter. Garabito sent a letter to Pedrarias that stated that Balboa intended to throw off his allegiance to the governor. He also claimed that Balboa never intended to marry Pedrarias' daughter but instead loved only an Indian girl.

In no time Garabito was called before Pedrarias. Garabito was quite pleased to repeat his damning story, which he had spread about in public places. A notary was sent out to gather up evidence against Balboa. Because Garabito had done a good job in spreading his lie, the notary came across quite a few people who said they had heard rumors that Balboa was plotting against Pedrarias. These people would later provide damaging testimony against Balboa.

Aclá & New Edinburgh

Balboa was on the Pacific coast with 300 loyal men at the time that the governor and Garabito were plotting their revenge. To lure Balboa to the Caribbean coast and away from his followers, Pedrarias sent him a fatherly letter begging him to come to Aclá to confer with him on a matter of great importance. Balboa fell into the trap, and soon he and his closest aides found themselves in chains facing charges of treason.

A farce of a trial was quickly held and appeals formalities brushed aside. It was clear to all that Balboa and his friends were to be sacrificed. Like sheep, first Balboa and then his four friends were led to the block and beheaded. Pedrarias witnessed the gory spectacle, but still filled with malice, he ordered that Balboa's head be placed on a pole and set in the plaza, where it remained for many days. Balboa was 42 at the time of his death.

Within a few years, the town of Nombre de Dios, to the west, had become the northern terminus of trade across the isthmus, and the residents of Aclá moved there to seek their fortunes. No one was left to stop the advance of the surrounding jungle, and it quickly swallowed up the site.

Aclá's exact location remained a mystery for more than 400 years. In 1985 eight young British explorers, aged 17 to 24, cut a 3m trench through a low artificial mound on what they suspected was the western end of the town. This revealed a circular structure made up of coral blocks and bricks thought to be the base of a 16th-century tower. The tower – the earliest European stone building found anywhere in the Americas – was abandoned yet again soon afterward and has since been reclaimed by the jungle.

Just east of Aclá is the overgrown site of New Edinburgh. No attempt by white people to found a settlement in the tropics was deadlier or more plagued by disaster than the Scottish effort at this site, on a peninsula at the mouth of a bay just a few kilometers from Aclá.

Today the peninsula is called Punta Escocés, but on November 3, 1698, the day the Scots landed and took possession of the site, it was named New Edinburgh. They erected a battery of 16 guns, called Fort St Andrew, to command the harbor. A cut was made through the narrowest part of the peninsula, only 180 paces in width, to let in the sea, thus converting New Edinburgh into an island and strengthening the defenses of the town and fort. A region that encompassed the bay and all the land within several days' walk from it was called Caledonia; today only a small island bears that name.

By April 1699 the Scots, who had never seen so much rain, were suffering badly. Of the 1200 men who had landed, already more than 200 had died of sickness, and the rest were hungry and living in constant fear of attacks by Spaniards, who viewed the Scots as invaders of their territory.

By June the Scots had had enough, and the 900 enfeebled survivors hurriedly evacuated New Edinburgh. The would-be settlers embarked in three ships, the *St Andrew*, the *Unicorn* and the *Caledonia*. Each captain selected his own course to hasten away from the ghastly settlement.

The *St Andrew* reached Jamaica, but not before losing another 100 people to disease. There the Scots continued to die, so there were too few seamen left to sail the ship back to Scotland. The *St Andrew* was deserted, and most of the Scots who had reached Jamaica aboard her never left the island. The *Unicorn* reached New York on August 14, losing about 150 people on the way. Here the survivors found the *Caledonia*, which had arrived 10 days earlier after losing about the same number.

Of the 900 Scots who left New Edinburgh in June, more than 400 died of disease and were tossed overboard en route to Jamaica and New York. In all, fewer than 500 of the men who had left

continued on page 344

Aclá & New Edinburgh

continued from page 343

Scotland for the New World on July 26, 1698, were alive 13 months later. Most of them never saw their homeland again.

Unaware of the situation in the Darién, the Scottish company that had financed the first expedition sent 300 more recruits in two vessels, the *Hopeful Binning* and the *Olive Branch*, in May 1699. To their surprise, they found New Edinburgh deserted. Knowing that a third expedition was being assembled, they resolved to await the arrival of that party.

The plan quickly changed a few days later, when a careless steward aboard the *Olive Branch* set fire to the ship while pouring a glass of brandy. The ship was entirely consumed, as were most of the provisions, which had been aboard. The *Olive Branch*'s passengers – about 100 people – were taken aboard the *Hopeful Binning*. The ship sailed to Jamaica, where most of the settlers rapidly sickened and died.

The third expedition consisted of 1300 people who sailed from Scotland on September 24, 1699, in four ships. By the time the ships arrived, 160 Scots had already perished. When the survivors arrived, they were hopeful that their luck would change, but the disease and death only increased. Two weeks after their arrival, nine sailors deserted in one of the ship's boats and were never heard from again.

Soon afterward, a plot to seize the leaders and ships and escape from the fateful spot was hatched and discovered. The suspected ringleader was condemned by court-martial and executed in Fort St Andrew.

In February 1700, Indians tipped the Scots that the much-feared Spaniards were coming to attack them. Instead of awaiting the assault, 200 Scots and 40 Indians who had befriended the settlers confronted the Spaniards at a site called Yoratuba. There the Scots had a short, sharp engagement with the much-surprised Spaniards, who fled, leaving their dead and dying on the field. Five Spanish survivors were taken prisoner.

The Scots' elation over their successful encounter was short-lived. The very next month a Spanish fleet entered the Bahía de Caledonia and prepared to level the fort and the huts that housed the Scots. Adding to the Scots' desperation, the Spanish located their source of fresh water and took possession of it. The Scots dug a well within the confines of their fort, but it produced only a brackish puddle.

Meanwhile hunger and disease killed the Scots like flies. In a single day 16 people were put in the ground. Spanish musketeers were advancing on the fort and the Scots were preparing to fight and die when the Spanish general offered the Scots a treaty. In return for their promise to leave, the Scots were given 14 days to prepare their departure and allowed to retain their arms. They sailed away with drums beating and colors flying. The Indians who had befriended the Scots were left at the Spaniards' mercy – and were brutally slaughtered.

The site was lost to jungle until 1979, when the Panamanian government invited British archaeologists to explore the area. The 30-member team spent three months at the site, clearing and cataloging about half of the fort. They identified remains of Scottish defenses, including a moat, earthen ramparts, bastions, cannon positions and palisades. They also found clay pipes, nails, pottery, various types of glass and bronze shoe buckles.

Like Aclá, New Edinburgh was again left to the forces of nature and has since been retaken by the jungle.

Darién Province

The Darién is one of the wildest *and* one of the most ravaged areas in the Americas. It is by far the biggest province in Panama (16,671 sq km) and the country's most sparsely inhabited with fewer than three people per square kilometer. It is home to Panama's most spectacular national park and to its worst scenes of habitat destruction. It is two worlds, really: one with roads and one without – the north and the south, respectively.

The northern Darién has been logged and has suffered serious environmental damage. Southern Darién Province – the vast area south of Yaviza – is the antithesis of the north. Here wildlife abounds and the only 'roads' are jungle-flanked rivers. In fact, most of the southern Darién is within Parque Nacional Darién – 576,000 hectares containing sandy beaches, rocky coasts, mangroves, freshwater marshes, palm forest swamps and four mountain ranges covered with double- and triple-canopy jungle.

The park is *the* attraction of the Darién. The bird watching here is among the world's finest. There are places in the park where you can sit back and watch four species of macaw fly by with outstanding frequency. The harpy eagle, the most powerful bird of prey on our planet, resides here, as do giant anteaters, jaguars, ocelots, howler monkeys, Baird's tapirs, white-lipped peccaries, caimans and American crocodiles.

The southern Darién is an adventurer's dream. It's the landscape of Indiana Jones movies, offering spectacular opportunities for rain forest exploration by trail or river. It's a place where the primeval meets the present – where the scenery appears much as it did a million years ago. Indians perfected the use of poison-dart guns here and still maintain many of their traditional practices. It's a place for travelers with youthful hearts, intrepid spirits and a yearning for something truly wild. If you've been growing old in a concrete jungle, spend some time in this verdant one – even if it's only for a few days. They'll be days you'll never forget.

Emberá & Wounaan Indians

Living within the boundaries of Parque Nacional Darién are the Chocóes, as they are commonly called. These Indians emigrated here from the Chocó region of Colombia, and they continue to live much the way they have for thousands of years.

Anthropologists place the Chocóes in two linguistic groups: the Emberá and the Wounaan. But with the exception of language, the two peoples' cultural features are virtually identical – no great surprise considering their shared origins and environment.

Highlights

- Parque Nacional Darién, crown jewel of Panama's parks, home to vast jungle, jaguars, crocodiles and Indians
- Lush Cana Valley, where macaws abound and jungle trails lead to abandoned mining trains
- Rio Sambú, where travelers can take a heart-of-darkness ride through primeval rain forest
- Pirre Station, a superior destination for birders, with unforgettable jungle trails
- Tropic Star Lodge, the legendary world leader in sport-fishing records

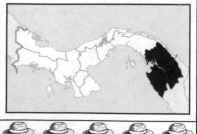

DARIÉN PROVINCE

DARIÉN PROVINCE

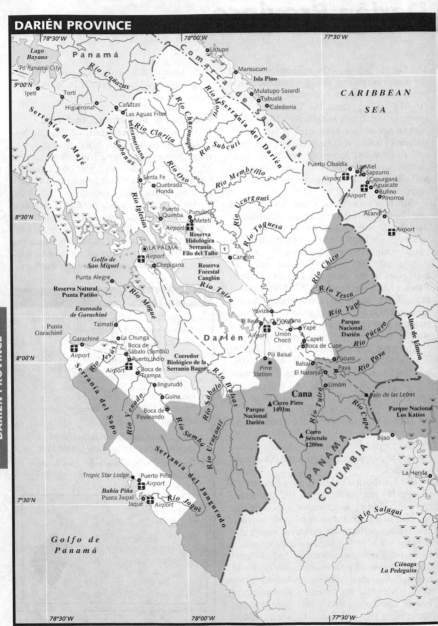

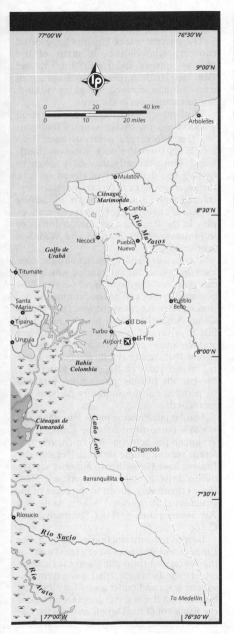

The external pressures placed on them (chiefly encroachment by white settlers and habitat destruction by loggers) are virtually identical as well. The tribes, however, prefer to be thought of as two separate peoples.

Some historians contend that the Emberá emigrated from northern Ecuador and southern Colombia beginning in 1830, and that the Wounaan emigrated from the Río San Juan area of Colombia (where the greatest concentration of them lives today) around 1910. Other historians say the tribes arrived much earlier. The Indians themselves aren't sure, as they have no written history.

In Panama, by far the greatest number of Emberá and Wounaan live in the Darién. They reside deep in the rain forest beside rivers, particularly the Ríos Sambú, Jaqué, Chico, Tuquesa, Membrillo, Tuira, Yape and Tucutí. They also live, in far smaller numbers, in Panamá and Colón Provinces. Their total population in Panama is estimated to be around 8200.

The Emberá and Wounaan practice subsistence agriculture, followed by hunting, fishing and poultry raising. To a lesser degree, they also create plantations to grow commercial crops appropriate to the areas in which they live. If a particular area is good for plantains or bananas, for example, the Indians grow those crops to sell. They also commercially cultivate rice and maize, but to a lesser extent.

Increasingly, the Emberá and Wounaan are replacing their traditional attire with Western wear. The men, but for a few older individuals, have set aside their loincloths for short pants and now prefer short-sleeved shirts to going around bare-chested. The women, who traditionally wore only a skirt, increasingly don bras, and some have taken to wearing shirts as well.

All of the women used to wear wide silver bracelets and elaborate necklaces made of silver coins, but that practice too is disappearing as tourists offer the Indians more money than they've ever seen to buy their family jewelry. Many Emberá and Wounaan still stain their bodies purplish black with juice from the *jagua* fruit, which

Danger on the Border

Travel beyond Yaviza toward the Colombian border is possible only on foot or by boat and is extremely risky. This area is known to be frequented by Colombian paramilitaries, drug traffickers, guerrillas and bandits. In recent years tourists have been shot, missionaries have been abducted, and local residents have been robbed, raped and murdered with machetes in towns east and southeast of Yaviza. Two British nationals traveling near the border in 2000 were held hostage by Colombian rebels for nine months before being released.

The area from Nazaret to Punusa is like a low-intensity war zone. The paramilitaries and rebels move in big groups armed with rocket launchers, flamethrowers and machine guns. Panamanian border police buzz the sky in helicopter gunships and tote AK-47s. Travel to the towns of Pinogana, Yape, Boca de Cupe and Paya is foolhardy at best. As of March 2001, however, the tourist haunts of Cana, Bahía Piña and Punta Patiño and the towns of El Real and La Palma remained unaffected by the hostilities.

is believed to have health-giving properties and to ward off insects.

Emberá and Wounaan homes are well suited to the environment in which the Indians live. Built on stilts 3m to 4m off the ground, the floors consist primarily of thin but amazingly strong strips of palm bark. The homes' stilts protect occupants and food from pesky ground animals and swollen rivers.

To permit breezes to enter, more than half of the typical Indian home is open-sided. The roof is made of thatch, which keeps the rain out and acts as good insulation against the tropical sun. The kitchen occupies one corner and has an oven made of mud. A log with stairs carved into it provides access to the home. Emberá and Wounaan grow medicinal plants and edible vegetables and roots around their homes.

Pigs and poultry are often raised in pens beneath the elevated houses.

The government of Panama has erected concrete schoolhouses in many of the Indians' villages. Today most Emberá and Wounaan children spend their mornings in class and their afternoons working the land. For fun, they swim in the rivers.

The Emberá and Wounaan are very good woodcarvers and basket weavers. Traditionally the men carved gorgeous boas, frogs and birds from the dark cocobolo hardwood. More recently they have taken to carving tiny figurines (typically of iguanas, turtles, crocodiles and birds) from the ivory-colored tagua nut. The women are among the world's finest basket makers. (See Shopping in the Panama City chapter for more information about Emberá and Wounaan products.)

The Emberá and Wounaan also produce incredibly fine dugout canoes, which they call *piraguas*. The boats have very shallow bottoms, so they can be used during the dry season, when the rivers run low. The Panama Canal Authority, which has the money to buy any rivercraft it wants, employs Emberá and Wounaan craftsmen to make the piraguas that Authority officials use to reach the higher parts of the canal's watershed. Most of the Indians' piraguas are powered by paddles, but the Authority piraguas are motorized.

Until it left Panama in the late 1990s, the US Air Force turned to the Emberá and Wounaan for help, but for an entirely different reason: jungle survival. Because the Indians have the ability to not only survive but to thrive in tropical wilderness, quite a few of them were added to the corps of instructors that trained US astronauts and Air Force pilots at Fort Sherman, near Colón.

Before the introduction of the gun, the Emberá and Wounaan were expert users of the *boroquera* (blowgun), and they envenomed their darts with lethal toxins from poisonous frogs and bullet ants. Many scholars believe that it was these people who forced the Kuna out of the Darién and into the Caribbean coastal area they now inhabit.

The Emberá and Wounaan are about the toughest people you'll ever meet, yet their smiles could melt silver. Emberá and Wounaan children are friendly and fun-loving; if you want to score points with them (and their parents), bring along a Polaroid camera and plenty of film. Lots of people take photos in Indian villages, but few ever leave the Indians with pictures of themselves.

Environmental Problems

Today the traditional cultures of the re-markable Emberá and Wounaan tribes appear doomed, because their land is under threat. For many years the Panamanian government was unwilling to construct the last section of the Carretera Interamericana (Pan-American Hwy) and thus close the Darién Gap – a 150km break in the other-wise unbroken 30,600km highway from Alaska to Chile – because it feared that hoof-and-mouth disease would spread from Colombia into Panama. The government was so afraid of the cattle disease that it created Parque Nacional Darién along the border as a buffer zone, and the Colombian government followed suit by establishing adjacent Parque Nacional Los Katíos on its side of the border.

In 1991 US officials monitoring the disease declared that it had been eradicated in Colombia. The governments of Panama and Colombia then revived efforts to close the Darién Gap. The last bit of highway would bisect the Darién and Los Katíos na-tional parks and would open up the forests of the Emberá and Wounaan to loggers, set-tlers and ranchers. The area's national-park status would not prevent such development. The only thing now preventing the road work is Colombia's civil war. When that conflict is resolved, the Gap will likely be closed.

To glimpse the future of the south, one needs only to look to the north. The Darién north of Yaviza (the town where the Inter-americana presently ends) was covered with virgin forest only three decades ago. But the highway was extended from Chepo to Yaviza 20-some years ago. At first only loggers used the extension, as the new stretch of highway was a dirt road with knee-deep ruts half the year and a mud road with zillions of small pools the rest of the year. But settlers and ranchers followed.

The loggers initially sought big trees within easy reach, felling all the giants near the highway and trampling young trees with their machinery. Once the giant trees were gone, the loggers cut roads perpendicular to the highway, which led into tall stands of hardwoods. After those stands were chopped down and removed, more roads were cut and yet more stands were leveled.

DARIÉN PROVINCE

ERIC L WHEATER

Many Emberá and Wounaan still stain their bodies with traditional patterns.

Today, even a person using binoculars can't see much Darién forest from the highway.

Right behind the loggers were settlers – thousands of them – poor people looking to eke out a living by turning into cropland the trampled vegetation left by the loggers. With the mature trees gone, all that was required to create cropland was an ax and a match; after some crackling and sizzling and a lot of smoke, the would-be subsistence farmers had fields for planting. Panamanian law encourages homesteading, and the settlers were *ery* encouraged; they burned and burned and burned.

As if to punish those who set fire to the forest, the topsoil that had been held in place by roots washed easily away in the rains. The earth beneath the topsoil proved nutrient deficient. After two or three years, the soil couldn't support a decent harvest and little more than grass grew on it. But grass is what cattle eat, so in came ranchers, buying fields that frustrated farmers could no longer use.

This succession of loggers, farmers and ranchers continues in northern Darién Province, although now the loggers must drive far up the side roads they've made to find trees. The farmers are still a step behind the loggers, unintentional nomads employing the slash-and-burn method so widespread in the Third World. And everywhere the settler-farmers go, ranchers move in behind them.

Today, nearly all that remains of the forests of northern Darién – complexly layered, fragile and wondrous ecosystems that had been evolving for *millions* of years – are cow pastures. Around these pastures are struggling farmers and loggers closing in on the last trees still standing.

As if bent on speeding the Darién's destruction, the Panamanian government is currently paving the Interamericana all the way to Yaviza (in 2001, the pavement ended at Lago Bayano in Panama Province). Gas stations, hotels and restaurants are already in place. The paving should be completed by late 2002 or early 2003. Regardless, the only road into the Darién offers travelers an interesting ride, though more for a firsthand look at mass habitat destruction than for anything else.

TO THE DARIÉN GAP

The 266km drive from Panama City to Yaviza along the Interamericana took six hours in 2001 during the dry season; travel time should be reduced to four hours once the road is entirely paved. Lodgings and food can be found in several small towns along the way.

The Interamericana passes through Chepo, El Llano, Cañita, Ipetí, Tortí, Higueronal and smaller, unmapped communities in Panamá Province before crossing into the Darién; see the Panamá Province chapter for details on those towns.

All of the towns to Yaviza are served by buses originating from Panama City's bus terminal. There are five buses daily to Yaviza, with the first departure at 4:15 am and the last at 2 pm (US$14, six hours). By looking at the map you can calculate approximately how long it will take you to reach any point along the way. Be sure to tell the bus driver your destination.

If you're coming from Yaviza and making stops as you head toward Panama City, simply ask a reliable-looking local at each stop when the buses to Panama City pass.

Las Aguas Frías

Near the border of Panamá and Darién provinces are the towns of Las Agua Fría Uno and Agua Fría Dos (3km southeast of Uno). There's no phone in either town. Agua Fría Dos has a gas station and a place with a sign out front that reads 'Pensión Interiorana,' but its rooms are only rented to longterm tenants. Agua Fía Uno is 7km southeast of Cañazas.

Santa Fé
pop 5754

In this town, 21km southeast of Agua Fría Dos and 3km from the Interamericana, there is *Motel Honee Kaiba*, which has six very basic double rooms with so-so beds, ceiling fans and private cold-water bathrooms for US$8/12. There are also four crappy rooms with shared bathroom for the same price.

As you continue into Santa Fé, you'll come across a large two-story building on the northern side of the road; *Casa La Esperanza* is painted on it in big letters. Upstairs are six tolerable rooms for US$10/18 with fan/air con. Downstairs at La Esperanza is a bakery and a general store.

Quebrada Honda

This tiny community 3.4km from Santa Fé is known for its tire repair shop. Tortí and Yaviza have got one as well.

Punulosa

pop 200

This community is notable for its border police checkpoint. Here, motorists traveling in either direction are stopped and asked where they are coming from and where they are going. Sometimes travelers headed southeast are asked to present their identifications; if you're a foreigner, your ID is your passport, not your driver's license or anything else. The soldier will return your identification to you in a few minutes. Occasionally, a soldier will give a foreigner a brief lecture about the dangers near the border. That's because it's fellows like him who are sent into the dangerous area to search for tourists every time one disappears.

(Technically, there are no soldiers in Panama, because Panama technically doesn't have a military, just a border police force that operates like an army. However, these guys wear combat fatigues and brandish AK-47s and 9mm automatics. For all practical purposes, they are soldiers. The term is used here instead of 'border police,' which suggests something far more civilized than these nail-hard, heavily armed men.)

Meteti

pop 6244

This town is 1km southeast of Punulosa. There's a gas station here, plus a public phone, a bank and a hotel. *Hotel Felicidad* (☎ 299-6188, 264-9985), above the Felicidad restaurant, offers 33 rooms with shared bathrooms/private bathrooms for US$8/15. Although there's one other hotel between here and Yaviza, this is the last decent place

before the end of the road. There are several restaurants in Meteti; *La Felicidad* is the best of them.

From Meteti, you can take a turnoff for Puerto Quimba, a port on the Río Iglesias; the road between Meteti and Puerto Quimba is paved and 19.7km long. At the time of writing, it was the only paved stretch of road in Darien Province. At Puerto Quimba it's possible to board a boat to La Palma, the provincial capital. Boats to La Palma leave hourly from 7:30 am to 6:30 pm (US$2.50); they depart from La Palma hourly from 5:30 am to 12:30 pm, and from 2 to 5 pm. There is a pickup truck shuttle service between Meteti and Puerto Quimba every 30 minutes from 6 am till 9 pm (US$1.25).

The boat ride is an excellent option to flying between La Palma and Panama City. The scenery along this river and two others passengers travel before reaching La Palma roughly 30 minutes later (the time varies with motor used, the number of passengers and the personality of the boatman) is of jungle and mangroves – very nice.

Yaviza

pop 3117

The Interamericana just kind of fizzles at the town of Yaviza. No sign announces that you've reached the famous Darién Gap. The highway ends and then there's just a narrow stretch of dirt road beside which trucks, buses and a few cars park. And the town seems filled with people who seem to have nothing but time on their hands.

There are a couple of awful-looking restaurants in this town at the meeting of the Ríos Chucunaque and Chico. There's one hotel, the *Hotel 3 Americas*, which has 10 rooms with fans, worn beds, stained walls and a common bathroom for US$8. There's a loud bar next door, and the town is hot as Hades. Welcome to the end of the road!

If you just want to see some of the Darién and don't have a compelling reason to be in Yaviza, you're encouraged to take the turnoff at Metití, proceed to Puerto Quimba and go by boat to La Palma. The scenes from the boat to La Palma will give you a good sense for wild frontier that still exists in much of Darién Province, whereas the views from the highway between Metití and Yaviza convey mostly destruction. From La Palma, restless spirits can travel deeper into the heart of Darién if they so desire.

EL REAL
pop 1185

El Real dates from the days of the early conquistadors. They constructed a fort here, beside the Río Tuira, to prevent pirates from sailing upriver and attacking Santa María. Gold from mines in the valley of Cana, to the south, was brought to Santa María and stored until there was a quantity sufficient to warrant assembling an armada and moving the bullion to Panama City.

Today, this hot and humid town is one of the largest towns in the Darién. It's nothing special, but it is home to the closest airstrip to the Pirre ranger station, south of town, which offers excellent bird watching (see Pirre Station, following). There's an ANAM office in town where you can get permission to visit Pirre Station. The best way to locate this office is to ask someone to point you toward it, as none of the wide paths in town have names. If you don't speak any Spanish, just repeat 'ANAM' a few times. See the Pirre Station section for permit requirements.

El Real has no bank. The only hotel, *El Mazareno*, has seven mildewy rooms with U-shaped mattresses and shared toilets that don't flush thoroughly for US$8 per person.

Aeroperlas (☎ 315-7500 in Panama City) flies from El Real to Panama City at 9:45 am on Monday, Wednesday and Friday (US$39, 75 minutes), with a stop in Sambú along the way. There's also a nonstop flight at 10:15 am on Saturday. Aeroperlas also flies from La Palma to El Real every Saturday.

PIRRE STATION

Pirre is an ANAM ranger station just inside the Parque Nacional Darién, 13km south of El Real as the lemon-spectacled tanager flies. It is, to steal a line from naturalist guide Hernán Araúz, 'Panama's foremost theater of life.' Pirre is of particular interest to

They Drove the Darién Gap

In 1960 – back when the Carretera Interamericana reached only as far as Chepo, 52km east of Panama City – a group of adventurers sought to become the first people to drive between North and South America. Their destination: Bogotá, Colombia, 433km from Chepo by land – 297km of it through primeval jungle in a region called the Darién. Those 297km then formed the Darién Gap.

The adventurers consisted of a distinguished crew of six men and two women, as well as nine local woodsmen – who were hired to cut a path through the jungle for the vehicles – a US-built Jeep and a British Land Rover. Also on board for most of the trip was Kip Ross, a *National Geographic* writer whose fascinating article on the expedition appeared in the society's March 1961 journal.

All told, the entire enterprise took four months and 28 days. The team crossed 180 rivers and streams and was forced to improvise bridges over 125 of them, built mainly from the trunks of palm trees. At times progress was slowed to 5km a day. Although several major vehicular mishaps occurred, no snakebites or serious injuries were sustained.

Among the group were historian Amado Araúz and his wife, Reina, the finest anthropologist Panama has produced. (Amado provided much of the information on the Emberá and Wounaan Indians that appears in this book.) Reina founded nine museums and wrote the definitive books on Panama's tribes before cancer took her life at the age of 48. Their son, Hernán Araúz, is now widely regarded as the country's top nature guide.

birders, although most of the bird species represented here can also be found in Cana Valley, an excellent bird-watching area that lies farther south. Specialties at Pirre include the crimson-bellied woodpecker, the white-fronted nunbird and the striped woodhaunter.

A Kuna artisan at work, Comarca de San Blás

Art is everywhere in Panama City.

Traditional Kuna mola, Comarca de San Blás

Moving art in Gamboa, Panamá Province

Kuna beaded leggings, Comarca de San Blás

Puente de las Américas mural, Panama City

Balboa, Panama City

Christ, Colón Province

Panama City's guardian

chocar – to collide

Be sure to try the local brew.

French tribute to early builders

You made it!

If you intend to visit Pirre Station, you must first get permission from the ANAM office in El Real (see El Real earlier) and pay US$3; if no one's at the office when you arrive, ask around for Narciso 'Chicho' Bristan, who can take care of business.

The area around Pirre is the most accessible section of the park, and the station's strength is that two good hiking trails originate from it. One trail leads to Pirre Mountain ridge, which takes most hikers two days to reach. Tents are pretty much a necessity. The other trail winds through jungle to a series of cascades about an hour's hike away. Neither trail should be attempted without a guide, as they are not well marked and if you get lost out here, you're finished. You can hire a ranger as a guide, or you can contact one of the tour operators listed in the Getting Around chapter.

Fifteen kilometers separate the station and Cana Valley, and between the two there's nothing but virgin rain forest. Unfortunately, no trails link Pirre Station and Cana, although trails lead from both sites to the Pirre Mountain ridge. Contact Ancon Expeditions of Panama (see the Getting Around chapter for contact information) if you're considering a Pirre-Cana trek.

At Pirre Station are barracks with a front room with fold-out cots for visitors, a dining area that consists of two tables and four benches beside a very rustic kitchen, a palapa with a few chairs, and one outhouse. Bathing is done in a nearby creek. There is no electricity at the station. Like Cana, Pirre is relatively cool and not very buggy.

If you plan on eating, you must bring your own food. Remember: This is a ranger station, not a hotel (though there is a US$10 per night fee to stay here). The rangers will cook your food for you (US$5 a day is most appreciated), but you must provide bottled water. However, if you've got a water-purification system or tablets, the water in the creek should be OK, and there are lots of lemon trees in the vicinity of the station (nothing beats cold lemonade after a hike).

Beware: Most of Parque Nacional Darién is prime fer-de-lance territory, and these very deadly snakes have been found near the station. Always wear boots when you're walking in camp at night or entering the forest at any time. This warning should not dissuade you from visiting the station; just be careful. The area surrounding Pirre Station has primeval lowland and premontane rain forest that's gorgeous and shouldn't be missed just because of the remote possibility of snakebite.

Be sure to try the *zapote* growing at the station. The fruit's as round as a softball, as hard as a rock and as green as an avocado, but it has a fleshy orange meat with the appearance, taste and texture of mango. It's absolutely addictive. With a lemonade chaser, life just doesn't get any better.

Getting There & Away

Pirre Station can only be reached by hiking or by a combination of hiking and boating. The hike from El Real takes three hours. You can also take a one-hour canoe ride from El Real to the village of Piji Baisal and then make a one-hour hike from Piji Baisal to Pirre Station.

First, you'll need to get to El Real, which can be reached by plane or boat (see the El Real section earlier). Then, if you prefer to hike, take the 'road' connecting El Real and Pirre Station. This road is covered with 2m high lemongrass and won't likely be cleared, as the only people who would clear it are Pirre's rangers, and they do not have vehicles or even enough money for gas. Hiking this barely discernible road takes about three hours and pretty much requires a guide. The ANAM station in El Real can help you find a local guide (expect to pay about US$20), and you have to go there anyway to get permission to visit the station.

The alternative is to hire a boatman to take you up the Río Pirre to Piji Baisal. Expect to pay about US$40 plus the cost of gasoline, which will vary depending on the size of your party, the size of the outboard motor and other factors. From Piji Baisal, it's a one-hour hike to the station. Again, you'll need a guide to lead you to the station, as no signs mark the way there.

CANA

Cana, a valley nestled in foothills on the eastern slope of Pirre Ridge, is the most isolated place in the Republic of Panama and home to some of the world's finest bird watching. About 60 Panamanian bird species can be found only in Parque Nacional Darién, and Cana is at the park's lush heart.

In addition to four species of macaw, Cana is known for its harpy eagles, black-tipped cotingas, red-throated caracaras, dusky-backed jacamars, varied solitaires, rufous-cheeked hummingbirds and golden-headed quetzals. Many bird species can be found much more easily here than elsewhere in Panama. Cana is also home to jaguars, pumas, ocelots, jaguarundis and margays, but you'd be extremely fortunate to see one of these cats. They avoid people and generally prowl at night – when it's cool and when they may cover several kilometers in their search for food.

Although the town of Santa Cruz de Cana, which was founded by Spaniards in the 16th century, has been completely overgrown, the valley is not entirely devoid of human habitations. There's an airstrip at the eastern end of the valley, and a short walk from it there's a border-police station, as well as an ANAM/Ancon field station (see Places to Stay later in this section).

History

A survey of Cana determined that a lake covered most of the valley's floor during prehistoric times. Experts speculate that the lake emptied when an earthquake created a divide that allowed the water to drain; such was the case at El Valle in Coclé Province. As you enter the valley by air, you can still see a marshy area and some ponds – remnants of the prehistoric lake.

During the early 16th century, Spaniards discovered gold in the valley, and in the years that followed they mined the heck out of the place using regional Indians as well as black slaves brought from Africa. Las Minas del Espíritu Santo (Mines of the Holy Spirit), as they were called, at one time filled the valley with 20,000 people. They lived in the town of Santa Cruz de Cana, which has long since been reclaimed by the jungle.

One of the longest rivers in the Darién, the Río Tuira, runs northward past Cana and out to the Pacific Ocean. The Spaniards used to send supplies to the Cana Valley via the Tuira, and they sent gold from the valley to Santa María, on the western bank of the river, for safekeeping until boats arrived to transport the precious metal to Panama City.

Naturally, the vast quantities of gold at Santa María attracted pirates, and the town fell numerous times. In some instances pirates came out of retirement to raid the place. In 1702, for example, a party of retired English buccaneers living in Jamaica sailed to the Darién, where they were joined by former colleagues who had married Indians and settled down. The come-back Kidds and 300 interested Indians drove the Spaniards from the valley and captured 70 black slaves, whom they kept at work for seven days. During that week, the raiders obtained about 36kg of gold from the mines. They set fire to the 900 houses in the valley when they left.

Another group of English pirates, these led by Sir Gregor MacGregor, attempted to take Portobelo in 1819, and the Spaniards managed to capture quite a few of them. Some were shot on the spot, but most were taken to Cana, where they were forced to toil in the same mines 'borrowed' by other Englishmen 117 years earlier. A few years later the Spaniards left Panama and the mines were abandoned.

An English outfit visited Cana in the early 20th century and discovered that there was still gold to be found in the hills. They ran train tracks from the valley to Boca de Cupe, 20km away as the toucan flies, and moved men, supplies and gold along them in small locomotives and in freight cars. When these Englishmen cleared out, 20 years later, they left their trains behind. Today you can find several rusting locomotives, numerous freight cars and many mines amid Cana's dense jungle.

Hiking

Three trails begin near the ANAM/Ancon field station: the **Cituro Trail**, the **Machinery**

Trail and the **Stream Trail**. The Cituro Trail begins at the northeastern corner of the station and winds a couple of hundred meters through secondary forest, paralleling some old railroad tracks and passing a rusted-out locomotive with the brand name 'Cituro' forged into it.

The Machinery Trail is a loop trail that begins at the western edge of the station and winds several hundred meters through secondary forest to the remains of another abandoned Cituro locomotive, a very overgrown smelter and other pieces of mining machinery.

The Stream Trail is the most glorious of all on a hot and humid day. It's a short one – only 50m – but it runs from behind the field station to a small creek where you can take a very refreshing dip.

Beside the valley's grass-and-dirt airstrip, which is about 100m from the field station, the mouths of two more trails disappear into the dense rain forest: the **Pirre Mountain Trail** and **Boca de Cupe Trail**.

The Pirre Mountain Trail, starting near the western end of the airstrip, offers a six-hour ridgeline hike to a campsite high above the Cana Valley. The campsite is in cloud forest, and it's quite cool and refreshing at night. The trail is arduous in spots, but it offers excellent birding in mostly virgin jungle. If you're traveling to Cana with a tour operator's assistance and want to camp along the ridge, let the operator know in advance so that it can arrange tents for you.

The Boca de Cupe Trail runs north from Cana to the town of Boca de Cupe. A person with good legs can reach Boca de Cupe via the trail in two to three days, depending on the trail's condition. However, because of bandits, guerrillas and paramilitaries in the vicinity of Boca de Cupe, use of this trail is not recommended. Be advised too that the trail crosses the knee-deep Río Cupe six times. It initially passes through secondary and thereafter only virgin jungle.

Please resist the temptation to explore the old mines in the area, even though some people may think it's a good idea to enter a mine that's been abandoned for many years and has who knows how many snakes, jaguars

or pumas living in it. At least one tourist who wandered into an old Cana mine developed a life-threatening respiratory illness after inhaling something nasty in the tunnel.

Places to Stay

The valley's *ANAM/Ancon field station* is a wooden structure that was built by gold workers during the 1970s and enlarged in mid-1998 by the wildlife conservation group Ancon. Tourists are welcome to stay at the barrackslike station, at the eastern end of Cana Valley, but to do so they must arrange their trips through Ancon Expeditions. Although Cana is managed by ANAM, the station is maintained by Ancon (parent to Ancon Expeditions), and Ancon does not allow other tour operators to use the facility.

Each room contains two or three firm beds and a shelf on which to place a candle at night, but nothing more. Food is provided for guests. There's no electricity and it's shared bathrooms only, but the place is clean and pleasant and cool at night. When you consider the awesome hiking and the bird-watching possibilities in the area, the station is wildly outstanding.

Getting There & Away

Except for a several-day hike, the only way into the valley is by chartered aircraft. Even if you arrive on foot, Ancon Expeditions has a monopoly on the valley's sole lodgings so you need to contact that company to make arrangements. At the time of writing, Ancon Expeditions offered an outstanding four-day, three-night package that included an English-speaking guide, all meals, accommodations (including tent camping along the Pirre Mountain Trail, with all provisions carried by porters) and transportation to and from Panama City. Contact Ancon Expeditions for rates.

LA PALMA

pop 3844

La Palma is the provincial capital and is also the most populous town in the Darién. La Palma is at the mouth of the Río Tuira, where the wide river meets the Golfo de San Miguel. It was actually the San Miguel gulf, not the much larger Golfo de Panamá, that Balboa saw when he became the first European to set eyes on the Pacific.

Despite its lofty position as capital of the largest province in Panama, La Palma doesn't offer much to see or do. It's pretty much a one-street town, with the street following the sweeping river bank. Every facility of possible interest to the traveler is on this street, within 300m of the airstrip. A good bit of this hot and muggy community went up in flames a few years back, which is why some of the best pieces of real estate in town have only charred pylons on them.

La Palma is home to the only bank in the Darién, the Banco Nacional de Panamá. There's also a hospital, a port and a police station (if you intend to go anywhere near the Colombian border and you speak Spanish, you should speak with the police here first), as well as three hotels, three bars and several food stands. By far the busiest places are the airstrip and the small port. The port is used mainly by people bringing produce out of the jungle via the Río Tuira, and by larger boats that take the produce from the port to Panama City.

Most travelers visit La Palma for one of two reasons: They're here to catch a plane to somewhere else or they're here to take a boat ride to somewhere else. The two most popular boating destinations are the Ancon nature preserve and lodge at Reserva Natural Punta Patiño and the Emberá villages along the banks of the Río Sambú; these fine trips are described later in this chapter.

You can visit these destinations on your own; if you speak Spanish, you can usually find someone near the dock who owns a boat and is willing to go on an adventure with you for the right price (US$120 to US$200 per day, gas included). Most people, however, prefer to make these trips with a guide, so that everything is conveniently prearranged (see the Getting Around chapter for information on Panamanian tour companies).

Places to Stay & Eat
The best of the three hotels in La Palma is *Hotel Biaquira Bagara* (*☎/fax 299-6224*),

which also goes by the name of Casa Ramady because the friendly Ramady family lives in a home beneath the 13 rooms they rent. Six rooms have cold-water private bathrooms that contain bathtubs – something rarely found in Panamanian hotels. The clean, fan-cooled rooms with shared bathroom/private bathroom cost US$15/20 and some have private balconies. Some beds are firmer than others; ask to see several rooms. There's also a lovely sitting area facing the river. This place is a godsend after a week or two in the jungle.

Pensión Tuira offers 11 small rooms with decent beds and fans for US$10 for a room with one single bed and US$15 for a room with two beds.

La Pensión Takela (*☎ 299-6490*) has nine fan-cooled rooms, three with private bathrooms and old TVs with lousy reception. Rates are US$10/12 with a shared bathroom and US$12/14 with private bathrooms. The hotel, which like the other two is at river's edge, is the worst of the three.

Refrequeria Guivi is owned and run by Viola Maria Avila, who's very friendly and a good cook. Among her offerings are chicken stew with spaghetti and rice (US$2), beer (60¢) and sodas (30¢). It's open 8:30 am to 8 pm daily.

Getting There & Away
Aeroperlas (*☎ 315-7500 in Panama City*) has flights from La Palma to Panama City at 9:40 am on Sunday (via El Real), at 9:55 am on Tuesday (via Garachine), and a nonstop at 9:55 am on Monday, Wedesday and Thursday (US$36).

Aviatur (*☎ 315-0307 in Panama City*) also flies between La Palma and Panama City.

RESERVA NATURAL PUNTA PATIÑO
Punta Patiño, on the southern shore of the Golfo de San Miguel 25km from La Palma, is known mainly for its 26,315-hectare **wildlife preserve**, which is owned by the conservation group Ancon. The only way to reach the preserve, short of hacking your way through many kilometers of trailless jungle, is by boat.

The boat ride is definitely part of the Punta Patiño experience. The ride begins at La Palma and takes you into the gulf but not too far from shore. You'll likely pass shrimp boats and fishermen in dugouts using nets. If you've never been on a shrimp boat and would like to see what they're all about, this is a good place to do it. If you speak some Spanish, just pull up beside a shrimper and ask if you can come aboard for a look. Unless you catch the shrimpers in a bad mood, they will welcome you. Shrimpers tend to view tourists as oddballs, so the request won't surprise or alarm them. If you are traveling with a guide, ask the guide to make the request.

After about 45 minutes, if you're traveling in a fairly fast boat, you'll pass the mouth of the Río Mogué, which is flanked primarily by virgin forest. There's an **Emberá village** on the bank of the Mogué, about 30 minutes upriver by boat. The village is home to about 400 people and remains fairly traditional. There are no other settlements on the river. The mouth of the Río Mogué is lined with black mangroves, which are interesting to look at and can make for intriguing and artistic photographs.

About 10 minutes after you leave the mouth of the Mogué and head south along the coast, you'll pass the small community of **Punta Alegre**. *Alegre* means 'happy,' and this does seem to be a pretty content community despite the poverty in which the 500 or so African-descent inhabitants live. Most of the adults make their living fishing from dugout canoes in the gulf. Their music, which relies heavily on bongo drums, is pure West African. If you're lucky, some of the men and women here will bring out their guitars and drums. It doesn't take much to put these people in a festive mood. Take a look at the simple boatyard near the center of town. Here you can see dugouts, called piraguas in the southern Darién, being mended.

There are no places to stay in Punta Alegre, but there are a couple of simple restaurants. Punta Alegre's food, which typically consists of fresh fish and prawns, is quite tasty.

A handful of Emberá families live at the southern end of Punta Alegre. Some of the Indians usually offer to paint visiting tourists with jagua-fruit juice, in the same manner that the Emberá paint themselves. The juice stains the skin for about a week and looks much like a tattoo. Consider getting painted if you're only days from going home and there's someone you'd like to surprise with your 'permanent tattoo.'

Continuing south another 20 minutes, you'll reach an expansive beach. A 400m long dirt road winds from the beach to the restaurant and cabins near the center of the Punta Patiño Ancon preserve, passing a swamp with several crocodiles and a meadow frequented by capybaras, the world's largest rodents (yes, bigger even than punk rockers).

The preserve contains lots of species-rich primary forest, but the jungle is a fair walk from the cabins and it's pretty buggy. The panorama of the gulf from the dining and viewing area, which is perched atop a ridge near the cabins, is spellbinding, particularly at daybreak. The cabins, all of which have private bathrooms, are quite comfortable. There's no good place to go swimming nearby, however.

Visitors to the preserve are treated to guided night and morning nature hikes. During the day, they can explore by boat the red and black mangroves lining the gulf, chat with fishermen at work (all are friendly but none speak English) or drop by Punta Alegre.

Getting There & Away

If you prefer, you can get to Ancon's preserve on your own without booking a guided tour through Ancon Expeditions, the organization's for-profit arm but you must notify Ancon Expeditions in advance so that it can reserve a cabin for you (see the Organized Tours in the Getting Around chapter for contact information). If you visit without Ancon Expeditions' help, lodging and three daily meals will cost you US$90 per person per day. You can hire boats in La Palma to reach Punta Patiño; expect to pay your boatman about US$120 to US$150 per day.

Ancon Expeditions offers a package tour to Punta Patiño that includes the roundtrip airfare between Panama City and La Palma, a boat ride up the Río Mogué to the Emberá village, a visit to Punta Alegre, hikes in the preserve, guide service and all meals. The three-day, two-night adventure costs about US$600 per person (party of two) and substantially less per person for larger parties.

RÍO SAMBÚ

The mouth of the wide, brown Río Sambú is 1½ hours by fast boat south of Punta Patiño. Traveling it is a heart-of-darkness experience: You pass through spectacular jungle inhabited by jaguars and mountain lions and Indians who until recently did most of their hunting with blowguns. The river meanders for many kilometers toward the Colombian border, passing Emberá villages along the way. The farther you go up the river, the more traditional are these Indian villages.

Boats and boatmen can be hired in La Palma, or you can travel with a guide (see Getting There & Away, below). When you reach the Río Sambú, you will need to hire a dugout canoe to get farther upriver. During the rainy season, the river is navigable by dugout all the way to Pavarandó, the most inland of the eight Emberá communities on the Sambú.

Prior to 1990 or 1991, the indigenous people living beside the river led traditional Emberá lives – they grew corn, rice, plantains and other crops; they fished the river and went about dressed in the manner of their ancestors (the women bare-breasted and wearing colorful knee-length skirts, the men wearing only loincloths).

Today, the Sambú continues to provide the Emberá with fish, traditional methods of agriculture are still practiced, and the Emberá still reside mainly in open-sided thatch-roof houses atop stilts. But western attire is replacing traditional dress, outboard motors are increasingly seen on the Indians' dugouts and Christianity brought by missionaries is replacing traditional Emberá religious practices.

At night, you can make camp where you please if you have a tent. However, unless you've brought an individual tent for your boatman, he will prefer an alternative – making a deal to sleep on the floor of an Emberá family's home. If you can speak Spanish, finding a family to move in with for the night isn't difficult, and even getting a hot meal is easy. Money talks, and it talks loudly in these Emberá villages. Expect to pay US$10 per person for shelter and US$5 for food.

Before you go to sleep, apply insect repellent liberally to avoid waking up with hundreds of bites. It's hard to say which are more annoying: the mosquitoes, chiggers or fleas. The trouble with chiggers is that they nestle before they bite – they burrow under your skin and hang out there, taking little nibbles of your flesh, for three or four days until they leave your body. Trying to remove them only makes them mad.

Be forewarned: A trip far up the Río Sambú is not everyone's cup of tea. Even before you reach the river, you will be on a boat rather a long time under a broiling tropical sun. And if riding in a boat that's loaded down with leaking gasoline cans bothers you, you should probably pass on the Sambú: You'll need to bring several large containers of gasoline along from La Palma to fuel the canoe that you'll hire upriver. There are no pumping stations on the Sambú.

There's nothing like a relaxing boat trip.

There are other minor hardships, like the lack of showers and toilets. But the Sambú offers you true adventure, something that may not even be possible anywhere in the Tropics 50 years from now. Even if you travel deep into the Amazon, you'd be hard-pressed to find such wilderness and such people these days.

Getting There & Away

If you speak Spanish, you can travel up the Sambú without the assistance of a tour operator. But if you or your traveling companions don't speak the language, you'll want to hire a guide. You will need to do this because the boat you'll hire in La Palma to reach the Sambú will sit too low in the water to navigate the upper portions of the river; to get any farther upriver, you must negotiate the use of a shallow dugout in one of the Emberá villages. If you don't speak fluent Spanish, these negotiations could prove futile. Be advised that when you rent a boat anywhere in Panama, you're also hiring its owner to operate the vessel. Remember too that you must bring enough gasoline from La Palma to fuel your dugout.

As for guides, only one name jumps to mind when the destination is the Darién: Hernán Araúz. Hernán is widely regarded as *the* guide for Panama's wild eastern province. The author has traveled with him here several times and was very impressed with his knowledge of the rivers, the Indians and especially the birds. He's a big guy who packs at least one big gun (legally), but he doesn't take unnecessary risks. He's about as levelheaded a person as you're ever likely to meet. Contact information for him appears in the Guides section of the Getting Around chapter.

TROPIC STAR LODGE

Overlooking Bahía Piña, near the southern tip of the Darién, is one of Panama's legendary institutions: Tropic Star Lodge (☎ *800-682-3424, 407-843-0125 in the USA*). This is the only lodge that serves Bahía Piña, and more International Game Fish Association (IGFA) world records have been broken in the bay than anywhere else.

Website: www.tropicstar.com

The facilities include stand-alone cabins, a wing of adjacent rooms, a pool, a restaurant, a bar and porch with lovely bay views, an impressive tackle room and even a so-called 'palace' that was built by a Texas oil tycoon as his home away from home in 1961. The facilities are on a manicured hillside overlooking the protected bay and the lodge's fleet of 31-foot Bertrams, the Ferraris of sport-fishing boats.

Tropic Star's owners and operators, Terri Kittredge Andrews and Mike Andrews, a married couple, enjoy 85% repeat client business. No surprise: Everything here is done just right. The multicourse dinners, for example, are a feast; offerings include baked Alaska, cherries jubilee, black bean soup, freshly baked pies and bread, ceviche and always the catch of the day. The mood here is festive, and there's a great sense of camaraderie among the guests, most of whom are millionaires and quite a number of whom are celebrities. (Tropic Star was one of John Wayne's getaways. Pierce Brosnan was here in 2000, looking surprisingly similar to James Bond.)

The Andrews' property covers more than 7000 hectares, most of it virgin rain forest. The birding is excellent, and there are also some lovely waterfalls with swimming pools on the grounds. There is a totally secluded white-sand beach a 45-minute hike away, and the bay lends itself well to sea kayaks, which the Andrews have purchased and brought to the lodge. There's even a healthy coral reef for snorkeling.

Tropic Star is only open from mid-December through July, in accordance with the fishing seasons. The prime black marlin season runs from mid-December to April. Pacific sailfish move in from April to July. Striped marlin season is mid-March to May. All species of billfish and nonbillfish can be caught year-round.

Note that reservations for fishing need to be made an entire year in advance. Per guests' requests, there are no phones at the lodge, nor are there TVs or radios.

Weekly and half-weekly packages are available; both options include the use of a boat with a captain and mate, all meals, and fishing tackle and leaders. Weekly per-person rates include seven nights of lodging and six days of fishing, and they vary with the number of people in a boat. From December through May 31: US$6200/3750 for one/two people in a boat and US$3025/2580 for three/four people in a boat. The rates fall in June and July. Half-weekly rates are also available. Discounts are available for stays of more than a week. Rates for people who don't want to fish are also available.

Getting There & Away
Aeroperlas (☎ 315-7500 in Panama City) flies from the capital to the Bahía Piña airstrip, which was built by Tropic Star, at 9:30 am every Tuesday, Thursday and Saturday (US$44). Planes that land here also stop at the town of Jaqué, 8km away. Which airstrip the plane lands at first seems to depend on the pilot's mood, so be sure to ask if you have arrived at Bahía Piña or Jaqué before you leave the aircraft. A short dirt road links the Bahía Piña airstrip to the Tropic Star Lodge.

The plane that brings you into the area also takes you back out, leaving Bahía Piña at 10:25 am and Jaqué at 10:45 am on Tuesday, Thursday and Saturday; it makes a stop at La Palma before continuing on to Panama City. Be sure to make a reservation at least a day in advance.

Aviatur (☎ 315-0307 in Panama City) also flies between Bahía Piña and Jaqué.

JAQUÉ
Unless you're here to surf out front of town or explore the Río Jaqué, there's no really good reason to come here. The small town, near the river's mouth, has an airstrip, and travelers can rent boats here. There's one ugly hotel in Jaqué, which wasn't out of business in 2001, but wasn't keeping regular hours either.

There are numerous Emberá villages along the river, the first four of which are fairly westernized. Unfortunately, traveling farther up river is foolhardy, due to bandits and guerrillas that occasionally move into the area. There are no hotels in these villages, but you should be able to negotiate food and a place to sleep if you speak Spanish.

If you make the trip, bringing a Polaroid camera and presenting the Indians with photos of themselves is a great way to score points with these very tolerant people, as noted earlier in this chapter. You could also buy a bag of candy at the Jaqué market. Emberá – adults as well as children – love candy, so handing some out when you arrive is a very nice way to greet them. Keep in mind too that the Emberá would probably close their villages to outsiders if tourists were to frequently pass through without giving anything or buying anything, but only taking photos and invading the Indians' privacy.

Language

Although Spanish is the most widely spoken language in Panama, travelers to the region will encounter indigenous languages. This chapter addresses such variations only briefly, mainly discussing the type of Spanish that is understood more or less throughout the region.

Every visitor to Panama should attempt to learn some Spanish, the basic elements of which are easily acquired (perhaps more so for speakers of English and Romance languages). A month-long language course taken before departure can go a long way toward facilitating communication and comfort on the road. Language courses are also available in Panama City. Even if classes are impractical, you should make the effort to learn a few basic phrases and pleasantries. Do not hesitate to practice your new skills – in general, Latin Americans meet attempts to communicate in the vernacular, however halting, with enthusiasm and appreciation.

Latin American Spanish

The Spanish of the Americas comes in a bewildering array of varieties. Depending on the areas in which you travel, consonants may be glossed over, vowels squashed into each other, and syllables and even words dropped altogether. Slang and regional vocabulary, much of it derived from indigenous languages, can further add to your bewilderment.

Throughout Latin America, the Spanish language is referred to as *castellano* more often than *español*. Unlike in Spain, the plural of the familiar *tú* form is *ustedes* rather than *vosotros;* the latter term will sound quaint and archaic in the Americas. In addition, the letters 'c' and 'z' are never lisped in Latin America; attempts to do so could well provoke amusement or even contempt.

Spanish in Panama

Think you know enough Spanish? Here's a quick rundown on some of the expressions and colorful colloquialisms you may hear while traveling:

salve	street slang for *propina*, or tip
tongo	street slang for cop
chota	street slang for police car
diablo rojo	literally, 'red devil'; refers to public buses
mangajo/a	someone who is filthy
mala leche	literally, 'bad milk'; means bad luck
buena leche	literally, 'good milk'; means good luck
salado/a	literally, 'salty'; refers to someone with bad luck
Eso está bien pretty.	refers to something nice
¡Eso está pretty pretty!	refers to something super-nice
¡Entonces laopé!	Hey, dude!
¡Hey, gringo!	Hey, white person! (friendly)
¡Juega vivo!	Be alert, look out for your best interests!
Voy por fuera.	I am leaving right now.
¡Ayala bestia!	Holy cow!
¡Chuleta!	common expression similar to 'Holy cow!'
pelao or *pelaito*	common expression for a child
Pa' lante.	Let's go now.
enantes	just now
Eres un comemierda.	refers to someone pretentious
¡Pifioso!	a showoff, or something that looks cool

Tas buena, mami. — You're looking good, mama.

Nos pillamos. — We'll see each other later.

una pinta or *una fría* — literally, 'one pint' or 'a cold one'; means a beer

Dame una fría. — Give me a cold one (a beer).

guaro — hard liquor

chupata — an all-out drinking party

¡Bien cuidado!
literally, 'Well taken care of!'; often used by a street person when asking for a tip for taking care of your car, normally in parking lots at restaurants, cinemas, bars, etc

Me estoy comiendo un cable
literally, 'I am eating a cable'; I'm down on my luck.

rabiblanco/a
literally, 'white tipped'; pejorative reference to a member of the socioeconomic elite; the term comes from *paloma rabíblano/a*, or white-tipped dove, a bird that walks with its head held out high and its chest thrust out in a seemingly pretentious way

racataca
also *meña*; both terms refer to women who wear lots of gold jewelry and are perceived as low class

chombo/a
an acceptable reference to a black person of Antillean descent

ladilla
literally, 'crab louse'; refers to an annoying person

nueve letras
literally, 'nine letters'; refers to Seco Herrerano (the second word has nine letters)

vuelve loco con vaca
literally, 'makes crazy with cow'; refers to drinking seco and milk

vaina
common word that substitutes for 'thing,' as in *Pasame esa vaina.* (Pass me that thing.)

yeye
refers to kids and adults who wear fancy clothes and maybe drive a fancy car and who pretend to be rich but who in reality are living well beyond their means for as long as they can

Phrasebooks & Dictionaries

Lonely Planet's *Latin American Spanish phrasebook,* by Anna Cody, is a worthwhile addition to your backpack. Another exceptionally useful resource is the *University of Chicago Spanish-English, English-Spanish Dictionary* – its small size, light weight and thorough entries make it ideal for travel. It also makes a great gift for any newfound friends upon your departure.

Pronunciation

The pronunciation of written Spanish is, in theory, consistently phonetic. Once you are aware of the basic rules, they should cause little difficulty. Speak slowly to avoid getting tongue-tied until you become confident of your ability. Of course, the best way to familiarize yourself with the pronunciation used in the area where you're traveling is to chat with locals, keeping an ear out for regional variations.

Traditionally, there were three Spanish letters that did not exist in English: 'ch,' 'll' and 'ñ.' These followed 'c,' 'l' and 'n,' respectively, in the alphabet, and had their own corresponding sections in the dictionary. However, in the mid-1990s, Spain's Academia Real de la Lengua Española abolished 'ch' and 'll' as separate letters; hence, newer Spanish dictionaries list them in their English alphabetical order. The practice varies from region to region, so look for a 'ch' section in the phone book if you can't find 'Chávez' under 'c.'

Vowels Spanish vowels are generally consistent and have close English equivalents.

a is like the 'a' in 'father.'

e is somewhere between the 'e' in 'met' and the 'ey' in 'hey.'

i is like the 'ee' in 'feet.'

o is like the 'o' in 'note.'

u is like the 'oo' in 'boot'; it is silent after 'q' and in the pairings 'gue' and 'gui,' unless it's carrying a dieresis ('ü,' as in *güero*).

Consonants Spanish consonants generally resemble their English equivalents. The following are the major differences in consonants.

b resembles the English 'b' but is a softer sound produced by holding the lips nearly together. When beginning a word or when preceded by 'm' or 'n,' it's pronounced like the 'b' in 'book' (*bomba, embajada*). The Spanish 'v' is pronounced almost identically; for clarification, Spanish speakers refer to 'b' as 'b larga' and to 'v' as 'b corta.'

c is like the 's' in 'see' before 'e' and 'i'; otherwise, it's like the English 'k.'

d is produced with the tongue up against the front teeth, almost like the 'th' in 'feather'; after 'l' and 'n,' it's pronounced like the English 'd' in 'dog.'

g before 'e' and 'i' acts as a more guttural English 'h'; otherwise, it's like the 'g' in 'go.'

h is invariably silent; if your name begins with this letter, listen carefully when immigration officials summon you to pick up your passport.

j acts as a more guttural English 'h.'

ll acts as a Spanish 'y,' although it is never a vowel; see Semiconsonant, below.

ñ is like the 'ny' in 'canyon.'

r is produced with the tongue touching the palate and flapping down, almost like the 'tt' of 'butter.' At the beginning of a word or following 'l,' 'n' or 's,' it is rolled strongly.

rr is a very strongly rolled Spanish 'r.'

t resembles the English 't' but without the puff of air.

v is pronounced like the Spanish 'b.'

x is generally pronounced like the 'x' in 'taxi' except for a few words in which it acts as the Spanish 'j' (as in 'México').

z is like the 's' in 'sun.'

Semiconsonant The Spanish **y** is a semiconsonant; it's pronounced as the Spanish 'i'

when it stands alone or appears at the end of a word. Normally, 'y' is pronounced like the 'y' in 'yesterday.'

Diphthongs Diphthongs are combinations of two vowels that form a single syllable. In Spanish, the formation of a diphthong depends on combinations of the two 'weak' vowels ('i' and 'u') or one weak and one of the three 'strong' vowels ('a,' 'e' and 'o'). Two strong vowels form separate syllables.

An example of two weak vowels forming a diphthong is the word *viuda* (widow; pronounced **vyu**-tha). The initial syllable of 'Guatemala' is a combination of weak and strong vowels. In contrast, the verb *caer* (to fall) has two syllables (pronounced ca-**er**). Other examples include the following:

ai	as in 'h**i**de'
au	as in 'h**ow**'
ei	as in 'h**ay**'
ia	as in '**ya**rd'
ie	as in '**ye**s'
oi	as in 'b**oy**'
ua	as in '**wa**sh'
ue	as in '**we**ll' (unless preceded by 'q' or 'g')

Stress Stress is extremely important, as it can change the meaning of words. In general, words ending in vowels or the letters 'n' or 's' have stress on the next-to-last syllable, while those with other endings have stress on the last syllable. Thus *vaca* (cow) and *caballos* (horses) are both stressed on their penultimate syllables, while *catedral* (cathedral) is stressed on its last syllable.

To indicate departures from these general rules, Spanish employs the acute accent, which can occur anywhere in a word. If there is an accented syllable, stress is always on that syllable. Thus *sótano* (basement), 'América' and 'Panamá' have the first, second and third syllable stressed, respectively. When words are written in capital letters, the accent is often omitted, but the stress still falls where the accent would be.

Basic Grammar

Although even colloquial Spanish comprises a multitude of tenses and moods, learning enough grammar to enable basic conversation is not particularly difficult. In general, Spanish word order in sentences resembles that of English.

Nouns & Pronouns Nouns in Spanish are masculine or feminine. In general, nouns ending in 'o,' 'e' or 'ma' are masculine, while those ending in 'a,' 'ión' or 'dad' are feminine. Of course, there are scores of exceptions to this rule: Both *día* (day) and *mapa* (map) are masculine, while *mano* (hand) is feminine. To pluralize a noun, add 's' if it ends in an unaccented vowel – eg, *libro* (book) becomes *libros* – and 'es' if it ends in a consonant or accented vowel – eg, *rey* (king) becomes *reyes*. Fortunately for speakers of English, there is no declension of nouns as in Latin.

The personal pronouns are *yo* (I), *tú* or *vos* (you, informal), *usted* (you, formal; abbreviated Ud), *el/ella* (he/she), *nosotros/nosotras* (we), *ustedes* (you, plural; abbreviated Uds) and *ellos/ellas* (they). Note that to use the feminine plurals *nosotras* and *ellas,* the group referred to must be entirely composed of females; the presence of even one male calls for the masculine pronoun. In common speech, the personal pronoun may be omitted when it is the subject of a sentence if the subject's identity is made clear by the verb ending: *estoy aquí* rather than *yo estoy aquí* (both mean 'I am here').

The possessive pronouns are *mi* (my), *tu* (your, informal), *nuestro* (our) and *su* (his/her/their/your, formal; singular and plural). As in English, possessive pronouns precede the noun they modify; however, they must agree in number and gender with that noun – not with the possessor. Thus we get *nuestro hombre* (our man), *nuestra mujer* (our woman), *nuestros novios* (our boyfriends) and *nuestras novias* (our girlfriends). *Mi, tu* and *su* do not change with gender, but add an 's' for plural nouns: *mis libros* means 'my books.'

The demonstrative pronouns are *este* (this) and *ese* (that). Gender and number also affect demonstrative pronouns. Consider the following examples:

this book	*este libro*
these notebooks	*estos cuadernos*
this letter	*esta carta*
these scissors	*estas tijeras*
that boy	*ese chico*
those guys	*esos muchachos*
that girl	*esa chica*
those gals	*esas muchachas*

Articles, Adjectives & Adverbs The definite articles ('the' in English) are *el, la, los* and *las*. These four forms correspond to the four possible combinations of gender and number. Similarly, the indefinite articles ('a,' 'an' and 'some') are *un, una, unos* and *unas*. In Spanish, the definite article is used more extensively than in English, while the indefinite article is utilized less. As in English, the articles precede the nouns they modify, eg, *el papel* (the paper), *unas frutas* (some fruits).

In contrast, adjectives in Spanish usually follow the noun they modify. Those ending in 'o' agree with the noun in gender and number (thus *alto* means 'tall,' while *mujeres altas* means 'tall women'); those ending in other letters merely agree in number. To form a comparative, add *más* (more) or *menos* (less) before the adjective. For superlatives, add the *más* or *menos* as well as *lo, la, los* or *las* (depending on gender and number). For example, *pequeño* is 'small,' *más pequeño* 'smaller' and *lo más pequeño* 'the smallest.'

Adverbs can often be formed from adjectives by adding the suffix *-mente*. If the adjective ends in an 'o,' convert it to an 'a' before affixing the ending. Thus *actual* (current) becomes *actualmente* (currently) and *rápido* (rapid) becomes *rápidamente*.

Verbs Spanish has three main categories of verbs: those ending in 'ar,' such as *hablar* (to speak); those ending in 'er,' such as *comer* (to eat); and those ending in 'ir,' such as *reir* (to laugh). Verbs are conjugated by retaining the verb's stem and altering the ending depending on subject, tense and mood. While most verbs follow a complicated yet predictable pattern of conjugation, there are scores of 'irregular' verbs, often the most commonly used, that must be memorized. For a more detailed explanation of verb conjugation, refer to Lonely Planet's *Latin American Spanish phrasebook*.

Greetings & Civilities

In public behavior, Latin Americans are often cordial yet polite and expect others to reciprocate. Never, for example, address a stranger without extending a greeting such as *buenos días* or *buenas tardes*. The usage of the informal second-person singular *tú* and *vos* differs from country to country; when in doubt, use the more formal *usted*. You must *always* use *usted* when addressing the police or persons with considerable power.

Hello.	*Hola.*
Good morning/Good day.	*Buenos días.*
Good afternoon.	*Buenas tardes.*
Good evening/Good night.	*Buenas noches.*
(The above three are often shortened to *Buenos* or *Buenas*.)	
Goodbye.	*Adiós* or *Hasta luego.*
Please.	*Por favor.*
Thank you.	*Gracias.*
You're welcome/It's a pleasure.	*De nada/Con mucho gusto.*
Excuse me. (when passing someone)	*Permiso.*
Excuse me.	*Discúlpeme* or *Perdón.*
I'm sorry.	*Lo siento.*
What is your name?	*¿Cómo se llama usted?*
My name is …	*Me llamo …*
A pleasure (to meet you).	*Mucho gusto.*

Useful Words & Phrases

yes	*sí*	before	*antes*
no	*no*	after	*después de*
and	*y*	soon	*pronto*
to/at	*a*	already	*ya*
for	*por, para*	now	*ahora*
of/from	*de/desde*	right away	*ahorita, en seguida*
in/on	*en*	here	*aquí*
with	*con*	there	*allí* or *allá*
without	*sin*		

I understand.	*Entiendo.*	What?	*¿Qué?* (use *¿Cómo?*
I don't understand.	*No entiendo.*		to ask someone to
I don't speak much	*No hablo*		repeat something)
Spanish.	*mucho castellano.*	Which (ones)?	*¿Cuál(es)?*
Is/are there …?	*¿Hay …?*	Who?	*¿Quién?*
I would like …	*Me gustaría*	Why?	*¿Por qué?*
	… or Quisiera …	How?	*¿Cómo?*
Where?	*¿Dónde?*	How much?	*¿Cuánto?*
Where is/are …?	*¿Dónde está/*	How many?	*¿Cuántos?*
	están …?		
When?	*¿Cuándo?*		

Emergencies

Help!	¡Socorro! or ¡Auxilio!	I've been robbed.	Me han robado.
Help me!	¡Ayúdenme!	They took my ...	Se me llevaron ...
Thief!	¡Ladrón!	money	el dinero
Fire!	¡Fuego!	passport	el pasaporte
police	policía	bag	la bolsa
doctor	doctor	Leave me alone!	¡Déjeme!
hospital	hospital	Go away!	¡Váyase!

Getting Around

plane	avión	pickup	camioneta
train	tren	bicycle	bicicleta
bus	camión, autobús	motorcycle	motocicleta
small bus	colectivo	hitchhike	un bote (a ride)
ship	barco, buque	airport	aeropuerto
car	auto or carro	train station	estación de ferrocarril
taxi	taxi	bus terminal	terminal de buses,
truck	camión		terminal de autobuses

I would like a ticket to ...	Quiero un boleto/pasaje a ...
What's the fare to ...?	¿Cuánto cuesta el pasaje a ...?
When does the next	¿Cuándo sale el próximo
plane/train/bus leave for ...?	avión/tren/bus para ...?
Are there student discounts?	¿Hay descuentos estudiantiles?/
	¿Hay rebajas para estudiantes?
first/last/next	primero/último/próximo
1st/2nd class	primera/segunda clase
one-way/roundtrip	ida/ida y vuelta
left luggage	guardería de equipaje
tourist office	oficina de turismocamión

Traffic Signs Keep in mind that traffic signs will invariably be in Spanish and may not be accompanied by internationally recognized symbols. Pay especially close attention to signs reading *Peligro* (Danger), *Cede el Paso* (Yield, or Give Way; especially prevalent on one-lane bridges) and *Hundimiento* (Dip; often a euphemistic term for axle-breaking sinkhole). Disregarding these warnings could result in disaster.

Adelante	Ahead
Alto	Stop
Cede el Paso	Yield/Give Way
Curva Peligrosa	Dangerous Curve
Derrumbes en la Vía	Landslides or Rockfalls (in the Road)
Despacio	Slow
Desvío	Detour
Hundimiento	Dip
Mantenga Su Derecha	Keep to the Right
No Adelantar/No Rebase	No Passing
No Estacionar	No Parking

No Hay Paso	No Entrance
Peligro	Danger
Trabajos en la Vía	Construction/Roadwork
Tránsito Entrando	Entering Traffic

Accommodations

hotel	*hotel, pensión, residencial, hospedaje*
single room	*habitación single/sencilla*
double room	*habitación doble/matrimonial*
What does it cost?	*¿Cuánto cuesta?*
Can you give me a deal?	*¿Me puede hacer precio?/¿Me puede hacer promoción?/*
	¿Me puede rebajar?
per night	*por noche*
full board	*pensión completa*
shared bath	*baño compartido*
private bath	*baño privado*
too expensive	*demasiado caro*
cheaper	*más económico/barato*
May I see it?	*¿Puedo verlo?*
I don't like it.	*No me gusta.*
the bill	*la cuenta*

Toilets

The most common word for 'toilet' is *baño*, but *servicios sanitarios* or just *servicios* (services) is a frequent alternative. Men's toilets will usually be signaled by *hombres, caballeros* or *varones.* Women's toilets will say *señoras* or *damas.*

Eating & Drinking

I (don't) eat/drink …	*(No) como/tomo …*
I'm a vegetarian.	*Soy vegetariano/a.*

water	*agua*	vegetables	*vegetales* or *legumbres*
purified water	*agua purificada*	fish	*pescado*
bread	*pan*	seafood	*mariscos*
meat	*carne*	coffee	*café*
cheese	*queso*	tea	*té*
eggs	*huevos*	beer	*cerveza*
milk	*leche*	alcohol	*alcohol*
juice	*jugo*		

Post & Communications

post office	*correo*	stamps	*estampillas*
letter	*carta*	phone call	*llamada (telefónica)*
parcel	*paquete*	collect call	*llamada a cobro*
postcard	*postal*		*revertido*
airmail	*correo aéreo*	public telephone	*teléfono público*
registered mail	*correo certificado*	local call	*llamada local*

long-distance call   *llamada de larga distancia*
person to person   *persona a persona*
email   *correo electrónico*

Geographical Expressions

The expressions below are among the most common you will encounter in Spanish-language maps and guides.

avenida	avenue	*estancia, granja,*	ranch
bahía	bay	*rancho*	
calle	street	*estero*	marsh, estuary
camino	road	*lago*	lake
campo, finca,	farm	*montaña*	mountain
fundo, hacienda		*parque nacional*	national park
carretera, camino,	highway	*paso*	pass
ruta		*puente*	bridge
cascada, salto	waterfall	*río*	river
cerro	hill	*seno*	sound
cerro	mount	*valle*	valley
cordillera	mountain range		

Countries

The list below includes only countries whose names are spelled differently in English and Spanish.

Canada	*Canadá*	Netherlands	*Holanda*
Denmark	*Dinamarca*	New Zealand	*Nueva Zelandia*
England	*Inglaterra*	Scotland	*Escocia*
France	*Francia*	Spain	*España*
Germany	*Alemania*	Sweden	*Suecia*
Great Britain	*Gran Bretaña*	Switzerland	*Suiza*
Ireland	*Irlanda*	United States	*Estados Unidos*
Italy	*Italia*	Wales	*Gales*
Japan	*Japón*		

I am from…   *Soy de…*
Where are you from?   *¿De dónde viene usted?*
Where do you live?   *¿Dónde vive usted?*0

Numbers

1	*uno*	9	*nueve*	17	*diecisiete*		
2	*dos*	10	*diez*	18	*dieciocho*		
3	*tres*	11	*once*	19	*diecinueve*		
4	*cuatro*	12	*doce*	20	*veinte*		
5	*cinco*	13	*trece*	21	*veintiuno*		
6	*seis*	14	*catorce*	22	*veintidós*		
7	*siete*	15	*quince*	23	*veintitrés*		
8	*ocho*	16	*dieciséis*	24	*veinticuatro*		

30	*treinta*	101	*ciento uno*	1000	*mil*
31	*treinta y uno*	102	*ciento dos*	1100	*mil cien*
32	*treinta y dos*	110	*ciento diez*	1200	*mil doscientos*
33	*treinta y tres*	200	*doscientos*	2000	*dos mil*
40	*cuarenta*	300	*trescientos*	10,000	*diez mil*
50	*cincuenta*	400	*cuatrocientos*	50,000	*cincuenta mil*
60	*sesenta*	500	*quinientos*	100,000	*cien mil*
70	*setenta*	600	*seiscientos*	1,000,000	*un millón*
80	*ochenta*	700	*setecientos*	2,000,000	*dos millones*
90	*noventa*	800	*ochocientos*	1,000,000,000	*un billón*
100	*cien*	900	*novecientos*		

Ordinal Numbers

As with other adjectives, ordinals must agree in gender and number with the nouns they modify. Ordinal numbers are often abbreviated using a numeral and a superscript 'o' or 'a' in street names, addresses, and so forth: Calle 1a, 2o piso (1st Street, 2nd floor).

1st	*primero/a*		
2nd	*segundo/a*	8th	*octavo/a*
3rd	*tercero/a*	9th	*noveno/a*
4th	*cuarto/a*	10th	*décimo/a*
5th	*quinto/a*	11th	*undécimo/a*
6th	*sexto/a*	12th	*duodécimo/a*
7th	*séptimo/a*	20th	*vigésimo/a*

Days of the Week

Monday	*lunes*		
Tuesday	*martes*	Friday	*viernes*
Wednesday	*miércoles*	Saturday	*sábado*
Thursday	*jueves*	Sunday	*domingo*

Time

Eight o'clock is *las ocho*, while 8:30 is *las ocho y treinta* (eight and thirty) or *las ocho y media* (eight and a half). However, 7:45 is *las ocho menos quince* (eight minus fifteen) or *las ocho menos cuarto* (eight minus one quarter).

Times are modified by morning *(de la mañana)* or afternoon *(de la tarde)* instead of am or pm. Use of the 24-hour clock, or military time, is also common, especially with transportation schedules.

What time is it?	¿*Qué hora es?*
It's one o'clock.	*Es la una.*
It's two/three/etc o'clock.	*Son las dos/tres/etc.*
At three o'clock...	*A las tres...*

Glossary

Note: For food and drink terms, see the Facts for the Visitor chapter. For additional terms and information on the Spanish language, see the Language section.

ANAM – Autoridad Nacional de Ambiente, Panama's national environmental agency
Ancon – National Association for the Conservation of Nature, Panama's leading private environmental organization
apartado – post office box (as in mailing addresses)
ATM – automated teller machine

bahía – bay
balboa – the basic unit of Panamanian currency
baños – restrooms
bohío – rustic hutlike accommodations
boroquera – blowgun once used by the Emberá and Wounaan Indians
bote – motorized canoe

caballeros – gentlemen
cabaña – cabin
cacique – Kuna tribal leader
campesino/a – rural resident, peasant
Carretera Interamericana – the Pan-American Hwy, the nearly continuous highway running from Alaska to Chile (it breaks at the Darién Gap)
casa de cambio – money exchange house
cayuco – dugout canoe
centesimos – cents; 100 centesimos equal one US dollar (or one Panamanian **balboa**)
cerro – hill
certificación de vuelo – certification of entry date into Panama
chitra – sand fly
chocosano – violent storm, or 'storm that comes form the east,' in Kuna
cine – cinema
cocobolo – a handsome tropical hardwood used for carving life-size images of snakes, parrots, toucans and other jungle wildlife
comarca – district

conejo pintado – raccoonlike animal abundant in Parque Nacional Volcán Barú
cordillera – mountain range
corredor de aduana – customs broker
corvina – sea bass
cuatro por cuatro – 4WD vehicle

damas – ladies
días feriados – national holidays

edificio – building

finca – farm
fuerte – fort

Gali-Gali – the distinct Creole language of Bocas del Toro Province; it combines English, Spanish and Guaymí
gringo/a – tourist, especially a North American tourist

habano – Havana cigar
haras – stables
hombre – man
hospedaje – guesthouse
huacas – golden objects made on the Panamanian isthmus in the pre-Columbian era and buried with Indians

iglesia – church
INAC – Instituto Nacional de Cultura, Panama's National Institute of Culture
IPAT – Instituto Panameño de Turismo, the national tourism agency
invierno – winter
isla – island

kilometraje – mileage

lago – lake
lavamático – laundromat
lavandería – dry cleaner

Merki – American, in Kuna
mestizo/a – person of mixed indigenous and Spanish ancestry

metate – flat stone platform used by Panama's pre-Columbian Indians to grind corn

migración – immigration

Migración y Naturalización – Immigration and Naturalization office

mirador – lookout point

molas – colorful hand-stitched appliqué textiles made by Kuna women

muelle – pier

museo – museum

PDF – the Panama Defense Forces, the national army under Manuel Noriega

piragua – canoe carved from a tree trunk

playa – beach

Patois – a blend of English, Spanish and Gali-Gali (a local dialect on the islands of Boca del Toro)

polleras – the intricate, lacy, Spanish-influenced dresses of the Península de Azuero; the national dress of Panama for festive occasions

pozos – springs

preservativos – condoms

prologa de turista – a permit that resembles a driver's license, complete with photo, and allows you to stay in Panama for longer than the 90 days permitted for tourists

punta – point

río – river

sendero – trail

serranía – mountain range

STD – sexually transmitted disease

tagua – an ivory-colored nut used for carving tiny figurines

tarjeta de circulación – vehicle control certificate

tarjetas – plastic phone cards

taxi marino – water taxi

típico – typical

típico – Panamanian folkloric music

tortuga – sea turtle

trucha – rainbow trout

urbano – local (as in buses)

verano – summer

volcán – volcano

waga – tourist, in Kuna

Thanks

Many thanks to the travelers who used the last edition and wrote to us with helpful hints, useful advice and interesting anecdotes:

Alexander Alexeev, Robban Anthony, Edward Berkovich, Steve Bibb, Sabrina Bini, Britt Blum, Stefan Bosshard, Joy Darley, Jean-Marc Dumont, Stan Eschmann, Becky Failor, Gary Foster, Martin Fuchs, Michael Gacquin, Tom Giles, Sheila Gobrien, Bing Goei, J Graal, Virginia Jane Harris, Hinsh, Joy Holl, Dirk Joris, Sharon Kalbarczyk, Rachael Keller, Bob Kelly, Kevin Kichinka, Jutta Kloeckner, Marianne Kronk, Jeff Lahann, Grant Landon, Bill Landwehr, Ted Lange, Jim Langer, Susan Larkin, Steve Lidgey, Tom Linhart, Panos Loupasis, Michael Marquardt, Allegra Marshall, Jan McDermott, Hugh Monahan, Laura Morse, Scott Muller, Jose Angel Murillo, Gavin Nathan, Olli Neuman, Dan Norvell, Chatea con Isabel Pisano, Monica Plata, Snapper Poche, Teresa Ramella, Mark Razook, Marna Reames, Nelson Rivera, Dennis Rogers, Don Rogers, Eduardo Rollox, Helen Ross, Susan Sanderson, Stacy Sayah, Lisa Schipper, Elizabeth Schmidt, Richard R Schrader, George Smartt, Savinder Soderstrand, Nilam Soni, Barbara Spaans, E Stevens, Mondo Taitu, Antonia Thomson, Lynwood Trowlane, Ray Umashankar, Chelsea & John Ursoleo, Marlies Van Hoef, Dennis & Cindy Veale, Rike Walkschmidt, Richard Warner, Andreas Wenck, Debby Werner, Colin Wilson, Brian Winder, Be Yeo and Yvon Zaugg.

LONELY PLANET

You already know that Lonely Planet produces more than this one guidebook, but you might not be aware of the other products we have on this region. Here is a selection of titles which you may want to check out as well:

Central America on a shoestring
ISBN 1 86450 186 3
US$21.99 • UK£13.99

Costa Rica
ISBN 0 86442 760 3
US$19.95 • UK£12.99

Latin American Spanish phrasebook
ISBN 0 86442 558 9
US$6.95 • UK£4.50

South America on a shoestring
ISBN 0 86442 656 9
US$29.95 • UK£17.99

Read This First: Central & South America
ISBN 1 86450 067 0
US$14.99 • UK£8.99

Healthy Travel: Central & South America
ISBN 1 86450 053 0
US$5.95 • UK£3.99

Available wherever books are sold.

Index

Boxed Text

Bold indicates maps.

MAP LEGEND

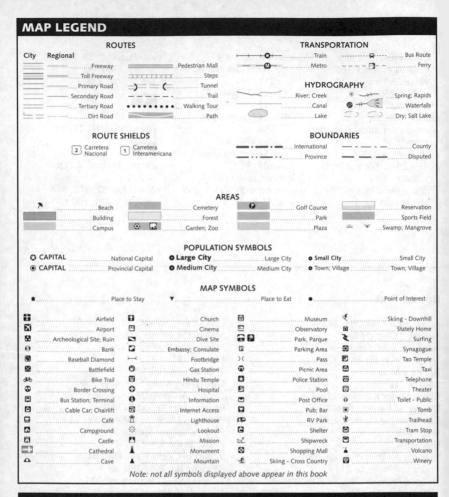

ROUTES

City   Regional

..........Freeway
..........Toll Freeway
..........Primary Road
..........Secondary Road
..........Tertiary Road
..........Dirt Road

..........Pedestrian Mall
..........Steps
..........Tunnel
..........Trail
..........Walking Tour
..........Path

ROUTE SHIELDS

2   Carretera Nacional
1   Carretera Interamericana

TRANSPORTATION

..........Train
..........Metro
..........Bus Route
..........Ferry

HYDROGRAPHY

..........River; Creek
..........Canal
..........Lake
..........Spring; Rapids
..........Waterfalls
..........Dry; Salt Lake

BOUNDARIES

..........International
..........Province
..........County
..........Disputed

AREAS

..........Beach
..........Building
..........Campus
..........Cemetery
..........Forest
..........Garden; Zoo
..........Golf Course
..........Park
..........Plaza
..........Reservation
..........Sports Field
..........Swamp; Mangrove

POPULATION SYMBOLS

○ CAPITAL ....National Capital
◉ CAPITAL ....Provincial Capital
● Large City ....Large City
● Medium City ....Medium City
● Small City ....Small City
● Town; Village ....Town; Village

MAP SYMBOLS

▪ ....Place to Stay
▼ ....Place to Eat
● ....Point of Interest

..........Airfield
..........Airport
..........Archeological Site; Ruin
..........Bank
..........Baseball Diamond
..........Battlefield
..........Bike Trail
..........Border Crossing
..........Bus Station; Terminal
..........Cable Car; Chairlift
..........Café
..........Campground
..........Castle
..........Cathedral
..........Cave

..........Church
..........Cinema
..........Dive Site
..........Embassy; Consulate
..........Footbridge
..........Gas Station
..........Hindu Temple
..........Hospital
..........Information
..........Internet Access
..........Lighthouse
..........Lookout
..........Mission
..........Monument
..........Mountain

..........Museum
..........Observatory
..........Park, Parque
..........Parking Area
..........Pass
..........Picnic Area
..........Police Station
..........Pool
..........Post Office
..........Pub; Bar
..........RV Park
..........Shelter
..........Shipwreck
..........Shopping Mall
..........Skiing - Cross Country

..........Skiing - Downhill
..........Stately Home
..........Surfing
..........Synagogue
..........Tao Temple
..........Taxi
..........Telephone
..........Theater
..........Toilet - Public
..........Tomb
..........Trailhead
..........Tram Stop
..........Transportation
..........Volcano
..........Winery

Note: not all symbols displayed above appear in this book

LONELY PLANET OFFICES

Australia
Locked Bag 1, Footscray, Victoria 3011
☎ 03 8379 8000 fax 03 8379 8111
email talk2us@lonelyplanet.com.au

USA
150 Linden Street, Oakland, California 94607
☎ 510 893 8555, TOLL FREE 800 275 8555
fax 510 893 8572
email info@lonelyplanet.com

UK
10a Spring Place, London NW5 3BH
☎ 020 7428 4800 fax 020 7428 4828
email go@lonelyplanet.co.uk

France
1 rue du Dahomey, 75011 Paris
☎ 01 55 25 33 00 fax 01 55 25 33 01
email bip@lonelyplanet.fr
www.lonelyplanet.fr

World Wide Web: www.lonelyplanet.com *or* AOL keyword: lp
Lonely Planet Images: lpi@lonelyplanet.com.au